THEGREENGUIDE
Scotland

Pipe band, Edinburgh © This is Edinburgh (edinburgh.org)

MICHELIN

THEGREENGUIDE **SCOTLAND**

Editorial Director	Cynthia Clayton Ochterbeck
Editor	Sophie Friedman
Principal Writer	Terry Marsh
Production Manager	Natasha George
Cartography	Peter Wrenn
Picture Editor	Yoshimi Kanazawa
Interior Design	Chris Bell
Layout	Natasha George
Cover Design	Chris Bell, Christelle Le Déan

Contact Us

Michelin Travel and Lifestyle North America
One Parkway South
Greenville, SC 29615
USA
travel.lifestyle@us.michelin.com

Michelin Travel Partner
Hannay House
39 Clarendon Road
Watford, Herts WD17 1JA
UK
&01923 205240
travelpubsales@uk.michelin.com
www.viamichelin.co.uk

Special Sales

For information regarding bulk sales,
customized editions and premium sales,
please contact us at:
travel.lifestyle@us.michelin.com

Note to the reader Addresses, phone numbers, opening hours and prices
published in this guide are accurate at the time of press. We welcome correcti
and suggestions that may assist us in preparing the next edition. While every
effort is made to ensure that all information printed in this guide is correct and
up-to-date, Michelin Travel Partner accepts no liability for any direct, indirect
consequential losses howsoever caused so far as such can be excluded by law.

HOW TO USE THIS GUIDE

PLANNING YOUR TRIP

The blue-tabbed PLANNING YOUR TRIP section gives you **ideas for your trip** and **practical information** to help you organize it. You'll find tours, practical information, a host of outdoor activities, a calendar of events, information on shopping, sightseeing, kids' activities and more.

INTRODUCTION

The orange-tabbed INTRODUCTION section explores Scotland's **Nature** and geology. The **History** section spans from Roman occupation to the establishment of a Scottish parliament. The **Art and Culture** section covers architecture, art, literature and music, while **Scotland Today** delves into the modern country.

DISCOVERING

The green-tabbed DISCOVERING section features Principal Sights by region, featuring the most interesting local Sights, Walking Tours, nearby Excursions and detailed Driving Tours. Admission prices shown are normally for a single adult. Last admission to most attractions, museums, etc., is usually one hour before closing time.

ADDRESSES

We've selected from the best hotels, restaurants, cafés, shops, nightlife and entertainment to fit all budgets. See the Legend on the cover flap for an explanation of the price categories. See the back of the guide for an index of hotels and restaurants.

Sidebars

Throughout the guide you will find blue, orange and green-colored text boxes with lively anecdotes, detailed history and background information.

😊 A Bit of Advice 😊

Green advice boxes found in this guide contain practical tips and handy information relevant to your visit or a sight in the Discovering section.

STAR RATINGS★★★

Michelin has given star ratings for more than 100 years. If you're pressed for time, we recommend you visit the ★★★ or ★★ sights first:

★★★ **Worth a special journey**
★★ **Worth a detour**
★ **Interesting**

MAPS

😊 Regional Driving Tours map, Places to Stay map and Sights map.
😊 Region maps.
😊 Maps for major cities and villages.
😊 Local tour maps.

All maps in this guide are oriented north, unless otherwise indicated by a directional arrow. The term "Local Map" refers to a map within the chapter or Tourism Region. A complete list of the maps found in the guide appears at the back of this book.

PLANNING YOUR TRIP

INTRODUCTION TO SCOTLAND

DISCOVERING SCOTLAND

CONTENTS

© imageBROKER/hemis.fr

Welcome to Scotland

There are few countries that offer so much popular imagery as Scotland: lochs and mountains, kilts and tartan, bagpipes, haggis and whisky. It fuels the traditional tourist trade, but infuriates progressive Scots who point to the new dynamic Scotland of adventure sports, buzzing music, Michelin-starred restaurants, 21C architecture, and more. Fortunately there's no need to choose – celebrate it all, both the old and the new!

SOUTHERN SCOTLAND

SCOTTISH BORDERS (pp77–107)

The Borders region makes a gentle, modest introduction in terms of topography, settlements and monuments. This is not to discount its many charms, nor beauty. This is a romantic land of abbeys and castles, and Sir Walter Scott, whose imagery still defines Scotland for many visitors.

AYRSHIRE (pp108–113)

Ayrshire is famous for its Robert Burns connections. Modern-day golfers tend to wax lyrical about the courses at Troon and Turnberry.

DUMFRIES AND GALLOWAY (pp114–131)

Dumfries and Galloway is Scotland's 'other' border region. Less trim and less well known than the Borders region, it nonetheless possesses many of the same attributes plus attractive towns, in the shape of Dumfries and Kirkcudbright ('cur-coo-bree').

Royal Edinburgh Military Tattoo, Edinburgh Castle

© Mauritius/Photononstop

EDINBURGH AND LOTHIANS (pp132–187)

Scotland's number one visitor destination rarely disappoints. With its year-round festivals, dramatic location, stunning architecture (past and present), glorious parks and gardens, and world-class museums and art galleries, it is a city for all people and all seasons.

GLASGOW (pp188–204)

Scotland's most populous city, with its industrial and port traditions, was named European City of Culture in 1990 and has not looked back since. Glasgow is a flourishing cultural centre, internationally acclaimed in the fields of art, design and music.

RENFREWSHIRE AND SOUTH LANARKSHIRE (pp205–212)

A pleasant wee jaunt from Glasgow, Renfrewshire is famous for its Paisley pattern while South Lanarkshire is home to New Lanark model village, a UNESCO World Heritage Site.

CENTRAL SCOTLAND

ANGUS AND DUNDEE (pp216–227)

The most famous attraction in Angus is Glamis ('glaams') Castle, of Macbeth and Queen Mother fame. Although Dundee's best-known 'citizens' are from its *Dandy* and *Beano* comics, Scotland's fourth largest city is making great strides in the tourist market. Inland, the Angus Glens offer some of Scotland's finest walking trails.

STIRLING AND ARGYLL
(pp228–259)

The hills and glens of the Trossachs, and the many glorious lakes, including bonnie Loch Lomond, offer a taste of picture-postcard Highland Scotland, within a day's coach trip of Edinburgh. Historic Stirling boasts a castle to match Edinburgh, while the Mull of Kintyre has figured large in popular media.

KINGDOM OF FIFE *(pp260–281)*

Fife's crown slipped some 400 years ago, but memories of kings and queens live on, most vividly at Dunfermline, Culross and Falkland Palace. One venerable Fife institution still going strong is St Andrews, the third oldest university in the English-speaking world, founded 1413. Around it has grown a charming seaside town with a world-famous golf course.

PERTHSHIRE *(pp282–302)*

Ancient Perth – gateway to the Highlands – was once the seat of kings, who came to be enthroned on the Stone of Destiny at Scone Palace. The throne (and power) has long been removed, but an air of nobility, or at least gentility, remains in the area's well-heeled towns. Perthshire is also now renowned as the adventure sports capital of Scotland.

NORTHERN SCOTLAND

GRAMPIANS *(pp306–339)*

The Grampians offers a wide range of diverse activities, from salmon fishing by the Dee to night clubbing in Aberdeen, to mountain climbing amid Arctic landscape. More accessible pursuits include visiting Old Aberdeen and seeking out the Grampian's many fine castles, fishing villages and whisky distilleries.

Jarlshof, Shetland

© Martin Zwick/age fotostock

HIGHLANDS *(pp340–369)*

Even if you've never visited Scotland you've already seen the Highlands – at the movies, on calendars, biscuit tins or jigsaw lids. It's a large region, and well worth the effort for its landscapes, romance, history and outdoor activities.

THE SCOTTISH ISLANDS

SKYE, MULL, OUTER HEBRIDES, CLYDE ISLANDS, SHETLAND AND ORKNEY
(pp370–425)

Scotland has almost 800 offshore islands gathered into five principal groups: The Clyde islands, the Inner Hebrides (which include the Isle of Skye and the adjacent Small Isles, the Isle of Mull, and the islands of Islay and Jura), the Outer Hebrides (also known as the Western Isles), Orkney and Shetland and Fair Isle. All hold special appeal in the hearts and minds of visitors. They are resplendent in their landscapes, culture, history, prehistory, flora and fauna, and together they can occupy a lifetime of exploration. Almost all are easily accessible, although the islands of St Kilda require fortitude, forward planning and good fortune with the weather.

Ring of Brodgar, Orkney
© Funkystock/age fotostock

Michelin Driving Tours

Use the DISCOVERING section to explore Scotland's hidden routes.

SOUTHERN SCOTLAND

"Scotland in Miniature" is the nickname for the Isle of Arran due to its topography, scenery and typical Scottish features. Our coastal route clings to its perimeter. Also on the west coast, Ayr is a good base from which to visit Burns Country, and see Culzane castle. Dumfries boasts rich Burns connections and is a good base for waterside excursions along the Nith estuary, and to the Solway Firth – to include romantic Sweetheart Abbey – or inland to the Lowther Hills. A little further southwest, Kirkcudbright ("cur-coo-bree") is a pleasant centre from which to explore Threave Castle and Gardens or maybe the bays south, including Whithorn, Wigtown and Galloway. We suggest Kelso as a good location from which to discover the Scottish Borders, the easterly part of the Southern Uplands: to Floors Castle, Mellerstain and Thirlestane Castle; into the Cheviot Hills, to Jedburgh and its abbey; and to Neidpath Castle via the abbeys of Dryburgh and Melrose, Scott's View, Abbotsford and Traquair House.

Duns, for a trip along the Lower Tweed valley, and Selkirk, to cover the wilder eastern Borders countryside, also make good touring centres.

Gritty post-industrial scenery can be explored along the Clyde estuary, while nestling in the Clyde valley, southeast of Glasgow, is the UNESCO World Heritage Site of New Lanark. The magnificent bridges of the Firth of Forth are close to Edinburgh, as are many coastal attractions heading south and along the coast. Historic Linlithgow and seaside Dunbar are useful bases.

CENTRAL SCOTLAND

From Dundee, a burgeoning cultural and artistic centre, you can explore the scenic hills and valleys of Angus, including Glamis ("glaams") of Macbeth fame. The coastal delights of Angus include the "Auld Red Town" of Arbroath, while East Angus includes beautiful Edzell Castle gardens. Nearby, the cultured festival town of Perth is the natural place for seeing the North Perthshire foothills of the Grampians including Glenshee and Dunkeld. Head west to Criff and Strathearn, and enjoy a wee dram at the Glenturret distillery.

Dunfermline – capital of ancient Scotland – is an apt base from which to explore the Kingdom of Fife and the charming time capsule that is Culross.

Ardvreck Castle, Loch Assynt, Northern Scotland

© Sebastian Wasek/age fotostock

From St Andrews, the ecclesiastical capital of the country, you can explore the East Neuk, with charming, historic fishing villages. Kirkcaldy ("curcoddy") is a good centre for seeing Central Fife including Falkland village, gardens and palace.

West, Stirling castle is just one of many iconic landmarks that you can explore in and around the historic city: the National Wallace Monument, Castle Campbell and Bannockburn are a short drive away. And just west are the ever-popular beauty spots of Loch Lomond and the Trossachs National Park.

Another good base is west-coast Oban, useful for Inverary, Loch Awe, Loch Fyne and the Crinan Canal. Close by is the Kintyre peninsula. North of the Trossachs but within easy reach is Pitlochry. West lies the wild splendour of Rannoch Moor.

NORTHERN SCOTLAND

Aberdeen, nicknamed Granite City, is cultured and cosmopolitan and the centre of "castle country". From here strike out along the Dee valley to the fortresses of Drum, Crathes, Braemar, Balmoral and the beauty spot Linn of Dee. There are two more castle routes to follow with breaks at Pitmedden Gardens and Haddo House. The coast road north runs through fishing villages and ports including Peterhead and Fraserburgh, the pretty town of Banff – featuring Duff House, the finest residence in the north east – Portsoy, and Cullen with its 16C Auld Kirk. A short drive west lie the mighty Cairngorms, Britain's finest mountain scenery, offering magnificent panoramas from many viewpoints, not least Cairngorm itself. For an extended stay choose bustling Aviemore as your base; for somewhere quieter head for Grantown-on-Spey.

Dufftown – home to Glenfiddich – is the start of the malt whisky trail, including Aberlour, Glen Grant, Cardhu, Glenfarclas, Glenlivet and Tomintoul. *Sláinte!*

On the north coast, Elgin is a good base for heading east – to Spey Bay, the fishing town of Lossiemouth, and Fochabers with its Baxters factory – or west along the Moray coast to visit the Pictish Sueno's Stone, and Brodie castle.

Inverness is the gateway to the Northern Highlands; the starting point southwards for "monster hunters" sailing Loch Ness, exploring the Great Glen, and the Nairn region, with place names such as Culloden, Cawdor castle and Fort George redolent in Scottish history and legend. Other excursions take in the Black Isle Peninsula, the Victorian spa resort of Strathpeffer and Royal Dornoch, famous for its golf and beaches.

The Atlantic seaboard of the Wester Ross area hosts arguably Scotland's finest mountain and coastal scenery and beauty spots. Our zigzag itinerary follows the lochs and bays of this spectacular coast with Gairloch and Lochinver as the main staging points. Eilean Donan Castle, exotic Inverewe Gardens, the Falls of Measach, Lochs Maree, Broom and Assynt, and Sandwood Beach are just a few highlights of this stunning part of the country.

You can still sail "Over the sea to Skye" either from Mallaig to Armadale, or Glenelg to Kylerhea, although the Kyle of Lochalsh road bridge is the quickest way. All three routes feed you onto Skye via Broadford. The "Road to the Isles", from Fort William to the fishing port of Mallaig, via Glenfinnan, charming Arisaig and the golden sands of Morar, is a delightful route, although you will have to deviate to visit Arisaig and Morar these days. Fort William is also a base, via the Corran ferry, for exploring the dramatic wild and dramatic landscapes of Morvern and Ardnamurchan, the westernmost point of the British mainland.

Thurso is the main town of the northernmost mainland; to reach the end of the line, head east to touristy John o' Groats, or west towards unspoilt Cape Wrath.

When and Where to Go

WHEN TO GO

The best time of year to visit Scotland, and especially the islands, is in the late **spring** and early summer when the natural beauty of the country is at its peak; the sunniest months are usually May and June. It is also the ideal time to enjoy all manner of outdoor leisure activities. The roads are not too busy and the midges (small, biting insects) are not very active until late June. The remaining months also have their special appeal. July and August are warm but can be wet. It is essential to pack **insect repellent** for trips into the countryside in midge season (*usually Jun–Sept*). Many events and festivals are held all over the country during these two months. Edinburgh and Glasgow are particularly lively centres for a short break or longer holidays, especially during the festivals. Be sure to take in the museums and art galleries and enjoy the relaxed atmosphere. In **summer**, the longest days may be enjoyed among the islands of Shetland and Orkney. September and October are also very pleasant months, but the temperature is cooler and the evenings shorter. The west coast – warmed by the Gulf Stream – enjoys a mild but wet climate while the east coast is cool and dry. In **winter**, the Grampians and Highlands offer cross-country skiing while Aviemore in the Cairngorms is the main winter sports resort. Winter is also a good time to visit Glasgow and Edinburgh when rates may be negotiable and the world-class galleries and museums, not to mention restaurants, bars and nightlife, are not dependent on weather.

WHERE TO GO

Scotland is a relatively small country and it's quite possible to stay in either Edinburgh or Glasgow and make trips as far afield as the Highlands. However, there's a lot to see and do in most of the regions, so the best strategy is to concentrate on two or three adjacent regions.

SHORT BREAKS

If you only have a few days in Scotland and you've not been here before then it's best to stay in either Edinburgh – most visitors' first choice – or Glasgow. Either one of these fascinating cities can comfortably occupy three or four interest-packed days (and nights), and their rich museum collections are a perfect introduction to the history and culture of the country. You can easily visit one city from the other (less than an hour by train) and they also make a good base for day trips to the Borders, the Kingdom of Fife (best from Edinburgh); Dumfries and Galloway, Ayrshire and Arran, Loch Lomond and the Trossachs (best from Glasgow).

LONGER BREAKS

Moving on from Edinburgh and Glasgow you will probably be looking at a touring itinerary. Scotland's other four major tourist cities are Stirling, Dundee, Aberdeen and Inverness and each of these makes a handy base for seeing the regions (though you may of course want to choose rural or village locations).

Winter walk in Glen Coe, Highlands

© dchadwick/iStockphoto.com

Stirling is the most southerly of the four, but northerly enough to enjoy the foothills of the Highlands, including the Trossachs and Loch Lomond. Heading west, Argyll and the islands are remote, rugged and beautiful, and although time consuming to get to and explore well worth the effort.

Dundee is a burgeoning cultural and artistic centre and perfect for exploring unsung Angus and the adjacent region of beautiful Perthshire (staying in Perth is also a good option). Aberdeen is cosmopolitan with spectacular architecture, fine museums, art and culture, and a lively social scene. It is also the gateway to the Grampians and spectacular Highlands scenery, and the seaways to Orkney and Shetland.

Inverness may be the least interesting city of the four, but with the Great Glen and Loch Ness on the southern doorstep, you probably won't spend much time in town anyway.

HERITAGE

National Trust for Scotland (NTS)
National Trust for Scotland, Hermiston Quay, 5 Cultins Road, Edinburgh EH11 4DF. ℰ0131 458 0200 (from outside the UK dial +44 131 458 0303). www.nts.org.uk.
The trust owns and conserves places of historic interest or natural beauty, including coast and countryside properties. Some properties host special events such as festivals, exhibitions and concerts (see website for details).

Historic Environment Scotland
Historic Environment Scotland, Longmore House, Salisbury Place, Edinburgh EH9 1SH. ℰ0131 668 8600. www.historicenvironment.scot.
Historic Environment Scotland (*formerly Historic Scotland*) restores, conserves and maintains over 150 properties representing Scotland's varied architectural heritage.
Explorer Passes to over 70 HES castles, cathedrals and palaces (and even an historic whisky distillery) are available online. *An Explorer Pass is valid for 5 or 14 consecutive days (⊜£35 and £45 respectively, 2019) and allows you to visit as many HES properties as you wish within that time at no additional cost.* The website gives an indication of the savings that can be made by purchasing an Explorer Pass. HES has reciprocal arrangements with English Heritage and Cadw (Welsh Historic Monuments).

SCOTLAND'S GARDENS
23 Castle Street, Edinburgh EH2 3DN. ℰ0131 226 3714. https://scotlandsgardens.org.
These are private gardens that open to the public in aid of charity. The handbook, **Open Gardens of Scotland**, is available via the website (*£7 inclusive of UK post and packaging*), or from major retail outlets (*£5*).

WHISKY TOURS
There are many distilleries open to the public, offering tours and samples of Scotland's national drink.
The Malt Whisky Trail winds its way through the Highlands, visiting seven working Speyside distilleries, including a fascinating cooperage and an historic distillery. These lie amid stunning settings, beautiful coastline and picturesque towns.
For more information visit www.maltwhiskytrail.com.
The Whisky Coast Trail, from Islay to Campbeltown, and from Mull to the Isle of Skye, brings together 16 distilleries, hotels, restaurants, golf courses and other attractions.
For more information contact the Scotch Whisky Association, Quartermile 2, 2 Lister Square, Edinburgh EH3 9GL. ℰ0131 222 9200. www.scotch-whisky. org.uk. ⓒSee INTRODUCTION: Whisky.

SCENIC ROUTES
Tourist information centres have leaflets on scenic routes. Scenic Route road signs have white lettering on a brown background with a blue thistle symbol.

What to See and Do

OUTDOOR FUN

Information on all the activities listed below is available from Visit Scotland either online (*www.visitscotland.com*) or in brochures from tourist information centres.

CYCLING

From dedicated mountain biking centres – Scotland is one of the best places in Europe for this sport – and forest trails, to quiet countryside lanes and miles upon miles of the National Cycle Network, Scotland is an excellent destination for cyclists.

Airlines, ferry companies and the rail network will transport accompanied bicycles. Tourist Information Centres will give advice on shops hiring out cycles in Scotland and provide leaflets on local cycling routes (*150 are available on the website alone*).

For more details go to the official Visit Scotland cycling website: http://active.visitscotland.com.

FISHING

Scotland is a world-class fishing destination. Salmon, sea trout and brown trout abound in the many lochs and rivers. Coarse fishing may be

Salmon fishing on the River Spey near Craigellachie, Moray

© JASPERIMAGESCOTLAND/iStockphoto.com

enjoyed in the southern part of the country.

The waters around the coast provide ample opportunities for sea anglers to test their skills. The main centres include Eyemouth, Arbroath, Stonehaven, Kippford, Ullapool and Shetland, where there is a ready supply of boats for hire. Sea angling festivals are regular features in some resorts.

For more information on the seasons, fisheries, price of licences and permits, boat and tackle hire and accommodation, go to the official Visit Scotland fishing website (*www.fishpal.com/VisitScotland*), where you can

Mountain Biking at Nevis Range near Fort William

© 22kay22/iStockphoto.com

Swilcan Bridge on the Old Course, St Andrews Links

© Luis Davilla/age fotostock

also download or request by post the brochure *Fish in Scotland*.
Fishing permits are available from local tackle shops, hotels, grocers and post offices.

GAELIC EVENTS

To find out information about Gaelic events visit An Comunn Gaidhealach, a voluntary organisation at Balnain House, 40 Huntly Street, Inverness IV3 5HR. ℘01463 709 705. www.ancomunn.co.uk.

GOLF

The traditional home of golf, Scotland has over 550 public and private courses in addition to the world-famous venues at St Andrews, Turnberry, Carnoustie, Muirfield and Dornoch. Most courses are open to the public on payment of a green fee, and golfers are admitted without introduction or the need to belong to a club. For more detailed information on golf courses, see the **Michelin** map 501, the red-cover **Michelin Guide Great Britain & Ireland** and go to the Visit Scotland website http://golf.visitscotland.com.

WALKING

Walk in Scotland is available as a brochure or to download from the Visit Scotland main website. It gives details on short walks, family walks and, at the other extreme, in-depth information sheets for individual long-distance walks. There are also leaflets, guides and maps detailing Scotland's three **long-distance footpaths**, the Speyside Way, the Southern Upland Way and the West Highland Way. Guides containing route maps are published by Cicerone Press Ltd. (*www.cicerone.co.uk*), and a free information and accommodation leaflet is available from **Scottish Natural Heritage** (♿*see below*). Another good contact is **Ramblers Scotland** (*Caledonia House, 1 Redheughs Rigg, South Gyle, Edinburgh EH12 9DQ. ℘0131 357 5850. www. ramblers.org.uk/scotland*).
"**Munro**" is the colloquial term for a Scottish mountain higher than 3 000ft/914.4m. There are 282 Munros, and climbing them all – "Munro-bagging" – is a popular pursuit among the climbing and hillwalking fraternity. Visit *www.munromagic.com* for more information.

WEST HIGHLAND WAY

This route runs 95mi/153km from Milngavie on the outskirts of Glasgow, north to Fort William. It follows the eastern shore of Loch Lomond, crosses remote Rannoch Moor and enters the mountains of Lochaber, passing Ben

Nevis on the way. *Visit www.cicerone. co.uk for their guide to the route.*

SPEYSIDE WAY

The route passes through varied countryside as it follows the river from the coast to the Cairngorms. Of the 60mi/96km from Tugnet on Spey Bay to Glenmore Lodge, east of Aviemore, only the northern section to Ballindalloch (30mi/48km) has been completed. In addition there is a spur from Craigellachie to Dufftown (3mi/5km) and a more arduous one (17mi/27km) from Ballindalloch to Tomintoul in the foothills of the Grampian Mountains. *Visit www.speysideway.org.*

SOUTHERN UPLAND WAY

This coast-to-coast footpath (212mi/341km) links Portpatrick, west, to Cockburnspath, east. Some of the longer stretches are arduous, covering remote hill country. *See www. southernuplandway.gov.uk.*

HORSE RIDING

A wide choice of centres throughout Scotland welcomes beginners or experienced riders for single day or longer holiday spells. Trekking and trail riding are good ways to discover the countryside. For more information, including residential centres and horse riding holidays visit *www. ridinginscotland.com.*

HUNTING

In Scotland you can hunt for roe buck, red stag, sika, red hind, pheasant, partridge, duck, pigeon and, most famously, grouse. The season for the latter starts on the Glorious Twelfth (12 August) until 10 December. Other birds and animals may also only be hunted seasonally. Perthshire is famous for grouse shooting, otherwise hunting takes place nationally.
A useful web portal for shooting, stalking/hunting and fishing is *www. countrysportscotland.com.*

MOUNTAINEERING

Scotland provides ideal country for hill walking, mountaineering, orienteering and rock climbing. Many Scottish peaks lie within easy reach of a public road, while some areas in the Cairngorms, Skye and Knoydart are very remote. The relatively low altitude of most peaks – only four are over 4 000ft/1 200m – is deceptive as rapid weather changes make them hazardous. All climbers should be aware of the potential dangers and equip themselves properly. Climbers are also advised to inform the police or another responsible person of their plans before venturing on hazardous climbs. Winter may present an entirely different environment from spring and summer.

Some of the principal climbing centres include Arran, Skye, Ben Nevis, Glencoe and the Cairngorms. There are more remote ranges and peaks in the Western and Northern Highlands. The more popular summits, especially Ben Nevis and Ben Lomond, have well-marked mountain trails.

The indoor **Edinburgh International Climbing Arena** at Ratho (*0131 333 6333. www.edinburghleisure. co.uk*) offers experienced climbers the opportunity to brush up on their skills without the danger or discomforts of the elements. Alternatively it can give complete beginners a taste of the sport with expert instructors on hand to advise on all aspects of climbing. With walls from 12m to 35m high, and routes from simple to complex, there is something for all levels and abilities. Keen climbers might like to visit the website of the **Mountaineering Council of Scotland** (*01738 493 942. www.mountaineering.scot*). Guided walking holidays and mountain courses in the Highlands are run by **Scot Mountain Holidays** (*01479 831 331. https:// scotmountainholidays.com*).

Sailing on the Sound of Mull

© DonFord1/iStockphoto.com

NATURE RESERVES AND NATIONAL FOREST PARKS

Scotland has numerous **nature reserves**, **country parks** and **forest parks** managed for public use and recreation. Nature conservation is the main aim of these reserves and most employ a warden. In general, visitors are welcome, with amenities that include visitor interpretation centres, nature trails and observation hides. The reserves provide the visitor with a good chance to see wildlife, though there are restrictions in some cases. In addition to bird sanctuaries on the cliffs and offshore islands (such as Bass Rock, Isle of May, Ailsa Craig), the Forestry Commission – Scotland's largest landowner – has created forest parks in areas of scenic attraction. These include Glenmore Forest Park, Queen Elizabeth Forest Park, Argyll Forest Park, Galloway Forest Park and Border Forest Park.

Timber growing is the main activity in these parks, but recreation is also encouraged. In addition to designated forest drives and marked trails there are picnic sites, camping and caravan sites and visitor centres.

On 1 April 2019 **forestry** was fully devolved and two new Scottish Government agencies accountable to the Scottish Parliament were created (♿*see below*).

For additional information apply to:

- ◆ **Scottish Forestry**, Silvan House, 231 Costorphine Road, Edinburgh EH12 7AT. ℘0131 370 5250. https://forestry.gov.scot.
- ◆ **Forestry and Land Scotland**, 1 Highlander Way, Inverness Business Park, Inverness IV2 7GB. ℘0300 067 6000. https://forestryandland.gov.scot.
- ◆ **Scottish Wildlife Trust**, Harbourside House, 110 Commercial Street, Edinburgh EH6 6NF. ℘0131 312 7765. http://scottishwildlifetrust.org.uk.
- ◆ **Scottish Natural Heritage**, 2 Great Glen House, Leachkin Road, Inverness IV3 8NW. ℘01463 725 000. www.nature.scot.
- ◆ **Royal Society for the Protection of Birds (Scotland),** 2 Lochside View, Edinburgh Park, Edinburgh EH12 9DH. ℘0131 317 4100. www.rspb.org.uk.

SAILING AND WATERSPORTS

Unsurprisingly, in a land where sea and freshwater lochs abound, there is no lack of sailing or watersports. The western seaboard with its many isles and sheltered waters is a safe playground. Many sailing centres hold local **regattas**; some of the main centres are Largs, Tobermory, Lamlash

World Heritage Sites

Over 500 sites of "outstanding universal value" are on the UNESCO World Heritage List. Sites may be exceptional natural locales; monuments with unique historical, artistic or scientific features; groups of buildings; or sites which are the combined works of man and nature of exceptional beauty. Scotland boasts five such sites: St Kilda; the Old Town and New Town of Edinburgh; Neolithic Orkney; New Lanark; the Antonine Wall.

Bay, Oban (Kimelford), Crammond Port, Aberdour, Helensburgh, Crinan and Tarbert. **Inland, sailing and watersports facilities** are good on Loch Earn, Loch Lomond and Loch Morlich. **Yachts** can be hired on the western seaboard and the Caledonian Canal. There are sailing marinas all round the coast of Scotland and on the inland lochs. All yacht clubs and sailing schools are linked to the **Royal Yachting Association Scotland**, Caledonia House, South Gyle, Edinburgh EH12 9DQ. ☎0131 317 7388. www.rya.org.uk/scotland.

SKIING

The main centres are:

- **Glenshee:** Cairnwell, Braemar, Aberdeenshire AB35 5XU. ☎013397 41320. www.ski-glenshee.co.uk.
- **The Lecht 2090 Ski Centre:** Strathdon, Aberdeenshire AB36 8YP. ☎01975 651440. www.lecht.co.uk.
- **Glencoe Mountain Resort:** Kingshouse, Glencoe, Argyll PH49 4HZ. ☎01855 851 226. www.glencoemountain.co.uk.
- **The Nevis Range:** Torlundy, Fort William, Inverness-shire PH33 6SQ. ☎01397 705 825. www.nevisrange.co.uk.
- **Aviemore:** Grampian Road, Aviemore. PH22 1RB ☎01479 861 261. www.cairngormmountain.org.

There are dry ski slopes all over the country; the longest in Britain is at the **Midlothian Snowsports Centre** (*Biggar Road, Hillend,*

Edinburgh EH10 7DU. ☎0131 445 4433; www.midlothian.gov.uk), south of Edinburgh. **Ski-Scotland** is the official ski site of Visit Scotland, https://ski.visitscotland.com. Here you can download e-brochures for full information about Scottish ski centres and winter sports.

ADVENTURE SPORTS

With its extraordinary range of adventure sports and activities Scotland has a justifiable claim to be Europe's adventure sports capital.

- On the **water**: adventure-tubing, bodyboarding, canyoning, diving (sub-aqua), kayak-surfing, kitesurfing, open canoeing, powerboating, river-bugging (riding a single person inflatable craft), sea-kayaking, surfing, wakeboarding, whitewater kayaking, whitewater rafting, windsurfing.
- On **land**: caving and potholing, land yachting, mountain biking, mountainboarding, scrambling, and weaselling (wriggling through an underground labyrinth of tunnels).
- **Adrenaline sports**: kart racing, off-road driving, paintball, quad biking, skateboarding, sphereing (hurtling down hillsides inside a large transparent inflatable ball).
- On **ice**: ice climbing, ski mountaineering, snowboarding, sled dog racing, telemark skiing.
- In the **air**: gliding, hang-gliding, hot air ballooning, microlighting, para-gliding, power kiting, sky diving.

WILDLIFE WATCHING

Scotland is home to a diverse range of species, from bottlenose dolphins that visit the Moray Firth to the capercaillie of the Central Highlands and the thousands of seals and puffins inhabiting the coastline.

For an excellent overview visit the official **Wildlife Scotland** website at *https://wildlife.visitscotland.com*. For reputable wildlife tour operators ask at tourist information centres.

SPAS

Scotland has a growing number of spas with many country house hotels and 4- and 5-star hotels in the cities now adding the latest luxury facilities. Recommended are:

- One Spa, 1 Festival Square, Edinburgh. www.marriott.co.uk.
- The Spa at Turnberry Resort, Ayrshire. www.turnberry.co.uk/ spa-at-turnberry.
- Stobo Castle, Stobo, Peebleshire. www.stobocastle.co.uk/spa.

ACTIVITIES FOR KIDS 👥

In this guide, sights of particular interest to children are indicated with a 👥 symbol. All attractions/tours offer discounted admission/tour fees for children and most have family tickets.

Scotland isn't the easiest place in the world to bring children, with a culture that has in the past not really catered for them and weather that often doesn't encourage them to play outside for long. The weather hasn't changed much, but things have improved immeasurably in recent years in other aspects, with, for example, museums and other interpretive attractions becoming far more hands-on.

Millennium cutting-edge attractions, such as Edinburgh's Our Dynamic Earth and Glasgow Science Centre, have been designed especially for the family. The big cities all cater well for family visitors and Edinburgh in particular is a wonderful place for children at festival time.

TRACING ANCESTORS

Before applying for professional help, eliminate any home sources of information that you may have to hand. Check out old letters, diaries, albums and newspaper cuttings and books with inscriptions, including the family Bible or school prizes.

Ensure that research has not already been done on the family with a visit to the **National Library of Scotland** in Edinburgh.

Birth, marriage and death certificates from 1855 onwards, Census Returns from 1801 and Parish Registers pre-1855 may be consulted in the **National Records of Scotland (NRS),** which was created on 1 April 2011 by the merger of the General Register Office for Scotland (GROS) and the National Archives of Scotland (NAS). The office holds property records (Sasines and Deeds Registers) and will furnish names of researchers experienced in using such documents. For those with titled or eminent ancestors, *Burke's* and *Debrett's Peerages,* the *Dictionary of National Biography* and *Who's Who* are useful sources. The names of professional genealogists can be obtained from the Scots Ancestry Research Society, which also furnishes the addresses of Clan Associations. There are organisations in Edinburgh and clan centres that can assist people of Scottish descent who wish to trace their ancestors. For information on clan gatherings, enquire at tourist information centres.

- **AncestralScotland.com** is Visit Scotland's official ancestral tourism site. www.ancestralscotland.com.
- **National Records of Scotland**, General Register House, 2 Princes Street, Edinburgh EH1 3YY. ✆0131 334 0380. www.nrscotland.gov.uk. Also see the **ScotlandsPeople Centre**; same address; ✆0131 314 4300. www.scotlandspeople. gov.uk, which is both and online and a walk-in research facility.

Shops are usually open Monday to Saturday 9am–5pm. In towns and cities as well as villages in holiday areas many shops will choose to open on a Sunday. Larger supermarkets usually open longer, some are even open 24 hours. Many stores remain open until late evening especially during the summer months and in the lead up to Christmas. Some stores operate late opening on Thursday evenings.

♦ **The National Library of Scotland**, George IV Bridge, Edinburgh EH1 1EW.
✆ 0131 623 3700.
www.nls.uk/family-history.

TARTANS

Tartan, a distinctive pattern of criss-crossed horizontal and vertical bands in multiple colours, originated in woven cloth, and is particularly associated with the clans of Scotland. The **Scottish Register of Tartans** is held at the National Records office in Edinburgh (☞ *see above and www. tartanregister.gov.uk*). The Scottish Register of Tartans was established by an act of the Scottish Parliament in 2008, to protect, promote and preserve tartan. The Register is a database of tartan designs, maintained by the National Records of Scotland.

SHOPPING

Glasgow and Edinburgh are wonderful places for shoppers whether in search of touristy souvenirs or the very latest in household and clothing fashions. There is much less choice in the provinces but here, too, the quality of merchandise has improved immeasurably over the last decade or so.

CRAFTS

Scotland boasts a host of homespun products including pottery, ceramics, weaving, lacemaking, knitting, basketmaking, metalwork, woodcraft, jewellery (Celtic designs are popular), tartan rugs, kilts, knitted jumpers from the islands, Caithness glass and Edinburgh crystal. These are on sale in many outlets from designer boutiques on the Royal Mile to craft studios in the Highlands and Islands where visitors are welcome to see craftsmen (and women) at work. You may also see demonstrations of obsolete crafts in folk museums, folk villages and at festivals.

Buchanan Street, Glasgow

© Arturo Cano Miño/age fotostock

TEXTILES

Scotland is renowned for a wide choice of woollen articles, in particular cashmere, Shetland and lambswool, as well as tweed and tartan garments, and you will find these on sale everywhere from the Borders to the islands. Mill outlet shops are a popular choice but their range is mostly designed for coach parties so expect mass market styles, albeit at reasonable prices. Handmade articles – available in both traditional and contemporary styles (look in the big cities for the latter) – will always command a premium, but are worth it.

OUTDOOR GEAR

If you are intent on any kind of outdoor pursuit in Scotland, the vagaries of climate and possibly also terrain, make it vital to be properly equipped. In recent years, outdoor gear shops have proliferated, but don't be tempted by products in cut-price discount stores. Your life may depend on the quality of your clothing and equipment: buy wisely.

REGIONAL FOOD AND DRINK

Scotch whisky (especially single malts), smoked salmon, marmalade, oatcakes, Dundee cake and shortbread are the staple items of most visitors' shopping baskets. Sample at source (at distilleries, confectioners, etc.) and, if your budget allows, buy here too, not only to support smaller regional ventures but to make sure you get the best quality. Stornoway black puddings are the finest the world has to offer, with legally origin-protected status.

Books and Film

BOOKS

Kidnapped – Robert Louis Stevenson (Cassell, 1886). Classic "boys' adventure novel" set in the 18C Scottish Highlands.

Whisky Galore – Compton Mackenzie (Penguin Books, 1957). Comic stereotypical novel but funny for all that: *see Films below*.

Orkney and Shetland – Eric Linklater (Robert Hale, 1965). The classic historical, geographical, social and scenic survey of the islands.

The History of the Highland Clearances – Alexander Mackenzie (Melven Press, 1986). An unhappy story of cruelty and eviction. The most authoritative work on the subject; a reprint of the 19C original.

The Story of Scotland – Nigel Tranter (Routledge and Kegan Paul Ltd., 1987). Legends, myths, stories and memories handed down from generation to generation.

Bonnie Prince Charlie – Fitzroy MacLean (Canongate, 1989). The definitive biography of the Young Pretender's struggle to rally the clans and restore a Stuart monarch to the British throne.

Robert the Bruce – Ronald McNair Scott (Canongate, 1989). Accounts of contemporary chronicles help tell the story of Scotland's most remarkable medieval king.

Scotland, A New History – Michael Lynch (Pimlico, 1992). Eighteen centuries of social and cultural history, from Picts to the 1980s.

Among Islands – Jim Crumley (Mainstream Publishing, 1994). A writer's eye and a poet's instinct come to bear on 25 years of island-lingering.

The Drove Roads of Scotland – A R B Haldane (House of Lochar, 1995). The long-established definitive book on these ancient lifelines in Highland and Island culture and economy.

The Military Roads of Scotland – William Taylor (House of Lochar,

1996). A complete, scholarly history of the military roads both in the Highlands and the southwest of Scotland.

Gulfs of Blue Air – Jim Crumley (Mainsream Publishing, 1997). The story of a journey across the Highland Edge from Rannoch Moor to Ardnamurchan.

The Islands of Orkney – Liv Kjørsvik Schei (Colin Baxter, 2000). A history of the islands of Orkney; folklore and tales of shipwrecks.

The Magic of the Scottish Islands – Terry Marsh (illus. Jon Sparks) (David and Charles, 2002 and 2008). The product of 18 months exploring the Scottish islands.

The Scottish Islands– Hamish Haswell-Smith (Canongate, 1996–2015). The most comprehensive guide to the Scottish islands – all of them.

Seton Gordon's Scotland: An Anthology – Hamish Brown (Whittles Publishing, 2005). An insight into the writings of one of Britain's greatest explorers.

A History of Scotland – Neil Oliver (BBC Books, 2009). A modern version of Scottish history from the popular BBC presenter, which explodes the myths of Scotland as the poor victim in its relationships with England.

Insurrection, Renegade and *Kingdom* – Robyn Young (Hodder and Stoughton). Splendid fictionalised trilogy about Robert the Bruce.

The Great Wood – Jim Crumley (Birlinn Ltd., 2011). Whatever happened to the Great Wood of Caledon, the historic native forest of Scotland?

The Makers of Scotland – Tim Clarkson (Birlinn Ltd., 2011). A narrative history of Scotland from the eve of the Roman invasion to the final phase of the Viking Age.

The Faded Map: Lost Kingdoms of Scotland – Alistair Moffat (Birlinn Ltd., 2014). A vivid portrayal of half-forgotten kingdoms that came and went during Roman times.

FILMS

Macbeth (1948)
Orson Welles directs and plays the tragic king; restructured, but the dialogue is Shakespeare's.

Whisky Galore! (1949)
A comedy classic of Scottish islanders trying to plunder whisky from a stranded ship.

Brigadoon (1954)
Two Americans on a hunting trip in Scotland discover a village set two hundred years in the past.

Ring of Bright Water (1969)
Tired of hectic, noisy city life, Graham Merrill moves to a small village in Scotland to fulfill his dream of being a writer...with an otter in tow. Screenplay by Gavin Maxwell.

Gregory's Girl (1981)
Romantic comedy of teens in love at a Scottish school in the 1970s.

Local Hero (1983)
An American oil company sends their representative to buy up an entire village where they want to build a refinery.

Highlander (1986)
An immortal Scottish swordsman pits himself against an equally immortal barbarian.

Braveheart (1995)
Mel Gibson plays William Wallace in an iconic role fighting English oppression.

Loch Ness (1995)
Heartwarming monster drama starring Ted Danson.

Rob Roy (1995). Liam Neeson plays Rob in a violent tale of treachery and revenge.

Trainspotting (1996)
Violent portrayal of Edinburgh drugs culture in the 1990s.

Mrs Brown (1997)
A touching look at Queen Victoria's platonic relationship with her Highland ghillie John Brown, starring Billy Connolly and Judi Dench.

Brave (2012)
Animation set in a fantasy medieval highland Scotland.

Calendar of Events

Listed below are a few of the more popular events among Scotland's many colourful customs and traditions. For more details on these and other events visit www.visitscotland.com, or ask at a local Tourist Information Centre.

♿*For a selection of Highland Games and Common Ridings, see INTRODUCTION: Traditions and Customs.*

JANUARY
Throughout Scotland —
Burns Night: Burns Suppers to celebrate the birthday (25 January) of the national poet, with haggis as the main dish.

Lerwick, Shetland — Last Tuesday **Up Helly Aa**: Torchlit procession followed by burning of Viking warship, singing and all-night dancing. www.uphellyaa.org.

Glasgow — **Celtic Connections**: Large festival of Celtic-inspired music throughout the city. www.celticconnections.com.

FEBRUARY–MARCH
Jedburgh, Scottish Borders — **Ba' Game** (mob or village football).

Inverness, Highlands — Inverness Music Festival. www.invernessmusicfestival.org.

Fire festivals, Shetland — in addition to the Lerwick festival, several fire festivals are held at other locations. www.visitscotland.com/blog/events/up-helly-aa-viking-fire-festival

MARCH
Lanark, South Lanarkshire — 1 March **Whuppity Scourie**: Children banish winter by beating each other with paper "weapons".

Edinburgh — Edinburgh Book Fair. www.pbfa.org/fairs/edinburgh-premier-fair-with-aba.

MARCH–APRIL
Edinburgh — **Ceilidh Culture**: Music, dance and story-telling. www.edinburghguide.com.

Kirkcaldy, Fife — Around Easter **Links Market**: Europe's longest (1mi/1.6km) annual street funfair. www.linksmarket.org.uk.

MARCH–OCTOBER
Pitlochry, Perthshire and Kinross — **Pitlochry Festival Theatre Season**. www.pitlochry.org.uk.

APRIL
Ayr, South Ayrshire — Mid-April **Scottish Grand National**. www.ayr-racecourse.co.uk.

JANUARY: Up Helly Aa, Lerwick, Shetland

© HelenL100/iStockphoto.com

APRIL–MAY
Lerwick, Shetland — Shetland Folk Festival. www.shetlandfolk festival.com.

MAY
Ayr, Alloway, Ayrshire — Mid–late May–early **June Burns and a' that**: A celebration of the life of Robert Burns with contemporary artists and performers. http://burns.visitscotland.com/festival.

Blair Castle, Perthshire and Kinross — Last weekend May Atholl Highlanders' Parade. https://atholl-estates.co.uk.

JUNE
Lanark, South Lanarkshire — Lanark Lanimers Festival. www.lanarklanimers.co.uk.

Kirkwall and Stromness, Orkney — Mid–late June St Magnus Festival. Arts festival. www.stmagnusfestival.com.

Ingliston, near Edinburgh — Royal Highland Agricultural Show. www.rhass.org.uk.

Glasgow — Late June–early July Glasgow International Jazz Festival. www.jazzfest.co.uk.

Edinburgh — Edinburgh International Film Festival. www.edfilmfest.org.uk.

JULY–AUGUST
Aberdeen — International Youth Festival of Music and the Arts. www.aiyf.org.

Edinburgh — Edinburgh Jazz and Blues Festival. www.edinburghjazzfestival.com.

Various venues — World Pipe Band Championship. www.rspba.org.

AUGUST
South Queensferry, West Lothian — Burry Man Festival: The "Burry Man" (clad in sticky burrs) tours the town on the last day of fair week. https://ferryfair.co.uk.

Mull of Kintyre — Mull of Kintyre Music Festival. www.mokfest.com.

AUGUST–SEPTEMBER
Edinburgh — Edinburgh International Festival, Military Tattoo and Edinburgh Fringe. Scotland's most famous festivals. www.edinburgh-festivals.com.

SEPTEMBER
Largs, North Ayrshire — Late August Largs Viking Festival. https://largsvikingfestival.org.

Highlands (various venues) — Blas Festival: The Highlands' traditional music festival. www.blas-festival.com.

OCTOBER
Various venues — The Royal National Mod: Scotland's premier Gaelic festival. www.ancomunn.co.uk.

Blair Castle, Perthshire and Kinross — Glenfiddich World Piping Championship. www.glenfiddich.com/uk.

NOVEMBER–DECEMBER
Edinburgh — Edinburgh's Christmas celebrations. www.edinburghs christmas.com.

Glasgow — Winterfest Glasgow. www.glasgowloveschristmas.com.

CHRISTMAS–NEW YEARS'S EVE
Kirkwall, Orkney — Ba' Games: Street/mob football. www.bagame.com.

Stonehaven, Aberdeenshire — Swinging Fireball New Year's Eve ceremony. www.stonehavenfireballs.co.uk.

Hogmanay — New Year's Eve celebrations: Nationwide but vibrant in Edinburgh and Glasgow. www.edinburgh shogmanay.com or www.glasgowloveschristmas.com.

Know Before You Go

USEFUL WEBSITES

www.visitscotland.com

The Official Scottish Tourist Board website. Accommodation, holidays, what to see and do, links to all geographical areas. Large sections on sports, culture, eating and other topics.

www.rampantscotland.com

This site claims over 13 000 Scottish-related links and over 3 700 webpage features on Scotland and the Scots, all regularly updated. Good for practical planning as well as browsing for fun.

www.scotland-info.co.uk

The 80 000-word Internet Guide to Scotland is a personal labour of love by a Scottish author, largely based on her personal travels. A very professional site with excellent suggestions on accommodation and much more.

www.undiscoveredscotland.co.uk

Despite its name, this site trawls mainstream Scotland attractions, hotels and restaurants, but does also unearth lots of facts on places that rarely get a mention on other sites.

www.visitscotland.com/see-do/active

An offshoot of the official visitor guide, this covers every sinew-stretching sport that you can do in Scotland. If it's just a wee gentle game of golf or curling you're after, stick to the mainstream sites.

www.aboutscotland.com

Clickable maps, good pictures, independently reviewed accommodation and lively articles about visiting Scotland.

https://edinburgh.org

Sooner or later every visitor to Scotland makes it to Edinburgh, and with good reason. You may as well know before you go, so click onto the official site of Scotland's favourite city.

https://peoplemakeglasgow.com

Though not quite so well known, nor visited, as Edinburgh, Scotland's second city (don't call it that while you're there!) definitely merits your time.

TOURIST OFFICES

BRITISH TOURIST OFFICES ABROAD

The **British Tourist Authority** (**BTA**) trading as Visit Britain provides assistance in planning a trip to Scotland and an excellent range of brochures and maps.

- ◆ **Australia**
  ℘61 9021 4401.
  www.visitbritain.com.au.

- ◆ **Canada**
  ℘1 416 646 6674.
  www.visitbritain.com/ca/en.

- ◆ **France**
  ℘33 1583 65089.
  www.visitbritain.fr.

- ◆ **New Zealand**
  ℘61 9357 6620.
  www.visitbritain.co.nz.

- ◆ **USA – New York**
  ℘1 800 462 2748.
  www.visitbritain.com/us.

- ◆ **USA – Los Angeles**
  ℘1 310 481 2989.
  www.visitbritain.com/us.

SCOTTISH TOURIST INFORMATION

Visit Scotland has a large network of local tourist boards and over 140 tourist information centres (TICs). The addresses and telephone numbers of the main TICs to be found in large towns and tourist resorts are listed in the *DISCOVERING section*. The centres can supply town plans, timetables and information on local accommodation, entertainment facilities, sports and sightseeing.

Visit Scotland – Ocean Point One, 94 Ocean Drive, Edinburgh EH6 6JH. www.visitscotland.com.

INTERNATIONAL VISITORS

CONSULATES

◆ **Australia**
5 Mitchell Street, Leith EH6 7DB.
℘0131 623 8666.

◆ **Canada**
5 St Margaret's Road, Edinburgh EH9 1AZ.
℘07702 359 916.

◆ **France**
11 Randolph Crescent, Edinburgh EH3 7TT.
℘0131 225 7954 or 220 0141.

◆ **Germany**
16 Eglinton Crescent, Edinburgh EH12 5DJ.
℘0131 347 9877.

◆ **Japan**
2 Melville Crescent, Edinburgh EH3 7HW.
℘0131 225 4777.

◆ **USA**
3 Regent Terrace, Edinburgh EH7 5BW.
℘0131 556 8315.

DOCUMENTS

It is essential for EU nationals to hold a **passport** or national identity card in order to enter the UK. Non-EU nationals must be in possession of a valid national passport. Loss or theft should be reported to the appropriate embassy or consulate and to the

---

☺ A Bit of Advice ☺

Medical Insurance
Visitors to Britain should take out medical insurance prior to departure as health treatment may be significantly more expensive.

---

local police. A **visa** to visit the United Kingdom is not required by nationals of the member states of the European Union and of the Commonwealth (including Australia, Canada, New Zealand and South Africa) and the USA. Nationals of other countries should check with the British Embassy and apply for a visa, if necessary, in good time.

CUSTOMS

Tax-free allowances for various commodities are governed by EU legislation. Details of these allowances and restrictions are available at most ports of entry to Great Britain.
British customs regulations and "duty free" allowances are posted online at www.hmrc.gov.uk (then Search "duty free").
US citizens should visit the US Customs and Borders Protection website, www.cbp.gov.

HEALTH

Visitors to Britain are entitled to treatment at the Accident and Emergency Departments of National Health Service hospitals.
For an overnight or longer hospital stay, payment will most likely be required.
Visitors from EU countries should apply to their own National Social Security Offices for a **European Health Insurance Card**, which entitles them to medical treatment under an EU Reciprocal Medical Treatment arrangement.
Nationals of non-EU countries should take out comprehensive insurance.

ACCESSIBILITY

Some of the sights described in this guide are accessible to disabled people. The red-cover **Michelin Guide Great Britain & Ireland** indicates hotels with facilities suitable for disabled people.

The charity **Tourism For All** (*1 Pixel Mill, 44 Appleby Road, Kendal, Cumbria LA9 6ES. ℘0845 124 9971. www.tourismforall.org.uk*) is the UK's central source of holiday and travel information and support for disabled people and their carers.

Disability Rights UK lists holiday facilities for disabled travellers (*Plexal, 14 East Bay Lane, Here East, Queen Elizabeth Olympic Park, Stratford, London E20 3BS. ℘0330 995 0400. www.disabilityrightsuk.org*).

Historic Environment Scotland produce an **Access Guide** to all their properties, available to download from *www.historicenvironment.scot*.

FACILITIES FOR DISABLED TRAVELLERS

The symbol ♿ indicates access for wheelchairs. However, because the range/scope/quality of facilities (also for impaired mobility, sight and hearing) is open to interpretation by site managers, and may also depend on staff availability at the time of visit, visitors are urged to telephone in advance to specify their requirements.

Getting There and Getting Around

BY PLANE

As airport security and baggage regulations change frequently, it is always advisable to check the rules before you fly. Allow plenty of time to pass through check-in and the security screening.

Visit www.gov.uk/browse/abroad for more information regarding UK airports. American travellers should visit www.tsa.gov/travel/security-screening.

International airlines operate flights to Edinburgh, Glasgow, Prestwick and Aberdeen. There are also low-cost flights from Europe and several parts of the UK to Inverness, Dundee and 11 small airports in the Highlands and Islands (♿*see www.hial.co.uk*).

All airports are linked by bus to the neighbouring towns. There are Fly-Drive schemes operated by most airlines, and taxis are generally available at airports.

BY SHIP

Details of passenger ferry and car ferry services to Scotland from Ireland can be obtained from travel agencies or from the carrier:

- ♦ **Stena Line** (Belfast, Northern Ireland to Cairnryan). ℘08447 70 70 70. www.stenaline.co.uk.
- ♦ **P&O Ferries** (Larne, Northern Ireland to Cairnryan). ℘0800 130 0030. www.poferries.com.

Ferry operators to the islands:

- ♦ **Caledonian MacBrayne Ltd.** ℘0800 066 5000. www.calmac.co.uk.
- ♦ **Northlink Ferries** – Orkney and Shetland services. ℘0845 6000 449 (UK), +44 (0)1856 885500 (International). www.northlinkferries.co.uk.
- ♦ **John o' Groats** John o' Groats to Burwick (Orkney). ℘01955 611 353. www.jogferry.co.uk.
- ♦ **Orkney Ferries** ℘01856 872 044. www.orkneyferries.co.uk.
- ♦ **Pentland Ferries**: Caithness to St Margaret's Hope, Orkney. ℘01856 831 226, or ℘0800 688 8998 (booking line). www.pentlandferries.co.uk.

Travel Michelin

Check **travelguide.michelin.com** to plan your route and find hotels and restaurants along the way.

BY TRAIN

- **ScotRail**
  ScotRail offers services through Scotland. *www.scotrail.co.uk*. If you are travelling from London Euston the Caledonian Sleeper departs from Euston just before midnight and arrives in Glasgow at 8.30am, with a connecting service to Edinburgh, arriving 10.01am.
- **Virgin Trains** – operate West Coast services from London Euston to Glasgow and Edinburgh. *www.virgintrains.co.uk*.
  In December 2019, this service will be taken over by First Rail. *https://www.firstgroupplc.com*.
- **London North Eastern Railway** – operate East Coast services from London King's Cross to Edinburgh, Glasgow Central, Aberdeen and Inverness. *www.lner.co.uk*.

For all rail service **timetable enquiries**: 03457 48 49 50, www.nationalrail.co.uk.

Discounts – Britrail and **Eurail**
Britrail passes are available to visitors from North America and certain Asia-Pacific countries including Australia. BritRail Passes are sold only overseas, so remember to purchase before you travel to Britain! For details visit *www.britrail.com*.
Eurail is a cooperation between 28 European railway companies offering discounted rail travel in Europe to non-European residents. Eurail passes are available to any person, except residents of Europe, the Russian Federation, Turkey, Morocco, Algeria and Tunisia. For details visit *www. railpass.com*.

BY COACH

National Express (0871 781 8181. *www.nationalexpress.com*) and **Scottish Citylink** (0871 266 3333. *www.citylink.co.uk*) operate a regular coach service throughout Scotland and between the major Scottish and English cities and towns.
Megabus (0141 352 4444. *www. megabus.com*) is a budget service operating from London (and other English cities) to Edinburgh and Glasgow, and onwards to Perth, Dundee, Aberdeen and Inverness.

BY CAR

DOCUMENTS

Nationals of EU and non-EU countries require a valid **national driving licence**. Visitors from non-EU countries can drive any small vehicle (e.g .car or motorcycle) listed on your full and valid licence for 12 months from when you last entered Britain; visitors from the EU have no such time restriction.

INSURANCE

Insurance coverage is compulsory in the United Kingdom.
Certain UK motoring organisations (*see below*) run accident insurance and breakdown service schemes. Drivers in the US should visit the American Automobile Association website: http://exchange.aaa.com, and click on International Travel.

HIGHWAY CODE

- The **minimum driving age** is currently 17 years old.
- Traffic drives **on the left** and overtakes on the right.
- **Headlights** must be used at night even in built-up areas and at other times when visibility is poor.
- There are severe penalties for driving after drinking more than the legal limit of **alcohol**, or while under the influence of **drugs.**
- There are also severe penalties for driving while using a **mobile phone.**

- In the case of a **breakdown** hazard warning lights are obligatory and a red warning triangle is advisable.
- On **single track roads** drivers should take extra care and use passing places to allow traffic to flow *in both directions*.
  But note that if the passing place is on the right-hand side of the road, do not pull over into it, but keep to the left and stop opposite the passing place in such a way that will enable traffic to pass.

SEAT BELTS

In Britain the compulsory wearing of **seat belts** includes rear seat passengers when rear belts are fitted, and all children under 14.

SPEED LIMITS

Maximum speeds are:
- 70mph/112kph: motorways or dual carriageways.
- 60mph/96kph: other roads (unless specified otherwise).
- 30mph/48kph: in towns and cities.

PARKING REGULATIONS

Off-street parking is indicated by blue signs with white lettering (Parking or P); payment is made on leaving or in advance for a certain period.
There are also parking meters, disc systems and Pay-to-Park zones; in the last case tickets must be obtained from ticket machines (small change necessary) and displayed inside the windscreen. Illegal parking is liable to fines and also in certain cases to the vehicle being clamped or towed away.
- Double red line/wide red line = no stopping at any time (freeway).
- Double yellow line = no parking at any time.
- Single yellow line = no parking for set periods as indicated on panel.
- Dotted yellow line = parking limited to certain times only.
- No stopping or parking on white zigzag lines before and after a pedestrian crossing, at any time.

Remember always to give way to pedestrians on crossings.

PETROL/GAS/ELECTRIC CHARGE

Dual-pumps are widespread with **unleaded pumps** being identified by green pump handles, and **diesel pumps** usually black or yellow. Connection points for electric cars, however, are few and far between throughout rural Scotland ((&see *www.zap-map.com/location-search/ scotland-charging-points*).

ROUTE PLANNING

Michelin Map 501 (scale 1: 400,000) and the **Michelin** *Road Atlas of Great Britain and Ireland* (scale 1: 300,000) show the motorways (M), major roads (A) and many of the minor roads (B) in Scotland and give highly detailed road information.

MOTORING ORGANISATIONS

The two long-established motoring organisations in Great Britain are the Automobile Association (AA) and the Royal Automobile Club (RAC). Each provides services in varying degrees for non-resident members of affiliated clubs. Similar (and cheaper) services are offered by Green Flag.
- **Automobile Association:** ℘0800 88 77 66 (breakdown assistance). www.theaa.com.
- **Royal Automobile Club:** ℘0330 159 8757 (breakdown assistance). www.rac.co.uk.
- **Green Flag:** ℘0800 400 600 (breakdown assistance). www.greenflag.com.

RENTAL CARS

There are car rental agencies at airports, railway stations and in all large towns throughout Scotland. Most companies will not rent to drivers aged under 21 or 25.
- **Avis** — www.avis.co.uk.
- **Budget** — www.budget.co.uk.
- **Europcar** — www.europcar.co.uk.
- **Hertz** — www.hertz.co.uk.

Where to Stay and Eat

Refer to the Addresses in the DISCOVERING section for local restaurant and accommodation listings. For coin ranges and for a description of the symbols used in the Address Books, see the Legend on the cover flap. The red-cover **Michelin Guide Great Britain and Ireland** is an annual publication that presents a selection of accommodation and restaurants. The range is wide, from modest guesthouses to luxurious grand hotels, and from centrally situated lodging to secluded retreats.

WHERE TO STAY

BOOKING A ROOM

The Scottish Regional Tourist Boards and Tourist Information Centres operate an accommodation booking service for a small booking fee.

BED AND BREAKFAST

Many private individuals take in a limited number of guests. Prices include bed and hot breakfast. Some also offer an evening meal.

UNIVERSITY ACCOMMODATION

During student vacations many universities and colleges offer low-cost accommodation in residence halls and dormitories in Dumfries, Dundee, Dunfermline, Edinburgh, Glasgow and Stirling.

YOUTH HOSTELS

There are many hostels in Scotland. Package holidays that comprise youth hostel vouchers, rail and bus pass or hostel vouchers, return rail fare and cycle hire are available by application to:

♦ **Hostelling Scotland,** 7 Glebe Crescent, Stirling FK8 2JA. ☎01786 891400. www.hostellingscotland. org.uk.
♦ **Scottish Independent Hostels** www.hostel-scotland.co.uk.

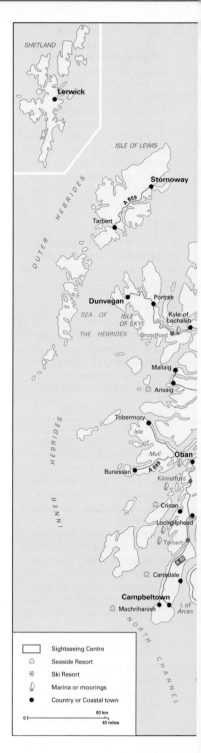

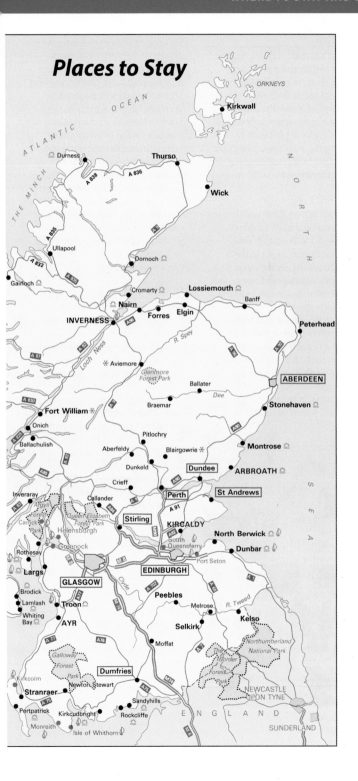

Places to Stay

ORKNEYS

OCEAN

Kirkwall

ATLANTIC

THE MINCH

☐ Durness

Thurso

A 838   A 836

Wick

Ullapool

A 835

Gairloch ☐

A 832

Dornoch ☐

A 835

Cromarty

Lossiemouth ☐

Banff

Nairn

Forres **Elgin**

INVERNESS

Peterhead

A 87

Loch Ness

R. Spey

A 82

✻ Aviemore

Glenmore Forest Park

A 630

ABERDEEN

Ballater

Dee

Fort William ✻

Braemar

Stonehaven ☐

Onich

Ballachulish

A 828

Pitlochry

Aberfeldy

Blairgowrie ✻

Montrose ☐

A 85

Dunkeld

Dundee

ARBROATH ☐

Crieff

Inveraray

Callander

Perth

St Andrews

A 83

Argyll Forest Park

Queen Elizabeth Forest Park

Stirling

A 91

Carrick Park

KIRCALDY

Helensburgh

South Queensferry

North Berwick ☐

Rothesay

Greenock

Port Seton

Dunbar ☐

Largs

GLASGOW

EDINBURGH

Brodick

Clyde

Peebles

A 1

Lamlash

Troon ☐

Melrose

R. Tweed

Whiting Bay ☐

AYR

Selkirk

Kelso

A 77   A 76

Moffat

Northumberland National Park

Galloway Forest Park

The Border Forest Park

Kirkcolm

Dumfries

Newton Stewart

NEWCASTLE UPON TYNE

Stranraer

Sandyhills

E N G L A N D

Portpatrick

Kirkcudbright

Rockcliffe

SUNDERLAND

Monreith

Isle of Whithorn

N O R T H   S E A

CAMPING

Scotland has many officially graded caravan and camping parks with modern facilities and a variety of additional sports facilities.

For a comprehensive list of sites visit *www.campsitesinscotland.co.uk*. Another useful organisation is The Camping and Caravanning Club (℘*024 7647 5426. www.camping andcaravanningclub.co.uk*).

WHERE TO EAT

Dining out in the UK has undergone a revolution in the last couple of decades and while changes may have taken longer to get to the farthest outposts, eating out in Edinburgh, Glasgow and many other major Scottish towns can be a very rewarding experience.

Thanks to its colonial past and its cosmopolitan present, the UK offers authentic tastes from all over the world. In particular Scotland's "Auld Alliance" (with France) has translated into a significant number of **French restaurants**. In recent years, as Indian and Asian restaurants have

Grassmarket, Edinburgh during Edinburgh Festival Fringe

© Christophe Boisvieux/age fotostock

burgeoned, Glasgow has become one of Britain's best places for **curry**. Whereas modern European cuisine is highly popular in London, the best Scottish restaurants, particularly in Edinburgh, feature top-quality Scottish ingredients married to European, Asian or even Pacific influences and flavours that produce a splendid hybrid cuisine known as **Modern Scottish**. Prices tend to be high compared to many other parts of the world, particularly in Edinburgh and Glasgow. Eating out in the big cities at lunchtime however, can be a bargain, as many restaurants offer very competitive pricing aimed at office workers.

DINING OUT

Restaurant hours are often flexible in the major cities but less so elsewhere. Most rural restaurants serve lunch noon to 2–2.30pm and dinner from about 7pm to 10pm. The rise of bistros, brasseries and continental-style cafés has brought all-day, pan-European eating and snacking to many places but these establishments are rare outside major cities and large towns. There are a growing number of "gastropubs", however, where the food is given top priority.

For guaranteed good food in a pub pick up a copy of **Michelin Eating Out in Pubs**.

FOOD

Scotland is renowned for the quality of its beef and its fish. Aberdeen Angus and Galloway beef are always reliable. Scottish seafood is equally famous; fish lovers can enjoy salmon or trout, either fresh from the stream or via the smoke house. Many coastal areas have fish farms, usually for producing salmon, mussels and oysters.

For more information on traditional Scottish cooking and produce, see INTRODUCTION: Food and Drink.

Basic Information

BUSINESS HOURS

Standard business and office hours are 9am to 5pm Monday to Friday. Museums and visitor attractions in the cities generally open year-round daily around 10am (noon on Sunday) to 5.30pm or 6pm.

Shops are usually open Monday to Saturday 9am–5pm. In towns and cities as well as villages in holiday areas many shops will choose to open on a Sunday. Larger supermarkets usually open longer, some are even open 24 hours. Many stores remain open until late evening especially during the summer months and in the lead up to Christmas. Some stores operate late opening on Thursday evenings. On the islands of Lewis, Harris and North Uist all shops are closed on Sundays.

Pubs generally open Mondays to Saturdays 11am–11pm, and Sundays 12.30–2.30pm and 6.30–11pm, though in the bigger cities and towns they may stay open much later and/ or all day.

ELECTRICITY

240 volts AC is the usual voltage; 3-pin flat wall sockets are standard. An adaptor or a multiple point plug is required for all non-British appliances.

EMERGENCIES

Dial 999 (free) for nationwide emergency assistance; ask for **Fire**; **Police**; **Ambulance**; **Coastguard**, etc.

MAIL/POST

Post Offices are generally open Mondays to Fridays, 9.30am to 5.30pm and Saturday mornings, 9.30am to 12.30pm.
Postcard/standard letter rate: UK 61p/70p (second/first-class); Europe and rest of the world (up to 10g) from £1.35. Check prices online at www. royalmail.com.

Stamps are also available from newsagents and tobacconists and even some supermarkets.
Poste Restante items are held for 14 days; proof of identity is required. Airmail delivery usually takes three to four days in Europe and four to seven days elsewhere in the world.

MONEY

Banks

Banks are generally open Monday to Friday, 9.30am to 3.30pm; some banks offer a limited service on Saturday mornings; all banks are closed on Sundays and bank holidays. Most banks have cash dispensers (ATMs) that accept international credit cards; most do not charge a fee for cash withdrawals (but be sure to check first). Exchange facilities outside these hours are available at airports, currency exchange companies, travel agencies and hotels. Some form of identification is necessary when cashing travellers' cheques in banks. Commission charges vary; hotels charge more than banks.

Credit Cards

The main credit cards (American Express; Access/Eurocard/Mastercard; Diners Club; Visa/Barclaycard) are widely accepted in shops, hotels, restaurants and petrol stations. Most banks have cash dispensers which accept international credit cards.

Currency

The official currency in Great Britain is the **pound sterling**. The decimal system (100 pence = £1) is used throughout Great Britain; Scotland has different notes including £1 and £100 notes, which are legal tender outside Scotland, though you may have difficulty getting some English shops to accept them; the Channel Islands and Isle of Man have different notes and coins, which are not valid elsewhere. The common currency, in descending order of value, is £50, £20, £10 and £5 (notes); £2, £1 (gold coins),

50p, 20p, 10p, 5p (silver coins); and 2p and 1p (copper coins). The Euro may be accepted in some stores in London, but always check in advance.

PUBLIC HOLIDAYS

The following are days when museums and other monuments may be closed or vary their admission hours:
+ 1, 2 January
+ Good Friday
+ Monday nearest 1 May
+ Last Monday in May
+ First Monday in August
+ 30 November (St Andrew's Day)
+ 25 December
+ 26 December

There are school holidays at Christmas, spring and summer, and half-term breaks in February and October.

REDUCED RATES

Discounts are generally available for senior citizens (over 65), students and youths (usually under 15/16) on visitor attractions and tours, public transport and other leisure activities such as movies. Proof of age may be required.

SMOKING

In the UK it is illegal to smoke (including vaping) in enclosed public spaces and some outdoor spaces, such as railway platforms.

TAXES

In Britain **Value Added Tax** (VAT) of 20% is added to most retail goods. Non-Europeans may reclaim this tax at the Customs office of the airport of their departure; each shop sets its own minimum purchase. See www.gov.uk/vat-rates.

INTERNATIONAL DIALLING CODES (00 + code)			
Australia	61	**New Zealand**	64
Canada	1	**United Kingdom**	44
Eire	353	**United States**	1

COMMUNICATIONS

Telephones

Public telephones, formerly housed in the iconic red telephone boxes, are available in many, and sometimes unusual, situations, Most require coins; some accept credit cards.

- ℘ 100: UK Operator
- ℘ 118 500: BT Directory Enquiries (£2.75 per call and £2.75 per minute, plus your phone company's Access Charge).

Mobile Phones

Mobile phone signals are restricted in coverage and often erratic – especially away from main urban centres. 2G coverage is reasonably wide-spread; 3G rather less so, and 4G (and soon 5G) mainly around cities and large towns. But it is improving at an impressive rate, and there are often seemingly bizarre and locations where reception is unexpectedly good.

You can check your own service provider's coverage on their website, but the reality is that you will not have a signal or connection in many parts of Scotland.

International Calls

To make an international call dial 00 followed by the country code, then the area code (without the initial 0) then the subscriber's number. Above are some of the more popular visitors home country codes. The codes for direct dialling to other countries are printed in telephone directories.

Internet

In urban areas, Wi-Fi is generally available at all hotels and hostels and in many cafes, pubs, and museums. In more rural areas, Wi-Fi may not always be available, and when it is, it can be very slow.

TIME

In winter, standard time throughout Scotland is Greenwich Mean Time (GMT). In summer (mid-March to late October) clocks are advanced by 1hr to give British Summer Time (BST).

CONVERSION TABLES

Weights and Measures

1 kilogram (kg) 6.35 kilograms 0.45 kilograms **1 metric ton (tn)**	**2.2 pounds (lb)** 14 pounds 16 ounces (oz) **1.1 tons**	**2.2 pounds** 1 stone (st) 16 ounces **1.1 tons**	*To convert kilograms to pounds, multiply by 2.2*
1 litre (l) 3.79 litres 4.55 litres	**2.11 pints (pt)** 1 gallon (gal) 1.20 gallon	**1.76 pints** 0.83 gallon 1 gallon	*To convert litres to gallons, multiply by 0.26 (US) or 0.22 (UK)*
1 hectare (ha) **1 sq kilometre (km²)**	**2.47 acres** 0.38 sq. miles (sq mi)	**2.47 acres** 0.38 sq. miles	*To convert hectares to acres, multiply by 2.4*
1 centimetre (cm) **1 metre (m)**	**0.39 inches (in)** 3.28 feet (ft) or 39.37 inches or 1.09 yards (yd)	**0.39 inches**	*To convert metres to feet, multiply by 3.28; for kilometres to miles, multiply by 0.6*
1 kilometre (km)	**0.62 miles (mi)**	**0.62 miles**	

Clothing

Women	EU	US	UK		Men	EU	US	UK
	35	4	2½			40	7½	7
	36	5	3½			41	8½	8
	37	6	4½			42	9½	9
Shoes	38	7	5½		**Shoes**	43	10½	10
	39	8	6½			44	11½	11
	40	9	7½			45	12½	12
	41	10	8½			46	13½	13
	36	6	8			46	36	36
	38	8	10			48	38	38
Dresses & suits	40	10	12		**Suits**	50	40	40
	42	12	14			52	42	42
	44	14	16			54	44	44
	46	16	18			56	46	48
	36	6	30			37	14½	14½
	38	8	32			38	15	15
Blouses & sweaters	40	10	34		**Shirts**	39	15½	15½
	42	12	36			40	15¾	15¾
	44	14	38			41	16	16
	46	16	40			42	16½	16½

Sizes often vary depending on the designer. These equivalents are given for guidance only.

Speed

KPH	10	30	50	70	80	90	100	110	120	130
MPH	6	19	31	43	50	56	62	68	75	81

Temperature

Celsius (°C)	0°	5°	10°	15°	20°	25°	30°	40°	60°	80°	100°
Fahrenheit (°F)	32°	41°	50°	59°	68°	77°	86°	104°	140°	176°	212°

To convert Celsius into Fahrenheit, multiply °C by 9, divide by 5, and add 32.
To convert Fahrenheit into Celsius, subtract 32 from °F, multiply by 5, and divide by 9.
NB: Conversion factors on this page are approximate.

Edinburgh from Calton Hill with Dugald Stewart Monument.
© Tim Gartside/age fotostock

INTRODUCTION TO SCOTLAND

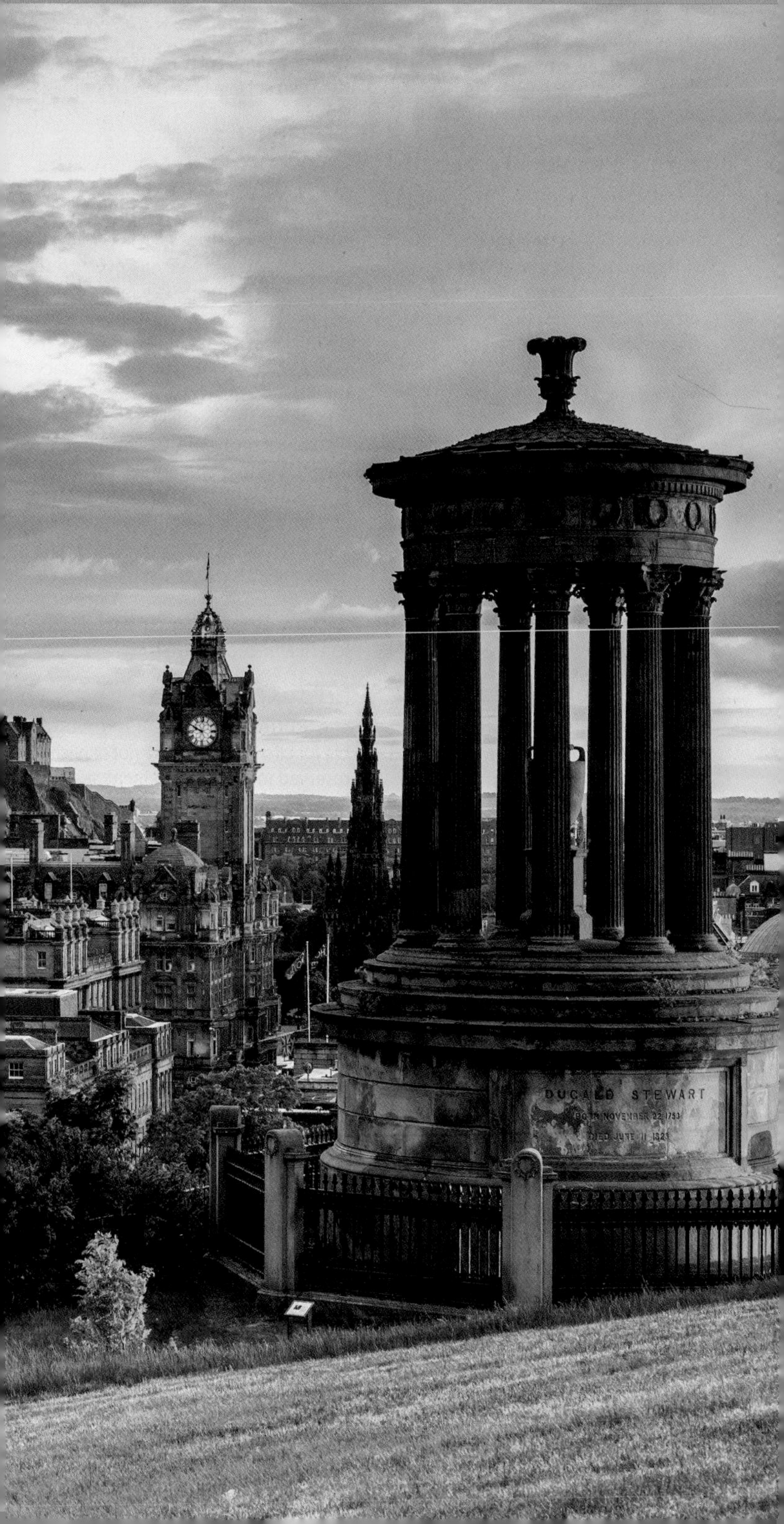

Scotland Today

As Scotland moves through the 21st century it's shaking off the old tourist stereotype of shortbread in tartan tins, bagpipers and haggis and is instead incorporating such icons into contemporary life, often with humour and verve. On the streets of Edinburgh, Glasgow and other major towns, there is a buzz and confidence equal to any modern European city, albeit with a definite Scottish twist.

21C SCOTLAND

BREXIT

On June 23, 2016, a referendum was held: should the UK leave the EU? This would be Brexit. Totalling votes across the UK, the Leave camp won 52% to Remain's 48%. In Scotland, however, Remain won 62% to Leave's 38%. Brexit was meant to take place on March 29, 2019, but as of this writing, no compromise has been reached. Likewise as of this writing, although no Scottish independence referendum is planned, it remains a possibility.

POPULATION

As of June 2017, Scotland's population is 5.425 million. Glasgow is the largest city with a population (2017) of 606 340 (985 290 in Greater Glasgow). The capital, Edinburgh, has 512 150, with Aberdeen next at 214 610.

Scotland's population peaked in the mid-1970s and was in decline until recent years, but there's now been a slow growth in people are moving from other parts of the UK to Scotland. Since 2004 and the expansion of the EU – offering economic migration without frontiers in much of Europe – incomers from countries such as Poland, Latvia, Lithuania and the Czech Republic have joined the local population.

Scotland has seen many waves of migration and, as a result, there are many more people with Scottish ancestry living abroad than the total population of Scotland. In the USA alone, 4.8 million people claim Scottish ancestry, while the figure for Canada is only slightly less.

HEALTH

It is a sad fact that the Scottish diet has long been the worst in Europe with Scots regularly topping the tables of degenerative disease such as cardiovascular disease and cancer. Poverty and health education are key issues being addressed in order to solve this, even though Scotland generally has a well-educated population with adult literacy rates over 99 percent. And, ironically, good food abounds. Farmers' Markets have never been more successful (albeit staged in more affluent areas such as Edinburgh and Perth) and, for tourists at least, Scottish cuisine has never been better, nor healthier. However, it is cheap supermarket foods, high in sugars, salts and artificial ingredients, that make up the daily diet of millions of less affluent, less health-conscious Scots.

GOVERNMENT

The Scottish Government is responsible for all matters that are not explicitly reserved to the UK Parliament at Westminster (by Schedule 5 of the Scotland Act 1998); devolved matters include the Scottish National Health Service, education, justice and home affairs, rural affairs, economic development and transport. Among areas which remain under Westminster control are the constitution, foreign policy, defence and national security, border controls and economic policy, including Scottish taxes, though the Scottish Parliament has limited power to vary local Income Tax (known as the Tartan Tax). The head of state in Scotland is still the British monarch.

SCOTTISH PARLIAMENT

Since the decline of Scottish industry in the 1930s, relations between Scotland and Whitehall worsened. In particular, economic decline and discontent about the lack of adequate benefits from North Sea oil fostered nationalist feelings. The remoteness of central government, the imposition of the Poll-Tax and local government reorganisation were all contentious issues.

In 1997, Whitehall granted Scotland a referendum to gauge support for the creation of a parliament for Scotland. The result was a resounding vote for devolution, and later that year – almost three centuries after the last parliament was dissolved – the Scottish Parliament was reopened.

The Parliament has responsibility over wide areas of Scottish affairs, though in theory at least, Westminster retains powers to amend or even abolish the Scottish Parliament. The new body, which is a single house legislature, has 129 members, 73 of whom represent individual constituencies (56 are regional MSPs) and are elected on a first-past-the-post voting system. The Executive consists of a First Minister and a team of ministers and law officers.

In 2005, the Scottish Parliament moved to the foot of the Royal Mile to take up their new permanent residence in Britain's most controversial post-Millennium building. Designed by the Spanish architect Enric Miralles (1955–2000), it arrived four years late and, most scandalously, 10 times over budget, costing over £430 million.

In 2000, tragedy struck the Parliament, when its recently elected first ever Scottish First Minister, Donald Dewar, died of a heart attack. His successor,

Henry McLeish, lasted just over a year before resigning over financial irregularities. He was succeeded by Jack McConnell, who was in turn succeeded by Alex Salmond in 2007, leader of the Scottish National Party, the largest political party in favour of full Scottish independence. Salmond, along with deputy first minister Nicola Sturgeon, campaigned for a "Yes" vote in the 2014 independence referendum. They failed in their bid; Salmond resigned and in a subsequent leadership election Nicola Sturgeon was elected to replace him. Salmond subsequently went on to stand successfully for the Westminster parliament in the 2015 election, when the Scottish National Party virtually wiped out all political opposition in Scotland. The SNP lost some of their seats in a snap 2017 election, when Alex Salmond was also defeated. Nicola Sturgeon continues (2019) as the First Minister of Scotland.

ECONOMY

The economy of Scotland has always been closely linked with the rest of the United Kingdom and in recent times also to the European Union. At the time of the Industrial Revolution Scotland was one of the powerhouses of Europe, famous for **shipbuilding**, as well as its thriving **coal mining**, **steel** and other manufacturing industries.

Scottish Parliament Building designed by Enric Miralles

© Yerbury Photography/Loop Images/Photononstop

As these traditional industries went into decline or moved to other parts of the world Scotland has become a **technology**- and **service**-based economy – it is estimated that around 80 percent of all Scotland's employees now work in services and this sector enjoyed significant rates of growth until 2008. Edinburgh was one of the top five **banking** and **financial services** centres in Europe but was badly hit by the crisis of 2009 with an estimated 10 000 lost jobs in banking alone.

The "**Silicon Glen**" corridor between Glasgow and Edinburgh is home to many blue-chip companies (such as Motorola, IBM, NCR and Honeywell) specialising in information systems, electronics, instrumentation, defence and semiconductors.

Scotland now produces about 30 percent of Europe's personal computers and 80 percent of its workstations. It provides almost half of the semiconductors made in the UK, with 10 000 employees in the semiconductor industry and almost double that in optoelectronics and communications technologies.

Despite the passing of its halcyon Clyde shipbuilding days, **Glasgow** still builds ships, is Scotland's leading seaport and is the fourth largest manufacturing centre in the UK. The city is also an important international banking centre and boasts the UK's largest commercial and retail district after London's West End.

In the late 1970s, the discovery and exploitation of **North Sea oil** and natural gas in fields around the Shetland Isles proved a massive boon to Scotland and to the Highlands and Islands in particular. Aberdeen is the nerve centre, with giants such as Shell and BP housing their European exploration and production headquarters in the city. Today, even though the best years of oil have passed, this sector continues to underpin a local economy which has barely survived – particularly in the islands – on traditional fishing and agricultural activities.

The new technology sector has also spread far north with modern Shetlanders and Orcadians more likely to be involved in software and microprocessors than fishing, crofting or crafts.

Knitwear and tweed, once traditional cottage industries, were brought into the 21C by names like Pringle which gave Scotland a presence on the international market. However, increasing competition from low-cost textile producers in Southeast Asia has meant that the workforce has been dramatically reduced over the last decade, including the loss of Pringle itself, which since 2008 has no longer been "Made in Scotland". Yet the sector still does employ more than 10 000 people in 665 companies, with a combined turnover of around £1 billion.

Whisky is probably the best known of Scotland's manufactured exports, contributing around £5 billion to the UK economy, supporting 40 000 jobs as well as adding £2 billion to the balance of trade, making it one of the UK's top five manufacturing export earners. The whisky industry also generates a substantial income for the government with around £1.6 billion raised in duty each year.

Another Scottish icon that is important to the economy is **shortbread**, which has evolved from a medieval biscuit bread recipe to the butter-laden delicacy known today around the world. Walkers Shortbread is the single biggest grossing branded Scots product. Exports account for 35 percent of the company's £89 million turnover.

And of course there is **tourism**, an important and growing area, which is responsible for sustaining around more than 200 000 jobs.

TRADITIONS AND CUSTOMS
CLANS

Clann in Gaelic means children or family. All members of a clan owed loyalty to the head of the family or the chief. In return for their allegiance, he acted as leader, protector and dispenser of justice. Castle pit prisons, gallows hills and beheading pits are all common features in clan territories. The ties of kinship created a powerful social unit which flourished north of the Highland

Line where Scottish monarchs found it hard to assert their authority. There the Lord of the Isles ruled as an independent monarch. As late as 1411, with the Battle of Harlaw, the monarchy was threatened by combined clan action. Clan ties ran deep and rivalries and feuds, often for land or cattle, were common. Scott popularised the Campbell–MacGregor feud in *Rob Roy*. The late 17C was marked by the Massacre of Glencoe. The mainly Catholic clans pinned their hopes on the "King over the water" and the Jacobite risings were based on clan support. Sweeping changes followed the Battle of Culloden (1746) with the passing of the Act of Proscription (1747–82). The wearing of tartan in any form and carrying of arms were banned and heritable jurisdictions abolished. This was the destruction of the clan system and the death knell came with the so-called Highland Clearances of the early 19C.

Battles and feuds, loyalty and traditions live on in legends and literature. Clan Societies and Associations are still active organisations, in Scotland and abroad. Some of them finance museums (Macpherson at Newtonmore, Donnachaid north of Blair Atholl); others undertake the restoration of clan seats (Menzies Castle) or building of clan centres (Clan Donald Centre, Armadale Skye).

TARTANS

The colourful clothing material, tartan, now so symbolic of Scotland, has ancient origins while clan tartans are an invention of the early 19C. In the Highlands a coarse woollen cloth (*tartaine* in French) was dyed using vegetable plant sources (bracken for yellow; blaeberries for blue; whin bark or broom for green). Originally patterns or setts corresponded to the district in which a particular weaver, with his distinctive pattern, operated. In early portraits it is common to see a variety of patterns being worn at one time. Some of the best examples are Francis Cote's splendidly defiant *Pryse Campbell, 18th Thane of Cawdor* (see CAWDOR CASTLE), *The MacDonald Boys* (c.1750),

Raeburn's series of Highland chiefs including *Macnab* and J Michael Wright's 17C *Highland Chieftain* at Holyroodhouse Palace.

The repeal of the Proscription Act (1782) led to the commercialisation of tartans and standardisation on a clan basis and a more rigid observation of clan or family tartans. The first tartan pattern books appeared at this time. George IV's 1822 visit, when the monarch wore a kilt, initiated the tartan boom of the 19C, a vogue continued by Queen Victoria and Albert with their interest in all things Highlandesque.

Colours

Any given **sett** or pattern may be woven in modern, ancient or reproduction colours. With the introduction of aniline dyes in the 19C the colours became bright and harsh and were termed **"modern"**. After World War I, an attempt was made, again using chemical dyes, to achieve the softer shades of the natural dyes. These were defined as **"ancient"** and created a certain amount of confusion on the tartan scene as some tartans, like the Old Stewart or Old Munro, already had "old" as part of their title. More recent developments include the invention of **"reproduction"** and **"muted"** colours. The introduction in the 19C of synthetic dyes gave vivid colours and the kilt began to lose its camouflage quality on the hills. **Hunting tartans** were created where the bright red backgrounds were replaced by green, blue or brown. The **dress tartan** was another innovation of the period. The clan tartan was given a white ground and used for men's evening dress.

A tartan exists for every occasion be it everyday, hunting or evening wear. The most common form is the kilt, which constitutes the principal item of Highland dress. By the 16C, a belted plaid *(feileadh mor)* was in use for everyday wear. The little kilt *(feileadh beag)* developed from this and was popular in the 18C. A proper kilt may use as much as 7m of tartan.

Making double width Harris Tweed

© The Harris Tweed Authority

The archives of the now defunct Scottish Tartans Society have been kept, since STS's closure, by the Scottish Tartans World Register. Their database comprises almost 3 000 tartan designs.

SPOKEN GAELIC

A steady decline in the overall number of Gaelic (that's Gah-lic, not Gay-lic) speakers in Scotland has slowed, according to the results of the 2011 census.

The majority of Gaelic speakers are bilingual. As a living language, Gaelic continues to flourish in the Northwest Highlands, the Hebrides, where 76 percent of the population are Gaelic speakers and Skye (58 percent). Outside these regions Glasgow has a pocket of Gaelic speakers.

One of the oldest European languages and a Celtic one, Scottish Gaelic is akin to the Irish version. The Gaeldom culture has given much that is distinctive to Scotland (tartans, kilt, bagpipes, music). An Comunn Gaidhealach (1891) with its headquarters in Inverness, promotes the use of Gaelic, its literature and music and organises an annual festival, the **Mod**, of Gaelic song and poetry (*see Calendar of Events, p23).

SCOTTISH CRAFTS

Craftsmen offer a wide variety of quality objects, which make perfect souvenirs of a visit to Scotland. Of the many traditional Scottish crafts, the best known is the **knitwear** of Fair Isle and Shet-

land. These include the natural colours of Shetland sweaters, the extremely fine lace shawls and the complicated multicoloured patterned Fair Isle jerseys. **Harris Tweed**, woven exclusively on handlooms in the Outer Hebrides, is a quality product well meriting its high reputation. **Tartans** are nearly all machine woven but **kilt making** has remained a handicraft.

Both **glass making** and **engraving** are thriving crafts today. The best-known products, other than cut crystal, are the engraving and handblown paperweights, in particular the delightful **millefiori**. Jewellery making includes the setting of semi-precious stones such as the Cairngorm or Tay pearls. Both serpentine and granite are employed for various ornaments and objects (paperweights, penholders) and granite is used for the polished curling stones.

The straw-backed and hooded **Orkney chairs**, white fleecy **sheepskin rugs** and **leather** and hornwork articles (cutlery handles and buttons) are also very popular.

Both individual craftsmen and larger firms usually welcome visitors to their workshops and showrooms. For further information apply to the local tourist information centres.

HIGHLAND GAMES AND GATHERINGS

Visitors are highly recommended to attend one of these colourful occasions

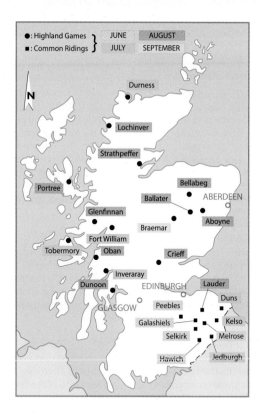

●: Highland Games	JUNE AUGUST
■: Common Ridings	JULY SEPTEMBER

where dancing, piping and sporting events are all part of the programme. As early as the 11C contests in the arts of war were organised to permit clan chiefs to choose their footrunners and bodyguards from the winners.

Following the repeal of the Proscription Act, Highland Societies were formed to ensure the survival of traditional dances and music. Today these events are popular with locals and visitors alike. Of particular interest and charm are those of the Grampian and Highland areas.

Traditional events include dancing, piping, athletics and the never failing attraction of massed pipe bands. The heavy events include putting the shot, throwing the hammer and tossing the caber as straight as possible and not as far as possible. The map opposite shows a selection of Highland Games, Gatherings and Common Ridings.

FOOD AND DRINK

Scottish cooking is characterised by the excellence and quality of the natural products from river, moor, sea and farm.

Often overlooked, Scottish produce is among the finest in Britain and there are few, if any, Scottish restaurants, even in remote places, that do not make full use of it in their menus.

For the visitor local food outlets and farm shops are growing in popularity as places to buy and try local produce, and are an excellent way of reducing food miles and so help the environment.

SOUPS

These number **Cock-a-Leekie** using fowl, cut leeks and prunes; **Scots** or **Barley Broth**, a vegetable and barley soup; **Game Soup**; **Partan Bree**, a crab soup; and **Cullen Skink** made with smoked haddock.

FISH

The harvest that comes from Scotland's rivers, lochs and coastal waters has long been one of the country's key attractions for visitors and locals alike.

Of the many varieties of fish, pride of place goes to the **salmon**, be it farmed or wild, from the famous fisheries of a dozen upwards. But the oysters that come from Croig on the Isle of Mull, and the Mull mussels from Inverlusa and Loch Spelve are second to none, and very cheap if you buy them direct from the lochside farm outlet to cook yourself. The **Tobermory Fish Company** on Mull (*www.tobermoryfish.co.uk*) may not be unique in its concept, but it has an online shop, and the finest smoked haddock you are likely to find anywhere.

GAME

The hills and moors provide a variety of game. The best known are the superb **red grouse** and **venison**. Venison in particular is low in cholesterol and fat content and an increasingly popular dish.

MEAT

With such first class beef cattle as the angus from Aberdeen and Galloway in addition to home-bred sheep, it is hardly surprising that the quality of Scotch **beef** and **mutton** is unsurpassed. Perhaps surprisingly, **water buffalo** produce a very healthy meat low in cholesterol and high in mineral content with less than half the total fat content of conventional lean beef, and can be found at a few farmers' markets and in restaurants. A herd of buffalo are raised in Deerness, Orkney. New breeds of **lamb, wild boar** and even **mutton** are appearing as a result of Scottish

the Tay, Spey or Tweed. Served fresh or smoked, it is a luxury dish. Try the flaky smoked salmon; it's quite a change, and available widely, even in supermarkets. **Trout** and **salmon-trout** with their delicately pink flesh are equally appreciated. Breakfast menus often feature the **Arbroath Smokie** – a small salted and smoked haddock; the **Finnan Haddie**, a salted haddock dried on the beach prior to smoking over a peat fire; and the **kipper**, a split, salted and smoked herring. The **Caledonian Oyster Company** near Oban (*www.caledonianoyster.co.uk*) has been producing **oysters** for years and can offer them in any quantity from half

Smoked salmon, Inverawe Smokehouse, Taynuilt near Oban

© David Lyons/age fotostock

Taste of Scotland

Taste of Scotland is a website (*www.taste-of-scotland.com*) devoted to selected restaurants, tearooms and other eating places which offer "a true taste of Scotland'" via their menus. It also includes information on Scottish food producers and Scottish farmers' markets.

restaurants demanding new, improved flavours.

Not just in Scotland, but around the world the term Scottish Lamb and Aberdeen Angus are synonymous with the best of meats.

Haggis is the national dish, traditionally served with "neeps and tatties" – swede or yellow turnip and potatoes, boiled and mashed separately.

Black pudding is a type of blood sausage widely eaten throughout Britain and made from pork fat or suet, pork blood and oatmeal. It is often grilled, fried, baked or boiled in its skin, and is a good source of protein, low in carbohydrate and high in zinc and iron. It is not recommended for anyone with cholesterol issues, however, but has been regarded in recent times as the new 'superfood'.

The black pudding produced in Stornoway on the Isle of Lewis is commonly regarded as the best in the UK and enjoys Protected Geographical Indicator of Origin (PGI) status.

DESSERTS AND SWEET THINGS

Succulent **soft fruits** (strawberries, raspberries and blackcurrants) ripened slowly make an excellent sweet. Keep an eye open for the more unusual such as tayberries, brambles and blueberries. Other cream sweets like **Cranachan** often incorporate one of the soft fruits. **Atholl Brose** is a mixture of honey, oatmeal, malt whisky and cream.

Up and down the country you can bring back memories of childhood with toffees, fudges, tablet (a medium-hard, sugary confection), macaroons, Edinburgh rock, butterscotch and puff candy.

CHEESE

Scotland is home to several very high-quality home-made cheeses. Cheese making continues to grow in popularity. The result is wonderful artisan cheese that rivals the best in the world. A fine example of this continuing fascination is the Strathearn Cheese Company at Comrie in Perthshire (*www.strathearncheese. co.uk*). Created in 2016 and operating from an old WWII prisoner of war camp, the company produces new cheeses flavoured with whisky, or wild garlic and truffle-infused rapeseed oil.

Both the **Dunlop** cheese from Orkney, Arran and Islay and the **Scottish Cheddar** are hard cheeses. **Caboc** is a rich double cream cheese rolled in oatmeal, while **Crowdie** is similar to a cottage cheese. And among the splendid artisan cheeses that visitors might seek out are Dunsyre Blue, Lanark Blue, Lanark White, Biggar Blue, Maisie's Kebuck and Cora Linn. **Caithness cheese** is widely available and includes smoked, chive, mustard, black pepper, garlic, chili, horse raddish, apricot and mature.

PRESERVES

Heather honey, and Scottish-made jams and marmalades are not only perfect at breakfast-time but also make ideal presents. Try to find Scottish chilli jelly as a way of heating up your breakfast.

WHISKY, THE WATER OF LIFE

Scotland's national drink, whisky – in Gaelic, *uisge beatha* (pronounced "ooshke bah"), meaning water of life – is thought to have begun centuries ago as a way of using up rain-soaked barley after a wet harvest. Whatever its origins, the highly competitive whisky industry is nowadays Scotland's biggest export and one of the government's main sources of revenue.

It is often asked, what makes a good whisky. The answer is that the quality depends essentially on a combination of factors, including barley (not always home grown); the water, filtered through peat or over granite; the equipment, and of course the experience and skill of the stillmen.

The Making of Whisky

A Troubled Past

Undoubtedly among the earliest distillers of whisky, the Scots have played a major part in the perfection of this art. In the 15C monks were distilling a spirit and soon after it became an everyday domestic occupation. The Union of 1707 brought exorbitant taxation, including the 1713 malt tax. Distilling went underground and smuggling became a way of life. From the illicit stills on the hillsides, the spirit was transported along a smugglers' trail from Speyside to Perth over 140mi/225km of hill country. Excisemen became the scourge of the Highlands. A succession of new laws in the early 19C did nothing to halt illicit distilling until the 1824 Act. The latter sanctioned distillation on payment of a licence fee and duty per gallon produced. Many famous distilleries were founded after this date. Whisky production developed rapidly in the 1880s as the replacement spirit for gin and brandy. Blending produced a more palatable drink which rapidly achieved universal success. Although blended whiskies still dominate the market, the subtler and finer qualities of a single malt are gaining recognition.

Malt Whisky

The original spirit was a malt or straight unblended product of a single malt whisky. There are around 116 single malts, classified into Highland, Lowland or Islay.

The subtle flavours of pure malt whisky distilled according to age-old methods are greatly prized by connoisseurs throughout the world. The distilleries on Speyside (Cardhu, Glenfarclas, Strathisla, Glen Grant, Glenfiddich, Tamnavulin, the Glenlivet and Dallas Dhu) enjoy a prestigious reputation and many welcome visitors to see the process and sample a wee dram.

Islay in the Hebrides produces distinctive smoky, peaty malts such as Laphroaig, Bowmore, Bunnahabhain.

There are also many lesser-known malt whisky distilleries close to Edinburgh and Glasgow and all over the Highland region which welcome visitors. The Scotch Whisky Heritage Centre in Edinburgh (*see EDINBURGH*) also provides a comprehensive introduction to the celebrated drink.

Blended Whisky

Grain whisky is made from a malted barley and other cereals. The blends are a mixture of a lighter grain with a malt. Blended varieties are subdivided into two categories: deluxe and standard.

Oak barrels, Glenfiddich Distillery, Dufftown

© Don Fuchs/age fotostock

Whisky Making

Scotch whisky is made from only three ingredients: malted barley, water and yeast. The processes have been refined down through the centuries but apart from the scale and complexity of the hardware, in essence they have remained the same for much of this time.

Malting

Best-quality barley is first steeped in water and then spread out on malting floors to germinate. It is turned regularly to prevent the build-up of heat. Traditionally, this was done by tossing the barley into the air with wooden shovels in a malt barn adjacent to the kiln.

During this process enzymes are activated which convert the starch into sugar when mashing takes place. After 6 to 7 days of germination the barley, goes to the kiln for drying. This halts the germination. Peat may be added to the fire to impart flavour from the smoke.

Mashing

The dried malt is ground into a coarse flour or grist, which is mixed with hot water in the mash tun. The quality of the pure Scottish water is important. The mash is stirred, helping to convert the starches to sugar. After mashing, the sweet sugary liquid is known as wort.

Fermentation

The wort is cooled and pumped into washbacks, where yeast is added and fermentation begins. After about two days the fermentation dies down and the wash contains 6–8 percent alcohol by volume.

Pot Stills

In some mysterious way the shape of the pot still affects the character of the individual malt whisky, and each distillery keeps its stills exactly the same over the years. The still is heated to just below the boiling point of water and the alcohol and other compounds vaporise and pass over the neck of the still into either a condenser or a worm – a large copper coil immersed in cold running water where the vapour is condensed into a liquid.

Distillation

The wash is distilled twice – first in the wash still, to separate the alcohol from the water, yeast and residue. The distillate from the wash still then goes to the spirit still for the second distillation. The more volatile compounds which distil off first, are channelled off to be redistilled. Only the pure heart of the run, which is about 68 percent alcohol by volume, is collected in the spirit receiver.

Spirit Safe

All the distillates pass through the spirit safe – whose locks were traditionally controlled by the Customs & Excise. The stillman uses all his years of experience to test and judge the various distillates without being able to come into physical contact with the spirit.

The origins of the spirit safe date from an 1823 change in duty laws which permitted small Highland distilleries to compete fairly with the much larger Lowland establishments. One of the main ways to rigorously enforce the laws was by requiring the use of the spirit safe, which prevented anyone siphoning off (to avoid paying duty on) the spirit.

The newly distilled, colourless, fiery spirit reduced to maturing strength, 63 percent alcohol by volume, is filled into oak casks which may have previously contained Scotch whisky, bourbon or sherry, and the maturation process begins.

Maturation

By law all Scotch whisky must be matured for at least three years, but most single malts lie in the wood for eight, ten, twelve, fifteen years or longer. Customs & Excise allow for a maximum of 2 percent of the whisky to evaporate from the cask each year – the Angels' Share. Unlike wine, whisky does not mature further once it is in the bottle.

Grain Whisky and Blending

Scotch grain whisky is usually made from 10–20 percent malted barley and then other unmalted cereals such as maize or wheat. The starch in the non-malted cereals is released by pre-cooking and converted into fermentable sugars. The mashing and fermentation processes are similar to those used for malt whisky.

While the distinctive single malts produced by individual distilleries are becoming increasingly popular, blending creates over 90 percent of the Scotch whisky enjoyed throughout the world.

Checking the levels in the spirit safe, Laphroaig Distillery, Isle of Islay

© David Lyons/age fotostock

By nosing samples in tulip-shaped glasses the blender selects from a wide palate – from the numerous Highland and Speyside malts to the strongly flavoured and peaty island malts, and the softer and lighter Lowland malts.

These malts are combined with grain whiskies – usually 60–80 percent grain whiskies to 20–40 percent malt whiskies, and are then left to "marry" in casks before being bottled as one of the world-renowned blended whiskies. A blend of a range of malt whiskies, with no grain whisky included, is known as a vatted malt.

To learn more about whisky in Scotland, visit the official website at www.scotland-whisky.org.uk. This gives details of places to visit, whisky festivals, tours, tasting guides and links to a whole host of other whisky-related websites.

History

TIMELINE

PREHISTORIC PERIOD: EARLY MIGRATIONS

4000–
2500 BCE Neolithic settlers arrive by the Atlantic route
2000 BCE Bronze Age
1000 BCE Agriculturalists arrive from the continent
800 BCE–400 CE Iron Age peoples from central Europe

THE ROMANS 1C–4C CE

The Roman conquest of **Caledonia** was never fully accomplished although there were two main periods of occupation. The initial one (c.80–c.100), which started with Julius Agricola's push northwards, is notable for the victory at **Mons Graupius**. The second period followed the death in 138 of the Emperor Hadrian (builder of the wall in the 120s). His successor Antoninus Pius advanced the frontier to its earlier limits but by the mid-160s the **Antonine Wall** was definitively abandoned.

55, 54 BCE Caesar invades Britain; conquest begins AD 43
71–84 Romans push north into **Caledonia**; Agricola establishes a line of forts between the Clyde and Forth
84 **Mons Graupius:** Agricola defeats the Caledonian tribes
142–c.145 Building of turf rampart, the **Antonine Wall** (39mi/63km long)
End 4C Roman power wanes

DARK AGES 4C–11C

The Barbarian invasions of Britain forced the Britons to take refuge in the barren mountains and moorlands of Cornwall, Wales, and even beyond Hadrian's Wall in southwest Scotland.

It was at Whithorn, in the native kingdom of **Strathclyde** with its main fortress at Dumbarton (*see GLASGOW: Driving Tour*), that the Romano-Briton St Ninian established the first Christian community in the late 4C. Over the next centuries, Christianity gained a firm foothold.

The early Scottish nation owed much to its western territories. The royal line descended from the Dalriadic royal house with the accession of Kenneth MacAlpine as king of Alba. Scottish kings had their ancient burial place, **Reilig Odhrian**, on Iona and the nation took its name from the western kingdom of the Scots.

In the 8C and 9C, the first Norse raiders arrived by sea. These were followed by peaceful settlers in search of new lands who occupied the Western Isles. Gradually the isles became independent territories over which the Dalriadic kings had no power. The kingdoms of the Picts and Scots merged, under the Scot Kenneth MacAlpine, to form **Alba**, the territory north of the Forth and Clyde which later became known as **Scotia**, while the western fringes remained under Norse sway. Territorial conflicts with the English and the Norsemen marked the next two centuries.

397 **St Ninian** establishes a Christian mission at **Whithorn**
563 **St Columba** and his companions land on **Iona**. The Celtic Church evolves in isolation until the **Synod of Whitby** (663/4) when certain Celtic usages were abandoned to conform with the practices of Rome
8C Beginning of Norse raids. The Western Isles remain under Norse domination until 1266, the Orkney and Shetland Islands until 1468–69
843 **Kenneth MacAlpine** obtains the Pictish throne unifying the Picts and the Scots

MEDIEVAL SCOTLAND

Under the influence of Queen Margaret, a pious English princess, and during the reigns of her sons, in particular Edgar,

Alexander I and David I, the Celtic kingdom took on a feudal character as towns grew and royal charters were granted. Monastic life flourished as religious communities from France set up sister houses throughout Scotland.

In 1098, King **Edgar**, the son of Malcolm III (Canmore), ceded to **Magnus Barefoot**, King of Norway (1093–1103), "...all the islands around which a boat could sail". Magnus included Kintyre having had his galley dragged across the isthmus. On the death of Magnus the native ruler of Argyll, **Somerled** (d.1164), seized power and assumed the kingship of the Isles and briefly of the Isle of Man, under the tutelage of Norway. Somerled died in 1164 fighting the Scots. Alexander II (1214–49) set out on a campaign to curb Norse rule but he died on Kerrera. It was his son **Alexander III** (1249–86) who, following the **Battle of Largs** against King Haakon IV, negotiated the Treaty of Perth in 1266 returning the Western Isles to Scotland.

Relations with England remained tense. In the 12C, after his defeat and capture at Alnwick, **William I the Lion** paid homage to Richard I the Lionheart. Northumbria remained a contentious issue until 1236 when Alexander II renounced his claim. The country enjoyed a degree of stability during the reign of Alexander III before plunging into centuries of conflict over rival claims to the throne and attempts to gain its independence.

1034	**Strathclyde** becomes part of the Scottish Kingdom
1058–93	**Malcolm III**; his second queen, **Margaret**, introduces the Catholic Church
1124–53	**David I**, last of the Margaretsons, reorganises the church, settles monastic orders and creates royal burghs, all of which increase the monarchy's prestige
1249–86	**Alexander III**, the last Canmore king; brief period of peace and prosperity
1263	**Battle of Largs**
1290	**Margaret**, the Maid of Norway, dies

WARS OF INDEPENDENCE

On the death in 1290 of the Maid of Norway, the direct heir to the throne, Edward I was instrumental in choosing from among the various **Competitors** the ultimate successor. In 1292 John Balliol became king and the vassal of Edward. Following Balliol's 1295 treaty with the French, Edward set out for the north on the first of several pacification campaigns. Strongholds fell one by one and thus started a long period of intermittent warfare.

The years of struggle for independence from English overlordship helped to forge a national identity. Heroes were born. The unknown knight **William Wallace** (1270–1305) rallied the resistance in the early stages achieving victory at Stirling Bridge (1297). He assumed the Guardianship in the name of Balliol. Wallace was captured in 1305 and taken to London where he was executed. The next to rally the opposition was **Robert the Bruce** (1274–1329), grandson of one of the original Competitors and therefore with a legitimate claim to the throne. Following the killing of **John Comyn**, who was the son of another Competitor and the representative of the Balliol line, Bruce had himself crowned at Scone (1306). Slowly Bruce

Statue of Robert the Bruce, Stirling Castle

© Rachelle Burnside /Dreamstime.com

forced the submission of the varying fiefs and even achieved the allegiance of Angus Og, natural son of the 4th Lord of the Isles. The victory at **Bannockburn** (1314) was crucial in achieving independence but formal recognition only came eight years after the **Declaration of Arbroath** (1320) with the **Treaty of Northampton**.

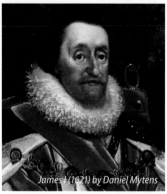
James I (1621) by Daniel Mytens
© Imagestate/Tips Images

1296	Edward I's choice, **John Balliol**, abdicates during the first of the Hammer of the Scots' punitive conquering campaigns in Scotland 1296, 1298, 1303 and 1307
1297	Wallace wins the **Battle of Stirling Bridge**; Falkirk, the following year, is a defeat
1306–29	Robert the Bruce kills the Comyn, is crowned at Scone, then starts the long campaign to free Scotland
1314	Battle of **Bannockburn**
1320	**Declaration of Arbroath**; the Treaty of Northampton (1328) recognises Scotland's Independence

THE STEWARTS (LATER STUARTS)

Following independence, royal authority was undermined by feuds and intrigue as bloody power struggles broke out among the clan chiefs; but the monarchy prevailed. The powerful Albany and Douglas clans were subdued in the 15C. The Scots supported France in its rivalry with England and as a result alliances were forged.

1406–37	**James I**; James takes the reins of power in 1424 after 18 years in English captivity
1410	Teaching begins at St Andrews University, officially founded 1412; confirmation by Papal Bull 1413
1437–60	Accession of **James II** following the assassination of his father at Perth
1440	**Black Dinner** at Edinburgh Castle
1451	Founding of Glasgow University
1455	Fall of the Black Douglases
1460–88	Accession of **James III** following the death of James II at the siege of Roxburgh Castle
1468–69	Orkney and Shetland pass to Scotland as the dowry of Margaret of Denmark
1488–1513	Accession of **James IV** following his father's death after Sauchieburn
1493	Forfeiture of the Lordship of the Isles
1495	Founding of Aberdeen's first university (King's College); Marischal founded 1593
1513–42	Death of **James IV** at the **Battle of Flodden**; accession of **James V**

In the 16C, to punish the Scots for refusing an alliance between the young Mary and Henry VIII's son, English troops, led by the Marquess of Hertford, invaded repeatedly and inflicted a harsh treatment on the country. The growing French influence at court was resented by the nobility and the Reformation gained ground. The regent Mary of Guise was deposed by Protestant leaders fired by John Knox's sermons; monastic houses were destroyed and Catholicism was banned. During her short tragic reign (1561–67) when conspiracies and violence were rife, the young queen advocated religious tolerance but murderous intrigues (&see

EDINBURGH: Hollyroodhouse), probably with Mary's tacit approval, caused great scandal. Rebellion broke out after her marriage to Bothwell, who was suspected of involvement in the murder of Darnley. Her flight to England, after her abdication in favour of her infant son and her escape from captivity, ended in imprisonment and execution by Elizabeth I to thwart the formation of factions around a rival claimant to the English throne.

1542–67	**Mary**, Queen of Scots
1544–47	**Rough Wooing** or Hertford's invasions
1548	The five-year-old Mary is sent to France for safety and affianced to the French dauphin
1559	Riot at Perth; the Lords of the Congregation set out from Perth on their campaign
1560	**Reformation**; death of Mary's French husband, François II
1561	Mary returns to Scotland as an 18-year-old widow; four years later she marries her cousin, Henry Stewart, Lord Darnley
1567	Murder of Darnley; Bothwell becomes Mary's third husband; she abdicates, and flees to England after the Battle of Langside (1568); executed after 19 years in captivity (1587)

THE STUARTS AND THE COMMONWEALTH

In the largely Protestant Scotland of the 17C James VI attempted to achieve a situation similar to that in England by re-establishing episcopacy. This implied royal control of the church through the bishops appointed by the Crown. His son Charles I aroused strong Presbyterian opposition with the forced introduction of the *Scottish Prayer Book*. By February of 1638 the **National Covenant** or Solemn Agreement was drawn up, which pledged the signatories to defend the Crown and true religion.

In 1643 the **Solemn League and Covenant** united the Covenanters and English parliamentary cause against Charles I. Many like the Marquess of Montrose were torn between their loyalty to the King and Covenant. In 1644 Montrose pledged to win back Scotland for the King. At the end of a year of campaigning with a largely Highland army he was master of Scotland. Defeat came at the **Battle of Philiphaugh** (1645) and Montrose was forced into exile. In England the struggle led to the execution of Charles I (1649).

The Covenanters were quick to offer Charles II the throne on his acceptance of the Covenant. Montrose was captured and executed. Cromwell marched north defeating the Covenanters' army at **Dunbar** (1650) and Scotland became an occupied country (1651–60) and part of the Commonwealth.

On the **Restoration** of Charles II, made possible by Monck's march on the capital, the king rejected his promise and restored episcopacy (1661).

The 1st Duke of Lauderdale ruled Scotland and the Covenanters suffered severe persecution. The years around 1685 were known as the Killing Times with Lord Advocate, Sir George ("Bluidy") Mackenzie responsible for much of the persecution.

The death of Charles II and the prospect of a new line of openly Catholic monarchs, with the accession of his brother James VII, inspired the ill-fated **Monmouth Rebellion** led by Charles II's natural son. The two landings, one in western Scotland under the 9th Earl of Argyll and the second in western England under Monmouth, both failed.

The Protestant Mary and William were invited to rule (1689). Viscount Dundee rallied the Jacobites or those faithful to King James VII who had already fled the country.

The initial victory at Killiecrankie (1689) cost the life of the Jacobite leader and the Highland army was later crushed at Dunkeld. The Act of Union guaranteed the maintenance of the Scottish legal system and church.

The Auld Alliance

The longstanding friendship between Scotland and France is known as the Auld Alliance. Its 700th anniversary was celebrated in 1995.

In the 12C, David I (1124–53) developed close ties with Normandy: many Normans settled in Scotland and the king himself owned land in the Cotentin. At his behest monastic houses were set up by French religious orders: Selkirk, Kelso, Arbroath. He also founded great Cistercian abbeys at Melrose, Dundrennan and Kinloss.

In 1295, Robert the Bruce signed the first treaty between Scotland and France as part of his fight to gain independence from England.

In the 15C, Scottish troops fought alongside the French army at the Battle of Vieux Baugé (1421) to drive the English from Angers.

During the 16C, France's reputation as a seat of learning attracted many Scots. In 1512 James IV signed a second treaty with France. James V married two French princesses successively. His second wife, Mary of Guise, gave birth to a daughter, Mary. In 1548 at the tender age of five Mary Stuart was sent to France where she lived at St-Germain-en-Laye until she reached the age of 16. In 1558 she married the dauphin François II and became Queen of France. A year after her husband's death (1560) she returned to Scotland at the age of 18 to live out her tragic destiny.

During the 17C, the Royal Scots Regiment was part of Louis XIII's royal guard; three centuries later they fought at the Battle of the Marne (1914). From 1688 to 1692 numerous supporters of James II (James VII of Scotland) went into exile in France. Further emigration occurred until the first half of the 18C especially after the Jacobite risings of 1715 and 1745.

1567–1625	**James VI** of Scotland reigns as **James I** of England
1582	Raid of Ruthven
1600	Gowrie Conspiracy
1603	**Union of the Crowns** with the accession of James VI to the throne of England
1625–49	**Charles I**; Scottish coronation ceremony in Edinburgh (1633)
1638	**National Covenant**; Glasgow General Assembly abolishes Episcopacy
1643	The **Solemn League and Covenant**
1645	Montrose loses the Battle of Philiphaugh
1650	Execution of Montrose following that of Charles I the previous year
1651	Cromwellian occupation, the **Commonwealth**
1660	General Monck and his regiment set out from Coldstream on 1 January
	1660 on the long march south to London which leads to the Restoration
1660–85	**Charles II**
1685–58	Accession of **James VII (James II of England)**: Monmouth Rebellion 1685
1688	James VII flees the country in late December
1689	William and Mary are offered the crown; **Battle of Killiecrankie**
1692	Massacre of **Glencoe**
1702–14	**Queen Anne**
1707	**Union of the Parliaments**

HOUSE OF HANOVER

The Jacobite uprisings of 1715 and 1745 aiming to restore the Stuarts to their throne reflected in some measure the discontent of post-Union (1707) Scotland. The rising ended at the indecisive Battle of **Sheriffmuir**. James VIII or the **Old Pretender** (1688–1766) not only arrived too late but also lacked the power to inspire his followers. His depar-

Crofting

Crofts are small agricultural holdings worked by tenant farmers. Crofting is a unique form of land tenure which became popular, especially on remote islands, in the 19C after the Highland Clearances. The Crofters Act of 1886 gave tenants security of tenure and other valuable rights. The 1976 Act allowed crofters to buy the land but they also lost many rights including grazing their herds on common land. The solution was to form a trust to buy the crofts and to rent the crofts back from the trust. Crofting is a hard life but holdings are in great demand as more and more people dream of escaping from large cities and living off the land.

ture by boat from Montrose was furtive and final. Following this, General George Wade set out to pacify the Highlands with a programme of road and bridge building to facilitate military access.

A generation later, the 1745 rising was led by **Charles Edward Stuart** or **Bonnie Prince Charlie** (1720–88) born five years after the first rising. After landing near Arisaig, the 24-year-old prince raised his standard at Glenfinnan and with an essentially Highland army won an initial victory at Prestonpans where he routed the government troops under Sir John Cope. At Derby his military advisers counselled retreat, which ended in the defeat of **Culloden** (1746). For five months the prince wandered the Highlands and Hebrides as a hunted fugitive with a £30 000 bounty on his head. Shortly after this, **Flora MacDonald** assisted him in escaping from the Outer Hebrides. The prince embarked for lifelong exile.

The aftermath rather than the failure of the '45 was tragic for the Highlands: Highlanders were disarmed, their national dress proscribed and chieftains deprived of their rights of heritable justice. Economic and social change was accelerated.

Eviction and loss of the traditional way of life ensued; this period became known as the **Highland Clearances**. Mass emigration followed for the many who faced abject poverty. A small number became crofters with no security of tenure. This uncertainty was later alleviated by the **Crofters Act**. The clearances were complete by 1860.

George IV's visit organised by **Sir Walter Scott** in 1822 made Highland dress and other accoutrements (bagpipes, arms) acceptable again. By making Balmoral Castle a favoured residence, Queen Victoria and Prince Albert later gave the royal seal of approval to the Highlands.

1714–27	Accession of **George I**
1715	**Jacobite Rising**, **Battle of Sheriffmuir**
1719	Jacobite Rising in Glen Shiel
1727–60	**George II**
1745	Jacobite Rising; The Year of the Prince opens with the raising of the standard at Glenfinnan
1746	**Battle of Culloden**
1747–82	**Proscription Act**
1760–1820	**George III**
1790	Opening of Forth Clyde Canal
1803–22	Building of the Caledonian Canal
1822	George IV State Visit
1843	The Disruption: founding of the Free Church
1871–78	Tay Railway Bridge; disaster the following year
1883–90	Forth Railway Bridge
1886	**Crofters Act**
1906–13	Home Rule Bills
1928	National Party of Scotland formed; SNP founded in 1934
1951	Stolen **Stone of Destiny** found in Arbroath
1964	Opening of the Forth Road Bridge; Tay Bridge opens two years later
1964–1970s	Discovery and development of major oil and natural gas fields in the North Sea with the subsequent growth of the North Sea oil industry.

1974–75	Reorganisation of local government; the old counties and burghs replaced by nine regions and island areas.
1979	Referendum on proposed Assembly failed to produce the necessary 40 percent.
1990	Glasgow nominated Cultural Capital of Europe.
1995	700th anniversary of the **Auld Alliance** between Scotland and France. Further reorganisation of local government – election of 29 unitary councils and three islands councils.
1996	After 700 years the **Stone of Destiny** is returned to Scotland, not to its original site, Scone Palace, but to Edinburgh Castle *(see p. 294)*.
1997	Second referendum approves the motion for a devolved tax-raising assembly.
1999	Opening of **Scottish Parliament** in a temporary home in the Church of Scotland Assembly Hall.
2005	**Scottish Parliament** transferred to Holyrood.
2008	Pro-independence **Scottish Nationalist Party (SNP)** elected to the Scottish Government, with Alex Salmond as First Minister.
2011	SNP win majority in parliament, a remarkable feat since Scottish voting system was designed to prevent single party governments.
2014	A referendum on independence from the UK ends with the 'No' side winning. Alex Salmond resigns as SNP leader. Nicola Sturgeon is elected.
2015	The SNP wins 56 of the 59 seats in the UK Parliament.
2016	A referendum is held asking if the UK should leave or remain in the EU. 52% voted to leave. As of this writing a withdrawal agreement has not been reached.
2017	The SNP lose seats in a snap election in which Alex Salmond is also defeated.

Famous Scottish Names

Mungo Park (1771–1806), explored West Africa; **David Livingstone** (1813–73), the first European to cross Africa from east to west; **Sir John Ross** (1777–1856), Arctic explorer; **John McDouall Stuart** (1815–66), explored Australian desert; **Alexander Mackenzie** (1764–1820), first European to cross North American by land (1783). **James McGill** (1774–1813), founded McGill University; **John Paul Jones** (1747–92), admiral in the American Navy; **John Muir** (1838–1914), founded the American National Parks; **Andrew Carnegie** (1835–1919), philanthropist and steel magnate; **John Hunter** (1728–93) and **William Hunter** (1718–83), leaders in anatomy and obstetrics. **Sir Joseph Lister** (1827–1912), pioneer of antiseptics; **William Thomson, Lord Kelvin** (1824–1907), formulated the second law of thermodynamics; **James Hutton** (1726–97) wrote *A Theory of the Earth* (1785) which formed the basis of modern geology; **Thomas Telford** (1757–1834) and **John Rennie** (1761–1821) built bridges, roads, canals, docks and harbours. **Robert Napier** (1791–1876) built the first Cunard steamships and ironclad battleships. Great inventions and discoveries: **John Napier of Merchiston** (1560–1617) – logarithms; **Sir James Simpson** (1811–1870) – chloroform as an anaesthetic; **James Watt** (1736–1819) – the steam engine; **Alexander Graham Bell** (1847–1922) – the telephone; **John Logie Baird** (1888–1946) – television; **Sir Robert Watson-Watt** (1892–1973) – radar; **Alexander Fleming** (1881–1955) – penicillin. Scientists at the **Roslin Research Institute** made history with the cloning of Dolly the Sheep in 1996.

Architecture

Shaped by Celtic beginnings, the early influence of invading Norsemen and the recurrent colonisation – peaceful or otherwise – by the English, the nation's culture has developed into a fascinating hybrid that is impossible to pin down. Rugged and romantic, traditional and modern, it is always evolving, yet manages to remain true to its roots.

ECCLESIASTICAL

CELTIC FOUNDATIONS

Mainland Scotland retains two of the earliest buildings erected by the Celtic clergy, the round towers of Brechin and Abernethy. Dating from the late 10C to early 11C these refuges or belfries are outliers of an Irish tradition. Although tangible remains are few, the Christian faith was an important unifying factor in Dark Age Scotland.

ANGLO-NORMAN PERIOD

Scotland of the mid-11C with its Celtic and Norse influences was soon to undergo a new and gradual Anglo-Norman colonisation. It was the west and north, the strongholds of the old cultures, that resisted the new imprint.

The 11C and 12C were a time of church reorganisation and all building efforts were concentrated on ecclesiastical works. **Queen Margaret** and her sons were the principal promoters. David I's church at Dunfermline has in the nave (12C) one of the most outstanding examples of Norman art. The parish churches of **Leuchars** and **Dalmeny** are equally well-preserved examples of this period.

GOTHIC TRADITION

Early monastic foundations included Arbroath, Dryburgh, Dundrennan, Holyrood and Jedburgh. Outstanding 13C Gothic buildings include Elgin, Dunblane and Glasgow cathedrals where the lancet window, pointed arch and vaulting are triumphant. War and strife brought building to a standstill and wreaked much havoc on existing buildings. Melrose Abbey, rebuilt in the 14C, is in the pure Gothic tradition. Prosperity returned to the burghs in the 15C and the great burghal churches were an expression of renewed wealth and civic pride (Holy Rude, Stirling; St John's, Perth; St Nicholas, Aberdeen and St Mary's, Haddington). The period also saw the flourishing of collegiate churches built by the baronial class (Dunglass, Seton, Tullibardine, Crich-

12C nave, Dunfermline Abbey Church

© Arturo Cano Miño/age fotostock

Plasterwork Ceilings

In England the Elizabethan period introduced plasterwork ceilings with their ornate strapwork. In Scotland the early 17C saw the introduction of ornate plaster ceilings as at Craigievar (1625), Glamis (1621), Muchalls (1624) and The Binns (1630). The ceilings were often accompanied by magnificent heraldic achievements (Craigievar and Muchalls) or elaborate fireplaces (Glamis).

This art evolved and was adapted by Sir William Bruce for the Classical interiors of Holyroodhouse and Thirlestane. The series at the latter include the magnificent Lauderdale eagles. All this is only a step away from the delicately detailed Neoclassical designs of Robert Adam (Mellerstain, Culzean and Hopetoun House).

ton and Dalkeith). The style was truly Scottish, with a martial influence where buttresses were stepped, towers crenellated, and roofs stone-slabbed. Some of the loveliest churches date from this last Gothic phase, such as Tullibardine and Kirk o'Steil.

The Late Gothic King's College Chapel in Old Aberdeen still has a splendid crown spire (&see ABERDEEN) as does St Giles', in Edinburgh.

SECULAR
CASTLES

The earliest predecessors of the Scottish castle were the enigmatic stone-built brochs of the 1C AD. An outstanding example is at Mousa in Shetland.

The feudalisation of Scotland was marked by the introduction of the Norman motte and bailey castles. Several imposing earthen mounds or mottes remain at Duffus, Inverurie and Invernochty. The earliest stone-built castles had a stone curtain wall, as a replacement for the wooden palisade, as seen at Rothesay, Sween and Dunstaffnage.

MEDIEVAL PERIOD

During the Wars of Independence **Edward I** altered a few strongholds including Kildrummy, giving it a Harlech-type gatehouse. From then on the gatehouse replaced the keep as the place of strength.

In 14C Scotland weak kings and a disunited kingdom encouraged turbulent and ambitious feudal lords to build fortresses. Early examples include Drum,

Threave, Castle Campbell and Craigmillar. The tradition continued with Cardoness and Newark.

The impact of the European Renaissance was limited to the royal works at Stirling, Falkland and Linlithgow.

POST-REFORMATION INNOVATION

The tower house reached its apotheosis in the late 16C and early 17C in the Grampian area, where a local school of architecture flourished. These **baronial** masterpieces – Craigievar, Crathes, Fyvie and Castle Fraser – all show a skilful handling of traditional features and a concentration on the skyline.

The 17C saw the infiltration of foreign influences as at Crichton with its Italianate façade, Edzell with its pleasance, at Huntly Castle, the Earl's Palace in Kirkwall and the inner courtyard façade of Caerlaverock.

The Restoration brought a new series of royal works, designed by the Architect Royal **Sir William Bruce** (c.1630–1710). Bruce excelled in the Classical style, which he used for the courtyard at Holyroodhouse Palace (1671), Hopetoun House and his own home, Kinross House. Bruce enlarged and remodelled the main front of the Duke of Lauderdale's principal Scottish seat, Thirlestane Castle. Bruce's successor as surveyor to the king in Scotland in 1683 was **James Smith** (c.1644–1731). Smith refitted the Chapel Royal and converted the old palace at Hamilton and the castle at Dalkeith.

GEORGIAN ELEGANCE

Apart from Smith the main exponent of this style in the early 18C was **William Adam** (d.1748), father of a family of famous architects. "Old Stone and Lime" dominated the period between the two Jacobite Risings. His better-known works are Hopetoun House, the House of Dun, Haddo House and Duff House. Of the sons **Robert Adam** (1728–1792) was the most famous and creator of the Adam style. With his brothers, he finished Hopetoun after the death of his father.

Following four years of travel in Europe in the entourage of Charles Hope and a period when he worked on a series of London mansions (Osterley, Syon and Kenwood), Adam returned to Scotland. From this period we have Mellerstain, a house of homely proportions with all the refinement of his Neoclassical interiors. Altogether more grandiose are Culzean, Seton and Airthrey castles.

19C

The Romantic movement was accompanied by a revival of medieval styles, as at Scone Palace, Abbotsford and Dalmeny House. David Bryce and Gillespie Graham both revived the baronial style in the Victorian period, notably at Blair and Brodick castles respectively. Balmoral Castle is the best-known example of the Scottish neo-baronial style. These imitations lacked the vigour and sculptural qualities of their 17C predecessors.

Mercat Cross, Aberdeen

20C AND BEYOND

At the close of the 19th century, **Charles Rennie Mackintosh** (1868–1928) revived the Scottish vernacular tradition in his design for the Glasgow School of Art. Mackintosh followed this early design in the Art Nouveau style with Hill House in Helensburgh, a work which even today, more than 100 years later, still seems modern. The Glasgow Herald building has been successfully converted into The Lighthouse, a Centre for Architecture and Design.

Another exponent of the distinctly Scottish style was **Sir Robert Lorimer** with his many restorations (Earlshall and Dunrobin castles) and creations (Thistle Chapel in St Giles', and the National War Memorial in Edinburgh Castle).

Contemporary landmark buildings have won acclaim for imaginative design: the Museum of Scotland, Dynamic Earth, International Conference Centre in Edinburgh, the Armadillo Conference Centre in Glasgow, and the Contemporary Arts Centre in Dundee. In 1999 Glasgow was celebrated as the UK City of Architecture and Design.

The first great Scottish building of the 21C is the Parliament Building at Holyrood. Designed by Spanish architect Enric Miralles (1955–2000) it is also destined to be one of the most controversial for many years to come for being massively over budget.

BURGHS

While several towns (Haddington, Elgin and Old Edinburgh) retain their medieval layouts, relatively few medieval buildings exist, in part due to their timber construction. As a rule the main street linked the castle and church and was the site of the market and tolbooth. Pends and wynds led off to closes with burgess plots extending back to the town wall pierced by gates or ports. The burghs tended to lavish funds on such symbols of civic authority and pride as the tolbooth and mercat cross, with the result that the townscapes of today are still enhanced by some fine examples.

Market Crosses

Known in Scotland as **mercat crosses**, these provided the focal point of the burgh, where goods for sale were presented, proclamations made and public punishment executed. Of the larger platform type an outstanding example is at Aberdeen, where a series of royal portrait medallions adorn the platform. Others are topped by the royal unicorn (Edinburgh, Cockburnspath). There is a rare pre-Reformation cross at Banff.

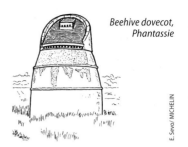

Beehive dovecot, Phantassie

E. Sevo/ MICHELIN

Tolbooth

Originally for collecting taxes, the booths gradually came to embody civic authority and house the council chamber, court and prison. Today they represent one of the most attractive elements of Scottish townscapes. Kelso and Haddington have handsomely elegant buildings reflecting periods of agricultural prosperity.

Tolbooths incorporated a tower (Glasgow, Aberdeen and Stirling) which was often adjoined by a later range of buildings.

Fine examples exist at Linlithgow, Crail, Culross, Dumfries and Old Aberdeen, Kirkcudbright, North Berwick, and the Canongate, Edinburgh. The most renowned of all was Edinburgh's now vanished Heart of Midlothian, as popularised by Scott's novel.

Cylindrical dovecot, Boath

E. Sevo/ MICHELIN

Lectern dovecot, Tealing

E. Sevo/ MICHELIN

Tron

Now a rare feature, the public weigh-beam was once a common sight. Both Culross and the village of Stenton still have examples.

DOVECOTS

Dovecots (doocots in Scotland) are a familiar and attractive sight in rural Scotland and are found in their greatest number in the rich farming areas of the Lothians, Fife, Angus and Moray where grain growing predominated.

Design

Most are stone-built. They vary in type from the fairly common beehive as at Phantassie, Craigmillar, Dirleton and Aberdour castles to the more typically Scottish lectern of Tantallon Castle and Tealing. Others were cylindrical (Lady Kitty's Garden, Haddington).

The majority were freestanding, although nesting boxes were incorporated into towers of certain castles (Hailes, Rothesay and Huntingtower) or even a church belfry (Aberlady, Stenton and Torphichen). 18C and 19C versions were built as part of farm buildings.

Ancient Monuments and Sculpture

Shaped by Celtic beginnings, invading Norsemen, Romans and Anglo-Saxons, Scotland has a rich legacy of ancient monuments and historical sites.

NEOLITHIC AGE (4400 BCE–2000 BCE)

The Orkney islands are particularly rich in sites, the jewel in its crown being **Maes Howe**, which is considered among the finest architectural achievements of prehistoric Europe.

Nearby **Skara Brae** is the best example of a Neolithic settlement where the local stone slabs have been used in every conceivable way. The settlers practised collective burials in chambered tombs, which took the form of either a galleried grave or passage grave.

Other Orkney examples are Unstan Cairn and the Tomb of the Eagles. Mainland sites include the Clava Cairns near Inverness, the Grey Cairns of Camster near Wick and Cairn Holy I and II in the southwest.

BRONZE AGE (2000 BCE–1000 BCE)

The Beaker people were continental agriculturalists who buried their dead in individual cists or graves. They erected the round cairns, stone circles and alignments as at **Callanish**, Ring of Brodgar, Hill o'Many Stanes and Cairnpapple.

IRON AGE (800 BCE–AD 400)

This period left the largest group of monuments. These include the hill forts and settlements (Traprain, Eildon Hill North, White Caterthun and Dunadd), crannogs or lake dwellings, earth houses or souterrains (Rennibister, Tealing) and wheelhouses (Jarlshof). This period is also marked by the enigmatic **brochs**. These tall hollow round towers of drystone masonry – in fact they are some of the most sophisticated examples of drystone architecture ever created – are unique to Scotland. The outstanding example, **Mousa Broch** in Shetland, dates from the 1C–2C.

ROMAN SCOTLAND

The Romans left a considerable heritage. Along the main road to York (Dere Street) were marching camps for Julius Agricola's army, intent on the subjugation of the native tribes. A chain

Skara Brae, Orkney

© Michael S. Nolan/age fotostock

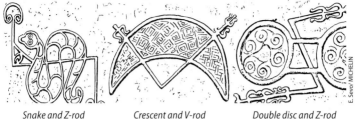

| Snake and Z-rod | Crescent and V-rod | Double disc and Z-rod |

of forts across the Forth–Clyde isthmus was built prior to his retirement to Rome. In the 2C Antoninus Pius built the turf **Antonine Wall** with walkway and ditch, along the Forth–Clyde line. Forts were placed at intervals along the wall. Both were abandoned c. 170. Vestiges of the wall may still be seen, however, around Dumbarton and very close to the present day Falkirk Wheel, an ingenious transportation device of which the Romans would no doubt have heartily approved!

EARLY RELIGIOUS SYMBOLS

The **Latinus Stone** (c.450) at Whithorn and a group of three other 5C–6C tombstones at Kirkmadrine, near Stranrar, are a few of the rare examples of this period when the Britons established the first Christian communities in the southwest.

ANGLO-SAXON INFLUENCE

The monumental **Anglian crosses** with their sculptured figures and patterns of vine scroll are the rich artistic heritage of the Northumbrian Kingdom. The 7C **Ruthwell Cross** near Dumfries is an outstanding example.

THE CELTIC TRADITION

The characteristic monument of the Scots was the **free-standing cross** with ring of glory, spiral patterns and high bosses. St Martin's and St John's Crosses (8C) on the **Isle of Iona** are among the better examples. The Scots brought with them their Celtic ornamental tradition, which they applied to stonecarving, metalwork and manuscript illumination. The tradition was continued to some extent in the art of the Picts and the influence is also clearly seen in the

works of the 14C–16C school of West Highland Sculpture (*see Architecture*).

PICTISH ART

In the Pictish Kingdom of the east and north, a flowering of this native culture produced the **Pictish Symbol Stones**. These incised and carved boulders and stones portray animal symbols (boar, fish, goose, snake and bull as at Burghead), or purely abstract symbols (mirror and comb, double disc and Z-rod, crescent and V-rod, snake and Z-rod). This art died out once the Scots had become rulers of Pictland c.843. **Sueno's Stone** near Forres remains a unique monument closely covered with sculpture of intertwined foliage and beasts and the serried ranks of troops on the shaft.

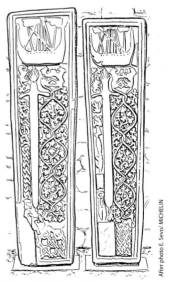

Tomb slabs, Kilmory Knap

61

Painting

Scottish painting is closely linked with the English artistic tradition as many artists worked in London. Some were also great travellers and were influenced by the evolution of artistic movements in Europe. Many artists, however, remained relatively unknown outside Scotland.

PORTRAITURE

In the 17C, the Aberdonian **George Jamesone** (1588–1644) was the leading portrait artist.

The 18C is marked by the portraitist **Allan Ramsay** (1713–1784), responsible for the founding of Edinburgh's first important art academy and painter to George III. His delicate portraits of women are notable. **Henry Raeburn** (1756–1823), George IV's Limner for Scotland, also has a well-deserved reputation as a portrait painter *(The Reverend Robert Walker skating, Sir Walter Scott, Mrs Lumsden, Mrs Liddell)*. These two artists painted the gentry and leading personalities of the period.

NATURAL AND HISTORICAL THEMES

Alexander Nasmyth (1785–1859), Ramsay's assistant, became a successful landscape artist *(Robert Burns, The Windings of the Forth, Distant Views of Stirling)*. The idealised treatment of nature is illustrated in *The Falls of Clyde* by the Neoclassical master Jacob More. **Gavin Hamilton** (1723–1798) painted vast historical compositions (illustrations of Homer's *Illiad*, *The Abdication of Mary, Queen of Scots*) and became very successful in Rome. In the 19C Walter Scott's novels brought about renewed interest in Scottish landscape: *Glencoe, Loch Katrine, Inverlochy Castle* by **Horatio McCullough** (1805–1867), who is famous for his Highland scenes. **David Wilkie**'s (1785–1841) artistry is evident in his realistic popular scenes *(Pitlessie Fair, Distraining for Rent)* and portraits *(George IV)*, which show Raeburn's influence. *The Gentle Shepherd* illustrates Ramsay's pastoral poem.

The Faed brothers (late 19C–early 20C), who were members of an artists' colony in Galloway, specialised in detailed genre scenes. The romantic landscapes and religious works of **William Dyce** (1806–1864) heralded the Pre-Raphaelites who influenced Noel Paton (1821–1901). Nature is depicted in great detail in the latter's fairy scenes *(Oberon and Titania)* and other paintings full of symbolism. The portraitist John "Spanish" Phillip (1817–1867) is better known for his exotic paintings.

In the Victorian era Highland scenery gained great popularity through the English artist **Edwin Landseer** (1802–1873), the official Animal Painter for Scotland, who is famous for his romantic depictions (stags at bay and other Highland scenes). Another Englishman **John Everett Millais** (1829–1896), who spent many years near Perth, painted romantic landscapes.

INNOVATION

The founding of the Scottish Academy in 1836 brought about a flowering of native talent. In reaction against Victorian conventions, **William McTaggart** (1835–1910) developed a highly individual style – bold brushwork, light effects, rich colours – evident in his dramatic seascapes *(The Storm, Dawn at Sea, The Fishers' Landing)* and landscapes *(Corn in the Ear, Spring, Rosslyn Castle: Autumn)*. In the second half of the 19C artistic activity in Glasgow was given a boost by rich art collectors and dealers. The works of the **Glasgow School** (James Guthrie, E A Walton, George Henry, E A Hornel, Joseph Crawhall, John Lavery among others under the leadership of W Y Macgregor) reveal the influence of Impressionism and other European movements (The Hague School). Their interest in Realism is expressed in an original decorative style: *A Galloway Landscape* (Henry), *Gathering Primroses* (Hornel), *The Gypsy Fires* (Guthrie), *Carse of Lecropt* (MacGregor), *The Tennis Party* (Lavery). Artists' colonies flourished at Brig o'Turk, Kirkcudbright, Cockburnspath and Cambuskenneth. *Tollcross 10* and *Girls at Play* are good examples of

J Q Pringle's original style. The **Scottish Colourists** (J D Fergusson, F Caddell, S J Peploe, L Hunter) were the next important group to emerge from Glasgow in the early 20C. Their canvases are striking with the strong lines and vibrant colours reminiscent of post-Impressionism and Fauvism: *Bathers, Le Voile Persan, Les Eus* (Fergusson), *The Red Chair* (Caddell), *The Brown Crock, Iona, Tulips and Cup* (Peploe). **Joan Eardley** (1921–1963) is an important artist who drew inspiration from slum life *(Street Kids)* and dramatic weather at sea.

The Glasgow School of Art nurtured many outstanding artists: R Colquhoun (1914–1962) – *The Dubliners, Figures in a Farmyard* showing the influence of Cubism – and R MacBryde (1913–1966) – *The Backgammon Player, Fish on a Pedestal Table* (original combination of unusual objects). **Anne Redpath** (1895–1965), well known for her still-life paintings, flower pieces, landscapes and church interiors *(Pinks, Red Slippers),* and William Gillies (1893–1973), who painted gentle landscapes *(Temple Village)* and still-life compositions, were both associated with the Edinburgh School of Art. The work of **Ian Hamilton Finlay** (b.1925) combines Classical allusions and form. Russell Flint's (1880–1969) watercolours celebrate the pleasures of life.

MODERN TRENDS

Another important group of artists was open to international influences. William Gear (1915–1997) and Stephen Gilbert (1910–2007) joined the CoBRA movement. Alan Davie (b.1920) became an exponent of Abstract Expressionism *(Jingling Space)* while William Turnbull's (b.1922) interest in modernist abstraction is expressed in geometrical or painterly compositions. **Eduardo Paolozzi** (1924–2005) creates collages in the Pop Art idiom using discarded artefacts of the consumer society and showing the influence of Dadaism and Surrealism. *Celebration of Earth, Air, Fire and Water* by William Johnstone is a good example of landscape abstraction. John Bellany (b.1942) tackles the inhumanity of people and the mysteries of existence and

Detail, A Ground Swell, Carradale (1883-1886) by William Mc Taggart, Aberdeen Art Gallery & Museums

© The Print Collector/age fotostock

human relations *(Woman with Skate).* The triptych *Journey to the End of Night* is a visionary creation.

The **New Image** group from Glasgow is blazing a trail on the contemporary scene. The influence of Fernand Léger and the Mexican muralists is evident in the graphic emphasis of the human figure and the raw vigour of the large compositions by **Ken Currie** (b.1960) – *The Glasgow Triptych* mural. Social realism is also tackled poetically by Peter Howson (b.1958). The works of Adrian Wiszniewski (b.1958) show great imaginative fantasy while Stephen Campbell (1953–2007) poses conundrums in natural philosophy. **Stephen Conroy** (b.1964), who seems to distance himself from human life, is famous for his strangely typecast characters depicted with flair and craftsmanship. Other artists making a name for themselves on the contemporary scene include Jock McFayden (b.1950) and the "Wilde Malerei" group (Fiona Carlisle, June Redfern, Joyce Cairns) who paint in lively, vivid colours.

Fife-born **Jack Vettriano** OBE (b.1951), known as "the people's painter", produces hugely popular romantic paintings, notably *The Singing Butler.*

Diana Mackie, a contemporary landscape artist based on the Isle of Skye, tries to capture the fleeting nuances of climatic change and the differing moods of the sea (*www.diana-mackie.co.uk*).

Literature

Scottish literature has a fabulous wealth. From the 18C onwards literary giants such as Robert Burns, Walter Scott, Robert Louis Stevenson and Arthur Conan Doyle wrote poetry and books that are still recited and read worldwide. Their characters are immortalised, not just in books gathering dust on the shelves, but in modern mainstream film too, with Sherlock Holmes only the most recent example. The legacy is carried on today by J K Rowling, Irvine Welsh and Ian Rankin.

EARLY TRADITION

Gaelic folklore celebrates the legendary 3C bard **Ossian** who was thought to be the author of *The Ossianic Fragments*; the poems were a literary fraud perpetrated by James Macpherson in the 18C which won great acclaim.

St Columba arrived in Iona in AD 563 and there is a tradition that the community's scribes and illuminators worked on the world-famous *Book of Kells* (now in Dublin), which would make it Scotland's oldest surviving manuscript.

The *Book of Deer* (now in Cambridge University Library) is a 10C illuminated Latin Gospel Book from Old Deer, Aberdeenshire, with early 12C additions in Latin, Old Irish and Scottish Gaelic. It is most famous for containing the earliest surviving Gaelic literature from Scotland. It may well be the oldest surviving manuscript produced in Scotland, if this honour does not fall to the *Book of Kells*. In medieval times learning was associated with monastic houses (Jedburgh, Dryburgh, Melrose, Arbroath, Dunfermline) but their treasures were lost following raids by the English and the religious conflicts in the 16C. **Thomas the Rhymer** (13C Scottish seer and poet) was famous for his verse prophecies. The wizard Michael Scott (1117–1232) won fame as a scholar and linguist at the court of Emperor Frederick II. **John Duns Scotus** (1266–1308), a Franciscan scholar, was a leading philosopher who dominated the European scene.

EVOLUTION

Printing was introduced to Scotland in 1507 and the earliest printed works included those of Bishop Gavin Douglas (1474–1522) who translated Virgil's **Aeneid** into Scots, and of the court poet William Dunbar (1460–1520). Both belonged to a group of poets known as the Makars, which also included Robert Henryson (1430–1506).

In the 16C Andrew Melville (1554–1622), a celebrated theologian, scholar and linguist, had a close association with the universities of Glasgow and St Andrews. The humanist George Buchanan (1506–1582) was the tutor of Mary, Queen of Scots and of James VI. The 16C was an era of religious ferment dominated by the reformer **John Knox** (1512–1572) who held famous debates with Mary, Queen of Scots and whose fiery sermons led to unfortunate excesses.

NATIONAL PRIDE

The Age of Enlightenment witnessed a flowering of talented men in all fields of endeavour who frequented clubs and learned societies. Leading figures included the prolific and influential poet and writer **Sir Walter Scott** (1771–1832), the revered bard **Robert Burns** (1759–96) who epitomised the national spirit, the poet Allan Ramsay (1686–1758) who fostered the use of the Scottish language in literary works (*The Gentle Shepherd)*, the writer James Boswell (1740–95), Dr Johnson's close friend and biographer, the novelist Tobias Smollett (1721–71), the philosophers David Hume (1716–86), Dugald Stewart (1753–1828) and Adam Smith (1723–90). James Hogg (1770–1835), the "Ettrick Shepherd", was known for his pastoral poetry. The first edition of the *Encyclopaedia Britannica* was published between 1768–71 in Edinburgh. Literary magazines (*Edinburgh Review, Blackwood's Magazine*) disseminated the new ideas and theories of the period.

In the 19C the essayist and historian **Thomas Carlyle** (1795–1881) was widely acclaimed and his seminal works (*The French Revolution, Oliver Cromwell*) wielded enormous influence. **James**

Barrie's (1860–1937) original works show great wit and imagination *(Peter Pan, The Admirable Crichton)*. **Robert Louis Stevenson** (1850–94) wrote thrilling tales of adventure *(Treasure Island, Master of Ballantrae)*. The gripping stories *(The Thirty-Nine Steps, Prester John, Greenmantle)* told by **John Buchan** (1875–1940) were much admired. Another famous figure was the poet Charles Murray (1864–1941) who penned his verses in the Doric (rustic Scotch dialect).

20C

The **Scottish Literary Renaissance** of the early 20C attempted to foster a national language and included the poet Hugh MacDiarmid (1892–1978), the journalist and poet Lewis Spence (1874–1955), Helen Cruickshank (1896–1973), the novelists Lewis Grassic Gibbon (1901–1935), Compton Mackenzie (1883–1972) and Neil Gunn (1891–1973) and the poet and literary critic E Muir (1887–1959). William McGonagall (1830–1902) took up the role of itinerant bard although he wrote verse that was at best indifferent, and today he has an almost cult-like following which hails him as the writer of the worst poetry in the English language!

John Joy Bell (1871–1961) wrote fiction, comic novels, travel books and recollections *(I Remember)*. George Blake (1893–1961) is known for his naturalistic treatment of life in Glasgow and Clydeside *(The Shipbuilders)*. The novelist and playwright Eric Linklater (1899–1974) *(The Man of Ness, The Dark of Summer, A Year of Space)* was born in Orkney. George Mackay Brown (1921–1997) drew his inspiration from the Norse tradition *(Winter Tales, Beside the Ocean of Time)*. Famous names on the modern scene include Muriel Spark (1918–2006) with her witty satirical novels *(The Prime of Miss Jean Brodie, Girls of Slender Means)*. Other notable writers of the late 20C include Alan Massie, William Boyd, James Kelman *(How Late It Was, How Late, The Bus-Conductor Hines)*, Alasdair Gray, A L Kennedy, and Russel D McLean.

Robert Louis Stevenson

© Stapleton Historical/age fotostock

CONTEMPORARY SCENE

The biggest name on today's bookshelves is **J K Rowling**, famed as the single mother who, famously, in five years went from welfare payments to become the 12th richest woman in Great Britain (reportedly outranking the Queen). Although English, Rowling has lived in Edinburgh since 1993 and wrote nearly all her Harry Potter series here.

At the opposite end of the realism spectrum are **Irvine Welsh** and **Ian Rankin**. Welsh is infamous for his no-holds-barred take on the sordid underbelly of contemporary Scottish life *(Trainspotting)* while Rankin is the UK's bestselling crime author, and creator of Edinburgh-based Inspector Rebus. In fact, crime writing is a rich vein for many other successful Scottish writers today, most famously **Alexander McCall Smith** *(No. 1 Ladies' Detective Agency)*. In 2004, Edinburgh – already home to the world's largest Book Festival – was declared the very first **UNESCO City of Literature**.

Glasgow-born poet **Carol Ann Duffy** was named Poet Laureate in May 2009 at a time when the Scottish literary canon was opening up to the idea of including women authors.

Music

ORIGINS

Scottish **folk music** has its roots in the Gaelic (Celtic) tradition. The *òran mor* (great song) comprises the Heroic Lays, the Ossianic Ballads and songs linked with pipe music (laments and pibroch songs). There were also songs which set the rhythm for daily chores, such as linen making, cloth fulling, reaping, spinning, churning, as well as lullabies, fairy songs, love songs and mourning songs *(coronach)*. *Puirt-a-Beul* (mouth music) was a popular form of vocal dance music, often with humorous lyrics.

Communities scattered in remote areas of the Highlands held gatherings *(ceilidhs),* when songs, music, dance and poetry were performed for entertainment. Itinerant musicians were always welcome.

TRADITIONAL INSTRUMENTS

The most ancient musical instrument is the **harp** *(clarsach)* as evidenced from stone carvings dating from the 9C, although no ancient harp music has survived in its original form.

The modern revival of the harp dates from 1892 when the first Mod Festival was held by The Highland Society (An Comunn Gaidhealach) to stimulate interest in Gaelic culture.

The fiddle, lute and flute were also popular instruments. There are many references to fiddlers from the 13C; music collections have been recorded from the 15C onwards with manuscripts and printed music collections from the late 17C.

BAGPIPES

These are now generally acknowledged as the national musical instrument, but are of uncertain origin. Already in use in 14C Scotland they developed from the original one drone instrument to the modern example with three drones, chanter (for the melody) and blow stick (mouthpiece). A 21C take on the instrument is provided by the hugely popular Red Hot Chilli Pipers.

REVIVAL

Robert Burns was active in collecting and rewriting Scottish songs which were published in *The Scots Musical Museum* (1787–1803) and *Select Scottish Airs* (1793–1818). Many of Burns' own poems were also set to music.

Scottish musical inspiration was at its lowest ebb in the 19C but a rebirth became evident in the late 19C with the formation of choral and orchestral societies, the changing attitudes of the church and the celebration of Scotland by native composers.

At the turn of the century, the philanthropist Andrew Carnegie donated organs to remote parishes to promote new interest in church music. 20C com-

Pipe band performing at The Muster, a regional gathering of Lowland and Border Clans, Bowhill House, Scottish Borders

© Loop Images/Photononstop

posers who adopted Scottish idioms include Eric Chisholm (1904–1965), Ian Whyte (1902–1969), Cedric Thorpe Davie (b.1913) and Lyell Creswell (b.1944). Celtic culture inspired two outstanding composers: Ronald Stevenson (b.1928) who wrote songs, piano works and concertos and Francis George Scott (1880–1958), who, together with his disciple Hugh MacDiarmid (1892–1978), promoted the **Scottish Renaissance**, a musical and literary movement in the 1920s.

Scotland's natural attractions have drawn several composers. The scenery of the Hebrides inspired Felix Mendelssohn to write the *Overture to the Hebrides*. Since 1970 Sir Peter Maxwell Davies, the avant-garde English composer, has written all his music on Hoy in the Orkney Islands and in 1977 inaugurated the **St Magnus Arts Festival** held every summer in Kirkwall and Stromness.

Celtic Connections, Glasgow

© Gaelle Beri/Glasgow Life

SCOTTISH FOLK MUSIC

Scotland underwent a roots revival in the 1960s. Ewan MacColl founded one of the first folk clubs in Britain and together with the likes of Alex Campbell, Jean Redpath, Hamish Imlach and Dick Gaughan, and groups like The Gaugers, The Corries, The McCalmans and the Ian Campbell Folk Group, created a booming folk scene. New Scottish bands who keep the folk spirit alive are the Battlefield Band, Boys of the Lough, Capercaillie, Runrig and Shooglenifty.

POP, ROCK AND THE CONTEMPORARY SCENE

Scotland has given the modern music world many best-selling and international stars. The first, in the 1950s, was Lonnie Donegan with his trademark skiffle brand of music combining blues and country. In the 1960s came Donovan ("Britain's Bob Dylan") and Ian Anderson, front man of Jethro Tull, though like Donegan, neither of these artists were perceived as being Scottish. The first real Scottish superstar was arguably Rod Stewart (though he too had been domiciled in the south since his early

years), while in the 1980s Simple Minds, Eurythmics and Big Country flew the flag. In the 1990s, Wet Wet Wet, Edwyn Collins, Texas and Garbage came to the fore. Most unmistakeably Scottish of all were the Edinburgh-raised Proclaimers (still going strong in 2010), with their distinctive accents and vocal delivery. However, it is Glasgow that spawned most of Scotland's contemporary musical energy during the last two decades of the 20C, including The Blue Nile, Jesus and Mary Chain, Belle and Sebastian. In the 21C Travis, Snow Patrol, the Fratellis, Franz Ferdinand, Paolo Nutini and Amy MacDonald have perpetuated and reinvented the sound of indie Glasgow. In 2008 the city was rewarded with the accolade **UNESCO City of Music**.

The title recognises Glasgow's musical riches, the vibrancy of its music scene and its role as a world player in music. The scene spans many genres, including both production and performance. In preparing its bid for UNESCO status, Glasgow counted an average of 130 music events a week ranging from pop and rock to Celtic music and opera. Whether it is contemporary, classical, Celtic or country, Glasgow has some of the most famous music venues in the UK and a thriving music industry. It also has some of the most recognised qualifications in higher education in music.

Nature

Scotland is renowned for its unspoiled natural state and the attractions of the great outdoors; from a majestic stag in Monarch of the Glen pose, or endearing shaggy Highland Cattle, to the humble thistle and purple heather, all are powerful icons of a land which has remained close to its roots.

TOPOGRAPHY

A FEW FACTS

The mainland of Scotland and the numerous fringing islands cover a vast area of 30 414sq mi/78 793sq km. The coastline is deeply penetrated by the Atlantic on the west and by the North Sea on the east; most places are within 60mi/96km of the sea.

Depending on how you classify them, there are just under 800 islands (fewer than 25% inhabited) and 6 214mi/ 10 000km of coastline. Ninety eight percent of Scotland is classified as countryside.

Although Scotland is generally recognised as a mountainous country, the infinite variety of landscapes is one of its major tourist assets. The country is traditionally divided into three areas, the Southern Uplands, Central Lowlands and the Highlands.

SOUTHERN UPLANDS

Here the hills are lower and more rounded than their northern counterparts. In the southwest the smoothly rounded forms of the Galloway Hills are dominated by the more rugged granitic masses of the Merrick (843m), Criffel (569m) and Cairnsmore of Fleet (711m). Both the **Clyde** and **Tweed** have their sources in the vicinity of the lead-bearing Lowther Hills. The Nith, Annan and Esk drain southwards to the Solway Firth.

Hill country continues eastward with the **Moorfoot** and **Lammermuir Hills**, which demarcate the **Southern Upland Fault**.

CENTRAL LOWLANDS

The **Highland Boundary Fault** extending from Stonehaven to the Isle of Arran, and the Southern Upland Fault, delimit this low-lying rift valley, which has little land below 122m and is not without its own hill masses – **Campsie Fells**, **Kilpatrick Hills**, **Ochils** and **Sidlaws**.

The Lothian plains fringing the Firth of Forth and stretching to the sea at Dunbar are interrupted on the southern outskirts of Edinburgh by the Pentland Hills. Lowland continues along the carselands of the Forth up through Strathearn to the Tay and the rich Carse of Gowrie, overlooked by the **Sidlaw Hills**. To the north the fertile sweep of **Strathmore** passes northeastwards, to become, beyond Brechin, the more restricted **Howe of the Mearns**. Dumbarton, Stirling and Edinburgh Castle rocks, North Berwick and the Bass Rock are associated with volcanic activity.

HIGHLANDS

Though altitudes are low by Alpine standards, much of this area lies above 600m. The **Great Glen Fault**, stretching from Loch Linnhe north to the Moray Firth, acts as a divide between the Grampian Mountains and the Northwest Highlands. The **Cairngorms** are an extensive tract of land above 1 000m punctuated by peaks rising to over 1 200m (**Cairn Gorm** 1 245m, **Ben Macdui** 1 309m and **Braeriach** 1 295m). West of the Spey are the Monadhliath Mountains, a rolling upland of peat and moorland.

Some of the highest peaks (**Ben Nevis** 1 344m, **Ben Lawers** 1 214m), finest saltwater (**Lochs Fyne** and **Long**) and freshwater lochs (**Lochs Lomond**, **Katrine**, **Awe** and **Tay**) and greatest rivers (Spey, Tay, Dee and Don) can be found here. The Buchan and Moray Firth (Laigh of Moray) lowlands fringe the mountains to the east and north.

The Highlands to the north and west of the Great Glen are a wilder and more remote area where isolated peaks rise above a plateau surface with an average height of 600m. Outstanding examples are the spectacular Torridon peaks of **Suilven** (731m), **Canisp** (847m) and **Quinag** (808m), and in Sutherland **Bens Hope** (927m) and **Loyal** (764m). The indented western coastline where sea lochs separate peninsulas is fringed offshore by the **Inner** and **Outer Hebrides**.

COASTLINE

Scotland's long coastline is deeply indented and largely rocky, although the east coast is generally smoother and straighter. The coastline is one of impressive cliff faces with offshore arches and stacks as at Hoy and Yesnaby in Orkney, Cape Wrath and St Abb's Head, or great stretches of dune-backed sandy beaches, the asset of such east coast resorts as Montrose, Aberdeen, Fraserburgh and Nairn.

ISLANDS

Mainland Scotland is fringed by almost 800 islands with the Hebrides, strung out along the western seaboard, as the largest group (500). The Inner Hebrides include such evocative isles as Skye, Mull, Iona, Jura and Islay. The Minch separates the mainland from the Outer Hebrides, an archipelago stretching 140mi/225km from the Butt of Lewis to Barra Head.

The principal islands in the Firth of Clyde are Arran, Bute and the Cumbraes. Beyond the Pentland Firth in the north are two important clusters of isles and islets, Orkney comprising 90 islands in all and farther north Shetland, a group of about 100. St Kilda and Rockall are isolated outliers of the western isles, while Fair Isle lies roughly mid-way between Shetland and Orkney. The majority are uninhabited, but it was on these distant isles that the Norse and Gaelic cultures resisted the longest. Today, each one has a jealously guarded character of its own.

THE MUNROS

A large percentage of Scotland lies above 250m and hills and mountains are an ever-present aspect of the landscape. In 1891 the Scottish mountaineer **Sir Hugh Munro** drew up tables of all the Scottish peaks over 3 000ft (914.4m).

Coastline of Unst, Shetland

© Matthias Graben/imageBROKER/age fotostock

With perfected surveying techniques the total is now 282, although the number varies from time to time as more accurate measurements are provided. To some climbers Munro-bagging, chalking off every single one, is a lifetime task. For more information on these visit *www.munromagic.com*.

CONSERVATION POLICY

The task of reconciling the increasing demand for public access and recreation with the conservation of the countryside and in particular the areas of outstanding scenic value is met in Scotland by the cooperation of numerous bodies. Agreements ensure the conservation of Scotland's scenic heritage with its wildlife. The National Trust for Scotland owns and administers some of Scotland's most important mountain areas – Balmacara-Kintail, Glencoe and Torridon – where ranger-naturalists meet the need for public access to the countryside.

In an attempt to reverse the destruction of native forests, Scottish Natural Heritage has launched schemes to regenerate woodland areas. Hawthorn, rowan and alder are planted to replace non-native tree species such as sycamore, larch and beech.

GARDENS

Somewhat surprisingly given Scotland's northern latitude, gardens are an important part of the country's natural heritage, both historically and horticulturally.

GULF STREAM GARDENS

For the foreign visitor these gardens are perhaps the most unexpected. In secluded spots all along Scotland's Atlantic seaboard gardens with a profusion of tropical and subtropical plants flourish.

The outstanding example is Osgood Mackenzie's woodland garden at Inverewe, in its perfect Highland setting. Moving southwards others include Crarae Woodland Garden, the Younger Botanic Gardens, Benmore and the Logan Botanic Gardens, to name a few of those open all year round.

GARDENS WITH A DIFFERENCE

The formal gardens at Pitmedden, Edzell and Drummond Castle reflect the spread of Renaissance ideas from the continent and from France in particular. Gardens came to be mere adornment for ancestral homes as at Brodick, Falkland and Kellie. The intimate enclosures at the garden at Crathes Castle are distinguished by colour, season and plant species.

WILDLIFE

Scotland is endowed with a rich natural heritage of wildlife, vegetation and land. Humans have been largely responsible for destroying certain habitats (deforestation and in particular the loss of the native pinewoods) and the extinction of the fauna. The first to suffer were the larger animals – reindeer, elk, brown bear and wild boar – which are extinct in Scotland in the wild. However, recent cooperation between government and specialised organisations is responsible

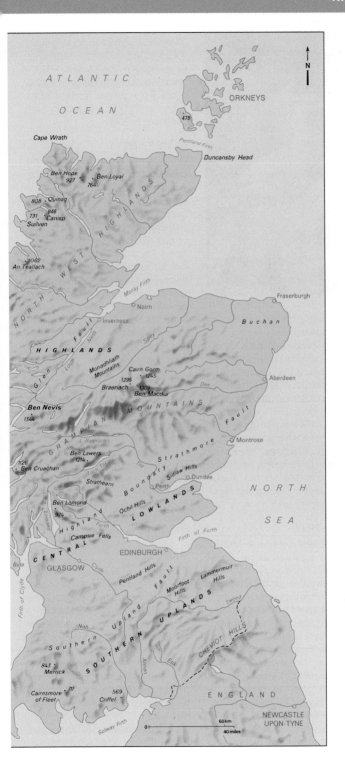

Gannets on Bass Rock

© SteveMartin/iStockphoto.com

20-year reintroduction programme by RSPB Scotland and Scottish Natural Heritage around the country. Since 1989, the graceful bird of prey has been reintroduced in four parts of Scotland, with a minimum of 149 Scottish pairs fledging 234 young in 2009.

GAME BIRDS

Of the better-known game birds the **capercaillie** (reintroduced c.1770), the biggest of the grouse family, has increased in number with the spread of forestry plantations. **Red grouse** thrive on the heather moors, with black grouse or blackcocks on forest edges and moors. The latter indulge in ferocious-looking mock battles at the lek or traditional display areas. The **ptarmigan,** the fourth member of the grouse family, with its successful white camouflage prefers the mountaintops. This is also the habitat of that colourful bird but reluctant flyer, the dotterel, and the elusive snow bunting.

SEA BIRDS

The offshore islands (Bass Rock, Ailsa Craig, St Kilda) and cliffs of Scotland are the haunts of a wide variety of sea birds from the comical puffin, to guillemots and kittiwakes, razorbills, fulmars and other members of the gull family. The Bass Rock, which is one of the easier gannetries to visit, gave the **gannet** its scientific name *Sula bassana*. Excursions from Anstruther take visitors to the Isle of May, thronged with sea birds.

MAMMALS

The early mammal population counted elks, northern lynx, brown bear, beaver, reindeer, wild boar, ponies, white cattle with black points (still found in some parks today) and the wolf (*see box opposite*). With re-afforestation Scotland has become the last British stronghold of otters, wildcats and the secretive pine marten. The fox is a newcomer to the northeastern coastal Lowlands and badgers have re-colonised most of the mainland.

Some of these animals can now be seen in the Highland Wildlife Park near Kin-

for the successful conservation of many habitats and wildlife.

Scottish Natural Heritage is responsible for establishing reserves to safeguard certain wildlife communities and the **Scottish Wildlife Trust** was founded in 1964 to combat the increasing dangers to Scotland's wildlife.

The official website to learn more about the country's wealth of species is http://wildlife.visitscotland.com. This excellent site also gives information on the best and most up-to-date locations for spotting creatures from osprey and capercaillie to dolphins and porpoises.

BIRDS OF PREY

The most majestic, if elusive, Scottish raptor is the **golden eagle**, found on Skye, Mull, the Outer Hebrides, Aviemore area, Deeside and Northwest Highlands, often in the former territory of the **white-tailed (sea) eagle** (reintroduced 1985). The fish-eating **osprey** is once again to be seen in Scotland, which is a major European stronghold for that other raptor, the hen harrier with its aerial acrobatics and unusual ground nesting habits. Both the peregrine falcon and buzzards are quite common sightings in the Highlands.

Red kites have reached a 150-year high in Scotland, after a hugely successful

The Big Bad Wolf...

Once common in Scotland, wolves were hunted to extinction by the late 18C, but now naturalists are calling for their reintroduction. The argument is that deer are close to reaching the maximum capacity that the local ecosystem (trees and plants in particular) can support. Culls by man would not be economically effective, so instead wolves would cull the deer. The negative side is that wolves may also cull farmers' livestock, most notably sheep. However, wolves do not typically slaughter whole flocks, but just take individuals when they are hungry. Farmers are cautious but are not completely averse to the idea provided they are adequately reimbursed for any lost stock. While the public are generally positive to the idea of wolf reintroduction, people living in rural areas are more sensitive. The debate rumbles on.

craig in Speyside or Edinburgh Zoo. Rare breeds such as the Soay sheep from the St Kilda group of islands are part of the Highland Wildlife Park at Kincraig while famously photogenic shaggy Highland cattle pasture the parklands of Scotland's castles.

In 2010, the first beavers to live in the wild in Scotland in over 400 years (they were hunted to extinction in the UK in the 16C) were released into a trial area in Knapdale Forest, Mid-Argyll for a time-limited period. This marked the first-ever formal reintroduction of a native mammal into the wild in the UK.

WHALES AND SHARKS

Minke whales are the commonest whale in Scottish waters, up to 10m long and up to 10 tonnes/10 000kg.

Orcas (killer whales), among the fastest sea creatures and the top predators in the ocean, can be seen in Scottish waters year-round. Males can grow between 6m and 7m and weigh over 5 tonnes. The huge dorsal fin can measure 1.8m high. Orcas are highly social and live in groups called pods. The only resident pod in Britain is the nine-strong group in Shetland. However, it is a cause of concern that the pod has not produced any calves for 20 years.

The **basking shark**, most frequently spotted in summer, is the second largest animal in the world, measuring 11m long and weighing up to 7 tonnes. It is usually seen swimming slowly near the surface.

DOLPHINS

Bottlenose dolphins may be seen all around the coast of Scotland in spring and summer – the Moray Firth colony is the most renowned. Their single nostril (blowhole) allows the dolphin to take in air when it comes to the surface. The distinctive bulging forehead contains an organ called a melon, which holds a mass of fat and oily tissue. This allows dolphins to echolocate food and to communicate with each other. The **harbour porpoise** is the most common cetacean in Scottish waters. It may be found year-round in any shallow seas and particularly around the Hebrides and Northern Isles. The animals tend to gather together in pods of two to five.

SEALS

Seals may be seen year-round. **Common seals** are often found around shallow inland waters, hauled up on sandbanks and around estuaries, but they will use rocky outcrops on the west coast. This species is roughly 1.5m to 2m long with the male (bull) weighing up to 250kg and the female (cow) around half that size. They fish over wide areas and breed between June and July.

The **grey seal** is slightly bigger and widespread on Scotland's rocky west coast. They feed on all types of fish, plus crabs, squid and sandeels, and breed in the autumn.

DISCOVERING SCOTLAND

Dunnottar Castle near Stonehaven, Aberdeenshire
© imageBROKER/hemis.fr

Southern Scotland

For visitors crossing Hadrian's Wall, the Borders is Scotland's welcome mat. An undulating verdant introduction to the country, this land of shires and streams is dotted with romantic ruined abbeys, gracious oft-forgotten country houses and comfortable little towns and villages. It is unmistakeably Scotland, if not stereotypically Scottish. Visitors in search of wilder Borders countryside should head to the hills of the west, or to the northeast and the dramatic cliffs of St Abb's Head.

Central Borders

This well-trodden route, from England to Edinburgh, is bisected by the River Tweed, tracing a silvery course from the hills to the sea, fed by many tributaries and providing some of the best fishing in Scotland.

The little towns of Melrose, Jedburgh and Kelso provide more than just welcome pit stops for weary drivers. Each is a base for keen walkers, fishermen and visitors interested in the fierce historical borderland strife that once ravaged this land, as witnessed by its many romantic ruined 12C abbeys – the Borders' iconic sights – and castle remains from the turbulent 16C and 17C.

If you see only one ruined abbey make it Melrose, which is also one of the Borders' loveliest towns. If the weather is good also make the time to divert briefly from here to enjoy Scott's View, and to nearby Dryburgh abbey, which enjoys a magnificent secluded setting. Jedburgh also boasts fine abbey ruins and an interesting Mary Queen of Scots Visitor Centre while Kelso abbey is worth a visit, though of less interest than the town itself.

Western Borders

The Western Borders is a land of scenic valleys and rounded green hills, home to the source of the River Tweed, famed for its salmon fishing. The river is at its most glorious around Peebles, as the number of walkers and cyclists attests. The handsome "royal burgh" of Peebles – just beside the Tweed – is a relaxed genteel town dating from Victorian times, good for a base or just a short stopover.

At Innerleithen, Robert Smail's Printing Works is a fascinating time-warp museum and nearby is the sulphurous spa water of St Ronan's Wells, made

Highlights

1 Walking or cycling the **Tweed valley** near Peebles (p80)

2 Discovering Sir Walter Scott's heritage at **Abbotsford** (p84)

3 Supping 400-year-old ale at **Traquair House** (p86)

4 A day at the races at picturesque **Kelso Racecourse** (p99)

5 A picnic in the grounds of romantic **Melrose abbey** (p106)

famous by Sir Walter Scott. The area's big draw, however, is Traquair House, the oldest continuously inhabited house in Scotland, little changed in half a millennium with gardens and a brewery, which are almost as venerable.

Eastern Borders

The Eastern Borders is a mixed landscape of wooded valleys, the low-lying Lammermuir Hills with their extensive grouse moors, and a short but very dramatic coastline. It may be off the beaten path but much of the area is excellent walking terrain.

From the various clifftop paths around St Abb's, there are spectacular views of the towering red cliffs and rocky outcrops of the rugged Berwickshire coast culminating at the sheer, sea-bird-nesting cliffs of St Abb's Head, rising some 100 metres above the water. On a sunny summer day – with more hours of sunshine than anywhere else in the country – the busy fishing port and beach of nearby Eyemouth is worth a look.

Away from the weatherbeaten coast the stately homes of Manderston, Floors Castle and, above all, Mellerstain provide historical interest.

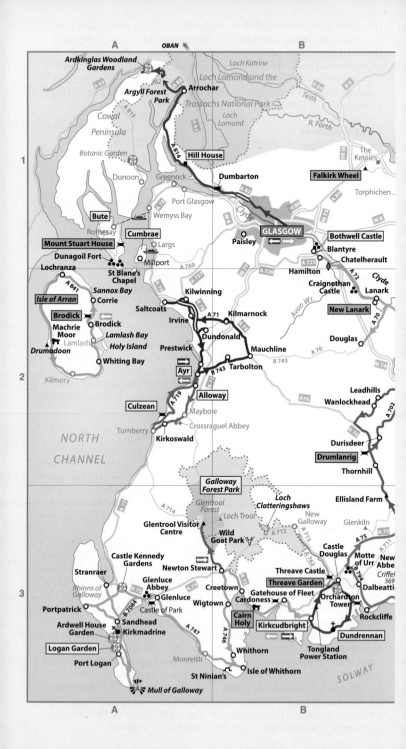

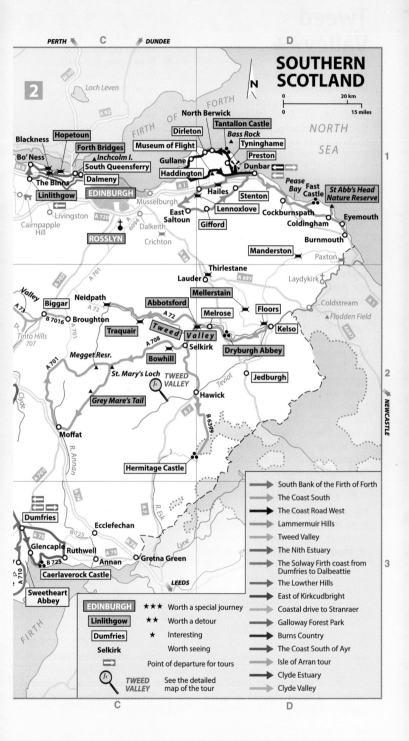

SOUTHERN SCOTLAND

2

Loch Leven

FIRTH   OF   FORTH

NORTH SEA

0 — 20 km
0 — 15 miles

N

Blackness
Hopetoun
North Berwick
Tantallon Castle
Dirleton
Bass Rock
Forth Bridges
Museum of Flight
Tyninghame
Bo' Ness
South Queensferry
Gullane
Preston
The Binns
Dalmeny
Haddington
Dunbar
Linlithgow
EDINBURGH
Hailes
Stenton
Pease Bay *Fast Castle*
St Abb's Head Nature Reserve
Musselburgh
Lennoxlove
Cockburnspath
Eyemouth
Livingston
East Saltoun
Coldingham
Burnmouth
Cairnpapple Hill
Dalkeith
Gifford
ROSSLYN
Crichton
Manderston
Paxton

Thirlestane
Laydykirk
Mellerstain
Lauder
Coldstream
Valley
Abbotsford
Floors
▲Flodden Field
Biggar
Neidpath
Melrose
Broughton
Tweed
Kelso
Tinto Hills 707
Traquair
Valley
Dryburgh Abbey
Selkirk
Megget Resr.
Bowhill
St. Mary's Loch
TWEED VALLEY
Jedburgh
Clyde
Grey Mare's Tail
Hawick
R. Annan
Moffat
Hermitage Castle
R. Esk
Dumfries
Ecclefechan
Lyne
Glencaple
Ruthwell
Annan
Gretna Green
LEEDS
Caerlaverock Castle
Sweetheart Abbey
FIRTH

NEWCASTLE

1

2

3

→ South Bank of the Firth of Forth
→ The Coast South
→ The Coast Road West
→ Lammermuir Hills
→ Tweed Valley
→ The Nith Estuary
→ The Solway Firth coast from Dumfries to Dalbeattie
→ The Lowther Hills
→ East of Kirkcudbright
⋯ Coastal drive to Stranraer
→ Galloway Forest Park
→ Burns Country
→ The Coast South of Ayr
→ Isle of Arran tour
→ Clyde Estuary
→ Clyde Valley

EDINBURGH ★★★ Worth a special journey
Linlithgow ★★ Worth a detour
Dumfries ★ Interesting
Selkirk Worth seeing
⇨ Point of departure for tours
TWEED VALLEY See the detailed map of the tour

Tweed Valley★★

The Tweed is one of Scotland's longest and most beautiful waterways, with long vistas and graceful curves. A series of famous landmarks and quiet, pleasant, well-to-do market towns adorn its banks.

A BIT OF HISTORY

A Rich Heritage – From earliest times the region has been favoured as an area of settlement. Iron Age remains, Roman forts and great monastic houses all chose its fertile haughlands as ideal sites. The area is best known for the troubled times (13C–16C) of Border raids and reiving as recounted in the ballads. The Border Laws accepted by both kingdoms were enforced by Wardens of the March, three for each country. It was the responsibility of these officers, often hereditary, to repel invasion and keep the peace.

The Tweed valley has a rich heritage from this period with the traditional Border peels or fortified tower houses. Some outstanding examples are Neidpath, Smailholm and Greenknowe. The memory of these times is also kept alive by the **Common Ridings** when groups of citizens ride the burgh boundaries.

A BIT OF GEOGRAPHY

River and Landscapes – The Tweed is the third longest Scottish river after the Tay and Clyde, and drains the Border region. The Tweed Basin is ringed by hills, with the Cheviots to the south, the Southern Uplands to the west and the Lammermuir Hills to the north. Tributaries include the Yarrow, Ettrick, Gala, Leader and Teviot.

In its upper reaches the Tweed cuts discordantly across the major structures and its valley is constricted and irregular. In its middle reaches, between the uplands and the Merse, it is broad with majestic curves, overlooked by ruined abbeys and prosperous Border towns.

Info: Tourist information about locations in the Tweed valley is available from www.visittweedvalley.co.uk, and from the individual websites of the towns within the area.

Location: The River Tweed rises in the Tweedsmuir Hills to the west of the Borders and flows eastwards, acting as the frontier with England for the latter part of its journey, ending at Berwick-upon-Tweed, some 97mi/156km later.
This section of the guide relates to the Middle Tweed valley.
For the description of sights along the upper reaches of the Tweed see MOFFAT and BIGGAR. For sights downriver see KELSO.

Don't Miss: Dryburgh Abbey, Scott's View, Abbotsford, Traquair House, Grey Mare's Tail waterfall. The **Glorious Tweed Festival** is a varied programme of events celebrating the Borders heritage.

Timing: Allow a full day.

The Tweed Today – The valley is noted primarily for its agriculture with hill sheep farming on the uplands and mixed arable farms on the flatter and richer till soils of the Merse. The traditional woollen and knitwear industries are of paramount importance to the Tweed towns. The Tweed, Queen of the Salmon rivers, and its tributaries provide several hundred miles of freshwater fishing with a possible catch of 16 different species of fish, and stillwater or loch fishing for trout, pike and perch.

🚗 DRIVING TOURS

🚗 1 MIDDLE TWEED, KELSO TO NEIDPATH CASTLE
40mi/64km.

This excursion is short on miles but long on history, taking in ancient castles, romantic abbey ruins and two of Scotland's most fascinating historic houses.

Kelso★ – *🦽See KELSO.*

▷ Leave Kelso by the A699, which follows the south bank of the river, heading in a southwesterly direction.

Floors Castle (*🦽see KELSO: Driving Tour*) enjoys an attractive terraced setting on the north bank. A visit to Mellerstain , norethwest of Kelso (*🦽see KELSO: Driving Tour*) is also very worthwhile. Pass on the left the site of Roxburgh Castle (*🦽see KELSO*).

St Boswells
This small village was once the site of an important livestock fair.

▷ Take the local B 6404 northeast across the Tweed.

Dryburgh Abbey★★
♿🕐*Daily: Apr–Sept 9.30am–5.30pm (rest of year 10am–4.30pm). 🕐25–26 Dec, 1–2 Jan. 🎫£6. 📞01835 822 381. www.historicenvironment.scot.*
Majestic and evocative, the extensive ruins of Dryburgh abbey stand in a splendid, secluded **setting★★★** on a sheltered meander of the Tweed. The mellow red tones of the Dryburgh stone amid the green swards of well-tended grass and majestic old trees, make this one of the most attractive of the Border abbeys.
Building began in 1150 and the abbey led a peaceful and prosperous existence with the monks (Order of Premonstratensians) tending the lands. The Wars of

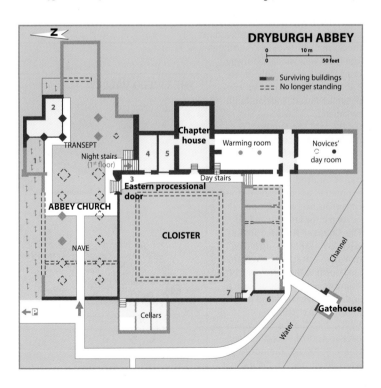

Independence and subsequent Border troubles resulted in destruction and fire damage on at least three occasions, 1322, 1385 and 1544; the latter also included the razing of the town of Dryburgh.

The religious life of the abbey ended at the beginning of the 17C. It was then inhabited by the Commendators (their descendants), which explains why the conventual buildings have been so well preserved.

Abbey church

Little remains of the mainly 12C and 13C church, dedicated to St Mary. The north transept and eastern chapel are the resting places of Field Marshal Earl Haig **(1)** and Sir Walter Scott **(2)**.

The south transept has the remains of a night stair leading to the first floor canons' dormitory and a door to the library and vestry.

Conventual buildings

These are among the best preserved of their kind in Scotland, and are laid out on the middle and lower levels, around the cloister, with two storeys on the east. The East Processional Doorway is an attractive example of late 12C work, still round-headed with dissimilar capitals and dog-tooth ornament.

On the left, the aumbry **(3)** or book alcove is complete with shelf grooves. The first door leads to the library and vestry **(4)**, a barrel-vaulted chamber later adopted as a family vault by the Earls of Buchan, while the parlour beyond is the Erskine vault **(5)**.

The **Chapter House** doorway with its flanking openings makes an attractive unit. Stairs lead down to the barrel-vaulted chamber, with its stone bench and attractive interlaced arcading on the east wall.

Next comes the day stair which gave access to the dormitory and treasury. Ahead, the doorway leads down steps to the lowest level where a door on the left opens onto the warming house (cale-factory) with two central pillars. The original fireplace was in the east wall as in the novices' day room across the passage.

Extending the full length of the eastern range, the **Dormitory** was altered following fire damage and in the 16C when dwelling rooms were made.

Lying on the south side of the cloister are the frater and subcroft, two barrel-vaulted chambers which were surmounted by the refectory. The cloister's most outstanding feature is the **wheel window (6)** in the west gable.

The west wall of the cloister has a lavatory **(7)**, a recess for hand washing before meals.

To the south of the frater on the far side of the water channel is the 15C **gatehouse** which was at one time connected to the main building by a covered bridge.

▶ Continue via the local B6356, which skirts Bemersyde Hill.

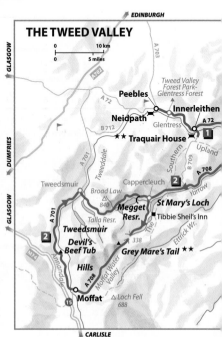

THE TWEED VALLEY

© J. Gibson/Loop Images/age fotostock

Scott's View

Scott's View★★

This panoramic view of typical Border scenery encompasses the Tweed valley with Melrose and Galashiels, the Eildons sloping down to Newtown St Boswells, then round to Minto, Rubers and Black Laws. In the near foreground is Bemersyde House, presented in 1921 by a grateful nation to Earl Haig, who is buried in Dryburgh abbey. Down on the Tweed meander is Old Melrose, the original site of the Cistercian settlement.

◗ Turn left on local road, then N on B6360 to join the main road left (S) to cross the river. At roundabout turn W on A6091, then take the B6361.

Note the 19-span Leaderfoot viaduct, and farther on, a monument marking

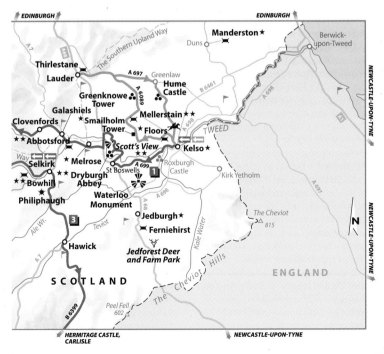

Sir Walter Scott

Born 15 August 1771, the youngest of 13 children of an Edinburgh solicitor, Scott's earliest contacts with the region began at **Sandyknowe**, his grandfather's farm (&see KELSO: Driving Tour). At the age of eight he attended Edinburgh High School and then the university where he qualified as an advocate. In 1799, he became Sheriff-Depute of Selkirkshire. To be nearer his work he acquired a property at **Ashiestiel** in 1804 and then in 1812, the small farmhouse of Cartley Hall, which he renamed Abbotsford, on the banks of the Tweed. He extended the building but later demolished the farmhouse replacing it with the present exuberant structure which reflects his romantic spirit.

Scott's narrative poems, *The Lay of the Last Minstrel, Marmion* and *The Lady of the Lake* were written before he came to Abbotsford, as were his Scottish novels: *Waverley* (1814), *Guy Mannering* (1815), *The Antiquary* and *Old Mortality* (1816), *Rob Roy* (1818), *The Heart of Midlothian* (1818), *The Bride of Lammermoor, Ivanhoe* (1820), *A Legend of Montrose* (1819) and *Redgauntlet* (1824). The literary reputation of Scott is largely based on these novels, where he shows a genius for character and a masterful handling of Scots dialogue.

the site of the Roman settlement of **Trimontium** &See MELROSE: Additional Sights.

Melrose★
&See MELROSE.

▶ Leave Melrose to the W by the A6091 and at the second roundabout follow signs to Abbotsford.

Abbotsford★★
&♿⊙*House, chapel and gardens:* Mar and Nov 10am–4pm; Apr–Oct 10am–5pm. *Visitor Centre and café:* Apr–Oct 10am–5pm; Nov–Mar 10am–4pm (Jan–Feb Wed–Sun only). 👝*House, chapel and gardens £11.20; Gardens only £5.60 (online discounts).* ℘01896 752 043. ✗. *www.scottsabbotsford.co.uk.*

Abbotsford, a fantasy in stone, is typical of **Sir Walter Scott** (1771–1832), the man who did much to romanticise and popularise all things Scottish. Here you can see souvenirs of the man, his friends and contemporaries, his literary works and his cherished collection of **"curiosities of small intrinsic value"**.

The visitor centre has an exhibition on the "life and legacy" of Scott, who on 7 January 1828 recorded in his journal, "It is a kind of Conundrum Castle to be sure and I have great pleasure in it for

while it pleases a fantastic person in the stile and manner of its architecture and decoration it has all the comforts of a commodious habitation." Scott lavished much thought and effort on the building of his beloved Abbotsford, bristling with turrets and gables in the baronial style, which was to house his collection of "gabions", a word he invented to cover "curiosities of small intrinsic value". They often related to some part of Scotland's chequered history. The small book-lined **Study** is almost entirely occupied by the massive writing desk and is adjoined by a "speak-a-bit" turret room.

The moulded ceiling in the **Library** is a copy of Rosslyn Chapel (&see ROSSLYN CHAPEL). The Chantrey bust of Scott is dated 1820, the year **George IV** knighted the author. The showcase in the bow window contains many of the treasured "gabions" including Rob Roy's purse and Burns' tumbler. The painting on the easel records the one and only meeting between Burns and the 15-year-old Scott. On the shelves are over 9 000 rare volumes.

The paintings in the **Drawing Room** include portraits of Scott's mother and father, and over the fireplace, **Henry Raeburn**'s *Portrait of Sir Walter* with his dog Camp, at his feet. In one of the wall alcoves (to the right of the fireplace) is the silver urn which Byron gave to

Entrance Hall, Abbotsford

© Patrick Dieudonne/age fotostock

Scott. It also figures in the Sciennes House painting.

What is now the **Armoury** was a smoking corridor in Scott's time; the items on display include a Highland broadsword with basket hilt by Andrea Farara, Rob Roy souvenirs, including his gun, a Landseer painting of *Ginger* (the companion portrait of his master is in the National Portrait Gallery in Edinburgh) and a still-life of the Regalia of Scotland, a reminder that Scott was instrumental in their rediscovery. The miniatures include one of **Bonnie Prince Charlie** and **John Graham of Claverhouse**.

It was in the **Dining Room**, where he could command a view of the Tweed to the last, that Scott died on 21 September 1832. His death was undoubtedly precipitated by the burden of overwork in his last years. Following a financial crisis in 1826, Scott produced a phenomenal three novels a year in an age when there were no mechanical aids.

Panelling in the **entrance hall** from Dunfermline abbey's church is surmounted by arms of the Border families, while the fireplace and statues are copied from details in Melrose abbey. Other souvenirs include people and events prominent in Scottish history.

Note the door in the South Court from the Heart of Midlothian, Edinburgh's Old Tolbooth.

Chapel and Grounds – Along with the neighbouring wing, the **Chapel** is a 19C addition. Ghirlandaio's *Madonna and Child* (c.1470) dominates the fireplace. Outside is a Walled Garden, a Woodland Walk and the chance to stroll down to the famous River Tweed.

▷ Return to the A6091 and turn L to join the A7 across the Tweed.

Galashiels

On the Gala Water river, this busy tweed and knitwear manufacturing and shopping centre is one of the largest Border towns. The **Braw Lad's Gathering** (*last weekend Jun*) is a famous Common Ridings. Local history can be traced at **Old Gala House** (◷*Apr–Jun and Sept Tue–Sat 10am–4pm; Jul–Aug Mon–Sat 10am–4pm, Sun 2–4pm; Oct Tue–Sat 1–4pm*); ✗ P ☎*01896 752611; www.galashiels. bordernet.co.uk/oldgalahouse*), a late-16C stone house with a 17C painted ceiling. **Lochcarron of Scotland** (☝◷*visitor centre: Mon–Sat 9am–5pm.* ☛*guided tours: Mon–Thu 10.30am, 11.30am, 1.30pm, 2.30pm;* ◷*public and local holidays;* ✗ P ☎*01750 726 100; www.lochcarron.co.uk*) is a working mill, museum and visitor centre with displays on the evolution of the town and its industries. Mill tours showing the process of tartan manufacture.

▷ Continue by the A72 to rise out of the constricted valley of the Gala Water to go round Meigle Hill.

Clovenfords

Clovenfords Hotel, once a coaching inn, was patronised by Sir Walter Scott who came to fish the Tweed. This hamlet was the site of the Tweed Vineries, where the Duke of Buccleuch's gardeners produced the famous Clovenford Tweed grapes.

▷ The A72 then follows the north bank of the Tweed closely as the forested valley sides move in.

Innerleithen

In a lovely setting at the meeting of Leithen Water with the River Tweed, wide and meandering at this point, the small woollen-textile town of Innerleithen has prospered from its beginnings as a modest rural village, following the opening of the first mill in 1790 by Alexander Brodie.

The medicinal merits of the historic spa waters from the mineral spring at **St Ronan's Well Interpretive Centre** (*St Wells Brae;* &♿⏱*Apr–Oct Mon–Fri 10am–1pm, 2–5pm; Sat–Sun 1–4pm.* P *☏01896 833 583*), although well known already, were popularised by Sir Walter Scott in his novel *St Ronan's Well* of 1824. The spring's heyday has long since passed, but the little pavilion above the

town has been restored and houses a museum recounting the spa's history.

On the High Street, **Robert Smail's Printing Works** (☏*Guided tours only: Apr–Oct Fri–Sat and Mon 11.30am, 2pm, 3.30pm; Sun 1.30pm, 3.30pm; ☞£7;* P *☏01896 830206; www.nts.org. uk/Visit/Robert-Smails*) is a fascinating time-capsule of a Victorian Letterpress Printing Works. The caseroom and machine room illustrate printing methods at the turn of the century and still produce commercial work today.

▷ Take the B 709 to the left.

Traquair House★★

♿⏱*Daily: Apr–Jun and Sept 11am– 5pm; Jul–Aug 10am–5pm; Oct 11am–4pm; Nov Sat–Sun only 11am–3pm.* ☞*£9; grounds only, £4.50.* ✕ P *☏01896 830 323. www.traquair.co.uk.*

The white walls of Traquair peep out from the tree cover on the south bank of the Tweed. The long and peaceful history of house and family, visited by 27 Scottish kings and queens and lived in by the Stuart family for over 900 years, is vividly illustrated by a wealth of relics, treasures, traditions and legends.

Royal Hunting Lodge – As early as 1107, Alexander I stayed at Traquair and it remained a royal residence up to the 13C, used initially as a hunting seat for

Traquair House

© Traquair House Charitable Trust

the surrounding forests. The favourite residence of William the Lion, it was transformed during the Wars of Independence into a Border peel or fortified tower. In the late 13C the tower was in English hands and both Edward I and II stayed here, but it was returned to the Scottish Crown in the early 14C. James III gave Traquair to his Master of Music, William Rogers, and he sold the property to James, Earl of Buchan, uncle to the King.

Tower House to Mansion – The Earl's son, **James Stuart**, inherited Traquair in 1491 and the present owners are direct descendants. James' plans to extend the property were cut short by his untimely death at Flodden in 1513 and it was not until the 16C–17C that the original peel was transformed into a mansion house. James' grandson, **Sir John Stuart**, 4th Laird of Traquair, was Captain of Mary, Queen of Scots' Bodyguard and played host to the Queen and Lord Darnley in 1566, which is why the house has so many personal belongings of Mary and associations with this period.

Another notable figure was **John Stuart, Ist Earl of Traquair** (1600–59), who rose to the high office of Lord High Treasure. He changed the course of the Tweed and added a storey to the house. It was during his son John's lifetime that the Catholic faith was adopted by the family, a tradition that has been maintained and which was to make Traquair an active centre for the Jacobite cause in the 18C.

Charles, 4th Earl (1659–1741), commissioned James Smith to make certain alterations (1695–99). The side wings were remodelled, a wrought-iron screen erected in the forecourt, and a formal garden was created and given two attractive pavilions with ogee-shaped roofs. Ever since then the exterior of Traquair has remained unaltered.

Visit

The oak armorial in the hall displaying Scotland's royal arms dates from Mary, Queen of Scots' 1566 visit. The corner cupboards in the panelled still room contain Chinese and English porcelain. The elm chairs are part of a Scottish-made set dating from around 1750. The main staircase leads off the hall. Note at the bottom the vigorously carved oak door from Terregles House.

Ascending to the first floor, the width of the drawing room gives some indication of the narrowness of the building. Other noteworthy features include the fragments of 16C painted beams, the 1651 Andreas Ruckers harpsichord, and portraits of the *4th Earl*, *Dryden* and another by George Jamesone (c.1620). Pass through the dressing room to reach the **King's Room**, dominated by the splendidly ornate yellow State Bed, again from Terregles and said to be the one used by Mary, Queen of Scots. The bedspread was the work of Mary and her companions, the four Marys, and the cradle was used by her son, King James VI. Beside the powder closet is the door giving access to the unevenly stepped, steep narrow stairs of the original 12C tower and the secret stairs.

The second floor may be reached by the secret stairs or main stairs. The **Museum Room** display includes a variety of historical documents, mementoes and other interesting items such as the 1530 fragment of wall painting and a collection of Amen glasses.

🐾 Return to the main stairs and go up another flight.

The **Library** remains almost intact, as formed in 1700–40, with books still bearing the mark of their shelf number and place. Adjoining is a second library with 19C works. At the end of the corridor the **Priest's Room** originally served as the chapel and it was in these cramped quarters that the chaplain lived his furtive existence, as testified by the hidden stairs, with the false cupboard entrance.

🐾 Return to the ground floor.

Take the passage to the left to see the **vaulted chamber** of the original construction. This is where the cattle used to be herded in times of raids.

South wing – In the Dining Room there is another group of family **portraits**, with Medina's one of the *4th Earl and Countess of Traquair* who had 17 children, and another of the Jacobite *Charles 5th Earl*. Above the fireplace is the *1st Earl* with the rod of office as Lord High Treasurer.

North wing – Following the Catholic Emancipation Act of 1829, the chapel replaced the priest's room as the place of worship. The set of 12 16C carved **wood panels** depicts episodes from the Life of Christ.

Next to the chapel is the reception centre and shop while above is a fully equipped washhouse. Take a tour around the **brewhouse**; one of the oldest working breweries in Britain, dating back to the 18C, its highly regarded Traquair House Ales are available to sample and purchase. Several independent craft shops occupy old buildings, and tea/coffee, cakes and lunch are served in The Garden Café, by the Walled Garden.

The site of the Well Pool marks the former bed of the Tweed and the grounds include a choice of woodland walks which boasts some of the oldest yew trees in Scotland.

The famous **Steekit Yetts (Bear Gates)** entrance, built in 1737–38, lies at the end of a grassy tree-lined avenue. Tradition has it that the gates were closed by the 5th Earl on the departure of **Bonnie Prince Charlie** with a vow to reopen them only on the Restoration of a Stuart monarch to the throne.

▶ Continue on the A72 to Peebles.

Peebles

🔲 *www.peebles-theroyalburgh.info.*
This pleasant and peaceful town makes a good excursion centre for exploring the Tweeddale countryside. It was a flourishing spa in the 19C, and today sits in an Area of Outstanding Natural Beauty. Made a Royal Burg by King David I in 1152, this charming market town is valued for its setting and unspoilt character. On the High Street the **Tweeddale Museum and Gallery** (⌖🕐*Mon–Fri 10.30am–12.30pm, 1–4pm; Sat 9.30am–*

12.30pm; 🕐*Christmas and New Year holidays;* ☎*01721 724 820; www.visitt-weedvalley.co.uk/museums*) presents a number of temporary displays throughout the year. Its "Secret Room" contains interesting historical plaster **friezes**.

▶ Take the A72 .5mi/8km W.

Neidpath Castle

This 14C tower house (⌖*closed to the public: www.neidpathcastle.com*) is dramatically situated on a rocky outcrop overlooking the Tweed. It is of the traditional Scottish L-plan and an interesting example of the adaptation of a rubble-built medieval tower house to 17C requirements.

🚗 ②YARROW VALLEY AND TWEEDSMUIR HILLS
78 mi/126km.

The Tweedsmuir Hills route climbs out of the Annan valley over into the wilder scenery of the Moffat Water valley, a classic U-shaped glacially deepened valley.

Selkirk

🔲 *www.visitsouthernscotland.co.uk.*
The imposing woollen mills that made Selkirk a thriving town are silent and boarded. However, the town's industrial background is reflected in the number of specialist tweed outlets, the Lochcarron Visitor Centre with mill tours (cashmere, woven and knitted goods), glass studios and the local glassworks, which offers the chance to see skilled craftsmen at work.

Sir Walter Scott served as Selkirk Sheriff for 33 years and his former courtroom features an audiovisual presentation of Scott's associations with the area.

▶ Head 3mi/5km west on the A708 Moffat/St Mary's Loch Road.

Bowhill★★

⌖🕐*House* by guided tour only: Aug at noon, 1pm, 2pm and 3pm: *Estate*: mid-Apr–Sept Fri–Sun 10am–5pm (Jul–Aug daily). ☞*House and estate £11; estate*

Bowhill House

© Bowhill House and Country Estate

and exhibition, £5.50. ✖. 𝒫01750 22204. www.bowhillhouse.co.uk.

On high ground between the Yarrow and Ettrick Waters, **Bowhill**, with its many treasures, is the Border home of the Scotts of Buccleuch.

The estate was formerly part of the ancient Ettrick Forest, which Robert the Bruce granted to the Douglas family in 1322. It then reverted to the Crown in 1450 for about 100 years before finally becoming the property of the Scott family. Henry, the 3rd Duke, married Lady Elizabeth Montagu, thus uniting the Scott and Montagu families and in 1810, Henry inherited the estates and titles of the Douglases of Drumlanrig (♘see DRUMLANRIG CASTLE) giving the present name, Montagu Douglas Scott.

Visit

The **entrance hall** is a 19C addition, hung with portraits of four Huntsmen of the Buccleuch Hounds, whose service totals 160 years.

The **Gallery Hall** rises through two storeys; the upper walls are hung with four 17C Mortlake tapestries, while an impressive array of family portraits overlooks the BQ monogrammed English carpet in the Savonnerie manner, and fine French furniture, including Aubusson-covered canapé and chairs.

Most of the portraits are by the Van Dyck school although *Lady Anne Scott* is by Peter Lely. The children are William II, Prince of Orange and Henrietta Mary Stuart, sister of Charles II.

The **Scott Room** houses a collection of portraits and mementoes of Sir Walter Scott. They include Henry Raeburn's (1808) *Sir Walter Scott and Camp* with Hermitage Castle in the background, and David Wilkie's *King George IV* in Highland dress; the king's state visit to Scotland in 1822 was stage-managed by Scott and started the vogue for Highland dress. Scott mementoes include the manuscript of *The Lay of the Last Minstrel*, which was dedicated to Harriet, the 4th Duke's wife. Other items recall the poet James Hogg, "the Ettrick Shepherd", a friend of both Scott and the Duke.

The **Monmouth Room** was built as the chapel but now contains a variety of Monmouth relics including his Dutch cradle, saddlery as Master of the Horse, execution shirt and coral teething ring. The wall opposite the doorway is hung with Lely's majestic portrait of *Monmouth* (c.1670) wearing the robes of a Knight of the Garter, and Kneller's fine family group.

Originally the billiard room, the **Italian Room** was renamed after its masterpieces, including scenes of his native

Venice by Francesco Guardi. There are two delightful 18C Dutch marquetry tables. The clock (c.1780) plays Scottish tunes. The highlight of the handsome **Dining Room** is the collection of paintings, in particular the family portraits, by Reynolds and Gainsborough.

The **Drawing Room** is resplendently rich under an attractively patterned ceiling and cornice, highlighted with gold are the red carpet, red silk brocade wall hangings (now faded to pink) and Aubusson-covered chairs and settees. The paintings include landscapes by Vernet (18C) and Ruysdael (17C).

There are fine pieces of French **furniture**: a table with Sèvres plaques, side tables with red tortoiseshell and brass inlay, parquetry and ormolu commodes. Between the two Boulle glazed cabinets with Sèvres and Meissen porcelain, is Reynolds' appealing portrait of *Elizabeth*, the Montagu heiress with her daughter Lady Mary Scott, and various family pets. Between the Claude landscapes is an early Kneller portrait.

The centrepiece of the **Library** is the white marble **fireplace** emblazoned with an A, for Duchess Anne, originally from Dalkeith Palace, with her portrait by William Wissing.

An impressive **collection of miniatures** is housed in the **Primrose Room**. Here are included works by such masters as Samuel Cooper, John Hoskins, Laurence and Nicholas Hilliard, and Peter and Isaac Oliver.

Philiphaugh

Ettrick Moor was the site of the Battle of Philiphaugh in 1645 between the Covenanters and the Royalist forces. The Royalists were routed and around 100 soldiers and 300 camp followers (including women and children) surrendered on the promise that they would be spared. The Covenanters promptly massacred them all.

At the **Philiphaugh Salmon Viewing Centre** (◷*Apr–Dec 9am–5pm;* ✕ ℘*01750 21766; www.salmonviewing-centre.com*) underwater cameras show salmon swimming against the river, and on the last leg of their epic journey, in season (either May to June or September to November, when the river is high) they can be seen leaping up the cauld (weir) a few minutes' walk from the centre.

St Mary's Loch

The handsome hill setting is reflected in the waters of the loch, which provides good sailing and trout fishing, and is the largest natural loch in the Scottish Borders, being 3mi/5km long and half a mile/1km wide. It was created by glacial action during the last Ice Age, and is today fed by Megget Water.

The area around the loch has great beauty and a depth of history that features Border Reivers, literary giants (James Hogg and Walter Scott) and the heart of the ancient Ettrick Forest, an ancient royal hunting ground and a place from whence William Wallace launched raids against the English. It is also has a place of legend with Merlin the wizard allegedly seeking sanctuary in the area after a bloody battle near Carlisle. The Southern Upland Way runs along the southern shore of the loch (◶*page 15*), which takes its name from a church that once stood on the southern shore. Between St Mary's Loch and the more southerly Loch of the Lowes, originally one, stands **Tibbie Sheils Inn**, the meeting place of a coterie of literary greats including James Hogg (1770–1835), "the Ettrick Shepherd", Walter Scott (1771–1832), Robert Louis Stevenson (1850–1894) and Thomas Tod Stoddart (1810–1880), the 'Angling Poet'. On the slope beyond the souvenir shop and café is a statue of James Hogg.

Grey Mare's Tail★★

The Tail Burn forms this spectacular waterfall as it plunges 61m from a superb example of a hanging valley to join the Moffat Water. The site, now part of a nature reserve, lies on an historic thoroughfare connecting southwest Scotland to Edinburgh, and the area generally has strong associations with the 17C story of the Covenanters. Two paths lead to the waterfall. The one on the left, the easier, leads to the bottom of the waterfall, while the one on the right, much steeper and stonier (⚠ *stout footwear needed*) climbs up to the valley and Loch Skeen.

▶ Follow the A708 southwest passing from the Borders into Dumfries and Galloway.

Moffat

🔖 *www.visitmoffat.co.uk.*

A small and attractive town at the head of Annandale, Moffat is set in the heart of beautiful countryside, and popular with tourists. The town is part of a Conservation Area with a rich heritage and history and a thriving cultural and creative scene, boasting theatres, art galleries, shops and eateries aplenty.

Once a flourishing spa in the 18C, the town is now principally a market centre for the surrounding hill sheep farming area and a tourist centre handily placed for the ample excursions into the hills around.

The town has a thriving music scene and stages numerous events throughout the year, including the annual July Moffat Gala and the renowned Moffat Sheep Races, held in August.

Moffat House

John Adam (1721–1792) built this mansion in 1761 as a residence for the 2nd Earl of Hopetoun, at a cost of £3 538. It is modest in comparison with other mansions designed by Adam. The severity of the design is relieved by the contrasting colours and textures of the building materials. It was during his stay as a tutor that James Macpherson (1738–1796) "translated" the Ossian Fragments. The property was converted into a hotel in 1950.

Colvin Fountain

The bronze ram by William Brodie on the fountain testifies to the importance of sheep farming in the area. The ram was presented to the town by William Colvin, a local businessman.

Moffat Museum

🕐 *Easter and end of May–Sept Mon–Sat (except Wed) 10.45am–4.15pm, Sun 1.15–4.15pm.* 📞 *01683 220 868; www.moffatmuseum.co.uk.*

Originally opened in 1984, the museum today tells the story of Moffat through the centuries with such topics as clan warfare, Covenanting, and its heyday as a spa.

▶ Leave Moffat by following the A701 N for around 6mi/9.5km.

Devil's Beef Tub

This steep-sided 150m-deep depression between the Tweedsmuir and Lowther Hills was so named after its use as a shelter for cattle stolen in reiving days, usually by the Johnstone clan, whose enemies called them the 'Devils'. It is one of the two main sources for the River Annan. In *Redgauntlet*, Walter Scott describes it as 'A d–d, deep, black, blackguard-looking abyss of a hole.'

A monument stands beside the road, at a viewpoint overlooking the hollow. It commemorates a fleeing covenanter, John Hunter, who tried to escape pursuit by running up its sides. He failed, and was shot dead on the spot, and is buried in Tweedsmuir churchyard.

▶ At Tweedsmuir turn right towards Cappercleuch and follow the narrow road beside the River Megget (no caravans).

Tibbie Shiels

Born in Ettrick in 1782, Isabella (Tibbie) Shiels moved into St Mary's Cottage when widowed in 1824. A spirited woman, she transformed the cottage into a welcome haven for wayfarers, and her spirit lives on. Somewhat presciently she said: 'Folk a' ken me best as Tibbie Shiels and I dar' say when I'm deid and gone this place will still be ca'ed Tibbie Shiels's'.

The Borders Textile Trade

It was a happy accident for the Borders that the word Tweed became synonymous with woven cloth when a London merchant misread the word "tweel" – a local form of "twill" – and placed the first order for "tweed". Today the textile trade is as closely associated with the Borders as the River Tweed itself. At first the rough homespun cloth was for domestic use and all knitting was done by hand until the introduction of the knitting machine in 1680. It was not until Sir Walter Scott astounded London society in the 1820s with his checked trousers, made from a black-and-white check derived from the plaids of the Peeblesshire shepherds, that the world first took to tweed. Around this period it is estimated that Hawick controlled around half of all the knitting in the country. Later, Prince Albert and Queen Victoria fuelled demand when they discovered the subtle shades that Border mills were introducing.

Today, Scotland boasts 450 textile companies with an annual turnover of around £1 billion and exports worth around £400 million. The industry employs more than 17 000 workers – around 4 400 of them in the Borders, accounting for 22 percent of Scotland's textile industry. Hawick is still the centre of the trade, famous for its fine woollens, cashmere and tweeds, and a number of internationally renowned firms which sell their high-quality knitwear from outlets in the town. At its peak there were over 50 mills here and so much manpower was required that Pringle alone brought in three busloads of employees from Kelso each day. However, the industry has shrunk dramatically during the past 20 years. Now, most of the mills are gone, including Pringle, and in the face of fierce competition from developing countries, the surviving companies face an uncertain future.

Megget Reservoir

With its curved grass-covered embankment the dam, the largest earth dam in Scotland, supplies Edinburgh and the Lothian region, and blends well into the landscape. There are good viewing points on the road running along the north shore of the reservoir.

③ SOUTH OF SELKIRK
59 mi/95km.

▷ Leave Selkirk on the A7.

This drive takes in some beautiful countryside, particularly south of Hawick.

Selkirk – *See above.*

▷ Follow the A7 for 11mi/17.7km.

Hawick
www.hawickonline.com/visit-hawick-tourism.
Hawick (it's pronounced "hoik"), the largest town in the Borders, is famous as a centre for knitwear, with big brands like Pringle, Lyle & Scott and Peter Scott, attracting visitors in search of bargains from its direct factory outlets.

Like most towns in the Borders, Hawick's history is marked by raids, fires and destruction. The **Common Riding** (early June) marks one such skirmish with the English – from which the locals emerged victorious – in 1514.

Borders Textiles Townhouse
1 Towerknow. Apr–Oct Mon–Sat 10am–4.30pm, Sun noon–3pm. Nov–Mar Mon, Wed–Sat 10am–4pm. 01450 377 615. www.heartofhawick.co.uk.
This former 18C inn – the oldest building in Hawick – began life as the sturdy Drumlanrig's Tower, built in the mid 16C. Now beautifully restored, it tells the stories and processes behind some of the world's most famous tweed and knitwear fashions, and interprets the Borders' industrial past in a lively hands-on exhibition.

Hawick Museum and Scott Art Gallery

Wilton Lodge Park. ♿🕐*Apr–Sept Mon–Fri 10–noon, 1–5pm, Sat–Sun 2–5pm. Oct–Mar Mon–Fri noon–3pm, Sun 1–3pm.* 📞*01450 364 747.*

Local industries and personalities plus 19C and 20C Scottish art are the staples on show here. There are usually some good touring exhibitions.

▶ Leave Hawick south on the B6399 towards Newcastleton. The road winds its way through an arid landscape for around 16 mi/26km.

Hermitage Castle★

🕐*Apr–Sept 9.30am–5.30pm.* 💷*£6.* 📞*01387 376 222. www.historicenvironment.scot.*

Set in splendid isolation amid wild Border country, this formidable-looking castle (once described as "the guardhouse of the bloodiest valley in Britain") conjures up the violent struggles for control of the Anglo-Scottish Border that once bedevilled this region. It was the seat of the Warden of the March (i.e. the Borders region) and controlled a strategic route defending the river and the main road between Hawick and England.

The castle would have been left to crumble had it not been for the writings of Sir Walter Scott, which caused the ruin to be preserved.

ADDRESSES

🛏 STAY

🛏 **Bellevue House Guest House** – *Bowmont Street, Kelso.* 📞*01573 224 588. www.bellevuehouse.co.uk. 6 rooms.* This Victorian House, five minutes from the town centre, offers good hospitality with individually decorated bedrooms and a choice of breakfast dishes.

🛏🛏 **Fauhope Country House** – *Gattonside, Melrose.* 📞*01896 823 184. www.fauhopehouse.com. 3 rooms.* Melrose Abbey is just visible from this stylish and charming 19C arts-and-crafts Country House B&B with antiques and fine furniture.

🛏🛏 **Tibbie Shiels Inn** – *St Mary's Loch, Selkirk.* 📞*01750 42231. 5 rooms.* Historic and atmospheric; a legend set amid outstanding scenery and a thriving charismatic local community.

🛏🛏 **Hartfell House Hotel** – *Hartfell Crescent, Moffat.* 📞*01683 220153. 7 rooms.* Impeccable and unpretentious guest house with restaurant (🛏🛏Lime Tree – ♿see below)

🛏🛏🛏 **Burts Hotel** – *Market Square, Melrose.* 📞*01896 822 285. www.burts hotel.co.uk. 20 rooms.* This some-time coaching inn on the main square is now a friendly family-run hotel with smart modern rooms. Its cosy clubby **restaurant** (🛏🛏🛏), with hunting scenes and rich tartans, serves modern Scottish cuisine featuring well-sourced local produce.

🛏🛏🛏 **Edenwater House** – *Ednam, Kelso.* 📞*01573 224 070. www.edenwater house.co.uk. 5 rooms.* 🍴. This charming house enjoys an idyllic rural location next to a 17C kirk, 2 mi/3.2km north of Kelso. Bedrooms and lounges boast antique furniture. Excellent modern Scottish cuisine is served in the elegant **dining room** 🛏🛏🛏.

🛏🛏🛏 **Ednam House** – *Bridge Street, Kelso.* 📞*01573 224 168. www.ednam house.com. 33 rooms.* Set on the banks of the Tweed, this Georgian mansion retains impressive period features and offers a bar, traditional bedrooms and a spacious **dining room** 🛏🛏 that overlooks the river and grounds.

🍴 EAT

🛏🛏 **The Hoebridge** – *Gattonside, Melrose.* 📞*01896 823 082. www.thehoebridge.com.* This charming rustic converted 19C bobbin mill serves top-class traditional Scottish fare with a modern twist.

🛏🛏 **Brodies** – *1–2 Altrive Place, Holm Street, Moffat.* 📞*01683 222 870. www. brodiesofmoffat.co.uk.* A large, laid-back, restaurant, gin and coffee lounge catering for all appetites from snacks and light lunches to substantial dinner and all-day brunch on Sunday.

🛏🛏 **Lime Tree** – *Hartfell House Hotel, Moffat.* 📞*01683 220 153. www.hartfell house.co.uk.* Small hotel restaurant serving dinner only (Tue–Sat); good value, weekly changing dishes that are full of flavour. 7 rooms (🛏🛏).

Jedburgh★

Known as "The Jewel of the Borders", the historic royal burgh of Jedburgh, lying astride the Jed Water, is on one of the main routes into Scotland, taken by the Roman Dere Street and the present A68. At one time the site of a castle and abbey, the town was granted royal burgh status in 1165 by William the Lion. However, it remained vulnerable in this troubled border region and its history reflects that of the area. It is now a peaceful market town, with some attractive vernacular buildings.

JEDBURGH ABBEY★★

⏱ Daily 9.30am–5.30pm (Oct–Mar 10am–4pm). ⏱ 25–26 Dec, 1–2 Jan. 🎟 £6. 📞 01835 863 925. *www.historicenvironment.scot.*

One of the most famous Border abbeys, Jedburgh was founded by **David I** in 1138 as a priory for Augustinian canons from Beauvais in France and elevated to abbey status 14 years later (1152). Work started at the church's east end in 1140 and continued for 75 years before the cloister buildings were commenced. A majestic building, it witnessed in its early days such royal events as the coronation of the founder's grandson, Malcolm IV (1153–65) and the marriage of Alexander III (1249–86) to his second wife, Yolande de Dreux. Constant attack and plundering were the fate of many of the great buildings in the region. The destruction of the 1545 raid ended abbey life although the church continued to be used as a place of worship until 1875.

Abbey church

The visitor centre gives a good introduction to the abbey, showcasing 8C carvings and artefacts excavated from the grounds. The mellow-toned stone building is roofless but otherwise comparatively complete. Seen from Abbey Close, the late-12C transitional **west front** is a powerful and most original feature. The main section with a deeply recessed, round-headed door-

▶ **Population:** 4 090.
♿ **Michelin Map:** Local map, see Tweed Valley.
ℹ **Info:** Murray's Green, Jedburgh; 📞01835 863 170; www.jedburgh.org.uk.
▷ **Location:** Jedburgh is just 10mi/16km north of the border with England on a main route north, the A68.
☺ **Don't Miss:** Jedburgh abbey; the view from the Waterloo monument.
🕐 **Timing:** Allow three hours for the town centre, including 30 minutes for the abbey.
👥 **Kids:** Children will enjoy the Jedforest Deer and Farm Park.

way crowned by three pedimented gables, has above a tall, fairly narrow window rising through the upper two sections to a rose-adorned gable, the whole being flanked by solid buttresses. Strength, originality and soaring height are its chief characteristics. The rhythm and regularity of the **nave** display the assurance of an art well mastered. The increasing number of elements per bay pulls the eye upwards from the pointed arches, through the triforium section of round-headed arches, sub-divided by two smaller lancets, to the clerestory and the serried ranks of lancets. The tower above the crossing is trimmed with a delicate balustrade. Beyond, the mid-12C east end, the earliest part of the church, is highly unorthodox. Massive round pillars rise upwards to the clerestory, buttressing the truncated arches of the main arcade.

Cloister Buildings

On a sloping site and now reduced to the foundations, these follow the usual pattern around the cloister, with, in the east range, the parlour, chapterhouse and treasury below, and dormitory above. The refectory, cellars and kitchens border the south side and offer a good view of the south elevation. Compare the Norman doorway giving access from the south aisle to the cloister, weathered but with a variety of sculptural motifs still discernible, to the replica on the left, resplendent with the full wealth of detail. In the middle is a herb garden, called a "garth", where herbs for medicine and cooking would have been grown by the cannons of the abbey.

ADDITIONAL SIGHTS
Mary Queen of Scots Visitor Centre★

Mar–Nov Mon–Sat 9.30am–4.30pm, Sun 10.30am–4pm. 01835 863 331. www.scotborders.gov.uk/museums.

This handsome 16C L-shaped tower house in the vernacular style, stands in its own well-tended garden. Originally the property of the Kerrs of nearby Ferniehirst, it took its present name following the lodging of Mary, Queen of Scots in 1566. Her stay was prolonged by ill health (to the point of fearing for her life) after an accident while visiting the injured Earl of Bothwell, her future husband, at Hermitage Castle.

The ground floor kitchen is cobbled and barrel vaulted. The window embrasures indicate the thickness of the walls. As in all Kerr houses, the spiral staircase is left-handed to allow this Kerry-fisted family to use their sword hands. Engraved glass panels, paintings, documents and relics tell the story of the hapless Queen's life. Portraits include her death mask and the Antwerp Portrait and contentious Breadalbane Portrait by George Jamesone.

Jedburgh Castle Jail and Museum

Late Mar–Oct Mon–Sat 10am–4.30pm, Sun 1–4pm. 01835 864 750. www.scotborders.gov.uk/museums.

This Georgian prison, built in the 1820s, was the site of the original Jedburgh Castle, a favourite residence of royalty in the 12C and well placed for hunting parties in the ancient Jed Forest. In the 15C, the castle was pulled down by the townsfolk to prevent it falling into English hands.

In 1823 the present building, a Howard Reform Prison, was considered one of the most modern of its time in the whole country. Three prison blocks arranged around the central governor's block were linked to the latter by first floor gangways. A top-floor terrace served as a surveillance point with a bell to sound the alarm in case of escape.

The three cell blocks had a similar disposition with cells leading off a central passage. Inmates' cells included two windows, a wooden bed and central heating – the grate at floor level covered

Jedburgh abbey

© hipproductions/iStockphoto.com

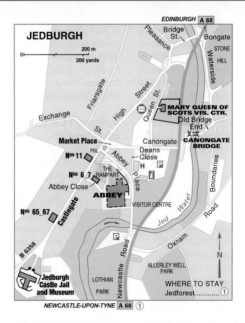

the hot air ducts, which were supplied by a stove in the windowless cell on the ground floor.

Some of the cells have displays evoking the life that went on in this "comfortable place of confinement", and there are exhibits on many aspects of local history.

Castlegate

Leading downhill to Market Place, the way to the castle is bordered by some attractive houses (restored). On the left, **Nos. 65** and **67** have incorporated into their walls two sculptures, one of which may well represent the Turnbull bull. Abbey Close, leading off down to the right to the abbey, is where in 1803 the Wordsworths received Scott who read them part of his *Lay of the Last Minstrel* (plaques **6** and **7**).

Continuing down Castlegate, No. **11** on the left is where Bonnie Prince Charlie lodged in 1745 when leading his Jacobite army into England.

Market Place

A plaque in the road marks the original site of the mercat cross around which clustered the stalls. The plaque on the County Buildings **(H)** commemorates Sir Walter Scott's first appearance as an advocate in 1793.

The Canongate continues down to the A68 which borders the Jed Water, bridged at this point by the **Canongate Bridge★**, a mid-12C triple-arched bridge. Stout piers with pointed cutwaters support the narrow bridge provided with pedestrian recesses.

EXCURSIONS

Waterloo Monument

3mi/5km north on the A68 and then the B6400. A path leads from the Harestanes Countryside Visitor Centre to the monument.
&⊙*Daily Apr–Oct 10am–5pm.*
℘*01835 830 306.*

Standing on the summit of Peniel Heugh (227m), the Waterloo Monument (o⊸*no access to viewing platform*), one of the Border's most prominent landmarks, was built to commemorate Wellington's victory of 1815. Formerly the site of pre-Roman camps, the craggy eminence offers a splendid **panorama★★** of the surrounding countryside: the fertile Teviot valley to the Cheviots in the south and east; great stretches of arable land and Smailholm Tower due north; the Eildon Hills to the northwest.

Ba' Games

© Rob Gray Photo/Shutterstock

Jedburgh Traditions

On the first or second Friday in July, a cavalcade of 200 or more riders depart on The Common Riding or **Jethart Callant's Festival**, from Jedburgh to Ferniehirst Castle, to recall how, in 1575, the fighting men of the two communities combined to break an English occupation of the castle. Another long-established local event is the mid-February Ba' Games when those born above the mercat cross, the Uppies, oppose the Downies, with the respective goals ("hails") being the Castle Jail grounds and Townfoot. This medieval ball game has been played here for over 250 years, using a leather ball stuffed with straw and decorated with ribbons. The game starts with the ball thrown into the waiting crowd which then gathers up and works together in a scrum to manhandle it through the streets.

Ferniehirst Castle

1.5mi/2.4km south on the A68.
&◗⌂*Guided tours only: Jul Tue–Sun 2–5pm.* ⌓*£5.50.* ☏*07900 152 986. www.ferniehirst.com.*
The original castle was built in 1450 and has been in the hands of the Kerr family ever since. Strategically important, it guarded the road to Otterburn and made an ideal base for the Wardens of the Middle March. The present building with its attractive rubble stonework dates from 1598: a visit includes the Border Clan Centre in the former chapel, the Kerr Chamber in the basement, the great hall hung with portraits, and the delightful turret room.

♣♦ Jedforest Deer and Farm Park

5mi/8km south on the A68.
☽*Easter–Aug 10am–5.30pm, Sept–Oct 11am–4.30pm.* ☏*01835 840 364. www.jedforestdeerpark.co.uk.*
This Borders farm (332ha) welcomes visitors with an array of rare breeds of sheep, cattle, pigs, goats and poultry. Beyond the belts of trees sheltering the farmstead paddocks from the wind are more extensive enclosures, the domain of muntjac, fallow and sika deer. Birds of prey displays are given each lunchtime.

ADDRESSES

🏨 STAY

🛏🛏 **Jedforest Hotel** – *3mi/4.8km south of Jedburgh. Children 12+ only.* ☏*01835 840 222. 8 rooms.* 7mi/11.2km north of the border, this handsome typical Scottish manor house sits amid 14ha of lovely grounds. Formal bedrooms are all en-suite. Wi-Fi. 🛏🛏 Fine bistro cuisine.

🍴 EAT

🛏🛏 **Ancrum Cross Keys** – *The Green, Ancrum (between St Boswells and Jedburgh).* ☏*01835 830 242. www. ancrumcrosskeys.com. Open for dinner Wed–Sun, and lunch Sat–Sun.* Carefully crafted dishes featuring pigeon and other local produce. Sit in the larger dining room and watch the chef at work.

Kelso★

Kelso stands at the confluence of the Tweed and its main tributary, the Teviot. A handsome market town, it is remarkable for its Georgian architecture and serves a rich agricultural hinterland. Although arable farming predominates in the rich Merse, the outlying hill regions maintain the tradition of hill sheep farming; however, the area is also known as horse country.

A BIT OF HISTORY

The original settlement grew up at a fording point, the first west of Berwick, and then developed round the abbey here in 1128. Kelso flourished when the nearby prosperous royal burgh of Roxburgh was destroyed in 1460 and her prosperity increased with the abbey's although she also suffered the fate of the abbey in 1545 when English troops led by the Earl of Hertford attacked. The town was raised to a burgh of barony in 1614 in favour of Robert Ker, 1st Earl of Roxburghe.

TOWN
Kelso Bridge

The attractive five-arched bridge, built (1800–03) by John Rennie, served as a model for his Waterloo Bridge. The lamp standards at the south end came from its London version when it was replaced in the 19C. The bridge offers a splendid **view★** upstream over the lazy flowing Tweed, of Kelso on the right with Floors in its fine setting and the mound of Roxburgh Castle on the left. An elegant toll house still stands on the north bank.

Abbey Court

The previous bridge opened onto this close, which is dominated by a church on the left and the white-harled 17C **Turret House**.

Abbey

The abbey was founded in 1128, the monks having moved from two previous sites at Selkirk and Roxburgh before finally settling here. With royal

▶ **Population:** 5 639.
Michelin Map: Local map, see Tweed Valley.
Info: Town House, The Square. ✆01573 223 464.
Location: Kelso is 23mi/37km southwest of Berwick-upon-Tweed via the A698 and B6350, and 10mi/16km from the Border with England.
Don't Miss: The Square; the views from Kelso Bridge, and (out of town) from the Maxwellheugh Road and Smallholm Tower.
Timing: Allow half a day for the town.

patronage the abbey grew and acquired extensive lands to become the richest in the land and the abbot claimed seniority among the Scottish clergy. The building itself, a vast edifice, took 84 years to complete. Following the death of James II while besieging Roxburgh Castle, the infant **James III** was crowned in the abbey. Time and again the abbey suffered from invading forces, the most destructive being that of Hertford's "Rough Wooing" in 1545 despite a desperate fight by the monks. By 1587 the abbey was officially defunct and in 1592 James VI granted it and the lands to Robert Ker of Cessford, 1st Earl of Roxburghe. From 1649 to 1771 the roofed-over transept served as parish church, then the ruins were pillaged for dressed stone. In 1919 the abbey was presented to the nation by the Duke of Roxburghe. The **ruins** date from the last quarter of the 12C. This once mighty abbey with its grandiose double transept plan was undoubtedly the largest and the most unusual of the Border group.

From the entrance only part of the south recessed doorway is visible, with a variety of sculpture on the arches, while rising above is the west transept tower, again massive in construction. Pass through to the abbey churchyard

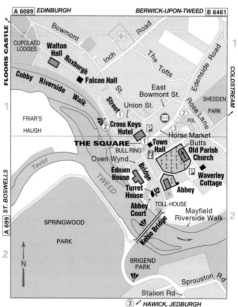

and turn around to admire the elevation. Three sections with round-headed openings rise above very attractively carved intersecting arcading.

The modern partial cloister (1933) by Reginald Fairlie is the Roxburghe family vault. The sculpture is interesting for the use of Celtic designs.

The **west front** and **tower** are best seen from the churchyard outside the abbey grounds. This is by far the most imposing part with its unique ordinance. In the transitional style, the recessed round-headed doorway with its pediment is surmounted by successive horizontal sections, each adorned with varying architectural elements. The whole is flanked by stout buttresses crowned with round turrets. The overall impression of this unique composition is one of soaring strength.

Pass through the churchyard to the car park. In the far corner is **Waverley Cottage**, the house, adorned with a statue of a dog, where Walter Scott spent some of his time while attending Kelso Grammar School.

Old Parish Church

The highly unusual and controversial octagonal-shaped church was built in 1773 by a local man, James Nisbet. The ground floor straight-headed windows and the round-headed ones above are all equipped with hood moulds, a common architectural feature of the region. The eight-sided roof is topped by a lantern.

Rams, Races and Rides

Kelso is famous for its Ram Sales (*September*), the Horse and Pony Sales (*April and September*), and an agricultural show, the Border Union Show (*July*).

Kelso Racecourse is one of the oldest in the country (established 1822) and was recently voted "Britain's Friendliest Racecourse" (*www.kelso-races.co.uk*). It is the home of National Hunt racing (steeplechasing) in the Borders. Point-to-point races are held across the river at Friarshaugh (*www.point-to-point.co.uk/go/courses/friars_haugh.html*). Kelso **Civic Week** has a varied programme including the Kelso Laddie leading his supporters on the Whipman's Ride.

Return to cobbled Bridge Street. Set back on the left is **Ednam House**, now a hotel. This fine Georgian mansion dates from 1761.

The Square★★

Spacious and elegant, this vast square is dominated by the 19C **Town Hall** which was built by public subscription and surrounded by a selection of 18C and 19C town buildings: three-storeyed, parapeted hipped roofs with dormers, straight-headed windows – some with straight hoods on scroll brackets, some in colourful harling, others of dressed stone, all a delight in summer with colourful hanging baskets and window box displays. On the west side the **Cross Keys Hotel** was one of the staging points on the Edinburgh–London coaching route. The names of the adjoining streets – Horsemarket, Woodmarket – are reminders of the original role of the square as the market place, as is the bull ring embedded in a star formation in the cobbles.

The restored Tudor building with oriel windows in Woodmarket (now home to a dental practice) was built in 1885 as the corn exchange.

Roxburgh Street

Leading off down towards the river is an alley that gives access to the **Cobby Riverside Walk**, affording pleasant views of the river, the weir, the eminence and former site of Roxburgh Castle, Floors Castle in its splendid setting, and the backs of a series of town houses. Climb back up to Roxburgh Street where on the left is the majestic entrance to Floors built in 1929 by Reginald Fairlie. Two lodges with cupolas are linked by grandly gilded gates.

Return to the town centre by Roxburgh Street passing **Walton Hall** behind massive wooden gates, the former home of James Ballantyne, a schoolfellow of Scott's and later business partner in his printing business. **Falcon Hall** is also noteworthy.

EXCURSION

Manderston★

🕐**House:** May–Sept, late May and Aug Bank Holidays, Thu and Sun 1.30–5pm. **Gardens:** 11.30am–dusk.
✕ ♿£10; gardens only, £6. ✆01361 883 450. www.manderston.co.uk.

Manderston is a sympathetically preserved Edwardian country house, in immaculate grounds, where the hallmark of extravagant splendour applies throughout. The long, low, two-storeyed building beneath a balustraded roof is interrupted on the south or garden front by two gracefully curved projections and a front porticoed entrance.

The supreme craftsmanship of **plasterwork ceilings**, doors, fireplaces and furnishings are matched by the quality of the materials – marble, rosewood, mahogany, alabaster, brass, silver and the refinement of the objets d'art. John Kinross' interior designs are in the manner of Robert Adam.

The impressively spacious **Hall** heightened by the dome, fringed by delicate plasterwork, opens into the Anteroom with alabaster panels, leading to the Dining Room. Completed in 1905 with an elaborate compartmented ceiling, it holds a unique Blue John collection. The Library, doubling as a billiard room, is hung with crimson silk damask. Double doors lead to the richly decorated **Ballroom** with embossed silk and velvet wall hangings, and century-old curtains woven with gold or silver threads. In the Tea Room a Lutyens painting shows the Miller children grouped round a dog by Landseer. Sir James, responsible for the house as it stands today, is on the left. The same luxury and attention to detail applies to bedrooms and bathrooms.

One of the more fascinating aspects of the visit is the vast domain of kitchen, scullery, five larders, housekeeper's room, linen store and servants' hall, a highly organised realm, where the housekeeper and the butler reigned supreme over an impressive army of domestic staff.

The south front overlooks terraced gardens and grassy slopes down to the lake with – on the far side – the

Country House or Fortress?

Floors Castle occupies a natural terrace overlooking the River Tweed and facing the Cheviot Hills (the heartland of the family's estate). It lies on the opposite river bank to Roxburgh Castle, once the strongest fortress along the former march with England. Formerly the lands of Kelso abbey, it was obtained by **Robert Ker of Cessford**, one of King James VI's courtiers, who was created 1st Earl of Roxburghe in 1616. **John, 5th Earl** (d.1740), an active promoter of the Act of Union (1707), was made a duke for his services to the Crown and it was during his lifetime that the house was built (1721) to **William Adam**'s designs.

William Playfair was engaged by **James, 6th Duke** (1816–79) to enlarge and embellish Adam's original building. He took his inspiration from the highly ornamented picturesque style of Heriot's Hospital in Edinburgh. The result is the romantic fairytale castle with its roofscape of turrets, pinnacles and cupolas, that we see today, though in fact it is a country house, and home to the Roxburghes.

Woodland Garden (rhododendrons and azaleas) and on a clear day the Cheviots as backdrop.

On the entrance front, manicured lawns and majestic trees precede gates to formal gardens. Beyond, the Marble Dairy, in the form of a chapter house, has an oak-panelled tearoom above. Nearby is the head gardener's house with its walled garden.

The refinement of the **stables★**, arranged around two courtyards, is all the more striking for being unexpected. Teak and brass predominate while in the mahogany panelled harness room both the floor and the central table are of marble. Traditional cream teas are served here.

Manderston is now the home of Lord and Lady Palmer, of Huntley & Palmers biscuit fame.

🚗 DRIVING TOUR

🚗 CASTLES AND STRONGHOLDS
50mi/80km.

▶ Leave Kelso on the A6089 towards Floors.

Floors Castle★
♿🕐*Easter–Sept daily 10.30am–5pm; Oct Sat–Sun 10.30am–5pm. Castle, Gardens and Grounds only, £11.50; Garden and Grounds only, £6.50.* ✗

☎*01573 450 331.*
www.floorscastle.com.
The highly distinctive pinnacled silhouette of **Floors Castle** (🕐*see Box above*) enjoys a superb terraced site overlooking the Tweed.

Exterior – On the north front, Adam's original castellated main block quartered by towers rises through three storeys and is flanked by Playfair's additions of wings at right angles, linked at ground level to the main building. The wings, again quartered by taller towers, repeat the pattern of the central block. The dramatic roofscape of cupolas, chimneys, battlements and turrets links and unifies the whole.

Interior – Many of the rooms were remodelled by **Duchess May**, the American wife (1876–1937) of the 8th Duke, to accommodate her outstanding collection of tapestries and fine furniture. From the windows of the **Sitting Room** may be seen a holly tree which marks the spot where James II was killed in 1460 by an exploding cannon while laying siege to Roxburgh Castle.

The **Drawing Room** was altered to accommodate Duchess May's handsome set of six 17C Brussels tapestries.

The **Needle Room** is said to resemble a room in Versailles. The fine post-Impressionist paintings include Matisse's *Corbeille de Fleurs* and a river scene by Bonnard.

The 17C Gobelins tapestries and dark panelling in the **Ballroom** are the background for some fine pieces of French furniture, porcelain and portraits.

The **Bird Room** is a small Gothic room designed by Playfair to house a collection of stuffed birds.

In the **Gallery** are mementoes and documents including a letter from Mary, Queen of Scots to her Warden of the Eastern Marches, the Laird of Cessford.

▷ Take the B6397 left, crossing rich arable farmland, and then turn left onto the B6404. Take the road signposted Sandyknowe Farm up to the right then branch left towards the steading (stables and farm outbuildings). Continue through the steading and over the cattle grid up to the car park at the foot of the tower.

Smailholm Tower★

🕑*Apr–Sept daily 9.30am–5.30pm.*
£6. 📞01573 460 365.
www.historicenvironment.scot.

Standing like a sentinel, this lone tower house (17m tall) captures the history of the Borders, when these marches were controlled by a day and night watch. This attractive 16C example is built of rubble masonry and contrasting red-standstone trims. Restored in the 1980s, the interior houses an exhibition ofcostumed figures and tapestries, representing characters from the Border ballads. The adjacent village of Sandyknowe was where the young Walter Scott spent his childhood years with his grandparents, listening to the rousing tales of the Border ballads.

The rocky outcrop at the base of the tower commands a **panoramic view★★** of the Border countryside over a patchwork of rich arable farmland with in the distance other local landmarks: the Waterloo Monument (*📖see JEDBURGH: Excursions*) on Peniel Heugh due south and two of the Eildon Hills to the west.

▷ Make for Smailholm village and then on to Mellerstain by the B6397.

Mellerstain★★

🕑*House: May–Sept Fri–Mon 12.30–5pm; Gardens and Café✕: 11am–5pm.*
£8.50; gardens only, £5.
📞01573 410 225. www.mellerstain.com.

Mellerstain is famous for the amazing detail and delicacy of the Robert Adam interior. Rarely did Robert Adam plan a house from beginning to end, as he did here; Mellerstain is even rarer in that Adam's father designed the wings.

Imposingly plain, the exterior comprises the yellow stone castellated centre by Robert Adam flanked at right angles by the two earlier wings by his father William. Although only 45 years separate, the constructions, the contrast in architectural styles is striking and best seen from the courtyard front. The wings of 1725 have a certain vernacular charm compared with the severity and plain-

Smailholm Tower

© DonnaVelcio/iStockphoto.com

Library, Mellerstain

ness of the castellated Gothic centre. Less grandiose than elsewhere (Culzean, Osterley, Syon) but nonetheless so typically Adam, it boasts a series of remarkable **ceilings★★★**, often with matching fireplaces, woodwork and furniture.

Part of the William Adam wing, the **Stone Hall** has a Delft tile-adorned fireplace. In the east corridor is an original copy of the National Covenant subscribed by the 2nd Earl of Haddington. In the eastern section of the main corridor are several portraits including that of *Lady Grisell Baillie* by Aikman (1717) and *Lady Murray*, her daughter, by Richardson.

Adam designed a Gothic ceiling and a fireplace with Dutch tiles for the **Sitting Room**. The furniture is principally from the Queen Anne period; the ornate mirror over the fireplace in the style of Adam. The **Library★★★** offers an initial impression of colour – pale green, ivory white, pink, blue-grey – and of an overall grand design with the delicately detailed ceiling as centrepiece, slowly giving way to a perception of constituent components: the Zucci roundels – *Minerva, Learning* and *Teaching* – vases, medallions, trophies and figure panels and recesses, with the unifying pattern echoed in the bookcases, frieze, fireplace, superbly carved doors and mirror cupboards of the window wall. The Roubiliac busts of Lady Grisell Baillie and her daughter face each other above the end wall doors. The **Music Room** was designed as the Dining Room; the plain claret-coloured walls provide a

sharp contrast to the highly decorative ceiling with plaster reliefs of urns, eagles, sphinxes, medallions, rinceaux and fan ornaments surrounding the central medallion. The end wall pier glasses are to Adam's designs; above the fireplace is *Patrick Hume* by William Aikman The **Drawing Room** is rich and ornate, with heavily patterned silk brocade wall hangings and Aubusson carpets and ormolu mounted furniture

Of the portraits, several are by Allan Ramsay, or Old Mumpy as Adam called him, including *Lady Murray, Lord Binning* and *Dr Torriano* (1738), one of the first paintings executed while in Italy.

Small Drawing Room – Originally a bedchamber, the Adam imprint is everywhere.

Small Library – This small room, originally two dressing rooms, has the distinction of having two different Adam ceilings.

Main Corridor – The ceiling design again differs from that of the eastern section and is decidedly Gothic in inspiration. The paintings include family portraits. A majestic double **staircase** climbs and unites to rise as a single flight to the first floor, where an early-16C Flemish hunting tapestry is displayed. Several bedrooms are open; note in particular in the Manchineel Bedroom, the 19C carpet, handwoven in Alloa.

Great Gallery – The final surprise, on the second floor, is a noble apartment with screens of Ionic columns at either end, alas unfinished. Adam's proposed design is on display, as is his father's project for

The Mellerstain Estate

The Mellerstain estate was purchased in 1642 by a Lanarkshire man and passed in 1646 to his son Robert Baillie, a staunch Covenanter. Imprisoned in Edinburgh's Tolbooth he was visited by his friend's daughter, Grisell Hume, who on that occasion met for the first time her future husband, the young **George Baillie** (1664–1738). Several years were to pass, including exile and hardship in Holland for both families, before a return in 1688 to their native Borders and the marriage of Grisell to George Baillie in 1692.

The remarkable **Lady Grisell Baillie** (1665–1746) was Mellerstain's heroine and mistress. She ruled her household with efficiency, unbounded energy and gentleness and lived to see the completion of the William Adam wings. On her death the estate passed to her grandson George Baillie, who engaged **Robert Adam** (1728–1792) to bridge the gap between the two wings.

the central block. *Lady Grisell Baillie* and *George Baillie* are portrayed by Medina. The enigma remains – what was the function of this gallery and why was it never completed?

Return to the Inner Hall; the mirror and table are Adam works. Among the canvases there is a beautiful conversation piece by Nasmyth.

Moving on to the **grounds and gardens**, in the vaulted halls of the old servants' quarters, is the **Mellerstain Art Gallery**. It offers temporary exhibitions of modern Scottish paintings. The Italian-styled terraced garden was laid out in 1909 by Sir Reginald Blomfield and has a glorious view overlooking the lake to the Cheviot Hills in the distance. A play area has recently been added.

Greenknowe Tower

After photo by E. Sevo/ MICHELIN

▷ Make for the A6089, turning left towards Gordon and at the road junction take the A6105 left, and continue for about half a mile/1km.

Greenknowe Tower

On an elevated site, surrounded by marshland, this 16C L-shaped tower house, now a roofless ruin, still stands sentinel. Over the entrance the lintel comprises the owner's coat of arms, dated 1581. Internally the layout is typical of such a building with cellar and kitchen on the ground floor, the laird's hall on the first and bedchambers above.

▷ Turn left onto the A6089 heading towards Lauder.

Thirlestane Castle

🕐 *Sun–Thu May–Sept 10am–4pm (grounds 5pm).* ❧*£9.50, grounds only, £4.* ✕ ☎*01578 722 430.* *www.thirlestanecastle.co.uk.*

The castle has been the home of the Maitland family from the 16C to the present day. The original tower, established on an ancient fortified site, was converted into a home by William Maitland, 1st Earl of Lauderdale and secretary to Mary, Queen of Scots.

The 2nd Earl of Lauderdale, John Maitland, was one of the most important and controversial Scottish figures of the late 17C. As a leading royalist, he was a confidant of King Charles II and spent nine years in the Tower of London under sentence of death. After the Restoration, he was appointed Secretary of State for Scotland. As such, he was virtually the uncrowned King of Scotland, wielded unrivalled power and influence and transformed Thirlestane Castle into a fitting palace from which to direct the affairs of Scotland. Sir William Bruce remodelled the castle, bringing Renaissance influences to the Scottish Baronial style. He also oversaw the transformation of the interior, the most remarkable feature of which is the rich **plasterwork★★** of the State Rooms.

▶ Follow the A68 north.

Lauder

Pronounced "Lorder", this market town is on the western edge of the Lammermuir Hills. If you have time, see its tollbooth and parish church, constructed in 1673 by William Bruce, architect of Thirlestane Castle.

▶ Take the A697 east until Greenlaw, then turn right on the A6105 towards Earlston, then left on the B6364 towards Kelso.

The imposing ruined edifice high on the right is **Hume Castle**. The present structure dates from the 18C. From its foot there are splendid views of the Merse.

▶ Continue on the A6089 to Kelso.

ADDRESSES

🖎 STAY

😑😑 **Cross Keys Hotel** – *36–37 The Square, Kelso. ☎01573 223 303. www.cross-keys-hotel.co.uk. 26 rooms and suites.* This imposing 18C hotel dominates the main square. Visitors can sample Scottish and international cuisine (😑😑).

😑😑 **Duncan House** – *Chalkheugh Terrace, Roxburgh Street, Kelso. ☎07980 809 774. www.duncanhouse.co.uk. 4 rooms.* This Georgian-style house by the Tweed is 2 min from the town centre and looks onto Floors Castle.

Cheviot Hills viewed from the Scottish Borders
© Jason Friend/age fotostock

😑😑 **Willow Court** – *The Friars, Jedburgh. ☎01835 863 702. 3 rooms.* A contemporary guest house looking out over the town's rooftops.

😑😑😑😑 **Roxburghe Hotel** – *Kelso. ☎01573 450 331. https://schlosshotel-roxburghe.com. 20 rooms.* Luxurious 19C neo-Renaissance country house hotel offering gourmet cuisine, a championship golf course, world-class fishing and shooting.

🍽 EAT

😑 **Caroline's Coffee Shop** – *45 Horsemarket, Kelso. Open Mon–Sat 8am–5pm. ☎01573 226 996.* Town centre café and tearooms, open for coffee, snacks and light meals.

😑 **Café U** – *45-47 Roxburgh Street, Kelso. Open daytime only. Closed Sun. ☎01573 225 177.* Café and shop specialising in organic, vegetarian and vegan food.

😑😑 **Lemon and Thyme** – *35–37 Horsemarket, Kelso. ☎01573 348 324. www.lemonandthymerestaurant.co.uk.* Fine dining in the centre of Kelso, with menus offering a combination of traditional Scottish dishes and internationally influenced fusion flavours. Small and cosy place.

😑😑 **Caddy Man** – *Mounthooly, Jedburgh. ☎01835 850 787. www.caddymann.com.* Family run restaurant with daily changing menus with an emphasis on local seasonal ingredients. Hearty portions.

Melrose★
Melrose Abbey and Eildon Hills

Grouped round its beautiful abbey ruins, in the middle reaches of the Tweed, Melrose is overshadowed by the triple peaks of the Eildons. This attractive town bustles with visitors in the summer and makes an ideal touring centre for exploring the surrounding countryside. The town's Summer Festival and the day of the Melrose Sevens (7-a-side rugby football tournament) are lively occasions.

- ▶ **Population:** 2 307.
- ✆ **Michelin Map:** Local map, see Tweed Valley
- **Info:** Abbey Street; ✆01896 822 283.
- ▶ **Location:** Melrose is in the heart of the Scottish Borders, 43mi/69km south of Edinburgh via the A68.
- **Don't Miss:** Melrose Abbey decorative sculptures; the panoramas from Eildon Hill North.
- ◷ **Timing:** One hour for the abbey, an hour for the town.

MELROSE ABBEY★★

◷*Daily 9.30am–5.30pm (Oct–Mar 10am–4pm).* ◷*25–26 Dec, 1–2 Jan.* ☞*£6.* ✆*01896 822 562.* *www.historicenvironment.scot.*

The fertile Tweed haughlands were traditionally the site of early settlers and the Cistercian monks who settled **David I**'s 1136 foundation proved no exception when choosing the site of their new abbey. The monks from Rievaulx built an original 12C church which was damaged by 14C raids, in particular by Edward II's retreating army of 1322. Robert the Bruce ensured the rebuilding of the abbey and it was here that his heart was buried. The community grew and prospered becoming probably the richest abbey in Scotland, a fact which was not to save it from the fate of most Scottish abbeys: passing into secular hands, decline of the community and subsequent decay of the building. The ruins date from the late 14C–early 16C and are in a pure Gothic style. It was Sir Walter Scott who initiated repairs between 1822 and 1826 securing for posterity some of the loveliest ruins and establishing them as a must for travellers in the mid-19C.

The harmony of the stone, with tints varying from ochre to red, the profu-

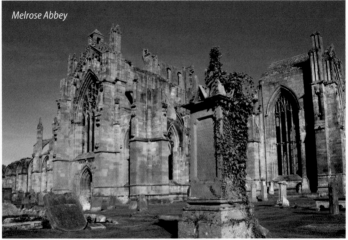

Melrose Abbey

© Carl Millar/Bigstockphoto.com

sion of decorative sculptural work, so uncharacteristic of the Cistercian order, and the purity of the Gothic style make for an extremely impressive and attractive group of ruins.

To appreciate fully the **decorative sculpture★★★** walk round the outside. The chapels of the south side are lit by a series of large pointed windows with elegant tracery, separated by pinnacled buttresses. The south transept gable is a profusion of detailed sculptural work. The pointed-arched, moulded doorway is surmounted by the great south window. The east gable with the great oriel and its fragile tracery is crowned with the *Coronation of the Virgin*.

A pulpitum divides the lay brothers' choir from the monks' choir. On the nave's south side the clustered piers support moulded pointed arches which open onto eight chapels. The **choir** beyond the pulpitum has later buttressing work and barrel vaulting, as this once served as parish church. The north transept still has statues of St Peter and St Paul above the west clerestory windows. The south transept frames the impressive **window**.

Cloister – Conforming to usual practice, buildings border the garth and walks on all sides. The east range housed the chapter house in the centre and dormitory above, the north the kitchens and refectory, the west the early frater with the lay brothers' cloister beyond. Note the arcading on the east wall and north processional doorway with a highly ornamental accolade.

Commendator's House – *Across the road and over the Great Drain.* A museum in this restored building contains sculptural fragments, explanations on construction methods, in addition to exhibits on Trimontium and Sir Walter Scott's associations with Melrose.

Priorwood Garden
Entrance on Abbey Street.
⚐⚐ *Apr–Oct Mon–Sat 10am–5pm, Sun 1–5pm.* ✄ ℘*01896 209 504.*
www.nts.org.uk.
Next to the abbey precincts this small garden specialises in flowers for drying;

their shop (*open all year*) sells the results of their labours. The roadside wall has attractive ironwork by Lutyens.

High Street
The street is bordered by some fine 18C buildings in the vicinity of the Market Square, with its 17C mercat cross.

ADDITIONAL SIGHTS
Trimontium Museum of Roman Scotland
The Ormiston, The Square.
⚐*Apr–Oct daily 10.30am–4.30pm.*
℘*01896 822 651.*
www.trimontium.co.uk.
Trimontium was the largest Roman fort in Scotland, built by Agricola in the 1C, at nearby Newstead. Finds made here in the early 20C (now kept at Edinburgh) gave an unparalleled insight into the life of the Roman soldier on this far frontier. The small museum features more recent excavations.

Eildon Hills
Leave Melrose by the Lilliesleaf B6359 road, turning left at the signpost Eildon Walk. Cross the bridge then follow the path leading up to the saddle between the two summits.
1h30 there and back. Wear sturdy shoes for the grassy slopes if it is wet.
The Eildons are of volcanic origin, but legend has it that this triple-peaked hill was the work of the 13C wizard **Michael Scott**, who is buried in Melrose abbey. Scott was in fact a mathematician, philosopher, doctor of theology and friend of the Emperor Frederick II. He figures in Dante's *Inferno* as Michele Scotto. The peaks are a conspicuous landmark in the region and the Eildon Hill North (404m), which was successively an Iron Age hill fortress and Roman signal station, now provides a magnificent **panorama★★★**: Melrose and its abbey, Leaderfoot viaduct, Smailholm Tower, the Cheviots, Peniel Heugh with its monument, round to the Tweed again and the Gala Water valley with Galashiels.

Aside from Burns' pilgrims and keen seaside golfers, few visitors have Ayrshire as a "must see" on their itinerary. Most of the visitors who come to the west coast are Irish (from just across the sea) though many American holidaymakers also make their first Scottish footfall just outside Ayr, at the confusingly named Glasgow Prestwick Airport. Most head east, to Edinburgh, but they could do much worse than turn west, and cross the water to the characterful Isle of Arran, for an equally fine introduction to Scotland.

Highlights

1 Visit the legendary **Tam o'Shanter Inn** (p109)

2 Following in the literary footsteps of **Robert Burns** (p110)

3 Visiting historic **Culzean Castle**, then relaxing on its beach (p113)

4 Spending a day or a night on the tranquil **Holy Island** (p377)

Ayr and South Ayrshire

The East Coast's premier holiday resort, Ayr is renowned for its sandy beaches, world-famous golf courses (Troon and Turnberry are close by) but above all, its links with the Scottish national poet and treasured icon, Robert Burns.

Burns was born in the neighbouring village of Alloway, lived part of his life here and took local inspiration for some of his most famous characters. A verita-

ble tourist industry has now grown up locally around the cult of the "Ploughman Poet", culminating in the nationwide – worldwide wherever there are ex-pat Scots – celebration of his birth on 25 January.

In April, Ayr is the venue for the country's top horseracing event, the Scottish Grand National. If you're here in July or August a trip aboard the paddle steamer *Waverley* – the last seagoing paddle steamer in the world – is a local treat.

South of Ayr are the region's other top visitor attractions: clifftop Culzean ("cullane") Castle – the finest stately home in the region, and Ailsa Craig – an offshore rock, halfway between Clydeside and Ireland, inhabited by 40 000 chattering gannets.

North and East Ayrshire

If the sun is shining, beat a path to the pleasant little seaside resort of Largs, and in any weather, pack your walking boots for a trek around the little island of Great Cumbrae, a short ferry ride away. From here there are great views back across the water.

Rainy day indoor excursions include the family-oriented Vikingar! which tells the story of the Battle of Largs in 1263, and the rather more substantial, though no less interesting, Scottish Maritime Museum outpost in Irvine. Another good family day out is provided by the often overlooked Dean Castle, set in 81ha of beautiful grounds.

Nearby Loch Doon is the largest inland loch in southern Scotland (8 miles/13km long by 3–4 miles/5–6.5km wide) surrounded by rugged mountains and unspoiled landscapes. Indeed, the "banks of braes of bonnie Doon" were the inspiration for one of Burns' poems.

© Scottish Maritime Museum, Irvine

Scottish Maritime Museum, Irvine

Ayr★

Ayr, the leading holiday resort on the Firth of Clyde coast, makes a good centre for exploring Burns country. This lively resort has a vast expanse of sandy beach backed by an esplanade, several delightful parks, traditional amusements and Scotland's premier racecourse. The latter is the venue for the Scottish Grand National (*see Calendar of Events*) and the Ayr Gold Cup.

A BIT OF HISTORY

The town grew up around its medieval castle to become the principal centre of Carrick, later an earldom. The original castle seems to have been obliterated by a huge citadel built by Cromwell of which a few fragments of wall remain. By the 16C and 17C the town was the busiest port on the west coast, just ahead of Glasgow for size. Trade was essentially with France until the late 17C when the West Indian and North American markets opened up. The railway age brought new life to Ayr, with the holidaymakers and commuting businessmen. At the beginning of the 19C Ayr expanded in a planned way southwards from its medieval core, and the orderly rectangular street pattern and many substantial terraced houses remain from this time. There are few traces left of an older Ayr.

Today, this market town, has a thriving tourist trade dependent on the proximity of the international airport at Prestwick, the reputation of nearby golfing centres (Turnberry, Troon) and its role as hub of Burns country.

SIGHTS
Auld Brig

This 13C bridge, immortalised by Burns, is said to have been financed by two sisters, one of whom had seen her fiancé drowned while trying to ford the river. The narrow cobbled bridge remains firm while its rival collapsed in the storm of 1870.

▶ **Population:** 47 190.
Info: 22 Sandgate; ✆01292 290 300; www.visitscotland.com.
Location: The town centre is a short walk from the seaside though you will need a car to visit the outlying historical attractions.
Don't Miss: Alloway for its Robert Burns connection.
Timing: Allow one to two days unless you are a "Burnsophile" or a keen golfer – in which case you will want to stay longer.

Tam o'Shanter Inn

A tavern in Burns' time, this is still a public house. It was from here that Tam set out on his famous ride one stormy night in Burns' immortal poem, one of his finest.

Burns' poem about Tam o'Shanter described how, on his homeward journey from a long evening at the inn, and riding his grey mare, Tam emboldened by "bold John Barleycorn", saw an "unco Sight! Warlocks and witches in a dance". Remembering that witches have no power to pursue anyone further than the middle of the next stream, Tam heads for the Brig o'Doon – the bridge spanning the River Doon. Tam manages to escape their clutches, but one witch grabs his mare's tail and pulls it off. Burns ends his tale with the lines:
Whene'er to drink you are inclin'd,
Or cutty-sarks run in your mind,
Think, ye may buy the joys owre dear
Remember Tam o'Shanter's mare.

EXCURSION
Alloway★
Leave Ayr south on the B 7024 for 2mi/3.5km.
Alloway is famed as the birthplace of Scotland's bard, **Robert Burns** (1759–1796). In his writing and poetry

the 13C **Brig o'Doon**, to which Tam was chased by the "hellish legion" and where his poor Meg lost her tail. A tiny pavilion contains jolly 19C statues of Tam, Souter Johnnie and Nanse and here too is the imposing neo-Classical **Burns Monument** and attached gardens.

Beyond, on the far side of the main road, stands **Alloway Kirk**, where William Burnes, Robert's father is buried. Robert dropped the 'e' from his surname to adopt the more common Ayrshire spelling of Burns.

DRIVING TOURS

① BURNS COUNTRY
60mi/97km. Allow at least a day.

▶ Leave Ayr heading NE on the A 77, A 719 and local roads for 7mi/11.5km.

Tarbolton

During the period when Burns' father farmed nearby Lochlea Farm (1777–84), Tarbolton was a muslin and silk weavers' village. Here Robert and some friends started a debating society in 1780.

The building today is known as the **Bachelors' Club** (◐*Apr–Sept Fri–Tue 1–5pm. ℘01292 541 940; www.nts.org.uk*). Downstairs, an early 19C kitchen adjoins the byre, while above is the hall where the debating club met. Burns' relics include his Masonic belongings.

▶ Take the B743, S and E.

Mauchline

Following the death of Burns' father, the family moved to Mossgiel Farm. Mauchline was where Burns met and eventually married a local girl, Jean Armour, by whom he had nine children.

On returning from his triumphant visit to Edinburgh in 1788, Burns leased an upper room in a Castle Street house, now the **Burns House Museum** (♿ ◐ *Tue–Wed 10.30am–1.40pm, 2–6pm; Thu 1.30–4.40pm, 5.40–8pm; Fri–Sat 10.30am–4pm; ℘01290 550 045; https://eastayrshireleisure.com*), for Jean and his children. Wed later in the

he became the spokesman for a nation and more than two centuries after his death his name is still invariably evoked wherever in the world two or more Scotsmen meet.

Robert Burns Birthplace Museum★

♿◐*Daily 10am–5pm. ◐25–26 and 31 Dec, 1–2 Jan. ⊛£10.50 (includes exhibition and Burns Cottage). ✗ ℘01292 443 700. www.burnsmuseum.org.uk.*

This roadside cottage, built by William Burnes, is where his eldest son Robert was born on 25 January 1759. Its simple ben, but and byre layout – a two roomed cottage with the but being the kitchen, and the ben being the sleeping area, and a byre tacked on to the end of the building to house the animals – evokes the spartan living conditions of the 18C. The museum has an extensive collection of Burns' manuscripts, letters, documents and other relics which shows the poet in the context of his life, work and travels in Ayrshire and beyond.

A footpath leads from the museum to highly manicured gardens overlooking

Burns Monument (right) and the garden

© louisemcgilvray/iStockphoto.com

Robert Burns

Robert "Rabbie" Burns was born in Alloway on 25 January 1759 of farming stock and through much of his life continued to work the land, thus earning him the nickname of the Ploughman Poet. He moved from his native Ayrshire to Edinburgh in 1786 where his writing blossomed, but returned to farm at Dumfries in 1788. Burns was a pioneer of the Romantic movement and in his writing encapsulated the patriotic fervour, the romance, hopes and beliefs of his countrymen like no other Scot before or since. As well as writing, Burns also worked tirelessly to collect and preserve Scottish folk songs, thus saving a huge amount of Scottish heritage. Today, a Scotland without Auld Lang Syne, Wha Hae, A Red, Red Rose; Tam o'Shanter, and Ae Fond Kiss would be like England without the works of Shakespeare. Burns died aged just 37 and is buried in Dumfries.

year, they all moved to Ellisland Farm (*see DUMFRIES: Excursion*). In addition to the Jean Armour Room upstairs, the museum has books, letters, documents and several personal items (including a watch and walking stick). Downstairs, a folk section includes 19C Mauchline ware and Cumnock pottery.

The house next door *(now the curator's, closed to the public)* was the home of Dr Mackenzie, who gave Burns a letter of introduction to Henry Mackenzie, editor of *The Lounger*, based in Edinburgh.

In the churchyard are buried four of Burns' children. On the far side of the churchyard is **Poosie Nansie's/Nanse Tinnock's Inn**, still a pub today, which figured large in his poetry of the period (*The Mauchline Lady, Mary Morrison, The Holy Fair, Holy Willie's Prayer, Address to the Devil*).

▷ Follow the A76 NW to Kilmarnock.

Kilmarnock

There's little to detain visitors in Kilmarnock itself, but just north of the city centre is **Dean Castle Country Park** (& ⊙*Park and grounds are open all year daily 11am–5pm. ☏01563 554 734; https://eastayrshireleisure.com*), covering over 81 ha, with woodland walks, adventure playground, pets corner, visitor centre, and a sturdy 14C castle housing fine collections of arms and armour★, tapestries and musical instruments★.

▷ Follow the A71 W to Irvine.

Irvine

Former royal burgh and one-time port for Glasgow, Irvine was designated a New Town in 1996. The Old Town centre with its skyline of church towers is no longer connected to the railway station by a stone bridge but by a huge shopping mall.

Harbourside

Close to where the River Garnock and River Irvine merge, the quayside is approached through an innovative and picturesque housing scheme, a good neighbour to the old buildings lining the waterfront.

The **Scottish Maritime Museum★** (*Mon–Sat 10am–5pm; £8.50; 01294 278 283; www.scottishmaritime museum.org*) captures Scotland's maritime history in a lively manner.

▶ Take the A737 north in the direction of Kilwinning and Dalry.

Kilwinning

The village contains two points of minor interest. On Main Street is **Kilwinning Abbey Tower** (*mid-May–mid-Sept Fri–Sun, 1–3pm; 01294 464 174; www. kilwinningheritage.org.uk*), built in the 19C on the ruins of a 12C abbey. From the top of the tower, there are excellent views.

Housed in the former Dalgarven Mill on Dalry Road is the charming **Museum of Ayrshire Country Life and Costume** (*Easter–Oct Tue–Sat 10am–5pm, Sun 11am–5pm; Nov–Easter Tue–Fri 10am–4pm; £4.50; 01294 552 448k*) complete with a working 16C water wheel and the machinery of a Victorian Grain Mill.

▶ Take the A738 SW towards Saltcoats.

Saltcoats

The **North Ayrshire Heritage Centre** (*Mon–Fri 9.30am–1pm, 2–5pm, Sat 10am–1pm, 2–5pm; 01294 464 174; www.north-ayrshire.gov.uk*) is an eclectic collection of social domestic and industrial objects (costumes, furniture, model ships), medieval carvings and temporary exhibitions.

▶ Take the A78 south towards Troon, then the A759 to Dundonald.

Dundonald Castle

Visitor centre and castle: daily 9.30am–5.30pm. £5; 01563 851 489. www.dundonaldcastle.org.uk.

Only the ruins of the fortress that was the cradle of the Stewarts now remains. This fortified tower house was built for Robert II on his accession to the throne of Scotland in 1371 and it was used as a royal residence by the early Stewart kings for the next 150 years.

▶ Return to the A78, S, and then take the A79.

Prestwick

The town is known for its international airport and its top-class golf course. It was on the Prestwick course in 1860 that the very first golf open was played for a Challenge Belt. The following year the competition was declared "Open to all the world".

2 THE COAST SOUTH OF AYR *20mi/32km.*

▶ Leave Ayr on the B7024 towards Maybole, then follow the A77.

Kirkoswald

The thatched and limewashed **Souter Johnnie's Cottage** (*Apr–Sept Fri–Tue 11.30am–5pm; 01655 760 603; www.nts.org.uk*) was the home of Scotland's legendary cobbler (souter), the "ancient, trusty, drouthy, cronie" of Tam o'Shanter, central figure in Burns' poem of the same name. Burns had met the real-life people (the cobbler John Davidson; and farmer Douglas Graham), of this rollicking narrative, during his 1775 summer stay at Kirkoswald when he came to study under the local dominie (schoolmaster-minister) Hugh Roger. In addition to the two rooms and cobbler's workshop is an original set of life-size figures by James Thom in the garden that depict Souter Johnnie, Tam, the innkeeper and his wife.

Douglas Graham (Tam) and his wife are buried in the local churchyard.

Culzean Castle

© DouglasMcGilviray/iStockphoto.com

▶ Continue as far as Turnberry then turn right (N) to follow the coast road.

Culzean Castle★

🕐*Castle*: Apr–Oct 10.30am–4.30pm.
👜£17; park only, £5. ✕ 🅿
📞01655 884 455. www.nts.org.uk.
Culzean (pronounced "cul-lane") Castle, in its dramatic clifftop **setting★★★**, provides testimony to "the taste and skill of Mr Adam".

Sir Thomas, the 9th Earl of Cassillis, inherited this traditional Kennedy family seat in 1744 and his brother, David, the 10th Earl (d.1792) commissioned **Robert Adam** (1728–1792) to transform the old castle. The work was executed in three stages. Initially there was the conversion of the tower house, then the creation of a magnificent suite of rooms on the seaward side with the construction of the oval staircase as the final project. Of Adam's castle houses of the 1780s this is perhaps the most spectacular. Adam was a confirmed Classicist, but the exteriors have, nevertheless, medieval touches in the mock battlements and arrow slits. The seaward front with the great drum tower is by far the most imposing. Begin your tour in the **Visitor Centre**, housed in converted buildings which were part of Robert Adam's Home Farm. It features an exhibition, an audiovisual presentation on the history of the castle, the Park Ranger Sevice, plus shops and a restaurant.

The Adam interiors characterise "The Age of Elegance". Delicately patterned ceilings – concentric or compartmented – with Antonio Zucchi paintings as focal points, are echoed in equally detailed friezes, chimney-pieces and furniture.

The centrepiece of the house and an Adam masterpiece is the **Oval Staircase★★** as it rises soberly elegant through three tiers of columns. Outstanding on the first floor is **The Saloon**, the epitome of disciplined 18C elegance. Adam-designed furnishings include the carpet, mirrors, wall sconces and a pair of semicircular side-tables.

In the **Armoury** is one of the most important collections of flintlock pistols (18C–19C) in the world. Also of interest are items that belonged to General (later President) **Eisenhower** who was invited by the 5th Marquess and the Kennedy family to accept the tenancy of a specially created guest flat on the top floor of the castle for his lifetime, as a gesture of Scottish thanks for America's support during World War II.

A series of **walks** have been designed around the castle's 229ha **Country Park** estate so that visitors can discover the seashore, the **walled garden** with its herbaceous border, the Swan Lake, the 19C Camellia House, Orangery and terrace garden.

DUMFRIES AND GALLOWAY

If Scotland has an unknown – or at least unsung – corner, then it is probably the western borders region of Dumfries ("dum-frees") and Galloway. Its settlements may be less polished than the tweedy country towns of its better-known neighbour, the Borders region, due east, but it has many of the same appealing ingredients as the Borders plus some truly wild areas, and a lovely coastline. Independent travellers may also be pleased to note that what it does lack are coach parties on the "Shortbread and Tartan" heritage trail!

Highlights

1 Following the final years of Robbie Burns in **Dumfries** (p115)

2 A sunny day's drive along the **Scottish Riviera** (p118)

3 Visiting **Drumlanrig Castle** for its setting and treasures (p120)

4 Discovering the charming arty delights of **Kirkcudbright** (p123)

5 A stroll around the gardens and castle at **Threave** (p126)

Dumfries town, East Dumfries and Galloway

Just across the border, Gretna Green may be the first taste of both Scotland and Dumfries and Galloway for travellers from the south, but those in the know keep on going and either head north to Moffat, which makes a good base for exploring the surrounding Southern Uplands, or divert a little way east to the lesser-known "Queen of the South" – Dumfries.

This attractive town is second only to Ayr for its associations with Robert Burns, who lived the final years of his life here. Just out of town is the Ploughman Poet's atmospheric Ellisland Farm, and, by contrast, the evocative medieval ruins of Caerlaverock castle and Sweetheart Abbey.

If you prefer your castle with its roof still on and its treasures intact, north of Dumfries is the impressive 17C Drumlanrig castle. The more workaday history of the region is illustrated in the nearby former lead mining settlements of Leadhills and Wanlockhead.

Central Galloway

The Galloway Heartland is a rich mixture of landscapes, from rolling farmland to the sandy coves of the "Scottish Riviera" Solway coast, and the glassy lochs, wooded hills and bare, rounded peaks of the Galloway Hills.

The region's main town is charming Kirkcudbright (pronounced "cur-coo-bree"); formerly a bustling port and subsequently an artists' retreat, it is now a tranquil, well-preserved little town with fine 18C and early 19C architecture, plus a rich artistic heritage.

The Galloway Hills are best experienced by visiting the huge Galloway Forest Park. Here amid beautiful moors, mountains, lakes and rivers, you are more likely to stumble across red deer than fellow human beings. By contrast lovely Threave Garden (and its castle) is the finest example of man's influence on the landscape.

West Dumfries and Galloway

This extreme southwest corner of Scotland is overlooked by most visitors but this very lack of crowds, plus its variety of landscapes and appealing towns and villages make it well worth the detour. At its westernmost point, the Mull of Galloway enjoys a microclimate that means palms can flourish outdoors at its famous Logan Botanic Gardens.

Two other "curiosities" are literary lovers' Wigtown, the self-styled "National Booktown" and Whithorn, a one-street town, known as the cradle of Scottish Christianity after St Ninian founded the first Christian church north of Hadrian's Wall here. Knockinaam Lodge, near Portpatrick, today a fine hotel, appealed to Sir Winston Churchill and General Eisenhower who chose to hold a secret meeting there during the Second World War to discuss the D-Day plans.

Dumfries★

and around

Known as the "Queen of the South" – the name was given by a local poet in 1857 and has been adopted by the town's football team – the attractive and bustling town of Dumfries has long been the southwest's most important town. Farming remains the principal industry with diversification provided by the administrative services of the regional headquarters and some manufacturing. The town has important historical associations with the national bard, Robert Burns and the national warrior hero, Robert the Bruce, as it was here that he slew Scotland's co-guardian, thus opening the second stage of the Wars of Independence.

▶ **Population:** 34 030.

🛈 **Info:** 64 Whitesands; ✆01387 253 862. www.visit dumfriesandgalloway.co.uk.

▶ **Location:** Dumfries is around 25mi/40km northwest of the border with England on the A75.

👁 **Don't Miss:** Sweetheart Abbey.

🕐 **Timing:** Allow a good half-day to see the town, at least a full day for excursions. The town has a fairly complex one-way system and it is advisable to visit on foot. Dumfries makes a good base for excursions.

🐾 WALKING TOUR

Burns Mausoleum

To the right, behind the prominent red sandstone church, rebuilt in 1745, is the mausoleum where Burns, his wife Jean Armour and several of their children are buried. A plan (to the right of the church) indicates where some of Burns' associates and friends are laid to rest.

▶ On leaving the church turn right into St Michael Street, and then bear right to follow Burns Street. Burns House is on the right.

Burns House

🕐*Apr–Sept Mon–Sat 10am–5pm, Sun 2–5pm; Oct–Mar Tue–Sat 10am–1pm, 2–5pm. ✆01387 255 297. www.dumgal.gov.uk/article/15733/ Robert-Burns-House.*

Burns spent the last three years of his life in this house, which now serves as a museum. The ground floor room has examples of the poet's correspondence. The small upstairs room with writing desk and chair retains the window pane engraved with the bard's name.

▶ Continue on Burns Street, turn left onto Shakespeare Street, then right onto High Street.

Midsteeple★

This imposing building makes a striking focal point for the High Street. The resemblance with Stirling's Tolbooth (👁*see STIRLING*) is not unexpected since the mason, Tobias Bauchop, had worked under Sir William Bruce on the Stirling project prior to erecting the Midsteeple in 1707 to serve as a prison and courthouse.

The royal coat of arms emblazons the front; there are also a standard measurement of the Ell – the universal measure for wool cloth (45 inches) –and a plan of the town in Burns' day.

Burns Statue

At the north end of the High Street, the 1882 statue commemorates Dumfries' most famous citizen.

A wall plaque on the buildings to the west of the statue marks the site of Greyfriars Monastery where Robert the Bruce killed his arch enemy John III Comyn, Lord of Badenoch ("the Red Comyn") in 1306.

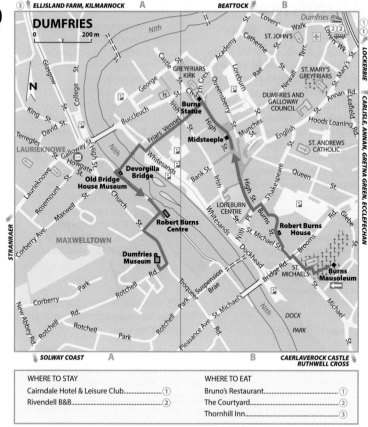

WHERE TO STAY		WHERE TO EAT	
Cairndale Hotel & Leisure Club	①	Bruno's Restaurant	①
Rivendell B&B	②	The Courtyard	②
		Thornhill Inn	③

◗ Take Friars Vennel to the river, and cross the pedestrian Devorgilla Bridge.

Devorgilla Bridge

This narrow six-arch bridge with pointed cutwaters built in the 15C replaced the original wooden structure built by Devorgilla (◖see SWEETHEART ABBEY, p119). The bridge is constructed of course red sandstone rubble, in parts dressed with horizontal drove lines. It is a well-worn bridge displaying masonry from many periods.

Old Bridge House

◷Apr–Sept Mon–Sat 10am–5pm, Sun 2–5pm. ℘01387 256 904.
Built in 1660 into the sandstone of the bridge, Dumfries' oldest house is now a museum of everyday life in the town. A Victorian house's family kitchen, nursery

and bedroom have been re-created, as well as an early dentist's surgery.

◗ Continue left along the riverside on Mill Road.

Robert Burns Centre and Film Theatre

&◷Apr–Sept Mon–Sat 10am–5pm, Sun 2–5pm; Oct–Mar Tue–Sat 10am–1pm, 2–5pm. ◉Free; audiovisual tour, £2.30. ℘01387 264 808.
The centre, which is housed in a restored 18C watermill, traces the bard's links with the town. The exhibition is illuminated by several original manuscripts and belongings of the poet.
There is a fascinating scale model of Dumfries in the 1790s and an atmospheric audiovisual presentation.

In the evening, the centre is Scotland's smallest art house **film theatre** (*www. rbcft.co.uk*), showing contemporary and world cinema.

▶ Turn down nearby Millbrae Street to meet Church Street. Turn left.

Dumfries Museum

&⏱*Easter (or 1 Apr)–Sept Mon–Sat 10am–5pm; Sun 2–5pm; Oct–Easter (or 31 Mar) Tue–Sat 10am–1pm, 2–5pm. Free; Camera Obscura, £3.60).* 🅿 ☎*01387 253 374. www.dumgal.gov.uk.*
A converted 18C windmill and later extensions house local collections of geology, archaeology and history, and includes the wildlife of Solway and the tools and weapons of prehistoric man. The mill also has displays of early Christian stones, country life and the origins of the museum, which was formerly an astronomical observatory. The original telescope (20cm), which still exists, was used to observe Halley's Comet in July 1836.

A **Camera Obscura** (⏱*Apr–Sept only*) installed on the top floor in 1836, gives a panoramic view of Dumfries and the surrounding countryside, and is said to be the oldest working instrument in the world.

EXCURSIONS

▶ Leave Dumfries by the A76.

Ellisland Farm

⏱*Early Jan–Nov Mon–Sat 10am–1pm, 2–5pm, Sun 2–5pm (Oct–Mar Tue–Sat). £5.* ☎*01387 740 426. www.ellislandfarm.co.uk.*
Burns leased this farm in June 1788. He introduced new farming methods but the soil was poor and his first crops failed. He accepted an appointment in the Excise in the district and in 1791, on being offered promotion, he gave up farming and moved to Dumfries as a full-time exciseman. His first house was in the Wee Vennel, now Bank Street.

It was at Ellisland, on the banks of the Nith, that Burns wrote what many consider to be his greatest work, *Tam o'Shanter*. One room of the farmhouse, which is still lived in, has a display of Burns relics with documents concerning family, patrons and friends. In the granary there is a video presentation of Burns' life.

Annan

15mi/24km SW of Dumfries. Leave Dumfries by the A780 and then A75.
On the east side of the River Annan, the town is just 8mi/13km from the English border, and began as a river port in the 14C, although most of modern Annan was built in the last 200 years.

The elegant Annan Bridge was built in 1826 by Robert Stevenson, and the local school attended by the Scottish writer Thomas Carlyle (&*See ECCLEFECHAN*). Annan is a Royal Burgh with a bustling high street and a good range of shops and restaurants.

Outstanding among its many sandstone buildings is Bridge House, built in 1780 and commonly regarded as one of the finest Georgian houses in Scotland. Annan's Old Parish Church dates from the same period; its interior is elegant and features a canopied Provost's pew.

Annan Museum (&⏱*Apr–Oct Mon–Sat 11am–4pm;* ☎*01461 201 384; www. annan.org.uk/museum*) houses an exhibition on the history of Annan.

Gretna Green

8mi/13km E of Annan.
Traditionally the first village in Scotland following the old coach road from London to Edinburgh, Gretna Green is renowned for its romantic tradition of elopement and marriage at the old village forge (now the very touristy World Famous Old Blacksmith's Shop Centre). The historical reason for this was a more lax legal approach to marriage in Scotland than in England – a situation which has long ceased to be, though Gretna still sees more than its fair share of (legal) weddings.

These runaway marriages are believed to have started in the 18C when a marriage act came into force in England that allowed that if a parent of a minor wishing to marry (i.e. then a person

Caerlaverock Castle

under the age of 21) objected, they could legally veto the union. The act did not apply in Scotland, where it was possible for boys to marry at 14 and girls at 12 with or without parental consent.

Ecclefechan

10mi/16km NW of Gretna Green.

Ecclefechan, in the Middle Ages part of the kingdom of Rheged, is the birthplace of Thomas Carlyle (1795–1881), essayist, historian, social reformer and great literary figure of his time.

Thomas Carlyle's Birthplace (☉*Apr–Oct daily 10am–5pm; ⌇£4. ✗ ℰ01576 300 666; www.nts.org.uk*) may be visited, as can the local cemetery where the "Sage of Chelsea" is buried. He refused a tomb in Westminster abbey because he wanted to be near his mother in death.

🚗DRIVING TOURS

🚗 ① THE NITH ESTUARY

33 mi/53km. Allow 1h driving time.

This tour follows the River Nith and cuts across dairy farming land.

▷Leave Dumfries by St Michael Street and head S on the B725.

Glencaple

This was once a bustling port where emigrants embarked for the New World and where Robert Burns worked as a Customs Office employee.

Glencaple today is a dormitory town for Dumfries, and best known for its marina.

Caerlaverock Castle★

⌆☉*Daily Apr–Sept 9.30am–5.30pm; Oct–Mar 10am–4pm. ⌇£6. ✗ (summer daily, winter Fri–Sun). ℰ01387 770 244. www.historicenvironment.scot.*
The substantial handsome ruins of Caerlaverock (lark's nest in Gaelic) is girt by a moat and earthen ramparts and stands in a green and pleasant setting on the north shore of the Solway Firth. Still formidable from the outside this medieval fortress and is an early example of the Scottish Renaissance style.

The present castle on the site was built in the late 13C (1290–1300). The defences were soon put to the test by Edward I's famous siege of 1300. By then it was the principal seat of the Maxwells, and alterations were made in the following centuries, the most important being the Renaissance façade of 1634, the work of the Philosopher Ist Earl of Nithsdale. Following a Protestant attack during the Covenanting Wars, the castle was abandoned for Terregles and then Traquair (⌆*see TRAQUAIR HOUSE*) and subsequently fell into disrepair.

Triangular in shape, the great keep **gatehouse** stands impressively at the apex with tall curtain walls receding to towers at the farther extremities, all with 15C machicolations. Inside the courtyard, the splendid **Renaissance façade★★** of the Nithsdale Building (1634) shows both a symmetry of design and refine-

ment of execution. The main elements, triangular or semicircular window and door pediments, are enriched with heraldic or mythological carvings.
An exhibition area features siege warfare, recalling the castle's violent past.

▷ Take the B725 and local roads.

Caerlaverock Wetland Centre
A rugged and beautiful 1 400 nature-filled acres looking out onto the Solway Firth that is perfect for birdwatching, especially during the winter migration. In summer wander through wildflower meadows looking for orchids, butterflies and dragonflies (www.wwt.org.uk).

▷ Continue E on the B725.

Ruthwell
Here in a small cottage, in 1810, Rev Henry Duncan founded the world's first savings bank based on business principles, paying interest on its investors' savings.
The cottage, the original Ruthwell Parish Bank, now houses the **Savings Banks Museum** (&. ◷Apr–Sept Tue–Sat 10am–4pm; Oct–Mar Thu–Sat 10am–4pm; ℘01387 870 640. www.savingsbanks-museum.co.uk). The museum houses a collection of early home savings boxes, coins and bank notes from many parts of the world.

Ruthwell Cross
Inside Ruthwell church this 7C cross is an example of early Christian art; the vivid and realistic sculpture tell the story of the Life and Passion of Christ. The artistic skill and craftsmanship of the 7C sculptor is most evident in the vine tracery intertwined with birds and other creatures. The margins are inscribed with runic characters. The many vicissitudes of the cross included its demolition on the orders of the General Assembly in 1642 and removal to the churchyard in 1780.
In 1823 the Rev Dr Henry Duncan rebuilt the cross in the grounds of the manse prior to its final installation and restoration in the church in 1887.

▷ Remain on the B725 as far as Carrutherstown, and join the A75 NW back to Dumfries.

☒ SOLWAY FIRTH COAST
47mi/75km. Leave Dumfries by either the A780 or A756 to join the A710 (New Abbey Road) heading S. Allow 1h30 driving time.

This route follows part of the Solway Coast Heritage Trail (the "Scottish Riviera") to the Mull of Galloway across an unspoilt countryside where mining villages nestle amid sandy bays and rocky coves with beautiful views over the Solway Firth.

New Abbey
The village of New Abbey, associated with the nearby Cistercian abbey, is a place of considerable charm and character. To the south, the land rises steadily to the magnificent summit of **Criffel** (*alt. 569m*) an easy ascent from Ardwall.

New Abbey Corn Mill
At the entrance to the village of New Abbey.
◷Daily Apr–Sept 9.30am–5.30pm; Oct–Mar Sat–Wed 10am–4pm. ◷1–2 Jan, 25–26 Dec. ◈£6. ℘01387 850 260. www.historicenvironment.scot.
This white-washed two-storey 18C mill produced oatmeal and animal feed until the World War II and its machinery remains intact and in working order. The overshot waterwheel is fed from a pond in a delightful village setting.

Sweetheart Abbey★
◷Apr–Sept daily 9.30am–5.30pm; Oct–Mar daily except Thu–Fri 10am–4pm. ◷1–2 Jan, 25–26 Dec. ◈£6. ☺ Part of the abbey is currently closed for safety reasons. ℘01387 850 397. www.historicenvironment.scot.
The beauty and charm of Sweetheart's ruins derive principally from the colourful contrast of the red sandstone and green of the surrounding lawns. Founded in 1273 by **Devorgilla**, wife of John Balliol, and colonised from nearby Dundrennan,

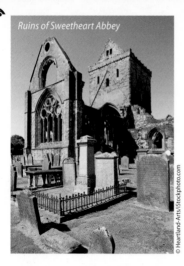

Ruins of Sweetheart Abbey

© Heartland-Arts/iStockphoto.com

Sweetheart was the last Cistercian foundation in Scotland. Walter Scott's novel *The Abbot* features Gilbert Brown, the last and most famous of Sweetheart's incumbents.

The whole is enclosed by a rare precinct wall which was originally interrupted by two gateways.

With the claustral buildings gone, the chief interest of the ruins is the completeness of its **church**. The stout tower above the crossing is adorned with rows of masks and heads supporting the battlements. The foundress Devorgilla was laid to rest in the presbytery, along with the casket containing the embalmed heart of her husband – thus explaining the unusual name.

▶ Continue on the A710 skirting the vast sandy beach of Sandyhills. At Colvend turn left towards Rockcliffe.

Rockcliffe

This resort nestles around a rocky cove facing **Rough Island**, an NTS bird sanctuary (⊘*not accessible May–Jul*).

▶ Return to Colvend and turn left towards Dalbeattie.

Dalbeattie

This small granite-built town is now a renowned mountain-biking centre, offering riders a choice of trails.

▶ Leave Dalbeattie on the B794 to Haugh of Urr.

Motte of Urr

A medieval earthwork, the Motte of Urr lies on the Urr Water to the north west of Dalbeattie. Dating from the 12C, it covers an area of about 2ha and has been described as one of the most impressive motte-and-bailey castle sites in Scotland

▶ Continue on the B794 to join the A75. Turn right to head back to Dumfries.

3 THE LOWTHER HILLS
72mi/115km. Allow 2h driving time.

Once a busy lead mining area the Lowther Hills is now an area of majestic beauty where the most frenetic activity is grazing sheep.

▶ Leave Dumfries north on the A76.

Thornhill

The broad main avenue of this village is dominated by a column erected by the 14th Duke of Queensberry whose ancestral home is the nearby Drumlanrig Castle.

Several walking trails criss-cross around the village.

▶ Continue north from Thornhill to Carronbridge, and remain on the A76 to the turning to Drumlanrig Castle.

Drumlanrig Castle★★

&⃝*Gardens and estate*: Apr–Sept 10am–5pm; *Castle*: Easter, May bank holidays and Jul–Aug. *Guided tours (1h) daily from 11am; last tour 4pm. ☞£12; gardens and park only £6. ℘01848 331 555.
www.drumlanrigcastle.co.uk.

With its theatrical skyline, Drumlanrig Castle, the seat of the Douglas family for generations, makes an arresting picture in a splendid setting. Inside, the grand reception rooms, magnificent staircases, ornate period features and cosy parlours give you an intimate sense of life through the centuries.

Drumlanrig Castle

© Drumlanrig Castle

History of Drumlanrig castle

As early as the 14C Drumlanrig was the site of a Douglas stronghold and son succeeded father until the late 18C. **William, 3rd Earl and 1st Duke of Queensberry** (1637–1697), a man of high position under the Stuarts and of an artistic nature, built in 1679–91 a mansion worthy of his status. However, it is said that he was so appalled by the total cost of the project that he spent only one night in his new palace before returning to the ancestral seat at Sanquhar. His son **James, 2nd Duke of Queensberry** (1672–1711) is known for his part in negotiating the Treaty of Union (1707). Since both his grandsons predeceased the 2nd Duke, the title passed to William (known as Old Q) in 1778 and he bled his Scottish estates dry with his profligate life in London. Through Jane Douglas, the 2nd Duke's sister and an heiress in her own right, her grandson Henry Scott, 3rd Duke of Buccleuch, inherited the estate in 1810.

The **visitor centre** in the stableyard provides visitors with an insight into how a large country estate is managed and the wildlife it supports. Live cameras are trained on the nests of resident red squirrels and barn owls. Inside is a superb collection of paintings, including Old Masters and family portraits, a varied selection of clocks and fine French furniture (mainly 17C and 18C) from the workshops of master cabinet makers. The Winged Heart motif on plasterwork ceilings, ironwork, wall hangings and woodcarvings is a reminder that Drumlanrig is a Douglas seat.

Ground Floor

In the **Hall** are paintings by Kneller and Thomas Hudson (1701–79). The splendid oak staircase with its barley sugar banisters rises in three flights from the **Staircase Hall**, where the highlights are a series of Old Masters, in particular Rembrandt's *Old Woman Reading* (1655). Compare this with the infinitely more detailed portraits (16C) by Holbein *(Sir Nicolas Carew)* and Joost Van Cleef *(François I, Eleanor of Austria)*.

In the splendid oak-panelled **Dining Room**, carved panels attributed to Grinling Gibbons alternate with 17C silver sconces and family portraits. *William, 1st Duke*, the builder of the castle in peer's robes (Kneller), is next to *William, 4th Duke of Queensberry* (Old Q) as an 18-year-old (Ramsay) and his heir *Henry, 5th Duke* (1746–1812). There are two of Monmouth (Kneller and Huysmans), one in a medallion with his mother.

First Floor

Both **Bonnie Prince Charlie's Bedroom** and the **Anteroom** are hung with 17C Brussels tapestries and graced by fine pieces of furniture.

In the **Drawing Room**, amid fine French furniture, are two outstanding **cabinets★** commissioned in 1675 for Versailles. The portraits include a series of full lengths: *King James VI* and his Queen, *Anne of Denmark* (Jamesone; the stance is similar to both the de Critz and Adam Colone portraits) with their grandson, *Charles II*, between them, and *Francis, 2nd Duke of Buccleuch* by Ramsay. The Porcelain Collection includes a delightful Meissen Monkey Band. The fine pier glasses are 17C.

From the **staircase gallery**, the superb 1680 **silver chandelier** is seen to its best advantage. On the panelled walls are magnificent Chippendale sconces and full length portraits. Fine Dutch and Flemish paintings (Teniers, Breughel, Cuyp) hang in the **Boudoir**.

In the **Principal Bedroom** are canvases by two 18C artists, Gainsborough and Hudson, of *Mary, Duchess of Montagu*, and *Kitty Duchess of Queensberry*.

Gardens

The gardens are extensive (16ha), and feature a Long Terrace Walk (183m) along a stone balustrade famous for growing climbing plants. There are Victorian glasshouses, heather houses, a rambling woodland garden amd rhododendron collection.

▶ On leaving the castle, return to the A76, turning right and immediately left onto a minor road leading to the A702.

Durisdeer

Located at the foot of the Lowther Hills, this hamlet is known for the **Queensberry Marbles**, housed in the parish church, built on a scale out of proportion to the vilage. The church houses an amazingly delicate marble monument in memory of James, 2nd Duke of Queensberry, by John Nost (1686–1729), which depicts the Duchess and Duke. It has a huge and intricately carved marble canopy standing on four marble columns

▶ Take the A702 to drive, via Elvanfoot, through the Lowther Hills. The highest point, Lowther Hill itself (*alt. 725m*) is one of the highest peaks in the whole region.

Leadhills

Set at 410m high the terraced miners houses are a reminder that this was once a flourishing lead-mining company town. Its library was founded in 1741 by the poet Allan Ramsay (1686–1758), author of *The Gentle Shepherd* and a pioneer in the use of the Scots language in poetry.

Leadhills is the home to the **Leadhills and Wanlockhead Railway**, Britain's highest narrow gauge adhesion railway, operating between Leadhills and Glengonnar (◷*Easter–Sept Sat–Sun; £5, child 3–16, £2.50; www.leadhillsrailway.co.uk*).

▶ Take the B797 south.

Wanlockhead

This scattered village has been a lead-mining centre as far back as Roman times. Gold was also mined here: reaching its peak in the 16C when much of the gold coinage of King James V and Mary Queen of Scots was minted in Edinburgh from gold from this area. It is said that local gold was also used in the crown of James V. In its more recent incarnation lead ore was mined and smelted locally between 1680 and 1934 – and there was still some mining activity here up until the 1950s.

The **Museum of Lead Mining** (&◷*Apr–Sept daily 11am–4.30pm. £12.90; ℘01659 74387; www.leadminingmuseum.co.uk*) tells the story of the local mines as well as the broader history of Scottish mining. Visitors can also try their hand at panning for gold, and be taught by experts.

▶ The road continues SW through the Mennock Pass to the A76. Turn left to return to Dumfries.

ADDRESSES

🏠 STAY

😋🍽 **Cairndale Hotel & Leisure Club** – *English Street.* ☎01387 254 111. *www.cairndalehotel.co.uk. 91 rooms. Restaurant (😋🍽) and café bar.* Occupying a large handsome building in the heart of town, this hotel has smart modern rooms and free access to a private leisure club offering gym, indoor pool, spa, sauna and steam room (*https://barracudaclub.co.uk*).

😋🍽 **Rivendell** – *105 Edinburgh Road.* ☎01387 252 251. *www.rivendellbnb.co.uk.* Very attractive Rennie Mackintosh-style villa with parquet floors, distinctive woodwork and brass fittings.

🍽/EAT

😋🍽 **Bruno's Italian Restaurant** – *3 Balmoral Road.* ☎01387 255 757. *www. brunosrestaurant.co.uk. Dinner only, closed Tue.* Bruno's is the town's original and authentic Italian restaurant, serving traditional freshly prepared dishes, run by the same family for over 40 years.

😋🍽 **The Courtyard (Station Hotel)** – *49 Lovers Walk.* ☎01387 254 316. *www.stationhoteldumfries.co.uk.* This atmospheric bistro is part of the Best Western Station Hotel; the menu changes according to the season.

😋🍽 **Thornhill Inn** – *103–106 Drumlanrig Street, Thornhill.* ☎01848 330 326. *www.thornhillinn.co.uk. Reservations recommended.* The picturesque village of Thornhill is 30 minutes drive from Dumfries and this rustic and laidback inn is worth travelling for. The menu is bursting with locally sourced produce.

Kirkcudbright ★
and around

Kirkcudbright, pronounced "cur-coo-bree", is set on the east bank of the Dee and derives its livelihood from farming, fishing and tourism (it is promoted as an "artists' town"). It was established as a Royal Burgh as long ago as 1455. The open waterfront was once a bustling port and this is the only town in the region to still have its fishing fleet. The lovely Georgian-Victorian town centre is well worth a visit.

A BIT OF HISTORY

The town became a Royal Burgh in 1455. Six years later, following defeat at the Battle of Towton, Henry VI of England cross the Solway Firth – a hazardous venture at the best of times, although guides (Sand Pilots) were available – and landed at Kirkcudbright in support of his wife, Margaret of Anjou, then resident at Linlithgow.

Kirkcudbright has a particularly long history of association with artists, 420 those of the so-called Glasgow Movement, which included the Glasgow

▶ **Population:** 3 420.

🛈 **Info:** Harbour Square; ☎01557 330 494; www.kirkcudbright.town.

🔘 **Location:** 28mi/45km southwest of Dumfries on the A75.

🕐 **Timing:** Allow 2–3 hours for Kirkcudbright, a full day for excursions, 3 hours for the coastal drive.

👫 **Kids:** Fish ladder at Tongland Power Station, Galloway Wildlife Conservation Park.

Boys and the Scottish Colourists, who based themselves in the area for over 30 years during the latter part of the 19C and early 20C.

SIGHTS

Broughton House and Garden

♿🕐*Apr–Oct daily 10am–5pm. The garden is also open Feb–Easter Mon–Fri 11am–4pm.* 👛£8. ☎01557 330 437. *www.nts.org.uk.*

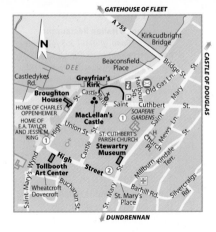

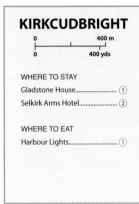

At the beginning of the century this 17C house became the home of the artist **Edward Atkinson Hornel** (1864–1933), known for his Galloway scenes and the originality of his bold and colourful style. It now contains the **Hornel Art Gallery** and the works on display include some of his Japanese paintings, the result of an extended visit to Japan.

MacLellan's Castle

🕐 *Apr–Sept daily 9.30am–5.30pm.*
♿ *There is currently restricted access at MacLellan's Castle to allow for maintenance works; check website for updates.* ✆ *£4.80.* ✆ *01557 331 856. www.historicenvironment.scot.*

In 1582 the former provost of the town, **Sir Thomas MacLellan**, quarried the adjoining ruined monastery to build his town residence, which is impressive for its sheer size. A spacious staircase, with straight flights, leads from the ground floor cellars and kitchen to the great hall where the massive fireplace is equipped with a **laird's lug** or spyhole. By 1752 the mansion was neglected and roofless.

Greyfriars Kirk

Formerly part of a 15C monastery, the kirk shelters the memorial of MacLellan, the castle builder, who is portrayed as a knight in full armour.

High Street

The west and south sides of this L-shaped street provide a mixture of styles, some with a vernacular flavour and others with a Georgian sophistication, interrupted by cobbled closes or pends. No. 14 was the home of the artist Charles Oppenheimer, while the mosaic on No. 44 commemorates the husband and wife artists team of E A Taylor and Jessie M King. At the far end are the 1610 mercat cross and the 16C–17C tolbooth, formerly the debtors' prison, now an art-centre, complete with jougs (iron rings used for holding offenders).

Tolbooth Art Centre

♿ *(except 2nd floor studio gallery).*
🕐 *Mon–Sat 11am–4pm.* 🅿 ✕ ✆ *01557 331 556. www.dumgal.gov.uk.*

In the late 19C–early 20C, Kirkcudbright had an active artists' colony, attracted here by the charm of the townscape, the unspoiled nature of the surrounding countryside, and the quality of the light. Their work and their contribution to the life of the town is celebrated in the handsome steepled 17C Tollbooth, where there is an audiovisual show, artists' studios and pictures. The tolbooth previously served as council offices and law courts.

Kirkcudbright in spring

© Gary Cook/age fotostock

Stewartry Museum

♿ *(ground floor only; stairs to second floor).* 🕯 *Mon–Sat 11am–4pm.* P
☎ *01557 331 643. www.dumgal.gov.uk.*
This small local museum, bursting with items, has particularly interesting exhibits on curling and quoiting, an old game played with iron rings resembling horseshoes, which used to be popular in every parish, and on local personalities such as Thomas Telford and John Paul Jones.

🚘 DRIVING TOURS

🚘 1 EAST OF KIRKCUDBRIGHT

30mi/48km.

This fascinating tour takes in a 21C power station, grand medieval ruins, and one of Scotland's finest gardens.

▷ Leave Kirkcudbright and head N for 2 mi/3.2km on the A711.

👤👤 Tongland Power Station (Galloway Hydros Visitor Centre)

🕯 *Visit by guided tour only, booking required.* ☎ *01644 430 238.*
Following the creation of a national grid system in 1926, Tongland was built in 1931–36 as headquarters for the Galloway Hydroelectric Scheme. The tour includes the turbine hall with original turbo generators, the arch and gravity dam (300m along its crest and 20m above the river bed), the overflow spillway, floodgates and popular **fish ladder**. Twenty-nine stepped pools and four resting ones allow salmon to move upstream to spawn.

▷ The A711 joins the A75; turn right towards Castle Douglas.

Threave Castle★

Threave Castle is on an island and is reached by passenger boat. 10min walk from car park; ring the bell for ferry.
🐦 *Parts of the castle may be closed during the bird breeding season.*
🕯 *Daily Apr–Sept 10am–4.30pm (last outward sailing); Oct daily 9.30am–3.30pm (last outward sailing).*
💲 *£6 (child 5–15, £3.60).* ☎ *07711 223 101. www.historicenvironment.scot.*
Ruined but still impressively grim on its island site in the Dee, Threave castle is a symbol of the turbulence and insecurity which reigned in medieval Scotland. This tower house was the stronghold of that most powerful and noble house, the **Black Douglases**.
Rising four storeys above its cellars, it was built in the late 14C by **Archibald the Grim**, 3rd Earl of Douglas (1330–1400). As part of a campaign against the Douglas ascendancy, James II besieged the castle in 1455. Additional defences

– the outer wall and towers – were built following Flodden in 1513. The castle was dismantled in 1640 when it fell into the hands of the Covenanters.

Threave Garden and Estate★★

&⚬*House:* Visit by guided tour only Apr–late Oct Wed–Fri and Sun 11.30am and 1.30pm; *Garden:* Apr–Oct daily 10am–5pm. £15; garden only, £9. ✕ ℘01556 502 575. www.nts.org.uk.

The estate comprises four farms, 49ha of woodland, a mansion and 26ha belonging to the house. Opened in 1960, the Threave School of Gardening welcomes eight students annually for a two-year course on all aspects of theoretical and practical gardening. The Victorian mansion serves as a school and the 26ha garden has evolved from the students' work.

Castle Douglas

Spaciously laid out to the north of Carlingwark Loch, this inland market town with its important auction market serves the local farming industry. The settlement assumed its present name and gridiron street plan in the late 18C. It was named after a local merchant, Sir William Douglas (1745–1809), who with the fortune he had made in the West Indies, bought local estates and established a cotton industry in the town. Beautifully kept, the garden, with its rich variety of flowers, plants, shrubs and trees, is a sheer delight with something for everyone. The main sections are roses (June and July), peat, rock, heather gardens, herbaceous borders, walled garden, glasshouses, patio, arboretum and woodland walk which boasts a mass of daffodils in April.

Carlingwark Loch

Beside the town, this lovely lake, dotted with islands, is a perfect place for a picnic or birdwatching. In summer there are boats for hire and you can even learn to sail (enquire at the tourist office).

▷ Leave Castle Douglas on the B736, heading S to its junction with the A711. Cross into local road opposite.

Orchardton Tower

⚬Apr–Sept 9.30am–5.30pm; Oct–Mar daily except Thu–Fri 10am–4pm. No charge. www.historicenvironment.scot.

This charming 15C ruin is unique, the only round laird's tower house built in late medieval Scotland. Circular towers, called donjons, were integral to great curtain-walled strongholds of the 1200s, where they were the focus of the lord's private accommodation. But after this time they disappeared, to be replaced by exclusively square and rectangular tower houses.

▷ Return to the A71 and turn left through Auchencairn to Dundrennan.

Dundrennan Abbey★

&⚬Daily Apr–Sept 9.30am–5.30pm. £6. ℘01557 500 262. www.historicenvironment.scot.

This Cistercian abbey was founded in 1142 by King David. The monastery prospered but by the time it passed into secular hands at the Reformation it was in a precarious state. In 1568 Mary, Queen of Scots halted here on her flight into England.

The ruins have a grandeur and austere simplicity true to the Cistercian tradition. The parts still standing include a section of the west wall, the transepts, chapter house and some outbuildings.

▷ Return to Kirkcudbright on the A71.

⚘ ② COASTAL DRIVE TO STRANRAER

134mi/216km. Allow two days with a stop overnight in Wigtown or Whithorn.

The drive follows the coast around Wigtown Bay, via Wigtown and Isle of Whithorn (the home of Scottish Chistianity); it turns into Luce Bay, then explores the southern arm of the Rhinns of Galloway right down to the extremity, the Mull of Galloway.

The countryside is rugged where small fields are enclosed by stone dykes and gorse abounds. Along the splendid coastline sandy beaches alternate with stretches of rugged cliffs and occasional

Cairn Holy

bays harbour peaceful villages and ports. Thanks to the Gulf Stream, the region enjoys Scotland's mildest climate.

▶ Leave Kirkcudbright on the A755 west and join the A75 near Gatehouse of Fleet.

Gatehouse of Fleet

This tidy and picturesque town is an example of late-18C town planning attributed to entrepreneur James Murray's decision to build a home there in 1765. The town takes its name from its position near the mouth of the Water of Fleet and from its former role as the "Gait House" or toll booth on the 18C stagecoach route from Dumfries to Stranraer.

Cardoness Castle

🕑 *Daily Apr–Sept 9.30am–5.30pm.*
🎫 *£6.* 📞 *01557 814 427.*
www.historicenvironment.scot.

This well-preserved, six-storey mid-15C tower house of the McCulloughs is prominently set on a rocky outcrop overlooking the tidal Fleet. A turnpike, linking the different floors, leads to the parapet (84 steps) which affords a view across the Fleet and the estuary with Wigtown Peninsula on the horizon.

The McCulloughs were a prominent Galloway family, who rubbed shoulders with royalty, but also noted for their lawlessness – even against their own family – and a long-running feud with their neighbours, the Gordons. In 1501,

Ninian McCulloch of Cardoness was prosecuted for breaking into a barn and stealing 1 500 animals, the property of his own mother!

▶ Continue on the A75 (the Newton Stewart road) which follows the coast. After 5½mi/9km, turn right off the main road to the Cairn Holy site.

Cairn Holy★★

🚶 *Park alongside the A75, and walk up the land towards the site of Kirkdale church.*

These two complete Neolithic chambered tombs are in a commanding site with a good outlook over the Wigtown Bay. Cairn Holy I has a splendid curving façade of standing stones, and is the more elaborate of the two. Cairn Holy II is believed to be the tomb of Galdus, a mythical Scottish king.

Few human remains have been discovered here, and artefacts are also scarce, but there is evidence that the tomb builders had widespread contacts. In the forecourt of Cairnholy I, a flake of pitchstone was found that can only have come from the island of Arran, while among the shards of pottery were fragments from a decorated bowl of a kind normally found in England. The most unexpected item, however, was a fragment of a ceremonial axe made of jadeite, a beautiful green stone imported into Britain from the Alps.

▶ Proceed for 1mi/1.6km.

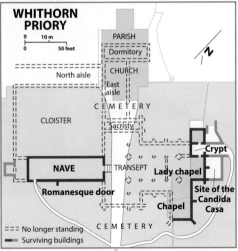

WHITHORN PRIORY

0   10 m
0   50 feet

PARISH

Dormitory

CHURCH

North aisle

East aisle

CEMETERY

CLOISTER

Sacristy

Crypt

NAVE   TRANSEPT   Lady chapel

Romanesque door   Site of the Candida Casa

Chapel

CEMETERY

=== No longer standing
▬▬ Surviving buildings

BRUCE STREET   MUSEUM

Carsluith Castle

The well-preserved ruin of a 16C tower house. It is similar to many L-planned tower houses built by the landed gentry throughout Scotland after the Protestant Reformation of 1560.

The 18C ranges of outhouses are still in use by a farmer. Note the waterspout carved with a human face at the southwest corner of the building.

Creetown

This delightful village was famous in the past for its granite quarries, and the **Creetown Gem Rock Museum** (&Apr–Sept daily 10am–5pm; Oct daily 10am–4pm; Nov–22 Dec and Feb–Mar Wed–Sun 10am–4pm; 23 Dec–31 Jan; £5. 01671 820 357; www.gemrock.net) features a dazzling collection of Scottish and worldwide specimens, alongside such items as a fossilised egg, dinosaur dung and a 4.5 billion years old meteorite.

▶ Return to the A75. At Newton Stewart, turn left onto the A714.

Wigtown

In 1998, this picturesque little place was designated "Scotland's National Book Town", a book lovers' haven (www.wigtown-booktown.co.uk). The two broad parallel avenues that form the town centre are lined with new and second-hand bookstores and it hosts a literary festival in late September–early October (www.wigtownbookfestival.com).

▶ Continue south along the A746.

Whithorn

🔲 www.whithorn.info

Whithorn, first known as Candida Casa, is the cradle of Scottish Christianity and predates the more famous shrine of Iona, by over 150 years. Today's unassuming town, with its wide main street, serves the surrounding dairy farming community of the Machars.

From the main street a path leads through the former priory gatehouse, built in the 15C, and emblazoned with the pre-Union Scottish coat of arms supported by two unicorns.

Whithorn Priory and Museum

Access through The Whithorn Story Exhibition. 45–47 George Street.
&Apr–Oct daily 10.30am–5pm.
Telephone for up-to-date prices.
01988 500 700.
www.historicenvironment.scot.
The museum houses a notable collection of **early Christian crosses★★**.

The earliest Christian memorial in Scotland is the **Latinus Stone** (No. 1,) dated to the year 450 and inscribed with the name of the relative who erected it. Typical of the more decorative Whithorn School is No 7. Later stones (Nos. 3 and 5) show a Northumberland influence. St Peter's Stone (No. 2) is 7C or early 8C. **Priory** – The ruins (nave, south and Lady Chapels), set on a knoll, are scanty and belong mainly to the medieval cathedral. The building to the left, originally the nave, served as a parish church until 1822. Note the reset Norman doorway in the south wall.

The rest of the structure is mainly 13C, much altered. To the right, the paved area and low walls mark the east end with crypts underneath. The probable site of the *Candida Casa* (St Ninian's original church) is beyond.

The Whithorn Dig

The exhibition in the visitor centre is a good introduction to the excavation programme, which has revealed evidence of more than 1 500 years of human occupation in the area. On a site to the south of the priory have been found traces of an early Christian community (5C), an 8C Northumbrian settlement – the ground plan of a church, burial chapel, hall and other buildings can be viewed – a graveyard (16C) and finally a market garden. The site of a Viking trading post to the west of the priory is also being investigated.

▶ Continue south, turn left onto the B7004 towards the Isle of Whithorn, then right towards St Ninian's Cave. A path (1.5mi/2.4km) leads to the cave.

St Ninian's Cave

This cave, with some crosses carved in the rock, is said to be St Ninian's place of retreat.

▶ Return to the main road and turn right towards the Isle of Whithorn.

Isle of Whithorn

The village, a popular yachting centre, is known for the ruined St Ninian's Chapel which stands on the rocky foreshore *(5min walk from pier)*. At one time thought to be the site of the *Candida Casa*, this 13C chapel with its enclosure wall may mark the site where St Ninian landed, or else was for the convenience of pilgrims arriving by sea.

▶ Continue on the road (B7004, then A747) towards Port William and on to Glenluce.

Glenluce

This small village is renowned for its nearby abbey, a disused Cistercian monastery. More recently, the town was served by Glenluce railway station from 1862 by the Portpatrick and Wigtownshire Joint Railway which provided a strategic link to Northern Ireland; the railway, like many others in this area, closed in 1965.

Castle of Park

This tower house, rising tall in a commanding site overlooking Luce Bay and glen, was built in 1590 by Thomas Hay, son of the last Abbot of Glenluce. The door has an inscribed **lintel**.

▶ Return to the main road and turn left after crossing the river. Continue for 1mi/1.6km up the valley.

Glenluce Abbey

Apr–Sept Sun–Tue 9.30am– 5.30pm. £6. www.historicenvironment.scot. The abbey was founded in the late 12C by Roland, Lord of Galloway, on a beautiful **site** in the Water of Luce valley. The outstanding features of the ruins are the 15C **chapter house** (*Wed–Sat*) with some fine sculptural work and the drainage system still in place. A Museum of Monastic life features objects excavated on the site.

▶ Return to the A75 and turn right towards Stranraer. Castle Kennedy Gardens entrance is on the right.

Castle Kennedy Gardens

♿ ⏱10am–5pm: Apr–Oct daily; Feb–Mar Sat–Sun. ⊙£5.50. ✕ 𝒫01776 702 024. www.castlekennedygardens.co.uk.
The natural beauty of the **site**, on a peninsula between two lochs, is an essential part of these gardens where vistas, sweeping lawns and tree-lined avenues are a delight.

The **ruins** are those of Castle Kennedy, former seat of the powerful Ayrshire family of the same name. It was the **2nd Earl** who created the gardens following the castle's destruction by fire (1716). He commissioned **William Adam** to create an informal garden to harmonise with the setting. In 1842, following years of neglect, the gardens were restored to their original aspect, using the Castle Kennedy ruins, the 19C baronial Lochinch Castle and several water features to form focal points, vistas and avenues. The garden is at its best during the rhododendron and azalea season (usually April–May).

▶ Take the B7084.

≛ Sandhead

A typical seaside village with great stretches of sandy beach overlooking Luce bay.

▶ Just S of the village, take the local road inland.

Kirkmadrine church

The glazed-in porch shelters some of Scotland's earliest existing **Christian monuments**. Three of the tombstones bear Latin inscriptions and the Chi-Rho monogram. They date from the 5C and 6C and are reminders of the early Christian mission established at Whithorn.

▶ Continue to the small village of Drummore from where the B7041 leads to the southernmost tip. The last part of the road is single track.

Mull of Galloway

🔼 Short walk from car park.
This rugged headland is fringed with cliffs some 61m–76m high. The waters offshore are notorious for strong tides.

Good **views** of the English Lake District and Ireland.

▶ Retreat on the B7041 as far as Damnaglaur, and there take the B7065.

Port Logan

Set on the far side of the bay, the 9m deep rock pool now known as **Logan Fish Pond ≛ and Marine Life Centre** (⏱daily 0am–5pm; ⊙£4 (child under 16, £3); 𝒫01776 860 606; www.logan-fishpond.com) was once used as a Victorian fish larder for Logan House. It is now stocked with trout, eels, plaice, rays and turbot and the coley can be fed by hand.

Logan Botanic Garden★

♿⏱Daily Mar–Oct 10am–5pm; 1–mid Nov 10am–4pm; Feb Sun only 10am–4pm. ⊙£7. ✕ 𝒫01776 860 231. www.rbge.org.uk/the-gardens/logan.
This annexe of the Royal Botanic Garden (⌖see EDINBURGH) has a large variety of well-labelled **exotic plants** which flourish in the warmth of the Gulf Stream. Impeccably kept, the garden has two main parts: walled and woodland. Outstanding among the many warm temperate regionwarm temperate region plants are the cabbage palms and the tree ferns.

▶ Take B7065 and then A716 to Ardwell and Sandhead, then take the B7042 and A77 to Portpatrick.

≛ Portpatrick

This popular west coast seaside village is the peninsula's most important community. The houses climbing the slopes at the back of the bay overlook the small harbour which in pre-steam days was the terminal for the Irish crossing.

The **Southern Upland Way** links Portpatrick to Cockburnspath on the east coast. Just south along the coast from Port Patrick, **Knockinaam Lodge**, now a luxury hotel, was the venue for meetings between Churchill and Eisenhower while planning the D-Day landings. The drive to the hotel features in John Buchan's Thirty-nine steps.

▶ Retreat along the A77 and continue to Stranraer.

Stranraer

At the head of Loch Ryan, the agricultural market town of Stranraer depends heavily on the ferry service to Larne (Northern Ireland). Although there's little of interest in the town itself, Stranraer is a good base from which to visit the Rhinns of Galloway Peninsula.

🚗 3 GALLOWAY FOREST PARK★

♿⏰*Daily, for full details of visitor centres visit https://forestryandland.gov.scot/visit/forest-parks/galloway-forest-park.* Set in one of the most beautiful parts of the Southern Uplands, this is the largest park in Britain, covering 300sq mi/116sq km.

To visit the southern section follow the Queen's Way (10mi/16km) via the A712. Begin at **Newton Stewart**, famous for its salmon fishing. Head towards New Galloway, through Kirroughtree forest, passing the Cairnsmore of Fleet (*alt. 711m*). The **Wild Goat Park** sanctuary at Craigdews is home to a flock of chamois. Next is the **Red Deer Range**. Lovely **Loch Clatteringshaws** is part of the Galloway hydro-electric Galloway scheme. Continue and look out for the sign to the **Raiders' Road**, a 10mi/16km long unpaved former drovers' road, popular with cyclists *(open to cars)*, with picnic areas and swimming in the Black Water of Dee.

Clatteringshaws Visitor Centre is a starting point for walks and cycle routes, one of which leads to **Bruce's Stone**, a giant boulder where Robert the Bruce is said to have rested after defeating the English.

Visit the northern section of the Forest Park via the **Glentrool Visitor Centre.**

ADDRESSES

🛏 STAY

KIRKCUDBRIGHT

⊜⊜⊜ **Gladstone House** – 48 High Street. ✆01557 331 734. https://

kirkcudbrightgladstone.wordpress.com. *3 rooms. No pets 🐾, and no children under the age of 12.* Former Georgian merchant's house, now a luxury B&B in the heart of Kirkcudbright. Comfort, charm and elegance.

⊜⊜⊜ **Selkirk Arms Hotel** – *High Street.* ✆01557 330 402. www.selkirkarmshotel. co.uk. *16 rooms.* Typical Scots hospitality at this attractive townhouse includes a fine dining restaurant (⊜⊜) and a bistro. Well placed to explore the western parts of Galloway.

PORT PATRICK

⊜⊜⊜⊜ **Knockinaam Lodge** – ✆01776 810 471. www.knockinaamlodge.com. *10 rooms.* Secluded country house hotel set in its own private cove with the sea at the bottom of the garden. Visited by Churchill and Eisenhower during World War II to discuss the D-Day landings. Excellent restaurant (**open to non-residents by reservation**) serving classic cuisine (⊜⊜⊜). The hotel is alluded to in *The Thirty-nine Steps* – John Buchan's classic murder mystery novel, made into a movie by Alfred Hitchcock in 1935.

NEWTON STEWART

⊜⊜⊜ **Kirroughtree House Hotel** – *Newton Stewart.* ✆07584 71 63 67. www. kirroughtreehouse.com. *17 rooms.* An impessive 18C mansion in mature gardens. Kirroughtree House was the Mansion House for the Kirroughtree Estate which was owned by the Heron family for well over 300 years. Vast open-fired hall and impressive staircase. Restaurant (⊜⊜⊜) serves Mull of Galloway lobster, Cree salmon, Kirroughtree venison, Wigtown Bay wild fowl.

🍴 EAT

KIRKCUDBRIGHT

⊜ **Harbour Lights** – *32 St Cuthbert Street.* ✆07565 55 62 26. This café-bistro-gallery in the centre of town makes the most of fresh local ingredients.

ISLE OF WHITHORN

⊜⊜ **The Steam Packet Inn** – *Harbour Row.* ✆01988 500 334. www. thesteampacketinn.biz. *7 rooms.* Set on the harbour, the Steam Packet specialises in local seafood and steaks served in one of the bars, the lower dinning room or the conservatory.

Edinburgh, the capital of Scotland, is a beautiful open and green city, dramatically sited on a series of volcanic hills. Both natural and man-made landmarks offer spectacular vistas. The city boasts a rich historic past and two contrasting town centres – Old and New. A wealth of tourist sights, rich museum collections, its prestigious arts festivals in season and its vibrant cultural life at any time of year are just some of the many great reasons to pay a visit.

Highlights

1 Breathtaking views of the city from **Edinburgh Castle** (p148)

2 Visiting the **State Apartments of Holyrood House** (p151)

3 **Royal Botanic Garden** in rhododendron season (p157)

4 Touring the floating palace of **Royal Yacht *Britannia*** (p159)

5 Retail therapy along George Street, or the **Farmers Market** at Castle Terrace (p162)

▶ **Population:** 512 150.

🅿 **Parking:** Difficult and expensive; don't drive in central Edinburgh.

ℹ **Info:** 3 Princes Street, S of Waverley station. ✆0131 473 3868. www.edinburgh.org.

👁 **Don't Miss:** The Royal Mile; an underground tour; the Scottish Parliament Building; the views from the Nelson Monument and Arthur's Seat; Charlotte Square; the Festival Fringe; Royal Museum and Museum of Scotland; Royal Yacht Brittania; Forth Bridges view from Queensferry.

🕐 **Timing:** Allow at least three days, preferably longer. It is best to explore on foot, particularly in the Old Town.

👫 **Kids:** A ghost tour; Edinburgh Zoo; Our Dynamic Earth; 3D Loch Ness Experience; Museum of Childhood; Brass Rubbing Centre; Royal Museum/ Museum of Scotland.

The **Festival City**

Held in August (until at least 2020) this prestigious annual **Edinburgh International Festival★★★** (*Ticket office: The Hub, Castlehill.* ✆*0131 473 2000; www.eif.co.uk*) provides an international quality programme of performances in all art forms.

The ever-popular **Military Tattoo** (*first 3 weeks Aug; tickets from The Tattoo Box Office, 1-3 Cockburn Street; see website for ticket details; postal bookings deadline mid-Nov;* ✆*0131 225 1188; www.edintattoo.co.uk*) provides a spectacle rich in colour, tradition, music and excitement under the floodlights of the Castle Esplanade. The capacity audience of 9 000 is entertained by a cast of approximately 600.

An integral part of the festival is **The Fringe** (*first 3 weeks Aug; ticket booking (Jun–Aug),* ✆*0131 226 0000; www.edfringe.com*) with over 700 productions covering a wide range of entertainment, from the avant-garde to just plain eccentric. The Fringe spills out onto the streets and squares of Edinburgh, which become the stage for a variety of entertainers from buskers and jugglers to musicians, dancers, mime artists and showmen of every imaginable kind in every imaginable venue and location. The **Edinburgh Jazz and Blues Festival** (*late-Ju; Ticket office: The Hub, Castlehill.* ✆*0131 473 2000; www.edinburghjazzfestival.com*) is also a very popular event.

When visiting Edinburgh during the festival it is absolutely essential to reserve accommodation well in advance. Many museums, galleries and houses

Royal Mile during Edinburgh Festival Fringe

extend their opening hours and organise special exhibitions during festival time.

A Bit of History

The Castle Rock no doubt proved to be a secure refuge for the earliest settlers, although the Romans preferred the attractions of Cramond. The name may in fact be derived from the Northumbrian King Edwin (Edwinesburg – Edwin's fortress) although he actually died before his people captured the site in 638.

As a residence, the Castle Rock site was associated with **Malcolm Canmore** and his **Queen Margaret**. Their son **David I** gave great preferment to the settlement by founding the Abbey of Holy Rood and the building of a small chapel to commemorate his mother. During the Wars of Independence, the strategic importance of the castle not only afforded protection to the growing burgh but also made it more susceptible to English attacks.

Medieval Golden Age – The first town wall dated from 1450. With the early Stewarts, Edinburgh slowly assumed the roles of royal residence, seat of government, important religious centre and capital. This Golden Age ended with Flodden when the host of Scots dead included the king and Edinburgh's provost. In haste the town started to build the **Flodden Wall**; although only completed in 1560 this was to define the limits of the Ancient Royalty for over two centuries confining expansion upwards in the characteristic lands (tenements) of as many as 10 and 12 storeys.

Mary, Queen of Scots and the Reformation – Two years after the proclamation of the infant Mary's accession, Henry VIII's army set out on the "**Rough Wooing**", creating havoc and destruction in the south and east of the country. Mary was sent to France for safety. Already the Roman Catholic church, wealthier than the Crown, was under attack and the ideas of the Reformation gained ground. The **Reformation** (1560) and the return of the Catholic Mary, Queen of Scots, a year later, made Edinburgh, during her short reign, the stage for warring factions, Protestant and Roman Catholic, pro-French and pro-English. With the departure of James and his court after the **Union of the Crowns** (1603), Edinburgh lost much of its pageantry and cultural activity.

Religious Strife – Relative peace ensued until Charles I, following his 1633 coronation at Holyrood, pushed through episcopacy (government of the church by bishops) – a policy inherited from his father. **The National Covenant** was drawn up in 1638 and signed in Greyfriars Church. The signatories swore loyalty to the King but fervently opposed his religious policy. A year later, following the General Assembly of Glasgow, episcopacy was abolished. Covenanters took the castle. By 1641 Charles had conceded to the Covenanters (defendants of the Reformed Faith) but the outbreak of the English Civil War brought a pact with the English Parliamentarians, the **Solemn League and Covenant** (1643). The Royalist campaign

GETTING AROUND

Transport for Edinburgh provides a high quality travel experience across the city, running highly integrated transport modes with a wide range of convenient and cost-effective ticketing options. Local bus services (run by Lothian Buses – www.lothianbuses.co.uk), are frequent and on time. SINGLEtickets, available from drivers, £1.70 (have correct fare ready, drivers do not give change). Download the Transport for Edinburgh app, an easy way of purchasing travel tickets. A DAYticket (£4), gives unlimited travel on day buses and Edinburgh trams, and a Ridacard for one week (£19) are money-saving options. Visit website for details. Edinburgh also has a fleet of 30 modern trams operating from York Place in the city centre all the way to Edinburgh Airport (www.edinburghtrams.com).

There are also sightseeing hop-on, hop-off bus tours. Visit www.edinburghtour.com for full details.

VISITOR INFORMATION

The main information office at 3 Princes Street (📞0131 473 3868. www.edinburgh.org) doubles as the Edinburgh and Scotland Information Centre, providing information on both the city and the country. It also offers an accommodation and theatre booking service, a bureau de change, bookshop and gift shop.

Scotland Explore Passes –

Formerly the Edinburgh Pass, the new Scotland Explore Pass offers free entry to 78 attractions. Available for 5 or 14 days, £35 or £45 per person. www.historicenvironment.scot.

suffered through fire. The Commonwealth was a period of uneasy peace in Edinburgh and much was the rejoicing at the Restoration in spite of the fact that it brought the reintroduction of the episcopal system and ruthless persecution of the Covenanters until opposition was finally eradicated.

In the late 17C Edinburgh flourished as a legal and medical centre. The failure of the Darien scheme – (to promote Scottish overseas trade and control trade between the Atlantic and the Pacific) gave rise to anti-English feelings. In 1707 Edinburgh lost its Parliament when the politicians headed south. The legal profession took over Parliament Hall and began to dominate Edinburgh society. Of the two Jacobite rebellions, that of 1745 saw the return of a brief period of glory to Holyroodhouse with the installation of the prince's court there.

The Enlightenment – In late-18C Edinburgh a circle of great men flourished, including philosophers David Hume and Dugald Stewart, economist Adam Smith, geologist James Hutton, chemist Joseph Black and architect Robert Adam. Clubs and societies prospered and it was in such a climate of intellectual ferment that plans were put forward for a civic project of great boldness and imagination.

Georgian Edinburgh – Old Edinburgh, on its ridge, was squalid and overcrowded. The earliest moves out were made to George Square in the south before plans for the New Town were drawn up, approved, enacted and accepted socially. The project was encouraged by the early establishment of public buildings in the new area; including the Theatre Royal (1767–8), and the Assembly Rooms (1784–7). Attractive as the elegant streets and squares were, it was to the markets, wynds and closes, taverns and clubs of the Old Town that many still went to earn their livelihood and spend their moments of leisure.

Today the contrast between the organic medieval Old Town and the planned Georgian New Town is recognised as a World Heritage Site which "provides a clarity of urban structure unrivalled in Europe".

led by the Marquess of Montrose ended with defeat at Philiphaugh (1645) and the final outcome of the Parliamentary victory at Marston Moor near York was the king's execution (1649).

Cromwell defeated the Scots at Dunbar (1650) and Montrose was executed. His troops entered Edinburgh and the palace and other buildings served as barracks; some like Holyroodhouse

Royal Mile★★

Daniel Defoe wrote, of the Royal Mile, in the early 18C, "This is, perhaps, the largest, longest, and finest street for buildings and number of inhabitants, not in Britain only, but in the world". The few original buildings which remain give some idea of what medieval Edinburgh must have looked like.

🔆 **Info:** www.royal-mile.com.

⊙ **Location:** The Royal Mile is a succession of streets: Castle Hill, the Lawnmarket, Parliament Square, the High Street and the Canongate, which run from the castle downhill to Holyrood.

👥 **Kids:** A ghost tour; Our Dynamic Earth; Camera Obscura & World of Illusions; Museum of Childhood; Royal Museum/ Museum of Scotland.

🐾 WALKING TOURS 1–6

1 THE ROYAL MILE

This is both quintessential and tourist Edinburgh, starting at the top of the hill, and then walking down, quite literally through a thousand years of history, from the castle, which dates back to the 11C, to the state-of-the-art 21C Parliament.

Edinburgh Castle
⊙See p148.

The Scotch Whisky Experience
354 Castle Hill. ♿⊙*Daily: Jan–Mar and Sept–Dec 10am–5pm; Apr 10am–6pm; May–Jun 10am–8pm; Jul 10am–8.20pm; Aug Mon–Fri 10am –5pm, Sat–Sun 10am–5.40pm.* ⊙*25 Dec.* ⊜*£16–£75.* ✕ ✆*0131 220 0441. www.scotchwhiskyexperience.co.uk.*
All tours begin with a journey through a replica distillery. Interactive exhibits and expert guides trace the whisky-making process from peat cutting to bottling and packaging. Tours conclude with a choice of tastings, ranging from a single dram (or soft drink) right up to a masterclass in whisky tasting.

👥 Camera Obscura and World of Illusions
Castle Hill. ♿⊙*Apr–Jun daily 9.30am–8pm; Jul–Aug daily 9am–10pm; Sept–Oct Sun–Fri 9.30am–8pm, Sat 9.30am–9pm; Nov– Mar Mon–Thu 9.30am–7pm, Fri and Sun 9.30am–8pm, Sat 9.30am–9pm.* ⊙*25 Dec.* ⊜*£16 (child 5–15, £12.* ✆*0131 226 3709. www.camera-obscura.co.uk.*

From its rooftop position in the Outlook Tower, the **Camera Obscura** presents a fascinating view of the city. Exhibitions and all kinds of interactive fun (including a vortex tunnel) deal with illusions, holography, magic, and light. There are telescopes on the roof.

The Church of Scotland **General Assembly Hall** stands on the site of Mary of Guise's Palace (destroyed 1861). Its blackened towers are a landmark to visitors walking up the hill to the castle. **Mylne's Court** is a picturesque 1970s reconstruction of what a court looked like once a narrow burgess strip had been built over. The narrow approach

Royal Mile
© Christophe Boisvieux/hemis.fr

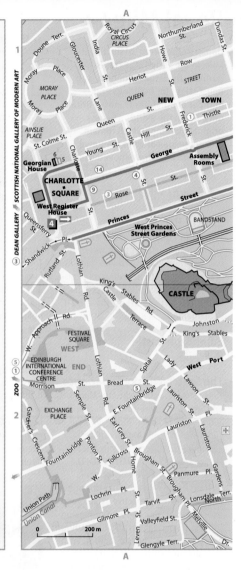

EDINBURGH

WHERE TO STAY

WHERE TO EAT

passages from the main street are known as closes or wynds with a "pend" at the entrance.

The Hub

Castle Hill. ⏱*Daily 10am–6pm.* ✕ 📞*0131 473 2015.* *www.thehub-edinburgh.com.* A tall steeple highlights this former Assembly Hall (later named the Highland Tolbooth), built in the mid-19C by James Gillespie Graham and Augustus Pugin and imaginatively refurbished as Edinburgh's Festival Centre. The ornate brightly coloured interior boasts contemporary sculpture, tiling and stained glass as well as a splendid sculpture hall. The Hub is a focal point for the city's festivals and a ticket office for the Edinburgh Festival. Its excellent **Café Hub** (⏱*Mon–Sat 9.30am–5pm, Sun 10.30am–5pm;* 📞*0131 473 2067*) is one of the Royal Mile's favourite meeting, eating and drinking places.

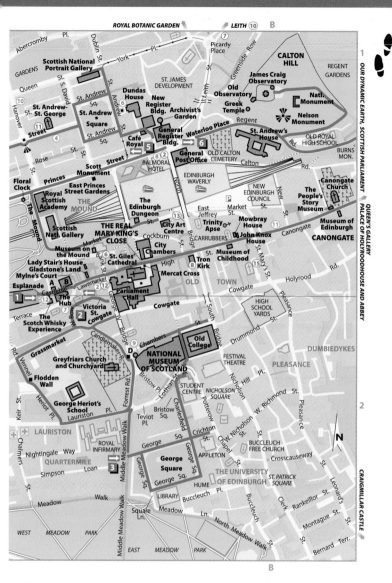

Gladstone's Land★

477b Lawnmarket. ⚓*Jan–Mar and Nov–Dec guided tours only 11am–4pm;* 🕐*Apr–Oct daily 11am–5pm.* 🕐*24–26 Dec.* 💺*£7.* 📞*0131 226 5856.* *www.nts.org.uk.*

This narrow six-storey "land" (tenement) is typical of 17C Edinburgh when all building was upwards.

The property was acquired in 1617 by merchant burgess Thomas Gledstanes, who traded in vinegar, honey, prunes and iron pots, rebuilt and extended it out towards the street.

The premises behind the pavement arcade are arranged as a shop with living quarters on the other floors. The first floor is a good example of a 17C town house with original **painted ceilings**, and carved Scottish bed and Dutch chests.

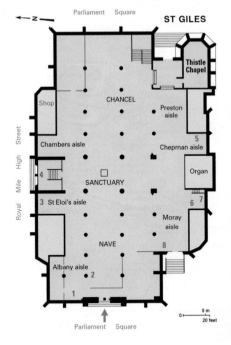

ST GILES

Parliament Square

Thistle Chapel

CHANCEL

Shop

Preston aisle

Chambers aisle

5

Chepman aisle

Organ

SANCTUARY

St Eloi's aisle

Moray aisle

NAVE

Albany aisle

Parliament Square

Royal Mile High Street

0   5 m
0   20 feet

Lady Stair's House

Down the close.
Built in 1622, this town house takes its name from an occupant of the late 18C, the widow of John Dalrymple, 1st Earl of Stair. It is now home to the **Writers' Museum** (*daily 10am–5pm; 0131 529 4901; www.edinburghmuseums.org.uk*) which displays manuscripts, relics and other memorabilia of three of Scotland's greatest literary figures: Robert Burns (1759–1796), Sir Walter Scott (1771–1832) and Robert Louis Stevenson (1850–1894).

St Giles' Cathedral★★

May–Sept Mon–Fri 9am–7pm, Sat 9am–5pm; Sun 1–5pm; Oct–Apr Mon–Sat 9am–5pm, Sun 1–5pm. 26 Dec and 1–2 Jan. £3 donation requested. ✕ 0131 226 0674. www.stgilescathedral.org.uk.
The present High Kirk of Edinburgh is probably the third church on this site. The first, dating from the 9C, was probably closer to the castle. It was replaced by a Romanesque structure in 1126 of which remain the four piers supporting the tower. This was burned down by the English in 1385 following which the present building was raised. Alterations and restorations have radically changed the character of the 15C church. The Reformation brought troubled times to St Giles', when many altars and images, including the precious relic and statue of St Giles, were swept away.

As the capital's principal church it served as meeting place for Parliament and the General Assembly and witnessed many great state occasions such as James VI's farewell to his Scottish subjects and, over 200 years later, George IV's 1822 state visit.

The Jenny Geddes stool-throwing incident (a protest against episcopacy – statue and plaque on the north side of the Moray aisle), although much disputed historically, preceded the signing of the National Covenant *(see the Linlithgow copy in the Chepman aisle)* and the ensuing religious strife. Twice during the 17C the church enjoyed a brief spell of cathedral status (1637–38 and 1661–89).

Exterior

Seen from the west, the church is dominated by the square tower raising aloft the delicate imperial or eight-arched **crown spire★★★** (1495), a most distinctive feature of Edinburgh's skyline. The church's exterior lost much of its original character when it was refaced (19C).

Interior

The original cruciform shape has been lost with the addition of aisle and side chapels. Although the interior was spared the systematic restoration of the exterior, details, and in particular monuments, provide the main points of interest.

Start in the northwest corner and proceed in a clockwise direction.

The flowing style and strong glowing colours of the north aisle window

(1) characterise the work of the Pre-Raphaelites, Burne-Jones and William Morris. In the north aisle stands a statue of **John Knox** (1512–1572) **(2)**, reformer and minister of St Giles'. The Albany Aisle with its Gothic vaulting was probably built in expiation for the murder of the Duke of Rothesay in 1402.

The aisle beyond contains the imposing 19C marble monument **(3)** to the 8th Earl and 1st Marquess of Argyll (1607–1661), who was executed only days after the body of his arch-rival the Marquess of Montrose had been rehabilitated and interred on the far side of the church. Move back into the south transept to admire Douglas Strachan's great north window **(4)**, a glow of blue above the carved stone screen. From here also admire the attractive 15C rib and groin vaulting of the chancel and compare it with that of the nave (19C).

In 1911 Robert Lorimer designed the **Thistle Chapel** in the Flamboyant Gothic style for the most Noble Order of the Thistle founded by James VII in 1687. Under a fan-vaulted ceiling and its multitude of carved bosses, are the richly carved stalls and canopies for the sovereign and 16 knights. It is a lavish display of 20C craftsmanship. Above are helmets, crests and banners.

Beyond the Preston aisle is the side chapel known as the Chepman aisle, the final resting place of the **Marquess of Montrose** (1612–1650) **(5)**, Covenanter and Royalist whose fame rests on his brilliant 1644–45 campaign. He suffered an ignominious fate at the hands of his enemy, Argyll. The Restoration meant rehabilitation for Montrose and a traitor's execution for Argyll.

The aisle beyond the organ has a 19C marble monument **(6)** to James Stewart, Earl of Moray (1531–1570), with an original 16C brass. Half-brother to Mary, Queen of Scots and Regent for her son, Moray was murdered in Linlithgow (&see LINLITHGOW) in 1570. A window **(7)** by Noel Paton relates the tale and shows Knox preaching at the funeral service of one of his strongest supporters. The low relief **(8)** at the end of the Moray Aisle portrays Robert Louis Stevenson

(1850–1894), offspring of a family of engineers, who achieved fame as an author.

The **Signet Library** to the rear of the cathedral dates from 1810–12. Near the Boehm statue of the 5th Duke of Buccleuch in Garter Robes is a heart shape set into the cobbles. This marks the site of the old tolbooth (1466–1817) made famous by Scott in *The Heart of Midlothian*.

Parliament House

&(&Mon–Fri 10.30am–4pm. &0131 444 3300. www.scotcourts.gov.uk.

Behind the imposing Georgian façade is the 17C Parliament Hall decreed by Charles I and designed by his master mason **John Mylne**. Where the Scottish Parliament met from 1639 to 1707, lawyers now meet under the carved and gilded **hammerbeam roof** and the gaze of their august predecessors. South of St Giles' is an equestrian statue of the Merry Monarch, Charles II (1685), the oldest in Edinburgh.

At the east end is the **Mercat Cross**, where merchants and traders congregated to transact business and the scene of celebrations, demonstrations, executions and royal proclamations. The 19C structure incorporates the shaft of the 16C cross.

City Chambers

The former Royal Exchange was built in 1753. To construct the building, the masons razed the upper floors of the old houses in **Mary King's Close** – a medieval alleyway which ran beneath it on the steep hillside – and made use of the lower floors as the foundation.

Closed off for centuries this underground warren was opened to the public in 1997 and renamed **The Real Mary King's Close★** (*2 Warrinston's Close, High Street.* &Apr–Oct daily 9.30am–9.30pm; Nov–Mar check website for details; the opening and closing times vary seasonally; &£16.50; &0131 225 0672; www.realmarykingsclose.com). Costumed guides re-create the dark and mysterious atmosphere of these four closes with real town houses, streets and rooms that date back to the 1600s. Plague epidemics in the insanitary cramped conditions were common and there are many reports of ghosts.

Tron Kirk

John Mylne built this church prior to undertaking Parliament Hall. It was built in the 17C and closed as a church in 1952. Having stood empty for over 50 years, it was used briefly as a tourist information centre. The spire is a 19C replacement.

⛉ Museum of Childhood

42 High Street. ♿⊙*Daily 10am–5pm.* ⊙*25–26 Dec and 1–2 Jan.* ☏*0131 529 4142. www.edinburghmuseums.org.uk.*
The Museum of Childhood is the first in the world dedicated to the history of childhood. Following extensive refurbishment, Gallery One features 60 rarely-seen objects relating to childhood life, learning and play. The museum now explores all aspects of British childhood from the mid-19Cto the present day, including a Queen Anne Doll dating from c.1740, a Raleigh Chopper bicycle from the 1970s, and Stanbrig Eorls, the largest dolls house in the museum's collection.

In Chalmers Close is **Trinity Apse**, the only surviving fragment of the Gothic Trinity College Church, founded about 1460 by Queen Mary of Gueldres, wife of James II of Scotland (*no admission*). Further along the street, 15C **Mowbray House** was the studio of the portraitist **George Jamesone** (1588–1644).

John Knox House

43–45 High Street. ♿⊙*Mon–Sat 10am–6pm (Jul–Aug also Sun noon–6pm).* ⊙*25–26 Dec and 1–2 Jan.* 👜*£6.* ☏*0131 556 9579. www.scottishstorytellingcentre.com.*
Located in The Netherbow, the halfway point in the Royal Mile and the site of Edinburgh's medieval Netherbow Port gateway, this picturesque town house was probably built prior to 1490. The original Netherbow bell, cast in 1621, and a carved stone plaque from the Port (gateway) have been reinstated in the

bell tower. The armorial panel on the west wall is that of one-time resident goldsmith James Mossman, whose father was responsible for redesigning the Scottish crown.

The **John Knox** connection is now much contested, but the house and its exhibits provide an insight into the man, his beliefs and Scotland during the Reformation. The main room on the second floor has a painted ceiling (1600).

Beyond the old Netherbow was the independent burgh of **Canongate** (gait or way of the canons) where the nobility, ambassadors and other royal officers built residences in close proximity to the royal palace of Holyroodhouse. Only a few of these mansions remain.

The People's Story Museum★

⊙*Daily 10am–5pm.* ☏*0131 529 4057. www.edinburghmuseums.org.uk.*
The tolbooth for the independent burgh of Canongate, this building with its turreted steeple was built in 1591 and is a fine example of 16C architecture.

The museum gives a moving insight into the daily life and work of the citizens from the late 18C to the present day with tableaux, documents, photographs, a video, and oral and written testimonies.

Canongate Church

This church was built in 1688 for the displaced congregation of Holyrood Abbey when James VII decided to convert the nave into a Chapel Royal for the Most Ancient Order of the Thistle. Above the south front is a stag's head bearing a cross, a reminder of the founding legend of Holyrood abbey.

Inside, the royal pew and those of officers of the Royal Household are indicated by coats of arms. Interesting memorials in the churchyard include that of Adam Smith and the young Edinburgh poet Robert Fergusson, whose tombstone was paid for by Burns. Another Burns connection is the plaque to Clarinda (east wall).

Museum of Edinburgh

&♿🕐*Daily 10am–5pm.* ✆*0131 529 4143. www.edinburghmuseums.org.uk.*
Three adjoined 16C mansions contain the main city museum of local history. Some of the rooms have 18C Memel panelling. The Edinburgh silver collection contains some particularly fine 18C pieces. but the museum's most coveted treasure is probably its original parchment of the National Covenant. Hidden in plain sight, this fascinating museum lifts the lid on the history of the city from its very beginnings up to the present day.

👥 Our Dynamic Earth

Opposite Palace of Holyroodhouse.
♿🕐*Feb–Oct daily 10am–5.30pm (Jul–Aug 6pm); Nov–Mar Wed–Sun 10am–5.30pm.* 🎟*£15.95 (child 4–15, £9.95) – online booking discounts.*
✗ ▣ ✆*0131 550 7800.*
www.dynamicearth.co.uk.
Against the dramatic backdrop of the Salisbury Crags, rises a striking building with a tented roof designed by Sir Michael Hopkins (1999). An innovative exhibition using state-of-the-art interpretative technology and two spectacular 360-degree films unravels the story of the planet: the Big Bang, the formation of the solar system, volcanoes and earthquakes, wild weather conditions, glaciers, the evolution of life, the extinction of animal and plant species, the beauty and power of the oceans. Life in the polar regions is dramatically contrasted with the environment of the tundra and rainforest.

Scottish Parliament★

♿🕐*Mon–Sat 10am–5pm, Tue–Thu 9am–6.30pm.* 🕐*Christmas period and February recess.* ✗ ✆*0131 348 5200 (Freephone 0800 092 7600).*
www.parliament.scot.
The Scottish Parliament has reinvigorated political life in Edinburgh. The dramatic cutting-edge design of this controversial building by Enric Miralles comprises clusters of small buildings shaped like upturned boats, connected by glass walkways.
Visitor areas usually include the dramatic vaults of the Main Hall, 'A Parliament for the People' exhibition, and the Parliament Shop and Café.

City Centre

② SOUTH OF THE ROYAL MILE TOUR – ROYAL MILE TO GEORGE HERIOT'S SCHOOL

Just off the beaten track, this walk takes in some of the city centre's most attractive little streets and squares with lots of quirky points of interest.

Victoria Street★

Descending in a curve to the Grassmarket, Victoria Street has graced many an Edinburgh picture-postcard and is lined with a very attractive series of boutiques, restaurants and small traditional shops.

▶ **Location:** This intriguing little corner of old Edinburgh lies at the foot of the Castle crags, beneath George V Bridge. By day it is bohemian and studenty, by night a little seedy, and by Greyfriars Kirkyard, more than a little spooky.

👥 **Kids:** Older kids will probably enjoy the bloody mayhem that is the Edinburgh Dungeon.

Grassmarket

The railed enclosure marks the site of the gallows where Captain Porteous was hanged (1736) and over 100 Covenanters were martyred.

New Town★★ 1767–1830

When the decision had been taken to extend the Royalty of Edinburgh, a competition was organised and was won by an unknown architect, **James Craig** (c.1740–1795). The North Bridge was thrown across the valley and the development of Edinburgh's New Town proceeded apace. The project was to be entirely residential at the outset – business and commerce were to remain in the Old Town centred on the Royal Exchange – and the winning plan had a grid-iron layout in which vistas and focal points played an important role.

The plan gave a succession of splendid squares and elegant streets, and people were quick to follow the example of Hume and Lord Cockburn in taking up residence.

When exploring Georgian Edinburgh look for the many decorative details which give the New Town so much of its character. The cast-iron work shows great variety of design (Heriot Row and Abercromby Place). Stretches of balcony spanning the frontages (Windsor Street and Atholl Crescent) alternate with window guards; the serried ranks of railings crested with finials are punctuated by lamp standards, brackets and extinguishers or link horns (Charlotte Square, York Place and Melville Street).

At the southwest corner, **West Port** marks the city's western gate. It was from a close nearby that the bodysnatchers Burke and Hare operated.

Cowgate

Although outside the original town wall, this was a fashionable quarter in the 16C. It is now a forlorn underpass.
Curving upwards, Candlemaker Row leads to George IV Bridge, passing the **statue** of a dog, Greyfriars Bobby (*see entry below*), on the left, at the top.

Greyfriars Church and Churchyard

Apr–Oct Mon–Fri 10.30am–4.30pm, Sat noon–4pm. 0131 225 1900. www.greyfriarskirk.com.
This early 17C church is famous for being the site where the **National Covenant** was signed in 1638. There is a copy inside the church together with an exhibition. The churchyard is highly atmospheric. Memorials include the Martyrs Monument (northeast wall) to the Covenanters taken at Bothwell Brig (1679) and imprisoned here for five months, and the grave of John (Jock) Macleod over which Bobby, his faithful Skye terrier, stood watch for 14 years (subsequently the story for a Walt Disney film). Inside

the church is the original portrait of "Greyfriars Bobby" painted by MacLeod in 1867.

▷ Take Forrest Road to Lauriston Place. During the daytime when the gate is open, the churchyard extension offers a shortcut to George Heriot's School.

George Heriot's School

Walk round the outside and into the courtyard.
This great Edinburgh school was endowed by **George Heriot** (1563–1624), goldsmith to James VI who nicknamed him "Jinglin Geordie". On his death, Heriot bequeathed the fortune he had made in London to the city fathers, for the education of "fatherless bairns of Edinburgh freemen". Construction was begun by William Wallace in 1628 but completion was delayed until 1659 when the building was used as a hospital by Cromwell's troops.
The symmetrical courtyard building is a good example of an early Renaissance edifice with abundant decorative stone carving and strapwork. The clock tower and statue of Geordie overlooking the courtyard are the work of Robert Mylne (1693).

A fragment of the **Flodden Wall** can be seen to the west of the school, at the head of the Vennel. Opposite is the 1879 Royal Infirmary.

▶ To reach George Square take Meadow Walk past Rowand Anderson's Medical School.

③ UNIVERSITY CAMPUS

George Square to Chambers Street. A stroll around the oldest part of Edinburgh and just beyond the Old Town.

George Square

The square, laid out in the 1760s, was the first major residential development outside the Old Town. Distinguished residents included Scott (No. 25 west side) and the Duchess of Gordon. The west side is the only complete example of the vernacular Classical style. The remaining sides are occupied by the university: library (1967) by Basil Spence, David Hume Tower (1963) for the Faculty of Social Sciences and the Science Faculty in Appleton Tower (1966).

Old University

The Old College was founded in 1581 and occupied premises within Kirk o'Field Collegiate Church (f.1450) outside the city walls. It was here that Lord Darnley met his death. In 1789 **Robert Adam** provided a grandiose design for a double courtyard building. Only the main front with impressive entrance overlooking South Bridge is his work. Playfair modified the design to one courtyard and completed the surrounding ranges. The **Talbot Rice Gallery** (♿⏲*Tue–Fri 10am–5pm, Sat noon–5pm; ☎0131 650 2210; www.ed.ac.uk/talbot-rice*) occupies Playfair's Georgian gallery, the original home of the Industrial Museum. The permanent Torrie Collection alternates with travelling exhibitions.

National Museum of Scotland★★★ ♿*See p153.*

Robert Louis Stevenson (1850–94)

A plaque inscribed with a verse of *The Lamplighter*, a poem for children, marks the site of Stevenson's childhood home at 17 Heriot Row *(private property)* in the New Town. He is famous for adventure stories such as *Treasure Island* and *Kidnapped* which have enthralled children through the years, and for his more sombre tale *Dr Jekyll and Mr Hyde* which is set in the Old Town. He took many trips abroad to warmer climes for health reasons including two to France which inspired him to write *An Inland Voyage* (1878) and *Travels with a Donkey in the Cévennes* (1879).

④ CHARLOTTE SQUARE TO THE EAST END OF PRINCES STREET

Students of Georgian architecture come from all over the world to bask in the grandeur of these squares and streets. And, for the non-architecturally inclined, they also house some of the city's finest shops, bars and restaurants.

Charlotte Square★★★

In 1791, **Robert Adam** was commissioned to design what is now the New Town's most splendid square. Elegant

Bute House, Charlotte Square

© rosn123/iStockphoto.com

143

frontages of a unified design frame the garden with a central equestrian statue of **Prince Albert** by Steell. The **north side** is a grand civic achievement where the vertical lines of the advanced central and end blocks are counterbalanced by the rusticated ground floor. The lines of straight-headed windows, round-headed doorway fanlights and occasional Venetian windows are happily juxtaposed. Note the wrought-iron railings, lamp holders, extinguishers and foot scrapers. The **centrepiece** comprises the ex-headquarters of the National Trust for Scotland (No. 5), Bute House, the official residence of the Secretary of State for Scotland (No. 6), and No. 7, **The Georgian House★** (*Mar and Nov daily 11am–3.15pm; Apr–Oct daily 10am–4.15pm, 1–mid-Dec Thu–Sun 11am–5.15pm; £8; 0131 225 2160; www.nts.org.uk*). The lower floors have been entirely refurbished by the NTS as a typical Georgian home of the period from 1790 to 1810. Some of the delights include the cheese waggon, rare wine rinsing glasses, lovely Scottish sideboard, moreen hangings, tea table and well-equipped kitchen and wine cellar. An introduction to Georgian Edinburgh is provided in one of the basement rooms.

A mirror image of the north side of the square, the south side has been comprehensively restored in as authentic a manner as possible by the National Trust. On the west side, St George's Church (1811–14) by Robert Reid provides the focal point for George Street and is now converted into part of the National Archives of Scotland annexe, **West Register House**. Famous residents included Lord Cockburn at No. 14, Lord Lister (No. 9) and Douglas Haig (No. 24).

George Street

The principal street of Craig's plan is closed at either end by Charlotte Square and St Andrew Square; it is 800m in length and 35m wide. Many of the houses of this originally residential street are now converted into banks, offices and a whole host of fashionable bars, restaurants and shops. Statues punctuate the street intersections – each of which has good views away to the Forth or down to Princes Street Gardens with the castle and Old Town as backdrop. Note in particular the **view** surveyed by George IV from his pedestal, with the successive landmarks perfectly positioned: Royal Scottish Academy, National Gallery, Assembly Hall and spire of the former Tolbooth Kirk.

Towards the east end are the **Assembly Rooms** (No. 54) built in 1784. This fine suite of rooms, with the Music Hall behind, is a magnificent setting for public functions.

St Andrew and St George Church (built in 1785), with its towering spire, was intended to close the George Street vista at the St Andrew Square end, but Dundas beat the planners to it.

Scottish National Portrait Gallery★

1 Queen Street. Daily 10am–5pm. 25–26 Dec. 0131 624 6200. www.nationalgalleries.org.

In the best Victorian tradition a munificent donation by the proprietor of

The Scotsman provided a building for the illustration of Scottish history. Rowand Anderson designed an Italianate Gothic, statue-decorated building to house the portrait collection founded in 1882. In 1890–91 the Antiquarian Society moved in from its premises in the Mound.

The initial aim of the National Portrait Gallery was to "illustrate Scottish history by likeness of the chief actors in it". Many of the portraits of persons of historic interest are masterpieces of portraiture. Scottish exponents of this tradition include the 16C George Jamesone (*self-portrait*), John Michael Wright, and the 18C masters, Ramsay (*David Hume* the companion portrait to the one of J J Rousseau) and Raeburn (*Scott*). In addition there are canvases by Wissing, Lely, Gainsborough and Lawrence. Some of the chief actors portrayed are royalty (*Mary, Queen of Scots, Lord Darnley, James VI, Charles I, Elizabeth of Bohemia* and *James VII*); statesmen formal and fine (*1st Earl of Dunfermline* and *Duke of Lauderdale*); 18C to 19C politicians (*Kier Hardie, Ramsay MacDonald* and *W E Gladstone*); literary figures (*Burns, Scott, Byron, Carlyle, Stevenson, Barrie*). By contrast modern portraiture of current Scottish personalities and heroes is also a very important part of the SNPG and this takes many formats in the exciting Contemporary Gallery where the traditional portrait canvas is largely eschewed.

St Andrew Square

Here **Henry Dundas**, Viscount Melville, better known as King Harry the Ninth for his management of Scottish affairs between 1782 and 1805, still dominates from his fluted column (46m high). The square, the home of banks and insurance companies, has none of the unified elegance of its counterpart, Charlotte Square, but has individual buildings of charm and splendour. On the north side Nos. 21 to 26 are examples of the vernacular Classical style of the first phase of New Town development.

Dundas House★ was built (1772–4) for Sir Laurence Dundas on what was originally intended to be a church site. Well set back, this three-storey mansion is adorned with a projecting three-bay pilastered, emblazoned, pedimented central section and a frieze at roof level. Step inside to see the splendours of the original entrance hall where capitals and roof bosses are highlighted in gold leaf. The building was purchased by the Royal Bank of Scotland in 1825 and the domed banking hall was added in 1858. West Register Street leads past the literary pub **Café Royal** with its oyster bar, to **New Register House** fronted by fine wrought-iron gates and crowned gateposts, indicating the offices of the Court of Lord Lyon with his Heralds and Pursuivants.

The Lord Lyon King of Arms regulates all Scottish armorial matters, adjudicates upon Chiefship of clans and conducts, and executes Royal Proclamations and state and public ceremonials of all descriptions in Scotland.

The east end of Princes Street is now dominated by Robert Adam's splendid frontage of **General Register House** (1774–1822), headquarters of the National Archives of Scotland. Changing exhibitions, relating to **ScotlandsPeople Centre** (family history) and the Historical Search Room (♿🕐*Mon–Fri 9am–4.30pm;* 🕐*some public holidays;* ☎*0131 314 4300; www.nrscotland.gov. uk*) are mounted in the front hall.

🏛Not many people know about the **Archivists' Garden**★ (🕐*during office hours*). The open courtyard between General Register House and New Register House has been transformed into a unique garden planted with more than 50 plant species – all connected in some way to Scotland's collective memory, through myth and folklore, heraldry, or by association with individuals.

The **General Post Office** stands on the site of the Theatre Royal built in 1768, as one of the first buildings in the New Town. During its heyday when Scott was a trustee, famous names such as Sarah Siddons and John Kemble performed here. The theatre closed in 1859 and was burned down in 1946. Opposite is the Balmoral Hotel with its famous clock tower landmark, and clock always set two minutes fast.

5 PRINCES STREET AND GARDENS

Princes Street

Edinburgh's famous shopping street was originally totally residential. Single sided, the street marked the southern extension of the New Town.

The 1770's town houses were modest but appreciated for the open view across the valley, which later became a private garden for residents. Following the laying of the railway (1845–46), commercial development slowly took over.

Princes Street Gardens★

The Nor'Loch valley was infilled during New Town excavation work and later laid out as private gardens for residents. With the coming of the railways, shops and hotels replaced houses and in 1876 the gardens were opened to the public. Today the gardens with their greenery, welcome benches and many monuments provide a pleasant respite from the milling crowds in Princes Street.

Scott Monument

Daily 10am–4pm. £8.
The spiral stone staircases (287 steps) are very narrow and can feel claustrophobic. 0131 529 4068. www.edinburghmuseums.org.uk.

This pinnacled monument dominating Princes Street is one of Edinburgh's most familiar landmarks. Following Scott's death in 1832, a successful public appeal was launched. Much controversy ensued as to the site and nature of the monu-

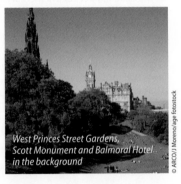

West Princes Street Gardens, Scott Monument and Balmoral Hotel in the background

© ARCO/J Moreno/age fotostock

ment; however, the foundation stone was laid in 1840. The neo-Gothic spire (61m tall) was designed by a joiner and draughtsman, **George Meikle Kemp**, who died before its completion. Steell's Carrara marble statue of Scott and his dog Maida is accompanied by 64 statuettes of characters from his novels (in the niches) and the heads of 16 Scottish poets (on the capitals). The monument became a major attraction. For the agile, four viewing platforms (*287 steps*) give good **views★** of central Edinburgh.

Dividing Princes Street Gardens into East and West are two imposing Classical buildings on the left: the National Gallery and the Royal Scottish Academy.

Scottish National Gallery★★

See p155.

Royal Scottish Academy

Mon–Sat 10am–5pm, Sun noon–5pm. Admission varies. 0131 225 6671. www.royalscottishacademy.org.

The Academy was custom built by William Playfair in 1826 to grace the north end of the Mound and counterbalance the Bank of Scotland's imposing building at the south end. Today, it is a world-class venue for temporary contemporary art exhibitions.

The Mound

The drained Nor'Loch area was initially crossed by stepping stones laid by an enterprising Lawnmarket clothier as a shortcut for his New Town clients. Later, excavated earth from New Town building sites was used to build up the Mound (1781–1805) as it stands today. Beyond, in West Princes Street Gardens, is the city's famous **floral clock** – composed of 20 000 annuals.

Museum on The Mound

Tue–Fri 10am–5pm, Sat–Sun and Bank Holiday Mons 1–5pm. Extended hours during the Festival: contact for details. 0131 243 5464. www.museumonthemound.com.

This "Mus£um" of money can hardly have chosen a more relevant time to open its doors. Art and design, technology, crime, trade and security are all examined. See what a million pounds really looks like and try your hand at cracking a safe. A visit here won't cost you a penny. Sadly, there are no free samples!

Edinburgh Dungeon

31 Market St. ♿☉*Daily, see website for variable opening times and ticket prices. Book online for the best deal, from £14.* ☎*0131 240 1001. www.thedungeons.com.*

Edinburgh has a bloodcurdling history which includes all manner of ghosts, vile executions and torture, bodysnatchers and even cannibalism. This is certainly no place for the squeamish, but older teens usually love the gorefest on show. Live actors and white knuckle rides pump up the adrenaline.

City Art Centre

2 Market Street. ♿☉*Daily 10am–5pm.* ⊜*Admission free to permanent exhibition.* ✗ ☎*0131 529 3993. www.edinburghmuseums.org.uk.*

Formerly part of the old Scotsman newspaper building, the CAC boasts a superb Fine Art collection of leading Scottish Artists, and showcases a wide range of contemporary Scottish and international artists with its temporary exhibitions.

⑥ CALTON HILL TOUR

At the east end of Princes Street rises Calton Hill (100m) with that familiar skyline of Classical monuments which gave rise to the name "Edinburgh's Acropolis". The James Craig **Observatory** was the initial building and development continued after 1815 when the ravine to the east of Princes Street had been crossed by Regent Bridge. The flanking porticoes and Classical façades of **Waterloo Place** provide a formal entry.

On the right, **St Andrew's House**, the former administrative centre of Scotland, stands on the site of two prisons.

Calton Hill★

Access by stairs from Waterloo Pl (Regent Road) or by a narrow road, leading opposite St Andrew's House.

Beltane Fire Festival

Since 1988 a festival marking the end of winter is held every year on Calton Hill (beltane.org). Until the beginning of the 20C this celebration, which is derived from an old Celtic tradition, took place on the site of St Anthony's Well on the eve of 1 May.

The main protagonists of this festival are: the May Queen and her retinue, a team of fighters known as the White Women, the Green Man and the Blue Man. Others such as the Red Men holding aloft torches process around a large bonfire to the sound of drums.

The most striking monument is the 12-columned portico of the **National Monument** to commemorate Scots who died in the Napoleonic Wars. It was intended as a replica of the Parthenon but construction was never completed. Adjacent is the **Nelson Monument** (☉*daily 10am–5pm;* ⊜*no charge, but £6 to climb the tower;* ☉*25–26 Dec, 1–3 Jan;* ☎*0131 556 2716; www.edinburghmuseums.org.uk*), a tiered circular tower, 32m tall. Atop it is a time ball, the original purpose of which was to enable ship's captains to set their chronometers accurately by observing the dropping of the ball at one o'clock Greenwich Mean Time.

Today, it still drops at exactly 1pm daily. The viewing gallery (*143 steps*) provides a magnificent **panorama★★★** of Edinburgh: up Princes Street, from the castle, to Holyroodhouse with Arthur's Seat in the background.

The circular Greek **temple** is Playfair's monument to Dugald Stewart, Professor of Moral Philosophy. The walled enclosure has at its southwest corner James Craig's 18C **Old Observatory**, itself succeeded by a new observatory on Blackford Hill, away from the bright city light just out of town.

Edinburgh Castle★★

This stately fortress, perched on its strategic site★★★ on Castle Rock, is impressive from all sides. The silhouette of the castle figures prominently on the skyline of most views of the city, and the castle's role has been of paramount importance throughout the city's history.

Info: ☏0131 225 9846; www.edinburghcastle.gov.uk. ⊙Daily Apr–Sept 9.30am–6pm, Oct–Mar 9.30am–5pm. ⊙25–26 Dec. £19.50 (online discounts).

Don't Miss: Fast track tickets online.

A BIT OF HISTORY

As early as the 11C the buildings atop Castle Rock were favoured as a residence by royalty, in particular by Margaret, the queen of Malcolm III, and her sons.

The castle subsequently alternated between Scottish and English forces and in 1313 suffered demolition by the Scots. In the late 14C, Bruce's son, David II, built a tower, of which there are no visible remains, on the site of the Half Moon Battery. The infamous **Black Dinner** of 1440 resulted in the execution of the two young Douglas brothers in the presence of their 10-year-old sovereign, James II, in an attempt to quell Douglas power.

In the 16C, Regent Morton did much to strengthen the castle's defences, which suffered again during Şir William Kirkcaldy of Grange's stout defence (1573) in the name of Mary, Queen of Scots. The end result was prompt execution for Grange and repairs and rebuilding to the castle. In the 1650s, Cromwell's troops took over and thus began the castle's new role as a garrison. The 18C saw two Jacobite attacks, the last by Bonnie Prince Charlie in person from his headquarters at the other end of the Royal Mile. The buildings we see today are basically those that have resulted from the castle's role as a military garrison in recent centuries.

CASTLE

Esplanade

Created as a spacious parade ground in the 18C, the esplanade is the setting for the festival's most popular event, the **Edinburgh Military Tattoo** (⊙see Calendar of Events), when the floodlit castle acts as backdrop. Before entering, note two of the castle's most imposing features from among the tiers of buildings, the appropriately named Half Moon Battery and the Palace Block towering up behind to the left.

Gatehouse

Beyond the ditch, started in the 1650s by Cromwell's troops, is the gatehouse, built as a suitably imposing entrance in the 19C. Two national heroes, Bruce **(1)** and Wallace **(2)** flank the entrance. Once through, the massive walls of the Half Moon Battery loom up ahead. These demarcate the line of the original outer defences. A plaque **(3)** on the left commemorates Kirkcaldy of Grange's stoic defence of 1573.

Portcullis Gate

The lower part, dating from Regent Morton's 1570s fortifications, has decorative features including Morton's coat of arms, while the upper part is a 19C addition.

Farther up, the two batteries, Argyle and Mill's Mount, both afford excellent **views★★** of Princes Street and the New Town. The **One O'Clock Gun (4)** is fired (Mon–Sat) from the upper battery.

Following the signs round to the left, on the right is the Governor's House (1742), with adjoining wings for the Master Gunner and Store-Keeper. The imposing building behind is the 1790s New Barracks for the castle garrison.

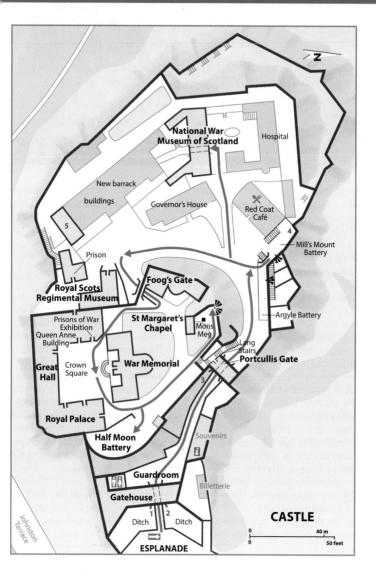

National War
Museum of Scotland

Hospital

New barrack
buildings

Governor's House

Red Coat
Café

5

4

Prison

Mill's Mount
Battery

Foog's Gate

Royal Scots
Regimental Museum

Prisons of War
Exhibition

Queen Anne
Building

St Margaret's
Chapel

Mons
Meg

Argyle Battery

Lang
Stairs

Portcullis Gate

Great
Hall

Crown
Square

War Memorial

3

Royal Palace

Half Moon
Battery

Souvenirs

i

Guardroom

Billetterie

Gatehouse

Johnston
Terrace

Ditch

1   2

Ditch

CASTLE

0   40 m
0   50 feet

ESPLANADE

Royal Scots Regimental Museum

&. ○ *Apr–Sept Mon–Fri 9.30am–5pm, Sat–Sun 9.30am–5.30pm; Oct–Mar Mon–Fri 9.30am–4pm, Sat–Sun 9.30am–4.30pm.* ○ *Christmas and New Year.* ☎ *0131 310 5015. www.theroyalscots.co.uk.*

The Royal Regiment is the oldest and most senior regiment of the British Army. Raised on 28 March 1633, the unit originally served under King Louis XIII of France where it earned the nickname "Pontius Pilate's Bodyguard". The regiment was finally recalled to Britain in 1676; two rooms of exhibits and an impressive display of medals trace the regiment's subsequent history: Corunna, Waterloo, Alma, Sebastopol, Marne.

Vaults

Two levels of great vaulted chambers (**5**), situated under the Crown Square buildings, housed French and American

149

Edinburgh Castle

© Pinkcandy/age fotostock

prisoners in the 18C and 19C. In the end chamber stands the 500-year-old siege cannon, **Mons Meg**. Commissioned by the Duke of Burgundy and forged in 1449 at Mons in Hainaut, it was given eight years later to his nephew James II. During an eventful career, Mons Meg is said to have served at Crookston (1489), Dumbarton (1489) and Norham castles (1497) and even to have spent time in the Tower of London. Sir Walter Scott petitioned for its return and in 1829 the huge medieval cannon was returned to Edinburgh.

St Margaret's chapel

The small rectangular building on the left incorporates remnants of the castle's oldest structure, and perhaps even Edinburgh's. This 12C chapel is dedicated to Malcolm III's Queen Margaret. Once surrounded by other buildings it served various purposes until the mid-19C when its original role was revealed and restoration ensued.

Inside, the chancel arch is Norman in inspiration with its cushion capitals and chevron decoration. The terrace in front offers an extensive **panorama★★★** of northern Edinburgh, in particular Princes Street and the gardens, and the geometric pattern of the New Town.

Half Moon Battery

The battery was built following the 1573 siege, which saw the destruction of David II's tower house. From here the strategic importance of the original tower with its command of castle approaches and entrance is evident.

The heart of the medieval fortress and one-time royal residence is marked by Crown Square. Of the four buildings overlooking the square today only the southern and eastern ranges are of historic interest.

Scottish National War Memorial

North side.

In the 1920s, **Sir Robert Lorimer** undertook the task of converting a mid-18C building into Scotland's War Memorial. The exterior, with a strong resemblance to the palace part of Stirling Castle, is in harmony with the earlier buildings. The interior achieves a suitable atmosphere of dignity and reverence. Wartime scenes are depicted in the stained-glass windows by Douglas Strachan. The low-relief sculptures depict the fighting men and other participants in the struggle. A casket containing the names of the fallen stands in the apse.

National War Museum

West side. East gallery in Palace Block.

Daily: Apr–Sept 9.45am–5.45pm; Oct–Mar 9.45am–4.45pm. 25–26 Dec, 1 Jan. £19.50 (includes admission to castle). 0300 123 6789. www.nms.ac.uk.

Displays of uniforms, medals, badges, colours and weapons illustrate the history of the Scottish regiments.

Great Hall

South side.

The hall was built in the late 15C for James IV and intended for great occasions. Its crowning glory is the **hammer-beam roof★★**. Boards and beams are attractively painted.

Palace Block

East side.

This range, which dates from the 15C, contained the royal apartments overlooking the old town. The interior was remodelled in 1617. Enter by the door nearest the Great Hall range. A room on the right has displays on excavations at Mill's Mount dating back to the Iron Age. Straight ahead, Queen Mary's Room is hung with family portraits of her son James VI, her grandson Charles I, her great-grandsons Charles II and James II, and her first husband François II. There is also a plaster cast from Mary's tomb effigy at Westminster Abbey. The adjoining small **chamber**, with its panelling and timber ceiling, is the room where James VI was born in 1566. The decoration dates from the 1617 refurbishing. Once in the square again, the doorway in the staircase tower leads to the Crown Chamber on the first floor where the Scottish crown jewels, known as the **Honours of Scotland★★★**, are displayed. Although of unknown age, the pearl and gem encrusted **crown** is Britain's only pre-Restoration crown to have escaped being melted down.

The **sceptre** and **sword** were gifts from two Popes to the Renaissance prince James IV, the former from the Borgia Pope, Alexander VI (1492–1503), and the latter from his successor, Pope Julius II (1503–13), a great patron of the arts. Pride of place is also given to the **Stone of Destiny**, the ancient symbol of Celtic kingship, which was returned to Scotland in 1996 after 700 years under the Coronation Chair at Westminster Abbey.

The other rooms (*East Gallery*) contain displays on the Royal Navy, Royal Air Force, the Royal Scots Greys, and the yeomanry regiments. Note the model of the pride of James IV's navy, the magnificent **Great Michael** (1507–11).

Palace of Holyroodhouse ★★

At the east end of the Royal Mile stands the Palace of Holyroodhouse, the Queen's official residence in Scotland, adjoined by the ruined nave of the abbey. In the background are the green slopes and rocky crags of Holyrood Park rising to Arthur's Seat. This is a wonderful place for breezy walks and the views back into town are unsurpassable.

A BIT OF HISTORY

Legend has it that **David I**, while out hunting, was thrown from his mount and wounded by a stag. In a defensive gesture he made to grasp the animal's antlers only to find he was holding a crucifix, the animal having made off into the forest. In recognition David founded the Augustinian Abbey of Holy Rood in 1128 and granted to the canons the right to their own burgh, Canongate.

The medieval abbey prospered and benefited from royal patronage in the 15C from the Stewart Kings. James II was born, married and buried here and broke with the Scone tradition to be crowned here. His three successors were all married in the abbey. It was during this period that the guesthouse was used as a royal residence in preference to the castle. James IV, intent on making Edinburgh his capital, started transforming the guesthouse into a palace.

> **Info:** ☏0131 556 5100; www.rct.uk. ⏰Daily: 9.30am–6pm (Nov–Mar 9.30am–4.30pm). Gardens open summer. ⏰Good Fri, mid-May, first and last week Jun, first week Jul, 25–26 Dec and during royal visits, see website. ⏣£15 (*Price includes an multimedia guide. A Royal Visit ticket – £24.50 – includes admission to the Palace, Queen's Gallery and a garden history tour.*

Palace of Holyroodhouse

© Tibor Bognar/age fotostock

The abbey buildings were despoiled at the Reformation and burned in 1650 by Cromwell's troops.

Charles II commissioned **Sir William Bruce** (1630–1710), the Architect Royal, to draw up designs; the final result is a handsome example of Palladian style.

PALACE

Exterior

Flanked by columns, the door is surmounted by carved stonework incorporating the Scottish coat of arms, a broken pediment, a cupola and crown. The inner court elevations are an outstanding example of classic Renaissance and one of Scotland's earliest examples.

Interior

The decoration of the State Apartments remains lavish. Highly intricate decorative plasterwork ceilings, lavishly carved woodwork (doors, doorcases, picture frames and swags) and inset canvases were all integral parts of the decor and of a very high standard of craftsmanship. The seven outstanding **plasterwork ceilings★★★** in high relief represent 10 years of labour by the "gentlemen modellers" **John Halbert** and **George Dunsterfield**.

Other than the ceilings, the most notable features of the **State Apartments** are: in the Adam-style Dining Room a

splendid portrait of *George IV in Highland Dress* by Sir David Wilkie. In the Throne Room, redecorated in the 1920s, are royal portraits of the brothers Charles II and James VII (the palace's first royal guest) with their respective queens, and Queen Victoria in her coronation robes. Carved door surrounds and 18C Brussels tapestries (market scenes, Asia, Africa) can be seen in the Evening Drawing Room. Finest of all is the Morning Drawing Room, sumptuously decorated with a Jacob de Wet medallion above the fireplace and 17C French tapestries (the Story of Diana). The King's Suite was on the east side, overlooking the famous Privy Garden of formal design on the site of the demolished cloister.

In the King's Chamber is a magnificent Red Bed (1672) and ceiling with a de Wet medallion. The Gallery walls are lined with fascinating (imaginary and real) portraits of every Scottish king from Fergus, in the 6C, to James VII. Jacob de Wet completed them in two years.

The **Historic Apartments** in the 16C round tower consist of similar suites on two floors. These were refurbished c.1672 when floor and ceiling levels were adjusted to correspond to the Bruce additions. There are many Mary, Queen of Scots associations. The antechamber has 17C Mortlake tapestries from the workshop founded by her son James VI. Upstairs are two exquisite **16C coffered ceilings**, the first adorned with painted designs. The small chamber adjoining the Bedchamber is closely associated with the murder of Mary's Italian secretary, Rizzio, in 1566. His body was found in the outer chamber (brass plaque marks the spot). Paintings depict Mary's second husband **Henry, Lord Darnley** (1546–67), as a 17-year-old youth with his brother. A second work shows his mourning family, including his son James VI, after Darnley's murder at Kirk o'Field.

A new display within the apartments focuses on **the Order of the Thistle**, the highest honour in Scotland. The order honours Scottish men and women who have held public office or who have contributed in a particular way to national life.

Shown alongside historic insignia is an example of the mantle worn at the Thistle ceremony at St Giles' Cathedral in Edinburgh, which The Queen attends during her visit to the Palace in July.

ABBEY

The roofless nave is all that remains of this once great abbey. It dates mainly from the late 12C and early 13C and there are some finely sculpted details. Queen Victoria rebuilt the royal burial vault following its destruction on the departure of the Roman Catholic James VII. The remains of David II, James II, James V and Lord Darnley are interred here.

QUEEN'S GALLERY

&⊙*Daily: 10am–5.30pm (late-Jul–Sept 9.30am–5.30pm. ✕ ℘0131 556 5100. www.rct.uk.*

Built in the shell of the former Holyrood Free Church and Duchess of Gordon's School, the gallery provides purpose-built, state-of-the-art facilities to show a programme of changing exhibitions of the most delicate works of art from the priceless Royal Collection.

HOLYROOD PARK

Holyrood Park, the largest area of open ground within the city, is dominated by Arthur's Seat (251m) and the Salisbury Crags, both volcanic features. A path from the car park on the Queen's Road, within the park, leads up to **Arthur's Seat** (*30min*) which affords a tremendous **panorama★★★** of the Edinburgh area.

At the foot of Arthur's Seat, the historic palace buildings are offset by significant structures reflecting the town's dynamic outlook following the devolution of power to Scotland: the futuristic **Our Dynamic Earth** (&*p141*); the spectacular Scottish Parliament building; another new building housing the offices of *The Scotsman*.

Beyond Dunsapie lies the lovely village of **Duddingston** in an attractive setting between park and loch (which acts as bird sanctuary). The 12C church has some good Norman features and its historic inn, **The Sheep Heid**, is worth the walk in its own right. One of the oldest pubs in Scotland, its name dates from 1580 when the landlord was presented with an embellished ram's head ("heid") by King James VI.

National Museum of Scotland★★★

The joy of the National Museum of Scotland is the magpie nature of its collection including exhibits from all over Scotland and beyond: Viking brooches, Pictish stones, ancient chessmen, medieval oak carvings and ornate quaichs (drinking cups); from Queen Mary's harp to Sir Jackie Stewart's F1 car, steam engines and spectacular silver to manuscripts donated by Ian Rankin and the Proclaimers. Yet despite this

▷ **Location:** Chambers Street.
▯ **Info:** &✕℘0131 225 7534; www.nms.ac.uk. ⊙Daily 10am–5pm (26 Dec and 1 Jan noon–5pm). Free guided tours available. ⊙25 Dec.
☺ **Don't Miss:** The many details by trying to rush it all in one visit!

seeming disparity, all are skilfully used to illustrate important aspects of "Scottishness", beautifully exhibited and very well explained in the nation's finest museum.

Grand Gallery,
National Museum of Scotland

© Jon Arnold Images/hemis.fr

A BIT OF HISTORY

After the Great Exhibition of 1851, museums and art galleries proliferated throughout England. In 1854, funds were allocated to Edinburgh to found its own museum of industry. Captain Fowke, known for his work on the Albert Hall in London, drew up a design combining iron and glass, and the museum was opened in 1861 by Prince Albert.

For 150 years this housed the collections of the **Royal Museum of Scotland**; an eclectic treasure trove of items collected by Scots during their world travels. In 1998, the brand new **Museum of Scotland**, dedicated to the history and culture of Scotland and housed in a brand new modern building, was integrated into the Victorian fabric. Resolutely modern, yet traditionally dressed in sandstone from Morayshire, the new building is dominated by a round tower overlooking Chambers Street and George IV Bridge.

Seek out the **Rooftop Terrace★** for a stunning panoramic view, as well as artworks by Andy Goldsworthy.

☺ Go up first thing in the morning for a truly peaceful experience.

Inside, is a striking diversity of spaces – some bright and light, others darker and more mysterious. Spiral staircases seem to be embedded in the thickness of the walls, while balconies, porches and windows look out onto different floors. Both buildings and collections are now known as the **National Museum of Scotland**.

Grand Gallery

The soaring pillars and high windows of the old Victorian building welcomes visitors with an eclectic collection of large-scale, often spectacular items, all with Scottish connections and contribution to world cultures.

Windows of the World

Also housed to stunning effect in the original section, rising up through the four storeys of the Grand Gallery, Window on the World is the largest single museum installation in the UK. It showcases a spectacular array of items to represent the diversity of the museum's collection.

Discoveries

The theme of Scottish ideas and innovations, travellers and collectors, and their impact and interaction across the globe continues in these galleries. They range from John Logie Baird and Alexander Fleming to the lighthouses of the Stevensons. A particular favourite is the amazing 10m-high **Millennium Clock Tower**. Watch it on the hour when it comes to life.

World Cultures

Showcasing some of the museum's oldest and most important historical collections, these eight very colourful galleries also demonstrate Scotland's international links. **Facing the Sea** is the only gallery in the UK dedicated to the cultures of the South Pacific. **Living Lands** moves across the deserts of Australia, to the coasts of Pacific North America and northern Japan, and over the high plateau of Tibet to the North American Arctic. **Looking East** highlights the museum's rich collection of Chinese, Japanese and Korean artifacts.

Natural World

The story of the earth and the wildlife upon it is the ambitious scope of this section. The awesome array of life-sized mammals and birds soaring through the Natural World galleries, from prehistory up to the present day is not to be missed. From a cast of Tyrannosaurus rex to a giant squid, whales and dolphins , animals from the depths of the oceans to the open skies "fly" all around.

Art and Design

These galleries trace innovations in style across the ages and around the world. They specifically focus on: **Ancient Egypt**; **Art and Industry**, from 1850 to the present day; **European Styles** and **Traditions in Sculpture**, from 1850 to the present day.

Science & Technology

Although all galleries feature interactive exhibits, this is the place for getting really hands-on. **Connect** takes visitors from early scientific instruments to Dolly the Sheep (cloning) and from steam engines to a real NASA space capsule. **Communicate!** gallery shows how we've progressed from jungle drums to mobile phones, while **Shaping Our World** looks at the ways in which scientific developments over the past 150 years, influenced by many Scottish scientists inventors and entrepreneurs, have revolutionised the way we live.

Scottish National Gallery ★★

The National Gallery Complex comprises two buildings: the Gallery which hosts the permanent collections, and the Royal Scottish Academy which stages temporary exhibitions. They are connected by an underground space, the Weston Link, which includes a café, restaurant, shop and a conference room.

A BIT OF HISTORY

The nucleus of the Gallery was formed by the Royal Institution's collection, later expanded by bequests and purchasing. Playfair designed (1850–57) the imposing Classical building to house the works.

VISIT

🔊 Start with Room 1 on the upper floor by taking the staircase opposite the main entrance.

The Early Northern and Early Italian holdings include the *Trinity Altarpiece*

▶ **Location:** The Mound.
📋 **Info:** ♿✕🔧☏0131 624 6200; www.nationalgalleries.org. 🕐Daily 10am–5pm (Thu 7pm). Times may change during festival. 🕐25–26 Dec.
🎨 **Don't Miss:** The iconic *Reverend Robert Walker Skating on Duddingston Loch*, and Rembrandt *Self-Portrait, aged 51*.

(c.1470s) by Van der Goes, a unique example of pre-Reformation art. When open, the panels represent James III and Margaret of Denmark with patron saints. *The Three Legends of St Nicholas* by Gerard David shows scenes from the life of St Nicholas of Myra (Santa Claus). Early Italian works introduce Raphael with his gentle *Bridgewater Madonna* and an excellent example of High Renaissance

© Hartmut Krintz/hemis.fr

Scottish National Gallery

portraiture by his contemporary, Andrea del Sarto (*Portrait of the Artist's Friend*). Downstairs, **Galleries I** and **II** introduce the principal figures of early-16C Venetian painting: Jacopo Bassano with the colourful *Adoration of the Kings* and Titian with his religious composition *The Three Ages of Man*. Two more examples of Titian's late style of mythological painting (1550s) are *Diana and Actaeon* and *Diana and Calisto*. The second generation of 16C painters on display include Tintoretto (*The Deposition of Christ*) and Veronese (*Mars and Venus, St Anthony Abbot*).

Gallery III displays a number of miscellaneous 16C and 17C European Cabinet Pictures (Cranach, Holbein, Clouet, Rubens and Avercamp). **Gallery IV** gathers together 17C works by Poussin, Claude Lorrain, El Greco, as well as an early work by Velázquez (*An Old Woman Cooking Eggs*). Poussin's admirable *Seven Sacraments* are enhanced by the gracious setting of **Gallery V**.

The diversity of 17C Dutch art is well represented in **Galleries VI**, **VII** and **IX**. Jan Weenix specialises in large hunting scenes. Cuyp's *View of the Valkhof, Nijmegen* introduces interesting light effects and Koninck's *Onset of a Storm* combines imaginary views with natural scenery. Alongside, the portraits of Frans Hals display a vitality and realism

which make them second only to those of Rembrandt, represented by his *Self-Portrait Aged 51*. In **Gallery VII** hang landscapes by Ruisdael, Hobbema and Philip Koninck.

Gallery IX (17C Flemish and Dutch painting) contains canvases by Rubens. The swirling movement of his *Feast of Herod*, a large banqueting scene full of colour and realism, contrasts with the staid formalism of Van Dyck's *The Lomellini Family*. Vermeer's early work *Christ in the House of Martha and Mary* shows Mary in an attentive mood.

The principal figures of 18C British art, Gainsborough, Reynolds, Romney, Raeburn and Lawrence, are introduced in **Gallery X**. Other 18C schools are represented by François Boucher, France's foremost Rococo painter; G B Tiepolo, the last exponent of the Venetian Renaissance tradition; and Gavin Hamilton, a pioneer in Neoclassicism.

19C British and American works (**Gallery XI**) include landscapes by Turner (*Somer Hill, Tunbridge*), Constable (*Vale of Dedham*), Ward (*The Eildon Hills and the Tweed, Melrose Abbey*) and Church (*Niagara Falls*). Next door in **Gallery XII** hang Sir Benjamin West's gigantic work *Alexander III of Scotland Rescued from the Fury of a Stag*, a colourful composition of frenzied action and a collection of full-length Raeburns.

Take the stairs between Gallery VI and IX to Rooms A2–6 located on the upper floor.

The smaller 18C and 19C paintings in **Rooms A2** and **A3** include works by Watteau, Greuze, Boucher, Guardi, Chardin, Hogarth, Allan Ramsay, Gainsborough, the early-19C landscapist John Crome and Wilkie. Precursors to the French Impressionists (**Room A4**) include the romanticism of Corot's landscapes and the realism of Courbet's everyday scenes.

In **Room A5**, note the preoccupation with play of light in the canvases of Monet (*Haystacks* and *Poplars on the Epte*), Sisley and Pissarro. The exoticism of Gauguin is typified by *The Visions* after the Sermon and *Three Tahitians*, Van Gogh's vigorous style and bright colours by the *Olive Trees* and Cézanne's rich tones by *La Montagne*.

▶ Take the stairs beyond Gallery VII down to the underground wing.

Galleries B1–8 illustrate Scottish painting 1600–1900. Portraiture dominates the early works. Beyond are numerous examples of Raeburn's works, including *Reverend Robert Walker Skating on Duddingston Loch*, and David Wilkie's realistic Scottish scenes, including *Distraining for Rent, The Letter of Introduction, Pitlessie Fair, The Gentle Shepherd*. Nasmyth's *Edinburgh Castle and the Nor'Loch, The Distant View of Stirling* are soft and atmospheric compositions.

William Dyce specialised in religious scenes and landscapes (*St Catherine, Christ as the Man of Sorrows*). The *Porteous Mob* by J Drummond is based on an historical episode in Scott's *Heart of Midlothian*.

McTaggart excelled in landscapes (*The Storm, The Young Fishers*) where bold brushwork and dramatic light introduced a sense of realism.

Outskirts

It's well worth allocating a day or two extra to your stay in Edinburgh to explore outside the centre. The Botanic Gardens, Zoo, Royal Yacht and Modern Art gallery are some of the city's finest attractions.

NORTHERN AND WESTERN EDINBURGH

Royal Botanic Garden★★★

1mi/1.6km from city centre by Broughton Street. 🅿 *West Gate, Arboretum Road.*
♿🕐*Daily Mar–Sept 10am–6pm, Feb and Oct 10am–5pm, Nov–Jan 10am–4pm.* 🕐*Glasshouses: Mar–Sept 10am–5pm, Feb and Oct 4pm, Nov–Jan 3pm.* 🍴*Garden free; glasshouses £7.*
✕✆*0131 248 2909. www.rbge.org.uk.*
The 28ha of the Royal Botanic Garden are a refreshing haven when you are weary of the city bustle. The Terrace Café enjoys a beautiful view.

Origins

In 1670, when Edinburgh was emerging as a centre for medical studies, a physic garden was established by Edinburgh University. The original plot was situated near Holyrood Abbey. In c.1820 the garden was moved to the present site.

▶ **Location:** The Botanic Garden, art galleries and Leith Walk are a very pleasant 30min walk (approx.), northwest of the New Town. Take the bus to Craigmillar Castle, Leith and the Edinburgh Zoo.

👪 **Kids:** Will love the Penguin Parade at Edinburgh Zoo.

Palm House, Royal Botanic Garden

© Wojtek Buss/age fotostock

157

Garden and buildings

The **rhododendrons** are a major attraction. The modernistic Exhibition Plant Houses (1967) provide unimpeded interiors where winding paths lead through a series of landscaped presentations. The Exhibition Hall is devoted to changing displays on various aspects of botany. The Tropical (1834) and Temperate (1858) Palm Houses have a more traditional, imposing architectural style. High in the centre of the gardens stands 18C **Inverleith House**, and from beyond the lawn a view indicator pinpoints Edinburgh's well-known landmarks.

CITY SUBURBS

🚻🧍 Edinburgh Zoo★★

3mi/5km from the city centre, on the A8.
♿🕐*Daily Apr–Sept 10am–6pm;*
Oct and Mar 10am–5pm; Nov–Feb
10am–4.30pm. 🎫*£19.95 (child 3–15,*
£9.95) – online discounts available.
✕ 🅿*£4.* ✆*0131 334 9171.*
www.edinburghzoo.org.uk.

The 32ha Scottish National Zoological Park is attractively set on the south slope of Corstorphine Hill. Barless and sometimes glassless enclosures for many of the species allow the visitor better views of the animals and their behaviour.

Since December 2011 the biggest draw here has been Tian Tian and Yang Guang the only two **giant pandas** in the UK. Such is the demand that a (free) time -ticketed system is in operation; booking in advance is recommended.

Before the arrival of the pandas the famous Edinburgh penguin collection (a colony of 30 kings and 100 gentoes) was the number one attraction with their daily **Penguin Parade**. Other highlights are: the **Budongo Trail** which allows visitors to see **chimpanzees** in what is claimed to be the world's most innovative, interactive chimpanzee enclosure;. **Living Links,** an indoor/outdoor facility that houses capuchin and squirrel monkeys; **Sun bears** Somnang and Rotana in their new state-of-the-art enclosure; the **Brilliant Birds** walkthrough aviary; the **White-faced Saki Monkey Walkthrough** enclosure;

The **view** from the hilltop (155m) shows the sprawl of Edinburgh and from the Pentlands to the mountains around Loch Lomond.

Craigmillar Castle★

3mi/5km southeast by St Leonard's Street and the A68.
🕐*Apr–Sept daily 9.30am–5.30pm; Oct–Mar Sat–Wed 9.30am–4pm.* 🕐*1–2 Jan and 25–26 Dec.* 🎫*£6.* ✆*0131 661 4445. www.historicenvironment.scot.*

Dramatically set on an eminence, even in ruins Craigmillar has an air of strength and impregnability. The 14C tower house rises massively above two curtain walls. The outer wall encloses a courtyard in front and gardens on either side. The inner curtain built in 1427 is quartered with round towers, pierced by gunloops and topped by attractive oversailing machicolated parapets.

Above the inner gate is the Preston family coat of arms. Straight ahead stands the L-shaped **tower house**. The **Great Hall** at first floor level is a grand apartment with a magnificent hooded fireplace. Climb to the top to get a view down over the other buildings and appreciate the strategic excellence of the layout.

It was here that Mary, Queen of Scots sought refuge after the murder of Rizzio and that the treacherous plot for the murder of Darnley was conceived.

LEITH

Some 2mi/3km north of the city centre, Leith has been Edinburgh's port since the 14C. In the second half of the 20C, with the decline of big ships and heavy industry, it slumped into inner city dereliction and acquired a very bad reputation – the tale of lowlife drug addicts in the 1991 film, *Trainspotting*, originated here. Since the mid-1980s however, it has been revitalised into a trendy dockland development area with the likes of media companies, and particularly the new Scottish Office Building, providing well-paid jobs. Loft homes have been created in run-down dockside warehouses, basic pubs have been gentrified and a rash of style bars, gourmet restaurants, a small number of hotels and nightclubs have sprung up.

Ocean Terminal (*www.oceanterminal.com*) is a large waterside complex devoted to eating, drinking and shopping, plus a multiplex cinema.

Royal Yacht *Britannia*★

🕐*Daily Nov–Mar 10am–3.30pm; Apr–Oct 9.30am– 4.30pm.* 🕐*25 Dec and 1 Jan.* ∞*£16.50.* ✖ 🅿 ✆*0131 555 5566. www.royalyachtbritannia.co.uk.*

The Royal Yacht *Britannia* was launched from the Clyde in April 1953. By the time she was decommissioned in December 1997, this symbol of post-Imperial royalty had sailed some a million miles, carrying Queen Elizabeth II and her family on nearly ,000 official visits. The roles *Britannia* played, from floating palace to venue for the promotion of British exports, are explained in a visitor centre, spacious enough to contain a royal barge afloat in a tank of water. Once aboard, visitors follow a trail through royal apartments, crew's quarters, bridge, wheelhouse and engine room, assisted by an entertaining audio tour.

Designed by Sir Hugh Casson in close consultation with the Queen and Prince Philip, the royal apartments have a cool but comfortable style, a subtle combination of country house luxury and shipshape practicality.

Water of Leith Walkway

This bucolic riverside footpath and cycleway links Leith to Dean Village with its two outstanding modern art galleries.

Scottish National Gallery of Modern Art★
Modern One

75 Belford Road. 🕐*Daily 10am–5pm.* 🕐*25–26 Dec.* ✖ 🅿 ✆*0131 624 6200. www.nationalgalleries.org.*

The Scottish National Gallery of Modern Art is in two buildings: Modern One and Modern Two (🕐*see below*). The first is an imposing neo-Classical building

and situated in large wooded grounds, which provide a fine setting for sculptures by Bourdelle, Epstein, Hepworth, Moore and Rickey.

The collection has two emphases: international and Scottish art of the 20C. If not fully comprehensive in its international collection, it does nevertheless have fine examples of most of the main artists and movements: Fauvism, German Expressionism, Cubism and its derivatives, Russian Primitivism and Abstract Art, Abstraction, School of Paris, Nouveau Réalisme, St Ives School, Pop Art, Minimal Art. The post-war collection features recent works by artists including Antony Gormley, Gilbert and George, Damien Hirst and Tracey Emin. The **Scottish Collection** is rich and comprehensive. It has particularly good holdings of the work of the Scottish Colourists (Peploe, Cadell, Hunter, Fergusson) and the Edinburgh School (Gillies, Maxwell, McTaggart and Redpath).

Modern Two

73 Belford Road.
♿ 🕐*Same as Modern One.*

Oriringally built in 1833, this imposing and idiosyncratic Greek Revival building makes a fine setting for the National Gallery's specialist collections of contemporary art.

The **Dada** and **Surrealist** holdings, based on the collections of Sir Roland Penrose and Gabrielle Keiller, include works by Ernst, Dalí, de Chirico, Magritte, Schwitters, Miró, Picasso, Magritte, Delvaux, Tristram Hillier and Henry Moore. Masks, skulls, other *objets trouvés* and the contents of Penrose's cabinet of curiosities help create the bizarre atmosphere favoured by the Surrealists.

The Paolozzi Gift consists of a large number of works by the Edinburgh-born sculptor **Eduardo Paolozzi** (1924–2005), among them the gigantic stainless steel *Vulcan* rising through two floors in the centre of the building. Beyond, a room containing a number of the artist's characteristic figures is a reconstruction of Paolozzi's fascinatingly crammed studio.

ADDRESSES

🛏 STAY

CENTRE

🛏 **Travelodge Edinburgh Central** –
*33 St Mary's Street. ℘0871 984 6137. www.
travelodge.co.uk.* It's modern, lacks style
and can be noisy, but it's also just a few
strides from the Royal Mile. Good value.

🛏🛏 **Apex Haymarket Hotel** –
*90 Haymarket Terrace. ℘0131 474 3456.
www.apexhotels.co.uk. 66 rooms.* This
impressive stylish modern hotel is
located in the West End, very close to the
New Town.

🛏🛏 **Castle View Guest House** –
*30 Castle Street. ℘0131 226 5784. www.
castleviewgh.com.* This is a spacious
penthouse apartment on the 3rd and
4th floors of an Edinburgh Georgian
town house in which Kenneth Grahame
(*The Wind in the Willows*) was born. There
are views to Edinburgh Castle and the
Firth of Forth.

🛏🛏 **Ibis Edinburgh** – *6 Hunter Square.
℘0131 240 7000. 99 rooms. www.accor
hotels.com.* Modern chain hotel with
small standardised rooms, located at the
heart of the old town.

🛏🛏🛏 **Fraser Suites** – *12–26 St Giles
Street. ℘0131 221 7200. https://edinburgh.
frasershospitality.com.* This sumptuous
boutique hotel boasts 75 luxurious
contemporary rooms and suites in a 19C
building just off the Royal Mile.

🛏🛏🛏 **DoubleTree by Hilton** – *34
Bread Street, Old Town. ℘0131 221 5555.
https://doubletree3.hilton.com. 139 rooms.*
This is possibly the most stylish medium-
sized hotel in the centre and enjoys
spectacular views of the castle.

🛏🛏🛏🛏 **Radisson Collection Hotel**
– *1 George IV Bridge. ℘0131 220 6666.
www.radissoncollection.com. 136 rooms.*
The exterior of Edinburgh's latest must-
stay hotel is elegant and modern; the
contemporary interior decor is the work
of Italian fashion house Missoni. Rooms
feature espresso machines and "rainwater
showers".

🛏🛏🛏🛏 **The Balmoral** – *1 Princes Street.
℘0131 556 2414. www.roccofortehotels.
com. 188 rooms.* Traditionally the haunt of
visiting royalty, rock stars and presidents,
who enjoy richly furnished rooms in
baronial style at this most central of city
landmarks. **Restaurant** (🍽🍽🍽🍽).

🛏🛏🛏🛏 **The Principal Hotel** –
*19–21 George Street. ℘0131 225 1251.
www.phcompany.com.* Beautifully
appointed, this classic New Town hotel
makes the most of Robert Adams'
listed 18C design. Printing Press bar and
restaurant (🍽🍽🍽🍽) is recommended.

🛏🛏🛏🛏 **The Bonham** – *35 Drumsheugh
Gardens. ℘0131 226 6050. www.
thebonham.com. 49 rooms and suites.*
A luxury boutique hotel in a quiet leafy
crescent just a short distance from the
main attractions. **Restaurant** (🍽🍽🍽🍽).

🛏🛏🛏🛏 **The Glasshouse** – *2 Green-
side Place. ℘0131 525 8200. www.
theglasshousehotel.co.uk.* Possibly the
city's most unusual and certainly one of
its trendiest places to stay, this boutique
hotels boasts ultra-modern styling set
behind the façade of a 19C church.

🛏🛏🛏🛏 **Kimpton Charlotte Square
Hotel** – *38 Charlotte Square, New Town.
℘0131 240 5500. www.kimptoncharlot-
tesquare.com. 198 rooms.* Set in one of the
finest squares in the city, this top-quality
hotel combines Georgian elegance with
contemporary decor and features.

🛏🛏🛏🛏 **The Scotsman** – *20 North
Bridge Street. ℘0131 556 5565. https://
scotsmanhotel.co.uk.* Occupying
the grand marble former offices of
Edinburgh's principal newspaper, this
stunning hotel has top leisure facilities
and superbly equipped bedrooms.

🛏🛏🛏🛏 **Tigerlily** – *125 George Street.
℘0131 225 5005. www.tigerlilyedinburgh.
co.uk. 33 rooms.* This ultra-stylish boutique hotel was voted "one of the coolest
65 hotels in the world" by *Condé Nast
Traveller.* Its **restaurant** (🍽🍽) and bar
have also drawn rave reviews.

🛏🛏🛏🛏 **Malmaison** – *1 Tower Place,
Leith. ℘0131 285 1478. www.malmaison-
edinburgh.com. 100 rooms.* The original
Malmaison Hotel in this stylish chain, this
imposing building, facing Leith Canal,
has been superbly restored and offers
atmospheric rooms.

🍴 EAT

CENTRE

🍴🍴 **Café Marlayne** – *76 Thistle Street,
New Town. ℘0131 226 2230. www.
cafemarlayne.com.* Cosy and intimate,
Marlayne offers imaginative refined
good value Franco-Scottish cuisine. The

Antigua Street branch is larger and has a more contemporary feel.

⊝⊜ **Dirty Dick's** – *159 Rose Street. ☏0131 260 9920.* This is the oldest (est. 1859) and among the most characterful of the many traditional pubs on Rose Street. Classic Scottish fayre.

⊝⊜ **Deacon's House Café** – *304 Lawnmarket, 3 Brodies Close. ☏0131 226 1894. http://deaconshouse1788.co.uk.* Atmospheric eatery off the Royal Mile, and well worth tracking down for its home-made goodies served at breakfast and lunch. Get there early; it's very popular.

⊝⊜ **First Coast** – *99–101 Dalry Road. ☏0131 313 4404. www.first-coast.co.uk. Closed Sun.* An informal little bistro near Haymarket Station with a short but interesting regularly changing menu of trad-modern favourites.

⊝⊜ **The Perch** – *110 Hanover Street. ☏0131 220 1208. www.theperchedinburgh. co.uk.* A modern restaurant serving Scottish cuisine with a twist. Exellent drinks menu in the bar.

⊝⊜ **The Dome** – *14 George Street. ☏0131 624 8624. www.thedomeedinburgh.com.* Featuring an enormous classic Georgian glass dome, this elegant 1900 building boasts two main dining rooms and a garden café. Perfect for coffee, cocktails, lunch or dinner, it is popular with locals and visitors.

⊝⊜⊟ **Forth Floor at Harvey Nichols** – *Harvey Nichols Department Store, 30–34 St Andrew Square. ☏0131 524 8350. www. harveynichols.com/forth-floor-edinburgh.* Stylish restaurant with delightful outside terrace offering views over the city and the Firth of Forth. Modern Scottish cooking with a choice between brasserie-style dining or a more formal setting.

⊝⊜⊟ **The Grain Store** – *30 Victoria Street. ☏0131 225 7635. www.grainstore-restaurant.co.uk.* Set on Edinburgh's prettiest street, diners sit beneath the cosy rustic stone vaulting and archways of the original storerooms. The kitchen serves authentic Scottish cuisine using local produce.

⊝⊜⊟ **Wedgwood** – *267 Canongate. ☏0131 558 8737. www.wedgwoodthe restaurant.co.uk.* Fine dining without pretentions is the essence of this popular, atmospheric bistro, hidden away at the bottom of Royal Mile.

⊝⊜⊟⊟ **The Witchery by the Castle** – *325 Castlehill, The Royal Mile. ☏0131 225 5613. www.thewitchery.com.* Next door to the castle, this magical place occupies a 16C merchant's house, re-created to appear as it was 500 years ago. It is probably the most atmospheric and spectacular dining destination in the city, and although it sounds like a tourist trap, the quality of food and service are impeccable. The à la carte menu is expensive but theatre suppers and lunch menus put it within the budget of most.

⊝⊜⊟⊟ **Number One** – *Balmoral Hotel, 1 Princes Street. ☏0131 557 6727. www. roccofortehotels.com.* A stylish, long-established restaurant well deserving of its Michelin star. Set in the basement of a grand hotel. Dishes are modern and intricate using prime Scottish ingredients. Richly upholstered banquettes give it a plush and luxurious feel.

⊝⊜⊟⊟ **Tower Restaurant** – *Museum of Scotland, Chambers Street. ☏0131 225 3003. www.tower-restaurant.com.* Wonderful rooftop views complement the game, grills and seafood at this popular contemporary brasserie-style restaurant.

LEITH

⊝⊜ **The Kings Wark** – *36 The Shore. ☏0131 554 9260. http://kingswark.co.uk.* This pleasant pub serves typical bar food and in its restaurant generous helpings of Scottish cooking.

⊝⊜ **The Shore Bar & Restaurant** – *3 The Shore. ☏0131 553 5080. www. fishersrestaurants.co.uk.* Fish and seafood are the staples in this unpretentious evergreen Edinburgh institution. Live folk and jazz in the bar area.

⊝⊜⊟⊟ **Martin Wishart Restaurant** – *54 The Shore. Closed Sun, Mon. ☏0131 553 3557. www.martin-wishart.co.uk.* Leith's most fashionable and gastrono-mically renowned restaurant serves the very best traditional and modern French cuisine in the city. Martin Wishart gave Edinburgh its first Michelin star in 2001 and this has been confirmed every year since.

⊝⊜⊟⊟ **Kitchin** – *78 Commercial Quay. ☏0131 555 1755. www.thekitchin.com.* Run by the eponymous chef, Tom Kitchin, this Michelin-starred restaurant promises dishes that are 'From Nature to Plate', reflecting a passion for the freshest and best quality Scottish ingredients.

SHOPPING

Princes Street is Edinburgh's busy high street, but these days has little to offer except national department stores – Marks and Spencer and John Lewis (St James Shopping Centre) – plus chains and discount shops. Only **Jenners** (*www.houseoffraser.co.uk*), the city's own famous department store, is a reminder of more elegant times on Princes Street. **George Street** (*www.edinburghgeorge street.co.uk*) is now *the* place to shop and be seen shopping, lined with trendy shops (Karen Millen, Space NK, White Stuff, jack Wills, Hobbs...). Just off George Street, on St Andrew Square is the famous "lifestyle" department store of **Harvey Nichols**(*www.harveynichols.com*).

Don't dismiss the **Royal Mile** (*www.royal-mile.com*) as "just for tourists". Among the souvenirs and kitsch, there are many high quality specialists selling clothes, gourmet foods and malt whisky.

Fashion boutiques and music shops are to be found in **Rose Street** (parallel to Princes Street), more famous for its many pubs and bars.

Antique shops are mainly in the area around the **Royal Mile**, **Victoria Street** and **Grassmarket** in the Old Town and in **Dundas Street** and **Thistle Street** in the New Town.

Quality garments in tweed, tartan, cashmere and wool are sold in Jenners, Burberrys, the Scotch House, Romanes & Paterson (Princes Street), The Cashmere & Kilt Centre in the Royal Mile and Kinloch Anderson (Leith).

Edinburgh's Farmers' Market (*www.edinburghfarmersmarket.co.uk*) is the largest of its kind in Scotland with around 55 stallholders, many of whom are also the primary producers. It is held every Saturday at Castle Terrace.

WALKING TOURS

Old Town Edinburgh must host more walking tours per square mile than anywhere else in the world. History tours, ghost tours, literary tours, crime tours, pub tours, food and drink tours... whatever you want, you'll find it here. For details enquire at the tourist office or look in *The List*. Easily the most popular are the many ghost tours, several of which explore the spooky hidden vaults and bricked over streets beneath the city's bridges and Old Town.

Mercat Tours (*www.mercattours. com*) and **Auld Reekie Tours** (*www. auldreekietours.com*) both specialise in these, while the **City of The Dead Mackenzie Poltergeist** tour (*www. cityofthedeadtours.com*) is probably the scariest of all. The most interesting offbeat walking tour is the humorous **Edinburgh Literary Pub Tour** (*www. edinburghliterarypubtour.co.uk*).

© Iain Masterton/age fotostock

Jenners

Removed from the bustle of city life, yet close to Edinburgh, the Lothians region is both dormitory town and countryside playground. East Lothian, officially the sunniest area of Scotland, provides beaches, golf and coastal scenery; Midlothian (formerly Edinburghshire) contributes the must-see sights of Rosslyn Chapel and the Forth Bridges, while West Lothian offers history and stately piles. Wherever you go in the Lothians you'll find excellent walking, pretty villages and reminders of a turbulent past.

East Lothian

The East Lothian coastline runs for around 40mi/64km, from Musselburgh to the traditional seaside town of Dunbar, comprising golden beaches, spectacular cliffs with dramatic castle ruins, and probably the world's finest selection of links golf courses. Birdies of a different kind can be spotted at North Berwick's award-winning Scottish Seabird Centre, and Bass Rock. The aerial theme continues where you can board Scotland's very own Concorde at the National Museum of Flight.

The bucolic charms of 16C Preston Mill contrasts with the savage windlashed beauty of nearby Tantallon Castle.

Inland East Lothian features picturesque villages, such as Gifford and Dirleton, and the red sandstone villages of the Lammermuir Hills. Haddington is the region's attractive county town, while nearby Lennoxlove is the pick of the region's stately piles.

Midlothian

The region's most famous and visited attraction, just 7mi/11km south of Edinburgh, is the mysterious, enchanted, richly decorated late-Gothic Rosslyn Chapel, which was catapulted to international fame by its role in the film and book *The Da Vinci Code*. Its legendary Apprentice Pillar is alone worth the detour.

Moving on from medieval wonders to the modern world, just as famous as Rosslyn Chapel, and viewed by many more people, are the iconic Forth Road and Rail bridges. The best place from which to view these equally monumental achievements is the charming little town of South Queensferry.

You can also take a boat trip from here to the monastic island of Inchcombe (the "Iona of the East") and contem-

Highlights

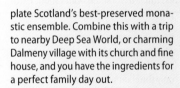

1 Cracking the codes in stone at **Rosslyn Chapel** (p164)

2 Soaring over 30m in the air aboard a boat at the **Falkirk Wheel** (p170).

3 Taking in grand homes on a **Firth of Forth** drive (p170)

4 Marvelling at the **Forth Bridges** from Queensferry (p174)

5 Playing a round of seaside golf at **Gullane** (p183)

plate Scotland's best-preserved monastic ensemble. Combine this with a trip to nearby Deep Sea World, or charming Dalmeny village with its church and fine house, and you have the ingredients for a perfect family day out.

West Lothian

Sandwiched between the major cities of Glasgow and Edinburgh, West Lothian is perhaps most often viewed through car or train windows. However, there's much to enjoy in this often overlooked area. The magnificent ruined royal palace at Linlithgow is famous for its connections with Mary, Queen of Scots while The House of the Binns and Hopetoun House bring the history of the Scottish nobility in the Lothians more up to date. There is some fascinating industrial heritage, too, including the unique experience of the Falkirk (boatlift) Wheel, and the restored railway at Bo'ness, both now converted into popular family attractions. For walkers, cyclist and boat owners the prettiest stretch of the recently upgraded Union Canal passes this way.

Rosslyn Chapel★★★

Set on the edge of the Esk valley, the 15C Rosslyn Chapel, famous for its stone carvings and legends, is a masterpiece of astonishing craftsmanship. Nonetheless, until the *Da Vinci Code* popularised the chapel in late 2005 (some of the final scenes were filmed here), this place was still a relatively well-kept secret. The following year visitor numbers quadrupled to more than 180 000. In response, a large modern visitor centre has opened, including interactive interpretative displays, and a coffee shop with outside terrace looking over Roslin Glen.

- **Michelin Map:** 7mi/11km south of Edinburgh, near Roslin.
- **Info:** ☎0131 440 2159; www.rosslynchapel.com. Jan–May and Sept–Dec Mon–Sat 9.30am–5pm, Sun noon–4.45pm; Jun–Aug Mon–Sat 9.30am–6pm, Sun noon–4.45pm. ☜£9.
- **Location:** Roslin Village is 8mi/13km south of Edinburgh, via the A701 towards Penicuik/Peebles. Bus 15 comes here direct.
- **Don't Miss:** To get the most from your visit take a free tour given by knowledgeable guides. These run Mon–Sat 10am, 11am, 12.15pm, 2pm, 3pm, 4pm; Sun 1pm, 2pm, 3pm.

A BIT OF HISTORY

The founder, **Sir William St Clair**, third and last Prince of Orkney (1396–1484) and lord of nearby Rosslyn Castle, assembled workmen from various European countries with the very intention of creating a unique work. This began in 1446 and came to a halt in 1486 two years after Sir William's death. Of the planned cruciform collegiate church only the choir was completed. Damaged in 1592, used as a stable for the horses of General Monck's troops in 1650, it was restored in 1861 and today serves as an episcopalian place of worship.

VISIT

Exterior

The pinnacled flying buttresses, window hood moulds, heraldic roof cornice, corbels and canopies of niches are covered with elaborate **decorative sculpture**.

Interior

A five-bay **choir** with clerestory above is bordered by north, south and east aisles, the latter being prolonged by a Lady Chapel stretching the full width of the building and raised by one step. The five compartments of the vaulted choir, spangled with stars, roses and other decorative paterae, are separated by sculptured ribs. In the side aisles, architraves between the pillars and outer walls separate pointed vaulting, with the apex running in a north-south direction, while the Lady Chapel has groined vaulting with pendants.

Amid this wealth of detail the outstanding feature is the **Apprentice Pillar★★★**. Legend has it that while the master mason was on a tour abroad prior to executing this work, the apprentice produced the pillar we see today. On his return the enraged master mason, in a fit of jealousy, killed the apprentice (☜*see* **30**, **29** *and* **27**). From the base with eight intertwined dragons, foliage winds up the column to the carved capital. The Stafford Knot is visible on the south side. Some of the scenes from this Bible of Stone are listed below and pinpointed on the accompanying plan.

North Aisle – **(1)** wall pillar to the right of the door: Crucifixion; **(2)** wall pillar: plaited crown of thorns; **(3)** pillar: imp; **(4)** pillar: lion's head; **(5)** wall pillar: shield; **(6)** wall pillar: shield displaying the arms of the founder and his wife; **(7)** architrave, east side: Our Blessed Lord

Vaulting, Rosslyn Chapel

© Nick Servian/age fotostock

seated in Glory; **(8)** windows: two of the Twelve Apostles; **(9)** arch: Samson pulling down the pillars of the House of Dagon.

Lady Chapel – **(10)** and **(11)** roof ribs: the Dance of Death is portrayed by a series of 16 figures; **(12)** pendant: Star of Bethlehem with eight figures evoking the Birth of Christ; **(13)** pillars: angels; **(14) Apprentice Pillar★★★**: carvings above include Isaac on the altar and a ram caught in a thicket; **(15)** and **(16)** roof ribs: eight figures.

South Aisle – **(17)** architrave: in Lombardic letters: "Wine is strong, the King is stronger, Women are stronger but above all truth conquers"; **(18)** window: two of the Twelve Apostles; **(19)** architrave; east side: The Virtues; west side: The Vices; **(20)** window arch: Nine Orders of the Angelic Hierarchy.

Choir – **(21)** niche: modern Virgin and Child replacing the statue destroyed at the Reformation; **(22)** floor: founder's burial slab; **(23)** pillar: human figures and animals; **(24)** pillar: Anna the Prophetess; **(25)** arch: Twelve Apostles and Four Martyrs each with the instruments of their martyrdom; **(26)** pillar: Jesus as the Carpenter of Nazareth, two men wrestling and Samson or David with a lion; **(27)** under

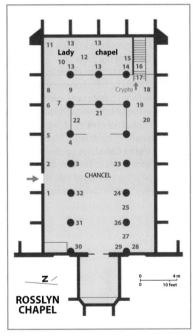

ROSSLYN CHAPEL

niche: the widowed mother; **(28)** pillar: crowned figure; **(29)** cornice level: the master mason; **(30)** cornice level: the apprentice with the scar on his left temple; **(31)** pillar: Prodigal son feeding the swine; **(32)** pillar: three figures looking north to **(1)**.

Linlithgow★★
and around

The historic burgh of Linlithgow gives little hint of its dramatic past, and is today a quiet residential town between Edinburgh and Stirling. Linlithgow Palace and St Michael's Church share a magnificent location, overlooking the Peel (park) and loch.

A BIT OF HISTORY

Royal Burgh – The history of the town is essentially that of its palace. The royal burgh grew up around the manor house and as early as Edward I's time its strategic role controlling the east-west route was appreciated. The burgh with its port at Blackness flourished and in 1368 its importance was such that it was included in the Court of the Four Burghs. With the rebuilding of both the palace and St Michael's, the 15C and 16C was a time of great prosperity which ended with the Union of the Crowns.

Despite the introduction of the leather industry during the Commonwealth, the smaller landward burghs like Linlithgow declined in the face of competition from the great industrial centres of the west coast flourishing on Atlantic trade. In 1822 the **Union Canal** was opened and prospered for 20 years. The barges were eclipsed with the coming of the railway in 1842, reviving the town's fortunes.

▶ **Population:** 13 260.

Info: Burgh Halls, The Cross. ☎01506 282720; www.edinburgh.org.

Location: Linlithgow is 22mi/35km east of Edinburgh via the M9.

Don't Miss: Linlithgow Palace fountain and the Great Hall with its hooded fireplace. The Falkirk Wheel.

Timing: Allow 2–3 hours.

Kids: A trip on the Bo'ness and Kinneil Railway, a boat trip (and lift!) at the Falkirk Wheel.

LINLITHGOW PALACE★★

⌖*Daily: 9.30am–5.30pm (Oct–Mar 9.30am–4pm).* ⏱*25–26 Dec, 1–2 Jan.* ⊞*£7.20.* ☎*01506 842 896. www.historicenvironment.scot.*

The formidably bare and vast form of the former royal residence – and birthplace of Mary Queens of Scots – dominates the town and loch of Linlithgow from its promontory site. The layout of this now roofless 15C–17C building with its many staircases and corridors is typical of a search for comfort and a more logical disposition.

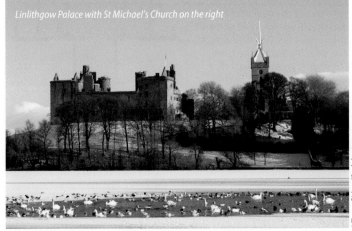

Linlithgow Palace with St Michael's Church on the right

© Thomas Dickson/iStockphoto.com

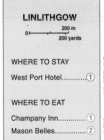

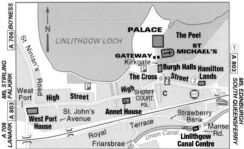

Manor House

Originally on an island site it was appreciated for its strategic location and for the good hunting in the surrounding countryside. The original manor house, accompanied by a conveniently near place of worship, was encircled by a wooden palisade by Edward I on his 1301–02 winter campaign. David II rebuilt the manor and it was his edifice that was gutted by a fire which ravaged the town, church and manor in 1424. On the return of the third Stewart king, James I, from 18 years' captivity in England, he undertook the first phase of construction from 1425 to 1435.

Favourite Royal Residence

It was during the reigns of James IV and V that Linlithgow became a favoured royal residence. **James IV** was responsible for another period of building and alterations (1490–1530) probably partly in preparation for his new bride Margaret Tudor, whom he married in 1503 and who spent most of her married life here. This was Scotland's Golden Age and their court was a glittering one with Linlithgow Palace fully participating in the round of merry pursuits. On 10 April 1512 the future James V was born here. Following this, the dowager queen left with her children for Stirling.

James V had his father's same love for Linlithgow Palace and often resided here. It was his second wife, Mary of Guise, who declared "she had never seen such a princely palace". Having lost two sons, Mary of Guise gave birth to the future **Mary, Queen of Scots** on 8 December 1542, only six days before the king died. As regent, Mary of Guise

continued to visit the great palace as did Mary, Queen of Scots on several occasions, but its heyday was past and decline set in with the removal of the court to London following the Union of the Crowns (1603).

The north wing was rebuilt, after the roof collapsed, from 1618 to 1620; later occupants included Cromwell and troops (1650–59). There was a fleeting visit by Bonnie Prince Charlie in 1745 and subsequently by the Duke of Cumberland's troops after whose stay fire gutted the palace leaving it the roofless ruin now standing.

Gateway★

The single-storey gateway, built by James V c.1535 at the head of the Kirkgate, gives access to the Royal Park wherein stand the palace and St Michael's Church. The town side of the gateway is adorned with four gaily painted orders, 19C representations of the originals, showing The Garter, The Thistle, The Golden Fleece and St Michael.

Courtyard

The centrepiece of the inner close is the magnificently intricate stone **fountain★★** built by James V in the 1530s. Octagonal in shape, the three basins decreasing in size are adorned by figures, buttresses, roundels, arms and various bearers.

The courtyard elevations present a variety of styles and decorative devices. Of the four ranges three are 15C–16C while the north one is 17C. On the east side above the round-headed arch of the former entrance, three canopied niches with angels above are surmounted by an elaborate moulding. The more strictly symmetrical north elevation (1618–20) with its regular string courses has window pediments sporting some of the national emblems.

Take the northeast spiral staircase to reach the main apartments on the first floor.

Interior at First Floor Level

To the left of the Screens Passage is the kitchen with its vast fireplace. The **Great Hall**, of impressive dimensions, runs the full length of the east range.

At the dais end is a superb **hooded fireplace**★★ with delicately carved ornamentation. Beyond the corner solar, the **chapel** retains four elaborately carved, but statueless, canopied niches between the windows. The remaining part of this wing is occupied by a hall followed by a corner chamber. Both of these ranges have the innovative feature of a corridor running along the courtyard side.

The apartments of the west range include the King's Hall, the Presence Chamber with an unusual window and, at the end, the King's Bed Chamber. The adjoining **King's** and **Queen's Oratories** have beautifully carved bosses figuring the unicorn. A wooden gangway leads through the shell of the range, remodelled by William Wallace in the early 17C. The new style is clearly visible in the decoration of the remaining fireplaces.

Look in the various ground floor cellars and guardrooms and take one of the turnpikes (*northwest*) for an overall view of the palace and its setting.

Exterior

The striking feature of the entrance façade is the group of five closely set **lancet windows** indicating the chapel. As one moves round to the east façade, the original entrance is flanked by elongated canopied niches with, above, the royal coat of arms. The Great Hall is identifiable by the great window and six fairly large windows slightly higher up. The openings of the 17C north front are more numerous and regular while on the plainer west face the corner towers are more easily distinguished.

ST MICHAEL'S CHURCH★

www.stmichaelsparish.org.uk.
The present building is essentially the 15C reconstruction of an earlier one destroyed by fire. This burgh church is one of the largest pre-Reformation ecclesiastic buildings and took over a century to complete. Construction started with the nave progressing to the choir (1497), the tower and finally the apse (c.1531).

Exterior

The most striking external feature of this aisled cruciform building with transeptal chapels and a polygonal apse is the west end tower with its **spire**, which however controversial, maintains the medieval tradition that any addition to a church should be in the style of the period to emphasise that it is both ancient and modern. The Geoffrey Clarke laminated timber and aluminium spire was erected in 1964 to replace an earlier crown spire. Also original is the **south porch** with an unusual oriel window above, flanked by a turret staircase. Farther round on the southwest buttress the only statue to survive the "cleansing" by the Lords of the Congregation in 1559 is a weathered, bewinged and armoured St Michael.

Interior

Pleasingly plain with little sculptural ornament, the pointed arcades and clustered piers of the five-bay **nave** continue for three bays into the chancel, separated only by the great chancel arch, and terminate with the tall windows of the three-sided apse. The elevation in both parts is similar excepting the blind triforium in the chancel. The nave, chancel and apse are roofed with a 19C plaster ceiling (replacing an 1812 oak roof) while the original rib vaulting still covers the aisles and transept chapels. Particularly worthy of attention are the **tracery** and **stained glass**.

Perpendicular tracery fills the three tall apse windows while the stained glass of the central one (eight lights)

The Feisty Tam Dalyells

Thomas Dalyell (1615–1685), better known as **General Tam**, is one of Scotttish history's most colourful characters (Dalyell is pronounced "dee-yell"). A military man and staunch Royalist, on the execution of Charles I (1649) he swore never to cut his hair or beard until the monarchy was restored. Following capture at the Battle of Worcester (1651) and imprisonment in the Tower of London, Tam eventually made his way to Russia where he served the Czar in a military capacity. He gained a fearsome reputation as the "Muscovy Brute", was accused of roasting his enemies in the Bake House oven at the Binns, and of introducing the thumbscrews into Scotland. Upon the Restoration Tam returned to command the king's forces in Scotland and proved to be an unrelenting opponent of the Covenanters, defeating their forces at Rullion Green.

The 11th baronet, the late Tam Dalyell (1932–2017), was a Scottish politician and an outspoken Labour member of the House of Commons 1962–2005. He was often his own party's fiercest critic, particularly when it came to foreign conflicts and in 1978–79 famously voted against his own government over 100 times. On 16 May 2009, the *Daily Telegraph* revealed that Dalyell had claimed £18 000 for three bookcases just months before his retirement from the House of Commons. The House of Commons' Fees Office, in fact, finally released £7 800.

portrays Psalm 104 (The Creation). The window overlooking the war memorial in the chancel's south aisle traces the history of the church and depicts three sovereigns: James IV, David I and Queen Victoria. Note, above, the stonemasons at work. Just before the transept chapel is a lovely Burne-Jones design (1899) in muted colours. The jewel of the church is the Flamboyant **window** in the south transept chapel with highly decorative and unusual tracery above the six lights. It was in this chapel that James IV was said to have seen the ghost forewarning him of impending doom at Flodden.

TOWN★

The town has conserved its medieval layout, with a long main street backed by its burgess plots, widening at the market place and closed by its ports. The arrival of the railway destroyed the town wall to the north.

The Cross

This is the former market place and in the centre is the **Cross Well**, a 19C replica of its predecessor.
On the north side is the grandly imposing **Burgh Halls** which dates from the 17C. Cromwell destroyed the origi-

nal. The present divided staircase is a 20C replacement for a wrought-iron loggia.
Stylishly refurbished in 2011 it how houses an art gallery, a tourist information centre, interpretive displays on the town and its surroundings and an garden cafe.

High Street

In East High Street **Nos. 40–48** are known as Hamilton Lands (o▬*not open to the public*). These rubblework, crow-stepped and gable-ended dwellings are typical of the late 16C–early 17C when Linlithgow was still at the height of its mercantile prosperity.
The narrow frontages corresponded to the width of the burghal lot (rig) and the round-arched pend was a typical feature of such layouts. There are more in West High Street.
A plaque on the wall of the Sheriff Court marks the approximate site of Archbishop Hamilton's house, from which the Regent Moray was shot in 1570. The latter died and the archbishop was later hanged for suspected complicity in this incident and the Darnley murder.
The new (2019) **Linthligow Museum** (◷*Mon and Wed–Sat 10am–4pm, Sun*

10am–4pm; 🅿 ☎01506 670 677), at the Linlithgow Partnership Centre includes a statue of Mary Queen of Scots and several trades' and fraternities' banners that have returned from conservation.

West Port House, as the name suggests, marked the site of the west gate. The three-storey, L-plan house dating from 1600 retains a turret staircase.

In a charming setting just above the town, at the Manse Street Basin, is the **Linlithgow Canal Centre** (🚻 ☉*early Apr–Sept, Sat–Sun 1.30–4.30pm; Jul–mid-Aug Mon–Fri 1.30–4pm*; ✕ 🅿 ☎*01506 671 215; www.lucs.org.uk*). There is a small museum here and boat trips can be made along the Union Canal to the 12-arch aqueduct over the River Avon, 2.5mi/4km to the west.

👥 FALKIRK WHEEL★★

Tamfourhill. 🚻☉*Daily Mar–Oct 10am–5.30pm; rest of year see website.* ☞*Boat trip £13.50 (child 5–15, £7.50).* ✕☎*0870 050 0208.* *www.thefalkirkwheel.co.uk.*

The Falkirk Wheel is one of Scotland's most ingenious modern engineering achievements, designed as a Millennium Project to relink the Forth and Clyde Canal to the Union Canal. The problem was that the latter lay 35m below the level of the Union Canal. Around 80 years ago the two were joined at Falkirk by a flight of 11 locks that stepped down across a distance of just under 1 mile (1.5km), but these were dismantled in 1933, thus breaking the link. The wheel, the world's first and only rotating boat lift, was thus created to lift a canal barge 35m high, from one canal to the other. Boat trips begin in the basin outside the Visitor Centre, boarding one of the specially designed boats. The journey starts by sailing into the bottom gondola of The Wheel, which then makes a graceful sweep, lifting the boat up to join the Union Canal 35m above. The ascent takes approximately 15min, allowing plenty of time to enjoy the views of the surrounding scenery. Once lifted, the boat sails smoothly from The Wheel onto the Union Canal. This passes along the aqueduct, through the 180m Roughcastle Tunnel and under the historic World Heritage Site, the Roman Antonine Wall. The boat then returns a gentle descent down to the Visitor Centre.

🚗 DRIVING TOUR

🚗 SOUTH BANK OF THE FIRTH OF FORTH

This 33mi/53km excursion takes in grand stately homes and Scottish industrial heritage in the form of the railways and the world-famous Forth Bridges.

▷ Take the A706 N towards Bo'ness.

👥 Bo'ness & Kinneil Railway & Museum of Scottish Railways

🚻☉*Trains run Jul–Aug daily; mid-Mar–mid-Oct, Sat–Sun. Phone or see website for schedule. Museum: Apr–Oct 11am–4.30pm.* ☞*£5.* 🅿 ☎*01506 822 298. www.srps.org.uk.*

A station and a track (3.5mi/5.6km) have been rebuilt by the Scottish Railway Preservation Society to become the **Museum of Scottish Railways**, Scotland's largest railway museum. Three large halls display locomotives, rolling stock and general railway paraphernalia. There is also a railway-themed activity area for children. The actual station complex, with booking office, footbridge, canopy and signalbox, evokes the era of the North British, one of the major Scottish railway companies. Steam trips run along the foreshore, inland to Birkhill station, and to the underground **Birkhill Fireclay Mine** (☛*not open to the public*).

▷ From Bo'ness, take the A993, then the B903 towards Blackness village.

Blackness Castle

☉*Daily: Apr–Sept 9.30am–5.30pm; Oct–Mar 10am–4pm.* ☉*25–26 Dec, 1–2 Jan.* ☞*£6.* ☎*01506 834 807.* *www.historicenvironment.scot.*

The now peaceful village of Blackness was once the flourishing seaport for Linlithgow. Likewise its castle, standing on a rocky promontory, jutting out into the

Firth of Forth, was formerly one of the most important in the kingdom. Following the Union of 1707, it was one of four Scottish strongholds (the others were Edinburgh, Stirling and Dumbarton) to be garrisoned. It has also served as a royal castle, a prison for Covenanters, an ordnance depot and latterly a youth hostel.

The stronghold was built in the shape of a ship. The south or "stern" tower is 16C with curtain walls of the same period enclosing a 15C central tower and meeting at the north or "bow" tower, reduced to serve as a gun platform. The latter affords a fine **view** across the Firth of Forth and its famous bridges.

▷ Retreat from Blackness, and turn down the B9109, and follow the signs to The Binns.

House of the Binns

🍃 *The house is open by special request and for tours by arrangement.* 👓*£10.50.* 📞*01506 834 255. www.nts.org.uk.*

This 17C hilltop house with fine views to the Forth is as colourful for its architecture as for the history of its famous owners, the Dalyell family (👣 *see Box p169*).

Despite successive alterations and additions, the present house retains much that dates from the 1630 reconstruction. Of particular interest are the **plasterwork ceilings**★ dated 1630, in the Drawing Room or High Hall and the King's Room. They are among the earliest examples of this kind of work in Scotland. Amid the many mementos of General Tam, his Russian boots and sword, huge comb and 1611 "Great She Bible", there are other family and regimental souvenirs. In the Dining Room hang Allan Ramsay's well-known portrait of *Christian Shairp* and a portrait of General Tam after the Restoration.

▷ Continue 3mi/5km east, and then follow signs for Hopetoun House.

Abercorn Parish Church

The old village church (refitted 1579, restored 1838) has a particularly fine example of a laird's loft. The **Hopetoun Loft**★★ is unusual in that when Sir William Bruce fitted it out in 1707–08 he included a suite of rooms comprising a retiring room with a burial vault underneath. The panelled loft, not unlike a theatre box, is decorated with Alexander Eizat's carvings and Richard Wiatt's highly colourful Hope coat of arms.

Hopetoun House★★

♿🕐*Apr–Sept daily 10.30am–5pm.* 👓*£10.50; grounds only, £4.75.* 🍴 📞*0131 331 2451. www.hopetoun.co.uk.*

This imposing monument stands in landscaped grounds with great vistas. Hopetoun House is the place to discover the contrasting exteriors of 17C Sir William Bruce and 18C William Adam and the different interior styles of Bruce and the Adam sons, Robert and James, the whole highlighted by fine furniture and a notable collection of paintings.

A Bit of History – The original mansion (1699–1703) by **Sir William Bruce** was altered shortly afterwards by **Charles Hope**, 1st Earl of Hopetoun, who commissioned **William Adam**, Bruce's former apprentice, to enlarge his residence. The result was the east front in the Roman Baroque manner which we see today. After William Adam's death in 1748 the sons **Robert** and **James** continued the work, in particular the interior decoration of the State Apartments.

Exterior – The square form of Bruce's mansion in his mature Classical style, with two main storeys on a rusticated basement, remains the centrepiece of the west front. In sharp contrast, the more theatrical and splendid **east front** moves outward from a central unit through curved colonnades to the advanced pavilions and is surely one of William Adam's masterpieces.

Interior – Again the more severe designs of Bruce, who used almost exclusively local materials, can be readily distinguished from the opulence of the Adam interiors of the State Apartments.

© Paweł Wysocki/hemis.fr

Yellow Drawing Room, Hopetoun House

Library – Two rooms were made into one to create this pine-panelled room now lined with bookshelves. In the small library with carved and gilded oak wainscotting and a Portsoy marble **fireplace** is a portrait by Sir Nathaniel Dance of *Charles, Lord Hope* (1740–66), who was one of Adam's companions on the Grand Tour.

Garden Room – Originally the entrance hall, this is an example of Bruce decoration at its best: handsome but sober oak panelling is enhanced by the gilded cornice, doorheads and pilaster capitals and a set of silver armorial candle sconces.

Bruce Bedchamber – The centrepiece of this sumptuously decorated room is the magnificent **bed** with red damask hangings. Painted decoration on a white background alternates with panels of red damask. The original suite included the dressing room and closet with an exhibition on Sir William Bruce, and beyond, the fireproof Charter Room.

Bruce Staircase – Octagonal pine wainscotting admirably carved by Alexander Eizat; oak handrail and banisters round an octagonal well.

West Wainscot Bedchamber – The room is hung with Antwerp tapestries (c.1700).

Yellow Drawing Room – The proportions of the State Apartments, now reordered, are undoubtedly those of William Adam while the interior decoration has the imprint of Robert Adam.

Above the walls hung with yellow silk damask, the coved **ceiling** is adorned with corner cartouches highlighted in gold and a matching central motif. The Cullen pier glasses and console tables between the windows are part of the original 18C dining room furniture. The Cullen commodes on either side of the fireplace came from the State Bedroom. In this room, in 1822 George IV knighted the portrait painter Henry Raeburn.

▶ Go back to the A904, and take the left turn to South Queensferry.

South Queensferry★

See p174.

▶ Continue beyond the M90 junction, and stay on the A904. At the junction with the A9000, keep forward onto Ferrymuir Road, and then follow signs for Dalmeny and Dalment House.

Dalmeny★

This charming village, set around several large greens, is graced not only by its 12C parish church, one of the finest examples of Norman architecture in Scotland, but also by Dalmeny House with its internationally renowned collections of porcelain and paintings.

St Cuthbert's church★

The church is set near the pilgrim route to Dunfermline, which has another Norman church and there is evidence to believe that the same masons worked at both places. The simple plan is clearly discernible from outside: a stout western tower, a 20C Lorimer addition, abuts the long nave, which in turn is prolonged by the shorter chancel and semicircular apse. Above the string course, round-headed and narrow windows are framed by chevron recessed orders but the jewel of the exterior is the superb **Norman south doorway★★**, originally the main entrance. Tall, narrow and round-headed without its carved tympanum, the recessed orders are intricately carved showing fabulous animals from the Bestiary, figures and heads. Above is a panel of interlaced arches.

Inside, seen from the west end, the two decreasing arches focus attention on the high altar. The handsome arches of the chancel and apse have orders of chevron mouldings, while the ribs of the chancel and apse vaulting spring from a series of **carved corbels** in the form of monstrous heads.

The Rosebery Aisle built in 1671 was remodelled in the 19C. The family arms are carved on the panel.

Dalmeny House★

2mi/3.2km east of the village.
♿🕐*Jun–Jul Sun–Wed 2–5pm.*
👓*£10.* 🍴 *📞0131 331 1888. https:// roseberyestates.co.uk/dalmeny-house.*
Sir Archibald Primrose (1616–1679) purchased the estate in 1662 and his son was created the 1st Earl of **Rosebery** in 1703. **Archibald, 4th Earl** of Rosebery (1783–1868), commissioned William Wilkins to build the Gothic Revival house we see today, still the family seat, presently home to the 7th Earl.

The family portraits in the hall include the *4th Earl of Rosebery*, by Raeburn and *The PM* by Millais. The set of five Madrid tapestries are after designs by Goya. The library has a painting by Stubbs and lotus-leaf furniture custom made by Wilkins. The Grecian interior of the Drawing Room is the setting for the Rothschild collection of 18C French **furniture and tapestries**. The carpet is Savonnerie while some pieces of furniture have the interlaced I's or dauphin stamp on them. In the corridor are 16C and 17C pieces of Scottish furniture.

The Napoleon Room was the work of the 5th Earl, a great historical collector who wrote Napoleon's biography. In the Dining Room there are Reynolds and Gainsborough portraits of such personalities as *Dr Johnson, Edward Gibbon, William Pitt the Younger* and *Henry Dundas, the first Viscount Melville*.

The Old Private Apartments, a suite of five rooms, include the 6th Earl's Sitting Room with the famous rose and primrose racing colours amid other racing mementoes. The Boudoir contains more of the Mentmore collection of furniture. Also on display is the **porcelain** collection, rich in Sèvres and Vincennes pieces.

ADDRESSES

🛏️ STAY

🛏️ **West Port Hotel** – *18–20 West Port, Linlithgow. 📞01506 847 456. www.west porthotel.co.uk. 9 rooms.* The rooms at this traditional pub are all decorated and furnished to a high standard. Weekends can be noisy, but the place has the vibrant atmosphere of a country inn. Great place to eat (🍴🍴), too.

🍴 EAT

🍴🍴 **Mason Belles Kitchen** – *52 High Street, Linlithgow. 📞01506 843 867. http:// masonbelles.co.uk.* Tucked away through a secluded archway, this family run restaurant offers trendy brunch, lunch, afternoon tea and elegant evening meals featuring seasonal produce with a twist.

🍴🍴🍴 **Champany Inn** – *Champany, Linlithgow. 📞01506 834 532. www. champany.com.* Traditional restaurant in a former flour mill, with emphasis on Scottish beef, and wine. There's also a laid-back 'Chop and Ale House' bar, as well as **16 rooms** (🛏️🛏️🛏️), should you want to stay overnight.

South Queensferry★

Former royal burgh and once a traffic-congested ferry port, this now quiet, small town nestles on the south shore of the Firth of Forth, overshadowed by the two Forth bridges.

> ▶ **Population:** 9 350.
> 🛈 **Info:** 3 Princes Street, Edinburgh; ☎0131 4733868.
> ◗ **Location:** 10mi/16km west of Edinburgh on the A90.

A BIT OF HISTORY

Forth Crossing – The narrowest point of the Forth, this has been the natural crossing point from earliest times. The first ferry, instituted by **Queen Margaret** – hence the town's name – for pilgrims travelling north to Dunfermline, was operated by the Dunfermline monks, then local seamen. By the 17C it was one of Scotland's busiest ferry crossings and was linked to the capital by one of the first turnpike (toll) roads. In the 18C, a tunnel was proposed to link the Hopetoun Estates on either side of the Forth and also a chain bridge.

Steam ferry ships were introduced in 1821 and in 1850–51, in the wake of the railway age, both the Forth and the Tay saw the inauguration of the first railway ferries in the world, albeit for goods traffic only. This service continued to operate until the building of the Tay Bridge in 1878 and the tay in 1890.

The Queen's ferry continued to ply between North and South Queensferry right up until 1964 when HM Queen Elizabeth II made the last crossing, in the electric paddle ferry *Queen Margaret*, after opening the New Road Bridge.

FORTH BRIDGES★★

The esplanade is an excellent **viewing point** for the bridges, in particular for the Rail Bridge, while the service area at the south end of the Road Bridge has a viewing terrace.

Queensferry Crossing

Built alongside the Forth Road Bridge, this newest of the Forth bridges opened to traffic at the end of August 2017. It is the longest three-tower, cable-stayed bridge in the world and also by far the largest to feature cables which cross mid-span. It has an overall length of 2.7km/1.7mi, and three towers each 207m (679 feet) high. The construction cost was in excess of £1.3 billion.

Forth Rail Bridge

Widely acclaimed as a great engineering achievement in its day, the familiar outline of this cantilever bridge is well

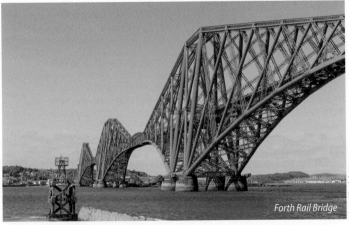

Forth Rail Bridge

© kruwt/iStockphoto.com

known as an icon of both Scotland and world-class bridge construction. Built between 1883 and 1890 at a total coast of £3 177 206, it was an intrepid endeavour in every way, but particularly so soon after the Tay Bridge disaster of 1879 (*see p218*). The construction of the Forth Rail Bridge also cost injury and loss of life – today monuments to those who died stand in North and South Queensferry. In 2015, the bridge was incribed by UNESCO as a World Heritage Site on the grounds of its outstanding universal value.

Forth Road Bridge

Upstream stands the slim elegant form of the suspension bridge with its amazing "curve". With two carriageways (7.3m wide), cycle tracks and pathways, the bridge took six years (1958–64) to complete at a total cost of £20 000 000.

ADDITIONAL SIGHTS
Hawes Inn

At the east end of the esplanade, part of this building dates from the 17C. It stands on the site of one of Queen Margaret's pilgrims' hospices and figures in novels by Scott and R L Stevenson.

Main Street

The winding street has been attractively repaved, setting off to advantage the many fine houses, some of which, built by the once-flourishing merchant community, give on to raised terraces reached by steps and ramps. Note in particular the elevated **terraces**, West, Mid and East, which are lined on the south side by houses which belonged to the flourishing merchant community. Note in particular **Black Castle** with its pedimented dormer windows, one of which bears the date 1626, a heart, loveknot and initials. The 17C tolbooth tower has several public clocks.

The little **Queensferry Museum** (*daily 10am–5pm; ☏0131 331 5545; www.edinburghmuseums.org.uk*) offers fine views over the Forth complete with telescopes and binoculars and relates the history of the road and rail bridges.

Inchcolm Abbey

© Alan Finlayson/Bigstockphoto.com

EXCURSIONS
🚶🚶 Deep Sea World
See DUNFERMLINE: Driving Tour.

Inchcolm

Hawes Pier. ⏰Call for sailing times and charges. ☏0131 331 5000. www.maidoftheforth.co.uk.
Known as the "Iona of the East", the island of Inchcolm lies 1.5mi/2.5km due south of Aberdour and is famous for its abbey ruins, the best-preserved group of monastic buildings in Scotland. The outward journey on the *Maid of the Forth* gives a good view of the south shore and Hound Point.

Inchcolm abbey

⏰Daily Apr–Sept 9.30am–5.30pm. 🚫From May–Aug, access may be reduced due to the aggressive behaviour of nesting gulls g. ✱£5.50. ☏07836 265 146. www.historicenvironment.scot.
In 1123 **Alexander I** was stormbound on the island and in gratitude for the hospitality he received from a hermit, he founded a monastery for Augustinian canons.
Despite many English raids the abbey flourished up to the Reformation when it passed to the Stewarts as commendators and finally the Earls of Moray. The conventual buildings are very well preserved and include a 13C octagonal **chapter house**, one of the few in Scotland, and 14C cloisters.

Dunbar

and around

This east coast holiday resort and day excursion centre takes its name from the once powerful stronghold, around which the town grew up.

A BIT OF HISTORY

Battles of Dunbar

Set on the main east coast road and in the path of invading armies, Dunbar has been the site of two important Scottish defeats. In the opening stages of the Wars of Independence, Edward I, on his first Scottish campaign, sacked Berwick in 1296 and then inflicted a defeat on the Scots army near Spott.

The 1650 Battle of Dunbar was part of Cromwell's campaign to subdue Scotland. The Covenanting General David Leslie, with a numerically superior army, abandoned a strong position on Doon Hill to fall prey to General Monck.

SIGHTS

Dunbar Town House Museum

High Street. ⏰*Apr–Sept daily 1–5pm.* ✆*01620 820 699. www.dunbar.org.uk/town-house-museum.*

Dunbar Town House was built around the end of the 16C. It is now home to an archaeology and local history centre, as well as temporary exhibitions about Dunbar and district.

▶ **Population:** 9 030.

ℹ **Info:** 143 High Street; ✆01368 866 030; www.visiteastlothian.org.

◗ **Location:** Dunbar is 12.5mi/20km SE of North Berwick via the B1346, A198 and A1087.

👥 **Kids:** The beach at Belhaven Bay.

Tolbooth★

The attractive 17C tolbooth with its steepled octagonal tower and crow-stepped gable is built of red rubblework sandstone.

John Muir's Birthplace★

High Street. ⏰*Apr–Sept Mon–Sat 10am–5pm, Sun 1–5pm; Oct–Mar Wed–Sat 10am–5pm, Sun 1–5pm.* ✆*01368 865 899. www.jmbt.org.uk.*

This was the birthplace and home for 11 years of **John Muir** (1838–1914), the pioneer geologist, explorer, naturalist and conservationist *par excellence*, who was responsible for the creation of America's National Park system. The flat, where he lived with his six brothers and sisters before emigrating to the States, is appropriately furnished while the rest of the house is devoted to the man and

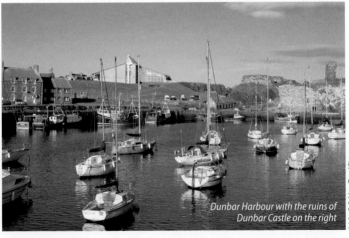

Dunbar Harbour with the ruins of Dunbar Castle on the right

© John D. Beldom/Travel Pictures

his work. The house is set within the **John Muir Country Park**. There is a clifftop walk which passes the harbour and ruined castle (🔒 see Harbour, below).

🏊 **Belhaven Bay** is a glorious, sandy beach fringed by low, sheltering sand dunes, rich salt marsh and colourful grasslands. From here there are splendid views across the Forth Estuary.

Dunbar castle

The jagged red ruins of what was once, strategically, one of the most important castles in the Middle Ages, rises above the waters of the harbour.

The castle was much fought over but it was the stout defence in 1339 by Black Agnes, Countess of March and Dunbar, against English troops led by Salisbury that stands out most clearly in its history. The orders to demolish came from the Scots Parliament in the same year that Mary, Queen of Scots, visited it with Lord Darnley (1567).

Harbour

The **New** or **Victoria Harbour** was opened in 1842 to accommodate the growing number of trading and fishing vessels. The arrival of the railway four years later, however, brought about a decline in the port's activities.

The pantiled, dormer-windowed house Yellow Craig, on the right, makes an attractive point of comparison for the Basil Spence housing complex between the harbours. The **Old Harbour** with its cobbled quays and rubble walls was built by Cromwell in 1650.

🚗 DRIVING TOURS

🚗 1 THE COAST SOUTH
50mi/80km

This coastal excursion leaves the Lothians and explores the craggy cliffs of the Borders, most notably Fast Castle and St Abb's Head.

▶ Leave Dunbar by the A1087 in the direction of Berwick-upon-Tweed,

---

The Making of John Muir

"When I was a boy in Scotland I was fond of everything that was wild ... I loved to wander in the fields to hear the birds sing, and along the shore to gaze and wonder at the shells and the seaweeds, eels and crabs in the pools when the tide was low; and best of all to watch the waves in awful storms thundering on the black headlands and craggy ruins of old Dunbar Castle." *John Muir*

then join the A1 after Broxburn. Leave the A1 for Cockburnspath

Cockburnspath

This charming village, known simply as "Coe-path", is the birthplace of John Broadwood (1732–1812), cabinetmaker and co-founder of the famous Broadwood piano makers, the oldest and one of the most prestigious piano companies in the world.

By the late 19C, the village had become the centre of a group of artists who were to become the famed Glasgow School (including James Guthrie, E A Walton and Joseph Crawhall).

The **Market Cross** was erected in 1503 to celebrate the marriage of James IV to Margaret Tudor; Cockburnspath formed part of the marriage dowry.

The village is also the eastern end of the Southern Upland Way (www.southernuplandway.gov.uk).

▶ Return to the A1, and take the road to Cove and continue to Pease Sands.

Pease Bay

Red sandstone cliffs overlook a beautiful sandy beach, unfortunately occupied by a mobile home campsite.

▶ Continue along the Pease road until it joins the A1107. Turn left (east). Fast Castle (and Dowlaw Farm) are signposted off here.

Fast Castle

2.3mi/3.7km off the A1107. A surfaced road leads to Dowlaw Farm.
Leave the car beyond the farm cottages. 15min walk down to castle ruins along a path, steep and stony in places.
⊙ Care is needed on the cliffs.

Once through the gate, the clifftop site affords a good **view** westwards of the coastline with ever decreasing red sandstone cliffs.

The few jagged remains of **Fast Castle** are perched in an audacious **site★★** teetering on a rocky crag high above the sea, where castle wall and cliff face merge into one another. This once impregnable stronghold dates from the 16C (*excavations are in progress to determine even earlier origins*) and figures as Wolf's Crag in Scott's *The Bride of Lammermoor*. A cave below the castle is reputed to have been used by smugglers.

In June seabirds (guillemots, razorbills, shags and kittiwakes) nest on the cliffs at the seaward end of the castle, and in November grey seals pup on the beaches at either side of the castle.

▶ Return to the A1107 and turn left.

Coldingham

This inland village is best known for its ruined **priory**, founded in 1098 by King Edgar for Benedictine monks. The present parish church occupies the choir of a 12C–13C building.

▶ In Coldingham take the B6438 towards the coast.

St Abb's

The church high on the clifftop pinpoints this attractive fishing village clustered round its harbour.

Walks in the area include the clifftop path south to the sandy beach of Coldingham Bay and north to St Abb's Head (*◔see below*).

St Abb's Head National Nature Reserve★★

Access road signposted to the left, off the B6438, just before entering St Abb's.

(*⊙Nature Reserve: daily. Nature Centre: Apr–Oct 10am–5pm. ✗ 🅿 (charge). ℘01890 771 443. www.nts.org.uk.*)

Eighty-one hectares in extent, the reserve covers a variety of habitats – coastal grassland, sandy and rocky shores and cliffs – and includes the man-made Mire Loch and the well-known landmark **St Abb's Head**. The cliffs, some of the finest on the eastern seaboard, rise to over 91m and provide myriad nesting ledges for seabirds (guillemots, razorbills, puffins, fulmars and gulls). The spectacle of entire cliff faces alive with diving, swooping birds to a background of piercing cries is a fascinating sight.

The knoll beside the lighthouse affords **views★** of the coastline south to Hairy Ness and north to Fast Castle's headland – with, on a clear day, views of the Bass Rock and Fife coast on the horizon. The reserve is a sanctuary for migrating birds in spring and autumn and an exhibition and ranger-guided walks interpret the site for visitors who are not specialist bird-watchers.

▶ Return to Coldingham and take the A1107 (left) to Eyemouth.

Eyemouth

A busy fishing port and popular holiday resort, Eyemouth stands on the Berwickshire coast at the mouth of the Eye Water.

Eyemouth Museum★

Auld Kirk, Manse Road. ♿⊙Apr–Oct Mon–Sat 11am–4pm. ⊚£3.50. ℘01890 751 701. www.eyemouthmuseum.org.

Displays give glimpses of rural life and attractive presentations touch on all aspects of local fisherfolk's lives: their homes and customs, the fish, the boats, gear and tackle and the ancillary crafts. The pride and joy of the museum however is the **Eyemouth Tapestry**, rich in symbolism, commemorating the terrible fishing disaster of 1881 (*see below*).

St Abb's Head

Harbour

The brightly painted boats lining the quayside and the busy **fish market** testify to the importance of fishing to the town. Ever since the 12C fishing has been the main activity in Eyemouth. In 1881, on "Black Friday", 14 October, 189 men were lost in the Great East Coast Fishing Disaster; 129 of those men came from Eyemouth. Nineteen boats were lost, almost half the fishing fleet of that time.

Old Fishing Village

The old fishing area still retains certain of the characteristics described by the Rev Daniel McIver: "Instead of rows of houses, we have clusters of houses, instead of gables facing gables, we have gables facing fronts and fronts facing back courts." Smuggling reached its height in the 18C and Eyemouth was an important centre in the illicit trade in wines, spirits, tea and tobacco.

Burnmouth

2mi/3.2km south.
⊘*The road down is steep and narrow; sound your car horn at the corner.*
Set on a rocky coastline, this attractive old fishing village, with its harbour at the foot of the cliffs, has the distinction of being the first settlement in Scotland after crossing the border with England.

2 THE COAST ROAD WEST

36mi/57km

This excursion takes in a wide range of natural and man-made sights, from bird colonies to Concorde, dramatic castle ruins to charming villages, Championship Golf courses and antique motors.

▶ Leave Dunbar on the A1087 to join the A199. Shortly leave the A199 for East Linton, and there turn right for Preston Mill along the B1407.

Preston Mill★

⊙*Easter, and May–Sept Thu–Mon 12.30–5pm.* ⊛*£6.50.* 🅿 *(charge).* ✆*01620 860 426. www.nts.org.uk.*
Picturesque 16C Preston Mill, with its red-pantiled roofs and rubble masonry, is one of Scotland's rare working watermills, believed to be of Dutch design. In the cone-shaped kiln, damp oats were dried on perforated metal plates before being transferred by chute to the mill.
In a field beyond (*5min walk*) is the oddly truncated, beehive-shaped **Phantassie Doocot** (*Fantasy Dovecot –* ⊘*See INTRODUCTION: Arts and Culture*). It is circular with two string courses – to prevent rats climbing up – and the south-facing side has a sloping roof and two sets of flight holes. Inside, the 500 nests are reached by a revolving ladder.

Scott's Tantallon

The dramatic setting of ruined Tantallon Castle is described by **Sir Walter Scott** in his narrative poem *Marmion*.

... Tantallon vast
Broad, massive, high and
stretching far,
And held impregnable in war
On a projecting rock it rose,
And round three sides the
ocean flows,
The fourth did battled walls
enclose ...

▶ Continue along the B1407. Turn left on the A198.

Tyninghame★

Most of the houses in this pretty estate village are single-storey pink sandstone with pantiled roofs. The original village situated in the grounds of Tyninghame House was removed in 1761.

Whitekirk

The parish church of St Mary's, a 15C mellow red-sandstone building, originally belonged to Holyrood abbey. The presence of a Holy Well made this a great pilgrimage centre, visited in 1435 by the Papal Legate, Aeneas Sylvius Piccolomini, later Pope Pius II. Burned by suffragettes in 1914, the church was restored by Robert Lorimer.

In the field behind, the 16C three-storey building was probably the tithe barn.

▶ Continue north. On the coastal side the massive Bass Rock suddenly appears, with Tantallon Castle close by.

Tantallon Castle★★

🕑*Daily Apr–Sept 9.30am–5.30pm; Oct–Mar 10am–4pm.* 🕑*25–26 Dec and 1, 2 Jan.* ✕ 🍴£6. 📞*01620 892 727. www.historicenvironment.scot.*

In its splendid **clifftop site★★★** facing the Bass Rock, the formidable ruin of

Tantallon Castle defies the pounding waves and howling easterly gales.

The Visitor Centre is the best introduction to exploring the castle. Two ditches and earthen ramparts defend the landward side and access to the bailey is by the now ruined Outer Gate. The lectern-type dovecot is 17C. The inner ditch stretches right across the headland at the foot of the curtain walls.

Dating from the late 14C, with 16C alterations, Tantallon is one of the great castles of enclosure. The massive curtain wall (15m tall) links the gatehouse and flanking circular towers and cuts off the impregnable promontory site. The attractively weathered red sandstone enhances the foreboding, stark ruin.

Mid Tower – In the late 14C a barbican, distinguished here by green stone with red string courses, was added to the gatehouse and followed by an outwork in the 16C. The Earl of Angus' coat of arms is high up on the forework. Pass through the passage to the original doorway. To the right is a guardroom and to the left a passage leading to a turnpike which gives access to the four floors above, each consisting of a single apartment with garderobe and small adjacent chambers.

The **well** in the close goes down to a depth of 32m.

East Tower – The five storeys are reached by a turnpike. At each level there are apartments with fireplaces, stone benches and mural garderobes.

Douglas Tower – Above the pit prison with a bedrock floor are six storeys of apartments similar to those in the East Tower.

Curtain Walls – Over 3.7m thick and 15m high, they connect the towers by a wall-walk and originally had their own independent stairways with mural chambers. The wall-walk was once roofed over and edged by a parapet wall.

Northern Courtyard Range – The western part included the Laigh and Long halls and was contemporary with the towers and curtain walls. It was altered in the 16C when the eastern part was added.

Tantallon Castle

© Martin McCarthy/iStockphoto.com

▶ Take the A198 west.

North Berwick

This ancient royal burgh is a popular holiday and golfing resort and provides a complete range of amenities – vast sandy beaches, golf courses and putting greens, sailing and sea-angling facilities. It faces onto the **Bass Rock**, world famous for its bird population. The town is also favoured by commuters with the railway giving rapid access to Edinburgh.

Auld Kirk

On the harbour promontory, dividing the two sandy beaches, are the scant remains of the town's first parish church (12C), notoriously associated with a gathering of witches in 1590 to plot the death of James VI. The burial place for the Lauder and Douglas families, it was abandoned in the 1680s on account of the expense of the upkeep of the connecting bridge, to what was then an island promontory.

Old Parish Church

Kirk Port. Now a ruin, this was the 17C replacement for the Auld Kirk. In the churchyard is a headstone commemorating **John Blackadder**, the Covenanting preacher who died in prison on the Bass Rock (&*see below*).

The Lodge

This 18C white harled building was the town house of the Dalrymple family. It has now been divided into flats and the grounds form a public park.

Town House

At the corner of Quality Street and High Street stands an attractive 18C building with outside stairs and a clock tower. The upper chamber still serves as a meeting place for committees and community councils.

Scottish Seabird Centre

&◷*Jan daily 11am–4pm; Feb–Mar and Sept–Oct Mon–Fri 10am–5pm, Sat–Sun 10am–5.30pm; Apr–Aug daily 10am–6pm; Nov–Dec Mon–Fri 10am–6pm, Sat–Sun 10am–5pm.* ◷*25 Dec.* ⊕*£9.95.* ℘*01620 890 202. www.seabird.org.*

This new birdwatching centre enjoys a stunning location overlooking the sea and islands of the Forth, most notably the famous **Bass Rock** (&*see below*). The latest technology in remote viewing, with cameras on the islands, beam back live panoramas and close-ups onto giant screens with such clarity that visitors can even read the rings on individual birds' feet.

In spring you can expect to see Bass Rock gannet, puffin and guillemot

The Gannet

The gannet comes to land on the Bass Rock during the breeding season only *(Feb–May)*. The single egg is protected, in turn, by the parents who cover it with first one then the other webbed foot. They leave in August and the deserted fledgling is driven by hunger down to the sea where it usually floats, protected by excess fat, for about 3 weeks before learning to fly. The birds are excellent divers capable of descending at least 15m for their prey.

huddled together like penguins on the sea cliffs and the fluffy white new-born seals on the Isle of May. There are wading birds along the shore in winter and the occasional rare and often spectacular sightings of dolphins, porpoises and whales in summer.

For a closer look take the **Seabird Safari** aboard a rigid inflatable boat (RIB). These speedy little craft depart from North Berwick Harbour, whisk visitors to Craigleith, home to the Centre's SOS Puffin project, then onto the Bass Rock.

North Berwick Law

1mi/1.6km south of the town centre by Law Road. Signposted path with occasional seats.

One of East Lothian's many volcanic hills and distinguishing landmarks, the Law, with the town spread out at its feet, has a commanding **panorama★★★**.

At the very top is a pair of ancient weathered whale's jawbones and a view indicator. On a clear day you can use it to pick out: St Abb's Head, inland to the Lammermuir Hills, the Traprain and the Garleton Hills backed by the Moorfoots and Pentlands, perhaps even as far as Ben Lomond on a really clear day; the Forth, the Ochils and the Grampians with the East Neuk of Fife on the northern shore of the Firth. The Law is the scene of an annual hill race in August.

Bass Rock

Boat trips May–end Sept subject to weather. Phone for details. ☎0131 331 4857. www.sulaboattrips.co.uk.

At the entrance to the Firth of Forth, 3mi/5km from North Berwick, the rounded form of this volcanic hill rises to 107m above sea level. It is now equipped with a lighthouse and foghorn for Forth shipping. Its role has varied throughout history: a retreat for St Baldred; a fortress; a Covenanters' prison; the last stronghold of the Stuart monarchy's cause to surrender (1691–4); and a present-day sanctuary of myriad seabirds. A boat trip makes it possible to observe the wildlife at fairly close quarters, depending on the weather. Every conceivable crevice and ledge of the vertical cliffs is the domain of some seabird, be it guillemot, razorbill, cormorant, puffin, tern, eider duck, gull or the famous **Gannet**, also known as Solan Goose, which takes its Latin name *Sula Bassana* from this island (*see Box*).

▷ Leave North Berwick west on the A198. Dirleton is just off the main road.

Dirleton★

A village full of charm, where highly individual 17C and 18C cottages and houses, enhanced by well-tended gardens, stand round two greens.

The church (built 1612) has at its gate the session house and schoolhouse, adjoined by the schoolroom. The pride of the village is its romantic ruined castle, which dates back to the 13C, and predated the establishment of the village and church.

Dirleton Castle and Garden★

Daily: Apr–Sept 9.30am–5.30pm; Oct–Mar 10am–4pm. 25–26 Dec, 1–2 Jan. £6. ☎01620 850 330. www.historicenvironment.scot.

Often in the mainstream of Scottish history, this stronghold was owned at different times by the de Vaux family, the Halyburtons and the Ruthvens. In 1650, it was besieged and destroyed by Commonwealth soldiers.

Dirleton Castle

© Douglas Houghton/age fotostock

The enchanting castle ruins, and the gardens, are today looked after by Historic Scotland.

The oldest **section** dates from the 13C (left of the entrance), and includes three towers, surrounding a lesser courtyard. Rising up out of a rocky mound, the castle is surrounded by attractive **gardens** that date from the late 19C to the early 20C. The North gardens (seen on the approach to the castle) feature the world's longest herbaceous border.

Also in the grounds is the **Ruthven Dovecot** – one of the best preserved pigeon houses in Scotland, housing over 1 000 nesting boxes.

▶ Return to the A198 and then continue west.

Gullane

With five golf courses, Gullane (pronounced "guillin" – with a hard "g") is a golfer's paradise, best known for the famous Muirfield Course, home of the Honourable Company of Edinburgh Golfers (founded 1744) and a regular venue for the British Open Championship. With its fine sandy beach the village has always been popular for day trips from the capital and recently it has been growing in popularity as a commuter haven too.

▶ Once over the Peffer Burn take the local road to the left, as the A198 swings west. Follow signs for Myreton Motor Museum.

👥 Myreton Motor Museum

♿🕐*Daily 10.30am–4.30pm.* 🚗*£7 (child, £3).* 🕐*25 Dec.* ✆*01875 870 288. www.myretonmotormuseum.co.uk.*
This privately owned, rather cramped collection presents a panorama of roadworthy vehicles, motorcycles and bicycles; it is a far cry from the spit and polish image of more traditional motor museums.

The cars, each with their individual case history, tell a story of misfortune and neglect or loving care and attention. They include the Galloway, with its thistle-adorned footplates – an exhibit at the 1926 Scottish Motor Show; a 14-seat charabanc from Ford (1920); *Eve* (1892) by A Benz – the oldest car in Scotland; the Standard Beaverette – with a name like a domestic appliance and looking like something out of a science fiction movie; the Bollee Motor Tricycle c.1896, which once belonged to the Hon C S Rolls of Rolls-Royce fame.

▶ Continue along minor roads to join the B1377. Turn left (east) and pass Drem to intercept the B1347. Turn right and follow signs to the Museum of Flight.

⚎ National Museum of Flight★

East Fortune Airfield. ○*Apr–Oct daily 10am–5pm; Nov–Mar Sat–Sun 10am –4pm.* ☞*£12.50 (child 5–15, £7.50).* ✖ ✆*0300 123 6789. www.nms.ac.uk/flight.*

In a vast hangar, this outstation of the National Museums of Scotland displays its superb collection of aircraft, ranging from a wooden D H Dragon biplane to Concorde. The model airship on show, **HM Airship R 34** ("Tiny"), set out from here on the historic first ever double Atlantic crossing in 1919.

In addition, two nationally significant Second World War hangars were opened in 2015. One hangar displays military aircraft; the other commercial and leisure aircraft.

Another hangar displays 18 aircraft including a Comet airliner and a Vulcan bomber. Hangar 4 is home to the pride of the museum, Concorde G-BOAA. Visitors can see her being reconstructed after her final voyage by land and sea from Heathrow. G-BOAA became the first of the British Airways fleet to fly commercially when she flew from London to Bahrain in January 1976.

▷ The B1347 back to East Linton, and then the A199 back to Dunbar.

⚎ ③ LAMMERMUIR HILLS

43mi/70km. Allow 1h30 driving time.

These rolling hills divide the Lothians from the Borders region. Along this excursion, the **northern foothills★** conceal a charming series of red sandstone pantiled villages and the region's finest stately home, Lennoxlove.

▷ Leave Dunbar on the A199 west, turn left towards East Linton. Before crossing the River Tyne turn left on local roads.

Hailes Castle

This ruined stronghold, which takes full advantage of the rocky outcrop overlooking the River Tyne, was owned at one time by the Hepburns, in particular James, 4th Earl of Bothwell. It is said

that Bothwell and Mary, Queen of Scots rested here en route for Dunbar Castle in April 1567.

To the south, the volcanic outcrop of **Traprain Law** (239m) rises abruptly from surrounding farmland. A good defensive site of early date, it was in all probability the capital of the British tribe, the Votadini. The Law is famous for the **Treasure of Traprain**, a hoard of Roman silver plate, buried in the 5C, rediscovered in 1919 and now in the Royal Museum of Scotland in Edinburgh.

▷ Follow minor roads to Haddington.

Haddington

♿*See HADDINGTON.*

▷ Take the B6369 south, and then branch onto the B6368.

Lennoxlove★

♿↝*Visit by guided tour only: Apr–Oct Wed, Thu and Sun 1.30pm, 2.30pm, 3.30 pm.* ☞*£10.* ✆*01620 823 720. www.lennoxlove.com.*

Lennoxlove is most famous for its Mary, Queen of Scots connections (♿*see Box, opposite*). It was built in the 1300s and retains its original tower. Today it is the residence of the 14th Duke of Hamilton.

Interior

Of special interest in the **Front Hall** are the portraits attributed to Mytens of *James, 2nd Marquess of Hamilton*, who accompanied James VI to England in 1603. The wall cabinets of the **China Hall** display 18C–20C armorial porcelain. By the entrance to the **Blue Room**, William Beckford (collector and author) is pictured as a boy. He was the father of the 10th Duchess. There is also a portrait by David Wilkie of the *10th Duke of Hamilton (1767–1852)*, known as "El Magnifico".

The **Petit Point Room** has an ebony and pewter Boulle cabinet. The damask wall hangings are appliqued with older petit point embroideries. In the **Yellow Room** a double portrait of the *2nd Duke of Hamilton* and the *Duke of Lauderdale* establishes the link between Lennoxlove original and present owners. There are

Mary, Queen of Scots slept here

A 16C four-poster bed, reputedly slept in by Mary, Queen of Scots, was unveiled at Lennoxlove in 2007. Made of black oak and beautifully refurbished, the bed is thought to have been used by the much persecuted Mary when under guard at Arden Hall in North Yorkshire. It is intricately carved and has been restored to the magnificent comfort and style that befitted a monarch at the time. It is draped in long, deep red velvet curtains which have been embroidered in the exact style of the Tudor times. In the 16C higher nobility literally travelled with their beds. Consequently, they were made very well and the framework of this bed is much as it was four centuries ago.

also portraits by Lely of the *Duke and Duchess of Lennox*. The **Stuart Room** is dominated by the inlaid tortoiseshell writing cabinet, Charles II's gift to La Belle Stewart. The **Great Hall**, which represented the original tower's whole living portion, was remodelled in 1912 by Robert Lorimer. The **Tower Room** has one of the four original death masks of Mary, Queen of Scots, and also her silver casket, a betrothal gift from her first husband François II of France. There's also a portrait believed to be of *John Knox*.

◐ Use minor roads to Pencaitland.

Pencaitland

Easter and Wester Pencaitland, a double village divided by the River Tyne, has a parish **church** with some unusual features. The octagonal portion of the tower once served as a dovecot. Note the three sundials on the buttress of the south side. The tombstones have lively depictions of the tools of the trade of the now defunct watch houses; these stand at each gateway and were built after a body-snatching raid in 1830 to prevent further incidents.

◐ Retreat from Pencaitland turn right onto the B6355.

East Saltoun

This village, with its imposing Gothic church and a line of model cottages, was the work of enterprising landowners, the Fletchers of Saltoun Hall.

◐ Continue on B6355 to Gifford.

Gifford★

This late-17C and early-18C village was re-sited before the enclosing of the park and rebuilding of Yester House. The main street goes from the church down to the mercat cross then turns to follow the magnificent avenue of limes leading up to Yester House (*private*), the former home of the Hays of Tweeddale.

◐ Leave by the B6355 and shortly afterwards branch left onto the B6370. Take a local road to the right to reach the village of Garvald.

Garvald

This is another attractive village of red-sandstone cottages. Many of these date from the 1780s when rebuilding followed a disastrous flood. The church, close by the Papana Water, has "jougs" (a kind of pillory) hanging on the west wall.

◐ Continue NE on B6370.

Stenton★

The village is overlooked by the old schoolhouse and adjoining single-storey schoolroom. On its east green is a now rare feature, a **tron** – for weighing wool. In the churchyard the 16C crow-stepped and saddlebacked tower, with a dovecot in its upper section, marks the site of the former church which was replaced in 1828 by William Burn's Gothic parish church. At the eastern end of the village is a 16C Rood Well.

◐ Continue on the B6370 to cross the A1 and join the A1087, right to Dunbar.

Haddington★

Haddington is a handsome market town where the triangular street plan testifies to its medieval origins. The many 18C town houses are witness to the prosperity occasioned by the agricultural improvements of the period. Set on the banks of the Tyne, the town serves the outlying agricultural area.

▶ **Population:** 9 130.
ℹ **Info:** 3 Princes Street, Edinburgh.
   ✆ 0131 473 3868; www.visiteastlothian.org.
▶ **Location:** The compact centre and riverside can easily be covered on foot.
▧ **Don't Miss:** High Street architecture; an excursion to the Lammermuir Hills.
◷ **Timing:** Allow 1 hour for Haddington.

A BIT OF HISTORY

The 12C town grew up around the royal palace in which Alexander II was born in 1198. Royal patronage was extended to the town itself, created a royal burgh by David I, who was responsible for the establishment of two monastic communities. To allow the royal burgh to exercise its foreign trading privileges, Aberlady, 5mi/8km to the north, was designated as the town's port.

By the 16C this was Scotland's fourth largest town. The Reformation saw the destruction of the monastic houses while ensuing strife led to the building of a town wall (c.1604).

The 18C, Haddington's golden age, was the direct result of increasing prosperity created by agricultural improvements.

TOWN CENTRE

The original market place of this royal burgh was the triangle formed by Market, Hardgate, High and Court streets. The burgesses built gable-ended houses onto this market place with long riggs leading back to the town wall and pends leading off. In the 16C, back-to-back housing was built in the middle, giving the present layout.

The houses themselves were often refronted, and in other cases new fenestration was fitted into a chimney gable end. The streets are lined with some rubblework buildings, some harled and painted, but all with a certain harmony of colour since the 1962 conservation programme. There is a variety of wrought-iron shop signs.

High Street★

The south side has a continuous line of frontages of varying heights, style and colour topped by roofs varyingly pitched, interrupted only by closes. The market cross with the Haddington goat is a 19C replacement.

Note in particular No. 27 with the decorative chimney, No. 31 with the roll skewputts of the dormer window, and Nos. 43 and 45 with the stair turret rising through three storeys.

Lodge Street

A continuation of the High Street, this short street mingles markedly contrasting styles. **Carlyle House** – a misnomer, with its highly ornate Italian palace-style façade of the 18C – is all the more striking for its direct contrast to the adjoining vernacular house and its attractive Venetian window. The intervening pend leads to the childhood home of Jane Welsh, wife of Thomas Carlyle.

Town House

This splendidly dignified William Adam building (1748), with pediment and pilasters framing a Venetian window, typified the civic dignity of a town prospering from the agricultural revolution. The steeple was an 1831 addition.

Court Street

Leading to the west port, this tree-lined street is bordered on the north side by splendid town mansions, such as the late-18C Bank of Scotland. Opposite are the 1854 Corn Exchange and William Burn's Gothic Council Buildings on the former site of the royal palace.

Market Street

Late-18C and early-19C three- to four-storey buildings line the north or original side of the triangle. Some gable ends were replaced by new front elevations. Survivals include No. 32 with its chimney gable. **Mitchell's Close** on the north side (restored 1967) is more typical of the 17C pattern with rubble masonry, pantiles, inset dormers, crow steps, turnpike stairs – a charming vernacular ensemble.

Hardgate

The most striking building is the white harled **Kinloch House** with its Dutch-style gable, a good example of an 18C laird's town house. The custom stone in front of the George Hotel marks the spot where customs dues were paid in medieval times.

RIVERSIDE
Church Street

On the right is a charming three-storey building, the Old Grammar School and library, combining Georgian formality with mellow rubblework and decorative patterns. The church opposite stands on the site of the original Lamp of the Lothian, which belonged to the Franciscan friary founded in 1138. No. 20, with its goat sculpture, has a corbelled corner. The street leads to the Sands and down to the riverside.

The sturdily solid 16C **Nungate Bridge**, with pointed cutwaters, offers a good view upstream of St Mary's Church in its riverside setting. The far bank was the site of the Cistercian Abbey from which it took its name.

The walled garden known as Lady Kitty's Garden has a cylindrical **dovecot** in one corner. This was a training ground for archery and bowling in the Middle Ages.

St Mary's Parish Church

♿🕐 *Easter weekend and May–Sept, Sun–Fri 1.30–4pm, Sat 11am–4pm.*
℘ *01620 823 109.*
www.stmaryskirk.co.uk.

The cathedral-like dimensions of this church (163m long and 34m at the transepts) are enhanced by its unencumbered setting in a spacious churchyard. The first church built in 1134 was rebuilt in the late 14C–early 15C and made a collegiate church in 1540. With successive floods and raids the fabric deteriorated. Extensive alterations were made in the early 19C and the choir was restored in 1971–3.

Restored to some of its original glory, the nave's 19C plaster vaulting replaces the original timber roof; the choir was covered with fibreglass vaulting.

The south window of the south transept is by Burne-Jones (1895). In the Lauderdale Aisle is the 17C marble **Lauderdale Monument** featuring the recumbent alabaster effigies of John Maitland, 1st Lord Thirlestane, his wife Jane Fleming, their son John, 1st Earl of Lauderdale, and his countess Isabella Seton.

In the floor of the choir is the commemorative slab by the great Scottish historian and essayist Thomas Carlyle (♿ *see ECCLEFECHAN*) to his wife Jane Welsh who was a native of Haddington.

Sidegate

The most notable building is the early 17C **Haddington House**. The street-side entrance was a later addition, the original one being under the turret stair on the garden side. **St Mary's Pleasance** has been re-created as a traditional 17C Scottish garden.

Poldrate Mill

Restored to serve as an Arts and Crafts Community Centre (℘ *07563 719 978; http://thepacc.org.uk*), this attractive biscuit-coloured stone 18C corn mill retains its undershot waterwheel, watermill, storehouses, barns and millers' cottages.

Scotland's most populous city, with its long-established industrial and port traditions, was named European City of Culture in 1990 and has never looked back. Now home to many of the country's most prestigious performing arts organisations, Glasgow is internationally acclaimed in the fields of contemporary art, design and music, and is a flourishing cultural centre.

Highlights

1 Admiring the pioneering design at the **Mackintosh House** (p197)
2 Dalí's *Christ of St John of the Cross* at the **Kelvingrove Art Gallery** (p197)
3 Exploring the **Riverside Museum** at the Glasgow Harbour (p199)
4 The **Science Centre** (p200)
5 The medieval architecture of **Glasgow cathedral** (p201)

▶ **Population:** 606 340.
🛈 **Info:** Glasgow iCentre, 156a/158 Buchanan Street. ☎0141 566 4083.
◗ **Location:** The city is situated on the River Clyde in the West Central Lowlands, 45mi/72km W of Edinburgh.
✿ **Don't Miss:** Glasgow Cathedral; Kelvingrove Art Gallery and Museum; Riverside Museum; an excursion to the Trossachs.
🕐 **Timing:** Allow at least 3 days in the city centre.
👫 **Kids:** Museum of Transport; The Mini Museum (for under 5s) at Kelvingrove Art Gallery and Museum; Glasgow Science Centre.

The City Today

Glasgow is one of Britain's fast changing cities, most evident at the docks with the new Riverside development, but also constantly regenerating and evolving its shopping, eating, drinking and nightlife which now matches the best in Europe. Its museums and galleries have long been recognised as world class and as a bonus are free to enter. Despite the changes, though, you'll rarely find a pretentious Glaswegian; the city retains its roots, local character and no-nonsense edge.

"Dear Green Place"

Although not the capital, Glasgow was part of the British Kingdom of Strathclyde which was bordered to the north by the Picts, to the northwest by the Scots and south by the Angles of Northumbria.

St Mungo came to this embattled kingdom in the mid-6C. Proclaimed bishop, he set up a wooden church and the fish and ring in the Glasgow coat of arms refer to a St Mungo legend when he saved an unfaithful wife from the wrath of her royal husband.

The 12C saw the consecration of the see and the new cathedral of Glasgow. Medieval Glasgow developed around its

Mackintosh Building, Glasgow School of Art

© Douglas Houghton/age fotostock

cathedral and its importance increased with the foundation in 1451 of Scotland's second university and the elevation to archbishopric in 1492.

In the religious troubles of the 17C, Glasgow was the scene of the General Assembly responsible for abolishing episcopacy (see INTRODUCTION: History) in Scotland. The town remained a strong supporter of the Covenanting cause, but the restoration of episcopacy brought renewed repression for the Covenanters. By the 17C, trade with the American colonies via Port Glasgow was a feature of Glasgow's commerce and early fortunes were made in sugar and rum.

Sugar, Tobacco and Textiles

Glasgow's growing prosperity in the early 18C depended largely on the tobacco trade. The outward cargoes of locally manufactured goods were paid for by the return loads of tobacco, which was then re-exported to the continent. The merchants, known as **Tobacco Lords**, played an important role in the city's economic and social life. With their traditional outfits of scarlet cloaks and black suits they provided a colourful scene on the plainstones, their exclusive trading patch in front of the Tontine Hotel at Glasgow Cross.

Today's street names, Jamaica, Virginia, Glassford, Dunlop, Miller and Buchan are reminders of this flourishing activity and its merchant families. The American War of Independence caused the eventual decline in the tobacco trade but by then many of the merchants had invested their accumulated wealth in other emergent industries (banking, textiles, coal mining and iron manufacturing).

Second City

Cotton manufacturing in particular was responsible for a large increase in the city's population. This trend continued with the impetus of the Industrial Revolution which brought in its wake the centralisation of heavy industries (coal, iron and steel) in the Glasgow area. Improved communications – building of the Forth-Clyde and Monkland Canals, arrival of the railways and deepening of the Clyde

which was made navigable up to Broomielaw – also played an important role in expansion.

Once Glasgow had become established as an area of heavy industry, the emphasis moved to shipbuilding with the development of iron ships and screw propulsion. Some of the world's greatest liners were Clyde-built.

The prosperity engendered by the Industrial Revolution gave the city its solidly prosperous Victorian face, becoming the workshop of the empire, second only to London.

The Glasgow School

Commercial prosperity begat a new generation of businessmen interested in art, some making bequests (Mitchell) and others (McLellan, Burrell, Sir William Maxwell Stirling) collecting. Out of this cultural activity a movement, known as the **Glasgow Boys**, emerged in the last quarter of the 19C partly as a protest against the traditions embodied by the Academicians of Edinburgh and the Victorian artistic conventions. The leading members were W Y MacGregor (the father of the group), James Guthrie, George Henry, E A Hornel and John Lavery. The artists sought to achieve realism – as an alternative to the prevalent romanticism, sentimentality and staidness – and nurtured the development of an Art Nouveau movement in the 1890s. The most brillant exponent was the architect and decorator Charles Rennie Mackintosh, largely responsible for a rebirth in fine and applied arts.

Glasgow is home to the **Scottish Opera**, the **Scottish Ballet** and is a rehearsal and recording base for the **Scottish National Orchestra**. The city hosts a busy calendar of international class festivals of classical and contemporary music, arts and dance and in 2008 Glasgow was named a UNESCO City of Music, reflecting its diverse musical riches and the vibrancy of its music performance and education scene.

VISITOR INFORMATION

Tourist Information Centre –
VisitScotland Glasgow iCentre
(*156a/158 Buchanan Street. ✆0141 566
4083; www.visitscotland.com*) offers an
accommodation and theatre
booking service. There is also a
bureau de change, a bookshop
and a souvenir shop.

GETTING AROUND

Glasgow's main sights are scattered,
so it is best to use public transport
including the underground railway.
Hop-on hop-off open-top tour buses
leave from George Square.
**Strathclyde Partnership for
Transport** (*✆0141 332 6811; www.
spt.co.uk*) SPT's travel centres provide
information about bus, coach,
rail, subway and ferry travel in the
Strathclyde area.
The **Daytripper ticket** (£22.50 for 2
adults and up to 4 children, or £12.70
for 1 adult and up to 2 children) gives
you unlimited travel for one day by
rail, subway, most buses, and some
ferries. **All-Day tickets** give you one
day unlimited travel on the subway
for just £4.20 per person.

🐾 WALKING TOURS

1 TOWN CENTRE

*This short walking tour (2km/1¼ mi;
allow 30 min) is a tribute to the genius of
Charles Rennie Mackintosh, Scotland's
greatest architect-designer (1868–1928)
who designed the Glasgow School of
Art.*

▷ Start from The Lighthouse in
Mitchell Lane, walking east.

The Lighthouse

*56 Mitchell Lane. ◷Mon–Sat
10.30am–5pm, Sun noon–5pm.
✖ ✆0141 276 5365.
www.thelighthouse.co.uk.*

The former offices of *The Glasgow Her-
ald*, designed by C R Mackintosh, have
been imaginatively converted into the
National Centre for Architecture and
Design including the award-winning
Mackintosh Centre and Mackintosh
Tower with stunning city views and a
stylish rooftop café-bar.

▷ Turn left onto Buchanan Street,
and soon pass the Willow Tea
Rooms (🏚*see Addresses*), a shrine to
Mackintosh design. Soon, turn right
into Exchange Place leading to Royal
Exchange Square.

Gallery of Modern Art★

*Royal Exchange Square. ♿◷Mon–Wed
and Sat 10am–5pm, Thu 10am–8pm, Fri
and Sun 11am–5pm. ◷25–26 Dec and
1–2 Jan. ✖ 🅿 ✆0141 287 3050.
www.glasgowlife.org.uk.*
Glasgow's collection of modern art
(GoMA) is the second most visited
contemporary art gallery outside
London. Built for the tobacco lord
William Cunninghame, this great neo-
Classical structure boasts a massive
Corinthian portico and a magnificent
main hall with a barrel-vault ceiling. At
the very heart of the commercial city,
it served for more than a century as
the Royal Exchange, the focal point of
Glasgow's business life, then as a library.
In the mid-1990s it underwent extensive
conversion and today comprises four
galleries which rotate an often thought-
provoking range of exhibitions, featuring
local, national and international
artists. Works on display include a
variety of media; painting, sculpture,
printmaking, photography, video,
installations... GoMA also explores
contemporary issues through a major
biennial social justice arts programme.

▷ Retrace your steps and turn right
onto Buchanan Street, and walk up
towards the concert halls, where
Buchanan Street swings left onto
Sauchiehall Street. Continue as far as
Dalhousie Street. Turn right here up to
Renfrew Street, and there turn left.

Glasgow School of Art★

167 Renfrew Street. ◐ Visit by guided
*tour only (1h); daily, see website
for schedule. Booking advisable.*
◐Christmas holidays–early Jan.
℘0141 353 4500. www.gsa.ac.uk.
This major landmark in the history of
European architecture was designed
by Charles Rennie Mackintosh when he
was only 28 years old.
The building was completed in
two stages, first in 1897–99 and then
in 1907–09, and nearly 100 years later
it remains highly functional while also
housing one of the largest collections of
Mackintosh furniture, designs and paintings. Of particular interest is the Library,
an architectural *tour de force* with its
three-storey high windows and sus-
pended ceiling and Mackintosh's most
original and celebrated interior. Visitors can also see his decorative stained
glass, metalwork, light fittings, etc. in
the Board Room, Director's Room and
the Furniture Gallery.

▷ Continue along Renfrew Street
and turn right into Garnet Street; cross
Hill Street and turn left into Buccleuch
Street.

The Tenement House

145 Buccleuch Street.
◐Mar–Oct daily 10am–5pm;
*Nov–23 Dec and 3 Jan–Feb Sat–Mon
11am–4pm.* ✆£7.50. ℘0141 333 0183.
www.nts.org.uk.
The housing demands of Glasgow's ever
increasing 19C population were met by
tenements built by speculative builders
keen to cash-in on Glasgow's industrial
boom. This tenement flat, built in 1892,
consists of two rooms, kitchen and bathroom; original fittings include the box-
beds, gas lamps and coal-fired ranges
with coal bin. Community life centred
on the close and back court.
This particular tenement house is an
important part of the city's heritage,
not only because it represents a typical
house that so many 19C Scottish people
used to live in, but also because it has
survived without any significant alterations for over a century.

ADDITIONAL SIGHT

The Mackintosh Church at Queen's Cross

*870 Garscube Road (not shown on
map;* ◐ *see website for location and
directions)*
◐◐11am–4pm: Apr–Oct Mon–Fri;
*Nov–mid-Dec and early Feb–Mar Mon,
Wed and Fri.* ◐mid-Dec–early Feb, and
on Good Friday, Easter Monday, May
Bank Holiday Mondays, Glasgow Fair
Monday. ✆£4. ℘0141 946 6600.
https://mackintoshchurch.com.
Mackintosh's innovative design for the
galleried, single-aisled church (1898–
99) was dictated by its corner site. The
spacious interior is enhanced by the
Art Nouveau furnishings. The church,
which houses the headquarters of the
Charles Rennie Mackintosh Society, is
now a visitor centre.

2 CATHEDRAL SQUARE

*This is quintessential Glasgow, from the
monied Merchant City around George
Square to the socialist People's Palace,
from the calm of the Necropolis to the
buzzing nightlife of the city centre.*

Cathedral Square

Prior to the Reformation this was the
very heart of the ecclesiastical city. The
cathedral, the Bishop's Castle and the
canons' manses all once overlooked
this focal point. The Bishop's Castle (a
stone in the Royal Infirmary forecourt
marks the site) was destroyed to make
way for the Adam brothers' 1792 Royal
Infirmary building. The present Royal
Infirmary is a 20C replacement. It was
in a ward of the original that Sir Joseph
Lister (1827–1912) pioneered the use of
carbolic acid as an antiseptic in the treatment of wounds.
The statues in the square include missionary explorer David Livingstone and
King William of Orange.

Necropolis

Behind the cathedral on the far bank of
the Molendinar Burn is the formal burial
garden dating from 1833. Pathways bordered by elaborate tombs lead up to the
highest point commanded by John Knox

191

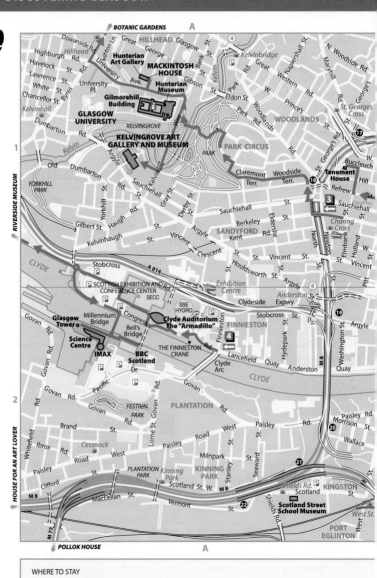

BOTANIC GARDENS · A

Dowanside Rd. · HILLHEAD · Glasgow

Highburgh · George · St.

Havelock · Hunterian · Gibson

Lawrence St. · Art Gallery · MACKINTOSH HOUSE

White · University · Hunterian Museum

Chancellor St. · Pl. · Gilmorehill Building

Kelvinhall · GLASGOW UNIVERSITY

Dumbarton · Rd. · KELVINGROVE

KELVINGROVE ART GALLERY AND MUSEUM · PARK CIRCUS

YORKHILL PARK · Old Dumbarton · Rd. · Claremont · Woodside · Terr.

Gilbert St. · Haugh Rd. · Sauchiehall · SANDYFORD

Kelvinhaugh · St. · Argyle · Berkeley · St.

CLYDE · Stobcross · A 814 · Houldsworth St. · Vincent

SCOTTISH EXHIBITION AND CONFERENCE CENTER · SECC · Exhibition Centre · Clydeside

SSE HYDRO · Stobcross · St. · Anderston Expwy.

Glasgow Tower · Millennium Bridge · Congress · Clyde Auditorium The "Armadillo" · FINNIESTON

Science Centre · Bell's Bridge · THE FINNIESTON CRANE · Lancefield Quay · Anderston Quay

IMAX · BBC Scotland · Clyde Arc · CLYDE

Govan Rd. · Pacific · FESTIVAL PARK · Govan Rd. · PLANTATION · Paisley Rd.

Brand · St. · West · Paisley · Road

Ibrox · Cessnock · Milnpark · St.

Paisley · Road · West · PLANTATION PARK · Kinning Park · KINNING PARK

Clifford · St. · Scotland St. · Scotland St. W. · Scotland · Scotland Street School Museum · KINGSTON

MacLellan · St. · Vermont · Shields Rd. · West St.

POLLOK HOUSE · A · PORT EGLINTON

RIVERSIDE MUSEUM

HOUSE FOR AN ART LOVER

WHERE TO STAY		
Abode .... ①	Apex City of Glasgow Hotel .... ③	Malmaison .... ⑤
Adelaides Guest House .... ②	Fraser Suites .... ④	

atop his column. There is a good **view★** of the city away to the southwest.

St Mungo Museum of Religious Life and Art

2 Castle Street. 🚪 🕐*Tue–Thu and Sat 10am–5pm, Fri and Sun 11am–5pm.* 🕐*25–26 Dec and 1–2 Jan.* ✗ ☎*0141 276 1625.*

www.glasgowlife.org.uk/museums. Since its opening in 1993 this museum has sparked controversy with its collections of religious artefacts. They are grouped in three main permanent galleries: Religious Art, Religious Life, and the Scottish Gallery. A fourth gallery houses temporary exhibitions.

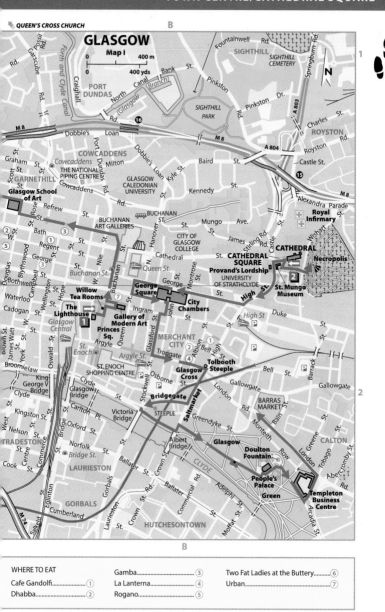

Provand's Lordship

♿ 🕐 *Tue–Thu and Sat 10am–5pm, Fri and Sun 11am– 5pm.* 🕐 *25–26 Dec and 1–2 Jan.* 📞 *0141 276 1625. www.glasgowlife.org.uk/museums.* Provand's Lordship, a former prebendal manse dating from 1471 is the oldest house in the city. This and the cathedral are the only survivors of the medieval town. The two lower floors are furnished with 16C–20C pieces.

▶ From Provost's Lordship, walk south along Castle Street, leading to High Street.

193

High Street

A plaque on the disused goods yard opposite College Street marks the site of Old College from 1632 to 1870 and the original Hunterian Museum prior to their transfer to Gilmorehill. At 215 High Street, the former British Linen Bank building is still crowned by the figure of Pallas, goddess of wisdom and weaving. The stained glass above the door portrays a flax boat.

▶ Turn right onto George Street and continue to George Square.

George Square

The heart of modern Glasgow, this busy square is lined by imposing 19C buildings. Development of the square and adjoining streets began in 1782 and by the beginning of the 19C it had become the city's hotel centre. The initial steps towards a change in character came with the building of the Merchants' House closely followed by the General Post Office and City Chambers.

On the north side is the only hotel to remain (now the Millennium Hotel). The Merchants' House (1869) on the west side, and today the home of the Glasgow Chamber of Commerce, is denoted by the Ship of Trade aloft, a replica of the one in Bridgegate. On the south are the Post Office buildings. Occupying the east side are the **City Chambers**★ (*Public tours are conducted twice daily, Mon–Fri 10.30am and 2.30pm; Tickets for tours can be obtained from the City Chambers reception desk 30 minutes prior to each tour. ✆0141 287 4018; www.glasgow.gov.uk*), another of Glasgow's magnificent Victorian buildings, a heritage from the time when Glasgow was the second city of the empire. Inside, grandeur and opulence reign supreme, particularly in the loggia, council and banqueting halls. Sir Walter Scott on the central column dominates a series of famous men: (clockwise) Peel, Gladstone, Lord Clyde, John Moore, Watt.

▶ Walk around the square by going left into Queen Street, and left again to go forward into Cochrane Street. Turn right into John Street, and then right, briefly, into Ingram Street. Take Glassford Street (first left), and continue until Trongate (third street on the left) and follow this to Glasgow Cross.

Glasgow Cross

Until Victorian times the Cross – at the junction of Trongate, High Street, Gallowgate and Saltmarket – was the heart of Glasgow. Defoe much admired the Cross, set as it was at the centre of a prosperous commercial area known as the "Golden Acre".

The **Tolbooth Steeple**★, in the middle of the street, is a striking reminder of this former elegance. The seven-storey tower was originally adjoined by the elegant tolbooth and then the Tontine Hotel. The mercat cross nearby is a 1929 replica.

▶ Turn into Saltmarket.

Saltmarket and Bridgegate

The Saltmarket was the main thoroughfare in the 19C. Its grey upper storeys contrast with its colourful ground floor windows.

▶ Turn into Bridgegate.

This now rather dismal street was once a fashionable main thoroughfare to the city's first stone bridge (1345). The 50m high steeple, rising out of derelict warehouses, is all that remains of the 1659 Merchants Hall (demolished 1818), the business and social meeting place for Glasgow's merchants. It used to serve as a lookout for cargoes coming up the Clyde. A new Merchants' House was built in 1877 in George Square.

▶ Continue along Bridgegate towards Victoria Bridge. Turn left into Clyde Street. Left in Saltmarket to enter Glasgow Green.

Glasgow Green

On the north bank of the Clyde this park is one of Glasgow's most historic sites. Successively or simultaneously it was a place of common grazing, bleaching, public hangings, military reviews and parades, merry-making at Glasgow Fair, and above all, of public meetings and free speech.

Alternating between fashionable and disreputable, it has always been most fiercely defended against encroachment and today lies within the GEAR (Glasgow Eastern Area Renewal Scheme) revitalisation programme, arguably the most determined attempt at inner city renewal in the UK.

Monuments on the Green include Nelson's Monument (pre-dating Nelson's column in London by three decades) and the nearby stone commemorating the spot where **James Watt** worked out his improvement to the steam engine. Formerly on the Green was the **Doulton Fountain** – a remarkable piece of pottery commemorating Queen Victoria's Golden Jubilee of 1887 – now moved a short distance in front of the People's Palace.

▷ Walk through the park to the People's Palace.

People's Palace and Winter Gardens

Enter by Morris Place. ♿⏰*Tue–Thu and Sat 10am–5pm, Fri and Sun 11am–5pm. Winter Garden daily 10am–5pm.* ⏰*25–26 Dec and 1–2 Jan.* ✕ ✆*0141 276 0788. www.glasgowlife.org.uk/museums.*

The People's Palace museum and Winter Gardens were opened in 1898 as a cultural centre for the east end. It is now a local and social history museum, where a wealth of historic artefacts, paintings, prints and photographs, film and interactive computer displays recount the story of Glasgow from earliest times to the present.

The **Winter Gardens** are a lovely place to stroll amid exotic plants and features a very popular cafe.

▷ Continue beyond the People's Palace onto Templeton Street, and turn right.

Templeton Business Centre

Overloking Glasgow Green, this highly unusual, colourful and richly decorated building, also known as Templeton on the Green, dates from 1889 and was modelled on the Doge's Palace. It originally housed a carpet factory and is now home to a varied mix of offices and business ranging from saddlemaking to biotechnology.

▷ Go round three sides of the building and follow London Road northwest. 🚇At weekends this is the home of the famous **Barras Market** (*Sat–Sun 9.30am–4.30pm; the shops are typically open Wed–Mon 10am–5pm; www.theglasgowbarras. com*) a mixture of street markets, indoor markets, shops and pubs, ideal for an assortment of goods at bargain prices.

On Sundays, visit the nearby **Barras Arts and Design Centre** (*11am–4pm; https://baadglasgow.com*) for a market within a market.

ADDITIONAL SIGHT
Scotland Street School Museum

225 Scotland Street (♿ *see map, p192).* ♿⏰*Tue–Thu and Sat 10am–5pm, Fri and Sun 11am–5pm;* ⏰*25–26 and 31 Dec, 1–2 Jan;* ✕ ✆*0141 287 0500; www.glasgowlife.org.uk/museums).*

This Mackintosh building (1906) is a superb example of his architectural style, featuring twin glass stair-towers, and fine stonework detailing. In the Mackintosh room visitors can study the architect's designs for the building. The museum covers education in Scotland over a hundred years, from the late 19C century to the late 20C.

Visitors get to see what school days were like in the reign of Queen Victoria, during World War II, and in the 1950s and 60s, in three reconstructed classrooms.

③ WEST END

The architecture and atmosphere of the West End's University District is quite different from that of the town centre, being altogether more elegant and bohemian.

▶ Begin from the point where Sauchiehall Street crosses above the M8 motorway. Once over the motorway, turn right into Woodside Terrace. Keep to the north side of a small park to enter Claremont Terrace. Go forward into Park Gardens and turn right towards Park Circus. Go left on Park Terrace, and then take to parkland pathways to descend to the Prince of Wales Bridge spanning the River Kelvin.

▶ Over the bridge turn right onto Kelvin Way, and left into University Avenue. Here you will find Glasgow University, the Hunterian Museum, the Hunterian Art Gallery and the Mackintosh House.

Glasgow University

University Avenue, Visitor Centre in Gilmorehill Building. ♿🚶Tours: *Tue–Sun 2pm.* 🚌up to £27. *𝒫0141 330 5360. www.gla.ac.uk.*
Bishop William Turnbull founded the university in 1451 and the first classes were held in the cathedral. The early university was greatly dependent on the church and the bishops and archbishops of Glasgow held the office of Chancellor until 1642. The university then acquired properties in the High Street which were used until 1632 when the Old College, a handsome building arranged around a double quadrangle, was built. The High Street premises were abandoned and destroyed in 1870 when the university moved to the present site on the estate of Gilmorehill in the west end of the city. The current imposing edifice remains the focal point of a complex of new (Adam Smith, Boyd Orr and Hetherington Buildings, Hunterian Art Gallery and Library) and refurbished buildings throughout the local streets. Today eight faculties (Arts, Divinity, Engineering, Law, Medicine, Science, Social and Veterinary Medicine) welcome over 13 000 students.

Gilmorehill Building – This massive Gothic Revival building, the oldest of the university's present buildings, was designed by George Gilbert Scott. The project was not completed owing to a lack of funds, and it was Scott's son, John Oldrid, who completed the design with Bute Hall (1882) and the tower (1887). The main façade overlooks Kelvingrove Park.

In Professors' Square at the west end of the main building is the Lion and Unicorn Staircase from the Old College, as are the staircase and Pearce Lodge facing University Avenue.

The **Visitor Centre** has informative displays and interactive computers.

▶ The Hunterian Museum is opposite.

Hunterian Museum

Main building, East Quadrangle, First Floor; enter from University Avenue side. ♿🕐Tue–Sat 10am–5pm, Sun *11am–4pm.* 𝒫0141 330 4221. *www.gla.ac.uk/hunterian.*
William Hunter (1718–1783), medical practitioner, anatomist and pioneer obstetrician, was also a great collector of coins, manuscripts, paintings, minerals, and ethnographical, anatomical and zoological specimens. Hunter bequeathed all to the university and in 1807 the Hunterian Museum was opened. It now contains more than 1 million items.

Highlights include the mummy of Lady Shep-en-hor; the 300 million year old Bearsden shark; the rare and fabulous map of the world prepared for the Chinese Emperor Kangxi in 1674 the 18C painting *A Lady taking Tea* by the French artists Jean-Siméon Chardin, and the Cleopatra coin, the best example in the world of such a coin.

Hunterian Art Gallery★★ and the Mackintosh House★★★

Hillhead Street. ♿🕐Tue–Sat 10am–5pm, Sun 11am–4pm. 🚌Gallery free; *Mackintosh House £6.* 𝒫0141 330 4221.

www.hunterian.gla.ac.uk.
The 1980 building provides a permanent home for the university's art collection which is particularly noted for the Whistler works, 19C and 20C Scottish art and the Mackintosh wing. Outstanding among the Old Masters is Rembrandt's *The Entombment.*

The **Whistler Collection★★★** is an important holding covering most periods of the career of James McNeill Whistler (1834–1903). The artworks comprise: 80 oil paintings; over 100 pastels; 120 drawings and watercolours; 14 sketchbooks; 150 lithographs and 390 etchings (excluding multiple states and duplicates); and 280 etching plates.

The remaining galleries present 19C and 20C Scottish art together with some French Impressionists. Breaking from the conventions of Victorian art, William McTaggart (1835–1910) developed his own bold style with vigorous brushwork and a sensitive approach to light. He was a precursor of the late-19C group, the **Glasgow Boys** – a response to the staidness of the Edinburgh art establishment and whose common denominator was realism. Acknowledged father of the group was W McGregor; other members included Hornel, Guthrie , Henry, Walton and Lavery.

Pringle's townscapes (*Tollcross*, 1908) in delicate pastel tones herald the Scottish Colourists: *Les Eus, Le Voile Persan* by Fergusson, *Iona, Tulips and Cup* by Peploe, *The Red Chair* by Caddell and works by Hunter. The modern section includes an atmospheric canvas by Joan Eardley (*Salmon Nets and the Sea*, 1960), Philipson's *Never Mind* (1965) and Davie's *Sea Devil's Watch Tower* (1960).

Mackintosh House

This wing of the Hunterian Art Gallery is a reconstruction of the Glasgow home of Charles Rennie Mackintosh's Glasgow home. He and his wife, artist Margaret Macdonald Mackintosh, lived at 78 Southpark Avenue (originally 6 Florentine Terrace) from 1906 to 1914. The house was demolished in the early 1960s but the original fixtures were preserved and have been reassembled, complete with the contents, as an integral part of the Hunterian Art Gallery.

The domestic interiors with highly distinctive decorative schemes are good examples of Mackintosh's pioneering work in modern architecture and design. Functional, with a restraint and purity of line, painted white woodwork is relieved by decorative motifs.

▶ Continue along University Avenue and turn right into busy Byres Road, the heart of the student West End. It's also worth the detour to Ashton Lane, a cobbled street lined with small white houses and pubs frequented by students (*On the right after joining Byres Road*).

Botanic Gardens

730 Great Western Road ⚠ 🕐 *Daily:*
Gardens: *7am–dusk.* ***Glasshouses:***
Apr–Sept 10am–6pm, (winter 4.15pm).
📞 *0141 276 1614.*
www.glasgowbotanicgardens.com.
These gardens are renowned for their collection of orchids, begonias and tree ferns. The spectacular recently refurbished Kibble Palace glasshouse, which houses the tree ferns and plants from temperate areas, is a magnificent example of a Victorian iron conservatory. The Main Range glasshouse contains the tropical and economic plants. A World Rose Garden is a recent addition.

▶ Return to the Hunterian Museum, and continue east on University Avenue back to rejoin Kelvin Way, a beautiful street running through Kelvingrove Park. Continue south to cross the River Kelvin once more.

Kelvingrove Art Gallery and Museum★★★

Argyle Street. ⚠ 🕐 *Mon–Thu and Sat 10am–5pm, Fri and Sun 11am–5pm.*
🕐 *25–26 Dec and 1–2 Jan.* ✕
📞 *0141 276 9599.*
www.glasgowlife.org.uk/museums.
Officially opened in 1902, this imposing red-sandstone building in Kelvingrove Park was partly financed from the profits

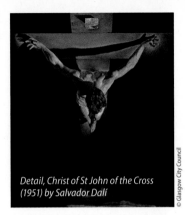

Detail, Christ of St John of the Cross (1951) by Salvador Dalí

© Glasgow City Council

of the 1888 International Exhibition on the same site.

The nucleus of the permanent collection was formed by the McLellan Bequest (1854) and ever since, prominent citizens and captains of industry have generously continued to bequeath their art treasures, creating 22 themed state-of-the-art galleries and a truly great British civic collection from art to animals, Ancient Egypt to Charles Rennie Mackintosh.

Ground Floor – The themes of Life and Expression are explored via their respective hands-on displays. Galleries on the ground floor include Looking at Art, featuring the work of the Glasgow Boys (👆 *see INTRODUCTION: Arts and Culture, Painting*). The Mackintosh and the Glasgow Style exhibition displays the work of Charles Rennie Mackintosh and his Glasgow contemporaries.

First Floor – The upper galleries are devoted to fine and decorative arts, particularly British and European paintings; from Italy, the Netherlands and France (the latter has a strong emphasis on 19C and early 20C works). The most famous painting on display is Dalí's stunning *Christ of St John of the Cross*. Scottish identity in art is also explored.

④ CLYDE WATERFRONT

This rapidly developing area just west of the town centre covers both banks of the Clyde, west of the town centre. Bridges

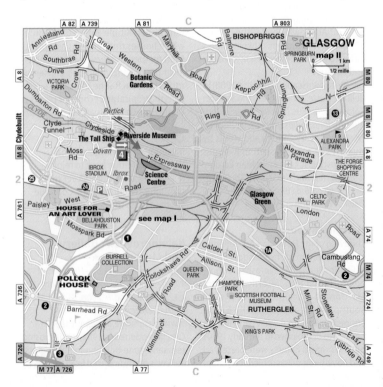

*link attractions and a promenade
for pedestrians and cyclists is under
construction.*

▷ Begin on the north bank of the
Clyde, at the foot of the elegant
arched Clyde Arc bridge and walk
towards the landmark "Armadillo".

Clyde Auditorium – SEC Armadillo

Built in 1997 by Foster & Partners, the
Clyde Auditorium is the futuristic section of the rather more prosaic SECC,
which in addition to trade fairs and
conventions hosts blockbuster concerts,
musicals and other events including the
Magners Glasgow International Comedy Festival. Resembling the middle
section of an armadillo (after which it
is nicknamed) and also called The Poor
Man's Sydney Opera House, the inspiration for the designer was in fact the ship
hulls with which the Clyde is historically
inextricably linked.

▷ Head west on the north bank
of the river.

👥 The Riverside Museum★★

100 Pointhouse Place.

♿ 🕐 *Mon–Thu and Sat 10am–5pm, Fri
and Sun 11am–5pm.* 🕐 *25–26 Dec and
1–2 Jan.* ✕ ♿ *No charge, but donations
welcomed.* ☎ *0141 287 2720.
www.glasgowlife.org.uk/museums.*

The Riverside Museum, Scotland's
national Museum of Transport and
Travel is a new iconic landmark project
on the banks of the River Clyde, at the
heart of the new **Glasgow Harbour
development**. It opened in spring
2011 and incorporates the much-loved
Museum of Transport, as well as the
Clyde Maritime Trust with its Tall Ship
Glenlee (🕐 *see below*) Both the building
and its displays – vehicles cling precari-
ously to walls and ceilings – have a real
"wow" factor. The museum's brief is also
much more than just antique vehicles.
There is an atmospheric re-created
street from 1895–1930 (including an
Edwardian photography studio, a 1930s
Italian cafe and a 1960s garage), plus

additional areas depicting shops from
the 1930s, right through to the 1980s,
giving a real insight into Glasgow's distant and more recent past. You can even
access the shops and subways.

Trams and Trolley Buses – Vintage
tramcars were an integral part of Glasgow's street scene from 1872 to 1962.
Arranged in chronological order they
include: No. 543, the horse-drawn one,
No. 1089, the 1926 single-deck car, and
No. 1392 of the type nicknamed the
Cunarder because of its comfort, the
last tram ever built in the UK (1952).
This extremely popular collection was
the nucleus around which the museum
was established. The trolley bus is an
example from the city fleet which operated from 1949 to 1967.

Railway Locomotives – Most of the
items on display are from the former
Scottish railway companies. There is
also a fascinating model railway, a spell
binder for all ages.

Scottish-Built Cars★★★ are the thing
here, with examples from manufactur-
ers such as Argyll, Albion and Arrol-
Johnston, who were all well to the fore
in the car industry of the early 20C.
The great traditions of Scottish car
manufacturing are represented here by
the 1902 Argyll Light Car, the 1906 Arrol-
Johnston TT Model 18, fast and powerful
for its time, and the Argyll Voiturette.
The 1963 Hillman Imp, IMP 1 was the
first Scottish-built car after a lapse of
30 years.

Horse-Drawn Vehicles – The varied
examples of horse-drawn vehicles
include the splendid Mail Coach (c.1840)
and the two Romany caravans, which
are brightly painted with traditional
decoration.

Bicycles and Motorcycles – Follow
the development of the bicycle from
the replica of MacMillan's 1839 bicycle
(on the wall) through boneshakers,
sociables and tricycles to the gleaming
lightweight road racers and fun cycles
of today.
The motorcycle section has early examples of British-designed machines from
the time when British makers dominated
the industry (Zenith, BSA, Triumph, AJS,

Beardmore-Precision, Norton, HRD/Vincent and Douglas).

Ship Models★★★ – This is a beautiful collection that includes the products of the Scottish shipyards through the ages, and in particular those of the Clyde. Side by side, visitors can view perfect models of sailing ships (the fully rigged *Cutty Sark*), Clyde River Steamers (*Comet*, *Columba* and other well-loved excursion steamers), cross-Channel steamers which were often Denny products, ocean-going passenger liners (*The Queens*), warships (HMS *Hood*), and yachts including Czar Alexander II's circular and unsinkable model.

The Tall Ship *Glenlee*

&⏷Mar–Oct 10am–5pm; Nov–Feb 10am–4pm. ≋No charge. ℘0141 357 3699. http://thetallship.com.
The *Glenlee* first took to the water as a bulk cargo carrier in 1896. She circumnavigated the globe four times and today is one of only five Clyde-built sailing ships that remain afloat in the world.

♟ Science Centre★

50 Pacific Quay. &⏷Apr–early Nov daily 10am–5pm; rest of year Wed–Fri 10am–3pm, Sat–Sun 10am–5pm). ≋Science Centre £11.50 (child 3–15, £9.50); Planetarium only £5.50. Additional charges: IMAX £2.50; planetarium £3; Glasgow Tower £3.50. ✕ ℘0141 420 5000. www.glasgowsciencecentre.org.
Directly across the water from the SEC (linked by the Clyde Arc footbridge) and reflecting the same style of architecture (designed 2001 by BDP), this is another bold step in the renovation of Glasgow's docklands.
The heart of GSC is the Science Mall housed in a gleaming titanium crescent. This is home to three floors with hundreds of interactive exhibits, the **Climate Change Theatre** and a **planetarium**, a spectacular state-of-the-art fulldome digital projection system. Two other important features are Scotland's only **IMAX cinema** and the 127m high **Glasgow Tower**, the tallest tower in the world capable of rotating 360 degrees from the ground up to the top.

Pollok House and Country Park★

3mi/5km southwest by the M77. &⏷Daily 10am–5pm. ⏷25–26 Dec and 1–2 Jan. ≋£7.50. ✕℗ ℘0141 616 6410. www.nts.org.uk.
The highlight of this 18C mansion (1752), set in spacious parkland, now a country park, is a superb collection of paintings acquired by the connoisseur and collector Sir William Stirling Maxwell (1818–1878), an authority on the Spanish School of painting. Highlights include works by El Greco, Murillo, and Goya, plus antique furniture, porcelain, silver and glassware.
Pollok House is where the National Trust for Scotland began, back in 1931. The discussions for the founding of the Trust took place inside Pollok's cedar-panelled smoking room.
The house interiors are imbued with the essence of country house living in the 1930s, during the twilight of the great era of stately homes in Britain. The ornate state rooms are lavishly decorated and prove to be a perfect backdrop for the Maxwell family's collection of fine art. The linrary contains no fewer than 7 000 books.
Pollok House also shows what life was like for the domestic staff who kept the house running: 48 servants to provide for just 3 family members!

EXCURSION
House for an Art Lover

10 Dumbeck Road, Bellahouston Park. &⏷Daily 10am–5pm (times for the Mackintoch exhibition vary; check website for details. ≋£6. ✕ ℘0141 353 4770. www.houseforanartlover.co.uk.
Set in the grounds of Bellahouston Park, this striking Charles Rennie Mackintosh villa is based on the architect's entry in a 1901 German design competition. The city council's bold project of implementing the design was completed in 1996 and the building is used by the Glasgow School of Art's postgraduate study centre. The house combines art gallery and exhibition space, events venue, café, and multipurpose artists studios.

Cathedral★★★

This majestic church in the heart of the city is the only medieval cathedral on the Scottish mainland to have survived the Protestant Reformation of 1560 virtually intact.

A BIT OF HISTORY

This is the fourth church on the site beside the Molendinar Burn, where St Mungo built his original wooden church in the 7C. The present building was consecrated in 1197, but the main part of the cathedral wasn't built until the 13C and 14C.

Construction progressed from the east end to the nave, and it was the 15C before the building took on its final appearance with the reconstruction of the chapter house and addition of the Blacader Aisle, central tower and stone spire, and the now demolished west front towers. Unusual features of the plan are the non-projecting transepts and two-storeyed east end.

Many of the cathedral's stained-glass windows are modern – note *The Creation* which fills the west window of the nave. This work is by Francis Spear and was installed in 1958. More recently, John K Clark was commissioned for *The Millenium Window*, which can be seen on the north wall of the nave. The theme of "growth" underpins this stunning work.

○ **Location:** Castle Street.
▯ **Info:** ✆0141 552 8198; www.glasgowcathedral.org.uk.
○ Apr–Sept Mon–Sat 9.30am– 5pm, Sun 1–4.30pm; Oct–Mar Mon–Sat 10am–3.30pm, Sun 1–3.30pm.

VISIT

The imposing Gothic building we see today stands hemmed in by the Royal Infirmary with the Necropolis behind. The best **view**★ of the cathedral as a whole is from John Knox's stance high up in the Necropolis where the verticality of the composition is best appreciated.

Nave

Stylistically this is later than the choir, and the elevation with its richly moulded and pointed arches, ever more numerous at each level, rises to the timber roof, which is medieval in design. The 15C stone screen or pulpitum, unique in Scotland, marks the change in level from nave to choir. The figures at the top of the screen depict the seven deadly sins; the human figures on the front of the altar platforms may represent 11 disciples.

Glasgow cathedral

© Crown Copyright HES.

Choir

The choir and the lower church, both dating from the mid-13C, are of the finest First Pointed style. The triple lancets of the clerestory are echoed in the design of the east window which depicts the Four Evangelists. Four chapels open out of the ambulatory beyond. From the northernmost chapel a door leads through to the upper chapter room, reconstructed in the 15C. It was there that the medieval university held its classes.

Lower Church

Access via stairs to north of the pulpitum. Here is another Gothic glory where light and shade play effectively amid a multitude of piers and pointed arches. This lower area was conceived to enshrine the tomb of St Mungo, Glasgow's patron saint. A cordoned-off area marks the site. The central panel of the St Kentigern Tapestry (1979) represents the Church and combines the symbols of St Mungo. On the south panel are the ring and salmon of the St Mungo legend. The Chapel of the Blessed Virgin is the area immediately to the east, distinguished by its elaborate net vaulting with intricately carved bosses.

The mid-13C lower chapter room was remodelled at the time of Bishop William Lauder (1408–25). The bishop's arms figure on the canopy. The 15C ribbed vaulting sports heraldic roof bosses including the arms of James I.

Blacader Aisle

Projecting from the south transept, this last architectural addition to the church, built around 1500, was designed as a two-storey extension by Glasgow's first Archbishop, Robert Blacader. Only the existing or lower part was finished. The Late Gothic style with its fully developed ribbed vaulting and brightly painted bosses against a white ceiling is striking. Look for the famous boss of a skull with worms and also for the carved boss (facing the entrance) recalling the legend of the hermit Fergus, who was found near to death by St Mungo. His body was placed on a cart yoked to two bulls with the intention of burying the hermit where they stopped. Tradition has it that this chapel marks the site.

Clyde Estuary★★

Once the home of Glasgow's world-famous shipbuilding yards, the banks of the Clyde near to the city are now largely derelict. The north bank of the Firth of Clyde however, is altogether more attractive, with its hinterland of Argyll countryside.

🚗 DRIVING TOUR

🚗 NORTH BANK AND COWAL PENINSULA

▷ Leave Glasgow on the A82.

Titan Clydebank
Garth Drive, Queens Quays, Clydebank.

♿🕐*Closed until 2020; check website for updates.* ✆*07538 842596. www.titanclydebank.com.*
An "A" listed giant cantilever Titan Crane – the oldest of its kind in the world – has a lift to take visitors up to the jib platform 46m off the ground. Here you can see the workings of the Titan wheelhouse and from the jib platform take in the stunning views over the River Clyde and the surrounding countryside.

▷ At Dumbarton, turn left onto the A814, in the direction of Helensburgh.

Dumbarton Castle
🕐*Apr–Sept daily 9.30am–5.30pm; Oct–Mar Sat–Wed 10am– 4pm.* 🕐*25–26 Dec and 1–2 Jan.* 💷*£6.* ✆*01389 732 167. www.historicenvironment.scot.*
This ruined castle enjoys a fine strategic **site★** perched on the basaltic plug

of Dumbarton Rock (73m), once the capital of the independent Kingdom of Strathclyde. The remaining fortifications are mainly 18C. Steps (*278 from the Governor's House*) lead up to the viewing-table on White Tower summit and then to the Magazine on the second summit (*an additional 81 steps*).

From the former viewpoint there is a vast panorama of the Clyde estuary and surrounding area.

◗ Continue northwest on the A814.

Hill House, Helensburgh★
Upper Colquhoun St.
Daily 10am– 5pm. 23 Dec–2 Jan.
£12.50. ✗ 01436 673 900.
www.nts.org.uk.
On a hillside overlooking the Clyde stands what is considered to be the best example of Mackintosh's domestic architecture. The house was built in 1902–04 as a family home for the Glasgow publisher Walter W Blackie. It was designed as a whole by Mackintosh down to the tiniest detail.

Every space, corridor, hall, bed or seating alcove was proportioned in itself as well as being part of a harmonious whole. Predominantly white or dark surfaces were highlighted by inset coloured glass, gesso plaster panels, delicate light fittings or stencilled patterns.

◗ Beyond Helensburgh remain on the A814, along the eastern shores of Gare Loch to Garelochhead, and there continue north, now along the shores of Loch Long, eventually to reach Arrochar.

Arrochar and Argyll Forest Park
Arrochar village is a popular climbing centre. The A83 passes through the picturesque landscapes of the Argyll Forest Park, and over the famous Rest and Be Thankful pass, which crosses the bounary into the Argyll and Bute region.

◗ Continue along the A83, through Glen Kinglas to Cairndow.

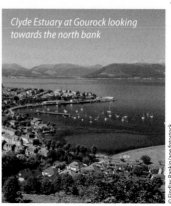

Clyde Estuary at Gourock looking towards the north bank

© Findlay Rankin/age fotostock

Ardkinglas Woodland Gardens
Cairndow. Daily dawn to dusk.
£5. 01499 600 261.
www.ardkinglas.com.
These gardens cover 10ha of hillside lying in a naturally sheltered pocket near the mouth of the River Kinglas, surrounded by wild Highland scenery. They are famous for their mature Champion trees (including the mightiest conifer in Europe) and an exceptional collection of rhododendron.

◗ From Cairndow return along the A83 for a short distance, then turn on to the A815 following this down the shores of loch Eck to the popular holiday town of Dunoon, which sees the Cowal Highland Gathering every August.

The Clyde Estuary by boat

In the 19C a succession of paddle steamers sailed the Clyde taking Glaswegians "Doon the watter" for the day. *The Waverley*, the last of these famous Clyde paddle steamers, still plies her home waters in the high season (*Not in service during 2019/early 2020; check website for updates. 0141 243 2224; www.waverleyexcursions. co.uk*) with departures from Glasgow, Helensburgh, Dunoon, Rothesay, Largs, Millport and Ayr.

ADDRESSES

🛏 STAY

Adelaides Guest House – *209 Bath Street.* ℘*0141 248 4970. 8 rooms.* Comfortable modern rooms set in a late-19C fully renovated former Baptist church. Quiet and friendly.

Fraser Suites – *1–19 Albion Street.* ℘*0141 553 4288. http://glasgow.frasers hospitality.com/en. 98 rooms.* Set in an elegantly restored historic building in the Merchant City, these hotel apartment-style suites offer large rooms, each with a corner kitchen.

Apex City of Glasgow Hotel – *110 Bath Street. www.apexhotels.co.uk.* ℘*0141 375 3333. 103 rooms.* This boutique-style hotel is in the heart of Glasgow's vibrant city centre – theatres and shops are only a short stroll away. The spacious rooms all feature plasma-screen satellite TV, a power shower and comfortable beds.

Abode – *129 Bath Street.* ℘*0141 221 6789. www.abodeglasgow.co.uk. 59 rooms.* Near Mackintosh's School of Art, this early-20C building is decorated with a daring modern palette, making it one of the most distinctive hotels in the city.

Malmaison – *278 West George Street.* ℘*0141 378 0384. www.malmaison-glasgow.com. 72 rooms and suites.* Former Greek Orthodox church with ultra-stylish rooms in bold patterns and colours. French themed **brasserie**.

🍴 EAT

Dhabba – *44 Candleriggs.* ℘*0141 553 1249. www.thedhabba.com.* In the heart of the Merchant City, this large, modern restaurant boasts bold colours and huge wall photos. Concentrates on authentic, accomplished North Indian cooking.

Willow Tea Rooms – *97 Buchanan Street.* ℘*0141 204 5242. www.willowtea-rooms.co.uk.* Inspired by the works of Charles Rennie Mackintosh, the Willow Tea Rooms is the place to go, modelled on Kate Cranston's Ingram Street Tea Rooms from the early 1900s.

Cafe Gandolfi – *64 Albion Street.* ℘*0141 552 6813. www.cafegandolfi.com.* Established in 1979 and famed for its interior Glasgow School of Art furnishings, this relaxed café's easy-going professionalism attracts locals and visitors who come for Scottish cuisine at affordable prices.

The Buttery – *652–654 Argyle Street.* ℘*0141 221 8188. www. twofatladiesrestaurant.com/buttery.* This comfortable Glasgow institution, the oldest restaurant in town, specialises in seafood, but also has a vegetarian menu.

Urban Bar and Brasserie – *23-25 St Vincent Place.* ℘*0141 248 5636. www. urbanbrasserie.co.uk.* Imposing 19C building in the heart of the city centre. Stylish, modern interior with individual booths and illuminated glass ceiling. Modern English cooking, with live piano at weekends.

Gamba – *225a West George Street.* ℘*0141 572 0899. www.gamba.co.uk.* This compact, bright basement with a cosy bar is the place to enjoy an enterprising range of seafood specials with well-priced lunches.

La Lanterna West End – *447 Great Western Road. Closed Sun.* ℘*0141 334 0686. http://lalanternawestend.co.uk.* One of the finest Italian restaurants to open in Glasgow. Authentic Italian cuisine is prepared using only the best seasonal and market produce.

Rogano – *11 Exchange Place.* ℘*0141 248 4055. www.roganoglasgow.com.* The Art Nouveau decor at this stylish seafood restaurant (oysters a speciality), opposite the Gallery of Modern Art, recalls the days of the great ocean liners. **Café Rogano**, in the basement, is cheaper and more casual.

SHOPPING

The glass-roofed **Princes Street** and **Buchanan shopping centres** in Buchanan Street display the latest fashions and Scottish items. **The Italian Centre** on the corner of John and Ingram Streets has on sale the finest Italian fashion and also offers bars, brasseries, restaurants and cafés in a beautiful decor. **The Scottish Craft Centre** in Princes Square displays fine items by Scottish craftsmen. **The Barras**, a large indoor and outdoor market, is the place to visit not only for a bargain but also for the spectacle.

These two counties border Glasgow to the south and west. Renfrewshire is most famous for its Paisley pattern, while South Lanarkshire is not only Glasgow's playground, but has also been put on the culture vulture's road map by its wonderfully restored 18C cotton mill village, New Lanark model village, a UNESCO World Heritage Site. South Lanark is also easily accessible from Edinburgh.

South Lanarkshire

By contrast to Glasgow (and North Lanarkshire), South Lanarkshire was never industrialised and the area is liberally dotted with scenic walks and nature trails amid some of the finest scenery in Lowland Scotland. The jewel in South Lanarkshire's historical crown is New Lanark, an 18C paradigm of social reform. There are excellent riverside walks upstream, including the scenic Falls of Clyde.

Bothwell Castle is Scotland's finest 13C fortification, while Hamilton's Chatelherault Country Park features the magnificent early 18C hunting lodge of the Dukes of Hamilton and is criss-crossed with miles of nature trails leading through 200ha of woods and the Avon River Gorge.

The old market town of Biggar is known as Scotland's Museum Town, boasting as it does no fewer than seven quirky museums.

From just beyond Hamilton, the Clyde Valley Tourist Route follows the meandering River Clyde towards Lanark, passing the many garden centres and pick-your-own orchards that are a feature of this fertile area.

Highlights

1 A tea and cake in bygone Paisley at **Sma' Shot Cottages** (p206)

2 **Bothwell Castle**, Scotland's finest 13C fort (p207)

3 Strolling **Chatelherault Park** (p209)

4 Taking a trip back to the 18C at **New Lanark Village** (p210)

5 Biggar's quirky **museums** (p211–212)

Renfrewshire

Paisley has long been the most important town in the county, first as a religious centre and then as a textile manufacturer of world importance. The medieval abbey, originally built in the 12C, experienced a turbulent and dramatic history but survives today as one of the few abbeys still in regular use as a place of worship.

In the Shawl Gallery at the Paisley Museum and Art Gallery, you can trace the growth and development of the famous Paisley pattern and shawls, showing the familiar pine cone (or teardrop) pattern from its humble beginnings to elaborate later incarnations.

Chatelherault Country Park

© BMPix/iStockphoto.com

Paisley

This industrial town, with its many fine examples of Edwardian and Victorian architecture, has long been famed for its Paisley shawls and thread production. The White Cart Water, a tributary of the River Clyde, runs through the town centre.

SIGHTS
Paisley Abbey
Mon–Sat 10am–3.30pm. ✖ *0141 889 7654. www.paisleyabbey.org.uk.*
Right in the heart of Paisley, unencumbered by encroaching buildings, the medieval abbey is an impressive sight. Founded in 1163, its monastery was once one of the richest and most powerful in Scotland. The present-day church is mostly 15C with a 13C west front doorway. The long choir, a 19C and 20C restoration, has Robert Lorimer furnishings. Here also is the tomb of Marjory Bruce the daughter of King Robert the Bruce. Tradition has it that she fell from her horse near Paisley Abbey and died.

Paisley Museum and Art Gallery
High Street. *Closed for refurbishment until 2022.* *0300 300 1210. www. renfrewshireleisure.com/museums.*
This 19C building houses a series of well-displayed collections, notably its **Paisley Shawl Section★** (*see Box*). The art gallery has a number of works by the Scottish School.

Info: *07947 894 948; www.paisley.org.uk.*
Location: Paisley is 9.5mi/ 15km W of Glasgow via the M8.

Coats Observatory
Closed for refurbishment until 2022. *0300 300 1210. www. renfrewshireleisure.com/museums.*
Built in 1883 this fine small observatory opens its array of telescopes to the public; displays include astronomy, meteorology and space flight.

Sma' Shot Cottages
Apr–Sept Wed and Sat noon–4pm, Fri 1–5pm. ✖ *0141 889 1708. www.smashotcottages.co.uk.*
These restored 18C and 19C weavers' cottages evoke bygone Paisley with photographs and artefacts. One of them houses a cosy tearoom.

EXCURSION
Kilbarchan Weaver's Cottage
5mi/8km west off the A737.
Apr–Sept Fri–Tue 1–5pm. *£7.50. *01505 705 588. www.nts.org.uk.*
This 18C weaver's cottage displays locally woven work including tartan. Handlooms in the basement are used for demonstrations.

Paisley Shawls

It was in 1805 that an Edinburgh manufacturer introduced the art of imitation Kashmir shawls to Paisley, where it prospered, initially as a cottage industry. Such was the success that all patterned shawls with the traditional "pine" or teardrop motif came to be known as Paisley shawls. With the introduction of the Jacquard loom in the 1820s the industry became more factory based, and intricate overall patterns with as many as 10 colours were popular. Printed shawls were introduced in the 1840s and were followed in the 1860s by the reversible shawl which never gained any real popularity.

The local museum has an excellent collection, demonstrating all the beauty and intricacy of these multicoloured, fine garments which were appreciated equally for their warmth, lightness and softness.

Clyde Valley

The Clyde may be better known for its utilitarian Glasgow shipbuilding heritage, but before this great river arrives in the city it forms the Clyde valley, a beautiful green hilly ribbon where both Glaswegians and other visitors can escape the city bustle.

🚗 DRIVING TOUR

▶ From central Glasgow go south to join the M74, and exit at J3a onto the A721 to Uddington on the B7071. Then follow signs for Bothwell Castle.

Bothwell Castle★

Uddingston, off the B7071, 8 mi/13km south east of Glasgow. ⓘ*Daily Apr–Sept 9.30am–5.30pm; Oct–Mar Sat–Wed 9.30am–5.30pm.* ⓢ*£5.* ℰ*01698 816 894. www.historicenvironment.scot.*
The ruins of this outstanding fortress – once Scotland's largest and finest 13C castle – remain impressive in a commanding site above the Clyde valley.
In the Wars of Independence it fell into English hands in 1301 and, after being retaken in 1314 after Bannockburn, it was dismantled. The castle was repaired during a second period of English occupation when Edward III made it his headquarters in 1336. By 1367 the Scots were

Info: Horsemarket, Ladyacre Road, Lanark; ℰ01555 661 661; 155 High Street, Biggar; ℰ01899 221 066; www.visitlanarkshire.com.

Kids: Biggar Puppet Theatre, Biggar Gasworks Museum.

again in command and Bothwell was again dismantled. The castle lay in ruin until it passed by marriage to Archibald the Grim, the 3rd Earl of Douglas, in 1362 and he made this his chief residence. The late 14C and early 15C saw additions.
Your first impression of this red sandstone ruin, all towers and curtain walls, will be one of sheer size, yet only part of the original 13C plan was executed. Take the stairs in the northeast tower to reach the courtyard enclosure. At the far end, the oldest and most impressive part, the 13C circular keep or donjon, designed to serve as the last bastion of defence, shows "masterly design and stonework". The keep itself is protected by a moat on the courtyard side, with the drawbridge giving access to the doorway, sheltering behind a beak construction. Walled up following partial dismantling, three storeys and a

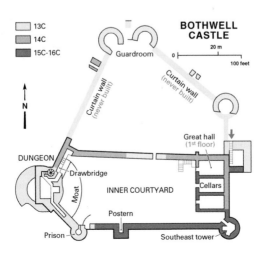

BOTHWELL CASTLE

- 13C
- 14C
- 15C-16C

Guardroom
Curtain wall (never built)
Curtain wall (never built)
Great hall (1st floor)
DUNGEON
Drawbridge
Moat
INNER COURTYARD
Cellars
Postern
Prison
Southeast tower

Bothwell castle

© BMPix/iStockphoto.com

fighting level rise above the basement. The tower communicates with the 13C prison tower and postern in the south curtain wall. In the southeast corner, the early-15C chapel, marked at first floor level by two pointed windows, communicates with the other great four storey tower, also 15C. Beyond, against the east curtain wall is the great hall with its succession of elegant windows.

▷ Take local roads to Bothwell village.

Bothwell

The town grew up in the shadow of its great castle at an important bridging point on the Clyde. Bothwell developed rapidly in the 19C when it was favoured by wealthy Glasgow merchants. The choir of the parish church belongs to the collegiate church founded in 1398. A fine example of the Decorated Gothic style, it has a unique stone slab roof.

A memorial beside Bothwell Bridge commemorates the battle of 1679 when the Covenanters suffered their worst defeat. 400 were killed and 1 200 taken prisoner. Most were imprisoned for several months in inhumane conditions in Greyfriars churchyard, Edinburgh, where many died from exposure and starvation.

▷ Leave Bothwell on local roads to join the A725/A724 to Blantyre.

Blantyre

David Livingstone Centre

1mi/1.6km from Main Street via Blantyre Mill Road and a footbridge over the Clyde. ♿ ⏱ *Sat–Sun noon–3pm.* ⊚ *£3.50.* 🅿 ☏ *01698 821 424.*
www.david-livingstone-trust.org.

The late-18C mill tenement, Shuttle Row, now a **David Livingstone Museum★**, vividly presents the missionary-cum-explorer, his life and achievements. Livingstone (1813–1873) was born in one of these single-room family homes which in their time were considered to be model accommodation. Like his father he worked in the local cotton mill. Young David also attended local evening classes and then medical classes at Anderson's Institution, Glasgow.

A man of strong religious beliefs, he set out as a medical missionary but soon embarked on the travels which were to make his name as an explorer. Pilkington Jackson's woodcarving, *The Last Journey*, is a moving tribute to both Livingstone and his faithful African followers.

▷ Return along the A724, and southeast to Hamilton.

Hamilton

Seat of the powerful Hamilton family (the first Dukes of Scotland), the town became a royal burgh in the 15C, then grew in the late 18C and 19C as an industrial centre thanks to the discovery and exploitation of local coal deposits.

Hamilton Low Parks Museum

129 Muir St. ♿🕐*Mon–Sat 10am–5pm, Sun noon–5pm.* 📞*01698 452 382. www.sllccameronians.co.uk.*

This former coaching inn retains its 18C banqueting hall and houses collections on local history, including transport and the 17C lace industry.

Low Park is also home to the **Cameronian (Scottish Rifles) Regimental Museum** celebrating an almost 300 years' history of the country's elite rifle regiment (disbanded in 1968). It occupies the old armoury of the Dukes of Hamilton.

In a separate adjacent building, on the site of the old Hamilton Palace (demolished in 1927 following the collapse of mine workings beneath), is the **Hamilton Mausoleum** *(details as for the museum)*. Alexander, 10th Duke of Hamilton (1767–1852), known as El Magnifico, ordered this imposing building in which he lies in an Egyptian sarcophagus. The mausoleum is renowned for its 15 second echo!

▶ Leave Hamilton via the A72, follow-ing the Clyde Valley Tourist Route signs.

Chatelherault Country Park

🕐*Visitor centre: daily 10am–5pm; Lodge House: Sun–Thu 10am–4.30pm.* 🕐*1–2 Jan and 25–26 Dec.* ✖ 📞*01698 426 213. www.slleisureandculture.co.uk.*

Pronounced "shat-le-row" this former hunting lodge of the Dukes of Hamilton is an outlying remnant of the old Hamilton Palace estate which covered many acres. The building has been renovated and its beautiful ceilings – by Thomas Clayton (c.1710–60), who also worked on Blair Castle, Hopetoun House and Holyrood House – have been restored to their original appearance.

In addition to housing the kennels (for the hunting dogs), the lodge also held an armoury, a pantry and an abbatoir for fresh meat for the kitchen. It is now the visitor centre (including a gift shop and café) for the Chatelherault Country Park, which covers part of the former palace estate.

The park stands at the edge of the densely wooded Avon Gorge, which boasts a history of unbroken wooded cover dating back at least 400 years. In spring and early summer it holds a wonderful array of woodland flowers. (*Pick up a Country Park Trails leaflet.*)

The ruins of 16C Cadzow Castle, the previous residence of the Hamiltons, stand on the other side of the Avon Gorge. Around the castle graze the very rare ancient breed of Cadzow Cattle with white coats and distinctive black muzzles, ears, feet and horn tips.

▶ Continue on the A72. At Crossford, follow the signs for Craignethan Castle.

Craignethan Castle

🕐*Apr–Sept 9.30am–5.30pm.* 💳*£5.* 📞*01555 860 364. www.historicenvironment.scot.*

Dating to around 1530, Craignethan is an important early artillery fortification with an exceptional residential tower and fine setting. The oldest part is the tower house built by James Hamilton of Finnart. The castle's defences include a rare caponier (a defence structure allowing the defenders to fire freely at a low angle on besieging forces) and a stone vaulted artillery chamber, also unusual in Britain.

▶ Return to the A72 and follow it to Lanark.

Lanark

Lanark is 31mi/50km southeast of Glasgow via the M74. New Lanark is 1.2mi/2km south of Lanark.

This busy market town has one of the biggest livestock markets in Scotland. Historically it boasts William Wallace associations and in sport possibly the oldest horse-racing trophy in the world, the Silver Bell. By far its biggest visitor attraction however, is the new model village of New Lanark.

New Lanark★★

Down on the floor of the deep gorge of the River Clyde, New Lanark is a fine example of an 18C planned industrial village. The Lanimer Festival *(June)* shouldn't be missed, with the traditional riding of the marches and the unusual "Whuppity Scourie" ceremony *(1 March)* (see Calendar of Events). Today, New Lanark is recognised as a World Heritage Site for its outstanding universal value.

Village

The best approach is on foot from the car park. Stop on the way down at the viewpoint with its orientation table. Visitor centre: ◷Daily Apr–Oct 10am–5pm; Nov–Mar 10am–4pm. ◖Guided tours daily 10.30am–4pm. £13.95. ℘01555 661 345. www.newlanark.org.

The centrepiece, New Buildings (1798), pinpointed by the bell tower, is prolonged to the right by the Nursery Buildings (1809) to house the pauper apprentices who worked and usually lived in the mills, and then the cooperative store (1810) – with an exhibition about Owen's original store and a period-style shop. The bow-ended counting house terminates a line of restored tenements which took its name, Caithness Row, from the storm-bound Highlanders on their way to America who were accommodated and subsequently settled here.

At the other end of the village, beyond Dale and Owen's houses, is more tenement housing, while between the river and the lade stands the massive mill, divided into units.

The Visitor Centre is home to working textile machines and the entertaining New Millennium Experience ride where visitors travel in time. There is also an interactive gallery of light, sound and colour *(Entry to the Interactive Gallery is £3.25 per child and valid only on date of purchase)*. The building which was Robert Owen's School for Children now houses Annie McLeod's Story, where the ghost of a mill-girl appears on stage. A Millworker's House shows living conditions of the 1820s and 1930s.

The Development of New Lanark

When the Glasgow tobacco trade collapsed owing to the American War of Independence (1776–83) cotton manufacturing was quick to take its place, exploiting a workforce skilled in linen making.

In 1783, a Glasgow manufacturer and banker, **David Dale** (1736–1806), brought Richard Arkwright, inventor of the spinning power frame, to the area to prospect suitable sites for a new factory. The present site was chosen and the smallest of the Falls of Clyde harnessed to provide water power for the mills. Building started in 1785 and by 1799 the four mills and associated housing comprised Scotland's largest cotton mill supporting a village population of over 2,000.

In 1800, Dale sold the mills to his future son-in-law, Robert Owen (1771–1858), a social reformer, who took over as managing partner and was to remain so for 25 years. The mills were a commercial success enabling Owen to put a series of social experiments into practice. He created the Nursery Buildings, the Institute for the Formation of Character, the village store and school. In an age of increasing industrialisation Owenism was widely acclaimed but was eventually eclipsed by government and employer resistance.

Cotton continued to be manufactured here until 1968. A major restoration programme followed; in 1986 the village was nominated a World Heritage Site and today New Lanark is one of the country's most popular visitor attractions.

New Lanark

© Mark Ferguson/Fotolibra

Mill No. 3 is the most handsome building and the only one to have been rebuilt by Owen, in 1826. Mill No. 1 was fully reconstructed in 1995 and has been converted recently into a hotel. The engine house gives access to a glass bridge – to the pattern of the original rope-race – which leads to mill No. 3.

Mill No. 2 is home to the Edinburgh Woollen Mill and on the very top of the building is a Roof Garden where a viewing platform gives a bird's-eye view of the village, woodland and Falls of Clyde.

◗ The riverside path leads upstream to the gorge section of the Clyde.

🐾 Falls of Clyde

The Old Mill Dyeworks, by the river, now serve as the **Falls of Clyde Visitor Centre** *with an audiovisual show and displays on the wildlife.* ♿🕐*Visitor centre: daily 10am–4pm.* 🕐*25–26 Dec and 1–2 Jan.* ☎*01555 665 262. https://scottishwildlifetrust.org.uk.*
This stretch of river boasts four spectacular falls – now used for hydro-electricity – and was once one of Scotland's most visited beauty spots, painted by Turner and described by Wordsworth, Coleridge and Scott. A viewpoint beyond Bonnington Power Station provides an excellent view of the highest falls, Corra Linn where the drop is 18m. These are spectacular on days when the water is turned on and thunders over the rocky lips down to a boiling mass below with a pall of vapour hanging above.

◗ Leave Lanark heading east via the roundabout beyond the railway station, and join the A73. Then take the A72.

Biggar★

30mi/48km south of Edinburgh.
This small, attractive market centre features a number of quirky museums around its attractive main street.

Biggar and Upper Clydesdale Museum★

156 High Street. ♿🕐*Apr–mid-Dec Tue–Sat 10am–5pm, Sun 1–5pm; Jan–Mar Sat 10am–5pm, Sun 1–5pm.* 👝*£5.* ☎*01899 221 050. www.biggarmuseumtrust.co.uk.*
Laid out as a shop-lined street, the museum presents an authentic record of local life a century ago. This entertaining presentation of various commercial premises passes from schoolroom to bank, ironmonger's to bootmaker's, photographer's studio and chemist's shop.
The museum now also houses the collections formerly housed in the Greenhill Covenanters' House.

Biggar Gasworks Museum

© Crown Copyright HES.

👥 **Biggar Puppet Theatre**
♿🕐*Most of the year, see website for performance times and admission charges.* ✆*01899 220 631.* ✉ *Booking essential. www.purvespuppets.com.*
The old coach house of a Victorian mansion has magically metamorphosed into an enchanting puppet theatre with Punch and Judy caryatids and a star-spangled ceiling. There are shows designed to appeal to all ages, while the history of puppetry is told in the little Puppet Museum.

👥 **Biggar Gasworks Museum**
🕐*Daily Apr–Sept Sat–Sun 1–5pm.* 👓*£5 (child 5–15, £3).* ✆*01899 221 070. www.historicenvironment.scot.*
This unusual industrial heritage site is typical of many small-town coal-gas works, common before the advent of natural gas. Today it is the only one surviving in Scotland. The oldest part of the works dates from 1839; it ceased supplying gas in 1973.

▶ Take the B7016 for 7mi/13km.

Broughton
Broughton is a tidy and colourful village with well-tended gardens, the **Beechgrove Garden** (🕐*all reasonable hours,* 👓*"honesty box"; www.beechgrove.co.uk*) being an example.

▶ To return to Glasgow go back to Biggar, take the A702 towards Abington then join the M74. Douglas is signposted off the motorway.

Douglas
The winding streets and alleyways maintain the pattern of the medieval village. The oldest structure here is **St Bride's church** (🕐*key available at No. 2 Clyde Rd. behind the hotel: Apr–Sept 9.30am–5.30pm; Oct–Mar Sat–Wed 10am–4pm; ✆01555 851 657; www.historicenvironment.scot*). The choir and south side of the nave is all that remains of the late-14C parish church. The choir contains three canopied monuments to the Douglas family, who during the 14C and 15C were just as powerful as the ruling Stuarts. These include the tomb of "Good Sir James" who was killed on Crusade while carrying the heart of Robert the Bruce.

Also buried here, beneath a pointed arch, is the 2nd Duke of Touraine and Marshal of France, recalling the "Auld Alliance" that Scotland and France have long held.

The cemetery offers a beautiful view across the River Douglas where once stood the castle which was the ancestral seat of the Douglas family. All that remains now are the ruins of a 17C tower, known as "Castle Dangerous", after the Walter Scott novel which took Douglas Castle as its inspiration. It was demolished in 1938 as a result of coal mining in the park causing subsidence.

ADDRESSES

🏨 **STAY**

⬤🛏️🛏️ **New Lanark Mill Hotel** – *New Lanark Mills.* ✆*01555 667 200. https://newlanarkhotel.co.uk. 38 rooms.* The hotel is part of the UNESCO World Heritage Site – the rooms and the rooftop garden both offer stunning views of the river and the surrounding Conservation Area. The hotel has spacious en suite rooms, a restaurant, bar and swimming pool.

Central Scotland

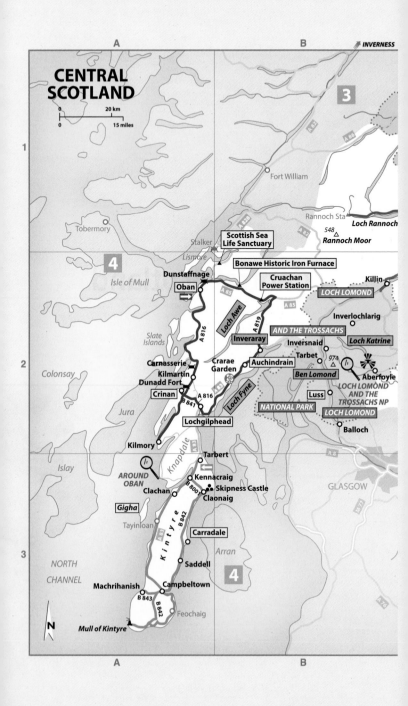

CENTRAL SCOTLAND

0 — 20 km
0 — 15 miles

INVERNESS

3

Tobermory

Fort William

Rannoch Sta

Loch Rannoch

Stalker

Scottish Sea Life Sanctuary

Lismore

548
Rannoch Moor

Isle of Mull

4

Dunstaffnage

Bonawe Historic Iron Furnace

Killin

Oban

Cruachan Power Station

A 85

A 85

LOCH LOMOND

Slate Islands

Loch Awe

A 816

A 819

Inverlochlarig

AND THE TROSSACHS

Loch Katrine

Colonsay

Inveraray

Inversnaid

Tarbet

974

Carnasserie

Crarae Garden

Auchindrain

Ben Lomond

Aberfoyle

Kilmartin

LOCH LOMOND AND THE TROSSACHS NP

Dunadd Fort

A 816

Jura

Crinan

B 841

Loch Fyne

Luss

LOCH LOMOND

NATIONAL PARK

Lochgilphead

Balloch

Kilmory

Knapdale

Tarbert

A 6

Islay

AROUND OBAN

Kennacraig

B 8001

GLASGOW

Clachan

● **Skipness Castle**

Gigha

Claonaig

Tayinloan

B 842

Carradale

Arran

4

NORTH CHANNEL

B 842

Saddell

Machrihanish

Campbeltown

B 843

B 842

Feochaig

N

Mull of Kintyre

Kintyre

214

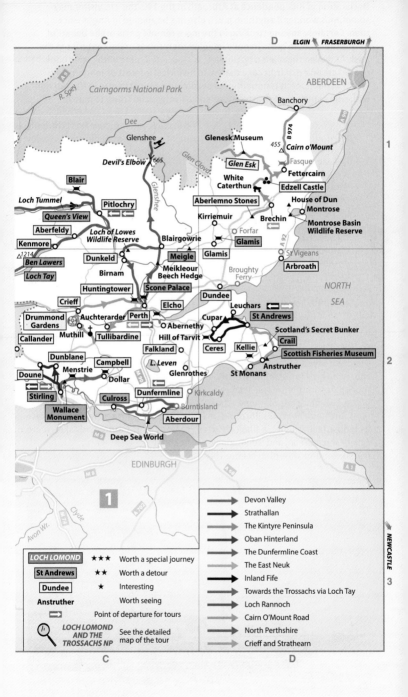

C · D

ELGIN ✈ *FRASERBURGH* ✈

R. Spey

Cairngorms National Park

ABERDEEN

Dee

Banchory

B 974

Glenshee

Glenesk Museum

455 △ *Cairn o'Mount* 1

Devil's Elbow 665

Glen Clova

Glen Esk

Fasque

Blair

Fettercairn

Glenshee

White Caterthun

Edzell Castle

Pitlochry

Aberlemno Stones

House of Dun

Loch Tummel

Kirriemuir

Montrose

Queen's View

Brechin

Montrose Basin Wildlife Reserve

Aberfeldy

Loch of Lowes Wildlife Reserve

○ Forfar

A 92

Kenmore

Blairgowrie

Glamis

△1214

Meigle

Glamis

St Vigeans

Ben Lawers

Dunkeld

Meikleour Beech Hedge

Arbroath

Loch Tay

Birnam

Huntingtower

Scone Palace

NORTH SEA

Crieff

Dundee

○

Elcho

Broughty Ferry

Drummond Gardens

Auchterarder

Perth

Leuchars

○

Cupar

St Andrews

Callander

Muthill

Tullibardine

○ Abernethy

Scotland's Secret Bunker

Hill of Tarvit

Kellie

Crail

Ceres

Dunblane

Falkland

Scottish Fisheries Museum

Campbell

L. Leven

Doune

Menstrie

Dollar

Glenrothes

Anstruther

St Monans

Stirling

Culross

Dunfermline

Kirkcaldy

Wallace Monument

Aberdour

Burntisland

Deep Sea World

EDINBURGH

NEWCASTLE ✈

1

Clyde

Avon Wr.

M8

M9

A72

A76

A1

3

C · D

Described in marketing parlance as Scotland's Birthplace, after the Declaration of Independence at Arbroath in the 14C, the 21C visitor may sometimes wonder if anything much else has happened in Angus since then. Certainly anyone strolling in the more remote parts of the beautiful Angus Glens could quite happily imagine themselves many centuries in the past. And even the main city, Dundee, is associated more with comic book characters and rich fruit cake than with historical interest or modern day visitor attractions. It is nonetheless becoming a tourist centre in its own right, with some cutting-edge attractions and a lively social scene to match.

Highlights

1 Reliving Captain Scott's voyage aboard *RRS Discovery* (p217)
2 Walking far from the madding crowds in the **Angus Glens** (p219)
3 Smelling the roses in the gardens of **Edzell Castle** (p222)
4 Discovering the treasures and mysteries of **Glamis Castle** (p223)
5 Puzzling over the Pictish past at **Meigle** (p224)

Dundee

Dundee is Scotland's fourth largest city and trying hard to break into Scotland's tourist destination major league. It boasts two first-class maritime attractions, the Verdant Works (focusing on its industrial heritage), a fine city art gallery and museum and a burgeoning restaurant and shopping scene. The Dundee Contemporary Arts centre will point you in the right direction to enjoy the buzzing cultural scene.

Angus

One of Scotland's lesser-known tourist regions, the most famous landmark of this agricultural area is the splendid castle of Glamis ("glarms"), the childhood home of the late Queen Mother and the setting for Shakespeare's *Macbeth*. Angus is also famous within Scotland for its Pictish remains, the best starting point for this being at Pictavia in the small cathedral city of Brechin. Nearby the attractive ancient fishing town of Arbroath is worth a visit to sample its famous "Arbroath Smokies" (smoked haddock) and its atmospheric Abbey ruins. The glory of Angus on a sunny day however, is arguably the beautiful gardens at Edzell Castle. Unless of course you are a golfer, in which case teeing off at Carnoustie takes some beating!

RRS Discovery, Discovery Point, V&A Dundee in the background

© Dundee Heritage Trust

Dundee★

Dundee enjoys a near perfect situation on the northern shore of the Tay with the Sidlaw Hills as a backdrop. In the Victorian era, prosperity accrued from the three j's: jute, jam and journalism. Modern, high-technology industries have now taken over, and the city centre reflects this with fine Victorian buildings and modern shopping facilities. Scotland's fourth city, Dundee is also a busy seaport, educational centre and capital of the Tayside region. The Dundee Contemporary Arts (DCA) centre heads a thriving cultural scene.

A BIT OF HISTORY

For the majority of people Dundee's most famous "sons" are Desperate Dan, Dennis the Menace, Korky the Kat and Our Wullie, comic characters from the Thomson publishing empire. Philatelists may also tell you it was home to **James Chalmers** (1823–1853), the inventor of the adhesive postage stamp.

Dundee took over as Britain's chief whaling port in the 1860s with a new generation of steamers for the whale and seal fisheries in the far north. The fleet spent eight months away from March to October. Crews were local but there was a tradition of hiring seamen from Shetland or Orkney as oarsmen for the whaleboats. The oil found a ready market in the burgeoning jute mills where it was used to soften the raw jute fibres. Whaling continued until World War I.

The museum in **Broughty Castle** *(just outside the city centre;* ○*Apr–Sept Mon–Sat 10am–4pm, Sun 12.30–4pm; Oct–Mar same hours but closed Mon;* ℘*01382 436 916)* has a section on whaling featuring whaling gear, paintings and prints.

🐾WALKING TOUR

This short tour by the river and city centre moves from the historic docks to the 21C Contemporary Arts centre.

▶ **Population:** 158 200.

🛈 **Info:** 16 City Square. ℘01382 527 527. www.angusanddundee.co.uk.

◑ **Location:** 22mi/35km northeast of Perth via the A85 and A90.

◉ **Don't Miss:** Discovery Point, the Frigate Unicorn, McManus Galleries, Verdant Works.

◔ **Timing:** Allow one to two days. All the main sights can be covered on foot though you will probably need a bus or taxi by the end of the day.

👫 **Kids:** The Science Centre, RSS *Discovery*, the Frigate Unicorn.

◑ Begin your tour at the waterside at Discovery Quay.

👫 Discovery Point★

Discovery Quay. ♿◔*Apr–Oct Mon–Sat 10am–6pm, Sun 11am–6pm: Nov–Mar Mon–Sat 10am–5pm, Sun 11am–5pm.* ◔*25–26 Dec, 1–2 Jan.* ⊛*£11.50 (child £6.40. Combined tickets: Verdant Works £18.65, child £10.50.* ✕🅿 ℘*01382 309 060. www.rrsdiscovery.com.*

Dundee is immensely proud of Captain Scott's Antarctic exploration vessel, the Royal Research Ship *Discovery*, built here in 1901 and commanded by him on the 1901–04 Antarctic Expedition. **RRS *Discovery*** returned to the Tay in 1986, and now, in dry dock, forms the centrepiece of an ambitious celebration of her historic voyage.

A tour begins in the visitor centre on the quayside, where no effort has been spared in preparing comprehensive displays to evoke the excitements of construction, the launch, the voyage, and the two winters spent in Antarctica. *Discovery* continued her career as a research vessel, and is presented as she was fitted out for a collaborative British/Australian/New Zealand expedition to the Antarctic in 1929.

During the tour, note the teak main deck with skylights (icebergs precluded portholes), the now empty engine rooms, laboratories, radio and chart rooms, storerooms, cold store, the mess deck for the 26 crew members and the teak-panelled officers' wardroom and adjoining cabins. The harsh environment of Antarctica is presented in the Polarama Gallery.

▷ Follow the path alongside the river to the Tay Road Bridge.

Tay Road and Railway Bridges

The Tay Road bridge, opened in 1966 two years after its Forth counterpart, is one of the longest road bridges in Europe at 1.4mi/2.3km long. It has 42 spans and carries two carriageways each way. The central walkway has observation platforms. Look upstream to see the Tay Railway Bridge which was completed in 1887, replacing the original which was only in use for 19 months. On a stormy night in December 1879, disaster struck as the bridge gave way and a train carrying 75 passengers plunged into the river with no survivors.The current bridge in fact made use of some of the original ironwork.

▷ Go forward below the bridge, and turn left at the first opportunity to South Victoria Dock Road. Turn right.

▲▲ The Frigate Unicorn★

Victoria Dock. ⏱*Daily Apr–Oct 10am–5pm; Nov–Mar Thu–Sun noon–4pm.* ⏱*25 Dec.* ▩*£6.55 (child 5–15, £3.15).* ✆*01382 200 900. www.frigateunicorn.org.*
This 46-gun frigate, now mastless, was commissioned by the Royal Navy in 1824. Visitors can explore her four decks, including the Captain's Quarters and the main gundeck where the 18-pounder cannon required nine gunners each to man them.

▷ Retrace your steps as far as the western end of the dock, and turn right into West Victoria Dock Road, left along the A991. Cross at the road

junction, and continue left, and soon turn right onto Commercial Street. Continue as far as Meadowside and Albert Square.

The McManus, Dundee's Art Gallery and Museum ★

Albert Square. ⏱*Mon–Sat 10am–5pm, Sun 12.30–4.30pm.* ✆*01382 307 200. www.mcmanus.co.uk.*
Sir George Gilbert Scott's fine Victorian Gothic building houses this very popular institution. There are 8 galleries laid out on 2 floors.
On the ground floor, the *Making of Modern Dundee* gives a good account of the activities that led to Dundee's late-19C and early-20C prosperity and includes memorabilia from the Tay Bridge disaster of 1879 (ℂ*see left*).
Upstairs the dark red walls of the Victoria Gallery set off the closely hung 19C portraits, landscapes and genre paintings, while the 20C Gallery contains an excellent survey of Scottish painting through a series of annually changing displays. This gallery hosts temporary and touring exhibitions, some brought in from external sources. The majority of the exhibitions feature contemporary arts and crafts.

▷ Continue along Meadowside, left onto Reform St and right onto High Street/Nethergate.

St Mary's Church

This is the oldest surviving building in Dundee. The Old Steeple is all that remains of the original 14C–15C parish kirk. Like many other churches it was subdivided after the Reformation. The east end has some fine stained glass by Burne-Jones and Morris.

▷ Continue along Nethergate.

Dundee Contemporary Arts

152 Nethergate. ⏱*Galleries: daily 10am–6pm (Thu 8pm).* ✖ ✆*01382 909 900. www.dca.org.uk.*
This excellent arts centre stages an eclectic programme of new film, literature, music, design and craft.

The Angus Glens

Lying to the north and northwest of the region, the Angus glens are a series of tranquil valleys penetrated only by single-track roads. They offer some of the most rugged and majestic landscapes of northeast Scotland.

Glen Shee is Scotland's biggest ski resort but, out of the snowy season, **Glen Clova** is, deservedly, the most popular. Wildlife is abundant, with deer on the mountains, wild hares, grouse and the occasional buzzard. The meadow flowers on the valley floor and Arctic plants on the rocks also make it something of a botanist's paradise. At the head of Glen Clova is **Glen Doll**, where ancient narrow roads and footpaths lead into the heart of the Cairngorms.

Hidden away behind a maze of country roads lies **Glen Lethnot**, where the local stream was once used by illicit distillers who secreted their stills in the corries – the track here is still known as the Whisky Trail. Another hidden gem is **Glen Prosen**, also perfect for walks and wildlife. Look out for the cairn dedicated to Wilson and Scott, the Antarctic explorers. Wilson lived in Glen Prosen, and it was here that Captain Scott planned his polar expedition.

Glen Esk is the longest of the glens, reaching as far as lonely Loch Lee and Glen Mark. **Glen Isla** is the westernmost of the Angus Glens, its upper reaches forming part of the dramatic Caenlochan valley.

ADDITIONAL SIGHTS

👥 Science Centre

Greenmarket. ♿🕐*Daily 10am–5pm.* 👓*£8.60 (child 4–15, £6.50).* ✖ 🅿 📞*01382 228 800.* *www.dundeesciencecentre.org.uk.* Discover how we use our five senses to explore the world around us at this exciting interactive Science Centre where everything is "hands-on".

Verdant Works★

West Henderson's Wynd. ♿🕐*Apr–Oct Mon–Sat 10am–6pm, Sun 11am–6pm; Nov–Mar Wed–Sat 10.30am–4.30pm, Sun 11am–4.30pm.* 🕐*25–26 Dec, 1–2 Jan.* 👓*£11.50 (combined ticket with Discovery Point £18.65).* ✖🅿 📞*01382 309 060. www.verdantworks.com.*

At its peak in the mid- and late-19C, when there was a huge growth in world demand for baling and packaging material, Dundee's jute industry employed 50 000 local people, many of them living and working in the close-packed Blackness district to the northwest of the city centre.

Developed from the late 18C onwards, this was one of Scotland's first industrial areas, but was still countrified enough for David Lindsay's factory of 1833 to be given the name of Verdant Mill. One of the best remaining examples of a Dundee jute mill, it has been converted into Dundee's Jute Museum. There are several ingenious exhibits and many audiovisual and hands-on displays which evoke the laborious processes involved in the conversion of the raw jute and some of the fascinating end uses; for example, the wagons rolling across the Wild West of the USA were covered in material made in Dundee.

👥 V&A Dundee – Design Museum

1 Riverside Esplanade. 🕐*Sat–Thu 10am–5pm, Fri 10am–9pm.* 🕐*25–26 Dec.* 📞*01382 411 611.* *www.vam.ac.uk/dundee.*

Opened in September 2018, V&A Dundee is a museum full of learning opportunities centred around design from gaming to fashion, architecture to product design.

Dundee Law

This volcanic plug (*alt. 174m*) affords a great **panorama** of Dundee and surrounding countryside. At the summit is a war memorial. Spread out below is Dundee with the Tay Bridges stretching across to Fife.

Brechin

and around

On the banks of the River South Esk, this small cathedral city developed around its original Celtic monastery at a convenient fording point. The city is known for its Round Tower and cathedral.

SIGHTS
Round Tower★

This Round Tower is one of only two of the Irish type in Scotland and dates from c.1000. The 32m structure (the spire is 14C) was originally free standing and may well have served as a belfry, lookout and place of refuge. The narrow **doorway** 2m above the ground is noteworthy for its carvings.

Cathedral

🕐*Daily 9am–5pm (3.30pm in winter).*
🕐*12 Jan.* 📞*01356 629 360.*
www.brechincathedral.org.uk.
Although the present church had its beginnings in the 13C, it has been much altered since. The west doorway is, however, a good example of 13C work. The square tower alongside is 13C–15C. Inside, there are two early **sculptured stones** (St Mary Stone – north wall of

▶ **Population:** 7 400.
ℹ **Info:** Pictavia Centre, Haughmuir. 📞01356 623 050.
◐ **Location:** Brechin is 26.5mi/43km northeast of Dundee on the A935.
◉ **Don't Miss:** The Round Tower and the Aberlemno Stones.
🧑 **Kids:** Brechin Castle Centre Country Park and Pictavia.

chancel arch, and Aldbar Stone – west end of south aisle), both good examples of Pictish art.

The hogback tomb is probably 11C. The stained glass is by such 20C masters as Douglas Strachan (War Memorial Window), Herbert Hendrie, Gordon Webster and William Wilson.

🧑 Brechin Castle Garden Centre and Country Park

♿🕐*Mon–Fri 9am–5pm, Sat–Sun 9am–6pm.* 💷*£5 (child 2–14, £7).* ✕ 📞*01356 626 813.*
www.brechincastlecentre.co.uk.
Brechin Castle Centre – confusingly a quite separate entry from the privately owned Brechin Castle, 1mi (1.6km) east – is also gateway to a 26ha country park, including a lake, children's play areas, a miniature railway, nature trails, wetland area, model farm and display of vintage farm implements.

EXCURSIONS
Aberlemno Stones★

6mi/10km to the southwest. Leave Brechin by the Forfar road (A935) and once past the castle gates turn sharp left to take the B9134. The stones are boarded up Oct–Mar.
The gently climbing road offers splendid views northwards over Strathmore and the winding South Esk, away to the ramparts of the Highland rim.
The village of Aberlemno has four **Pictish sculptured stones**★ (🔆*see INTRODUCTION: Art and Culture*) dating

Pictish symbol stone, Aberlemno

After photo E.Sevo/MICHELIN

from the 7C–9C. Of the roadside stones, the one nearest to the village hall bears a cross with flanking angels and on the reverse, a hunting scene with Pictish symbols.

Other examples of these enigmatic symbols are discernible on the roadside face of the eastern stone. A road to the left leads to the churchyard with its **stone★**, another outstanding example of this Dark Age art form. On one side a cross with intricate interlacing is flanked by intertwined beasts while on the second, a battle scene evolves.

Arbroath★

14.5mi/23.3km south via the A933.
Known as the "Auld Red Town" because of the distinctive stonework of its close-packed fishing quarter, Arbroath is famous for the lovely ruins of its abbey church and for its cured herrings. Expansive shoreline parklands and promenades recall the town's mid-century aspirations as a seaside resort.

Arbroath abbey★ (🕐 *daily: Apr–Sept 9.30am–5.30pm; Oct–Mar 10am–4pm);* 👓*£9;* 📞*01241 878 756; www.historicenvironment.scot*) found a place in history as the site of the drawing up of the **Declaration of Arbroath** on 6 April 1320 during the Wars of Independence.

William the Lion (1143–1214) founded a priory here in 1178 in memory of his childhood friend Thomas à Becket, murdered in Canterbury cathedral eight years previously.

By 1233, the building was finished and in 1285 was accorded abbey status. Tironensian monks from Kelso (👓*see KELSO*) maintained a wealthy and influential establishment, which flourished until the early 17C. Thereafter neglect led to decay and today it is a romantic ruin. A visitor centre provides an insight into the abbey's history and an exhibition on the Declaration is within the abbey.

Brown and White Caterthuns

5mi/8km northwest. Leave Brechin to the north towards Menmuir.
Two Iron Age hill forts – Brown and White Caterthuns – stand either side of the road about 1km apart. They are two of the most impressive hilltop enclosures in Scotland (*www.historicenvironment.scot*). The **White Caterthun** (🚶*400m by a grassy track*) is the nearer and better.

🚗 DRIVING TOUR

🚗 CAIRN O'MOUNT ROAD★

50mi/80km from Brechin to Banchory. Allow 1h for the drive, excluding visits.

This scenic route follows one of the most popular passages over the hills to Deeside. Livestock drovers, whisky smug-

Ruins of Arbroath abbey

© Gannet77/iStockphoto.com

glers, royalty and their armies have all marched this way, including Macbeth, who fled north to his final defeat.

○ Leave Brechin centre by the B966 (Southesk Street). Cross below the A90, and continue to Edzell.

Edzell Castle and garden★

&○*Daily Apr–Sept 9.30am–5.30pm. ⊕£6. ℘0131 668 8800. www.historicenvironment.scot.*
The small village of Edzell was resited to its present location from the original settlement in the vicinity of the castle, whose attractive ruins are unique for their formal walled garden, or pleasance. The present entrance leads to the cobbled courtyard of the late-16C mansion. Now in ruins, this extension was never completed.

The great hall in the tower house affords a bird's-eye view of the pleasance.

The Pleasance★★★ – This glorious formal walled garden was created in 1604 by **Sir David Lindsay** (c.1550–1610). Influenced by what he had seen abroad, he created a remarkable work displaying elegance and refinement without parallel in Scotland. When the roses of the flower beds and the blue and white lobelia of the wall boxes are in bloom against the rich red of the walls these gardens are a blaze of colour.

The heraldic and symbolic **sculpture** on the walls rewards a closer inspection. Between the wall boxes representing the Lindsay colours and arms are panels portraying the Planetary Deities (*east wall*), Liberal Arts (*south wall*) and Cardinal Virtues (*west wall*). The design is completed in the southwest corner by a bath house, a luxury in 17C Scotland, and a summer house.

○ Stay on the Fettercairn road (B966) out of Edzell. Once across the River North Esk it is possible to detour left into Glen Esk as far as Tarfside.

Glen Esk★

Go up the valley (*15km/9.25mi*) to reach the **Glenesk Retreat and Folk Museum** (&○*closed until 2020 for restructuring; check website for updates, or call. ℘01356 648 070; www.gleneskretreat.scot*). This popular museum and art gallery gives a fascinating account of close-knit life in the glen, and is locally famous for its restaurant and tearoom. The road continues up to just before the ruin of Invermark Castle, a Lindsay stronghold.

○ Return to the B966 and continue to Fettercairn.

Fettercairn

This charming red-sandstone village boasts a picturesque square; its imposing arch commemorates Queen Victoria's 1861 visit while staying at Balmoral.

Fettercairn is home to the **Fettercairn distillery**, owned by Whyte and Mackay Ltd. that produces the "Fettercairn 1824" single malt whisky (○*mid-Apr–Sept Tue–Sat 10am–4pm;* ⏚*tours £7.50; www.fettercairnwhisky.com*).

○ Take the Cairn o'Mount road (B974) andcontinue through the foothills to Strachen.

Shortly after passing the Fasque Castle Estate (⟳ *closed to the public*), away to the right, a green mound is all that remains of Kincardine Castle, once a royal residence. The road then follows a glen up to the Clatterin Brig. Keep left to climb rapidly through moorland to the **Cairn o'Mount** (*alt. 455m*). From near the top there is a splendid **view★★**.

The road descends to Deeside along the course of an old military road through hills and forests with several narrow bridges, then over the Water of Dye, with some steep gradients to negotiate.

○ Cross the Water of Feugh at the village of Strachan (pronounced Struan), then turn right to follow the B974 to Banchory on the River Dee.

Glamis ★

and Strathmore

Set in the rich agricultural countryside of Strathmore this attractive village (pronounced "glaams") stands on the periphery of the Glamis Castle policies (estate). Its 18C cottages make it an outstanding conservation area.

GLAMIS CASTLE ★★

Guided tours only: Apr–Oct 10am–4.30pm. £15.50. 01307 840 393. www.glamis-castle.co.uk.

Set in the rich Vale of Strathmore, Glamis is the epitome of a Scottish castle with the added interest of many royal connections – it was the childhood home of Her Majesty Queen Elizabeth, the Mother of Queen Elizabeth II, and the birthplace of HRH Princess Margaret – literary associations (Macbeth was Thane of Glamis, as well as Cawdor) and a ghost in residence. Originally a hunting lodge, Glamis has been the seat of the same family since 1372. In 1376 the Chamberlain of Scotland, Sir John Lyon, married Joanna, the widowed daughter of Robert II. The family fell out of favour during the reign of James V, and after a long period of imprisonment during which

Info: 16 City Square, Dundee. 01382 527 527; www.angusanddundee.co.uk.

Location: Glamis is 12mi/19km north of Dundee.

Timing: Early July sees the Scottish Transport Extravaganza (*www.svvc.co.uk*) when around 800 vintage vehicles turn Glamis Castle grounds into a carnival of yesteryear.

Don't Miss: Early Christian monuments in Meigle Museum.

the sovereign occupied the castle, James had Lady Glamis burned as a witch. Her ghost, "The Grey Lady", is still here.

Seen from the end of the tree-lined avenue, the castle is grandly impressive. Its central part rises upwards bristling with towers, turrets, conical roofs and chimneys, with windows seemingly placed at random. The 15C L-shaped core has been added to and altered through the centuries, creating the present building.

Interiors of various periods, family and other portraits and a variety of interesting

Glamis Castle

items highlight the guided tour. The west wing was destroyed by fire in 1800 and in the rebuilding, the **Dining Room** was given its ornate plaster ceiling. Family portraits include the grandparents and brothers of Queen Elizabeth, the Queen Mother.

In the stone-vaulted **Crypt**, which was the main hall of the original tower, Jacobean furniture, armour and weapons are displayed.

The Crypt is the supposed location of the castle's famous "Secret Room" (ⓒ*see Box below*). This opens onto the great circular staircase, a later addition, the central shaft of which served as an early heating system.

The splendour of the **Drawing Room** is enhanced by a beautiful vaulted ceiling with **plasterwork decoration** (created in 1621) and a magnificent fireplace (possibly by Inigo Jones) built to commemorate the 1603 Union of the English and Scottish Crowns.

The **Chapel**'s panelling is decorated with 17C paintings depicting the Twelve Apostles and 15 scenes from the Bible. The paintings are by **Jacob de Wet** (1695–1754), a Dutch artist who also worked at Blair and Kellie castles and Holyroodhouse. The intriguing feature is the painting showing Christ wearing a hat. The chapel is the haunt of the Grey Lady (ⓒ*see above*).

The 20C ceiling of the **Library** makes a good comparison with the 17C one in the drawing room. The finely worked (17C) tapestries were woven at the Mortlake factory founded by James VI, and *The Fruit Market* is a combined composition by Rubens and Frans Snyders. Delicately worked hangings, a plaster ceiling and coat of arms, an unusual fireplace and armorial porcelain are the chief points of interest in **King Malcolm's Room**. The most notable features of the **Royal Apartments** are the hangings of the four-poster bed embroidered by Lady Strathmore and the Kinghorne Bed (1606) made for Patrick, 1st Earl. **Duncan's Hall**, the oldest (and eeriest) part, has literary associations with Shakespeare's *Macbeth* written during the reign of James

VI, though in historical fact Macbeth did not murder Duncan here. Here also are a pair of portraits of the castle's royal occupants during the unfortunate "Grey Lady" Glamis' imprisonment.

Grounds – Statues of James VI and his son Charles I flank the end of the drive. Beyond a fine spreading chestnut tree is the delightful **Italian Garden**.

ADDITIONAL SIGHTS
Glamis Graveyard and St Fergus Well

According to local legend St Fergus established the local kirk at Glamis, and it was here in the early 8C that he baptised the earliest converts to Christianity in Strathmore in the well which still exists to this day.

Various Pictish stones, together with gravestones describing the trades of long-deceased locals, reinforce the importance of Glamis as a holy place. Water from the Well of St Fergus trickles into the Glamis burn, and baptism and marriage ceremonies still take place in this isolated and atmospheric spot.

In the graveyard can be found the headstone of **Margaret Bridie** of Glamis. She made the original bridies (meat-and-potato filled pastries, similar to Cornish pasties) in the village and then sold them at the Buttermarket in Forfar. Forfar Bridies are still enjoyed all over the region today.

EXCURSIONS
Meigle Sculptured Stone Museum★★

7mi/11.3km west via the A94.
♿�*Daily Apr–Sept 9.30am–5.30pm.*
🎫*£6.* ℘*01828 640 612.*
www.historicenvironment.scot.

The former village school houses an outstanding collection of Old Red Sandstone **Early Christian monuments★★** (7C–10C), all found in the vicinity. Cross-slabs, recumbent gravestones and a variety of fragments vividly illustrate the life and art of the Picts. Although the exact purpose of the monuments remains obscure the car-

The Secret Room

It is said that somewhere in the crypt is a room that harbours a dark secret. One Saturday night Earl Beardie was a guest at Glamis castle. After a heavy drinking session with Lord Glamis, he demanded a partner to play him at cards. A servant reminded him of the lateness of the hour and that it was almost the Sabbath. "I care not what day of the week it is," he roared, and raged that he would play with the Devil himself. At the stroke of midnight there was a knock at the door, and a tall man in dark clothes came into the castle and asked if Earl Beardie still required a partner. The Earl agreed and the two started to play cards. There was a great commotion and when one of the servants peeped through the keyhole to establish the cause of the noise, he saw a bright beam of light, blinding him in one eye. The Earl burst from the room and when he returned, the stranger, who was the Devil, had disappeared along with the Earl's soul, lost in the card game.

ving everywhere is full of spirit and vitality and shows a high degree of skill. The stones are all numbered. Subject matter includes enigmatic Pictish symbols, Celtic-type crosses with associated complex interlace, fretwork, spiral and key patterns; pictorial scenes (including Daniel in the Lion's Den), and fabulous animals and human figures.

Kirriemuir

5 mi/8km north of Glamis via the A928.
The small town of Kirriemuir, with its narrow winding streets lined by red-sandstone houses, has a certain charm. Set on the slopes of the Highland rim overlooking the great sweep of Strathmore, Kirriemuir is at the heart of raspberry growing country and was the birthplace of the playwright J M Barrie. It is the fictional village, Thrums, portrayed in his books.

J M Barrie's Birthplace

9 Brechin Road.
Apr–Sept Fri–Mon 11am–4pm.
£7. 01575 572 646. www.nts.org.uk.
The four-roomed cottage was where **James Matthew Barrie** (1860–1937), the playwright, author and creator of *Peter Pan*, was born. It was here that he grew up. immersed in the culture and traditions of a small weaving community, which provided the inspiration for his work.
The ground floor room with albums and other memorabilia was no doubt where

Barrie's father originally had his linen-weaving hand-loom.
Upstairs is the Barrie kitchen and the bedroom with a portrait of the St Bernard, Porthos, the model for Nana. Of particular interest are the two historic Peter Pan costumes: one with the shadow and the second with the detachable "kiss".
The small wash-house outside served as a makeshift theatre and likely provided the inspiration for the Wendy House built by the Lost Boys.
The house next door, No. 11, is home to an imaginative exhibition about Barrie's life and works, as well as a garden with a living-willow crocodile.
Barrie's grave is signposted at the nearby **cemetery** *(turn left off Brechin Road to take Cemetery Road right to the top)*. The short walk has good views of the agricultural patchwork of Strathmore below.

Camera Obscura

Barrie Pavilion, Kirriemuir Hill.
Apr–Sept Sat–Mon 11am–4pm.
07825 408207.
www.kirriemuircameraobscura.com.
Gifted by J M Barrie, this is one of only four camera obscuras in Scotland. It offers excellent views of the Highlands north and south over Strathmore to Dundee.

Montrose

The east coast town of Montrose sits on a peninsula between a tidal basin and the sea. The steeple of the parish church pinpoints the town from afar. Ever popular with summer visitors, the town has a vast stretch of golden sand, several golf courses and scenic countryside nearby to explore. Montrose has always been a busy shopping centre and market town for the rich agricultural hinterland and a thriving port. Increased prosperity has accrued from North Sea Oil with the establishment of an oil base on the River South Esk.

▶ **Population:** 13 320.
🛈 **Info:** 2 Bridge Street; ℰ01674 672 000;. www. angusanddundee.co.uk.
▶ **Location:** Montrose is 29mi/47km NE of Dundee on the A92.
🕐 **Timing:** Allow 2 hours.
👥 **Kids:** The town's golden beach and sand dunes.

A BIT OF HISTORY

In the difficult times leading up to the Reformation, Montrose had more than its fair share of martyrs, most notably David Straton (d.1534) and **George Wishart**, whose execution at St Andrews (ℰsee ST ANDREWS) in February 1546 sparked off reprisals which resulted in the stabbing of Cardinal Beaton.

Protestant connections continued with John Knox who was a regular visitor to John Erskine at the nearby House of Dun. Erskine was the town's provost and one of the first Moderators.

The tradition continued with Knox's follower, the scholar and linguist **Andrew Melville** (1554–1622), and his nephew James, who led a determined fight against James VI's policy to introduce episcopacy. The former is remembered for his admonition to James VI that he was but "God's silly vassal".

HIGH STREET

The elongated triangular layout is medieval and many of the original wynds and closes between the burgess plots still remain. Interspersed between the substantial 17C and 18C buildings are a number of gable-ended houses from which the Montrosians acquired their nickname "gable endies". This feature is a relic of trading days with the Low Countries.

The **Old Town House** – 18C with a 19C extension – has an elegant arcade on the High Street side. It faces the statue of local worthy, Joseph Hume (1777–1855), a radical politician and reformer.

The Gothic steeple (67m) of the **Old Church**, a notable landmark, was added to this 18C church by Gillespie Graham in the 19C. The famous Panniter Panels in the Museum of Scotland in Edinburgh came from the earlier church on this site. At the south end of the High Street is castellated **Castlestead**. It was the site of a 13C castle which later became the town house of the Graham family and it may have been here that the town's most colourful historical character, James Graham, 5th Earl and 1st Marquis of Montrose, was born in 1612. Accomplished in many fields, elegant, fastidious and vain, he was a natural military commander and fought as a Covenanter before switching his allegiance to the Royalist cause. He was betrayed however, and executed in Edinburgh in 1650. The building is now used as offices.

ADDITIONAL SIGHTS

Montrose Museum

Panmure Place (just off the south end of the High Street).
♿🕐*Tue–Sat 10am–5pm.* 🕐*25–26 Dec and 1–2 Jan.* 🅿 ℰ*01674 907 447. http://archive.angus.gov.uk.*

The collection includes sections on the town's activities in the past (salmon fishing, 18C tobacco trade and whaling), natural history dioramas and biographical sections on famous citizens from James Graham, Marquis of Montrose, leader of the Royalist party, to the politician and reformer Joseph Hume, and William Lamb, the 20C sculptor. Note in particular the bust of his contemporary Hugh McDiarmid; one of Scotland's finest 20C poets, he was editor of the local paper in the 1920s.

William Lamb Studio

Market Street (running parallel to the north end of the High Street).
&♿☉*Jul–Aug Tue–Wed 1.30–4.30pm (The opening dates are advisory – others might be added at short notice).* ℘*01674 662 660. http://archive.angus. gov.uk.*

In this small studio is a display of sculptures, paintings and sketches by the relatively unknown but highly talented artist **William Lamb** (1893–1951) – "one of the few original minds in Scottish art of this century". The bronzes have a verve and sureness of touch which is all the more remarkable given Lamb's history. Following a war wound to his favoured right hand, he taught himself to work anew with the left. One of his life-size works, *The Seafarer*, cast posthumously, stands down by the harbour.

Montrose Air Station Heritage Centre

1mi/1.6km north of High Street off A92 (continuation of High St). Entry via Broomfield Road, follow brown tourist signs.
&♿☉ *Apr–Jun and Oct–early Nov Wed–Sat 10am –4pm, Sun noon–4pm; Jul–Sept Mon–Sat 10am–4pm, Sun noon–4pm.* ⊜*£5.* ℘*01674 678 222. www.rafmontrose.org.uk.*

Britain's first operational military airfield was set up in Montrose by the Royal Flying Corps in 1913. This small collection of memorabilia, artefacts and pictures tells its story from the origins of flight, through the two world wars.

EXCURSIONS
House of Dun and Montrose Basin Nature Reserve

3mi/5km west on the A935 Brechin Road.
&♿☉*House:* 👣 *hourly guided tours*

only: Apr–late Oct Sat–Wed 11am–3pm; late Oct–Nov Sat–Sun 11am–3.30pm. **Garden and estate:** *daily 9am–dusk.* ⊜*£12.* 🅿*(charge).* ✕ ℘*01674 810 264. www.nts.org.uk.*

William Adam built this fine Palladianstyle mansion in the early 18C for the Erskine lairds of Dun to replace an earlier castle. The house was remodelled in the 19C. The **reception rooms** show decorative features typical of "stone and lime": the garlands, swags, regalia, armorial trophies and allegorical scenes in the **Saloon** are by Joseph Enzer (1742–43).

On the first floor the decoration of the private rooms and the bedrooms re-creates the 19C setting. The Red Bedroom and the Tapestry Room contain 17C Flemish tapestries. The domestic rooms give an insight into life below stairs. The gardens are also being re-created. The parkland offers stunning views of the adjacent **Montrose Basin Nature Reserve** with access to wigeon and shellduck bird hides.

Montrose Basin Visitor Centre and Wildlife Centre

Rossie Braes.
1mi/1.6km southwest by A92.
&♿☉*Daily mid-Feb–Oct 10.30am–5pm; Nov–mid-Feb Fri–Mon 10.30am–4pm.* ☉*25–26 Dec and 1–2 Jan.* ⊜*£4.50.* ✕🅿 ℘*01674 676 336. https://scottishwildlifetrust.org.uk.*

This striking visitor centre, built by the Scottish Wildlife Trust, perches on the southern rim of the splendid tract of sheltered tidal water known as the Montrose Basin.

The wetlands of the relatively unpolluted and undamaged basin are of great conservation interest and of first importance for up to 50 000 migratory birds. Displays explain the ecology of tidal basins while the wildlife can be observed through the high-powered binoculars that are provided and also by live video footage.

This is the most romanticised area of all Scotland, in both fact and fiction. Who hasn't heard of "the bonnie bonnie banks" of Loch Lomond, Rob Roy, Scott's "Lady of the Lake", Bannockburn and – as recently as the late 20C – Mull of Kintyre and "Braveheart" William Wallace? The scenery is familiar from chocolate boxes and jigsaws: the hills and glens of the Trossachs and the many glorious lochs make for unmissable Scottish viewing.

Highlights

1 Gazing up to, and down from, **Stirling Castle** (p230)

2 The Achray Forest Drive Hilltop Viewpoint of the **Trossachs** (p247)

3 A boat trip on **Loch Katrine**, viewing Rob Roy Country (p248)

4 Exploring the glorious interiors of **Inverary Castle** (p251)

5 Take a trip to the **Mull of Kyntyre** and visit **Campbeltown**, setting for Denzil Meyrick's crime novels (p258)

Stirling and Around

With a glorious castle, once the residence of Scottish kings, perched atop a long-extinct volcano, and a charming Old Town lining the cobbled streets trailing down from the castle, it is hardly surprising that the centre of Stirling draws so many comparisons with Edinburgh. From the castle heights you can gaze out over centuries of tumultuous Scottish history, to the Wallace Monument, and in the direction of Bannockburn.

The magnificent cathedral at Dunblane, dramatically sited Castle Douglas and Doune Castle are very worthwhile short excursions from Stirling.

The Trossachs and Loch Lomond

The hills of the Trossachs mark the dividing Highland–Lowland Line and, though their peaks may be modest compared to those further north, these verdant uplands still dwarf the plains to the south. Scotland's first great travel writer, Sir Walter Scott, was captivated by the beauty of the area and, while the gateway villages of Callander and Aberfoyle may be busy with tourist fripperies, and in high summer the roads thronged with visitors, in essence it has changed little since his day. Don't miss Loch Katrine, the inspiration for Lady of the Lake and home to Rob Roy. Loch Lomond, the largest inland lake in the British Isles, is just as beautiful in reality as it is in verse.

Oban and around

The sweeping mountains of Lorn create the perfect backdrop to the picturesque and bustling town of Oban, capital of the West Highlands, and, as the main port for ferries departing to the Inner Hebrides, also Gateway to the Isles. South of Oban lie the islands of Seil, Easedale and Luing that are ideal for quiet days off-the-beaten-track. To the north, Ganavan Bay is a sandy beach much favoured by locals.

Mid-Argyll and Kintyre

At every turn, the sea-fringed West Highland landscape of Mid-Argyll is steeped in history, from prehistoric sculptures to mighty castles. Inveraray enjoys a wonderful lochside setting and is a perfect base for exploring glorious Loch Fyne.

A few miles north Loch Awe is equally impressive in terms of natural beauty. The Kintyre peninsula is joined to the Argyll mainland by a narrow isthmus (*tarbert* in Gaelic) from which the lively fishing village and sailing haven of Tarbert takes its name. Swept by the warm Gulf Stream and studded with quiet inns and hamlets, the Mull of Kintyre has deservedly been immortalised in song by Sir Paul McCartney and Wings.

Stirling★★

Strategically important from time immemorial as focal point for all Scotland, the long and eventful history of the town has been essentially that of its famous stronghold and former royal residence.

A BIT OF HISTORY

Strategic Location – The site of Stirling has always been of paramount strategic importance, controlling a crossing of the Forth at its tidal limit, a passage northwards between the Ochils and Gargunnock Hills, and being fortuitously endowed with a superb and nigh impregnable strongpoint, the crag. It comes as no surprise then that so many important battles have been fought in the vicinity: Stirling Bridge 1297; Falkirk 1298, 1766; Bannockburn 1314; Sauchieburn 1488; Kilsyth 1645; and Sheriffmuir 1715.

Early Royal Connections – Royal associations began in 1124 with the death of Alexander I. In 1126 his brother, David I, granted the settlement royal status and the ensuing privileges ensured the town's subsequent prosperity and growth, becoming, in the 12C, one of the "Court of the Four Burghs" along with Berwick, Edinburgh and Roxburgh. It was from here that David I no doubt supervised the building of his abbey at Cambuskenneth (founded 1147) down on the carselands of the Forth.

Wars of Independence (1296–1305) – Owing to its vital strategic importance the castle was attacked and counter-attacked by both the English and Scots during this turbulent period, which figures largely in the castle's own history and features two of Scotland's most famous heroes, **William Wallace** and **Robert the Bruce**. The castle was recaptured from Edward I's garrison following **William Wallace**'s victory at the **Battle of Stirling Bridge** (1297), which was no doubt fought upstream from the present bridge. In 1304, the castle was the last Scottish stronghold in Wallace's hands and after capitula-

- ▶ **Population:** 49 830.
- **Info:** Old Town Jail, St John Street. ✆01786 475 019. www.visit scottishheartlands.com.
- ▶ **Location:** Stirling is 43mi/69km northwest of Edinburgh via the M9. All the sights are clustered tightly together in the Old Town, adjacent to the castle. Regular bus services run to Bannockburn and the National Wallace Monument.
- **Don't Miss:** Stirling Heads in the Castle; view from the National Wallace Monument.
- **Timing:** Allow a day to see the town and Wallace Monument.
- **Kids:** Old Town Jail and the Stirling Ghost Tour; Blair Drummond Safari and Adventure Park.

tion there followed 10 years of English occupation. The castle again became the centre of a struggle in 1313, and the **Battle of Bannockburn** (☞see DRIVING TOURS below) the following year was fought in the short term for possession of Stirling Castle with, as long-term aim, the achieving of independence from the English.

Royal Abode of the House of Stewart – With the accession of the Stewarts, Stirling Castle became a permanent royal residence. James III (1451–88) strengthened the defences and built the gatehouse to the castle of his birth, as well as building the Great Hall as a meeting place for Parliament and other State occasions. Stirling's Golden Age corresponded with the reigns of James IV and V (1488–1542). **James IV**, a true Renaissance prince, initiated the building of the Palace Block.

A notable escapade in the merry round of festivities, which was an important

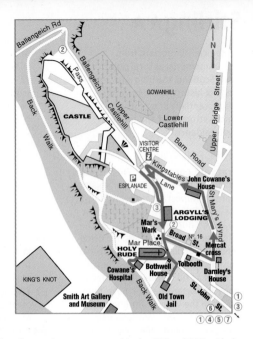

feature of his court, was that of a courtier named Damian, who thought he would attempt to emulate Icarus. Winged only with cocks' feathers he launched himself from the battlements and surprisingly he survived his maiden flight!

On James' death at Flodden his queen, Margaret, brought her son to Stirling where he was crowned in the chapel (21 September 1513) as James V. Thirty years later his daughter, **Mary, Queen of Scots** (1542–87), was crowned in the old Chapel Royal on 9 September 1543. Her infant son James was baptised in 1566, with the absent Elizabeth I as royal godmother. At this time, Mary was already estranged from her husband, Darnley. The following year, prior to his mother's abdication, the 13-month-old prince was crowned in the parish church and it was here that he lived under the stern tutorship of George Buchanan. James rebuilt the Chapel Royal (1594) for the baptism of his own son, Prince Henry, in the same year. With the departure of James VI to Whitehall, Stirling's role as a royal residence ceased.

A Prosperous Royal Burgh – This royal burgh, with its exclusive trading privileges and the stimulus of the court, greatly prospered in the 15C and 16C, with the town itself spreading downhill from its august neighbour.

Stirling was once again to play its military role of garrison town during the Covenanting troubles and the Commonwealth. Associations with the Jacobite rebellion included the Battle of Sheriffmuir which, although indecisive, ended the 1715 campaign, while the 1745 links are even more numerous since Bonnie Prince Charlie wintered in the area prior to his final defeat at Culloden (*see INVERNESS: Driving Tours*).

The 19C saw the growth of textile, coal mining and agricultural engineering industries. In 1967 Stirling was chosen as the site for a new university and the electronics industry is now so firmly established in the Central Belt that it has acquired the nickname "Silicon Glen". The town is also a leading agricultural service centre with a modern cattle market.

STIRLING CASTLE★★

Daily: Apr–Sept 9.30am–6pm; Oct–Mar 9am–5pm (1 Jan 11am–5pm).
25–26 Dec. £16 (child 5–15, £9.60) – advance purchase discounts are

© Jon Arnold Images/hemis.fr

Stirling Castle

available. ✕ 🅿 *£4 (for 4h).* ✆ *01786 450 000. www.stirlingcastle.gov.uk.*

With a magnificent **site★★★**, high on a crag dominating the Forth carselands, Stirling Castle was once one of Scotland's strongest and most impregnable fortresses. The castle is approached, up the tail formation of the crag, through the old town. Standing sentinel on the esplanade is Robert the Bruce's statue. Begin your visit at the **Castle Exhibition Centre** and, after crossing the ditch and first gateway, continue upwards passing through the Inner Gateway. On the left are the **Queen Anne Garden**, once a bowling green, the ramp up to the terrace, and the **Casemates**, where there is an entertaining exhibition area.

The 15C **Entry and Portcullis House**, the work of James IV, opens onto the Lower Square.

Lower Square

This is overlooked on the left by the ornate **façade★★★** of the palace, with the Great Hall straight ahead and the Grand Battery to the right.

Palace★

Begun in 1496 by **James IV**, the palace was completed by 1540 in the reign of his son and is a masterpiece of Renaissance ornamentation. However Stirling and the other royal residences of Falkland and Linlithgow remain isolated examples of the then current European Renaissance ideas and were to have little direct effect on Scottish architecture in general. A £12 million refurbishment has re-created the palace to appear as it did in its heyday in the mid 16C. With the help of costumed actors, visitors are invited to step into a world of plots, passion, intrigue and high fashion with the people of the palace.

External Elevations

The outstanding architectural feature of the palace, which is simple in plan with four buildings round a courtyard, is the elaborate design of the external elevations (♿ *for further details see Upper Square, below*). Turn left into the covered passageway, passing the entrance to the Lion's Den **(1)**.

Lady's Hole (2)

This terrace has good **views** to the west and in particular of the **King's Knot** below. Now all grass, the outlines of this garden can still be distinguished as laid out in 1627 by William Watt within the confines of the royal park.

Away to the left the flagstaff of the rotunda at Bannockburn (♿ *see Bannockburn Heritage Centre p237*) pinpoints another historic site.

Royal Lodgings (Apartments)

This area has recently undergone major refurbishment to present the Royal Lodgings based on the latest historical research and archaeological evidence

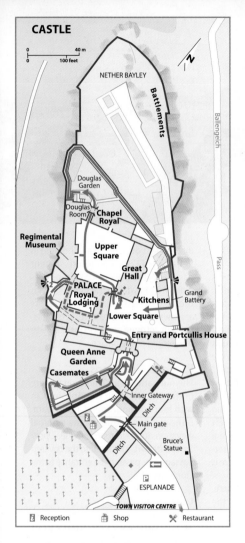

CASTLE

0 — 40 m
0 — 100 feet

NETHER BAYLEY

Battlements

Ballengeich

Douglas
Garden

Douglas
Room — **Chapel
Royal**

**Regimental
Museum**

**Upper
Square**

Pass

**Great
Hall**

**PALACE
Royal
Lodging** — **Kitchens** — Grand
Battery

Lower Square

Entry and Portcullis House

**Queen Anne
Garden**

Casemates

Inner Gateway

Ditch

Main gate

Ditch

Bruce's
Statue

ESPLANADE

TOWN VISITOR CENTRE

Reception — Shop — Restaurant

Of the original 56, roughly a quarter are missing, three are in the Royal Museum of Scotland in Edinburgh and the rest are at Stirling awaiting reinstatement. Set in circular frames the medallions portray kings and queens, courtiers, and mythical and Biblical figures. (As part of the ongoing refurbishment of the castle, a Renaissance Gallery on the upper floors of the palace will eventually house the original Stirling Heads.)

Great Hall

This free-standing building was sadly much altered when used as a barracks in the 18C. However, an important programme of restoration has recreated the former splendour of this chamber to the period when it was used by the Stewart court. A fine example of late-Gothic domestic architecture, it was described by Defoe as "...the noblest I ever saw in Europe". The original arrangement of the Gothic chamber included a dais at the south end flanked by magnificent oriel windows, with the screens and minstrel gallery at the opposite end. The hall with its oak **hammerbeam roof** was lit by paired windows.

using materials and craftsmanship of appropriately high quality.

The Palace Block has cellars below with the royal apartments on the main floor and accommodation for the courtiers above. The Queen's Outer and Own Halls are two nobly proportioned chambers where examples of the famous 16C **Stirling Heads** are on display. This series of oak medallions is an extremely fine and rare example of Scottish Renaissance woodcarving. The medallions were originally set into a compartmented ceiling in the King's Presence Chamber (Own Hall).

Upper Square

This courtyard provides a good vantage point for comparing the **facades★★★** of the Great Hall (1460–88), the Palace (1496–1540) and Chapel (1594) showing clearly how styles changed in under 150 years.

The original front of the Great Hall had four pairs of deeply embrasured windows with, below, a lean-to roof protecting outside stairs leading up to the main chamber. Above the cornice was a crenellated parapet with wall-walk. The **palace façade** by contrast has a variety of unusual sculptured decoration: between the windows, recessed and cusped arches are the setting for carved figures (*left to right*: James V; young man holding cup; Stirling Venus; bearded man; woman in flowing drapery) which are on the baluster wall shafts.

Chapel Royal

The present church was hurriedly erected on the site of an earlier chapel by James VI for the baptism of Prince Henry. In the early classic Renaissance style, the courtyard front is most pleasing with three pairs of round-headed windows on either side of the elaborate **doorway**. The interior has elaborate wall decoration.

Argyll and Sutherland Highlanders Regimental Museum

Closed until 2020.
Battle Honours, Colours, medals, peace and wartime uniforms, documents and pictures, all tell the story of nearly 200 years of regimental history and its heroic moments: The Thin Red Line at Balaclava 1854 and the Relief of Lucknow. The regiment is the proud possessor of an outstanding **collection of silver**.
Pass through to the Douglas Garden. It was in the building (Douglas Room) on the left that Black Douglas was treacherously murdered in 1452 by **James II**.

Battlements

The wall-walk round the battlements on the east side offer fine **views** of the Forth carselands. From the **viewpoint** at the Grand Battery, pick out below the medieval Stirling Bridge bestriding the Forth with, in the middle distance, the tower of Cambuskenneth Abbey, the Wallace Monument and the Ochils.

The Great Kitchens

Steps from the Lower Square lead down into the Great Kitchens, where, lit by fires and flickering torchlight, there is a vivid recreation of the chaos and confusion involved in the preparation of a right royal medieval feast.

✦✦WALKING TOUR

OLD TOWN

Explore the Old Town on foot starting from the castle esplanade.
The medieval town with its steep streets and narrow wynds spills downhill from the castle to the centre of present-day Stirling.

▷ Walk down the hill.

Argyll's Lodging★

Castle Wynd. ⊙*Closed until further notice for essential maintenance; check website for details.*
www.historicenvironment.scot.
Scotland's most splendid and complete example of a 17C town house was built in 1632 by Sir William Alexander, founder of Nova Scotia. On his death the property passed to the Argyll family when alterations and extensions were made. The street side of this courtyard mansion is enclosed by a screen wall pierced by a fine rusticated Renaissance gateway. The courtyard façades are rich with Scottish **Renaissance decoration★**: strapwork on dormer and window heads, and an armorial panel above the entrance.

▷ Continue downhill, now on Par Place.

Mar's Wark

Ruined but nonetheless impressive, the **façade** is all that remains of this stillborn palace, with ornamental sculpture and heraldic panels adorning the street front. It was started in 1570, for John Erskine (1510–72), Regent and Ist Earl of Mar, but never completed.
As Hereditary Keeper of the castle and guardian of Prince James, it was thought only appropriate that his Grace should have a private residence close at hand. It is said that Cambuskenneth Abbey (*see Driving Tours, below*) was quarried for the stone which went towards Mar's Wark. The unusual name comes from the fact that in the 1730s the town council made plans to convert it into a workhouse.

Church of the Holy Rude★

This burgh church was built in stages on the site of an earlier church destroyed by fire. The oldest parts, the nave and lower part of the tower, date from the first half of the 15C. Of interest in the nave, with its round piers supporting pointed arches, is the original 15C oak **timber-work roof**. Almost a century older, the choir and pentagonal apse (1507–46) were partitioned off from the rest between 1656 and the 1936–40 restoration. The **east end** is most impressive when seen from St John's Street, looming up massively with sloped intake buttresses between the great windows, characteristic of the Scottish Gothic style. It was here that the infant James VI was crowned in 1567 and John Knox preached the sermon.

▷ On leaving the church, follow signs to Cowane's Hospital.

Cowane's Hospital

Not open to the public.

Until recently used as the Guildhall, and this city instiution was founded by **John Cowane** (c.1570–1633) as an almshouse to accommodate 12 "decayed" brethren. Built between 1633 and 1639 the premises included a refectory with sleeping accommodation above. The donor, a member of the Council of Royal Burghs and Scots Parliament, a man of some substance, stands jauntily above the doorway. The figure is said to come to life at Hogmanay!

▷ Rejoin St John Street.

St John Street

At No. 39 is **Bothwell House** (also known as Bruce Of Auchenbowie's House) a three-storey rubble stonework house with a projecting tower.

Nearby stands the **Old Town Jail**, first opened in 1847, and used as the only military prison in Scotland from 1888 until 1935. Today it is a place where visitors can get an idea of the harsh treatment meted out as punishment to prisoners (*Tours Jul–early Sept daily from 10.15am until 5.15pm. 01786 46 40; http://oldtownjail.co.uk/tours*). There are fine **views** of Stirling from the rooftop of the jail.

The **Stirling Ghost Tour** walk departs from the jail (*Jul–Aug Tue–Sat 8.30pm; Sept–June Fri–Sat 8pm; £6, child £4; 01592 874 449; www.stirlingghost-walk.com*).

Broad Street

Once the centre of burgh life, Broad Street with its **mercat cross**, marks the site of the market and place of execution. **Sir William Bruce** designed the elegant **tolbooth** (1701–04), shortly after his release from Stirling Castle where he had been held for Jacobite sympathies. The design is unusual in that the stairs climb internally over the cells and up to the panelled rooms. The crowning feature of the six-storey tower is an unusual pavilion with delicate crestings. Across the street at No. 16 the narrow gable-ended house has inscribed window pediments.

At the bottom of Broad Street is **Darnley's House**, a four-storeyed town house where Lord Darnley is supposed to have stayed while Mary, Queen of Scots attended to affairs of state at the castle. Farther down in St Mary's Wynd is the now roofless **John Cowane's House**.

ADDITIONAL SIGHT

Smith Art Gallery and Museum

Dumbarton Road.

Tue–Sat 10.30–5pm, Sun 2–5pm.
01786 471 917.
www.smithartgalleryandmuseum.co.uk.
Founded by Thomas Stuart Smith (1814–69), a local collector and painter of portraits, landscapes, oils and watercolours, this enjoyable small gallery and museum contains collections relating the history of the royal burgh, 19C artwork, and oddities such as the world's oldest football, dating from the 1540s made from a pig's bladder.

🚗 DRIVING TOURS

🚗 ① DEVON VALLEY★

29mi/46km.

This tour includes sites rich in history and of great symbolic importance to the nation.

▶ From Stirling station follow Goosecroft Road (B8052), north. It later becomes Cowane Street. Turn right into Union Street and at the roundabout follow the A9.
While crossing the Forth look left to admire the Old Bridge, dating from the 15C, now only for pedestrian use.
At the junction with the A907 (Alloa Road) turn right and then follow signs and local roads to Cambuskenneth Abbey.

Cambuskenneth Abbey

Apr–Sept daily 9.30am–5.30pm. www.historicenvironment.scot.
Access is across a field that can become muddy in wet weather and is used for grazing cattle.
The remains of this once-great Abbey lie within a loop on the flat and fertile carselands of the Forth. Around 1147 King David founded an Augustinian monastery which grew to become one of the most prosperous and influential houses, and its abbots were often statesmen of note. Proximity to Stirling meant royal patronage and the abbey was used for meetings of the Scottish Parliament. The remains include an attractive, free-standing 13C **belfry** which rises through three storeys to a height of 24m. Within the church there is a 19C monument marking the graves of **James III** (1451–1488), victim of the rebel lords after the Battle of Sauchieburn (1488), and his Queen, Margaret of Denmark.

▶ Return to the A907 and turn left. At the roundabout turn right onto the B998.

National Wallace Monument★★

Shuttle bus or 10min walk from the car park. *Daily: Jan–Feb and Nov–Dec 10am–4pm; Mar 10am–5pm; Apr–Jun and Sept–Oct 9.30am–5pm; Jul–Aug 9.30am–6pm.* *25–26 Dec, 1 Jan.* *£10.50.* *01786 472 140. www.nationalwallacemonument.com.*
A famous landmark, the 19C Wallace Monument stands sentinel on Abbey Craig (110m) to commemorate the patriot, **Sir William Wallace** (1270 –1305), responsible for rallying Scottish forces against English rule in the period from 1297 to 1305. Hero of the hour at the Battle of Stirling Bridge (1297), he became Guardian of Scotland, prior to the introduction of a collective system of rule. Following the Scots submission in 1304, Wallace was hunted and captured and died a traitor's death in London the following year.

The 19C cult of Wallace was unexpectedly revived towards the end of the 20C, with the popular success of Mel Gibson's film *Braveheart*, a highly

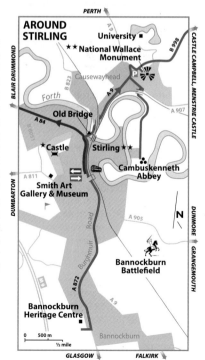

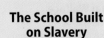

The School Built on Slavery

Dollar Academy is the oldest co-educational school in Britain and is claimed to be the oldest co-educational boarding school in the world. In terms of academic results it is frequently the best-performing school in Scotland. It was founded in 1818 at the bequest of John McNabb, a former slave trader who bequeathed his fortune to provide "a charity or school for the poor of the parish of Dollar where I was born".

floor is a museum and a National Trust for Scotland shop. Exhibits on the former Scottish colony of Nova Scotia relate to the fact that Menstrie was the birthplace of the founder of the colony, **Sir William Alexander**, 1st Earl of Stirling (1567–1640). The title was created to further the development of the colony and replenish impoverished royal coffers, as, in return for a payment, each Earl was granted land in eastern Canada. The project ceased when Nova Scotia was returned to the French in 1631 – even though charters continued to be granted until 1637!

▷ Continue on the A91.

Dollar

The fame of this small residential town, at the southern edge of the Ochil Hills in Clackmannanshire, lies in its Academy (⚘ *see Box above*) and nearby Castle Campbell. The town name probably derives from "doilleir", Gaelic for dark or gloomy – its Castle Campbell was originally known as Castle Gloom.

Castle Campbell★

*1.25mi/2km from the main street up Dollar Glen. The road up is narrow and winding with a limited number of parking places (*P*). Thereafter it is a 5-minute walk to the castle.*
🕙 *Apr–Sept daily 9.30am–5.30pm; Oct–Mar Sat–Wed 10am–4pm.*
🕙 *25–26 Dec and 1–2 Jan.* 💷*£6.*
📞 *01259 742 408.*
www.historicenvironment.scot.

Castle Campbell occupies a magnificent site★★★, on a promontory, with burn-filled clefts on either side, dominating Dollar Glen and Dollar, with the Ochil Hills as a backdrop. The builder of the tower house, one of Scotland's finest surviving examples, was **Colin Campbell, 1st Earl of Argyll** (d.1493) and Lord High Chancellor to James IV. The castle was adopted as the Campbell Lowland seat conveniently close to the various royal residences. Alterations and extensions in the 16C and 17C included the creation of an enclosed courtyard and additional domestic ranges and

romanticised and historically wayward account of the hero.

An upper chamber within the monument contains Wallace's War Tent, with a gripping audio-visual presentation of his conflict with the English. Another chamber, the Hall of Heroes, is lined with the busts of such figures as Sir Walter Scott, Robert the Bruce and Robert Burns. The viewing platform (*246 steps*) has a tremendous **panorama★★** of Stirling in the flat carselands of the Forth.

Also visible is the **University of Stirling** in its lake and parkland setting, with the Ochils as backdrop. Airthrey Castle, another of Adam's castle houses in the baronial style, serves as administrative centre while the **Macrobert Centre** is the focus of cultural activity for both town and gown.

▷ Return to the B998 and turn right and join the A91. Follow the Mill Trail tourist route along the A91 towards St Andrews. This follows the steep southern slopes of the Ochil Hills (*highest point Ben Cleuch, alt. 721m*) and the beautiful wooded Devon valley. In Menstrie follow the castle signs (on the main street).

Menstrie Castle

🕙*Easter Sun and May–Sept Wed and Sun 2–5pm.* 📞*01259 213 131.*
Built in the 16C, Menstrie castle has been partially converted into holiday apartments while part of the ground

gardens. The Campbell family was staunchly Presbyterian and legend has it that John Knox visited the castle and preached here in 1556. The personal animosity between Archibald, 8th Earl of Argyll (1607–61), and the Marquess of Montrose, no doubt made the estate a target for raids but it is doubtful if the castle was attacked. Damage more probably came nine years later during General Monck's campaign and by the late 19C the castle was in a considerable state of disrepair.

The main part of the castle is the late-15C four-storey **tower house** which rises to an overhanging parapet. Prior to the construction of the turnpike stair, access was by a stair in the thickness of the wall or by an outside stair or ladder to first floor level. The vaulted great hall with its massive fireplace has a vaulted cellar below and two chambers above. The topmost room is noteworthy for its ribbed barrel vault and two unusual grotesque masks. The parapet walk (*84 steps from the courtyard*) provides an excellent **view**★ away over Dollar to the Forth valley and Pentlands in the distance.

▶ To complete the tour, rejoin the A91 and return to Stirling, leaving the town south on the A872.

Bannockburn Heritage Centre

👤⌚*Site:* all year daily until dusk; *Visitor Centre and Exhibition* daily: Apr–Sept 9.30am–6pm; Oct–Mar 10am–5pm. ⌚*25–26 Dec, 1–2 Jan.* ✆£11.50 (child £8.50). ✕ 🅿 ☎01786 812 664. https://battleofbannockburn.com. The equestrian statue (1964) of King **Robert the Bruce** (1274–1329) marks Bruce's command post on the eve of the historic **Battle of Bannockburn**, 24 June 1314. Although numerically superior, the English forces, led by Edward II in person, were routed and Bannockburn was a turning point in the **Wars of Independence** (⌚*see HISTORY*).

Since his coronation at Scone in 1306 and Edward I's death in 1307, the Bruce had been steadily regaining his king-

dom and by 1314 Stirling castle was the most important stronghold remaining in English hands.

The **Visitor Centre** harnesses 3D technology to give a presentation on the battle and exhibitions on the Kingdom of the Scots, Robert the Bruce and the Struggle for Independence.

🚗 ② STRATHALLAN★

13mi/20km – one way. This short tour through the wide river valley of Strathallan takes in Dunblane's splendid cathedral, Doune's fine castle and a Red Kite sanctuary.

▶ Leave Stirling following signed routes NW to join the M9 N towards Perth. At the end of the motorway take the B8033 (an old military road) into Dunblane.

Dunblane★

This mainly residential town, on Allan Water, is famous historically for its lovely 13C Gothic cathedral, set in its close. Unfortunately the town gained national and worldwide notoriety on 13 March 1996 when a crazed gunman entered a school, killing 16 children and their teacher. It was Britain's worst gun tragedy and precipitated drastic new gun ownership laws in the United Kingdom. A modern memorial in the cathedral commemorates the victims.

Dunblane Cathedral★★

☎01786 825 388. www.dunblanecathedral.org.uk. Although Dunblane was already an ecclesiastical centre in Celtic times, it was David I who created the bishopric c.1150. The cathedral led a peaceful existence and numbered among its bishops Clement (1233–58), the builder of the cathedral, and that rare ecclesiastic. Despite a chequered history of 15C alterations, neglect following the Reformation (albeit no pillaging) and several 19C and 20C restorations, the cathedral remains a fine example of 13C Gothic architecture.

Adjoining the nave on the south side to the left of the entrance is a 12C **tower**

Dunblane cathedral

© O. Forir/MICHELIN

which belonged to the early Celtic building. Continue round to the west end overlooking the Allan Water where the masterful design of the **west front★★** combines a deeply recessed doorway with a tall triplet of lancets and Ruskin's small vesica (oval window).

The building (64m long) passes from nave to choir uninterrupted by transepts or crossing. Built after the Lady Chapel, the pointed arcades of the eight-bay nave descend onto clustered columns and are surmounted by a double clerestory where window tracery is repeated inside the gallery.

This device is copied at the west end, where the great window shows the Tree of Jesse (1906). Below are two sets of the canopied 15C **Chisholm stalls**, deeply and vigorously carved with a wealth of detail.

The misericords are of great interest. Around the pulpit are the carved figures of St Blane, who gave his name to the

town, King David I, Bishops Clement and Leighton, and John Knox.

The glory of the building is the **choir** with its great height emphasised by soaring lancets. Level with the high altar are the early-15C **Ochiltree stalls**, showing a similar verve of execution. The present stalls and organ case were designed by Robert Lorimer during his 1914 restoration of the choir. Three stone slabs in the floor mark the burial places of the Drummond sisters, allegedly poisoned in 1501 to prevent Margaret, the eldest, from becoming James IV's Queen in preference to Henry VIII's sister, Margaret Tudor. The effigy in the north wall tomb recess is said to be that of Clement, the builder bishop. The oldest part, the **Lady Chapel** opening off the north side of the choir, has ribbed vaulting with carved bosses.

The Dean's House (1624) contains the **Dunblane Museum** (&◷*Apr–mid-Oct Mon–Sat 10.30am–4.30pm; Feb–Mar Sat 12.30–3.30pm; ℘01786 825 691; www.dunblanemuseum.org.uk*); note the collection of Communion Tokens, the predecessors of today's communion cards.

Within the manse grounds is the 1687 home of Bishop Leighton's personal library, the oldest private library in Scotland. **Leighton Library** (◷*May–Sept Mon–Sat 11am–1pm; ℘01786 822 296; www.leightonlibrary.org.uk*)

Ruskin's Praise

The great Victorian art critic John Ruskin said of Dunblane cathedral: "I know not anything so perfect in its simplicity and so beautiful, in all the Gothic with which I am acquainted."

houses 4 500 books in over 80 languages printed between 1504 and 1840. Here you can browse through some of the country's rarest books, including a first edition of Sir Walter Scott's *Lady of the Lake*.

From the northeast corner there is a lovely view along the north side of the cathedral.

▶ Leave Dunblane heading W on the Doune Road (A820) which crosses the A9 as you head for Doune.

Doune★

Strategically set on one of the main routes into the Central Highlands, this neat little burgh, famed in the past for its pistol making and cattle and sheep fairs, is now known for its impressive castle ruins.

Doune Castle★

Access by car from the A820. ⏱*Daily: Apr–Sept 9.30am–5.30pm; Oct–Mar 10am–4.30pm.* ⏱*25–26 Dec and 1–2 Jan.* ⊜*£9.* ☏*01786 841 742. www.historicenvironment.scot.*

This formidable castle overlooks Ardoch Burn and the River Teith. It was built in the late 14C by the regents, Robert Duke of Albany and his son Murdoch. On the latter's execution it passed to the Crown and was used as a dower house by successive Queens before becoming the property of the Stewarts.

The key to the defence of this 14C fortified castle is the keep-gatehouse. The castle was unusual for its period in that consideration was also given to the provision of practical living quarters.

The **keep-gatehouse** (29m high) rises through four storeys and is flanked to the right by the range of buildings containing the halls. The well-defended portal gives onto a vaulted passage flanked by prison, guardroom and cellars. The latter and the well chamber have hatches allowing victuals to be hoisted upstairs in the eventuality of a siege. Curtain walls with wall-walks enclose the **courtyard** on three sides; the keep-gatehouse, adjoining range and second tower form the fourth.

Doune or Highland Pistols

In the 17C and 18C the village was renowned for the manufacture of fine pistols. The trade originated in the mid-17C and catered mainly for the Highland cattle drovers. Doune pistols are recognisable by their shape and decoration: a ram's horn butt, fluted breech, flared muzzles and rich embellishment. They were manufactured in pairs for left- or right-hand use. The **1747 Proscription Act**, which prohibited the wearing of Highland dress and the carrying of arms, destroyed the traditional market.

A well-defended outside staircase – compare to the second one – climbs to the first floor lord's hall. The portcullis was operated from a window embrasure here. Steps beside the double fireplace lead down to the lord's private chamber with escape hatch, and up to the solar and other apartments of the keep-gatehouse, a truly self-contained and secure unit. From the courtyard, take the second outside staircase up to the retainers' hall where the soldiers were garrisoned. From here access is gained to the impressive **kitchen** area in the second tower.

▶ Leave the A820 in Doune, heading roughly NE on a minor road for Argaty.

Argaty red kites

2.5mi/4km northeast of Doune. ⏱*Ranger-led visit to hide daily 2.30pm (late Oct–late Feb 1.30pm). Prebooking essential.* ⊜*£6; guided walk and visit to hide.* ☏*01786 841 373. www.argatyredkites.co.uk.*

Around 130 years ago the red kite became extinct in Scotland. It was re-introduced in 1996, and numbers are now growing again. To enable the public to see this magnificent bird at close quarters, the Argaty viewing centre places a small amount of food daily near the hide (though it should be emphasised that the birds are still wild and do not rely on it for survival).

ADDRESSES

⌂ STAY

Number 10 – *Gladstone Place. ℘01786 472 681. www.cameron-10.co.uk. 3 rooms.* Set in a pleasant suburb within walking distance of the old town, this Victorian terrace house is deceptively spacious and offers smart and modern-traditional bedrooms.

Castlecroft B&B – *Ballengeich Road. ℘01786 474 933. www.castlecroft-uk.co.uk. 5 rooms.* This modern B&B is a 20min walk from the centre, perched immediately below Stirling Castle with fine views one way to the castle and to the scenic northwest, the start of the Highlands. Request a room with a patio.

Victoria Square Guest House – *12 Victoria Square. ℘01786 473 920. www. victoriasquareguesthouse.com. 10 rooms.* Detached 1880s house in the shadow of Stirling Castle; spacious bedrooms, some with four-poster beds.

Allan Park Hotel – *20 Allan Park. ℘01786 475 336. https:// theallanparkstirling.co.uk. 9 rooms.* Set in a quiet street a short walk from the centre of town, this is a simple pub, restaurant and coffee house with rooms.

The Park Lodge Hotel – *32 Park Terrace. ℘01786 474 862. www.park lodge.net. 9 rooms.* This charming Georgian house, with splendid castle views, was built in 1825. Its bedrooms (some include four-posters), have style and period furnishings, and there is a lovely walled garden. Terrific value.

Golden Lion Hotel – *8–10 King Street. ℘01786 475 351. www.thegoldenlion stirling.com. 67 rooms.* Stirling's oldest hotel (est. 1786) is in the heart of the old town in the pedestrianised zone. It mixes contemporary comforts with historical character in its newly refurbished rooms and in the timeless elegance of the stunning Regency Ballroom.

Stirling Highland Hotel – *Spittal Street. ℘01786 272 727. www.thecairncollection.co.uk. 96 rooms.* Formerly owned by Barceló, this is the finest hotel in Stirling and occupies old college buildings very close to the castle. Health and beauty facilities include a pool and there is a good **restaurant** (⊜⊜⊜). Several of the bedrooms enjoy wonderful views.

⅋ EAT

Hermann's – *Mar Place House, Broad Street. ℘01786 450 632. www.hermanns-restaurant.co.uk. Reservations advised on Sat.* Austrian favourites such as schnitzel and strudel meet fine Scottish cuisine at this cosy smart restaurant run by Tyrolean owner Hermann Aschaber.

The Portcullis Hotel – *Castle Wind. ℘01786 472 290. www.theportcullis hotel.com.* This pub-hotel near the castle was built in 1787 and has a nice garden. Sirloin steak and Highland chicken are the favourite dishes in its convivial restaurant. There are four bedrooms (⊜⊜⊜), some of which enjoy views over the town and to the Ochil Hills beyond.

Henderson's Bistro – *Albert Halls, Dumbarton Road. ℘01786 469 727. www. hendersonsstirling.co.uk.* Located within Albert Halls, this trendy bistro offers a good range of mainstream dishes – steak, chicken, duck, sea bass, risotto – based around seasonal produce.

NIGHTLIFE

The Tolbooth – *Jail Wynd; ℘01786 274 000. www.stirling.gov.uk/tolbooth* is the town's most popular venue for music and the arts, staging comedy, folk, jazz, world music and more in the beautifully restored former jail and courthouse. Large windows and an eighth floor terrace look out over the town. A short walk away the **Albert Halls** (*Albert Place; ℘01786 473 544; http://alberthalls.stirling. gov.uk*) is the venue for bigger names and more mainstream acts including comedy and tribute bands. It includes a bistro.

The Trossachs★★★

and Loch Lomond★★★

One of Scotland's most beautiful regions, the Trossachs conjure up an idyllic landscape of great scenic value where rugged, lofty mountains, and their often wooded slopes, are reflected in the sparkling waters of the lochs.

A BIT OF HISTORY

> *"So wondrous and wild, the whole might seem The scenery of a fairy dream."*

Sir Walter Scott put the Trossachs on the map in the early 19C with his novels *Lady of the Lake* and *Rob Roy*, and its untamed peaks, glens and deep forests have attracted visitors from England and Scotland (thanks in no small part to its proximity to the great urban populations of the latter) ever since.

LOCH LOMOND & THE TROSSACHS NATIONAL PARK

20 Carrochan Rd, Balloch, Alexandria
℘*01389 722 600.*
www.lochlomond-trossachs.org.
The Trossachs is part of the **Loch Lomond & the Trossachs National Park**. It embraces the deep waters of Loch Lomond, the wild glens of the Trossachs, Breadalbane's high mountains and the sheltered sea lochs of the Argyll forest.
Despite the fact that Balloch is the southern gateway to the lake, the main National Park Visitor Centre is at Balmaha (*see panel*). The centre contains state-of-the-art interpretation, exploring the nature, geology and social history of the National Park and a peaceful outdoor area with accessible walks down to the loch. Children's activities and a play area. Various events are held here.

The area described here under the heading Trossachs has been extended towards Loch Lomond in the west and in

Info: www.lochlomond-trossachs.org.
Visitor Centres:
Aberfoyle: Trossachs Discovery Centre, Main Street. ℘01877 381 352.
Balloch: Old Station Building; ℘01389 753 533.
Balmaha: Main car park. ℘01389 722 100.
Callander: 52–54 Main Street. ℘01877 330 342. https://incallander.co.uk.

Location: The Trossachs are bounded by the head of Loch Achray in the east, the foot of Loch Katrine to the west, Ben An (*alt. 533m*) to the north and Ben Venue (*alt. 729m*) to the south. The term is more generally taken to cover a wider area from Loch Venachar in the east to the shores of Loch Lomond.

Don't Miss: The Hilltop viewpoint panorama; a boat trip on Loch Katrine.

Timing: Allow a day for the round tour including visits and boat trip. To appreciate to the full the solitude and scenic splendours, it is advisable to visit early in the morning when the coaches are not yet about and driving on the narrow roads is less demanding.

Kids: Go Ape at the Queen Elizabeth Forest Park.

the south to the Lake of Menteith for the convenience of the round tour described below, which has Callander as its starting point.
An alternative day tour combining boat and bus trips and covers the western part of the area, starts from Balloch.

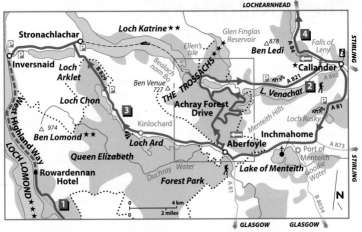

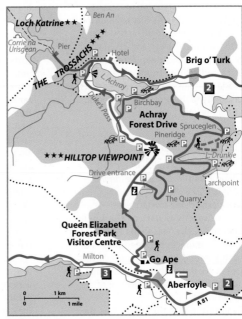

THE TROSSACHS

🐾 Picnic Area

🚶 Forest footpath

🚗 DRIVING TOURS

🚗 ① LOCH LOMOND★★★

Whether you take the high road, or the low road, a drive around the bonny bonny banks of the loch is a highlight. The legendary beauty of the "Queen of Scottish Lochs", so often celebrated in song and verse, is one of blue waters flanked by shapely mountains or fringed by pastoral wooded shores. This freshwater loch, straddling the geologically important Highland Boundary Fault Line, is 23mi/37km long and 5mi/8km at its widest and has a maximum depth of 199m; its surface area is 27 sq mi/70 sq km. Within the United Kingdom, it

Loch Lomond

© Liz Leyden/iStockphoto.com

is surpassed only by Lough Neagh and Lower Lough Erne in Northern Ireland The water discharges into the Firth of Clyde by the River Leven.

The ruggedly mountainous scenery of the narrow northern end gives way in the south, having crossed the Highland Boundary Fault, to a more pastoral setting of wooded islands and shores.

For walkers, part of the **West Highland Way** from Milngavie to Fort William follows the eastern shore (&see www. cicerone.co.uk for guide).

The loch is featured in a well-known song first published around 1841, which includes the chorus:

Oh, ye'll tak' the high road, and I'll tak'
the low road,
And I'll be in Scotland afore ye;
But me and my true love will never meet
again
On the bonnie, bonnie banks o' Loch
Lomond.

Parking can be difficult in high season and it is advisable to avoid summer weekends as the west shore road is often very busy.

Islands of Loch Lomond

The majority of the loch's islands are private, but some can be reached by ferry.

Cars are allowed along the eastern shore but only as far as Rowardennan.

Several of the islands appear to be crannogs – partial or entirely artificial islands built in prehistoric periods and used as dwellings over five millennia from the European Neolithic period.

Inchmurrin

The largest of the 30+ islands speckling the wider southern part of the loch. Indeed, Inchmurrin is the largest island in a body of freshwater in the British Isles.

At the southern tip are the ruins of what was once a Lennox stronghold.

Inchcailloch

Nature Reserve. Balmaha lies on the line of the Highland Boundary Fault where mountains suddenly rise out of the gentler Lowlands to the south.

Balloch

Balloch, at the southernmost point of Loch Lomond, is 20mi/32km northwest of Glasgow via the A82. The name comes from the Gaelic word for village or hamlet – bal–loch means the village on the loch. Given its prime location at the southern end of Loch Lomond, Balloch is an important centre for tourism.

Cruise Loch Lomond ship, Luss

© josefkubes/iStockphoto.com

Boat Trips

By far the best way to discover the charms of Loch Lomond is to take to the water. Boat trips depart from Balloch with **Sweeney's Cruises** (*12.30pm and 3pm: May–Sept daily; Apr and Oct Sat-Sun only. £20, child 12–15 £18, under 12, £12, under 5, free. 01389 752 376; www.sweeneyscruises.com*). **Cruise Loch Lomond** offer an 'Island Explorer' trip sailing from Luss to Inchcailloch (*late May–early Nov; 10am, 11.30am, 1.15pm; £13, child £7; 01301 702 356; www.cruiselochlomond.co.uk*).

Loch Lomond Shores

Ben Lomond Way, Balloch. Daily 10am–5.30pm. 01389 751 031. www.lochlomondshores.com.
This spectacular visitor centre on the water's edge is the perfect introduction to the Loch and National Park. It hosts a range of shops (including a branch of Edinburgh's famous department store, Jenners) plus family activities and attractions including the **Loch Lomond Sea Life Centre** (*daily Mar–Oct 10am–5pm; Nov–Feb 10am–4pm (1 Jan 11am–4pm); 25–26 Dec. £9.95, online discounts available; 0871 423 2110; www.visitsealife.com*), with its rays, turtles, otters and giant pacific octopus.

The complex is also home to a small Help Centre, though more comprehensive information is available at The Old Station Building in Balloch.

Return to Balloch to join the A82 and then drive north along the western shore.

Western Shore

Luss★

A small, attractive conservation village with mellow sandstone and slate cottages. A settlement has stood on this site since medieval times, although most of the present village dates from the 18C and 19C. A large car park here is a popular halt for visitors to the area and those heading further north.

There is a seasonal charage for parking, and for the use of toilets.

There is another car park and toilets (free), also with ready access to the shores of Loch Lomond a short distance farther north at Firkin Point.

Beyond Luss the loch begins to narrow and the mountains close in; more so once Tarbert is reached.

Tarbet

Tarbet lies at the head of a short valley which leads southwestwards to Arrochar. The Vikings are said to have hauled their galleys over this neck of land to claim sovereignty over the peninsula. Queen Victoria described Tarbert as "a small town [with] splendid passes, richly wooded and the highest mountains rising behind".

From just above (and east of) Arrochar there is indeed a splendid and inspiring **view**, across the tip of the loch, of the so-called Arrochar Alps on the far shore: left to right the craggy shaped **Cobbler**

Rob Roy

Often referred to as Scotland's Robin Hood, Rob Roy MacGregor (1671–1734) – unlike his English counterpart – was a real person, born at Glengyle, at the head of Loch Katrine. His name is in fact an anglicisation of his given Gaelic name, Raibeart Ruadh, meaning Red Robert, on account of young Rob's red hair. Rob, together with his father, a senior clan chief, joined the Jacobite rising led by Viscount Dundee to support the Stuart King James who had been deposed by William of Orange. They fought at the Battle of Killiecrankie on 27 July 1689 and, although defeated, managed to escape.

Statue of Rob Roy in Stirling

© W. Buss/De Agostini/age fotostock

Rob became a respected cattleman and borrowed a large sum of money to increase his own cattle herd. Unfortunately his chief herder, entrusted with the money to bring the cattle back, betrayed Rob who consequently defaulted on his loan and was therefore branded an outlaw. His principal creditor, James Graham, 1st Duke of Montrose, seized his lands. His wife and family were evicted from their house at Inversnaid, which was then burned down (it is also claimed Rob's wife was raped and branded). It was this that caused Rob to wage a bloody feud against the duke, raiding his lands and cattle as reparation for his loss. Rob died in his house at Inverlochlarig Beg, Balquhidder, on 28 December 1734, after a short illness, and his grave in the churchyard can be visited today. Much of the Trossachs was MacGregor country and is closely associated with Rob – the most popular Rob Roy locations are around Loch Katrine but if you read the books you will find many more.

First Daniel Defoe, in *Highland Rogue* (published in 1723, while Rob was still alive), then Sir Walter Scott's famous *Rob Roy* (1818) embellished his exploits and gave birth to a legend, revived more recently in the eponymous 1995 movie starring Liam Neeson. A short film on Rob Roy is shown in the visitor centre in Balloch.

MacGREGOR DESPITE THEM

COLL. DIED 1735.
ROBERT, DIED 1754.
SONS OF ROB ROY.

Rob Roy's grave in Balquhidder

© David Carton/Fotolibra

(Ben Arthur) then a group of three: Beinn Ime (at the far head of Allt a'Bhalachain glen), Ben Narnain, and A'Chrois.

Eastern Shore

Rowardennan Hotel

The loch's eastern road ends at this 17C hotel. It's well worth the visit for the drive up along the eastern shore and to enjoy, at various points, the tranquil loch shore. (🅿 *Parking charges apply.*)

A path leads from near the hotel to the summit of Ben Lomond, but it is neither a casual nor genteel ascent.

Ben Lomond★★

In the care of the National Trust for Scotland, the shapely form of this 974m peak rises above the eastern shore behind Rowardennan. This is the most southerly of the Munros.

The higher regions of the mountain support an alpine tundra ecozone, hosting bird species including peregrine falcon, merlin, ptarmigan, red grouse and golden eagle. Much of Ben Lomond is designated a Site of Special Scientific Interest (SSSI) for the range of upland habitats present at all altitudes. The **Ardess Hidden History Trail** (*www. nts.org.uk*) gives a detailed explanation of the rich cultural and archaeological heritage of the area.

There is a **fell race** to the summit and back in early May each year; the current male record (set in 1983) is 1hr 2min and 16 seconds; the female record is 1hr 11min and 57 seconds! (*www. scottishhillracing.co.uk*)

⟵ 🚗 ② CALLANDER TO ABERFOYLE★

26mi/42km (without the Achray Forest Drive loop)

Known to millions of older television viewers as the Tannochbrae of Dr Finlay's Casebook, Callander is a busy summer resort on the banks of the River Teith. Astride one of the principal routes into the Highlands, the town was built on Drummond lands confiscated after the 18C Jacobite risings. Its popularity has grown ever since, owing in large part

to its proximity to the Trossachs. Before beginning this tour, visit Callander's curious toy collection.

👥 Hamilton Toy Collection

11 Main Street. 🚻 🕐 *Easter–Oct Mon– Sat 10.30am–5pm, Sun noon–5pm.* ⬛ *£3; child £1.* 📞 *01877 330 004. www.thehamiltontoycollection.co.uk.* This charming small museum-shop takes parents (and grandparents) back to their childhood days, while children are fascinated to see the things that were fashionable then.

▷ Leave Callander on the A81.

Lake of Menteith

On the northern edge of Flanders Moss, the lake is the venue for The Bonspiel, or Grand Match, an outdoor curling tournament between teams from the north and south, which historically has drawn tens of thousands of participants. However, it is only played when the ice is sufficiently thick enough (more than 18cm) to make it safe to do so – the last time was in 1979! In fact, it has been staged only three times since 1945.

The Lake of Menteith is often thought of as the only body of water in Scotland that is referred to as a lake rather than a loch, but in fact there are at least four others, all artificial.

There are a number of small islands in the lake. On Inchmahome, the largest, is Inchmahome Priory, an ancient monastery that served as refuge to the infant Mary, Queen of Scots, in 1547 (ℓ *see below*).

▷ Just before passing the lake turn left (south) on the B8034. The car park is 800m down the road, on the right.

Inchmahome Priory

This is an island monastery. 🕐 *Apr–Sept daily first ferry 10am, last ferry 4.15pm; Oct 3.15pm;* ⬛ *£9 (includes ferry fare);* 📞 *01877 385 294; www.historicenvironment.scot.*

The mid-13C ruins include the church of the Augustinian priory with its deeply recessed west doorway strongly resembling the one at Dunblane and the chapter house, which shelters an unusual **double effigy★** tomb monument. In 1547 Mary, Queen of Scots was brought here for her own safety – she was only four years old at the time – after the battle of Pinkie Cleugh and stayed for three weeks prior to embarking for France.

▷ Return to the A81 and turn left to follow it westwards. Turn onto the A821 to reach Aberfoyle.

Aberfoyle

Aberfoyle was made famous as the meeting place of Rob Roy and Nicol Jarvie. Today, it is busy with tourists in summer, many of whom throng the sales floor of **The Scottish Wool Centre** (⬥🕐daily 9.30am–6pm (5.30pm over Easter weekend); ✕. ℰ01877 382 850; www.ewm.co.uk). The story of 2 000 years of Scottish wool is told by means of an entertaining live show featuring sheepdogs and ducks; there are also Birds of Prey to see, with flying demonstrations on certain days.

▷ Leave Aberfoyle to the west on the B829 towards Duke's Pass.

Queen Elizabeth Forest Park Visitor Centre and Go Ape

Lodge Visitor Centre, Duke's Pass, Aberfoyle. ⬥🕐*Daily from 10am, closing from 3pm–6pm depending on season.* ✕ 🅿£1–£3. ℰ0300 067 6615. https://forestryandland.gov.scot.
The audiovisual presentation in the Visitor Centre is an excellent introduction to the forest park. A variety of walking **trails** are open to the public including the Fairy Trail on Doon Hill, the site from where the Rev Robert Kirk was spirited away (⬥see Box, p248).
Between March and September the wildlife room in the visitor centre offers a chance to see ospreys with a live CCTV stream showing these magnificent birds in their natural habitat.
The centre is also the base for **Go Ape** (⬥🕐*Feb–Nov, see website for dates and times, booking in advance required;*

🕐*min height 1.4m; weight and adult supervision restrictions apply;* 🅿 ; ℰ01603 895 500; https://goape.co.uk/days-out/scotland/aberfoyle*). This is an exciting treetop trail for children and adults, traversing a series of rope ladders, bridges, Tarzan swings, trapezes, stirrup crossings and zip wires, including two of the longest zip wires in Great Britain (426m).

▷ The road descends into Aberfoyle leaving behind the mountainous rim of the Central Highlands.

Achray Forest Drive

This forest road (7mi/11km long, and diverting from the main itinerary) makes an excellent outing for those wanting an afternoon away from it all (*ample parking and picnic places with a choice of walks*) but since it is through forested countryside it has few views of the surrounding countryside.

Hilltop viewpoint★★★

Park at the roadside; 5min climb to viewing table.
From here there is a wonderful **panorama** of the Trossachs, encompassing Ben Venue, Loch Katrine with its mountain ring, Ben A'an, Finglas Reservoir, the great shoulder of **Ben Ledi** (*alt. 879m*) with Brig o'Turk at its feet, **Loch Venachar** (*4mi/6.4km long; parking and picnic places*) and due east round to the Menteith Hills. In the immediate fore-

Scott's Trossachs

Sir Walter Scott popularised the Trossachs in his writings on Rob Roy and his romantic poem, *The Lady of the Lake*. Such was the public desire to follow in the footsteps of Scott's characters that the Duke of Montrose built **Duke's Road** in 1820, a connecting road north from Aberfoyle. Famous visitors who came this way included the Wordsworths and Coleridge in 1830, following which Wordsworth wrote *To a Highland Girl*.

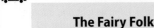

The Fairy Folk

Local folklore includes such mythical creatures as the Water Bull of Loch Katrine and the Water Horse of Loch Venachar, the latter made into a movie, *The Water Horse* (2008). An Aberfoyle minister, the Reverend Robert Kirk, published *The Secret Commonwealth of Elfs, Fawns and Fairies* (1691) and another supernatural tale is that of *The Water Witch,* the name taken by the first commercial steamboat to ply the waters of Loch Katrine.

ground is Loch Drunkie in the heart of Achray Forest.

▷ Follow the sign to Loch Katrine along the A821, driving next to the shore of Loch Achray for a while.

Loch Katrine★★

1mi/1.6km from A821 to the pier and car park. No access round loch for vehicles. Other than hill walking, the only (very rewarding) way to discover this famous loch is to take a **boat trip** on board the *Sir Walter Scott* or the *Lady of the Lake* (*operates 1h and 45min cruises daily from Trossachs Pier, late Mar–early Nov, see website for times and prices;* ℰ*01877 376 315; www.lochkatrine.com/cruises*). The loch (10mi/16km long and 2mi/3.2km at its widest) has been Glasgow's water supply since 1859, when Queen Victoria officiated at the inauguration. On the northeastern slopes of the twin-peaked Ben Venue are Corrie na Urisgean (Goblin's Cave), the traditional meeting place of Scotland's goblins, and Bealach nam Bo (Pass of the Cattle), a route much favoured by the drover Rob Roy when returning home with cattle. Ellen's Isle (Eilean Molach) figures in Scott's *The Lady of the Lake.*

Glen Gyle, at the head of Loch Katrine, was the birthplace of Rob Roy and on the north shore is a MacGregor burial place. Factor's Isle, another Rob Roy haunt, is where the outlaw held the

Duke of Montrose's factor, Baillie Nicol Jarvie, in reprisal for having evicted Rob Roy's family.

▷ Rejoin the A821 towards Callander, and passing Loch Achray Hotel on the shores of the loch.

Brig o'Turk

This widely scattered village at the mouth of Glen Finglas is closely associated with the Victorian art critic John Ruskin, who with his wife and John Everett Millais, the famed painter, spent an extended holiday in the area together in 1853. Brig o'Turk was also one of the early summer haunts of the Glasgow Boys art movement.

Once across the Finglas Water, the road enters the **Achray Forest**, part of the Queen Elizabeth Forest Park (ℰ *see main entry, above*). After Loch Achray, the second tallest peak of the area, **Ben Venue** (727m) stands out in the distance with the white form of Loch Achray Hotel at its feet. Pass on the right the castellated 20C reconstruction of the Trossachs Hotel.

▷ Continue on the A821, and at the junction with the A84, turn right to return to Callander.

3 ABERFOYLE TO LOCH LOMOND

16mi/26km

This **scenic road**, ending beside Inversnaid Hotel on Loch Lomond, makes a pleasant drive through the southwest of the Queen Elizabeth Forest Park.

▷ From Aberfoyle, take the single-track B829 to the west.

Loch Ard

The road along the north shore runs close to the water's edge of Loch Ard described by **Queen Victoria** in 1869 as "...a fine long loch with trees of all kinds overhanging the road, heather making all pink, bracken, rocks, high hills of such fine shape and trees growing up

© Jon Arnold/hemis.fr

them as in Switzerland. Altogether the whole view was lovely". The **scenery** has lost none of its attraction with the southern shore clothed with the trees of Loch Ard Forest. The prominent outline of Ben Lomond looms large on the horizon. There is a fine **view** of Loch Chon, backed by the "Arrochar Alps" in the distance.

Loch Chon

This is the smaller of the two lochs.

◗ At the road junction the branch to the right leads to Stronachlachar.

Stronachlachar

On the western shore of Loch Katrine. The *SS Sir Walter Scott* and the *Lady of the Lake* make occasional stops here in summer (♿*see Loch Katrine above*).

◗ Return to the junction and carry straight on.

Loch Arklet

This artificial loch (reservoir) lies in a glacially created hanging valley.
The ruins to the right are those of Inversnaid barracks built in the early 18C to curb the MacGregors.

Inversnaid

On Loch Lomondside, the Inversnaid Hotel overlooks the pier and is one of the stopping places for steamer cruises. The far side of Loch Lomond (♿*see LOCH LOMOND*) is dominated by the peaks of The Cobbler, Bens Vorlich, Vane and

Ime. The 92-mile **West Highland Way** follows this shore of Loch Lomond (♿*see www.cicerone.co.uk for guide*).

◗ Return towards Aberfoyle, leaving to the east. At the junction with the A81 turn left. The road skirts the great rounded spine of the Menteith Hills.

☛ 4 ROB ROY COUNTRY

The valley west of Balquhidder – the home ground of Rob Roy (♿*see p245*) – provides a pleasant change from the bustle of the main road. The scenery is wilder but less dramatic.

◗ Leave Callander by the A84 and continue as far as Kingshouse. Here, turn left on a minor road to Inverlochlarig (11.5mi/18.5km from the main road). The road is single track with passing places.

Balquhidder – Pronounced "bal-whidder" the railed enclosure in the churchyard marks the last resting place of Rob Roy MacGregor, his wife Helen, and two of their sons. The defiant tombstone inscription "MacGregor Despite Them" – referring to the king's banning of the MacGregor clan name – was not added until the 1920s.

Loch Voil – This peaceful stretch of water is overlooked to the north by the rounded outlines of the Braes of Balquhidder, and the much higher Stob Binnein (1 165m) and Ben More (1 174m), with lower forest-clad slopes to the south.

Inverlochlarig – At the road end, one mile above the head of Loch Doine, is the site of Rob Roy's house, where he died. Rob moved here from Glen Gyle, the latter being too near for comfort to the recently established garrison at Inversnaid. This is the departure point for several hill walks with paths leading north to Glen Dochart and west to Glen Falloch.

ADDRESSES

🏠 STAY

🛏 **Oak Tree Inn** – *Balmaha, Loch Lomond. ℰ01360 870 357. www. theoaktreeinn.co.uk.* Close encounters with folk of the West Highland Wayfaring kind are possible in this family run B&B, **restaurant** (🛏🛏), bar, village shop and coffee shop with ice cream parlour.

🛏 **Lubnaig House** – *Leny Feus, Callander. ℰ01877 330 608. www. lubnaigguesthouse.com.* Built in 1864 on the outskirts of town, this characterful house boasts well-kept, large mature gardens and homely bedrooms – two in converted stables.

🛏🛏 **Lodge on Loch Lomond** – *Luss. ℰ01436 860 201. www.loch-lomond.co.uk. 48 rooms.* This luxury hotel merges the traditional and the contemporary to provide luxury accommodation and has hosted two US presidents. **Colquhouns restaurant**🛏🛏 is recommended.

🛏🛏 **Macdonald Forest Hills Hotel and Spa** – *Kinlochard, Aberfoyle. ℰ0344 879 9057. www.macdonaldhotels. co.uk/foresthills.* This luxury country-house hotel spa is in a lovely location overlooking Loch Ard, with extensive leisure facilities and individually-styled rooms. Look online for some bargain deals. The **Garden Restaurant**🛏🛏 enjoys glorious Scottish views to complement its Modern-Scottish cuisine.

🛏🛏🛏 **Cameron House**, *on Loch Lomond, Alexandria* – *ℰ01389 310 777. www.cameronhouse.co.uk.* Extensive Victorian house in a picturebook setting on the loch among wooded parkland. Luxurious rooms (monsoon showers, iPod docking stations…) and superb leisure facilities (including spa and golf course). 🐾 *The hotel, the Leisure Club, the Great Scots Bar and Cameron Grill will be closed until autumn.*

🛏🛏🛏 **Roman Camp Country House** – *Main Street, Callander. ℰ01877 330 003. www.romancamphotel.co.uk. 15 rooms and suites.* A very peaceful part-17C hunting lodge built for the Dukes of Perth, in extensive gardens replete with antiques and fine *objets d'art*. Opulent public rooms include a secret chapel. Bedrooms are decorated in comfy country-house style. Two dining rooms 🛏🛏 .

🍴 EAT

🍽 **Mhor Fish** – *75-77 Main Street, Callander. ℰ01877 330 213. www.mhor.net.* On the one hand a take-away chippy; on the other a funky caff. Great for something quick and easy.

🍽 **Callander Meadows** – *24 Main Street, Callander. ℰ01877 330 181. www. callandermeadows.co.uk. Closed Tue–Wed.* The Meadows, a lovely early 19C town house with charm and character. Expect high-quality bistro-style dishes with fresh, seasonal produce sourced locally. They also offer three elegant, trad-modern rooms (🛏🛏), one of which is a four-poster.

🍽 **Lade Inn - pub and restaurant** – *Kilmahog (east of Callander). ℰ01877 330 152. www.theladeinn.com.* Bright lively attractive trad-modern pub where they brew their own beer (three choices) and cook up modern variations of pub classics. Eating and drinking options include a bright garden room and a lovely outdoor space. Regular live Scottish folk music.

🍽🍽 **The Restaurant** – *Roman Camp Country House, Main Street, Callander. ℰ01877 330 003. www.romancamphotel. co.uk.* Attentive staff serve skilfully prepared modern Scottish cuisine on crisp linen-covered tables in a vibrant modern dining room.

🍽🍽🍽 **Martin Wishart at Loch Lomond** – *Cameron House Hotel, Loch Lomond. ℰ01389 722 504. www. mwlochlomond.co.uk.* A refined elegant restaurant, awarded a Michelin-star in 2011, using notably fine local ingredients, served in superb lochside surroundings. 🐾 *Closed until Spring 2020.*

Inveraray★★

Reflecting in the waters of beautiful Loch Fyne, the delightful small Georgian whitewashed town of Inveraray enjoys a lovely setting. A gateway to the Highlands and Islands, it has plenty of interest on its doorstep.

A BIT OF HISTORY

Neil Campbell, one of Robert the Bruce's most faithful supporters, acquired the forfeited MacDougall lands in the 14C and in the 15C the Campbells came to Inveraray. The medieval settlement arose at the mouth of the River Aray, around the Campbell stronghold.

The town achieved royal burgh status in 1648 but remained isolated in an area where there were no roads.

The military road from Dumbarton arrived in 1745. Building work on the castle took 12 years (1746–58), with Roger Morris as architect and William Adam as clerk of works, although the town took the better part of 100 years to complete.

CASTLE★★

◷ *Daily Apr–Oct 10am–5.45pm.*
⊷ *£12.50.* ✖ 🅿 ✆ *01499 302 203.*
www.inveraray-castle.com.

A castle at Inveraray has been standing on the shores of Loch Fyne since the 15C, although the neo-Gothic castle seen today – the ancestral home of the Duke of Argyll, Chief of the Clan Campbell – was the result of a fire in 1877, which resulted in an additional floors and conical roofs on the corner towers.

Exterior

Roger Morris' original Gothic Revival edifice was altered externally in the 19C with the addition of a range of dormers at battlement level and conical roofs to the corner towers. On the four fronts, pointed Gothic windows predominate with a tiered central **keep** rising above the general roof line.

▶ **Population:** 560.
🏠 **Info:** Front Street.
✆ 01499 302 063;
www.inveraray-argyll.com.
▶ **Location:** Inverary lies 37mi/60km southeast of Oban on the A85 and A816.
👁 **Don't Miss:** The castle interior and the town itself.
🕐 **Timing:** Allow around an hour for the castle.
👥 **Kids:** Visit the Inverary Jail.

Interior★★★

During the 5th Duke's late-18C redecorations the original long gallery was subdivided to give two main rooms on either side of a small entrance hall.

Dining Room – This room is a masterpiece of delicately detailed decoration where roof and walls are perfectly matched. The compartmented **plasterwork ceiling** by a London craftsman is complemented by Clayton's frieze and cornice, and matches admirably the superb painted work of Girard and Guinand (grisaille roundels over doors and in wall panels). The 18C chairs are of Scottish fabrication after a French design and are covered with 18C Beauvais tapestry.

Resplendent under the Waterford chandelier (1800) and on the Gillow table are several German silver gilt nefs (c.1900) – elaborate table centrepieces used for holding salt.

Tapestry Drawing Room – The outstanding set of 18C Beauvais **tapestries** and decorative panels and overdoors by Girard rival the compartmented ceiling based on Robert Adam's design. Off this room, the China Turret has an impressive display of porcelain.

Armoury Hall – The hall rises through several storeys to the **armorial ceiling**. The plain pastel-coloured walls provide the ideal background for the impressive display of arms (pole-arms, Lochaber axes and broadswords).

Loch Fyne Oysters

Loch Fyne is renowned for the quality of its seafood, particularly its oysters. This reputation is based on the eponymous business which started life as a small oyster bar on the banks of the loch. They started with one idea – to grow oysters in the clear, fertile waters of Loch Fyne, which they first did successfully in 1980. From the humble beginnings of a small, roadside stall on the banks of Loch Fyne, a group of businesses have developed based on the principles of good food, sustainably sourced. The original **Loch Fyne Oysters Bar and Shop** began life in a small shed at the head of Loch Fyne. In 1985, it moved into the old cow byre at Clachan Farm, Cairndow, 9mi/14.5km north of Inveraray, (◷*9am, last orders Mon–Thu 5.45pm; Fri–Sat 6.15pm, Sun 4.45pm; ℘01499 600 482; www.lochfyne.com*); it offers excellent value and claims to sell more oysters than anywhere else in the country. Not surprisingly it is often in great demand, so booking ahead is recommended.

From one of these balconies the Duke's personal piper awakes the household with a medley of Campbell tunes.

Saloon – The main family **portraits** hang here, namely Pompeo Batoni's *8th Duke of Hamilton* and Gainsborough's portrait of *Conway*, enlarged to match the former. Among the relics in the show cases are some belonging to the Duke, the Marquess of Montrose's arch-enemy.

North West Hall and Staircase – Of the portraits note the *3rd Duke* by Allan Ramsay and the *5th Duke* (Gainsborough) and his Duchess Elizabeth Gunning.

TOWN★★

The tidy township has a showpiece waterfront facing the loch head. The parish church has a prominent site in the axis of the main street, a classic example of an 18C planned town, and a beautiful display of Georgian white-washed buildings with black window casings.

Inveraray Bell Tower (All Saints Episcopal Church)

◷*Mon–Fri Jul–mid-Sept 10.30am–4.30pm.*
www.inveraraybelltower.co.uk.
The 10th Duke conceived the idea of building this tower as a memorial to all Campbells who had fallen in war.
An exhibition in the base of the tower covers the history, the bells and their ringing. A spiral staircase leads to the ringing chamber and then on to the bell chamber. From here the magnificent peal of 10 bells can be seen close up. A total of 176 stairs will bring you out on the roof of the tower where you are rewarded with spectacular views of Inveraray, Loch Fyne and the surrounding mountains.
Each of the 10 bells of the peal is named after a Celtic saint. St Mund, the patron saint of Clan Campbell, is number three (*there are regular bell ringing sessions*).

🚹🚺 Inveraray Jail

♿*(restricted access)* ◷*Daily Apr–Oct 9.30am–6pm; Nov–Mar daily 10am–5pm.* ◷*25–26 Dec and 1 Jan.* ➥*£12.25 (child (5–16, £7.50). ℘01499 302 381. www.inverarayjail.co.uk.*
This lively attraction re-creates the harsh living conditions of a century or so ago in a real 19C prison.
Engaging costumed actors and guides re-enact trials in the courtroom and the punishment meted out to prisoners. Children are both entertained and horrified to learn about the draconian punishments doled out to children here including Hector MacNeil, aged 13, who was found guilty of stealing a turnip from a field, sentenced to 30 days' imprisonment, and Margaret Cowan, who, aged 11, stole a pair of shoes and was sentenced to 40 days' imprisonment followed by three years at reformatory school.

ADDRESSES

🛏 STAY

🛏🍽🍽 **Brambles Hotel** – *Main Street East and West, Inveraray.* ✆*01499 302 252. www.inverarayhotel.com.* Individually styled rooms that combine stunning traditional Scottish hotel features with a modern finish. The **Brambles Café and Bistro** (🍽🍽🍽) offers a choice of dining options.

🛏🍽🍽 **Inveraray Inn** – *Front Street, Inveraray.* ✆*01499 302 466. www.inveraray-inn.co.uk. 36 rooms.* Built in 1750 at the gates to Inveraray Castle, the Inveraray Inn, formerly the Argyll Hotel, offers unrivalled views over Loch Fyne and Benn Bhuidhe to the castle. It is the oldest inn in Inveraray, and has large well appointed rooms (including four-posters). Enjoy fine dining in the **restaurant** (🍽🍽🍽) overlooking Loch Fyne.

🛏🍽🍽 **The George Hotel** – *Main Street East, Inveraray.* ✆*01499 302 111. www. thegeorgehotel.co.uk. 17 rooms, plus 8 rooms in the adjacent* **First House Hotel**.

Built in 1770, originally as two private houses as part of a project to build a whole new town. Managed by the same family since 1860, over the last 6 years all the rooms have been restored in keeping with the building's history and architecture.

🛏🍽🍽 **Loch Fyne Hotel and Spa** – *Inveraray.* ✆*01499 302 980. www. crerarhotels.com/loch-fyne-hotel-spa. 67 rooms.* Guestrooms are traditional and comfortable. Many feature loch views and all have that little twist of tartan. Integral **Clansman Restaurant** (🍽🍽🍽) serves the finest seafood.

🍽 EAT

🍽🍽🍽 **Loch Fyne Oyster Bar** – *Clachan, at the head of Loch Fyne.* ✆*01499 600 236; www.lochfyne.com.* Having started in a small shed in the early 80s, this seafood restaurant is now frequented by politicians, celebrities, film stars, royalty and touring visitors alike (♿*see panel opposite*).

Oban★

and Kintyre

Scotland's most popular west coast holiday town is built round Oban Bay and is backed by a ring of low hills. Much of the town's activity is concentrated in and around the harbour, where fishing vessels, ferries, excursion steamers and a variety of pleasure craft find refuge, protected by the island of Kerrera.

A BIT OF HISTORY

Oban has long been a service centre as a livestock market and fishing port for the outlying area and islands. The town became a fishing port in the 18C and really developed a century later with the arrival of the steamboats and then the railway, giving Oban its present very Victorian aspect.

▶ **Population:** 8 490.
🛈 **Info:** 3 North Pier. ✆01631 563 122; www.oban.org.uk.
◉ **Location:** Looking across to the Isle of Mull, 44mi/71km south of Fort William, Oban makes an ideal West Coast touring centre, by land and sea.
◉ **Don't Miss:** Loch Awe; Loch Fyne. If you are here during late August visit the Argyllshire Highland Gathering (*visit www.oban games.com for details*).
◉ **Driving:** The town is very busy in summer with long traffic queues.
◉ **Timing:** Allow two hours to see the town, and at least a full day for excursions.
👥 **Kids:** The Scottish Sea Life Sanctuary.

Kilchurn Castle, Loch Awe

© krzych-34/iStockphoto.com

🚗DRIVING TOURS

🚗 ① OBAN HINTERLAND★★
105mi/168km (excl. the 24mi/38km diversion to Kilmory).

This tour includes two of Scotland's most beautiful lochs and fascinating historical and modern industrial visitor attractions.

▶ Leave Oban N on the A85. Turn left at Dunbeg and continue on a minor road for 1mi/1.6km.

Dunstaffnage
🕐*Apr–Sept daily 9.30am–5.30pm; Oct–Mar Sat–Wed 10am–4pm.* 🕐*25–26 Dec, 1–2 Jan.* 💷*£6.* ✆*01631 562 465. www.historicenvironment.scot.*
This impressive 13C castle, one of the principal seats of the MacDougalls, rises out of a rocky outcrop on a promontory commanding the entrance to Loch Etive. The thick curtain walls are punctuated by three towers and a 17C tower house. It was captured by Robert the Bruce in 1309 and remained in royal possession for some years. In fact, it is claimed that Dunstaffnage was the home of the Scots court prior to Kenneth MacAlpine's unification of the country and removal of the seat of power to Scone (🔎*see SCONE PALACE*).
Flora MacDonald (🔎*see ISLE OF SKYE*) was held prisoner here on her way to The Tower of London in 1746.

▶ Continue by the A85 to Taynuilt and bear left onto the B845.

Bonawe Historic Iron Furnace★
🕐*Daily Apr–Sept 9.30am–5.30pm.* 🕐*25–26 Dec, 1–2 Jan.* 💷*£6.* ✆*01866 822 432. www.historicenvironment.scot.*
The most complete charcoal-fuelled ironworks in Britain, Bonawe was founded in 1753 and in production until the 1870s. Displays bring to life the industrial heritage of the area and illustrate how pig iron was made.

▶ Return to the A85 and proceed east.

Cruachan Power Station★
Dalmally. 🔦*Guided tours: Apr–Oct daily 9.15am–4.45pm; Nov–Mar Mon–Fri 9.15am–3.45pm.* 🕐*Mid-Dec–early Feb.* 💷*Tour £7.50 (child 5–15 £2.50.* ✖ ✆*0141 614 9105. www.visitcruachan.co.uk.*
Lying deep within the mountain of Ben Cruachan, on the shores of Loch Awe, is one of the country's most amazing engineering achievements, a power station buried over half a mile below ground. At its centre lies a massive cavern, high enough to house the Tower of London, where enormous turbines convert the power of water into electricity. Part of the Awe scheme, the Cruachan power station, opened in 1965, has an annual output of 450 million units of electricity. The pump turbines are reversible and are used to pump water from Loch Awe to the high-level reservoir in the corrie on Ben Cruachan, which in turn feeds,

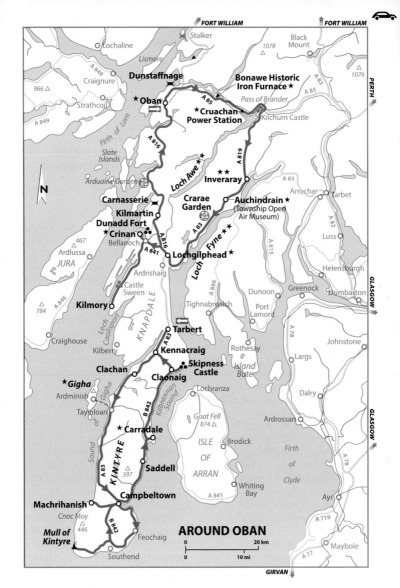

AROUND OBAN

| 0 | 20 km |
| 0 | 10 mi |

by means of two shafts, an underground power station in the heart of the mountain. A road tunnel (1mi/1.6km long) leads to the Generating Hall.

A visitor centre on the surface provides an introduction to this ambitious scheme. Once inside the mountain, visitors walk past subtropical plants that grow well in the warm humid conditions, and then onto the viewing gallery looking into the mighty main hall.

▶ The road follows Loch Awe, skirting the lower slopes of Ben Cruachan.

Loch Awe★★

This is Scotland's longest loch, stretching over 25mi/40km. It drains via the River Awe and the Pass of Brander where the former is harnessed for hydroelectric power. This is the heart of Campbell country with the family seat formerly

McCaig's Tower

Dominating the Oban skyline, high on the hill above, is a replica of the **Colosseum**, known as McCaig's Tower, or McCaig's Folly. The project was initiated in 1897 by the philanthropic Oban banker John Stuart McCaig in order to relieve unemployment and act as a family memorial. It cost around £5 000, an enormous sum at the time. He planned it to include a museum, art gallery and central tower, but the building has remained incomplete since McCaig died in 1902.

It's a short if steep walk to its viewing platform and well worth the effort. Go at sunset to enjoy the Mountains of Morvern providing a spectacular backcloth for the isles of Kerrera and Lismore, the Maiden Isle and Mull.

situated on Innischonnail Island, then at Kilchurn, at the head of Loch Awe.

▶ Turn right onto the A819 towards Inveraray and enjoy the views of 15C Kilchurn Castle, jutting into Loch Awe.

Loch Fyne★★

This splendid lake begins in the central Argyll mountains and extends south to the sea just north of Arran. At the height of the herring fishery industry in the 19C it was dotted with up to 600 boats setting out from several lochside villages. These have now all but gone though at the southern end of the loch, **Tarbert**, once the centre of the herring industry, is still a working fishing village, landing catches if not daily then every weekend. And recently Loch Fyne has also become renowned for its oyster fishery.

The main settlement on the loch is **Inveraray** (*see INVERARAY*).

▶ Leave Inveraray on the A83 southwest, in the direction of Lochgilphead. Continue for 8mi/13km.

Auchindrain Township Open Air Museum★

Apr–Oct daily 10am–5pm. Nov–Mar open most weekdays, 10am–4pm, except Christmas and New Year. £8. *01499 500 235. www.auchindrain.org.uk.*

This open-air folklife museum township evokes everyday life as it was for the ordinary people of the West Highlands. Communal tenancy, where a group of tenants hold and work a farm, was the commonest kind of farm in Scotland. This system lasted the longest in the Highlands. Auchindrain is a very ancient settlement, with a history dating back over 1 000 years.

Start in the visitor centre which gives details on the way of life (field patterns, domestic interiors and occupations), then visit the township where cottages, longhouses, barns and byres have been restored and furnished as museum pieces.

▶ Continue for 2.5mi/4km on the A83.

Crarae Garden

Visitor Centre: daily Apr–Aug 9.30am–5pm; Sept–Oct Thu–Mon 9.30am–5pm. Gardens: daily 9.30am–dusk. 24 Dec–2 Jan. £7.50. 01546 886 614. www.nts.org.uk.

This delightful Himalayan-style woodland garden (40ha) occupies a steep sloping site overlooking Loch Fyne. The beautiful natural setting in a small glen with its rushing burn and waterfalls is complemented by judicious planting and includes the national collection of southern beech trees.

The garden is at its best in spring, particularly for its rhododendrons, or in autumn when the leaf colours are a blaze of russet shades. The winding climbing paths afford splendid viewpoints and glimpses of the loch and mountains.

▶ Continue southwest on the A83.

Loch Fyne at Inveraray

© JoeDunckley/IStockphoto.com

Lochgilphead★

This planned village was created in 1790, not long following the completion of the road from Inveraray to Campbeltown. Once the Crinan Canal was completed in 1801, the village became an important link across the Kintyre peninsula. Today, it is a useful base for exploring this out-of-the-way corner of Scotland, and is one of the venues for the annual March Mid-Argyll Music Festival.

▷ Take the A816, right. Continue onto the B841.

Crinan★

This charming hamlet stands at the western end of the Crinan Canal (9mi/14.5km long) which links the Sound of Jura and Loch Fyne. The canal, with its 15 locks, was opened in 1801 to save fishing boats the long sail round the Mull of Kintyre. Today, yachts and pleasure craft make a colourful spectacle as they manoeuvre and jostle for position in the holding pool and locks.

▷ At this point you can choose to make a 24mi/39km detour to Kilmory (leave the B841, south, at Bellanoch) to visit Kilmory Chapel which shelters MacMillan's Cross, a 2.4m high 15C Celtic cross. A long drive on minor roads towards the Point of Knap.

▷ Return to the A816 and continue north.

Dunadd Fort

Access by the farm road to the left.
The rocky eminence rising abruptly out of the flatlands of the Great Moss was a Dark Ages fortification.

▷ The road enters Kilmartin Glen, leading through a pass to reach the southwestern end of Loch Awe.

Kilmartin

There are over 350 ancient monuments within a 6mi/10km radius of the village of Kilmartin, of which 150 are prehistoric. This extraordinary concentration and diversity of monuments distinguishes **Kilmartin Glen** as an area of outstanding archaeological importance. **Kilmartin House Museum** (🕐*daily Mar–Oct 10am–5.30pm; Nov–23 Dec 11am–4pm; ⊘£7, child under 16, £2.50;* ✕ 🅿 🖍*01546 510 278; www.kilmartin. org*) is an award-winning world-class centre for archaeology and landscape interpretation.

In Kilmartin churchyard is a fine collection of **sculptured stones** dating from the 14C to 16C. Inside the church, **Cross No. 3** (16C) is outstanding.

▷ Follow the A816 2mi/3.2km north.

Carnasserie Castle

On a strategic site commanding the route northwards to Loch Awe, the remains of this 16C castle are remarkable for their carved detail and mouldings.

> Follow the A816 back to Oban.

② KINTYRE PENINSULA
134mi/216km. Begin at Tarbert.

Kintyre is the southern part of the long west coast peninsula. The western shores are pounded by the great Atlantic rollers while the east coast looks over the sheltered Kilbrannan Sound to Arran. The varying scenery and seascapes make for a fine drive. The western (A83) road is wider and faster with good views of Ireland, while the eastern route is single track with passing places.

Tarbert
At the head of East Loch Tarbert, this small town marks the isthmus dividing Kintyre from Knapdale to the north. The houses fringe the harbour and bay, lively with fishing boats and yachts in summer. There are scant overgrown remnants of Bruce's castle. In imitation of the 11C King Magnus of Norway, Bruce dragged his boats across the isthmus on his way to attack Castle Sween in 1315.

> Leave Tarbert south on the A83 towards Campbeltown.

Western shore
Pass **Kennacraig**, the ferry port for Islay and Jura. Near **Clachan** is **Ronachan Point** where grey seals may be seen basking offshore. Tayinloan is the ferry port for the small island of **Gigha**, lying 3mi/5km off the Kintyre coast.
It is known for the remarkable woodland **gardens** at Achamore (*daily, dawn–dusk; Admission charge through donations; 01583 505 390; www.gardens-of-argyll.co.uk*). The rhododendrons, azaleas and camellias burst into colour in late spring.

Gigha★
This small island off the west coast of Kintyre has been continuously inhabited since prehistoric times, and is the ancestral home of the Clan MacNeill. There are several standing stones on the island along with other archaeological sites. The island has a long history of private ownership, but in 2002, the islanders purchased the island for themselves, and now manage it through the Isle of Gigha Heritage Trust.
A ferry service links the island's only village, Ardminish, to Tayinloan on the Kintyre peninsula of the Scottish mainland.

Campbeltown
The main market and shopping town of the peninsula, Campbeltown is also a quiet holiday centre. In the 19C it boasted a large fleet based on the Loch Fyne herring fishery and over 30 distilleries producing a variety of malt whiskies. Both sectors have declined drastically, although they are still represented. The cross near the pier dates from the 15C. Campbeltown is the fictional Kinloch in Denzil Meyricks' crime novels.

> Head southeast, in the direction of Feochaig, towards the Mull of Kintyre.

Mull of Kintyre
The Campbeltown Pipe Band and, of course, Paul McCartney and Wings, brought worldwide publicity to this headland (only 13mi/21km from Ireland) with the eponymous song in 1977.
The Mull is the southwesternmost tip of the Kintyre peninsula and an important landbridge throughout history thought to have been used by early humans on their journeys through Britain from Europe, to Ireland.
The lighthouse was the second commissioned in Scotland by the Commissioners of the Northern Lights, designed and built by Thomas Smith and completed in 1788.

> Head back towards Campbeltown on the B842, then at Stewarton turn left onto the B843 towards Machrihanish.

Machrihanish
Machrihanish is known for its huge sandy beach (6mi/10km long) and 18-hole golf course.

A nearby farm was the home of artist **William McTaggart** (1835–1910) who was inspired by local landscapes.

▶ Return to Campbeltown and head north on the B842.

Carradale★
This small village fringing the tiny fishing harbour shelters a busy fishing fleet.

Saddell
Overgrown ruins are all that remain of this once important West Highland abbey founded c.1207. The founder Reginald, who was the ruler of Kintyre and Islay, is said to be buried here. In the churchyard a collection of **14C–16C grave slabs★** displays warriors, weapons and galleys.

Claonaig
Pier for the ferry to Lochranza on Arran (*summer only*).

Skipness Castle and Chapel
Castle & chapel open year round; tower open Apr–Sept.
This vast courtyard fortress incorporates an early-13C hall house and a 16C tower house. This stronghold marked the southern limit of Campbell territory.

▶ Take the B8001 and rejoin the A83 back to Tarbert.

ADDRESSES

🏠 STAY

🛏️🛏️ **Alltavona House** – *Corran Esplanade, Oban.* ✆*01631 565 067. www. alltavona.co.uk. 10 rooms.* This elegant 19C villa is set on a smart esplanade with fine views of Oban Bay across to the Isle of Mull. The attractive interiors and fittings are contemporary to the house.

🛏️🛏️ **The Old Manse** – *Dalriach Road, Oban.* ✆*01631 564 886. www.obanguest house.co.uk. 5 rooms.* Set just outside the town this former manse is perched on the hillside with views out to sea. Rooms are spacious and well equipped.

🛏️🛏️ **Glenburnie House** – *Corran Esplanade, Oban.* ✆*01631 562 089. www.glenburnie.co.uk. 12 rooms.* Located on the main esplanade with great views. Comfy, good-sized bedrooms.

🛏️🛏️ **Premier Inn** – *Shore Street, Oban.* ✆*0163 170 5129. www.premierinn.com.* The latest addition to Oban's hotel range, close to Oban Distillery and Glencruitten Golf Club. Premier Inns is a chain hotel offering standardised facilities in comfy and peaceful rooms, always with a no frills eatery nearby, in this instance Thyme bar and grill (🛏️🛏️).

🛏️🛏️🛏️ **The Barriemore** – *Corran Esplanade, Oban.* ✆*01631 566 356. www.barriemore.co.uk.* A gabled 1890s house with fine views over the town (a 10min walk away) and islands, this is a comfortable mix of modern and period styling.

🛏️🛏️🛏️ **Manor House** – *Gallanach Road, Oban.* ✆*01631 562 087. www.manorhouse oban.com. 11 rooms.* A country house-style interior with traditional comforts. and delightful bay and harbour views. Formal dining room.

🛏️🛏️🛏️ **Oban Bay Hotel** – *Corran Esplanade, Oban.* ✆*01631 564 395. www.crerarhotels.com/oban-bay-hotel. 79 rooms.* Fully equipped rooms in a splendid setting. Beauty treatment rooms, free parking; dog friendly.

🍴 EAT

🍽️🍽️ **Coast** – *104 George Street, Oban.* ✆*01631 569 900. www.coastoban.com. Closed Sun lunch.* The appealing and reasonably priced modern menu at this former bank building in the centre of town include plenty of fish and shellfish. Attractive minimalist contemporary interior.

🍽️🍽️ **Ee-Usk** – *North Pier, Oban.* ✆*01631 565 666. www.eeusk.com. (No children under the age of 12 after 5.45pm)* This smart modern award-winning fish restaurant ("ee-usk"is fish in Gaelic) enjoys excellent views over the bay and harbour.

🍽️🍽️ **Waterfront Fishouse Restaurant** – *1 The Pier.* ✆*01631 563 110. www. waterfrontfishouse.co.uk.* Set on the pier with great views over the bay and the comings and goings in the harbour, this converted quayside mission is stylish but not fussy.

Fife's regal connections began with the 4C Kingdom of the Picts and ended with the Union of the Crowns in 1603. Ever since then the "Kingdom of Fife" has been a relative backwater, with its many castles and cathedrals testament to a rich history. St Andrews' (Scotland's oldest university town) is a major tourist destination and the quaint fishing villages of East Neuk and the Fife Coastal path are other big draws. Several islands of the Forth are home to thousands of seabirds, with vast numbers of puffins found on the offshore Isle of May.

Highlights

1 Putting at **St Andrews**, right next to the Old Course (p261)

2 Tucking into a fishy feast by the harbour in **Crail** (p267)

3 Exploring **Kellie Castle**, an example of 16C architecture (p268)

4 Visiting the wonderfully preserved village of **Culross** (p274)

5 Exploring **Falkland Palace**, its gardens, and the village (p279)

South and West Fife

Linked as it is to Edinburgh and the Lothians by the three Forth Bridges (see p174), West Fife is most visitors' first introduction to the "Kingdom". Indeed the first settlement of any size across the Forth is Dunfermline, the Scottish capital from the mid-11C until 1603. Nowadays the quiet "auld, grey toun" is dominated by its impressive abbey and ruined palace but it is largely a dormitory town for Edinburgh.

West of the famous bridges sits Culross (pronounced "coo-ross"), one of Scotland's most picturesque settlements. Much of what can be seen today is the 17C village, its whitewashed, crow-stepped-gabled and red-tiled buildings, beautifully renovated by the National Trust for Scotland.

Along Fife's south coast is what is optimistically termed the "Fife Riviera" – a cluster of seaside holiday centres including Aberdour, Burntisland and Kinghorn with excellent beaches, watersports, golf and sailing. The Fife Coastal Path is a waymarked walking trail that picks its way for over 50mi/80km along the coast.

North Fife

Spread across the lower slopes of the Lomond Hills, Falkland's narrow streets are lined with well-preserved 17C and 18C buildings. The village grew up around the majestic Falkland Palace, a favoured royal residence from the mid-15C until the mid-17C. Its gardens are charming and boast the oldest tennis court in Britain.

Cupar, the capital of Fife, has retained some of its medieval character from the days when it was a bustling market centre. From here you can visit the Edwardian mansion, Hill of Tarvit, the Scottish Deer Centre and the picturesque village of Ceres.

Fife's biggest visitor attraction is St Andrews, famed nationally as Scotland's oldest university town, and internationally as the home of golf, host to the world-famous Royal and Ancient golf club. The town itself is possessed of ancient buildings and a youthful (rather elite) student population – leading to comparisons with Oxford and Cambridge – who add a social buzz and healthy cultural scene.

The East Neuk

Fife's East Neuk (as in "nook", meaning corner) is famous for its picturesque fishing villages: Crail, Anstruther, Pittenweem, St Monans and Elie. Their old cottages and merchants' houses, all crow-stepped gables and tiled roofs, huddle round stone-built harbours, and are well patronised by holidaymakers and weekenders from Scotland's central belt, who come to feast on the freshly landed seafood in the various restaurants.

Exploring the olde-worlde streets of Crail and the excellent fishing museum in Anstruther are equally satisfying treats.

St Andrews★★
The East Neuk and Inland Fife

St Andrews, on the Fife coast, is famous both as a seat of learning and the home of golf. As the former metropolitan See of Scotland, the city was in the mainstream of Scottish history and its rich heritage includes a 12C cathedral, 13C castle and 15C university. Today it has a quieter charm, detached from national matters, although it is a buzzing holiday resort in summer, and reverts to the role of a university town in term time with a very busy social and cultural scene.

A BIT OF HISTORY

The Celtic settlement of St Mary on the Rock, associated with the relics of St Andrew, grew in importance with the founding of the St Regulus Church, a priory in the 12C and finally a grandiose cathedral.

The monastic establishment renowned as a seat of learning was the precursor of the university. With a growing university attracting scholars and students of a high calibre, 15C St Andrews was an active and prosperous burgh well meriting the attribution of a national role as ecclesiastical capital of Scotland in 1472. Prosperity and the population declined in the 17C, owing in part to the loss of the archbishopric (in the 1689 Revolution), the changing trading patterns (now with the American colonies), as well as the political changes after the 1707 Act of Union. The 18C was one of general decline for St Andrews.

The 19C saw the beginning of the growth of golf as a sport and by the turn of the century the town had achieved renown as a mecca of golf. Its popularity as a holiday and golfing resort has gone from strength to strength.

St Andrews University – Founded in 1410 by **Henry Wardlaw**, Bishop of St Andrews, this was the first university in Scotland and third in Britain after Oxford and Cambridge.

▶ **Population:** 17 580.

🛈 **Info:** 70 Market Street. ℘01334 472 021; www.visitstandrews.com.

▶ **Location:** St Andrews is 54mi/87km NE of Edinburgh, across the Firth of Forth. The town centre is compact and can be covered on foot. Open-top bus tours *(late Jun to Aug)* go to outlying sites.

⊚ **Don't Miss:** The view from the cathedral tower in St Andrews; the West Port; an excursion to the East Neuk villages.

🕐 **Timing:** Allow at least half a day plus a day for excursions.

👪 **Kids:** The Scottish Deer Centre; St Andrews Aquarium; Craigtoun Country Park.

CATHEDRAL★

♿🕐*Daily: Apr–Sept 9.30am–5.30pm; Oct–Mar 10am–4pm.* 🕐*25–26 Dec, 1–2 Jan.* ✆*£6 (joint ticket with St Andrews Castle, £12).* ℘*01334 472 563. www.historicenvironment.scot.*

Bishop Robert founded the **priory** c.1159 and his successor Bishop Arnold began work on the cathedral, consecrated in 1318 by Bishop Lamberton in the presence of Robert the Bruce. Only the 12C east end, the late-13C west gables and the south wall of the nave remain of this once immense building with its 10-bay nave. Following the depredations of the Reformation, neglect and 17C quarrying for stone, the cathedral was reduced to its present ruined state.

To the south were the buildings of what must have been one of the most powerful monastic establishments in Scotland. The 16C precinct wall encloses the cathedral ruins and the imposing **St Regulus church** that may well have been the shrine built to shelter St Andrew's relics.

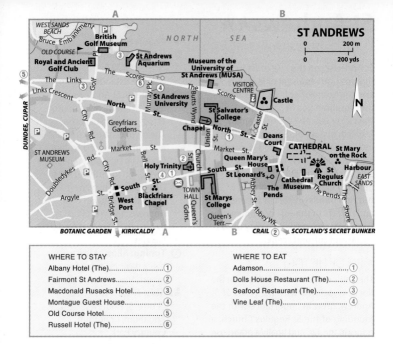

Queen Margaret's son, Alexander I, nominated Robert, Prior of Scone as Bishop of St Andrews, and it was he who built the church between 1127 and 1144. **St Rule's Tower** (*33m, 151 steps*) offers a magnificent **panorama★★** of St Andrews and its main monuments. The **museum** has a good collection of early and later medieval sculpture and other relics found on the site.

CASTLE

&⟲*Daily: Apr–Sept 9.30am–5.30pm; Oct–Mar 10am–4pm.* ⟲*25–26 Dec, 1–2 Jan.* ⟲*£9 (joint ticket with St Andrews Cathedral £12).* ✆*01334 477 196. www.historicenvironment.scot.*

A Powerful See

Overlooking the foreshore, the castle ruins once formed part of the palace and stronghold of the bishops and archbishops of St Andrews.

Founded c.1200, it suffered greatly during the Wars of Independence. Bishop Henry Wardlaw, founder of the university, was tutor to James I and it is possible that his young charge spent time here prior to his captivity in England. Bishop Kennedy taught James II how to break the power of his nobles by comparing them to a bundle of arrows, with the suggestion he snap each one individually.

Many reformers suffered imprisonment here, including George Wishart whom Cardinal Beaton had burned at the stake in front of his palace, and Patrick Hamilton, another martyr.

Following the martyrdom of Wishart, a group of Protestants seeking revenge gained admission to the castle disguised as stonemasons and stabbed Cardinal Beaton to death (⟲*see MONTROSE*). They were besieged in the castle for a year and were joined at intervals by others such as John Knox; the siege was only lifted when the garrison capitulated to the French fleet. The defenders were taken to France and Knox was sent to the galleys.

The late-16C entrance range with the central Fore Tower, originally flanked by two round towers, was the work of Archbishop Hamilton and it was supposedly from this façade (the exact spot is con-

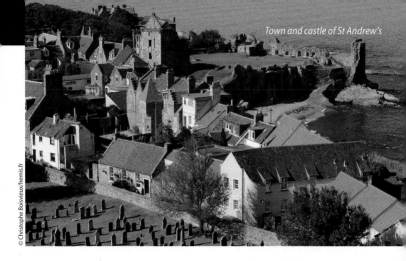

Town and castle of St Andrew's

© Christophe Boisvieux/hemis.fr

tested) that the body of Cardinal Beaton was displayed to the crowd.

The buildings were arranged around a courtyard. In what remains of the north-west or Sea Tower is the grim **Bottle Dungeon** of late-14C construction; it is 7.3m deep and was hewn out of the solid rock. The body of Beaton was dropped into here.

The other interesting features are a **mine** and **counter mine** (*enter from the ditch in front of the entrance building*) excavated during the 1546–47 siege.

In the pavement in front of the castle are carved the initials "G W", for George Wishart, marking the spot where he was burned at the stake in 1546.

UNIVERSITY

Tours usually only open to prospective students and guests. The exteriors of the following buildings are open for viewing at any reasonable hours. ℘*01334 462 245.*

St Salvator's College

St Salvator's was founded in 1450 by Bishop James Kennedy. The chapel and tower, above the entrance archway, form the North Street frontage and are a good example of 15C Gothic ecclesiastical style. The two ranges around the quadrangle are 19C reconstructions.

St Salvator's Chapel was, according to Dr Johnson, "...the neatest place of wor-

Golf, a Royal and Ancient Game

Since the 15C St Andrew's has been a place for playing golf or at least the early ball and stick version of the sport. So popular was the game that by 1457 an Act of Scottish Parliament was passed requiring that "futeball and the golfe be utterly cry it down" in favour of church attendance and archery practice. Mary, Queen of Scots played and her son, **James VI**, popularised golf in England.

Founded in 1754, the Society of St Andrews Golfers had the title **Royal and Ancient** conferred on it by **William IV** in 1834 and is now recognised as the sport's ruling body. To meet the increasing popularity of the game, new courses (New 1895, Jubilee 1897, Eden 1912) were laid out, supplementing the Old Course, which was established several centuries before.

By the beginning of the 20C, St Andrews was firmly established as Scotland's golfing heartland, and the town regularly hosts the British Open, and many big money tournaments which draw the stars of the professional circuit, bringing huge crowds despite television coverage.

Mere mortals can take in the atmosphere at the Ladies Putting Club (no booking required) cheek by jowl with St Andrews Links Club House, where the green is known locally as the Himalayas due to its lumpy bumpy nature!

ship he had seen". The collegiate church was restored in the 19C and 20C. Inside is the **founder's tomb**, an amazingly intricate 15C work of art in the Gothic style. The pulpit opposite, with the preacher's hourglass, is supposedly the one used by John Knox.

The initials "P H" laid in the pavement before the entrance mark the spot where **Patrick Hamilton** (1504–28), an early reformer, was burned on 29 February 1528.

Museum of the University of St Andrews (MUSA)

7a The Scores. ⓒCurrently closed for refurbishment and the building of a new extension; check website or call for updates. It is due to be completed in late 2019. ℘01334 461 660. www.st-andrews.ac.uk.

Opened in 2008, for the first time in its history, some of the many treasures among the university's priceless collection of over 112 000 artefacts is on display to the public. These include medieval silver maces, rare books, a changing selection of the university's art collection, and an 18C "cabinet of curiosities". There are four galleries, the child-oriented "Learning Loft", and a viewing terrace with panoramic views over St Andrews bay.

St Leonard's Chapel

The chapel belonged to the college of the same name. The original buildings were a hospital for pilgrims to St Andrew's shrine, then a nunnery, before being acquired to form the nucleus of the new St Leonard's College.

When St Leonard's and St Salvator's were united in 1747, the chapel was neglected while the buildings and grounds were eventually taken over by the girls' school. The 1950s restoration re-created the medieval layout with a screen and organ loft.

St Mary's College

Archbishop James Beaton founded St Mary's College in 1537. The buildings on the west side of the quadrangle are 16C.

On the ground floor, College Hall has portraits of past principals including Cardinal Beaton. Up two flights of stairs is one of the original student chambers with box beds. On the north side is the old **University Library**, on the site of the original Pedagogy, which is now refurbished as the Psychology Department.

On the street front there are a series of arms of University Chancellors. The two Joseph Knibb longcase clocks flanking the fireplace of the 19C Senate Room were part of Gregory's equipment.

The Upper Hall (1612–43) is a galleried room panelled with pale Baltic pine. This was where **Gregory**, the Astronomer (1638–1675) and inventor of the reflecting telescope, worked. The ground floor Parliament Hall completed in 1643 is where the Scottish Parliament sat in 1645–46 following the Battle of Philiphaugh.

ADDITIONAL SIGHTS
The Town

The town has retained its original layout with three main streets – South Street, Market Street and North Street – converging on the cathedral.

The main entrance to the old town **West Port★** was built in 1589 and opens onto **South Street**. A few yards on the right is **Blackfriars Chapel**, all that remains of a mid-15C foundation for Dominican friars. The chapel dates from the 16C. The imposing building behind is part of Madras College.

The medieval **Holy Trinity Church** (*www.holyt.co.uk*), rebuilt in 1410, was modified in the late 18C and restored in the 20C. The corbelled tower with the stone steeple is 15C. Inside, Archbishop Sharp's monument graphically records his death in 1679 on Magus Muir.

A little further on **Queen Mary's House** is an attractive 16C building in attractive rubble stonework with a pantile roof.

Cut through to **North Street**, which runs parallel to South Street. Sixteenth century **Deans Court** is now a student hall of residence at the University of St Andrews. It is possibly the oldest dwelling house in town. At the top of South Street, by the cathedral, **The Pends** is a 14C vaulted gatehouse which was the main entrance to the priory. The road follows the precinct wall down to the **harbour**, which was rebuilt in the 17C with stone from the castle and cathedral. Beside the harbour, the **Church of St Mary on the Rock** was the site of the 12C Celtic settlement, which was gradually superseded by St Regulus and the new cathedral and priory.

Royal and Ancient Golf Club

Club members only.

The imposing 1854 clubhouse overlooks the 1st and 18th holes of the Old Course and is the headquarters of the Royal and Ancient Golf Club (see Box, p263).

British Golf Museum

Apr–Oct Mon–Sat 9.30am–5pm, Sun 10am–5pm; Nov–Mar daily 10am–4pm. 24–26 and 31 Dec, 1 Jan. £8.50. 01334 460 046. www.britishgolfmuseum.co.uk.

Five centuries of golf history, both in Britain and abroad, come alive by means of audio-visual displays and interactive screen presentations including the origins of the game, the development of the equipment and famous golfing events and personalities.

Running on the Beach

The famous stirring opening sequence to the movie *Chariots of Fire* (1981), with the athletes running in slow-motion to the music of Vangelis, was filmed on the West Beach beside the Aquarium.

St Andrews Aquarium

The Scores. Daily 10am–6pm. 25–26 Dec, 1 Jan. £11 (child, £9). 01334 474 786. www.standrewsaquarium.co.uk.

By the cliffs with great views of the famous West Beach (*see Box*), the aquarium has one of the best locations in town. Stingrays, sharks, conger eels, piranha, catfish, mudskippers and many other exotic fish and marine creatures come under the spotlight in this lively place. It's not all sea creatures; poison dart frogs, large spiders, scorpions and snakes fascinate the kids and you can also book to feed meerkat (*1.30pm and 4.30pm daily*), as well as penguins (*4pm*) and seals (*10.30am*) in the outdoor seal pool.

Botanic Garden

The Canongate. Daily Apr–Sept 10am–6pm; Oct–Mar 10am–4pm. £6 (Tropical Butterfly Experience, Apr–Sept +£2.95). 01334 476 452. www.standrewsbotanic.org.

Attractions here include the rhododendrons of the Peat Garden, the colourful Heath Garden, the alpine varieties of the Rock Garden, the Water Garden with exotic species and moor plants, and the glasshouses.

EXCURSION
Scotland's Secret Bunker

10mi/16km southeast on the B9131 and the B940. Daily late Feb–Oct 10am–5pm. £12.95 (child 4–16, £8.95). 01333 310 301. www.secretbunker.co.uk.

Deep below the surface of Fife's farmlands, the sinister chambers and corridors

Crail harbour

© lucentius/iStockphoto.com

of this once top-secret installation evoke all the menace of the Cold War era.

The bunker was built as one of a chain of early warning radar stations along Britain's eastern coastlines. Redundant in this role, it was then modified to become a nuclear command centre, one of several regional seats of government which would have administered what was left of the country following an atomic holocaust. Following the disappearance of the Soviet threat, it was opened to the public in 1994.

Set in an excavation (40m deep), protected by 3m of reinforced concrete and approached down a corridor (153m long), the bunker is entered via the guardhouse, cunningly designed to resemble a traditional farm building. All stages of its 40-year operational existence are brought hauntingly to life.

Contemporary films and videos recall the Orwellian atmosphere of possible nuclear attack, while figures with dishevelled hair plot the extent of fallout and members of the emergency services communicate with the contaminated surface. The Secretary of State's office with its bedstead overlooks the Operations Room. In the chapel, a plaque commemorates "those who gave their lives keeping the peace throughout the Cold War".

🚗 DRIVING TOURS

🚗 EAST NEUK★★

37–43mi/60–70km. Allow half a day for Crail, half a day for Anstruther and half a day for the rest (excluding boat trips).

A car is best to explore the four villages, even though the distances between them are small.

The East Neuk is the group of fishing villages and their hinterland on the most northerly part of the Firth of Forth. The East Neuk (meaning east corner, as in "nook and cranny") is one of the main attractions of Fife, a stretch of coastline dotted with a series of delightful fishing villages, each clustered around its harbour.

As early as the 11C Fife was the hub of the nation, with Dunfermline as the political and St Andrews as the ecclesiastical centres. The villages flourished as active trading ports with the Hanseatic League and the Low Countries.

King James VI described Fife as "a beggar's mantle with a fringe of gold". It was the royal burghs along the coast, with their profitable activities of trading, fishing and smuggling, which were the "fringe of gold". With the development of the transatlantic routes, the villages concentrated on fishing.

▶ Head south out of St Andrews on the A917.

Crail★★

This busy resort is the most attractive East Neuk burgh. The older heart of the burgh is clustered down by the harbour while the upper town is altogether more spacious.

Upper Crail★ – Standing alone in a prominent position overlooking the spacious market place, the tolbooth (1598), a tiered tower, is graced by an attractively shaped belfry.

The weather vane, a gilded capon (dried haddock), is a reminder that capons were the town's staple export. Behind the tolbooth at Nos. 62–64 is a **Crail Museum and Heritage Centre** (&○*Apr–Oct Mon–Sat 11am–4pm, Sun 1.30–4pm (May Sat–Sun and bank holidays only);* ✆*£3;* 𝄞*01333 450 869; www.crailmuseum. org.uk*), which gives an insight into the burgh's history, its main buildings and activities. The tree-lined Marketgate is bordered by elegant two- and three-storey dwellings. Of particular note are Nos. 30 and 44 on the south side and Auld House (16C) and Kirkmay House (early 19C) opposite. The "Blue Stone" just outside the churchyard on the left is said to have been thrown by the Devil from the Isle of May in an attempt to destroy the church.

Take Kirk Wynd to pass the 16C circular dovecot, the sole remnant of a priory. Follow the path round to Castle Walk which skirts the few remains of what was a royal stronghold. Among the landmarks visible across the Forth are St Abb's Head, the Bass Rock, Tantallon Castle and the Isle of May.

Old Centre★★ – Sloping down to the harbour, Shoregate is bordered by an attractive group of cottages (Nos. 22–28). Crab and lobster boats still use the inner harbour with its attractive stonework. On the waterfront is the three-storey Customs House (No. 35). Note the boat carving on the lintel. The adjoining group of buildings surround a paved courtyard. On the way up, note No. 32 Castle Street and the delightful 18C No. 1 Rose Wynd with its forestair and attractive door surround.

▶ Continue southwest on the A917 with the Firth of Forth on your left.

Anstruther

This linear settlement includes the once independent communities of Cellardyke, Anstruther Easter and Anstruther Wester. There is still some creel-fishing (for lobster and crab) and white fish activity from Anstruther, but most of the fishermen now operate from Pittenweem, a mile to the west.

On the harbour front, housed in a group of 16C–19C buildings around three sides of a cobbled courtyard, the **Scottish Fisheries Museum★★** (&○*Apr–Sept Mon–Sat 10am–5.30pm, Sun 11am–5pm;*

Small port of Anstruther

© O. Forir/MICHELIN

Oct–Mar 10am–4.30pm, Sun noon–
4.30pm; ⊕£9; ✕ ℗ ♪ 01333 310 628;
www.scotfishmuseum.org) includes 19
actual boats, the largest being the 24m
Zulu, and recounts the history of Scottish fisheries, including the hard life of
fisherfolk.

The West Room and West Gallery house
"Days of Sail" exhibition, illustrated by
paintings, model boats, tableaux of life-
size figures at work and fishing gear. In
the Long Gallery is a map of Scotland's
fishing communities; ancillary trades
tableaux showing women gutting and
packing herring and making barrels.

"Whaling" follows, illustrating a once-
important sector of Scotland's industry.
The "Days of Steam" gallery is devoted
to the era of the steam drifter, with
paintings, models, an original mural
and examples of gear and fishing techniques. Model boats, fishing equipment,
paintings and photos from the advent
of motor power to the present day are
found in the "Fishing into the Future"
Gallery.

The Courtyard and Gallery contain
examples of heavier items of machinery,
actual small fishing boats, nets, anchors
and a fully equipped wheelhouse.

The 16C Fisherman's Cottage & Loft,
once the property of the monks from
Balmerino, has been renovated as a
fisherman's home c.1900 (a period of
relative prosperity).

Berthed in the harbour opposite is the
museum's own veteran sea-going 1902
Fifie, *Reaper*. The *Reaper* houses a small
display describing life on board the fishing vessel. A 19C Bauldie, *White Wing*, is
also currently being refitted.

Pittenweem

The burgh of Pittenweem is set on two
levels. Kellie Lodge (*private*) in the High
Street is the 16C town house of the Earls
of Kellie from Kellie Castle. Corbelled,
pantiled and crow-stepped, it is a
fine example of the vernacular style.
St Fillan's Cave and Holy Well is said to
have been the sanctuary of the 7C Christian missionary Fillan.

Take any one of the six wynds down to
the harbour, which is today Fife's busiest

fishing port. Of particular interest on the
waterfront are The Gyles at the east end
and No. 18 East Shore, a three-storeyed
building with its Dutch-style gable.

St Monans

The village is tightly packed around its
small harbour. Wynds and closes lead
off into the usual maze of lanes, back
alleys and yards; a smuggler's paradise.
The church was probably begun in the
11C by Queen Margaret. A large part of
it is 13C and the choir was rebuilt by King
David II in 1346.

Inside, look for the hanging ship, the
coats of arms and the painted panel
from the laird's loft.

ADDITIONAL SIGHT
Kellie Castle★

&⊙*Castle: Apr–May and Sept–Oct
Sat–Thu 11am–5pm; Jun–Aug daily
11am–5pm. Garden and estate: daily
9am–dusk. ⊕£10.50. ℗£3. ✕ ♪ 01333
720 271; www.nts.org.uk.*

This unspoiled laird's house is a fine
example of authentic 16C and 17C Scottish traditional Lowland architecture.

Once home to the youngest daughter of Robert the Bruce, in 1613 Kellie
Castle passed to the Erskines or Earls
of Mar and Kellie. It is said that the 1st
Earl saved the life of King James I, and
the 5th Earl, who fought on the side of
the Jacobites at the Battle of Culloden,
spent the entire summer of 1746 hidden
in an old beech tree here in the garden
where his butler secretly brought him
food every day.

The castle and lands were dissociated
in the late 18C and a period of neglect
followed from 1830 until a lease was
granted in 1876 to Edinburgh Jurist
Professor James Lorimer. The castle
stayed in the Lorimer family, and was the
childhood summer home to the internationally renowned architect Sir Robert
Lorimer, and his brother the accomplished artist John Henry Lorimer. Sir
Robert's son, Hew, an acclaimed sculptor, took over the lease in 1937, refurbished it and bought the castle in 1957.
It has since gradually been restored to

Kellie Castle

its former glory by the National Trust for Scotland.

Castle – Built of rubble sandstone to a T-shaped plan, each wing of the T forms a tower. Around 1573 a second, quite separate tower was added to the east. The southwest tower, containing the entrance door, is a splendid work.

Interior – The late-17C plasterwork ceilings are notable, in particular the Vine Room ceiling. Typical of the period is the Memel pine panelling in the Withdrawing Room painted with over 60 romantic landscapes.

Grounds – The Arts and Crafts garden is filled with scent of old roses and the beautiful herbaceous borders. The walled garden includes formal gardens and orchards and a summerhouse exhibits a display on the history of the walled garden. Woodland and meadow walks offer extensive views of the Firth of Forth and the Bass Rock.

🚗 INLAND FIFE★

34mi/55km.

This tour through the agricultural hinterland of St Andrews offers a varied selection of places of interest to visit.

▶ Leave St Andrews to the northwest by the Cupar Road (A91). Once over the Eden turn right onto the A919 in the direction of Guardbridge.

Guardbridge

This small village features a narrow 15C bridge and landmark paper mill that went bust in 2008 but revitalised by a St Andrew's University project.

Leuchars

Leuchars is synonymous with its RAF station and also Leuchars Junction, the railway station for St Andrews. However, its most eminent building is its parish **church★**, dedicated to St Athenase, which dominates the village from its elevated position and is regarded as Fife's finest surviving example of Romanesque arechitecture. The 12C chancel and semicircular east end are exceptional examples of Norman work. On the external walls, under the cornice of grotesque heads, are two fine bands of arcades.

▶ Return to the A91 and turn right, heading SW towards Cupar.

Cupar

Formerly the county town of Fife, Cupar boasts some interesting buildings including two 17C survivors, Preston Lodge and Chancellor's House – the birthplace of John Campbell who became Lord Chancellor in 1859.

♿♿ The Scottish Deer Centre

2mi/3.2km west of Cupar on the A91. Rankeilour Park.

♿⊙*Daily 10am–4.30pm (Jul–Aug 5.30pm).* ⊙*25 Dec, 1 Jan.* ⊕*£9.50 (child £6.50).* ☐ ✆*01337 810 391. www.tsdc.co.uk.*

Deer are normally associated with the Highlands, but were once common in Lowland Scotland too, before woodland clearance and farming drove them away. This Georgian farmstead and its surrounding parkland are now used to introduce the public, particularly children, to these fascinating creatures.

In the 20ha of paddocks there are not only red deer but 13 other species totalling around 140 deer in all. These are supplemented by rare breeds, such as a black Highland cow and Soay sheep. There are native red foxes and in the wolf wood (segregated from the deer!) visitors can watch the wolves feeding time (*3pm*). There are also daily bird-of-prey demonstrations and children are allowed to feed the otters. Rangers give regular guided tours.

▶ Return to Cupar and take the A914 southeast, then fork second left onto the A916.

Hill of Tarvit Mansionhouse and Garden

⊙*Mansion: Apr–Oct Sat–Tue 11am–4pm; Garden and grounds: daily 9am–dusk.* ⊕*£10.50.* ✗ ✆*01334 653 127. www.nts.org.uk.*

This elegant Edwardian country house was commissioned by Frederick Bower Sharp (d.1932), a jute manufacturer and financier from Dundee. In 1904 Sharp purchased the estate that included the original house, Wemysshall (1696) – attributed to Sir William Bruce – and the 16C Scotstarvit Tower. Sharp was an art collector of note and his remodelled family residence was designed as a suitable setting for his important private collection of fine French and Chippendale-style furniture, Old Masters, tapestries, Chinese porcelain and bronzes. Visitors can sample the "Upstairs, Downstairs" nature of the Edwardian period, the grandeur and charm of the main rooms, the fascination of the kitchen with its old utensils, and the laundry in the garden.

A nature trail leads through the wild garden to the hilltop (211m) with viewpoint indicator and a panorama of Fife and beyond.

First established in 1924, **Kingarrock Golf Course** gives golfers a chance to play the only remaining 9-hole hickory golf course in the UK (*9-hole £45, 18-hole £60; fee includes all equipment and a post-game refreshment of ginger and shortbread;* ✆*01334 653 421; www.kingarrock.com*).

Scotstarvit Tower

⊙*Apr–Sept, daily 9.30am–5pm. Access to the parapet must be arranged in advance. Call to organise:* ✆*01334 653 127. www.historicenvironment.scot.*

This L-shaped tower house dates from c.1579 and rises through five storeys. The vertical accommodation, consisting of six chambers with a well-lit main hall on the first floor, is reached by a turnpike (circular spiral) stair.

▶ Once through Craigrothie turn left onto the B939 towards St Andrews.

Ceres★

This picturesque village with its arched bridge and village green is the home of the **Fife Folk Museum** (⊙*daily Apr–Oct Wed–Sun 10.30am–4.30pm;* ✗ ▱ ☐ ✗ ✆*01334 828 180; www.fifefolkmuseum.org*), with comprehensive displays of everyday items, the living room of a cottar (farm labourer) and a tool and agricultural section.

▶ Continue along the B939 past Pitscottie. At the Strathkinness junction turn right. Once up the hill a signpost to the right indicates the footpath to Magus Muir (5min).

Magus Muir

When level with the railed enclosure in the field, veer right towards the pyramid-shaped monument. This marks the spot where Archbishop Sharp of St

Andrews was assassinated by a group of Presbyterian Fife Lairds in 1679.

👥 Craigtoun Country Park

🕐 *Jul–Aug daily 10.30am–5.30pm; Sept–Jun daily 10.30am–5pm.*
✕ *𝒫01334 472 013.*
http://friendsofcraigtoun.org.uk.
Originally laid out as parkland attached to adjacent Mount Melville House, this has been a country park since 1947. Much of the formal design, including the avenue of Lawson Cypress, the Italian Garden and the much loved Dutch Village are part of the original design. Little ones will enjoy the adventure playground, miniature railway, trampoline, bouncy castle, boating, putting, crazy golf, pets' corner and aviaries.

ADDRESSES

🏨 STAY

ST ANDREWS

🍽🛏 **The Albany Hotel** – *56 North Street. 𝒫01334 477 737. www. albanyhotelstandrews.co.uk. 22 rooms.* An elegant well-run Georgian town house with casual but high quality bedrooms. The homely firelit lounge is stocked with books and a bar.

🍽🛏 **Montague Guest House** – *21 Murray Park. 𝒫01334 479 287. www. montaguehouse.com. 8 rooms.* This traditional late 19C Victorian townhouse boasts charm and original features. There's a large communal living room to meet other guests.

🍽🛏 **The Russell Hotel** – *26 The Scores. 𝒫01334 473 447. www.russellhotelst andrews.co.uk. 10 rooms.* This charming small hotel is set in a Victorian terraced town house by the sea (four rooms have sea views). Restaurant🍽🛏.

🍽🛏 **Fairmont St Andrews** – *St Andrews Bay. 𝒫01334 837 000. www. fairmont.com/st-andrews-scotland. 209 rooms.* Set on a 210ha estate with a wonderful coastal setting, this is one of Scotland's most prestigious hotels, host of the G20 Summit for the world's top financial leaders in November 2009. It features two of its own championship golf courses and a spa.

🍽🛏🛏 **Macdonald Rusacks Hotel** – *Pilmour Links. 𝒫0344 879 9136. www. macdonaldhotels.co.uk/rusacks. 68 rooms.* This is one of Scotland's finest golfing hotel locations, within a sand wedge of the 18th hole on the world-renowned Old Course. Luxurious accommodation and the finest food and drink is enjoyed against a backdrop of the world's most photographed golf course, with views out to sea and the famous West Sands.

🍽🛏🛏 **Old Course Hotel** – *Old Course. 𝒫01334 474 371. www.oldcoursehotel. kohler.com. 144 rooms, including 35 suites.* This luxury establishment borders the renowned 17th "Road Hole" of the Old Course.

EAST NEUK

🍽🛏 **The Grange** – *45 Pittenweem Road, Anstruther. 𝒫07904 974420. 4 rooms.* This spacious Edwardian house is just outside the village. It features snug lounges, a charming sun room and neat traditional bedrooms.

🍽 EAT

ST ANDREWS

🍽🛏 **The Doll's House Restaurant** – *3 Church Square. 𝒫01334 477 422. www.dolls-house.co.uk.* Specialising in traditional Scottish and French cuisine and with a terrace on the square in front of Holy Trinity Church, this is a charming informal restaurant.

🍽🛏 **The Vine Leaf** – *131 South Street. 𝒫01334 477 497. www.vineleafstandrews. co.uk. Open Tue–Sat dinner only.* The Vine Leaf undoubtedly serves some of the best Scottish food in town.

🍽🛏 **The Seafood Ristorante** – *Bruce Embankment. 𝒫01334 479 475. www. theseafoodrestaurant.com.* Floor to ceiling glass on all four sides of this award-winning restaurant ensures everyone gets a sea view.

🍽🛏 **Adamson** – *127 South Street. 𝒫01334 479 191. www.theadamson.com.* A stylish modern brasserie and cocktail bar in a house owned by 19C photographer John Adamson, and 20C post office.

EAST NEUK

🍽🛏 **Cellar** – *24 East Green, Anstruther. Booking essential. 𝒫01333 310 378. www.thecellaranstruther.co.uk.* Near the harbour, this seafood restaurant has a warm ambience with open fires and exposed brick and stone.

Dunfermline★
and the Dunfermline Coast

The "auld grey town", formerly the capital of Scotland, figures large in Scottish history, mainly in association with its great abbey and royal palace. From earliest times it was a thriving industrial centre with coal mining and later linen weaving; the tradition is maintained today with a variety of new industries. The naval dockyard at Rosyth (3mi/4.8km south) was originally built as a port for Dunfermline.

▶ **Population:** 74 380.

Info: www. visitdunfermline.com.

Location: Dunfermline is 17.5mi/28km northwest of Edinburgh via the A823, and the A90 across the Forth Road Bridge.

Don't Miss: The Norman nave of the abbey church.

Timing: Allow 2 hours to see the city centre. The main sights can easily be covered on foot.

Kids: Deep Sea World.

A BIT OF HISTORY
Margaret and Malcolm

In the 11C, **Malcolm III** or Canmore (c.1031–1093) offered hospitality in his Dunfermline Tower to the English heir to the throne, Edgar Atheling and his family, on their flight from William the Conqueror and the Norman Conquest (1066). Edgar's sister **Princess Margaret** (c.1045–1093), a devout Catholic, married the Scottish king in 1070 and was largely responsible for introducing the religious ideas of the Roman Catholic Church, which were gradually to supplant the Celtic Church. Together with her husband, she founded the church in 1072. Three of Queen Margaret's sons ascended the throne: Edgar, Alexander I and David I; it was Alexander who proclaimed the town a royal burgh between 1124 and 1127 and David I (c.1084–1153) who founded the Benedictine abbey. The town prospered as the abbey grew in importance.

Following the untimely deaths of Alexander III and Margaret of Norway, Edward I, during his tour as mediator in the struggle for succession, visited the town and on his departure in 1304, the monastic buildings were a smouldering ruin.

Robert the Bruce (1274–1329), the great national hero, helped with the reconstruction and is buried in the abbey. His heart is in Melrose abbey.

Royal Palace

The guesthouse was refurbished for James V's French wife but it was James VI who gave the abbey and palace to his **Queen, Anne of Denmark**. Once more Dunfermline was the home of royalty and three royal children were born here: Elizabeth, the ill-fated Charles I and Robert, who died in infancy. With the Union of the Crowns (1603), the court departed to London. James VI subsequently made two fleeting visits to the town as did Charles I in 1633, and

Famous Citizen

The philanthropist and steel baron, **Andrew Carnegie** (1835–1919), was born in Dunfermline, the son of a hand loom weaver. In 1848, the family emigrated to America and young Andrew passed from bobbin boy and telegraphic messenger to working in the railroads before dealing in iron and then the new steel industry. By 1881 he was the foremost steel baron in the USA and in 1901, following the sale of his steel companies, he retired and set about spending his fortune in public benefactions. His many gifts to his home town included the Carnegie Baths, the Library, the Lauder Technical School and Pittencrieff Park.

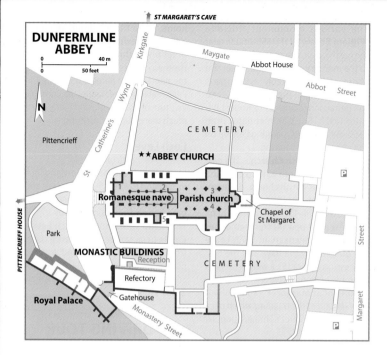

DUNFERMLINE ABBEY

ST MARGARET'S CAVE

Kirkgate

Maygate

Abbot House

Abbot Street

Pittencrieff

CEMETERY

★★ABBEY CHURCH

Romanesque nave Parish church

Chapel of St Margaret

Street

Park

Margaret

MONASTIC BUILDINGS

Reception

CEMETERY

Refectory

Royal Palace

Gatehouse

Monastery Street

PITTENCRIEFF HOUSE

his 20-year-old son Charles II to sign the Dunfermline Declaration.

PALACE AND ABBEY★

Apr–Sept daily 9.30am–5.30pm; Oct–Mar Sat–Wed 10am–4pm.
25–26 Dec and 1–2 Jan. £6.
01383 739 026.
www.historicenvironment.scot.

The original Celtic church was replaced and dedicated by Malcolm Canmore and Queen Margaret in 1072. Their son David I accorded it abbey status in 1128 and rebuilt the monastic church. The abbey with its extensive lands, property, coal pits, salt pans and ferry dues, accrued enormous wealth and its prestige was enhanced by the fact that it was a royal establishment becoming the "Westminster Abbey of Scotland", where 22 royal persons were buried.

The 13C saw the addition of St Margaret's Chapel holding the remains of Malcolm and his consort. The abbey was damaged by fire by Edward I and, although restored by Robert the Bruce, it never attained its former glory. It was during the 14C that a new royal residence was built. At the Reformation the abbey declined and was no longer used as a place of worship; the east end fell into ruins and only following the collapse of the central tower was the east end rebuilt (1818–21).

Abbey church★★

Norman Nave – The nave of David I's (1128–50) church was restored by William Schaw, Master of Works to Anne of Denmark. The north porch, northwest tower, west front and massive buttresses are all his work.

The interior presents one of Scotland's finest Norman naves with close affinities to both Durham and St Magnus', Kirkwall, where simple massive forms and round-headed arches predominate. Great cylindrical pillars, four of which have chevron and spiral motifs, separate the seven-bay nave from the aisles and support semicircular arches. Marked on the floor are the outlines (blue on the plan) of the original Celtic church and Queen Margaret's 1072 Church of the Holy Trinity.

The various monuments include **William Schaw's (1)** (1550–1602), near the north porch, erected by Queen Anne to the memory of her Chamberlain and Master of Works who ably restored parts of the building in the 16C and17C, and the Renaissance one **(2)** to Robert Pitcairn (1520–84), Commendator from 1560–84, with 16C paintings above on the panels of the vaulting.

East End or Parish Church – The east end was rebuilt from 1818 to 1821 and now serves as parish church. A memorial brass **(3)** marks the tomb of Robert the Bruce (1274–1329), Scotland's hero. The new royal pew **(4)** commemorates the 900th anniversary in 1972. Leave the building by the nave and the East Processional Door **(5)**, a well-preserved example of Norman work.

Chapel of St Margaret – Foundations only remain of the building which once enclosed St Margaret's Shrine, a popular pilgrimage centre.

Monastic Buildings

Of the once great ensemble of abbatial buildings which extended to the south of the abbey church, there remain four walls of the refectory, with chambers below, joined by the gatehouse bestriding the pend to the kitchen and former royal palace.

Royal Palace

In the 14C a new royal palace was built adjacent to the 13C guesthouse. A single wall remains to recall the splendour of this building. Charles I and his sister, the Winter Queen or Elizabeth of Bohemia, were both born here.

ADDITIONAL SIGHTS

Andrew Carnegie Birthplace Museum

Moodie Street. & ☉*Mid-Feb–Oct Mon–Sat 10am–5pm, Sun 1–4pm (Jul–Aug daily 10am–5pm); Nov Mon–Sat 10am–4pm, Sun 1–4pm.* 🅿 ✆*01383 724 302. www.carnegiebirthplace.com.* On the left is the cottage where Andrew Carnegie (1835–1919) was born, arranged as a typical weaver's

home, while the adjoining Memorial Hall houses exhibitions illustrating the great philanthropist's life and work. His many trusts and endowments are too numerous to name but include The Peace Palace in the Hague, the Carnegie Institute of Pittsburgh, and many other much more humble institutions.

Loch Leven

12mi/19km north on the M90.
Loch Leven is the largest lowland loch in Scotland (some 5.5sq miles/14sq km) and is of international importance for breeding and wintering wildfowl.
The island stronghold of **Loch Leven Castle** (*ferry service from Kinross*) dates from the 14C to the 16C and was the place of imprisonment of Mary, Queen of Scots from June 1567 until her escape on 2 May 1568.

🚗 DRIVING TOUR

🚗 DUNFERMLINE COAST★
42mi/67km.

This tour takes in the West Fife settlements of Culross and Aberdour, as well as Scotland's national aquarium.

▶ Leave Dunfermline to the SW on the A994 and, from Cairneyhill, continue W on the A985 in the direction of Kincardine. After High Valleyfield, follow signs for Culross.

Culross★★

Culross (pronounced "coo-ross") is an attractive small Scottish burgh of the 16C and 17C on the north shore of the Firth of Forth, 15mi/24km west of Edinburgh city centre off the A985. A programme of restoration has ensured the preservation of its essential charm, a wealth of Scottish vernacular architecture.
16C–17C Industrial Royal Burgh – Legend has it that this was the landing place and subsequent birthplace of St Kentigern (Mungo of Glasgow) following his mother's flight from Traprain in Lothian. The 13C saw the founding of a Cistercian house high on the hill, beside the then main road. In the 16C coal mining, salt

Culross Palace with a view to the Forth estuary

panning and trade with the Low Countries were the principal activities. The port of Sandhaven was a flourishing one and the ensuing prosperity was followed by royal burgh status in 1588, accorded by James VI. The golden age continued until the end of the 17C, the decline setting in with the growth of transatlantic trade and developing industrial centres in the west and central belt.

The village was forgotten for almost 200 years. Its renaissance was triggered off by the purchase of The Palace in 1932 by the National Trust for Scotland only shortly after its own foundation in 1931. An extensive restoration programme has since followed, and in 1981 to mark The Trust's Golden Jubilee, Culross was twinned with Veere in the Netherlands, re-creating a link of the past. The village as it stands gives a glimpse of an east coast burgh of the 16C and 17C.

Vernacular architecture – The visitor may enjoy the details and richness of Scottish domestic architecture with a walk through Culross: white or pale colour-washed harling or rubble stonework, dressed stone window and door trims, red pantiles with the occasional glass one, half or pedimented dormer windows, gable ends, crow stepping, skewputts, decorative finials, inscribed or dated lintels and forestairs.

The Palace★★

🕐*Palace and Gardens: Apr–Sept daily 10am–5pm; Oct–Mar Fri–Mon 10am–4pm.* 👓*£10.50.* ✕ 🅿
📞*01383 880 359. www.nts.org.uk.*

Built between 1597 and 1611 by George Bruce, the Palace is a monument to both a period and a man. James VI's reign (1578–1625) was a time of economic change when merchants such as Bruce, Danzig Willie Forbes and Provost Skene of Aberdeen acquired wealth from trade, which financed the construction of substantial dwellings (The Palace, Craigievar Castle and Provost Skene's House).

The man, **Sir George Bruce** (d.1625), was an enterprising merchant, a burgessman at the height of the burgh's prosperity, with interests in the local coal mines, salt panning and foreign trade.

Despite the fact that many of the materials (pantiles, Baltic pine, Dutch floor tiles and glass) were obtained by Baltic barter, the buildings are a superb example of 16C and 17C domestic architecture.

The interior provides an insight into the domestic surroundings of a prosperous merchant of the period. Rooms are small with Memel pine panelling for warmth and have interesting examples of the decorative painting typical of the late 16C and early 17C. Surprisingly, 21 fires burned coal rather than logs as elsewhere, but this was perhaps only natural for a coalmine owner.

West Wing – To the left of the main courtyard is the earliest building with George Bruce's initials and the date 1597 on one of the dormer pediments. The

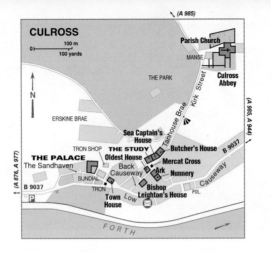

initial lodging was later extended to the north and to the south with the creation of the Long Gallery. On the ground floor the Nomad's Room for passing travellers has a **painted ceiling** (1620, *not restored*) with beyond, one of the rooms of the domestic quarters paved with perforated Dutch tiles. In the northern extension alongside the inner court are the kitchen and bakery with the wine cellar across the passage.

Outside stairs give access to the first floor where the **Long Gallery** is now subdivided. The term "palace" (it was neither royal nor episcopal) may come from the word *palatium*, meaning long hall, which was a typical feature of Elizabethan or Jacobean houses in the south. The Lady's Drawing Room at the south end is panelled with Baltic pine while the Sun Room beyond derives its name from the tempera paintings. Commanding a view of the port, the Business Room where Bruce received his captains has half-shuttered and half-glazed windows – a window-tax dodge. In the adjoining fireproof Strong Room, glazed Dutch tiles pave the floor and wall safes and iron doors ensure security.

On the second floor in the West Bedroom, the insertion of the occasional glass pantile is again a window-tax dodge. The second panelled room has the **allegory ceiling** – a fine example of decorative painting – on the pine barrel vaulting.

North Wing – A separate building, this extension dates from 1611 and the initials SGB commemorate Sir George's knighthood. The three-storey building has a stables, byre and hay loft.

The rooms are panelled and both ceiling and wall paintings, although faint, can be deciphered: in one first floor room the painting depicts the Judgement Steps of King Solomon while in the other rooms there are more 400-year-old paintings, depicting heraldic devices, fruit and geometrical patterns.

Village★★★

Moving away from The Palace along the Sandhaven, note, on the left, the sundial at first floor level on the gable end, with the tron in front, then look up the close to see the Tron Shop with its forestair.

Town House – The Sandhaven is dominated by the stone and slate Town House which contrasts with the white harling and red pantiles all around. Built in 1625, with the tower dating from 1783, the edifice has a strong Flemish influence. The exhibition and audiovisual presentation are a must before visiting the burgh of Culross. The former council chambers on the first floor have typical 16C interiors. The Back Causeway is a cobbled way with a central line of paving stones slightly higher than the rest. Known as the "crown o'the causie", it was reserved for notables. Note the corbelled tower of the study.

Culross village with Town House

© John Butterfield/iStockphoto.com

The Study★

This delightful example of Scottish burgh architecture dates from 1610. The main room has a restored original painted ceiling and original 1633 panelling. The marriage cupboard is Norwegian and the imposing portrait is of the town's merchant hero, George Bruce. Opposite is the **oldest house** in Culross with, in front of its gable end, a replica of the 1588 **mercat cross**. On the left on Tanhouse Brae, a former **Sea Captain's House** has a window lintel with a Greek inscription.

The wall plaque on the **Butcher's House** displays the tools of the occupant's trade. The road climbs up to the present parish church and remains of the abbey; through the gaps in the wall you can admire the **view** across the Forth and glimpse Abbey House (*private*), built in 1608 for Sir George's brother and one of Scotland's earliest Classical mansions. Little remains of **Culross abbey** (⏱*freely accessible; www.historicenvironment.scot*), founded in 1217 by Malcolm, Earl of Fife. The eastern parts of the abbey church are incorporated in the present **Parish Church** (⏱*daily 10am–sunset*). In the Bruce vault off the north transept stands Sir George Bruce's **funeral monument** – with alabaster effigies of Sir George, his wife and eight children – a type that is unusual in Scotland. The churchyard has some interesting tombstones.

Go downhill again to the square, noting the 17C **Nunnery** in Wee Causeway marked by its forestair and statue, and pass the **Ark**, a former seamen's hostel, then **Bishop Leighton's House**.

▶ Leave Culross on the East Fife Coastal Road (B9037/A985), heading east with the Forth on your right. Cross below the M90 motorway onto the A921, and at Inverkeithing, follow the signs to Deep Sea World.

👥 Deep Sea World

♿⏱*Mon–Fri 10am–5pm, Sat–Sun 10am–5.30pm.* ⏱*25 Dec and 1 Jan.* 🎟*£15.55 (child 3–12, £11 (online discounts).* ✕ ☎*01383 411 880. www.deepseaworld.com.*

This spectacular and extremely popular aquarium succeeds in its aim of informing and entertaining including large-scale shark and piranha displays and an "underwater safari" along a transparent underwater tunnel.

▶ Return to Inverkeithing and take the A921 NE towards Aberdour.

Aberdour★

Aberdour, a small resort on the Fife shore of the Forth Estuary, is famous for its castle and silver sands, which make it a popular destination for day trips from Edinburgh or as a base from which to explore the Forth valley.

Aberdour Castle and Garden

🕐 *Apr–Sept daily 9.30am–5.30pm; Oct daily 10am–4pm; Nov–Mar Sat–Wed 10am–4pm.* 🕐 *1–2 Jan, 25–26 Dec.* 🎫 *£6.* ✕ ☎ *01383 860 519. www.historicenvironment.scot.*

Initially granted by **Robert the Bruce** to his nephew, Thomas Randolph, Earl of Moray c.1325, it passed to William Douglas in 1342.

Regent Morton, James Douglas, 4th Earl of Morton (1516–1581), inherited Aberdour in 1548. Morton, who played an active part in the overthrow of Mary, Queen of Scots, is remembered for his iron rule as Regent (1572–78) during James VI's minority when he achieved peace in a time of religious strife. Forced to resign the regency in 1578 he was tried, convicted and beheaded in 1581 for complicity in the murder of Darnley 14 years earlier.

In 1642, Aberdour became the principal Morton family seat. Extensions and improvements followed. By 1725 the castle was abandoned in favour of nearby Aberdour House.

Today the castle consists of the original 14C west **tower**, which was rebuilt in its upper part in the 15C. A rectangular extension was added in the 16C to the southeast. This is distinguished by Renaissance decoration on the windows overlooking the courtyard. The internal layout was innovative in that a corridor served the rooms on both levels. The L-shaped extension to the east was built for William, 6th Earl and contained a picture gallery on the first floor. In accordance with the fashion of the time this was in all probability panelled with a painted timber ceiling.

To the east is the **walled garden** which was once a typical 17C formal garden. It became a bowling green and its lawn is now fringed with herbaceous borders. The pediment over the kirk lane entrance displays the monogram of the 6th Earl and his wife and the date 1632. The sloping ground to the south of the castle was once laid out as formal terraces, with a dovecot and orchard beyond. The late-16C terrace gardens have been reinstated. It is interesting to note that two of the family's near relations in the late 16C/early 17C included the owners of other famous gardens, namely Edzell and Glamis.

👥 Silver Sands

This attractive sandy Blue Flag beach is a popular spot in summer with a play area and bouncy castle for the kids and watersports for the grown ups.

Beyond Silver Sands walkers can follow the Fife Coastal Footpath and cliff top walks at Hawkcraig, which boast magnificent views across the Forth to Edinburgh.

▷ Continue on the A921 towards Burntisland to enjoy the view of Edinburgh across the Forth, then return to Dunfermline on the A909/A92/A907.

Aberdour harbour

© Douglas Houghton/age fotostock

Falkland ★

The Dutch engraver, John Slezer's description of Falkland in the 17C, "a pretty little Town ... a stately Palace", sums up the town of today. Tucked away at the foot of the Lomond Hills, safe from the depredations of war and strife so endemic to Scottish history, Falkland has retained the peaceful charm of a royal burgh of yesteryear.

FALKLAND PALACE AND GARDEN ★

&♨○*Mar–Oct Mon–Sat 11am–5pm, Sun noon–5pm (Jul–Aug Mon–Sat 10am–5pm, Sun noon–5pm).* ✆£13 (Gardens only £6.50). *℘01337 857 397. www.nts.org.uk.*

The palace was partially destroyed by fire after Cromwell's troops stayed here during his conquest of Scotland. Abandoned, the palace fell into a state of disrepair. In the late 19C the Hereditary Keeper carried out restoration work. The palace, although still royal property, is now under the guardianship of the National Trust for Scotland.

South Range: Street Front

This range, built by James IV, consists of two very distinct parts: on the extreme left is the twin-towered gatehouse, which was completed in its present form in 1541 and provided accommodation for the Constable, Captain and Keeper. The corbelled parapet, cable moulding and gargoyles link this with the range to the east where massive buttresses are adorned with canopied niches. The statues are the work of Peter the Flemishman (1538). The street front is a good example of Scottish Gothic.

South Range – From the entrance hall of the gatehouse, climb to the Keeper's suite on the second floor. The bedroom is dominated by James VI's magnificent canopied bed and the room is hung with copies of full length royal portraits. Adjoining are the Dressing Room with the Bute Centenary Exhibition and the small panelled Bathroom.

▶ **Population:** 1 150.

🄸 **Info:** The Merchant's House, 339 High Street, Kirkcaldy. ℘01592 267 775. www.visitstandrews.com.

◖ **Location:** 11mi/18km north of Kirkcaldy.

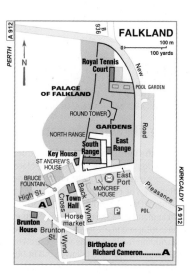

▶ Go down one flight to the Drawing Room.

The Drawing Room was restored by the Marquess of Bute in the 1890s. The oak ceiling is emblazoned with the coats of arms of the Stuart Kings and the different Keepers of the palace. The paintings include James VII and Mary, Queen of Scots, Charles II and Catharine of Braganza. The outstanding features of the 16C interior of the Chapel Royal are the oak screen between chapel and ante-chapel and the painted ceiling redecorated for Charles I's 1633 visit. The Tapestry Gallery is hung with 17C Flemish tapestries and furnished with 16C–17C replica pieces of furniture. The 19C heraldic glass shows sovereigns and consorts closely associated with the palace.

Chapel Royal, Falkland Palace

© Sandro Vannini/age fotostock

The Stewart Monarchs at Falkland Palace

Fife, the Centre of the Royal Kingdom

The original castle belonged to the Macduffs, the Earls of Fife, and its early history was marked by the mysterious death in 1402 of David, Duke of Rothesay, heir to Robert III, while staying with his uncle, Robert, Duke of Albany. David's brother, James I of Scotland, on his release from imprisonment in England in 1424, set out to restore the power of the monarchy. His revenge was total and in the following year the Albanys were beheaded. Their property, including Falkland, passed to the Crown. James II gifted the castle to Mary of Gueldres in 1451 and followed this in 1458 by raising the town to a royal burgh and the castle to a palace.

Royal Residence (15C–16C)

The hunting seat of Falkland became one of the Stewarts' favourite royal palaces. James II built an extension, the north range, which originally contained the Great Hall, and it was here that Margaret of Anjou and her son took refuge when Henry VI was imprisoned. The future James III (1451–1488) spent his childhood here.

James IV (1473–1513), a typical monarch of the Renaissance, re-established royal authority, and with his Queen, Margaret Tudor, entertained a splendid court. Poet **William Dunbar** (1465–1530) dedicated *The Thistle and the Rose* to his royal patrons. James, who loved to hunt in the Falkland Forest and hawk on the Lomond Hills, built the south range.

James V (1512–1542) made extensive alterations in preparation for his marriage, initially to Magdalene, daughter of François I, then after her untimely death, to Mary of Guise in 1538. French workmen prepared the palace for a French bride and included the Renaissance ornament on the courtyard façade of the south range. A radical departure from the Gothic of the time, this stylistic flourish was in fact the earliest of its kind in Britain.

James' two sons died as infants and it was to Mary, Queen of Scots that the throne went, when she was just a baby. In later years, Falkland was a favourite with Mary, who came here to hunt. Her son James VI of Scotland and I of England visited on his 1617 royal progress, as did her grandson, Charles I and great-grandson, Charles II.

◗ Take the turnpike (stairs) up a level.

The Old Library has memorabilia of the 20C Keepers, the Crichton Stuarts.

◗ Return to the corridor level before crossing to the East Range.

East Range

This was built at the same time as the south one, to contain the royal apartments with the king's suite on the first floor and queen's above.

This level affords a good view of the delightful courtyard front of the South Range, so different from the Gothic street front. The Renaissance influence is most evident in the buttresses embellished with engaged pilasters and pronounced mouldings and the sets of paired medallions. The latter are not unlike Wolsey's terracotta medallions at Hampton Court and the Stirling Heads. The King's Bed Chamber in the cross house projecting from this range (rebuilt 19C) has been restored. The windows have shutter boards below and leaded glass above and the painted ceiling is resplendent with the monograms of James V and Mary of Guise. The Golden Bed of Brahan is of early 17C Dutch workmanship. James V died here in 1542 several days after learning of the birth of his daughter Mary, Queen of Scots, when he pronounced "It came wi' a lass, and will gang wi' a lass."

Gardens★

The foundations of the North Range and Round Tower of the original Macduff stronghold can be seen in the gardens. The gardens were replanted after their use as a potato field in the World War II effort. Designed by Percy Crane, the 20C gardens, ablaze with colour, include shrubs, herbaceous borders and a more formal garden.

Beyond, in the gardens, lies the original real (or Royal) **tennis court**, built in 1539 for James V. It is the world's oldest tennis court still in use.

VILLAGE★

A stroll around Falkland shows off its fine vernacular architecture and gives an insight into the houses and offices of the court officials, royal servants and tradesmen who once resided in the village. Of particular interest are the many lintel and marriage stones.

On the south side of the High Street, 17C Moncreif House sports a thatch of Tay reeds, a marriage lintel and inscribed panel proclaiming the builder's loyalty to his monarch.

The hotel next door features further panels, and beyond Back Wynd stands the **town hall** (1801), adorned with a sculptured panel of the burgh arms.

On the far side of the street next to the palace is **Key House** with its lintel dated 1713 with, as neighbour, the harled and red pantiled 18C St Andrew's House. The Bruce Fountain is 19C.

Cross Wynd is lined by a row of single-storey cottages, interrupted on the left by the cobbled Parliament Square. Glance up Horsemarket to see the building with forestairs.

Dominating Brunton Street is the imposing three-storeyed **Brunton House** (1712), which is the home of the Royal Falconers. Back in the main street, the birthplace of the "Lion of the Covenant", **Richard Cameron** (1648–1680), is marked by another inscribed lintel. He headed the extremist Covenanting group, the Cameronians, the nucleus of which was later to form the regiment of the same name.

EXCURSION
Glenrothes

6mi/10km south of Falkland on the A912 and the A92.

Glenrothes is one of five new towns created in Scotland after World War II. The architectural style of the conventional residential suburbs is offset by a range of outdoor artworks, mostly by local artists, since 1968. The exhibits, from colourful murals to spectacular sculptures of flowers, animals or characters, are constantly renewed to stimulate the imagination.

Situated in the very heart of Scotland, Perthshire boasts some of the finest and most accessible scenery anywhere in the Scottish Highlands. This is Big Tree Country – home to Europe's oldest tree, the widest conifer in Britain and the sole survivor from Shakespeare's Birnam Wood. It has long been a retreat for the royal and well heeled – from ancient Scone Palace to modern Gleneagles – and nowadays is also a draw for adrenaline junkies who take on a wide range of outdoor white-knuckle activities.

Highlights

1 Rhododendron season at the charming **Branklyn Garden** (p287)

2 Touring magnificent **Scone Palace** (p293)

3 Learning the art of whisky production at **Blair Atholl Distillery** (p296)

4 Catching the May **Atholl Highlander Parade** (p302)

Perth and North

This small provincial bustling city, renowned for its parks and gardens, enjoys a charming position on the banks of the Tay, and an historic walk is recommended. Although it is no longer regal, Perth was once capital of Scotland, as witnessed by Scone Palace on the town outskirts. Here many Scottish kings were crowned on the legendary Stone of Destiny, from Robert the Bruce to James I. The town retains an affluent air, thanks in no small part to its position at the heart of one of Scotland's richest food producing areas (including Aberdeen Angus beef and soft fruits) with excellent shopping, outdoor markets and fine dining restaurants, popular with visitors and locals alike.

Amid some of the finest woodlands in Scotland, distinguished Dunkeld – with its majestic cathedral ruins, brightly coloured 18C houses, and specialist shops – and Birnam, famous for its oak, and Beatrix Potter connections, are two small towns of great character. On the outskirts of Dunkeld, the Loch of the Lowes nature reserve is home to breeding osprey. "Big Tree Country" is all around.

East Perthshire

Blairgowrie, the shire's second largest town, is the focus of the soft fruit growing industry (especially raspberries), and the gateway to Glenshee, famous for its skiing but also catering for year-round sports including, golf, mountain biking, abseiling and paragliding.

Aberfeldy, Loch Tay and Strathearn

Aberfeldy is a popular holiday town where visitors come to enjoy the "Birks" (falls) and visit Dewar's World of Whisky. Nearby is the natural beauty of Loch Tay and the conservation village of Kenmore; with its unique Iron Age re-creation. Perthshire's highest mountain, Ben Lawers, and Scotland's longest glen, Glen Lyon, invite climbers and walkers to sample wonderful scenery.

The Strathearn area of south Perthshire sees rolling Lowland landscape meet majestic Highland terrain. Crieff is the attractive bustling county town.

Highland Perthshire

Pitlochry is the Gateway to the Highlands. There are wonderful walks along the River Tummel. An unusual attraction is the salmon ladder by Pitlochry Dam. Downstream is the renowned Pitlochry Festival Theatre.

North of Pitlochry, at the Pass of Killiecrankie, the visitor centre tells the story of the famous battle in this tree-lined gorge, spectacular in autumn.

A drive to Rannoch Moor and Loch Rannoch shows Perthshire's wildest face – indeed the famous moor is renowned as one of the most remote and isolated parts of all Scotland.

The jewel of North Perthshire is Blair castle, the region's finest stately home enjoying one of Scotland's finest settings in extensive woodlands.

Perth★

and around

Perth, "the Fair City on the Tay", is pleasantly situated beside the river between two vast parklands, and although this former royal burgh has few historic buildings, it has succeeded better than most in retaining the atmosphere of a Scottish county town. Within driving distance of many major Scottish cities and attractions, Perth is an ideal touring centre.

A BIT OF HISTORY

Royal Burgh – The town achieved royal burgh status in the 12C and both William the Lion and Robert the Bruce gave confirming charters. During the reign of James I, Perth became the meeting place on several occasions for Parliament. The town would no doubt have become the centre of government or national capital had the king not been murdered in Blackfriars Monastery. By the 16C the walled town was a prosperous burgh, and the various trades and crafts are remembered today by street names: Cow Street, Meal Street, Flesher's Street, Cutlog Street, Baxter's (Bakers) Street, Mercer Terrace, Glover Street and Skinnergate.

Inland Port – From earliest times the Tay was important in bringing trade to the town and river traffic included both foreign and coastal vessels. Between 1814 and the 1930s a steamboat service plied the river between Dundee and Perth. Today, Perth's port, situated downstream, imports and handles fertilisers, with grain, timber, malt and potatoes as the main exports.

The Tay is known as a salmon river, but also boasts pearl fishing. The gems obtained from freshwater mussels range in colour from grey to gold and lilac.

🐾 WALKING TOUR

The city centre is flat and can easily be covered on foot. Begin on the corner of Shore Road/Tay Street and Marshall Place.

▶ **Population:** 47 430.
🛈 **Info:** 45 High Street;
   ℘01738 450 600.
   www.perthshire.co.uk.
▶ **Location:** The town centre is compact and can be covered on foot, with bus tours to outlying sites.
👁 **Don't Miss:** The city's Georgian terraces; Perth Museum and Art Gallery; an excursion to Scone Palace; the view from Glenshee.
🕐 **Timing:** Allow two hours for the town centre.

Marshall Place is a beautiful Georgian thoroughfare, punctuated by the crown tower of St Leonard's-in-the-Fields, that has dominated the green lawns of South Inch for over 200 years.

Fergusson Gallery

🕐*Apr–Oct Tue–Sun 10am–5pm.*
℘*01738 783 425.*
www.culturepk.org.uk.
Formerly the city's water works, this handsome circular building is girdled by a balustrade, crowned by an elegant dome and guarded by an urn-topped tower. Now home to the gallery, which exhibits in rotation the works of J D Fergusson (1874–1961), a leading member of the Scottish Colourists.

The muted tones of his early landscapes and portraits contrast with the vibrant colours and luminous quality of later scenes, which reflect the influence of Fauvism. There may also be on display at any one time some of his striking female nudes, in vivid colours with dark outlines. Fergusson's Scottish paintings include Highland landscapes and Glasgow scenes. The gallery also holds the entire collection of Fergusson's lifelong partner Margaret Morris (1891–1980), a pioneering dancer, choreographer and artist in her own right. Her artwork and costumes are on display.

Tay Street, Perth

▶ Walk beside the river and just before you turn left onto South Street admire the fine view of Perth Bridge.

Tay Street

The colonnaded frontage of the **Sheriff Court** (1820) is typical of Robert Smirke's Greek-inspired work.

A plaque to the left commemorates and represents the once magnificent Gowrie House (1520). It was the scene of the mystery-shrouded **Gowrie Conspiracy** (August 1600) when the descendants of the Ist Earl of Gowrie were murdered. Theories abound on whether this was an attempted regicide, kidnapping, or a plot on the part of James VI (♿ *see Box below*).

St John's Kirk

♿ 🕐 *Daily May–Sept 10am–4pm (more limited hours during rest of year).* 📞 *01738 638 482.* *www.st-johns-kirk.co.uk.*

With its steepled tower, this is an example of the great burgh kirks. Founded in the 12C, this mainly 15C church was restored in 1925–26 to house a war memorial. It was probably from this church that Perth took its early name of "St John's toun", perpetuated today by the name of the local football team (St Johnstone).

At the junction with South Street, a plaque on the building on the left marks the former site of the Bishops of Dunkeld's house. **The Salutation Hotel**

The Gowrie Conspiracy

Who knows what really happened on 5 August 1600 at Gowrie House? The basic facts are that King **James I** and a small retinue visited John Ruthven, 3rd Earl of Gowrie, and his brother Alexander. There ensued a fight, during which John and Alexander were both killed. On the Royalist side it was claimed that the king was lured here falsely, then threatened with kidnap, and the deaths of the Ruthvens were as a result of self-defence. But it is also clear that the Ruthvens were known to be disloyal to James and, moreover, owed him a large sum of money, so James had at least one motive to get rid of them. Whether it was the king or the Ruthvens who engineered the situation may now never be known.

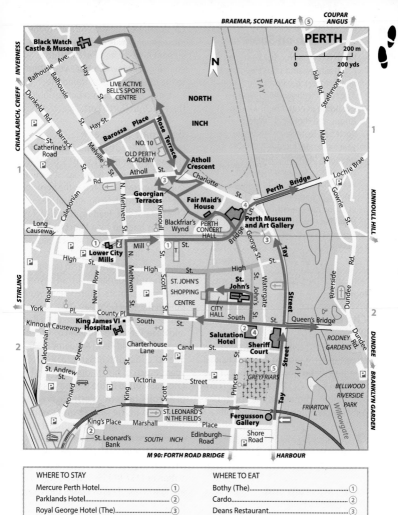

(1699) with its Venetian-style window was used by Bonnie Prince Charlie.

▶ Continue along South Street and pause on the corner where it meets South Methven Street (on the right). Look to your left across the street.

King James VI Hospital

In 1429 James I founded the only **Carthusian Monastery** in Scotland on this site. The murdered founder, his Queen, Joan Beaufort, and Margaret Tudor, James V's Queen, were all buried within its walls. The monastery was destroyed in 1559. The present four-storeyed, H-plan building, now divided into flats, was founded by James VI in 1587 originally as a hospital.

▶ Turn from South Street, right, onto South Methven Street, and again, when you reach the corner, with Mill Street, pause and, this time, look left.

City Mills
West Mill Street.
A fine group of early industrial buildings straddles Perth's Town Lade, the channel bringing water from a tributary of the Tay. The Upper City Mills have been converted into a hotel and the Lower City Mills is now home to the tourist office.

▶ Continue on Mill Street (in the opposite direction of the tourist office).

Perth Museum and Art Gallery★
♿ ◷*Tue–Sun 10am–5pm.* ◷*25 Dec, 1 Jan.* ☏*01738 632 488.*
www.pkc.gov.uk.
This is one of the oldest museums in the UK with more than half a million objects. In addition to displays on History, Natural History and Art there are particularly interesting sections on the local glass (Monart and Vasart ware), silver and clock-making industries. The art gallery includes works by **John Millais**, Cadell, and Henry and David Wilkie. At the woodland display you can see and listen to red squirrel and capercaillie, and marvel at the 64lb/29kg salmon, a British record, caught by a Miss Ballantine on the Tay in 1922.

▶ Continue past the entrance to the museum and walk halfway across the elegant nine-arched **Perth Bridge**, enjoying the views. Retrace your steps to the museum and go round the building, turn right into Castle Gable, then left into North Port.

Georgian Terraces★
North Port leads to **The Fair Maid's House**, the home of Scott's heroine, Catherine Glover; it is the oldest secular building in town, and today the home of the Royal Scottish Geographical Society. Charlotte Street, leading round to Tay Street, is backed by a short Georgian row, the last house of which has an attractive fire plaque.
On the completion of Perth Bridge in 1772 the town began to spread beyond the medieval limits. Entire streets were built in the new Georgian style, such as **Barossa Place** with its substantial villas, and **Rose Terrace** dominated by its centrepiece, the Old Perth Academy (1807). The art critic John Ruskin (1819–1900) spent much of his childhood at no 10. Continue round to the delightful curve of **Atholl Crescent**, which was the first extension in the New Town development. A plaque on the southwest corner of Blackfriars Street marks the site of Blackfriars Monastery. Founded in 1231, this was the scene of James I's assassination in 1437. In 1559 it was destroyed along with all of Perth's other monastic establishments.

North Inch
This 40ha park, extending northwards along the west bank of the Tay is mainly given over to sports facilities. Its outstanding feature is the domed form of Bell's Sports Centre built in 1978. It was on the North Inch that the great **Clan Combat** took place in 1396 between 30 champions from clans Chattan and Kay. There were few survivors in this event, which Scott describes in his novel *The Fair Maid of Perth*. Robert III and his Queen spectated from the Blackfriars Monastery, which once stood at the south end of the park.

Black Watch (Royal Highland Regiment) Castle and Museum★

Daily Apr–Oct 9.30am– 4.30pm; Nov–Mar 10am–4pm. Christmas and New Year period. £8.50. Guided tours daily at 11am and 2pm, £15. ℘01738 638 152. www.theblackwatch.co.uk.

Balhousie Castle, the former home of the Earls of Kinnoull, is now the setting for the Black Watch Regimental Museum. The origins of the regiment date back to the early 18C when General Wade was given the task of bringing peace, law and order to the Highlands.

During his subsequent programme of road and bridge building, Wade enlisted and armed groups of Highlanders to keep the peace. These companies were known as **The Black Watch** for the watch they kept on the Highlands and for their dark tartan, a direct contrast to the red of the government troops. The regiment was formed in 1739.

This well-presented museum is organised chronologically to unfold the regimental history through its battles and campaigns with paintings, silver, Colours and uniforms, plus medals, including those won in battle this century.

OUTSKIRTS

Branklyn Garden★

Apr–Oct 10am–5pm. £6.50. pay and display. ℘01738 625 535. www.nts.org.uk.

"Small is beautiful" aptly applies to Branklyn, which began life in 1922 as a private garden on the east bank of the Tay, overlooking Perth. It is only 0.8ha but it has a wide variety of plants. Branklyn is famed for its rhododendrons, which start to come into colour as early as February, frosts permitting, and many species are still in bloom in July in the most vibrant of colours. Another speciality is the lovely blue Himalayan poppy.

Kinnoull Hill

Take Bowerswell Road; 20min walk from Braes Road car park to the view indicator. The summit (*alt. 241m*) commands an extensive **view★**, away from the High-

land rim, over Perth, to the New Friarton Bridge, then follows the Tay round into the Carse of Gowrie with the Ochils and Lomonds in the distance. The craggy cliffs of Kinnoull, towering 213m above the Tay, are dominated by the follies of Kinnoull Watchtower and its counterpart 1mi/1.6km to the east on Binn Hill, both of which are imitations of Rhineland castles.

EXCURSIONS

Scone Palace★★

2mi/3.2km NE via the A93. See SCONE PALACE.

Huntingtower Castle★

3mi/5km northwest on the A9 and then the A85.

Apr–Oct daily 9.30am–5.30pm; Oct–Mar Sat–Wed 10am–4pm. 25–26 Dec, 1–2 Jan. £6. ℘01738 627 231. www.historicenvironment.scot.

Originally known as the Castle of Ruthven, this was the hunting seat of the family of the same name and scene of the **Raid of Ruthven** in 1582. William, 4th Lord Ruthven, created Earl of Gowrie the previous year, invited the 16-year-old James VI to the castle, where he was held captive for 10 months by a group of nobles resentful of the influence the Earl of Arran and Duke of Lennox exercised over the young monarch. Although officially pardoned, the Earl of Gowrie was beheaded in 1584 at Stirling, on charges connected with an attack on Stirling Castle. Revenge was to follow with the counterplot, the Gowrie Conspiracy (*see Gowrie Conspiracy Box p284*) in 1600. The castle was confiscated, its name changed to Huntingtower and the family name of Ruthven proscribed. In 1643 the castle passed into the hands of William Dysart, "whipping-boy" for Charles I and father of Elizabeth Dysart, Duchess of Lauderdale.

This typical 15C–16C tower house consists of two towers, which were joined in the 17C to provide more commodious accommodation. Both towers have three storeys plus a garret served by turnpikes. Note in particular the roofline with corbelled wall-walk, corner turrets, punctuated by chimneys and crow-stepped gable ends. The **painted timber ceiling** on the first floor of the eastern tower is one of the earliest of its kind (c.1540). An unusual feature is the dovecot in the garret of the western tower.

◗ Leave Perth by the A912 and before the motorway turn left onto a local road in the direction of Rhynd.

Elcho Castle★

Signposting leads down to the castle by a farm road and through the steading.
Daily Apr–Sept 9.30am– 5.30pm.
£6. 01738 639 998.
www.historicenvironment.scot.
Overlooking the Tay, the Earls of Wemyss' family seat is reputedly on or near the site of an earlier stronghold and former retreat of William Wallace. Built in the second half of the 16C, Elcho Castle is a handsome and remarkably complete 16C fortified mansion with three projecting towers. Above the plain walls, pierced by windows with wrought-iron grills and gun ports, the wallhead is an intriguing composition of decorative elements: pediments, roll-moulded window surrounds, corbelled turrets, crow-stepped gables and chimney stacks. The north and west fronts are good examples of the imaginative Scottish masons at their best.
The southwest tower has an unusually elegant and spacious **staircase**.

Abernethy

8mi/13km southeast by the A912 and A913.
Happily the main road by-passes the old centre of this peaceful village on the lower slopes of the Ochils. As the village stood at the heart of the Pictish kingdom, some claimed this was the early capital. Later it was the site of a Celtic settlement; a relic of its ancient past is its **11C Round Tower★**. This Irish-type tower served the dual purpose of place of refuge and belfry. Standing alone at the kirkyard gate the tower (23m tall) tapers slightly. Two periods of construction are clearly visible. Note the elevated position of the door (a defensive feature) the jougs (rings) attached to the wall and the Pictish symbol stone at its foot.

🚗 DRIVING TOURS

🚗 1 NORTH PERTHSHIRE
95mi/152km. Allow 2h30 driving time.

This tour allows you to enjoy the foothills of the Grampians and visit the pretty village of Dunkeld.

◗ Leave Perth to the north by the A93. You can stop at Scone Palace before continuing further north.

Scone Palace★★
See SCONE PALACE.

Meikleour Beech Hedge
This remarkable hedge (30.5m high) was planted in 1746.

◗ Continue towards Blairgowrie.

Blairgowrie
Set in the heart of an area famous for soft fruit growing, in winter Blairgowrie becomes the main ski centre for the resort of Glenshee (*see below*).
The road follows the Black Water up Glenshee, a typical Angus Glen, as far as the Spittal of Glenshee.
The final ascent to the Cairnwell Pass (665m) was famous for the zigzag bend, appropriately called the **Devil's Elbow**, now by-passed by a new stretch of the A93.
In the romantically wooded valley of the River Ericht just upstream from Blairgowrie stands **Keathbank Mill**. Once a flax and jute mill with the largest wheel in Scotland, the imposing structure is now private housing.

Glenshee
The Glenshee ski area lies to either side of the A93.
This is the busiest **ski resort** in Scotland. The season generally commences around late December and runs until Easter, but can be longer or shorter depending on snow cover.

Ski slope, Glenshee

During winter, the lifts run from December to April, with 22 ski tows and two chair-lifts operating on three peaks, giving access to 36 ski runs ranging from easy to expert (*for more information contact the Ski Centre: ☏013397 41320; www.ski-glenshee.co.uk*).
At the summit of The Cairnwell (*alt. 933m*) there is a **panorama★★** which encompasses Ben Macdui, Beinn à Bhuird, Lochnagar and Glas Maol on the far side of the valley, plus several more Munros. The **Cairnwell Chairlift** runs from mid-May–Oct (*☜£10 return*).
In summer Glenshee is a centre for hang-gliding and mountain biking.

▶ Retrace your steps to Blairgowrie, and from here, take the A923 towards Dunkeld.

Loch of Lowes Wildlife Reserve

♿☉*Mar–Oct daily 10.30am–5pm; Nov–Feb Fri–Sun 10.30am–4pm. ☜£4.50. ☏01350 727 337. www.scottishwildlifetrust.org.uk.*
The reserve (98ha) covers the freshwater Loch of Lowes and its fringing woodland and has a consequently rich flora and fauna. Visitor access is limited to the south shore, the visitor centre and the observation hide. From the latter, the treetop eyrie of a pair of ospreys – one of only two nests accessible to the public in Scotland – can be observed (*binoculars are provided*) from early April to late August.

▶ Continue on the A923 to Dunkeld.

Dunkeld★

The particular charm of this modest village on the north bank of the Tay is its ruined cathedral and attractive precinct.
Metropolitan See – As early as the year 700, this was the site of a monastic establishment which was to become, for a brief spell, the kingdom's principal ecclesiastic centre under Kenneth MacAlpine in 843.
Confirmed during the reign of Alexander I, the bishopric was held by such historic figures as William Sinclair and the scholar poet Gavin Douglas (1474–1522). The settlement which developed around the majestic cathedral (14C–16C) never grew to any great size.
By 1650, the cathedral itself was a ruin and in 1689 the village was burned to the ground in the aftermath of the Battle of Killiecrankie.

Dunkeld Cathedral

☉*Daily Apr–Sept 9.30am–5.30pm; Oct–Mar 10am–4pm. ☏01350 727 601. www.dunkeldcathedral.org.uk.*
In a lovely riverside setting surrounded by tree-shaded lawns, the cathedral is divided into two distinct parts, a roofless ruined nave, and the choir.
Choir – Begun in 1315 by Robert the Bruce's bishop, William Sinclair, building continued until 1400. In 1600 the choir of the ruined cathedral was renovated to serve as parish church. There have

been several restorations since. Inside, recumbent effigies portray Bishop Sinclair (headless), and Alexander Stewart, the Wolf of Badenoch, in an impressive suit of armour. The 15C chapter house serves as Atholl mausoleum and houses the small **Chapter House Museum** covering town and church history. At the choir's west end is a copy of the 1611 Great She Bible.

Nave – Dating from the 15C, work was begun by Robert Cardney whose effigy lies in the Chapel of St Ninian. The windows of the triforium level are unusual. The Late Gothic tower (1469–1501) was the last addition. Inside are two mural paintings, while the platform offers a good view.

From the grounds can be seen Telford's bridge (1809). The imposing cathedral gates (1730) came from Dunkeld House (*now a hotel*), once the Atholl ducal seat.

Cathedral Street and The Cross★

Cathedral Street and the square known as The Cross were rebuilt to the original street plan after the destruction of 1689. Many of the 17C houses were derelict by the 1950s. An extensive restoration programme, by the National Trust for Scotland and the local authority, has recaptured the 17C–18C aspect of these streets, thus providing an attractive approach to the cathedral.

Cathedral Street is lined with houses where the characteristic door and window trims set off the pale coloured harling, and pends interrupt the succession. **No. 19**, Dean's House, was where **Gavin Douglas** (1474–1522), the poet and scholar of the Scottish Renaissance, was consecrated Bishop of Dunkeld in 1516. Apart from his politicising for the Douglas faction, Douglas is remembered for his translation of Virgil's *Aeneid* into Scots.

Occupying pride of place on the west side of the cross is the National Trust for Scotland's **Ell Shop**, named after the ell or weaver's measure fixed to one of its walls. At the heart of the cross is the restored Atholl Memorial Fountain, erected in 1866 by public subscription in memory of the 6th Duke of Atholl.

Birnam

Resting on the opposite bank of the River Tay is the Victorian village of Birnam. In the centre is the modern **Birnam Arts & Conference Centre**, home to **The Beatrix Potter Exhibition & Garden** ♿♨ (♿🕙*daily 10am–4.30pm;* 🕙*Christmas and New Year;* ✕ ✆*01350 727 674; www.birnamarts. com*).

Beatrix Potter, the English author and illustrator (1866–1941) developed her interest in wildlife, drawing and painting during her childhood summers spent at Dalguise House near Dunkeld.

Characters from her books were inspired by local personalities, the most famous being Mrs Tiggywinkle, modelled on the Potters' Dalguise washerwoman, Kitty MacDonald

▷ 2mi/3.2km to the west of Dunkeld is The Hermitage, just off the A9 heading north.

The Hermitage

The **Hermitage** (1758), a woodland walk along the banks of the River Braan, has been a famous beauty spot for over two centuries. It overlooks the Falls of Braan, where this Highland torrent rushes through the cleft and under the bridge. Further on is Ossian's Cave, another folly of the same period as the Hermitage. Britain's tallest tree, a 65m Douglas Fir, can also be seen here.

▷ The A9 south will return you to Perth. At Dunkeld you can reach Crieff along the A822.

⬅ ② CRIEFF AND STRATHEARN

60mi/96km.

This tour of the heartland of Scotland takes in the principal sights around the market town of Crieff.

▷ Leave Perth on the A9 in the direction of Stirling, and later branching onto to A824 towards Auchterarder.

Auchterarder

This little town has a long history. A very popular 11C hunting ground, it later became the chief town of County Strathearn. It was destroyed in 1715 after the Jacobite retreat from the Battle of Sheriffmuir. The town is now famous for its proximity to the famous **Gleneagles Hotel**, a name synonymous with 5-star luxury (it hosted the 2005 G8 summit) and championship golf.

▶ Take the A823 towards Muthill. On the way, stop at Tullibardine Chapel.

Tullibardine Chapel★

ⓘ*Apr–Sept daily 9.30am–5.30pm.*
www.historicenvironment.scot.
One of the most complete and unaltered small medieval churches in Scotland, this attractive red sandstone church stands on its own in the middle of rich agricultural land, sheltered by a couple of gnarled and windswept trees. It was founded in 1446, enlarged c.1500 and has survived unaltered ever since.

▶ Rejoin the A823 and then take the A822 towards Muthill.

Muthill

This Strathearn village, destroyed in 1715 after the Battle of Sheriffmuir, is dominated by its 21m high 12C **tower**, one of a group in the area. The saddle-backed and crow-stepped tower is now embedded in the west end of the ruined 15C church.

▶ From the centre of the village, follow the signs to Drummond Castle.

Drummond Castle Gardens★

2mi/3km south of Crieff.
ⓘ*Easter weekend and May–Oct daily 1–6pm (Jun–Aug 11am–6pm).* ⊛*£6.*
℘*01764 681 433.*
www.drummondcastlegardens.co.uk.
The Drummond family seat (*closed to the public*), consisting of a 1491 tower and later buildings, is set high on a rocky eminence. Laid out below in a series of terraces, these lovely **formal gardens** are in the form of St Andrew's Cross. Against the background of lawns and gravel areas, boxwood hedging and the many shaped and pruned trees and bushes present a medley of greens and shapes and detailed patterns.

▶ Continue on the main A822 road, crossing the Machany Water and just before reaching the heart of town is the Crieff Visitor Centre.

Crieff Visitor Centre

Muthill Road.
⚐ⓘ*Daily 9am– 5pm.*
✗ ℘*01764 654 014. www.crieff.co.uk.*
This is best known as the home of **Caithness Glass** (*www.caithnessglass. co.uk*) who produces beautiful hand-made paperweights, crystal and arty studio pieces. A visitor's gallery lets you see the whole production process. You can also watch master craftsmen at the **Buchan Pottery**, which makes decorative flagons for many of Scotland's leading whisky distillers, as well as its distinctive range of "Thistle" stoneware. The **Highland Drovers Exhibition** (*free*) tells the story of the cattle drovers who made Crieff the crossroads of Scotland at the turn of the 18C.
The centre also includes a large shop, restaurant and garden centre.

Crieff★

Located at an important crossroad from the north, Crieff was once a centre of the cattle trade and one of the great cattle trysts. Burned down by the Jacobites after the 1715 rising, the town was rebuilt by the Crown Commissioners and by the end of the 18C it had become a minor spa resort. The railway arrived in 1856 and by the late 19C Crieff Hydro was flourishing.
The face of Crieff today testifies to its Victorian popularity as a spa. Set on the Highland rim, with fine scenery all around, it makes an ideal touring centre. The **Crieff Highland Gathering** with the official Scottish Heavyweight Championship is always a popular event.

▶ From Crieff, make the short round trip along the A85 towards Comrie.

Glenturret Distillery (Famous Grouse Experience)

Just outside Crieff on the A85 Comrie road. ♿🚻*Guided tour hourly from 10.30am: Apr–Oct 10am–6pm; Nov–Mar 10am–5pm.* 🕐*25–26 Dec and 1 Jan.* 🎫*Distillery Experience Tour £10–£40.* ✖ ☎*01764 65 65 65. https://theglenturret.com.*

On the banks of the Turret, the Glenturret distillery (est. 1775, the oldest in Scotland) still employs traditional methods. A choice of three tours quite literally caters for most Scotch whisky tastes. The "entry-level" Experience Tour is enough for most visitors and includes a BAFTA-award winning interactive show and two drams. Two other tours progress in levels of sophisticatiion and expense.

▶ Complete the circuit back to Perth by leaving Crieff on the A85, heading east.

ADDRESSES

🛏 STAY

🚪🍽 **Mercure Perth Hotel** – *West Mill Street.* ☎*01738 481 607. www.accorhotels. com. 76 rooms.* Comfortable modern city-centre hotel set in and around a restored 15C watermill. Lovely gardens.

🚪🍽 **Taythorpe** – *Isla Road.* ☎*01738 447 994. 3 rooms.* An immaculately kept modern guest-house, a short walk from the city centre and close to Scone Palace, with cosy bedrooms, an inviting lounge and communal breakfasts.

🚪🍽🍽 **Parklands Hotel** – *2 St Leonard's Bank.* ☎*01738 622 451. www.theparklands hotel.com. 14 rooms.* Near the station, this hotel has recently won national awards for its accommodation (contemporary decor, free Wi-Fi) and its bistro (with terrace tables in summer).

🚪🍽🍽 **Salutation Hotel** – *30-34 South Street.* ☎*01738 630 066. www. strathmorehotels-thesalutation.com. 84 rooms.* One of the oldest hotels in Scotland, the Salutation has been welcoming guests, including Bonnie Prince Charlie, since 1699. Some rooms have four-poster beds – those in the main part of the hotel are the best.

🚪🍽🍽 **The Royal George Hotel** – *Tay St.* ☎*01738 624 455. www.theroyal georgehotel.co.uk. 45 rooms.* Dating from 1770 and patronised by royalty, including Queen Victoria, this is the most prestigious hotel in Perth. Its **restaurant** 🍽🍽 is also recommended for afternoon tea and dinner (no evening meals on Sunday, but High Tea served in lieu at 5pm).

🍴EAT

🚪 **Cardo** – *38 South Street.* ☎*01738 248 784 (and 2 Princes Street; ☎01738 628 152). https://cardo.restaurant.* An innovative reataurant, pizzeria and bakery in which everything is baked freshly each day.

🚪🍽 **Post Box** – *80 George Street.* ☎*01738 248 971. www.thepostboxperth.co.uk.* Striking building with bright red doors, formerly the first post office in Perth. Classic lunches and more up-market modern dishes in the evening. Cellar bar hosts live jazz and blues on Fridays and Saturdays.

🚪🍽 **The Bothy** – *33 Kinnoull Street.* ☎*01738 449 792. www.bothyperth.co.uk.* Smart modern bistro with a traditional feel, just as good for drinks, snacks and cocktails as its full menu of traditional and modern Scottish dishes.

🚪🍽 **Deans Restaurant** – *77–79 Kinnoull Street. Closed Sun, Mon.* ☎*01738 643 377. www.letseatperth.co.uk.* Vibrant, modern Scottish cuisine with a firm focus on flavour and seasonability in a relaxed setting, a short walk from the town centre.

🚪🍽🍽 **63 Tay Street** – *63 Tay Street.* ☎*01738 441 451. www.63taystreet.com.* Light and airy, this modern restaurant close to the riverside serves well-priced modern cuisine. The philosophy is local, honest, simple.

Scone Palace★★

Situated on the edge of the city of Perth, overlooking the Tay, Scone Palace (pronounced "skoon") is not only one of Scotland's most hallowed historic sites, but also one of Scotland's most popular visitor attractions.

A BIT OF HISTORY

Heartland of a Pictish kingdom – Although the exact role of the site in Pictish times is unsure, its considerable importance is in no doubt. The tradition was perpetuated by Kenneth MacAlpine in the mid-9C when he made Scone the centre of his new Pictish Kingdom. From this time on Scottish Kings were ceremonially enthroned on the **Stone of Scone**, also known as the **Stone of Destiny** (&see Box on following page). Robert the Bruce was the first of many Scottish kings to be crowned here, right up to James VI, the last being Charles II in 1651. Such was the stone's importance that in 1296, Edward I, following his defeat of the Scots and imprisonment of King John Balliol, had the stone and other regalia carried off to Westminster Abbey where it has been part of the Coronation Chair ever since, except for a notable interlude in 1950–51. In 1996 the stone was transferred to Edinburgh Castle in acknowledgement of its symbolic importance. It will be returned to Westminster Abbey for future coronations.

Religious Centre – The original Celtic community was superseded when Alexander I founded an Augustinian priory c.1120, the first of that order in Scotland. The abbey and abbot's palace, as was the custom, served as a royal residence. In 1559, during the early days of the Scottish Reformation the abbey fell victim to a Protestant mob from Dundee motivated by the great reformer John Knox. The abbey was badly damaged despite Knox's attempt to calm the mob.

🛈 **Info:** &🕐Apr–Oct 10am–4pm (May–Sept 9.30am–5pm). Grounds close at 5.45pm. 💷£21.50 (grounds only, £7.50). 📞01738 552 300. www.scone-palace.co.uk.

▶ **Location:** Scone Palace is 2mi/3.2km north of Perth via the A93. Buses run here from the city centre.

🕐 **Timing:** Allow 1½ hours.

&️ **See Also:** North Perthshire Driving Tour.

Despite this setback Scone abbey was repaired and continued to function for another 90 years. It became the property of the Earls of Gowrie who built a 16C house, Gowrie Palace, using the old palace stones. Following the Gowrie Conspiracy (&see PERTH) and the forfeiture of their property in 1600, James VI bestowed the estate on the Murray family, later the Earls of Mansfield. The 3rd Earl commissioned William Atkinson to build a neo-Gothic palatial mansion (1802–08).

Scone Palace

© Angus Forbes/Scone Palace

Romancing the Stone

Replica of the Stone of Scone, Scone Palace

© FLPA/Wayne Hutchinson/age fotostock

The Stone of Scone, also known as the **Stone of Destiny**, is an oblong block of red sandstone, which measures around 66cm by 41cm by 27cm and weighs approximately 153kg. At each end of the stone is an iron ring, presumably for carrying, or perhaps securing it.

Legends abound as to its provenance. It is said to have been Jacob's Pillow when he saw the angels of Bethel; another story suggests it was brought to Scotland by Scotia, daughter of an Egyptian pharaoh; and yet another theory is that it was a portable altar used by St Columba in his missionary work in Caledonia. The most likely explanation is that it was a royal stone used by the early Irish kings, brought from Antrim to Argyll and then to Scone in 838 from Dunstaffnage (&see *OBAN: Driving Tours*) by Kenneth MacAlpine.

Its recent history is hardly less colourful. On Christmas Day 1950, a group of four Scottish students managed to steal the stone from Westminster Abbey – no mean feat given its size and weight. However, in the process of removing it they broke it into two pieces. The stone was passed to a pro-Nationalist senior Glasgow politician who arranged for it to be professionally repaired by a Glasgow stonemason. Meanwhile a nationwide hunt continued for the stone.

On 11 April 1951, over 15 months after its disappearance, the stone was found on the altar of Arbroath abbey, the site of the signing of the Declaration of Arbroath and a hallowed site for Scottish Nationalists. A relieved and red-faced government hastily returned it to Westminster. Meanwhile rumours circulated among Scottish Nationalists that a copy had been made of the stone while it was in hiding, and that the block of sandstone now sitting in Westminster was not the real thing. An adventure comedy movie of this escapade, *Stone of Destiny*, starring Robert Carlyle, was released in 2008. In 1996, the stone was transferred to Edinburgh Castle in acknowledgement of its symbolic importance. It will be returned to Westminster Abbey for future coronations.

VISIT
Interior

Throughout the richly furnished State Rooms in neo-Gothic style are superb pieces of French furniture and a series of unusual and interesting timepieces. Outstanding in the Dining Room is the beautiful dining table and chairs which were commissioned by the Earl for Queen Victoria's visit in 1846, these were locally made in the Chippendale style.

His Grace the **Hon. William Murray** (1701–1779), the eminent lawyer, politician and embellisher of Kenwood House (Hampstead Heath, London), is portrayed here, as is the Ist Earl In the adjoining **Anteroom**

Sir David Murray, the Cup Bearer to James VI, was the lucky recipient of the forfeited Gowrie lands and palace.

In the **Drawing Room**, against the 18C Lyons silk-hung walls, are a series of **portraits**, including Allan Ramsay's pair of royal portraits (1765) of *King George III* and *Queen Charlotte*, and Reynolds' portrait of the *1st Earl of Mansfield*, William Murray as Lord Chief Justice of England (1776). One of the greatest lawyers of his day, he was known as "Silver-Tongued Murray" and was the lifelong opponent of William Pitt the Elder.

The Pierre Bara set of French fauteuils with fine needlework are dated 1756, and flanking the fireplace are two Boulle

Long Gallery

commodes. However, the finest piece is Marie Antoinette's exquisite Riesener (1734–1806) **writing table**. The magnificent array of fine **porcelain** in the **Library** was collected by the Ist and 2nd Earls. The 1st Earl's portrait shows his prized possession, Bernini's bust of Homer which Alexander Pope had given him, and flanking this is Rysbrack's bust of the Lord Chief Justice.

The **Ambassador's Room** is named after the 2nd Earl, politician, statesman and ambassador, who served in Dresden, Vienna and subsequently Paris, where he became the confidant of Louis XVI and Marie Antoinette and acquired much of the fine French furniture now in the house. The bed was a royal piece commissioned for *His Grace the Ambassador*, who is portrayed here by Pompeo Batoni. Zoffany's portrait of the ambassador's daughter, *Lady Elizabeth Murray*, shows her in the grounds of Kenwood, the Earl's English country house and permanent home after rioting crowds destroyed his Bloomsbury residence.

Stretching 51m, the **Long Gallery** retains its original oak and bog-oak flooring but sadly has lost its painted ceiling. Outstanding among the paintings and fine furniture is a unique collection of **Vernis Martin** *objets d'art*, all made of papier mâché.

David Wilkie's *The Village Politicians* formerly in the Long Gallery now hangs in the Inner Hall beside the Siberian bears.

Grounds

Facing the palace is **Moot Hill**, now occupied by a 19C chapel. Explanations for the name Moot are various. The Gaelic derivation (*Tom-a-mhoid*) would have it as a place where justice was administered, while another version, **Boot Hill**, though more unlikely on first hearing, is perhaps the more credible. It was said that when the earls, chieftains and other men of consequence came to swear fealty to the Lord High Ardh, they carried earth in their boots from their own lands – since fealty could only be sworn for their land while standing on it! Having taken the oath they then emptied the contents on the spot.

The avenue opposite the main entrance leads down to the **Old Gateway**, emblazoned with the arms of James VI and the Ist Viscount. Beyond was the original site of the village of Scone, before it was moved during 19C alterations to the palace.

The Victorian **pinetum** (20ha) has some of the oldest firs including the Douglas species. The first such tree was sent by its namesake the celebrated botanist, David Douglas (1798–1834) who was born at and worked on the estate.

For children there is a playground and the unique "tartan" **Murray Star Maze**. This was designed by the world-renowned maze designer, Adrian Fisher, in the shape of the five-pointed star that features in the Murray family crest, and comprises 2 000 beech trees, half copper and half green, planted in a way to create a tartan effect.

Pitlochry★
and Lochs Rannoch and Tay

Set in the lovely Tummel valley, this holiday resort makes an ideal touring centre from which to enjoy the magnificent scenery of the surrounding countryside. The busy main street is a succession of hotels, guesthouses, restaurants, cafés, and tweed and Highlands craft shops.

A BIT OF HISTORY

One of the main drove roads from the north followed the alignment of the Tummel valley and in the 1720s and 1730s **General Wade** (1673–1748) built one of his first military roads from Dunkeld to Inverness through Pitlochry. Prior to this the main settlement was Moulin, and as late as the 1880s Pitlochry numbered barely 300 people. The town's growth was due in large part to its popularity as a health resort in Victorian times, and more recently as a tourist centre situated astride the Great North Road.

SIGHTS
Blair Athol Distillery

Atholl Road/Perth Road. Guided tours only, daily: Jan–Jun and Oct–Dec 10am–5pm; Jul–Sept 10am–6pm. £9.50–£75. 01796 482 003. www.malts.com.
Guided tours take visitors through the different stages of whisky production with a wee dram at the end.

Pitlochry Power Station Visitor Centre

Daily 9.30am– 5.30pm. 01796 484 111. https://pitlochrydam.com.
Part of the North of Scotland Hydroelectric Board's Tummel Valley Scheme, the dam (16m high and 139m long) retains Loch Faskally to even out the flow of water. There is an interactive exhibition which includes videos on the Tummel Scheme and the life cycle of the salmon. The main attraction is the **Salmon Ladder**, which permits salmon to move upstream to their spawning grounds between April and October: 34

▶ **Population:** 2 950.
Info: 22 Atholl Road. 01796 472215. www.perthshire.co.uk.
Location: Pitlochry is 27mi/43km north of Perth on the A9.
Don't Miss: The Queen's View panorama.
Timing: Allow at least a day and a night here.
Kids: The Salmon Ladder at The Hydro Electric Story.

pools, three of which are "resting pools", rise up in steps to the level of the loch. The salmon can be observed at close quarters through windows in the observation room. The artificial Loch Faskally (3mi/5km long) is stocked with salmon and trout. It provides good angling and boating facilities and a pleasant walk (*1h*) around the shores.

🚗 DRIVING TOURS

1 LOCH RANNOCH
75mi/121km. Allow half to a full day.

This tour can easily be taken in reverse order, depending on whether you want to divert to Blair Castle and how much time you want to spend in your car.

▷ Leave Pitlochry north to join the A9. Beyond Garry Bridge, leading to Lochs Tummel and Rannoch, the river, road and railway all run parallel to negotiate the narrow Pass of Killiecrankie.

Killiecrankie Visitor Centre
End Apr–24 Dec Thu–Sun 10am–5pm. P (charge). 01796 473 233. www.nts.org.uk.
The centre interprets the rich natural history of the pass (famous for its spectacular autumn colours) and the story of the **Battle of Killiecrankie** (27 July 1689). This was the major event in the first of the Jacobite uprisings, fought on high ground to the north of the

pass. The Jacobite followers were rallied by **John Graham of Claverhouse, Viscount Dundee** (c.1649–1689), who, having seized Blair Castle, moved south to meet the government troops under Mackay. The encounter was brief, and a decisive victory for Dundee even though he was mortally wounded in the fray. Yet a month later the leaderless Highlanders were beaten at Dunkeld. The final Jacobite saga ended in 1746 with Culloden. From the Visitor Centre a path (signposted) leads to **Soldier's Leap** where a fleeing government soldier is said to have jumped an 5.5m gap to escape from his Jacobite pursuers. A second path leads down through the wooded Pass of Killiecrankie to the car park beside Garry Bridge.

▷ You can continue north along the A9 to visit Blair Castle (&see *BLAIR CASTLE*) on the outskirts of Blair Atholl village, or head south towards Pitlochry and then turn right onto the B8019 and continue west on the B846.

Loch Rannoch

The larger of the two lochs is almost 10mi/16km long and is on average 0.79mi/1.2km wide.

The road runs close to the loch side. On the south shore are the remains of the native pine forest, the Black Wood of Rannoch.

Beyond the head of Loch Rannoch the B846 continues a further 6mi/9.7km to Rannoch Station, on the West Highland Railway (Glasgow–Fort William). The terrain is hummocky with glacial debris and erratics all around. The Gaur is a typical Highland river with a boulder-strewn course.

Once over the watershed, Rannoch Moor stretches away to the horizon.

Rannoch Moor

The vastness of this desolate wilderness is legendary. At an average height of 305m the granite floor is mainly covered with blanket bog and lochans with the peat in places reaching a depth of 6m. The moor was a centre of ice dispersal during the Ice Age, with glaciers radiating outwards and gouging, among others, the troughs of the Rannoch-Tummel valley and Glencoe in the west.

▷ Unless you take the train, Rannoch Station is a dead end, so go back along the B846. After 24mi/39km, you'll reach Tummel Bridge. From here you can go south to Aberfeldy for the following driving tour to Loch Tay. Otherwise, drive east beside Loch Tummel.

Loch Tummel

Hydroelectric works in the vicinity have been responsible for increasing the size of the original loch from about 3mi/4.8km to 7mi/11.3km in length and its depth by 5m. The power station at the Tummel Bridge end is powered by water from the Loch Errochty reservoir, high in the mountains to the north, which arrives by a 6mi/9.7km tunnel.

Queen's View★★

Access from the Forestry Commission car park and information centre.

This famous viewpoint, named after Queen Victoria's 1866 visit, has a truly royal vista up Loch Tummel, which is dominated by the conical shape of Schiehallion (1 083m).

2 TOWARDS THE TROSSACHS VIA LOCH TAY

40mi/64km.

▷ Leave Pitlochry on the A9 heading south towards Perth. At Ballinluig, take the A827 towards Aberfeldy, 2mi/3.2km northeast of Aberfeldy, signposted off the A827. Take the farm road up to Pitcairn Farm.

St Mary's Church, Grandtully

Behind the farm buildings, this low unassuming whitewashed 16C church is now in the care of Historic Scotland (*www.historic-scotland.gov.uk*) on account of its extraordinary 17C **painted ceiling★**. The elaborate design includes heraldic devices of local Stewarts and colourful Biblical scenes.

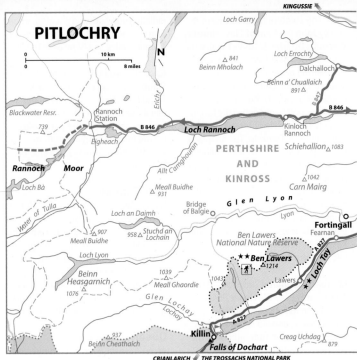

PITLOCHRY

0 ——— 10 km
0 ——— 8 miles

N

Loch Garry

△ 841
Beinn Mholach

Loch Errochty

Dalchalloch

Beinn a' Chuallaich
891 △

B 846

Blackwater Resr.

Rannoch
Station

B 846

Loch Rannoch

Kinloch
Rannoch

739
△

Eigheach

Erichd

Allt Camghouran

PERTHSHIRE
AND
KINROSS

Schiehallion △1083

Rannoch   Moor

Loch Bà

Water of Tulla

Loch an Daimh

△ 907
Meall Buidhe

958 △ Stuchd an
Lochain

Meall Buidhe
931

Bridge
of Balgie

Glen   Lyon

Lyon

△1042
Carn Mairg

Fortingall
Fearnan

Ben Lawers
National Nature Reserve

★★ Ben Lawers
△1214

Lawers

★★

Loch Tay

A 827

Loch Lyon

Beinn
Heasgarnich

1076

1039
△
Meall Ghaordie

1043△

Glen Lochay

Lochay

△ 937
Beinn Cheathaich

Killin

Falls of Dochart

A 827

Creag Uchdag

879

CRIANLARICH   THE TROSSACHS NATIONAL PARK

Aberfeldy★

This small town, pleasantly set in Strath Tay, was immortalised by Burns, who wrote: "Come let us spend the ... days, In the birks of Aberfeldy." The deep pools and majestic waterfalls of the **Birks** (birches), just outside the town, remain one of its most popular attractions.

The Water Mill

Daily Mon–Sat 10am–5pm, Sun 11am–5pm. 25–26 Dec, 1 Jan. ✕
01887 822 896.
www.aberfeldywatermill.com.
In the centre of the town The Watermill brings together the UK Independent Bookshop of the Year (2012), a contemporary art gallery, a music shop and café, all set in the lovely surroundings of an early-19C watermill.

Water from the Birks (falls, *see above*) is channelled through a 500m tunnel to power the big overshot waterwheel of the restored mill. Atmospheric rumblings and creakings accompany the grinding of oats.

General Wade's Bridge

This elegant five-arched bridge was built by Wade to carry his military road north from Crieff to Dalwhinnie.

Black Watch Monument

The kilted figure, dressed in a uniform of the time, commemorates the formation of the Black Watch Regiment in 1739 and marks the site of the first parade.

Dewar's World of Whisky

Apr–Oct Mon–Sat 10am– 6pm, Sun noon–4pm; Nov–Mar Mon–Sat 10am–4pm. Tours from £10.50. ✕
01887 822 010. www.dewars.com.
Just on the edge of town is one of Scotland's most famous drinks brands. The tour does a good job of explaining the process while a video and exhibition tells you Dewar's history. And of course there is a tasting session, which may be upgraded to include sampling superior whiskies.

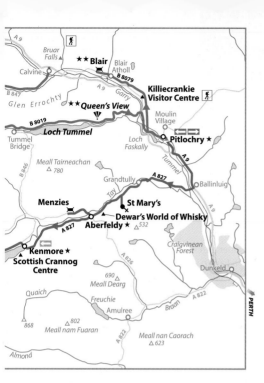

From Aberfeldy, you can make a short (3mi/5km) side trip to Castle Menzies on the B846.

Castle Menzies

1.5mi/2.5km to the west. Leave by the B846 crossing General Wade's Bridge. Take the second entrance.

Apr–Oct Mon–Sat 10.30am–5pm, Sun 2–2pm. £7 (includes entry to the Castle's Walled Gardens and the Old Kirk of Weem). ✕ *01887 820 982. www.castlemenzies.org.*

This 16C Z-plan castle – repeatedly besieged – was the chief seat of the Menzies (pronounced "Mingus") until some 80 years ago when the bloodline eventually died out. There are two fine plasterwork ceilings.

Leave Aberfeldy on the B827, which takes you along the south bank of the Tay to Kenmore.

Kenmore★

The sites of 18 crannogs have been discovered in Loch Tay. A crannog is an artificial or modified natural island, found throughout Scotland and Ireland, the oldest dating back some 5 000 years. Many crannogs were built as defensive homesteads and represented symbols of power and wealth.

The multi-award-winning **Scottish Crannog Centre** (♿ daily Feb–Oct 10am–5.30pm; £10; *01887 830 583; www.crannog.co.uk*) features a unique reconstruction of an early Iron Age loch dwelling, based on the excavation evidence from a 2 600-year-old site. Iron Age actor-guides help bring the site alive for visitors.

From Kenmore, there is a road either side of Loch Tay. The A827 to the north is the quickest, and skirts the base of Ben Lawers; the southerly road is more narrow and winding, offering fine views of the surrounding hills.

Crannog, Loch Tay

© Lukasphoto/iStockphoto.com

Loch Tay★★

Allow half a day for the north shore tour, plus a full day if ascending Ben Lawers.

Loch Tay is an attractive freshwater loch in a mountain setting with Ben Lawers rising to majestic heights on the north shore. It measures over 14mi/22.5km long from Killin to Kenmore, but is never more than 1mi/1.6km wide. The loch is fed by the Dochart and Lochay, and at the east end, by the River Tay.

The biggest island in the loch, the Isle of Loch Tay, is just north of Kenmore. When Alexander I's Queen Sybilla died in 1122, the king granted her burial place, the isle, to the monks of Scone. A nunnery succeeded the monastery until the late 15C.

▶ Ben Lawers can be accessed along a 2.5mi/4km single track road heading uphill from the B827.

Ben Lawers★★

The summit (*alt. 1 214m*) and southern slopes of the mountain are a National Nature Reserve, and access is controlled in order to protect the fragile ecology of the area.

A **nature trail** (*1h30*) introduces visitors to some of the fascinating plants and makes clear the need for careful conservation of their vulnerable habitat. On the descent the road provides good **views** of Loch Tay.

Killin

At the head of Loch Tay, Killin is busy with passing trade in summer. To the west (best seen from the bridge) the River Dochart tumbles into the **Falls of**

Dochart, towards the loch. On a rocky outcrop overlooking the loch stand the tree-sheltered and overgrown ruins of **Finlarig Castle**, seat of Black Duncan of the Cowl, the ruthless chief of **Clan Campbell**. Finlarig was notorious for its beheading pit.

To the north is **Glen Lyon** – at 34mi/55km, the longest enclosed glen in all Scotland. It shelters the hamlet of **Fortingall**, which claims to be the birthplace of Pontius Pilate, son of a Roman officer who was temporarily based here. It is also home to the Fortingall Yew, a tree 3 000 to 5 000 years old that is believed to be the oldest living thing in all of Europe.

▶ From Killin, you can take the A85 south to reach the Trossachs.

ADDRESSES

🛏 STAY

🍽🍽 **Beinn Bhracaigh** – *Higher Oakfield. ☏01796 470 355. www.beinnbhracaigh.com. 12 rooms.* This restored Victorian country house has panoramic views of the Tummel valley. It has been extended and decorated with a blend of antique and contemporary style.

🍽🍽 **Dunmurray Lodge** – *72 Bonnethill Road. ☏07783 462 625. www.dunmurray.co.uk. 4 rooms.* This charming, immaculately kept, 19C cottage has a homely sitting room and smallish but cosy bedrooms, all in soothing shades of cream. Good value.

🍽🍽 **Torrdarach** – *Golf Course Road. ☏01796 472 136. www.torrdarach.co.uk. 6 rooms.* This beautiful and very popular Edwardian country house lies in secluded wooded gardens with views over the Tummel valley. Rooms are equipped to a very high standard and offer excellent value.

🍽 EAT

🍽🍽 **Auld Smiddy Inn** – *154 Athol Road. ☏01796 472 356. www.auldsmiddyinn.co.uk.* Housed in a former blacksmith's forge and serving traditional cuisine, the Auld Smiddy has a pleasant simplicity with slate floors and wood-burning stoves.

Blair Castle★★

The great white form of Blair Castle, bristling with turrets, crow-stepped gables, chimneys and crenellated parapets, shines out against green forested slopes, occupying a site that was once of great strategic importance, commanding a route into the Central Highlands. The castle, the family and the nation's history are closely interwoven.

A BIT OF HISTORY

Kingdom, Earldom, Dukedom – The original ancient province or kingdom of Atholl had its main stronghold at Logierait. Cumming's Tower was built on the present site in 1269 and it became the seat of the Atholl earldom, eventually dukedom, held successively by the Stewart and Murray families.

The castle has been considerably altered over the years. The Murrays were given the castle in 1629. It was in the lifetime of the Royalist 1st Earl that Montrose raised the king's standard at Blair (1644). This act of rebellion was paid for by a Cromwellian occupation in 1652.

In the early 18C further troubles ensued as the Hanoverian 1st Duke, John Murray, had several Jacobite sons. Four members of the family raised regiments of Athollmen in the '15 rising. In 1745

⚐ ♿🕑Apr–Oct 9.30am–5.30pm. 🎟House and grounds £13 (grounds only, £7.70). ✕✆01796 481 207. www.blair-castle.co.uk.
▶ **Location:** The castle is on the outskirts of Blair Atholl village, 8mi/13km northwest of Pitlochry on the A9 and B8079.
🕐 **Timing:** Allow 1h30.
👥 **Kids:** The formidable display of weaponry in the Entrance Hall.

it was one of the former, **Lord George Murray** (1694–1760), an able military tactician, who became Bonnie Prince Charlie's Lieutenant-General and subsequently laid siege to his own home (1746).

Following the 1745 rising the 2nd Duke made many improvements such as the larch plantings and transforming the castle into a Georgian mansion house. In the 19C Sir David Bryce added features in the baronial style to the castle.

VISIT

Many of the 30 rooms open to the public have outstanding 18C interiors and

Blair Castle

© David Lyons/age fotostock

The Atholl Highlanders

The Duke retains the only private army in the British Isles, known as the Atholl Highlanders. The 80-strong army, composed mainly of estate workers, still fulfils certain ceremonial duties. It is the sole survivor of the clan system of pre-army days, when the king relied on each chief to bring out his clan forces in order to raise an army. The annual parade is on the last Sunday in May.

furnishings, Clayton plasterwork, family portraits, arms and porcelain.

Stewart Room (1) – Stewart relics, 16C and 17C furniture and portraits depicting *Mary, Queen of Scots*, her son *James VI* and her parents, *James V and Mary of Guise*.

Earl John's Room (2) – Note in particular one of four original copies of the National Covenant (1638); the 17C bed and lovely walnut chairs; and portraits.

Entrance Hall and Picture Staircase

The dual-purpose **Entrance Hall** was designed under the direction of the 7th Duke, to serve also as an ornamental armoury. Weapon displays were a feature of the Scottish Baronial style, and this is one of the finest examples, with almost every square inch of the panelling bristling with arms. It includes targes (shields) and muskets which were used at the Battle of Culloden.

The large **stag** who presides over the hall was a park favourite, Tilt, who died fighting in 1850.

The 2nd Duke employed Thomas Clayton for over nine years on the interior decoration, during his alterations on the castle and the **Picture Staircase**, including the stucco ceiling, is his tour de force. Between panels and frames of stucco decoration hang the portraits of the 2nd Duke's grandparents, *John, the 2nd Earl* as Julius Caesar (Jacob de Wet) and *Lady Amelia Stanley* (Lely).

Rooms 5–13

The main room in this section of the house is the **Dining Room (7)** which was formed during the 18C from the 16C Great Hall. It incorporates more of Thomas Clayton's plasterwork, while ceiling roundels show the four seasons, and local landscape scenes by Charles Stewart, an artist patronised by the 3rd Duke.

In the **Small Drawing Room (5)** note the unusual set of mahogany chairs (1756) and in the **Tea Room (6)** the 18C china cabinets are Chippendale and Sheraton.

In the **Blue Bedroom (9)** there is a portrait of the 7th Duke's wife, the Victorian beauty *Louisa Moncrieffe*, who had six children, none of whom had an heir!

Drawing Room to Ballroom

After the Ballroom, the **Drawing Room (16)** is the largest room in the castle and represents the pinnacle of the 2nd Duke's aspirations to grandeur.

The ceiling and cornice represent Thomas Clayton's very finest work, set off by the exquisite marble chimney-piece by Thomas Carter.

Tapestry Room (18) – On the top floor of Cumming's Tower, this chamber is hung with Brussels tapestries entitled *Atalanta and Meleager*. The magnificent state bed (1700) with Spitalfields silk hangings originally came from Holyroodhouse.

Ballroom (29) – A 19C addition, it is decorated with arms, antlers and portraits, including Henry Raeburn's painting of *Neil Gow*, the legendary fiddler to the dukes.

It is still used for its original purpose: Highland balls, wedding receptions, corporate hospitality, private dinners.

Grounds

Walk via Diana's Grove and over the Banvie Burn, passing towering 18C larches, to the ruins of St Bride's.

Northern Scotland

NORTHERN SCOTLAND

0 ___ 30 km
0 ___ 20 miles

CAPE WRATH

Faraid Head

Smoo Cave

Sandwood Beach

Durness

A 838

Oldshoremore

Handa Island

927 △
Ben Hope

Scourie

Point of Stoer

Kylesku

Stoer Peninsula

B 869

Loch Assynt

Lochinver

Loch Shin

Achiltibuie

A 837

Gruinard Island

WESTER ROSS

Ullapool

Rubha Réidh

A 832

Loch Broom

INVEREWE GARDENS

Poolewe

Falls of Measach

Gairloch

A 835

LOCH MAREE

Victoria Falls

WESTER ROSS

Fearnmore

Strathpeffer

A 896

DRIVING TOURS AROUND INVERNESS

Torridon

A 890

Beauly

Applecross

Lochcarron

Drumnadrochit

Plockton

Urquhart Castle

Kyle of Lochalsh

Eilean Donan

Loch Ness

The Cuillin
△ 993

Glen Shiel

Fort Augustus

Armadale

Point of Sleat

Mallaig

Caledonian Canal

Laggan

Morar

Glenfinnan

Neptune's Staircase

Commando Memorial

Arisaig

Lochailort

A 830

Spean Bridge

Eigg

Fort William

Ben Nevis

Sanna Bay

Tioram Castle

△ 1344

Glen Nevis

Ardnamurchan Point

Glenmore

Strontian

Corran

Glencoe

Coll

Kilchoan

Buachaille Etive Mór

Glenborrodale

A 861

Glen Coe

Kingshouse

Bidean nam Bian
1141

△ *Meall*

Lochaline

Gualachulain

Glen Etive

Rannoch Moor

Tiree

ISLE OF MULL

A 85

LEWIS

A 857

Stornoway

A 858

A 859

Tarbert

HARRIS

Uig

OUTER HEBRIDES

UIST

Glendale

Portree

ISLE OF SKYE

THE MINCH

BENBECULA

BARRA

N

↓ **GLASGOW**

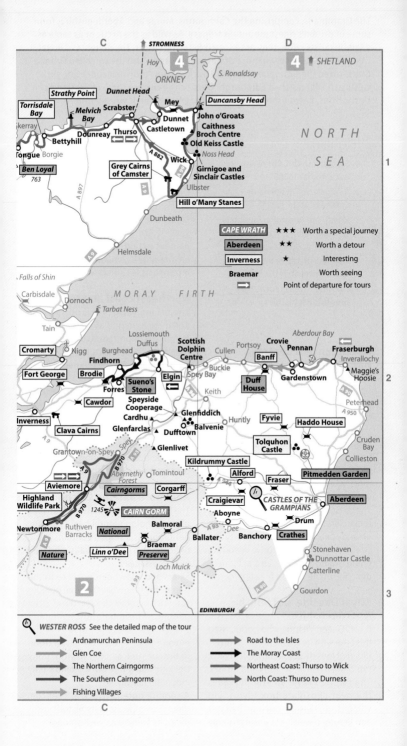

STROMNESS

SHETLAND

ORKNEY

Hoy

S. Ronaldsay

C 4 **D** 4

Strathy Point

Torrisdale Bay

Melvich Bay

Dunnet Head

Scrabster

Mey

Dunnet

Duncansby Head

Castletown

John o'Groats

Kerray

Dounreay

Thurso

Caithness Broch Centre

Old Keiss Castle

Bettyhill

Tongue Borgie

Ben Loyal
763

A 882

Noss Head

A 897

Grey Cairns of Camster

A 9

Wick

Girnigoe and Sinclair Castles

Ulbster

NORTH

SEA

1

Dunbeath

Hill o'Many Stanes

Helmsdale

CAPE WRATH ★★★ Worth a special journey

Aberdeen ★★ Worth a detour

Inverness ★ Interesting

Braemar Worth seeing

⇨ Point of departure for tours

Falls of Shin

Carbisdale

Dornoch

M O R A Y   F I R T H

Tarbat Ness

Tain

Lossiemouth

Scottish Dolphin Centre

Aberdour Bay

Cromarty

Nigg

Burghead

Duffus

Cullen

Portsoy

Crovie

Pennan

Fraserburgh

Inverallochy

Fort George

Findhorn

Brodie

Spey Bay

Buckie

Banff

Maggie's Hoosie

Elgin

Sueno's Stone

Duff House

Gardenstown

2

Forres

Cawdor

Speyside Cooperage

Keith

A 950

Peterhead

Inverness

Clava Cairns

Cardhu

Glenfiddich

Huntly

Fyvie

Haddo House

Cruden Bay

A 9

Glenfarclas

Dufftown

Balvenie

Colliestone

Grantown-on-Spey

Spey

Tolquhon Castle

Glenlivet

Abernethy Forest

Tomintoul

Kildrummy Castle

Pitmedden Garden

⇨

Aviemore

Cairngorms

Corgarff

Alford

Fraser

Highland Wildlife Park

1245

CAIRN GORM

Craigievar

CASTLES OF THE GRAMPIANS

Aberdeen

B 970

Drum

Newtonmore

Ruthven Barracks

National

Balmoral

Aboyne

A 93

Dee

Banchory

Crathes

Stonehaven

Dunnottar Castle

Nature

Linn o'Dee

Preserve

Braemar

Ballater

Loch Muick

Catterline

Gourdon

2

3

EDINBURGH

🔍 *WESTER ROSS* See the detailed map of the tour

➡ Ardnamurchan Peninsula

➡ Glen Coe

➡ The Northern Cairngorms

➡ The Southern Cairngorms

➡ Fishing Villages

➡ Road to the Isles

➡ The Moray Coast

➡ Northeast Coast: Thurso to Wick

➡ North Coast: Thurso to Durness

C   D

305

GRAMPIANS

The Grampians, comprising the Cairngorms, Moray and Aberdeenshire, form some of Britain's finest mountain scenery. As wild as the Arctic or as tame as a family railway ride, they are accessible to any visitor. The delights of Royal Deeside are well known, those of Aberdeen less so, and the so-called Granite City is often the Grampians' surprise package; few tourists expect city-slick culture this far north of Edinburgh! Outside the city are some of Scotland's best castles, finest fishing villages and a tempting malt whisky trail.

Highlights

1 Discovering **Old Aberdeen** and its cathedral (p308)

2 A sunny stroll in the gardens at **Crathes Castle** (p314)

3 Skiing, snowboarding, or simply walking, around **Aviemore** (p330)

4 Standing on top of the region at **Cairn Gorm** (p331)

5 Enjoying a wee dram at the **Glenfiddich distillery** (p338)

Aberdeen and Central Aberdeenshire

Cosmopolitan, oil-rich Aberdeen lives up to its billing as Scotland's third most important metropolis. By day, explore the fine architecture of Old Aberdeen, particularly its cathedral, and its captivating museums and splendid art gallery. There's good shopping too. By night, the city boasts first class restaurants, a vibrant nightlife and a thriving year-round cultural calendar.

The coast around Aberdeen moves from rocky cliffs in the south to a long stretch of sandy beach that starts at the city and stretches north. A short drive inland are grand Grampian castles and, at Pitmedden, one of the north's finest gardens.

Royal Deeside and South Aberdeenshire

It was Queen Victoria who popularised this area with its characteristic Scottish blend of moody mountains, lofty crags, tumbling rivers and moors and forests. The rarefied royal air still pervades the neat chocolate box towns and villages of Deeside, such as Ballater and Braemar, which are unsurprisingly

thronged with tourists in season. The finest castle and gardens of all belong to Crathes. Braemar is famous for its Highland Gathering – one of Scotland's best. It's easy to escape the crowds as Deeside offers excellent opportunities for outdoor activities such as walking, biking and wildlife watching. Bustling, seaside Stonehaven, with its pretty harbour setting, is the main town in the area. Nearby is Dunnottar Castle with its incomparable clifftop setting.

Northeast coast and Moray

The fishing villages and ports of the north are as varied as historic Fraserburgh, still important to the Grampian fishing economy, to picturesque Pennan, location star of the 1983 comedy-drama film *Local Hero*.

The pretty town of Banff features Duff House, the finest residence in the northeast. South and west into Moray, the cathedral city of Elgin is worth exploring, while just south are the famous Speyside distilleries, known the world over for the quality of their malt whisky.

Aviemore and the Cairngorms

The Cairngorms National Park is an area of outstanding natural beauty by any definition. The region contains some of Scotland's highest peaks, and vast wilderness areas.

Skiers and snowboarders take to the slopes in winter, while there are outdoor activities on offer all year round, from gliding and climbing to cycling and sailing. Less extreme pursuits in the region include some of the best walking in Britain, golf, salmon fishing, pony trekking and a ride on Scotland's only mountain railway.

A sombre note is struck at Glencoe, though even without its historic resonance its scenery is awe inspiring.

Aberdeen★★

The "Granite City" lies between the Don and the Dee, backed by a rich agricultural hinterland and facing the North Sea oilfields which has given her a new role, that of Offshore Capital of Europe.

A BIT OF HISTORY

Twin Burghs – The present city developed from two separate fishing villages on the Dee and Don. By the 12C, Old Aberdeen was the seat of an episcopal see. The cathedral city acquired burgh status in the 12C, and in the late 15C Bishop Elphinstone founded a university. The second distinct burgh grew up around the king's castle (13C) to become an active trading centre based on coastal and Baltic trade. While the Reformation brought ruin to Old Aberdeen, the city centre continued to prosper, acquired its own university (1593) and by the late 17C had started to break out of its medieval bounds.

The Granite City – Following Edinburgh and Perth, Aberdeen implemented its own plan for expansion with the laying out of Union and King streets (1801). Local architect **Archibald Simpson** (1790–1847) was responsible for giving the city much of its present character by his masterly use of Aberdeen granite as a building material. He gave his buildings a simplicity and dignity fully

▶ **Population:** 214 610.

▯ **Info:** 23 Union Street; ☎01224 269 180 www.visitabdn.com.

◗ **Location:** Most of the major attractions are clustered in Old Aberdeen and the city centre.

⊙ **Don't Miss:** The heraldic ceiling in St Machar's Cathedral, Aberdeen Art Gallery, Grampian castles.

🕑 **Timing:** Allow 1 hour to stroll around Old Aberdeen. Allow another 2 hours to see the sights of the city centre.

👥 **Kids:** The maze at Hazelhead, Alford Valley Railway.

✦ **See:** The signed routes of the Victorian Heritage Trail; Scotland's Castle Trail; the Coastal Trail, and the Malt Whisky Trail, which includes famous distilleries and coopers (barrel makers).

in keeping with the nature of the stone. The streets were lined with dignified public buildings (Medical Hall, 29 King Street: 1818–20, Assembly Rooms now the Music Hall, Union Street: 1822) and there were imaginative private ventures,

North Sea supply vessels, Aberdeen harbour

© atzee/iStockphoto.com

such as the Athenaeum and a successful design for the Clydesdale Bank at the Union and King Street corner site. Until the middle of the 20C, Aberdeen continued to be built in granite, giving its townscape a rare homogeneity, though few of its later suburbs can match the harmony of Simpson's essay in town planning centred on Bon Accord Square, Terrace and Crescent to the southwest of the city centre.

Maritime Past – The tradition of shipbuilding has always been strong in Aberdeen as the yards produced vessels for whaling and line fishing. Then came that age of international fame, the **clipper ship era** when the city's boatyards specialised in fast sailing ships. With the legendary and graceful tea clippers, *Stornoway*, *Chrysolite* and *Thermopylae*, Britain gained supremacy in the China tea trade. Wooden clippers gave way to composite and finally iron built vessels in the 1870s. Sail yielded to steam. Throughout, the local shipbuilding industry remained to the fore and continues today as an important aspect of the city's economy, although now geared to the oil industry.

The earliest fisheries included whaling (1752–1860s) and line fishing. Aberdeen became a fishing port with the herring boom (1875–96) and by 1900 had converted to trawling; it remains Scotland's premier white fishing port. The decline in trawling has in some way been counteracted by the increase in oil activities and today Aberdeen is one of Scotland's more vibrant cities, with a wide choice of good eating, drinking and cultural opportunities of all kinds.

OLD ABERDEEN★★

Old Aberdeen became a burgh of barony in 1489 under the patronage of the bishops and retained its separate burghal identity until 1891.

Today, the quarter stretching from King's College Chapel to St Machar's cathedral is part of a conservation area where the old burgh's essential character has been well retained. The medieval streets – College Bounds, High Street, Don Street and the Chanonry – are now bordered by a variety of single- and double-storey cottages, and some more substantial detached mansions; a happy mix.

King's College Chapel★

&🕐Mon–Fri 10am–3.30pm.
📞01224 272 137.
www.abdn.ac.uk/chaplaincy/chapel.
Of the university founded in 1495 by **Bishop Elphinstone** (1431–1514), the beautiful chapel, in its campus setting, is the only original building. The chapel in the Flamboyant Gothic style (1500–05) is famous for its attractive Renaissance **crown spire★★★** of great delicacy. It was restored in the 17C following storm damage. The bronze **monument** in front of the chapel is a 19C tribute to the founder. The tinctured arms on the buttresses of the west front are those of the sovereign James IV, his Queen Margaret Tudor, the founder Bishop Elphinstone, and a royal bastard, Archibald of St Andrews.

Inside is an extremely rare ensemble of **medieval fittings★★★**: rood screen, canopied stalls, pulpit and desk all richly and vigorously carved. The plain Tournoi marble tomb is that of the founder and the plaque commemorates the first principal of the college, Hector Boece (c.1465–1536).

The square Cromwell Tower in the northeast corner of the quadrangle was designed in 1658 to serve originally as student lodgings.

King's Museum

17 High Street.
🕐Tue–Fri 1– 4.30pm. 📞01224 274 330.
www.abdn.ac.uk/kingsmuseum.
This is the new home of the former Marischal Museum, host to a series of temporary exhibitions, drawn from the University collections.

The collections range from contemporary art, social history and ethnography to archaeology, scientific instruments and natural history.

Old Town House

🕐 *Tue–Fri 1– 4.30pm.* 📞 *01224 273 650.*
www.abdn.ac.uk/oldtownhouse.

The attractive Old Town House, built in 1788, was the hub of the burgh and the focal point for a busy trading community. Recently restored by the University of Aberdeen it is now the visitor information point for Old Aberdeen, as well as being the gateway to both the university and its charming medieval campus.

The old Aberdeen coat of arms above the door belonged to an earlier building dating from 1702.

The Chanonry

The layout of this once walled precinct is still apparent. Within this area were grouped dependent residences, from the Bishop's Palace to the manses of the secular canons and dwellings of the choir chaplains. On the left are the university's **Cruickshank Botanic Gardens**.

St Machar's Cathedral★★

🕐 *Daily Apr–Oct 9.30am–4.30pm;*
Nov–Mar 10am–4pm. 📞 *01224 485 988.*
www.stmachar.com.

The twin spires of St Machar's have long been one of Old Aberdeen's most famous landmarks. Its highly individual style – so very Scottish – reflects the nature of the granite building material. The present edifice, which dates from the 14C and 15C, overlooks the haughlands of the Don. According to legend, the original Celtic (c.580) settlement was established by St Machar slightly to the west so as to overlook the "crook" of the Don and comply with instructions from **St Columba**. When the bishopric was transferred from **Mortlach**, now **Dufftown**, to St Machar's in 1131, a programme of rebuilding was undertaken. The present building is the nave as finally completed in the 15C.

Exterior – The **west front★★★**, the cathedral's most distinctive feature, is immediately impressive for the austerity and strength of its unusual design, where the role of the doorway is reduced to a minimum. Buttressed and crenellated towers, topped by tapering sandstone spires, flank the majestic seven-light window. The whole is devoid of decorative details.

Move round past the south porch (*entrance*) to the east end. The church was truncated at the transept crossing when the choir was demolished at the Reformation and further shortened in 1688 when the central tower and spire collapsed, destroying the transepts. Here are to be found the **tombs** of two of the bishop builders: in the north transept that of Bishop Henry Leighton (1422–40) – his effigy is inside the cathedral – and in the south, now glazed over, that of Bishop Gavin Dunbar (1518–32).

Interior – *Enter by the south porch.* (⚲*Take binoculars to examine the heraldic ceiling*). A majestically simple but effective interior is the setting for this 16C **heraldic ceiling★★★** attributed to the enterprising Bishop Gavin Dunbar. The flat, coffered oak ceiling is decorated with 48 brightly tinctured coats of arms arranged in three rows of 16 each running from east to west. Ingeniously designed, this unique ceiling presents a vision of the European scene around 1520 and a strong assertion of Scottish nationalism.

The central axis representing the Holy Church, until then the traditional unifying force in Europe, is headed by the arms of Pope Leo X followed by other ecclesiastical arms. The absence of York and Trondheim is significant.

On the right are the King of Scots (closed crown) and his nobles while on the left, headed by the Holy Roman Emperor, are the other Kings of Christendom. The King of England comes fourth after his fellow monarchs of France, Scotland's traditional ally, and Spain!

The stained glass is all 19C and 20C: the west window with cusped round arches and the Bishops Window (third from east end in the south aisle) 1913, an early example of Douglas Strachan's work showing the three great builder bishops, are noteworthy.

Brig O'Balgownie★
Approach via Don Street.

This early 14C bridge, one of Aberdeen's most important medieval buildings, is set astride the Don. The single span bridge with its pointed Gothic arch has cobbled approaches and a defensive kink at the south end.

Farther downstream is the **Bridge of Don**, by Aberdeen's first city architect, John Smith, with modifications by Thomas Telford (1827–30). The cost of building was financed by its illustrious neighbour's 17C maintenance fund.

The development of the North Sea oil industry brought conversion to the building of oil supply and fishery protection vessels.

CITY CENTRE

Maritime Museum★
Provost Ross's House, Shiprow.
♿🕐*Mon–Sat 10am–5pm, Sun noon –3pm.* 🕐*25–26, 31 Dec, 1–2 Jan.*
✕ 🖉*01224 337 700. www.aagm.co.uk.*

The museum is housed in two 16C town houses bordering Shiprow, one of the medieval thoroughfares winding up from the harbour. Provost Ross's House was owned by a succession of wealthy merchants, provosts and landed gentry. The museum has recently been enlarged and redeveloped with the introduction of interactive displays (touch screen, computerised visual databases, hands-on exhibits) complementing the ship models, paintings and artefacts tracing the story of the fishing, shipping and oil industries.

Castlegate
The gait or way to the castle on Castle Hill (marked by two high-rise blocks behind the Salvation Army Citadel) was the medieval market place. Near the paved area known as the "plain-stones" stands the Mannie Fountain (1706), a reminder of Aberdeen's first piped water supply.

Marischal Street, leading to the harbour, was laid out in 1767–68 on the site of the former tenement of the Earls Marischal. The new street was given a uniform design of three storeys and an attic. In the middle of the Castlegate is the splendid **mercat cross★★** dating from 1686. The unicorn surmounts the cross, which rises from the roof of an arcaded structure. The decoration includes a frieze of oval panels containing 10 portraits of the royal **Stuarts** from James I to James VII and the series is completed by the royal and Aberdeen coats of arms.

Northwards along King Street the integrated design of the various buildings was the result of collaboration between **John Smith** and **Archibald Simpson**. On the north side of Castle Street, the 19C **Town House** dominates all. Rising from behind this relatively recent façade is the tower of the 17C **Tolbooth** (🕐*Mon–Sat 10am–5pm, Sun noon–3pm;* 🕐*25–26, 31 Dec, 1–2 Jan;* 🖉*01224 621 167; www.aagm.co.uk*) which features displays on local history and the development of crime and punishment through the centuries. Spiral stairs and cramped passageways lead to chambers and cells with lifelike figures. The tower is best viewed from the opposite side of Castle Street.

Provost Skene's House★
🔒*Closed until 2020 for redevelopment; check website for details.*
🖉*01224 641 086. www.aagm.co.uk.*

This 17C town house is named after a wealthy merchant and one-time provost of the town, **Sir George Skene** (1619–1707). His portrait by Medina hangs in the 17C bedroom. Although title deeds go as far back as 1545, the house acquired its present form under the ownership of Skene.

Following restoration in the 1950s, a series of tastefully furnished period rooms were created.

Original features include plasterwork ceilings (Cromwellian, Restoration and 17C bedroom), panelling (1732, Regency) and stone flagging (Georgian Dining Room). Outstanding, however, is the **Chapel** or Painted Gallery with its 16C **painted ceiling★★**.

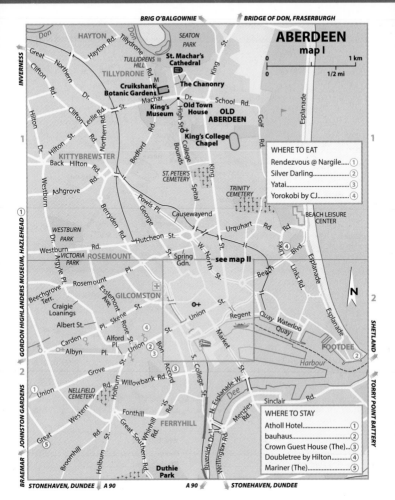

ABERDEEN
map I

WHERE TO EAT
Rendezvous @ Nargile.....①
Silver Darling.................②
Yatai............................③
Yorokobi by CJ.............④

WHERE TO STAY
Atholl Hotel.........................①
bauhaus..............................②
Crown Guest House (The)...③
Doubletree by Hilton...........④
Mariner (The)......................⑤

Marischal College★

The striking, if controversial, granite façade (1905) overlooking Broad Street was the latest extension to Marischal College. In 1593 George Keith, 5th Earl Marischal founded a college in the buildings of Greyfriars Monastery, appropriated following the Reformation. Marischal was to be the counterpart of King's – older by a century – and for over two and a half centuries the two universities coexisted, a situation unique in Britain.

St Nicholas Kirk

Enter from Correction Wynd and the south transept. &. ○ *Jun–Sept Mon–Fri noon–4pm.* ✆ *01224 643 494. www.kirk-of-st-nicholas.org.uk.*

The once vast medieval burgh church was divided into two at the Reformation. The medieval transepts now serve as vestibule. In Drum's Aisle or south transept are the reclining figures of the Irvines of Drum Castle (**⌖** *see DEESIDE*) and a tablet to Edward Raban, master printer to the city and universities in the 17C.

St John's Chapel celebrates the contribution made by the oil industry to the life of the city with striking contemporary stained glass and furniture. At the far end in Collison's Aisle is the effigy of Provost Davidson who fell at Harlaw.

West Church – The church was rebuilt c.1752 by the Aberdonian architect, **James Gibbs** (1682–1754), the desi-

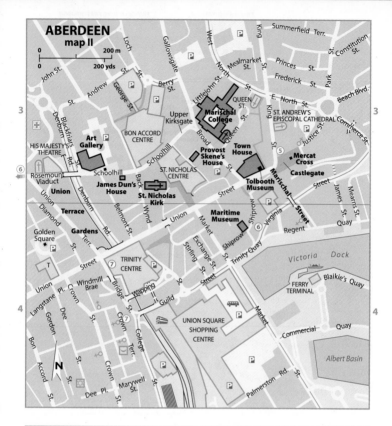

ABERDEEN
map II

WHERE TO STAY		WHERE TO EAT	
Ibis, Aberdeen Centre	⑥	Fusion	⑤
Travelodge, Aberdeen Central	⑦	La Lombarda	⑥
		Royal Thai	⑦

gner of St Martin-in-the-Fields, London. The interior has dark oak pews and galleries with a splendid canopied "Council Loft".

East Church – Originally designed by Archibald Simpson (1835–37), the church was restored by William Smith after fire damage in 1875 and has recently been subject to major archaeological excavations . Steps lead to the restored 15C **St Mary's Chapel**. The transepts are also 15C. The central roof boss depicts the legend of St Nicholas.The Gothic spire (1876) has a carillon of 48 bells and is used for concerts.

James Dun's House – This late-18C house takes its name from its builder

James Dun (1708–1789). He was the rector of the Old Grammar School which stood nearby and was attended by Byron.

Aberdeen Art Gallery★★

○━ *Closed for major redevelopment; check website for latest information.* ℘03000 200 293. www.aagm.co.uk. [Original text] The permanent collection has a strong emphasis on contemporary art, work by the Impressionists and the Scottish Colourists. The sculpture court and adjoining rooms contain the larger works of sculpture, while additional pieces are also on display throughout the first floor rooms. Foreign sculptors (Degas, Rodin and Zadkine) and British artists (Hepworth, Moore and Butler) are represented by a variety of techniques and materials.

The first floor features the **Scottish collection**. **William McTaggart** (1835–1910) provided a turning point on the 19C Scottish scene, when he broke with the grandeur of the Romantics and commercial sentimentalism of the genre artists in his search for realism. Inspired by nature, his works are notable for their clarity and vitality culminating in his own personal "impressionist" style (*A Ground Swell*-1). Other works in Room 1 include those of the versatile William Dyce (1806–1864), another Aberdonian with an international outlook. Dyce's *Ferryman* and Titian's *First Essay in Colour* are first and foremost figure compositions with the landscape playing a secondary role. They also show his care for detail and naturalism in outdoor scenes, as does *A Scene in Arran* where the figures are reduced to a minor role while the treatment of landscape anticipates the Pre-Raphaelites.

The **MacDonald Collection**★★ of British artists' portraits in Room 2 numbers 92, many of which are self-portraits. This unique series is a highly revealing survey of the art world in the 19C. It includes the patron himself, Alexander MacDonald. Room 3 presents some of the earliest Scottish portraitists, including a self-portrait by Aberdeen's own **George Jamesone** (1588–1644), *Mrs Janet Shairp* by Allan Ramsay (1713–1784), and works by Raeburn (1756–1823), who was Knighted by George IV.

A selection of works by the French Impressionists is displayed among the 19C foreign works in Room 4, while an array of mostly British prints and watercolours are hung in Room 5. The 20C British paintings hung in Room 6 and on the balcony include works by Nash, Spencer, Nicholson, Peploe, McTaggart, and Joan Eardley.

The Gordon Highlanders Museum

♿ 🕐 *Feb–Nov Tue–Sat 10am–4.30pm.* 🎫 *£8 (online discounts apply); Gardens, admission free.* ✕ 📞 *01224 311 200.*

Winter Gardens, Duthie Park
© Gannet77/iStockphoto.com

www.gordonhighlanders.com.
This stirring collection traces the 200-year long history (1794–1994) of one of the most famous regiments in the British Army.

It includes uniforms, silver, weapons, textiles, art and a vast archive of papers, diaries and documents, as well as over 4 000 medals and 12 Victoria Crosses. Interactive maps, original film footage, scale reproductions, life-size models, touch screens, regimental colours, uniforms, medals and weapons are featured in a constantly evolving exhibition.
After your visit you can take tea in their lovely gardens.

Parks and Gardens

Known as "The Flower of Scotland", the city has been many times winner of the Britain in Bloom competition, and Aberdeen's parks and gardens are justly worthy of a mention. Take the time to visit at least one, be it **Union Terrace Gardens** (off Union Street) with their celebrated floral displays including Aberdeen's coat of arms, the unrivalled Winter Gardens in **Duthie Park**, the Rose Garden, the delightful **Johnston Gardens** and the university's **Cruickshank Botanic Gardens**.

At **Hazlehead Park** (👪🚻✕🕐 *daily 8am–1h before dusk.* 📞 *01224 219281 www.aberdeencity.gov.uk*) you can explore the oldest **maze** in Scotland, two formal rose gardens, and take in a pets' corner (⏰*from 10am*), two golf courses, a mini zoo, heather and conifer garden, azalea garden and children's playground.

🚗 DRIVING TOURS

🚗 1 DEESIDE★★

Aberdeen to Braemar, one way. 64mi/103km.

The Dee, a splendid salmon river, flows from its source 1 219m up on the Cairngorm plateau at the Wells of Dee through the Lairig Ghru and then due east to the sea at Aberdeen. Scenically attractive with its many fine castles and its royal associations which have earned it the title of "Royal Deeside", this beautiful valley is a tourist honeypot and very busy in summer. Travelling by car is the best way to see Deeside though there is no circular route; you have to backtrack from Braemar.

Allow at least a day for the following driving tour, though two would be much better. Alternatively, Stagecoach Bluebird Bus 201 from Aberdeen services the A93, calling at many of the main towns and attractions featured below. Beware of crowds in the summer holidays.

▷ Leave Aberdeen heading SW on the A93.

Drum Castle

♿⏰*10.30am–4pm: Nov–Mar Sat–Sun (Nov–22 Dec 11am–4pm); Apr–May and Sept–Oct Thu–Mon; Jun–Aug daily. Grounds: All year, daily dawn–dusk.* ⏰*23 Dec–4 Jan.* 🎫*£13 (walled garden only £4.50).* ✖ 🅿 *(charge).* 📞*01330 700 334. www.nts.org.uk.* Robert the Bruce granted the lands to his armour bearer William de Irwin and the castle remained in the same family until 1976 when it was donated to the National Trust for Scotland. The massive rectangular **tower**, dating from the 13C is the oldest intact tower in Scotland. The walls taper from 3.7m at the base to

1.8m near the parapet and are rounded at the corners.

External stairs lead up to the first floor entrance and the interior, which was divided by timber roofs into three vaulted chambers. Ninety steps in all, including a ladder, lead to the battlements. In addition to the tower there is the Jacobean wing with attractively furnished rooms and a 17C family chapel in the grounds. The property is famous for its tradition of beautiful and varied gardens and its **garden of historic roses** is a special feature which alone attracts many visitors.

▷ Return to the A93 and turn right (SW) to Crathes.

Crathes Castle★★

Located 16mi/26km southwest of Aberdeen, the 16C tower house of Crathes castle is an impressive example of the traditional architectural style, enhanced by a series of delightful gardens. The interiors include some outstanding painted ceilings and some particularly fine early vernacular furniture. The castle is the ideal place to see the home and lifestyle of a 16C–17C Scottish laird.

Visit

⏰*Castle, guided tours only: Jan–Mar and Nov–23 Dec Sat–Sun 11am–4pm; Apr–Oct 10.30am–5pm. Grounds: All year, daily dawn–dusk.* ⏰*Christmas and New Year holidays.* 🎫*£13 castle and gardens.* ✖🅿 *(charge).* 📞*01330 844 525. www.nts.org.uk.*
Exterior – The roof line is enhanced by a variety and quality of decorative detail – spot the many gargoyles – making it one of the best examples of the local baronial style. Also note the series of coats of arms.

Interior – The tour starts with three vaulted kitchen chambers where family documents are on display and passes by the prison hole and the **yett**, now remounted outside.
The construction is typically Scottish with an ingenious system of interwoven bars reversed in diagonally oppo-

Crathes castle

© Alan Crawford/iStockphoto.com

site corners giving great strength to the yett.

Upstairs, the barrel-vaulted **High Hall** has armorial paintings on the window embrasures and three unusual stone pendants. Above the fireplace is the family's most prized heirloom, the delicate **Horn of Leys**, the original token to tenure (1322) given by Robert the Bruce. The motif is found throughout the castle. The family **portraits** by George Jamesone (1588–1644) include the most well-known family member, Bishop Burnett, author of *A History of My Own Times* and adviser to William of Orange. Note on the great marriage chest the portraits of Alexander, 12th laird, and his wife.

In the **Laird's Bedroom** is the outstanding oak bed (1594), resplendent with the carved heads of Alexander and Katherine, their heraldic devices and colourful crewel work. The highlight of the **Room of the Nine Nobles** is the lovely **painted ceiling** (1602). As was usual, the composition was drawn in black and then colourfully filled in. This bright and lively form of decoration was common on the east coast, no doubt influenced by trading contacts with Scandinavia where similar techniques flourished. Plasterwork ceilings superseded this form of decoration. The Crathes examples are some of the best in existence (restored). The figures of the Nine Nobles (Hector, Alexander the Great, Julius Caesar, Joshua, David, Judas Maccabeus, King Arthur, Charlemagne and Godfrey de Bouillon) are portrayed on the ceiling boards with Biblical quotations on the sides of the beams. In view of the foreignness of their costumes it is supposed that they were copied from a continental source, as were the garden sculptures at Edzell (💷 see *EDZELL CASTLE*). Beside the 1641 inlaid bed with its colourful crewel work hangings are two lovely carved chairs dated 1597 with the initials of Alexander and Katherine.

The **Green Lady's Room**, which is said to be a haunted chamber, has another ornate ceiling where the figures (ceiling boards) and decorative patterns (underside of beams) bear no relation to the maxims and Biblical quotations (sides of beams). Stairs again lead upwards.

The **Long Gallery**, running the entire width of the house, is unique for its oak-panelled roof decorated with armorials and the horn motif. Documents illustrate the 600 years of family history. The gardens may be admired from this good vantage point.

Proceed to the **Muses Room** which boasts another vividly painted ceiling showing the nine muses and Seven Virtues. The tapestry is a William Morris commission (1881). Look for the mouse trademark on the stool by Robert Thompson (1876–1955).

Gardens★★★

Full of variety and beauty, the gardens at Crathes were the lifetime achievement of the late Sir James and Lady Burnett. The whole is composed of a series of distinct and separate gardens where the visitor is lured on by yet another secluded enclosure beyond. The shape, colour, design and fragrance defy description but here the expert gardener and amateur alike will be enthralled by the display. The yew hedges dating from 1702 separate the **Pool Garden** (yellows, reds and purples) from the formal **Fountain** (blues) and **Rose Gardens**. In the lower area a double herbaceous border separates the Camel and Trough Gardens with, beyond, the White and June borders and a Golden Garden as a memorial to Lady Burnett.

Woodland walks offer the chance to discover the natural life of the Crathes estate. Well signposted, they start from the shop and vary in length from 1mi to 5mi (1.6km to 8km).

▶ Before reaching Banchory, the A93 passes the Royal Deeside Railway.

The Royal Deeside Railway

Inaugurated in 1845 the Royal Deeside Railway was one of the region's most scenic railway lines and for many years was used by members of the Royal Family en route to Balmoral Castle. It became uneconomical however and closed in 1966 and its tracks were taken up. A group of enthusiasts have relaid about 1 mile of the line and a service now runs from Milton of Crathes station (*Sun and some Sat Apr–Oct, plus a few additional days; see website for details and fares; www.deeside-railway.co.uk*).

▶ The A93 links the following three sights as you head west towards the Linn o'Dee.

Banchory

Banchory, Deeside's largest community, is mainly residential.

The South Deeside Road branches off to the left forking from the Cairn o'Mount road (B974) to Fettercairn.

At the **Bridge of Feugh**, the Water of Feugh negotiates a narrow gorge giving spectacular falls and the chance for salmon to display their leaping abilities.

▶ Proceed along the A93 which follows the course of the Dee.

Aboyne

This popular summer centre is set around a large green, the venue for the **Highland Games**. Part of the traditional pageantry is the ceremonial entry of the self-styled Cock o'the North, the Chief of clan Gordon attended by his chieftains. The **Burn o'Vat** (*2mi/3.2km from the main road*) is a popular picnic site. As the valley becomes more enclosed this marks the beginning of the upper reaches, and the change to Highland scenery begins with the Cambus o'May defile. Ahead is the rounded form of Craigendarroch, pinpointing the site of Ballater.

Ballater

This dignified little town developed as a watering place in the 18C and became the railway terminal in 1863. The line closed in 1966 but the **Old Royal Station** with its unique Royal Waiting Room has been restored and contains displays on its 100-year history of royal use.

The Royal Saloon railway carriage, as used by Queen Victoria to journey between Ballater and Windsor in the late 19C, is also here and open to visitors. Ballater is a lively resort in summer, famous for its **Highland Games** and its unique hill race.

▶ Continue alongside the river on the A93.

Crathie Kirk

The church (*http://braemarandcrathie-parish.org.uk/crathie-kirk*), which is attended by the Royal Family, is the fifth

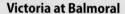

Victoria at Balmoral

In her journals Queen Victoria described Balmoral as "my dear paradise in the Highlands". When the Queen – at the time, ruler of the largest empire the world had ever seen – first arrived she was greeted by a crowd of locals estimated to be 80 000 strong. Not everyone was enthusiastic – the local press complained that the area was to be "desolated by cockneys", but over the years most locals have become fiercely protective of the royal connection, as embodied in the 1997 movie *Mrs Brown* (&*see CRATHIE CHURCH*). Many of the Queen's visitors from London were unimpressed by the rustic nature of the royal retreat and some foreign dignitaries were particularly scathing. Czar Nicholas II complained "the weather is awful, rain and wind every day" and a Prussian Count thought it "astonishing that the Royal Power of England should reside amid this lonesome, desolate mountain scenery".

on the site. The foundation stone for the church was laid in September 1893 by Queen Victoria. In the churchyard is a memorial to John Brown, the Queen's manservant, made famous in the 1997 film *Mrs Brown*.

Balmoral Castle

Car park to the left of the main road.
&ⓞ*Apr–Jul daily 10am–5pm.*
⊜*£11.50.* ✕ ℘*013397 42534.*
www.balmoralcastle.com.
Purchased by Queen Victoria in 1848, the Balmoral Estate is the Scottish home of the British Royal Family. Visitors are allowed into the formal and vegetable gardens, and there are exhibitions in the Carriage Room and the Ballroom. All other rooms are private.

Royal Lochnagar Distillery

ⓞ*Jan–Feb Mon–Fri 10am–4pm, Sun noon–4pm; Mar–Jun Mon–Sat 10am–5pm, Sun noon–5pm; Jul–Aug Mon–Fri 10am–6pm, Sat 10am–5pm, Sun noon–5pm; Sept–Oct Mon–Sat 10am–5pm, Sun noon–5pm; Nov–Dec 10am–4pm, Sun noon–4pm.* ⓞ*25–26 Dec and 1–2 Jan.* ⊜*£9–£150.*
℘*01339 742 700. www.malts.com.*
Next to Balmoral Castle the Lochnagar Distillery has been on this site since 1841. Only three days after Victoria had moved into Balmoral the distillery invited her to visit. To their delight and surprise, the next day she did, and the distillery received a Royal Warrant of Appointment as supplier to the Queen.

▷ The road now follows the alignment of the Old Military Road. Cross the Dee at the Invercauld Bridge which replaces Telford's bridge downstream.

Braemar Castle

ⓞ*10am–5pm: Apr–Oct Wed–Sun (Jul–Aug daily).* ⊜*£8.* ℘*013397 41219. www.braemarcastle.co.uk.*
This L-plan tower house, set back from the roadside, was built in 1628 by the Earl of Mar as a hunting seat. Burned by Farquharson of Inverey, ancestor of the present owners, the castle was rebuilt and strengthened with a star-shaped curtain wall and crenellations to serve as a military post for Hanoverian troops after the '45 rising. Guided tours (*45 mins*) take in 12 furnished rooms.

Braemar

This scattered village is a busy summer resort in fine mountain scenery. The two original villages grew up at a strategic convergent point of the routes from the south via the Cairnwell Pass, from Atholl by Glen Tilt (of marble fame) and from Speyside via Glen Feshie. Each year on the first Saturday in September the popular **Braemar Highland Gathering** (&*see Calendar of Events*) is attended by members of the Royal Family.

▷ Take the secondary road out following the south bank of the Dee as it winds along the flood plain.

Linn o'Dee★

This famous beauty spot is where the placid river suddenly tumbles through a narrow channel to drop into rocky pools. Salmon may be seen leaping here.

⮐ 2 HILLSIDE GRAMPIAN CASTLES★

71mi/113km.

Aberdeen's hinterland is rich in castles with examples from all periods. These range from the earliest Norman motte and bailey to the formidable strongholds (Kildrummy), which were the centres of government in the troubled Middle Ages. The golden age of castle building (16C–17C) is well represented. In this far from rich area, stability engendered prosperity and encouraged lairds to build castles worthy of their newly acquired status or wealth. A flourishing native school produced the baronial style. Master masons skilfully worked the local stone creating a native tradition unparalleled elsewhere. This tour takes you close to The Cairngorms or the centre of whisky production, Dufftown.

▷ Leave Aberdeen heading W on the A944. At Dunecht, turn right onto the B977, and then left on a minor road to Castle Fraser.

Castle Fraser★

🕙 *Mar and Nov–mid-Dec Sat–Sun 11am–2pm; Apr–Oct Mon–Sat (guided tours) 10am–4pm, Sun (open guiding) 10am–4pm.* ⊙£12. ✖ 🅿£2. ℘01330 833 463. www.nts.org.uk.

Completed in 1636 Castle Fraser is a typical product of the Scottish golden age of castle building.

Exterior★★ – The glory of Castle Fraser, reminiscent of a French château, lies in its elevations. Here, bare lower walls contrast with the flourish of decorative detail at roof level while harling sets off the sculptured granite work. As you approach from the car park, the layout of this largest and most elaborate of Scottish castles, built on the Z-plan design, becomes apparent. The **central block**, distinguished by a magnificent heraldic achievement, is adjoined by towers, one round and one square (Michael Tower) at diagonally opposite corners. The two-storey service wings, flanking the cour-

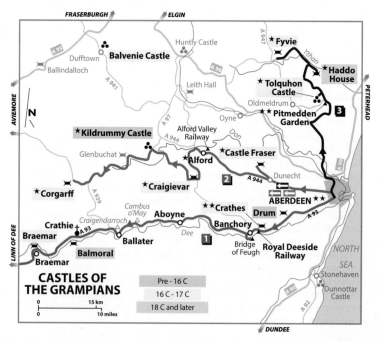

CASTLES OF THE GRAMPIANS

0   15 km
0   10 miles

Pre - 16 C
16 C - 17 C
18 C and later

tyard, serve to emphasise the height of the main buildings.

Above the stepped and highly decorative corbelling, a variety of traditional features – turrets, conical roofs, crow-stepped gables, chimney stacks, decorative dormers and gargoyles – is deployed to achieve a harmonious composition. The lantern and balustrade are essentially Renaissance features but the decorative effect as a whole is Scotland's unique contribution to Renaissance architecture.

Interior – The visit is arranged to include those rooms which have been restored. Of particular note are the **Great Hall** and the suite of rooms in the Round Tower reserved for the laird's family.

The rooftop balustraded area (*101 steps*) affords an excellent **view** of the surrounding farmland and of the walled garden, and in the distance the **Bennachie Hills** (*see below*).

▶ Return to the A944, and continue west to Alford.

Alford★

This market town lies 28mi/45km west of Aberdeen on the A944 in the Howe of Alford, a rich arable basin encircled by hills, notably the Correen Hills to the northwest and Bennachie to the northeast.

Grampian Transport Museum

Beside the main car park. &.*Apr–Oct 10am–5pm (Oct 4pm).* £10. ✗
01975 562 292. www.gtm.org.uk.
The main collection evokes the transport (cars, cycles and carriages) history of the Northeast amid a variety of side exhibits. Look out for the "sociable safety cycle", which was anything but safe, and the Craigievar Express, a local postman's 19C steam tricycle. There is a fine collection of Scottish-built cars.

▶ Leave Alford by the A944 and the A980.

Craigievar Castle★

Access by guided tours only, on a first come, first served basis with a

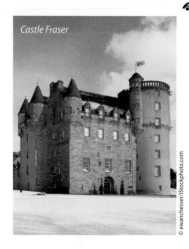
Castle Fraser
© ewanchesser/iStockphoto.com

maximum of 10 on each tour. Tours run approximately every 30 minutes. Apr–May Fri–Tue 10.30am–4pm; Jun–Sept daily 10.30am–4pm; Oct Sat–Sun 10.30am–5pm. £13. **P** (£2).
01339 883 635. www.nts.org.uk.
A quintessential example of Scots Baronial architecture Craigievar is a fairytale-like tower house, among the best preserved in Scotland. It boasts fine 17C plaster ceilings.

▶ Turn right out of the castle grounds and right again up the single track road to Ley.

▶ Follow more minor roads W towards Glenkindie on the A97, where you can turn right to Kildrummy Castle, or left further along the Don valley to see the changing scenery of its upper reaches at Corgarff.

Kildrummy Castle★

South of Kildrummy village.
Apr–Sept 9.30am–5.30pm. £6.
01975 571 331.
www.historicenvironment.scot.
Now in ruins, Kildrummy was once the mightiest of the Highland castles, and dominated Strathdon as the stronghold of the mighty Earls of Mar.

The initial castle was built in the 13C. Edward I of England stayed at Kildrummy twice, in 1296 and 1303. The ground plan of Kildrummy's great twin-towered

Highland Gathering

On Games Day in August the tiny village of Bellabeg in Upper Donside is the scene of a 160-year-old tradition, the **March of the Men of Lonach**. The Men of Lonach, traditionally Forbeses and Wallaces, resplendently attired in full Highland dress with pikes aloft, march proudly through the strath to the scene of the Gathering in the park at Bellabeg. Traditional games, pipe music and dance create a lively atmosphere (http://lonach.org).

gatehouse is so remarkably like that at Edward's great castle of Harlech (in north Wales) that it is possible this part of Kildrummy may well have been built for the "Hammer of the Scots". However in 1306, it was not the English king but Robert the Bruce who considered it a safe enough haven to provide shelter for his queen and her attendants. Besieged by the future Edward II of England, the castle was burned down, rebuilt, then taken again in 1335, and annexed by the Crown in 1435.

In later centuries, the castle became a residence of the Elphinstones, before resuming its role as seat of the Earls of Mar after 1626. It was abandoned in 1716 following the failure of the Jacobite rebellion, confiscated and dismantled. Behind the great defensive walls the sparse remains of the outbuildings include the great hall flanked by a bedroom and kitchen.

The most outstanding features to survive are the twin-towered gatehouse – possibly a legacy of Edward I – and the chapel windows – three elegant mid-13C lancet chapel windows.

In a medieval quarry below the Castle – the ruin of which provides a wonderful backdrop – are **Kildrummy Castle Gardens** (◷Apr–Oct noon–5pm; ℘01975 571 203; ⊜£4.50; www.kildrummy-castle-gardens.co.uk) featuring an attractive **alpine garden**.

▷ Continue on the A97 to its junction with the A944, and there turn right. Continue for 11mi/18km, turning right onto the A939.

Corgarff Castle★

◷Apr–Sept daily 9.30am–5.30pm.
⊜£6. ℘01975 651 460.
www.historicenvironment.scot.
In a lonely moorland setting near the source of the Don, and controlling a ford across the road from the valley of the Spey, this 16C tower house was once a hunting lodge for the Earls of Mar. After the insurrection of 1745 it was transformed into a garrison for government troops, surrounded by a distinctive star-shaped perimeter wall. Abandoned in the early 19C, it was once again garrisoned from 1827 to 1831 to fight against the whisky smuggling trade; there is an exhibit of a reconstructed whisky still.

③ CASTLES OF ABERDEENSHIRE★
45mi/72km.
The great expanse of countryside north of Aberdeen is dotted with cows, sheep agricultural crops and numerous castles. Indeed, the soil around here is so rich and fertile that the gardens of the castle are sometimes their finest features.

▷ Leave Aberdeen on the A96 towards Inverurie, turning right onto the A947 to pass the airport and cross the Dee. At Whiterashes, head right on minor roads to Pitmedden.

Pitmedden Garden★★

⚹◷Garden and Museum of Farming Life: 10.30am–4.30pm: Apr–Sept daily; Oct Fri–Mon. Grounds: daily dawn to dusk. ⊜£8; grounds only, free. ✕ ℙ ℘01651 842 352. www.nts.org.uk.
The formal Great Garden at Pitmedden is a rare jewel in the northeast area and a magnificent sight in summer when the extravagant scale of its planting is revealed in a riot of colour. Allow at least two hours in July or August, when over 30 000 flowers are in bloom.

© Tom Mackie Images Ltd/Travel Pictures

Pitmedden Garden

The Creator – In the early 17C the Pitmedden Estate was acquired by the Setons. When John, the 3rd laird, was killed at the Battle of Brig O'Dee (1639) his two young sons were entrusted to a relative, George Seton, 3rd Earl of Winton. An improving laird and man of advanced tastes, he had established gardens at Winton and Pinkie. It was Sir Alexander Seton (c.1639–1719), the younger brother, who in 1675 began to transform this treeless and stony area into an extraordinary formal garden.

Re-Creation – By 1951, when the donation of the garden was made to the National Trust for Scotland, time had all but effaced the formal designs and the lower area was a vegetable garden. The original plans had been lost when Pitmedden Castle was burned in 1818. New designs were established based on Charles II's garden at Holyroodhouse.

The Gardens Today – Pitmedden features over 5mi/8km of box hedging arranged in intricate patterns to form six parterres, made from trim boxwood hedges. Each parterre is filled with plants bursting with colour in the summer months. The initial impression is of immaculately tended gardens where neatly clipped yews, neat hedges and shaven lawns edge masses of colour and contrast with the more natural exuberance of the extensive herbaceous borders and a spectacular lupin border. The **walled garden** is planned on two levels. An upper western half, mostly lawns and hedgaes with a herb garden, overlooks the lower formal garden area. Honey-

suckle, jasmine and roses create a succession of fragrances, while fountains, topiary, sundials and a fascinating herb garden add to the sense of discovery around the walled garden. A belvedere provides a good **viewing point**. The colour is provided by annuals, coloured gravels and green turf paths. Three of the designs are geometric while a fourth represents the armorial display of Sir Alexander Seton. Also part of the original plan are two gazebos with their ogee-shaped roofs, the central fountain (rebuilt) and the entrance staircase linking the two levels.

Over 80 varieties of apple trees adorn the high granite walls, offering a spectacular show of blossom and scent in spring. On the last Sunday in September harvest celebrations feature dancing and music, and fruits harvested from the gardens are on sale.

Grounds – In the surrounding area, a woodland walk and nature trail shows off rare breeds of livestock and endangered species. It also takes in ponds, rhododendrons, a lime kiln and a nature hut with information about the wider estate. The outbuildings house a **Museum of Farming Life** with implements, artefacts and domestic utensils from a bygone era. The farmhouse, bothy (unmarried farm servant's home) and the stables, with a display on the era of the horse, are of particular interest.

> Follow the signs to Tolquhon Castle along the B999.

Tolquhon Castle★

🕐 Apr–Sept Fri–Wed 9.30am–5.30pm.
💷£6. 📞01651 851 286.
www.historicenvironment.scot.
Pronounced "tol-hoon", this is one of the most picturesque castle ruins in the Grampians. The oldest part is the stump of an early 15C tower house, probably built by one of the Prestons of Formartine, who once held the barony. However, the castle visitors can see today was built by Sir William Forbes in 1574. Its gatehouse is a gem, built not to deter, but to impress – which it still contrives to do.

The main house is a charming composition at the far end of the courtyard, with a good "below stairs" and family rooms above to explore. There is a secret hiding-place in the laird's bedchamber on the second floor, a hidden compartment below the floor where Sir William hid his valuables.

In the nearby parish church in the village of Tarves, Sir William also built the **Tolquhon Tomb** burial vault. This one of the best examples of Scotland's so-called "Glorious Tombs" from the Jacobean age, finely decorated with beguiling stone effigies of Sir William Forbes (d.1596) and Elizabeth Gordon.

▶ Continue on the B999 to Tarves, and B9170 to Methlick, and then follow the signs to Haddo House.

Haddo House★

♿🚻🚌 Guided tours only: Apr–Oct Mon–Fri noon–2pm, Sat–Sun 11am–3.30pm; Nov–Mar Mon and Fri noon–2pm, Sat–Sun 11.30am–3.30pm.
🕐 23 Dec–11 Jan. 💷£12. ✗
📞 01651 851 440. www.nts.org.uk.
This 18C mansion, set in lovely wooded grounds, is the ancestral seat of the Gordon Earls of Aberdeen.

The estate was acquired by a Gordon in 1469 and, in the 17C, William, 2nd Earl of Aberdeen (1679–1745), commissioned William Adam to design a mansion house to replace the earlier family seat destroyed by Covenanters.

The house was an expression of the prosperity caused by agricultural improvements. Unfortunately, the next incumbent, George, nicknamed the "wicked earl", dispersed the wealth. A spendthrift of great energy, he established three mistresses in residences as far apart as Fraserburgh and Wiscombe Park in Devon, and maintained their offspring, all at the cost of Haddo.

George Hamilton Gordon, 4th Earl (1784–1860), rose to high office as Prime Minister (1852–55) of a coalition government at the time of the Crimean War. A man of many talents, he nevertheless devoted much time to the improvement of the estate, landscaping the parkland and repairing the house which was by then derelict. Of his three sons, two inherited; the eldest, the "Sailor Earl", and the youngest, the latter, John Campbell Gordon, 7th Earl (1847–1934), embarked on a programme of alterations and refurbishment.

Today the house is in the care of the National Trust for Scotland, with the south wing as a private residence for the Gordon family.

Interior – The interior of this Palladian country house was entirely transformed when the 1st Marquess refurbished it in the Adam Revival style. The well-lit, elegant reception rooms are a perfect setting for the many family mementoes. From the ground floor entrance hall with its **coffered ceiling**, the staircase leads up to the main apartments. The striking portrait halfway up is Pompeo Batoni's elegant presentation of Lord Haddo as the Grand Tourist. His son, the Prime Minister Earl, is commemorated by many souvenirs in the Ante-Room with its 18C panelling and carved overdoors. Alongside Sir Thomas Lawrence's Byronic portrait of the 4th Earl are portraits of one of his guardians, Sir William Pitt the Younger, as well as other political contemporaries such as Sir Robert Peel and the Duke of Wellington (the 4th Earl was Foreign Secretary to both). The bust of Queen Victoria was a personal gift to the former Prime Minister. The Queen's Bedroom was in fact used by the sovereign on her 1857 visit to Haddo.

In the Dining Room the group of family **portraits** includes the 7th Earl in his

Thistle Robes and the 4th Earl's actor friend *John Philip Kemble.* Part of the 19C alterations included the transformation of a hay loft into the splendid cedar-panelled **library**. The creators of the Library, *We Twa*, are depicted above the fireplaces. The architect G E Street designed the chapel with its Burne-Jones east window.

Grounds – The **Terrace Garden** features geometric rosebeds and fountain, a lavish herbaceous border and secluded glades and knolls. A magnificent avenue of lime trees leads to adjacent **Haddo Country Park**. The 73ha of parkland with their splendid trees are the result of the 4th Earl's planting programme. The landscaping includes two vistas, Victoria Avenue from the entrance front, and a second on the east side beyond the formal garden, reaching away to the lake, the focal point.

Haddo House Choral and Operatic Society

Originally a community centre, a custom-built wooden hall serves as home for various productions (concerts, opera and drama) which attract many visiting artists of international repute and are open to the public (visit *https://hhcos.org.uk* for details).

▷ Return to Methlick and then take the B9005 west to Fyvie.

Fyvie Castle★

&. ⏱ *Castle: Apr–May daily 11am–4pm; Jun–Sept daily 11am–4.30pm; Oct–mid-Dec Fri–Mon 11am–3pm.* ⏱ *Mid-Dec–Mar. Grounds open daily 9am–sunset.* ⏣ *£13.* ✕ ✆ *01651 891 266.* *www.nts.org.uk.*

This imposing baronial pile, with eight centuries of history, is the ideal place to discover the opulence of an Edwardian interior

The original royal stronghold passed in 1390 to the Preston family and then in 1433 to the Meldrums. In 1596 Sir Alexander Seton, later Chancellor of Scotland, purchased Fyvie and remodelled the castle to incorporate the already existing Preston and Meldrum towers. He created the spectacular **south front** (46m long), a striking example of 17C baronial architecture, and the great wheel staircase. In 1889 the castle was sold to Alexander Forbes-Leith, a man with local origins who had made his fortune in the American steel industry. Lord Leith refurbished Fyvie and assembled a collection of paintings with family or castle connections.

The spacious 17C **wheel stair** is liberally spangled with the Seton crescent of its

Interior, Fyvie Castle

© Andrea Pistolesi/hemis.fr

Local Hero

Thousands of film fans have made the pilgrimage to **Pennan** to have their photographs taken next to the red telephone box which features in the film *Local Hero* (1983). In fact it was a movie prop, set up because the actual phone box was not in the best position for filming. The hotel in the film was also faked, with interiors from elsewhere used. But don't let any of that put you off visiting or bringing your camera; the phone box and the hotel exterior still look very much the part!

builder and rises through five floors. In the Dining Room, with its 19C plasterwork ceiling, are portraits of the first Lord Leith. Other works are by Raeburn, Romney and Opie. Up another floor, the original high hall, now the Morning Room, boasts a 1683 plasterwork ceiling from the Seton period.

The Back Morning Room is the unpretentious setting for the Fyvie portraits, masterpieces by **Raeburn**. *Mrs Gregory* is claimed to be his finest female portrait. In the Library the John Burnet painting of the *Trial of Charles I* recalls the royal association. Charles as a four-year-old boy spent time at Fyvie.

The Drawing Room in the Gordon Tower has Pompeo Batoni's memorable portrait (1766) of *The Hon William Gordon* as a Grand Tourist.

There are other notable works by Lawrence, Hoppner, Romney, Reynolds and Gainsborough.

4 FISHING VILLAGES

33mi/53km.

This drive through farming country and fishing villages includes stories of local characters, such as Maggie Duthie, generations of lighthouse keepers and even a village that was a "local hero".

Fraserburgh

Though the great days of the Scottish herring fishing industry were in the 19C and early 20C, this austere town on the northeastern tip of Aberdeenshire (Scotland's northeasternmost town) is still home to a fleet of around 220 fishing boats. The original harbour was the creation of the Fraser family in the 16C and it was they who built the grandiose castle on Kinneard Head; a mansion in fact whose top floor was adapted in 1787 as a base to house Scotland's very first lighthouse.

Some 5mi/8km east along the B9033 at Inverallochy is **Maggie's Hoosie** (⊙*Mon–Thu 2–4pm;* ℰ*01346 514 761).* The twin fishing villages of Inverallochy and Cairnbulg are extraordinary agglomerations of single-storey granite cottages placed gable-end to the rocky shore. Many have been modernised, but Maggie's Hoosie has been renovated to evoke the simple and harsh life led by local fisherfolk in the late 19C. A tour guide shows visitors around the rooms, and talks about the village fishing community in bygone years, Maggie's family and, of course Maggie and her "hoosie". Maggie Duthie was born in 1867 and died in 1950. She spent her life preparing and baiting fishing lines, curing, smoking, salting and drying the fish and then selling it (or bartering it for other produce) around the countryside.

The floor is maintained as it would have been in Maggie's day – beaten down earth covered in fresh sand from the beach. There was no electricity and no running water – Maggie and her family used the local well and then the pump. Neither was there a toilet; a bucket would be used in the shed.

Museum of Scottish Lighthouses

Kinnaird Head. ⓺⊙*Regular tours (45min) to Kinnaird Head lighthouse at 11am, 1pm, 2pm and 3pm (also noon and 4pm Apr–Oct).* ⊚*£8.80.* ✕ ℰ*01346 511 022. www.lighthousemuseum.org.uk.* This museum tells the fascinating story of the "Northern Lights", which have protected shipping from the perils of the country's long coastline with ever-increasing technological sophistication since the first fire tower was lit on the Isle of May in 1636.

Crovie

© Nachteule/iStockphoto.com

There are models, maps, drawings and all kinds of objects associated with light-house-keeping, but the most compelling exhibits are the great lenses of the lighthouses themselves, gigantic jewels of Art Deco allure. Human interest is not absent. The lives of lighthouse-keepers – a disappearing race due to modern automation – is well evoked with tales such as the mystery of the Flannan Isles lighthouse where three men literally vanished without trace. Also recorded is the extraordinary achievement of five generations of the Stevenson family who between them built around 100 lighthouses.

On Kinnaird Head, on the far side of a fishermen's net drying area, is a cluster of structures including keepers' cottages and the original lighthouse of 1787.

▶ Leave Fraserburgh by the B9031 in the direction of Sandhaven, looking out to your right for the superb beach at Aberdour bay.

Pennan

Hairpin bends and steep gradients lead down to this attractive village of white-painted cottages with their gable ends on to the rocky shore. Pennan figures as "Ferness" in Bill Forsyth's celebrated film *Local Hero* (♨ *see Box*). For a longer excursion, from Pennan continue along the picturesque road B9031

which runs inland before rejoining the coast at Rosehearty to Fraserburgh.

Crovie

On the east of Gamrie Bay, the cottages of this tiny picturesque village stand, gables on to the sea, only a path's width from the shore.

Troup Head (*no access*), with its 90m cliffs, is a prominent rocky headland. Just to the east is **Castle Point**, an exhilaratingly exposed headland, fortified and refortified since about 700 BCE, most recently in the 18C, when **Fort Fiddes** was added. There are magnificent **views**★★ of Pennan, of the cliffs and headlands of this splendid coastline, and of Hell's Lum, a cleft in the cliffs leading to a sea tunnel.

Gardenstown

A winding narrow road leads down to this village, which is terraced on the cliffs of the south side of Gamrie Bay. The small harbour is still the base for lobster boats.

▶ Continue along the B9031 to Macduff.

Macduff

Facing Banff across the river Deveron, Macduff – formerly called Doune – was renamed in the 18C by the 1st Earl of Fife when he built the harbour. Today the town still boasts an active fishing fleet,

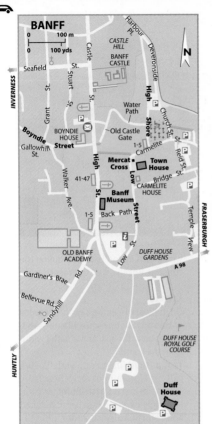

BANFF

0 — 100 m
0 — 100 yds

CASTLE HILL
BANFF CASTLE
Seafield
Castle St.
Stuart St.
Grant St.
Harbour Pl.
Deveronside
Deveron St.
Water Path
High Shore
Church St.
Old Castle Gate
BOYNDIE HOUSE
Boyndie Street
Gallowhill St.
Carmelite St.
Reid St.
Mercat Cross
Town House
High St.
Low St.
CARMELITE HOUSE
Banff Museum
Walker Ave.
Back Path
Bridge St.
Temple View
OLD BANFF ACADEMY
DUFF HOUSE GARDENS
Low Rd.
A98
FRASERBURGH
Gardiner's Brae
Bellevue Rd.
Sandyhill
DUFF HOUSE ROYAL GOLF COURSE
Duff House
INVERNESS
HUNTLY
41-47
1-5
1-5
N

fish market and boat building yards, owing in large part to its deep water harbour and the silting up of the Banff one. Another attraction is the open-air swimming pool at Tarlair, amid the rocks.

▷ Facing Macduff on the other bank of the Deveron is Banff.

Banff★

Set at River Deveron's mouth, Banff is a distinguished small coastal town. A royal burgh as early as the 12C, it had at one time both a castle and a monastery, but most notable today is its wealth of 18C buildings, a reminder of the days when Banff was a winter seat for wealthy local landowners.

Duff House★★

&. ☉Daily Apr–Sept 9.30am–5.30pm; Oct–Mar Fri–Sun 10am–4pm. ☉25–26 Dec, 1–2 Jan. ☞£9. ✕ ℘01261 818 181. www.historicenvironment.scot.

The most sophisticated country house in the northeast of Scotland, this splendid Baroque mansion was designed around 1735 by William Adam for William Duff MP, Lord Braco and Earl of Fife.

Unfortunately the architect and patron fell out, and a prolonged lawsuit was settled only shortly before Adam's death in 1748. The embittered Duff never took up residence.

The house was sold in the early 20C and, during World War II, Duff House accommodated Norwegian and Polish troops as well as German POWs. Resplendently restored, it now houses paintings from the Scottish National Gallery, which, together with a rich array of loan furnishings and fittings, has re-created something of the atmosphere it enjoyed in its heyday.

Exterior – With its four corner towers Duff House rises dramatically from level parkland in the valley of the River Deveron just inland from its mouth between Banff and Macduff. The mansion consists of a great central block rising over a basement and entered by a double curving staircase above which Corinthian pilasters support a richly decorated pediment. Adam's proposed flanking pavilions and colonnades were never built, but the house is held in place visually by mature trees. Upstream the river emerges from a gorge whose woodlands conceal an ice house and a mausoleum ornamented with an effigy taken from St Mary's Church at Banff.

Interior – The centre of the building is occupied by the vast and sumptuous spaces of the **Vestibule** on the first floor and the **Great Drawing Room** on the second, contrasting with the more intimate rooms to either side which served as boudoirs, bedrooms, libraries and closets. The Vestibule is dominated by William Etty's grandiose painting entitled *The Combat, Woman Pleading for the Vanquished – an Ideal Groupe*, while the Drawing Room is hung with a superb set of Gobelins **tapestries**.

Other fine paintings in first floor rooms include an early portrait by Ramsay, fragments of a large picture by Cuyp and a magnificent **El Greco** of *St Jerome in Penitence*.

The Great Staircase is densely hung with portraits and other pictures, but the most remarkable object here is a porphyry lion's paw and marble wine cooler mounted on a dense black block of polished anthracite. On the second floor, the North Drawing Room has a number of Raeburn portraits, while the pier-glass over the mantelpiece is the sole surviving item of the house's original fittings. The Libraries are hung with portraits of Kings of Scotland, exiled monarchs and Pretenders.

The house also holds a regular programme of **temporary exhibitions** throughout the year including at least one from the National Galleries of Scotland in Edinburgh, which showcases a masterpiece.

Upper and Lower Towns

Low Street – Of particular interest are the 18C Carmelite House, the only reminder of the town's former monastery, and the **town house** with its unusual steeple. On the plainstones in front of the house is a rare pre-Reformation **mercat cross★**.

High Shore – Nos. 1 to 5 on the left are an attractive group of 18C buildings. The doorway of No. 3, with its straight-headed pediment and grotesque, contrasts with the more vernacular inn with its pend.

Boyndie Street – On the north are two examples of 18C town houses. The first, Boyndie House, has a date stone and curvilinear gable.

High Street – On the west side Nos. 47 to 41 are more fine examples of 18C buildings. Farther along on the other side is Abercrombie Tower House, an attractive rubblework mid-18C town

house. At the south end are more 18C houses, Nos. 5 to 1 with the Old Banff Academy beyond.

Banff Museum (🕐 *Thu–Sat 10.30am–2pm; 🞄01771 622 807; www.livelifeaberdeenshire.org.uk/museums/banff-museum*) is the oldest museum in Scotland north of Perth, founded in 1828. It includes award-winning natural history displays and an important collection of Banff silver.

ADDRESSES

🏨 STAY

ABERDEEN

🛏**The Crown Guest House** – *10 Springbank Terrace. 🞄01224 586 842. www.crownguesthouse.co.uk. 7 rooms.* Smart family-run guesthouse with a pleasant garden.

🛏🛏 **Ibis Aberdeen Centre** – *15 Shiprow. 🞄01224 398 800. www.accorhotels.com. 107 rooms.* In the centre of town, this popular chain hotel offers simple comfortable contemporary designed guest rooms.

🛏🛏 **Travelodge Aberdeen Central** – *9 Bridge Street. 🞄0871 984 6117. www.travelodge.co.uk. 97 rooms.* This standard chain hotel offers good value in the city centre; look out for promotional deals on its website.

🛏🛏🍽 **Atholl Hotel** – *54 King's Gate. 🞄01224 323 505. www.atholl-aberdeen.co.uk. 34 rooms.* This Baronial-style hotel is set in the leafy suburbs. Rooms are light and airy with Tartan decor. Its popular restaurant serves fresh local produce; the lounge bar has a wide selection of local drinks.

🛏🛏🍽 **bauhaus** – *52-60 Langstane Place. 🞄01224 212 122. www.thebauhaus.co.uk. 39 rooms.* This modern hotel is just off the main street; its functional minimalist design is in keeping with the Bauhaus school of thought. First-floor **restaurant** (🍽🍽🍽) offers modern classics and avoids the need to go out for dinner.

🛏🛏🍽 **Doubletree by Hilton** – *384 Beach Boulevard. 🞄01224 633 339. www.doubletreeaberdeen.com. 168 rooms.* A 10min walk from the centre this is the most comfortable hotel in central

Aberdeen. Its excellent facilities, include a fully equipped Leisure Club with swimming pool.

☺☺🛏 **The Mariner** – *349 Great Western Road.* ℘*01224 588 901. www. themarinerhotel.co.uk. 25 rooms.* A nautical theme welcomes visitors to this elegant hotel set in a residential district, a 5min drive from the city centre. Bedrooms are spacious and colourful with extensive facilities. Good restaurant.

DEE VALLEY

☺☺🛏🛏 **Norwood Hall Hotel** – *Garthdee Road, Cults (3mi/5km from Aberdeen).* ℘*01224 868 951. www. macdonaldhotels.co.uk. 73 rooms.* At the heart of an ancient wooded estate this Victorian mansion, now a hotel and conference centre, offers trademark MacDonald Hotels luxury.

BANCHORY

☺☺🛏 **Banchory Lodge Hotel** – *Banchory.* ℘*01330 822 625. https:// banchorylodge.com. 28 rooms.* A tranquil setting for this Georgian manor house on the banks of the Dee.

GRAMPIAN CASTLES REGION

☺☺🛏 **Pittodrie House** – *Chapel of Garioch.* ℘*0344 879 9066. www. macdonaldhotels.co.uk/pittodrie. 27 rooms.* Set within its own ancient 970ha estate extending as far as the eye can see, this luxury hotel offers a tranquil retreat with romantic Scots Baronial turrets, mysterious passageways and stone spiral staircases. **Restaurant**☺☺🛏.

☺☺🛏 **Kildrummy Castle** – *Kildrummy, Alford (9.5mi/15km from Alford).* ℘*01975 571 288. 16 rooms.* This splendid country retreat mansion lies in the grounds of a real ruined castle. Lovely gardens, recommended **restaurant**☺☺🛏.

♈/ EAT

ABERDEEN

☺☺ **La Lombarda** – *2–8 King Street.* ℘*01224 640 916. www.lalombarda.co.uk. Open Mon dinner, and lunch and dinner Tue–Sun.* Claimed to be the oldest Italian restaurant in the UK (est. 1922), Lombarda serves classic Italian dishes, pasta, pizzas, meat and seafood dishes, mainly sourced from local suppliers, in a friendly, traditional atmosphere.

☺☺ **Rendezvous@Nargile** – *7106-108 Forest Avenue.* ℘*01224 323 700. www. rendezvousatnargile.co.uk. Open daily noon till late.* This stylish modern restaurant serves authentic contemporary Turkish cuisine, from snacks to full meals, with flair.

☺☺ **Royal Thai** – *29 Crown Terrace. Closed Sun.* ℘*01224 212 922. www.royal thaiaberdeen.co.uk. Open Sun dinner, and lunch and dinner from Mon–Sat.* The city's longest running Thai restaurant (est. 1992). Fresh seafood is a vital ingredient here with daily deliveries to the kitchen.

☺☺ **Fusion Bar and Bistro** – *10 North Silver Street. Dinner only and Sat lunch.* ℘*01224 652 959. www.fusionbarbistro. com.* Fashionable and modern in modernised granite townhouse.

☺☺ **Silver Darling** – *Pocra Quay, North Pier.* ℘*01224 576 229. www. thesilverdarling.co.uk.* At the port entrance, atop the former customs house. Classical dishes and excellent quality seafood.

☺☺ **Yatai** – *53 Langstane Place.* ℘*01224 592 355. www.yatai.co.uk. Closed Sun–Mon.* Atmospheric Japanese restaurant offering authentic and tasty dishes, including sushi, sashimi and maki.

☺☺ **Yorokobi by CJ** – *51 Juntly Street.* ℘*07528 235094. www.yorokobibycj. co.uk. Closed Sun–Mon.* A justly popular Japanese restaurant serving flavoursome and authentic Japanese and Korean dishes; a perfect excuse to try one of the sizzling platters or a Korean pot dish.

CRATHES

☺☺ **The Milton Brasserie** – *Milton of Crathes, Crathes.* ℘*01330 844 566. www. miltonbrasserie.com.* Set in a stone barn in a craft village next to Crathes Castle this smart, highly acclaimed modern restaurant serves a range of eclectic contemporary dishes.

BALLATER

☺☺🛏 **Auld Kirk** – *31 Braemar Road.* ℘*01339 755 762. www.theauldkirk.com.* This fine old church has been tastefully converted into a restaurant with high vaulted ceilings, cathedral windows and ornate chandeliers provide a very unusual experience.

The Cairngorms★★
and Aviemore

This granitic mountain range between the Spey valley and Braemar is an area of wild and dramatic scenery. It lies mainly above 915m and the highest point is Ben Macdui (1 309m) although three other peaks top the 1 220m mark, including Cairn Gorm. The summits have been planed down by glacial erosion to form flat plateaux while glaciers have gouged the trough of Loch Avon and River Dee.

FLORA AND FAUNA

The severe climate of these high-altitude plateaux and summits, so often windswept, allows only an Arctic-Alpine flora to flourish. Lichen, heather and moss serve as background to the brilliant splashes of colour provided by the starry saxifrage and moss campion. These windswept tracts are the domain of such elusive creatures as the snow bunting, dotterel and ptarmigan.

The objectives of the **Cairngorms National Nature Reserve**, designated in 1954, are to protect the scientific, scenic and wilderness values of its 125 900ha.

The national park is home to 25 per cent of Britain's threatened species and includes extensive areas of wild land, moorlands, forests, rivers, lochs and

- **Info:** National Park Authority, Grantown-on-Spey; ☎01479 872 478. http://visitcairngorms.com. There are 9 visitor centres in total around the national park.
- **Location:** There are 9 National Nature Reserves in the Cairngorms. Aviemore is the base for sports and most outdoor activities.
- **Don't Miss:** Spectacular views (on a clear day) from the top of Cairn Gorm.
- **Walkers and climbers:** It is essential to follow the mountain code and always leave a note of route and expected time of return with someone responsible. Proper clothing and mountain equipment are vital.
- **Timing:** Depending on how sporty you are (and, in winter, the weather conditions), you could easily spend several days here.
- **Kids:** The Cairngorm Reindeer Centre and Strathspey Railway.

Red deer, Cairngorms National Nature Reserve

© Nature in Stock/hemis.fr

glens. Sites designated as of importance to natural heritage take up 39 per cent of the land area – two thirds of these are of Europe-wide importance.

The area, however, has long been associated with osprey, which arrive from Africa in late March-early April, and depart again in August and September. Their story and its ups and downs is both prolonged and fascinating.

Finding a capercaillie, or for that matter any of the remarkable wildlife species that inhabit these Speyside forests and moors, is never easy at the best of times. But doing so can be made more likely by visiting the **British Wildlife Watching Club** (*www.bwwc.co.uk*), a dynamic set-up established in 2008, and operated by and from the Grant Arms Hotel in Grantown-on-Spey (&see ADDRESSES). It is a unique enterprise that provides guests and other visitors with information on what has been seen recently, and where visitors might go to watch for wildlife. The club, which enjoys dedicated rooms in the hotel, including a natural history library and 100-seat lecture room, exists for anyone interested in wildlife, from those who come armed with a telescope and a list of "Must see" species, to those who simply wish to enjoy a good walk with the chance of seeing wildlife along the way.

Those keenly interested in wildlife should visit **Speyside Wildlife**'s evening mammal watching hide deep in the Rothiemurchus forest on one of the dusk watches, for the chance of close up views of pine marten, badger, red deer and more (*www.speysidewildlife.co.uk*).

Mountaineering and Walking

No roads suitable for motor vehicles traverse these wild and awesome mountains and their very remoteness makes them all the more attractive to the mountaineer or hillwalker. 😊 *Only experienced and well-equipped climbers and walkers should take on this terrain however.* If you are planning your own itinerary, get a copy of the Scottish Mountaineering Club's *Climber's Guide to the Cairngorms* for advice on staying safe in the Cairngorms.

Skiing

The northern and western slopes of Cairn Gorm (&see opposite) provide Scotland's top ski area. The ski slopes are within easy reach of all Spey valley towns and villages. The main access road passes Loch Morlich before dividing to serve the two distinct skiing corries, Coire Cas and Coire na Ciste. Chair-lifts and ski tows transport the skiers to the various ski runs ranging from easy to difficult. There is also skiing off the Lecht Road on the eastern side of the Cairngorms.

AVIEMORE★

Set in the Spey valley on the western fringes of the Cairngorms, Aviemore is Scotland's premier all-year sports resort. The building of the Aviemore Centre in the mid-1960s transformed this small

---

The Big Grey Man

The slopes and corries of **Ben Macdui** are a wild primeval place and legends of a strange presence had long been known when, in 1899, Professor Normal Collie, an acclaimed climber (who lies buried on the Isle of Skye), confirmed he, too, had felt the presence of the Big Grey Man. "I was returning from the summit in a mist when I began to think I heard something else than merely the noise of my own footsteps. Every few steps I took I heard a crunch, as if someone was walking after me but taking steps three or four times the length of my own. As I walked on and the eerie crunch, crunch sounded behind me I was seized with terror and took to my heels. Whatever you make of it I do not know, but there is something very queer about the top of Ben MacDhui and will not go back there again by myself I know."

Cairngorm Mountain Railway

© Peter Burnett/iStockphoto.com

village, which had grown up around the railway station into a bustling centre offering day and night entertainment and indoor and outdoor sports and pastimes. Attractions include indoor swimming pools, ice rink, watersports centre and a dry ski slope.

Strathspey Railway

Steam trains operate from the main station in Aviemore (15min single journey to Boat of Garten, 40min to Broomhill). See website for full timetable and prices. 01479 810 725. www.strathspeyrailway.co.uk.
The sounds and smells on this 5mi/8km steam-driven journey between Aviemore and Boat of Garten are evocative reminders of bygone times.

EXCURSIONS

Cairngorm Reindeer Centre

Located close to the Forestry Commission's visitor centre in Glenmore Forest Park.
Exhibition and Paddocks: early-Feb–early-Jan (weather permitting); Daily Hill Trips (except early Jan–early Feb) depart at 11.00am . Paddock only Apr–early-Jan £3.50 adult, £2.50 child; Hill trips (includes Exhibition and Paddocks) £15, child £9; Wear warm and waterproof clothing and sturdy footwear; 01479 861 228; www.cairngormreindeer.co.uk.

The centre has an exhibition and paddocks with a small number of deer (*Easter to early Jan*), but most visitors make the short journey out into the wild to where a guide takes them to the only reindeer herd in Britain which ranges freely in the open. The deer are very friendly and can be stroked and hand-fed.

Cairn Gorm★★★

12mi from Aviemore to the Cairn Gorm car park. By car, take the B970 or by public transport take bus No 31.
For the non-hillwalker or skier, the funicular **Cairngorm Mountain Railway** (*daily (weather permitting) 10am–5.30pm; Funicular and Exhibition check website for times and charges;* 01479 861 261; www.cairngormmountain.org) is an ideal way of discovering the area's austere beauty.
The railway transports visitors to two levels. The first is Base Station, with a Mountain Garden. The Ptarmigan Top Station, nestled just below the summit of Cairn Gorm, includes a shop, a bar, the excellent Ptarmigan restaurant and a mountain exhibition. Allow two hours for your full visit including transport.
The already excellent view from the car park unfolds further as the train ascends. At the terminal, at 1 100m, there is an extensive **view★★★** westwards of the Spey valley.

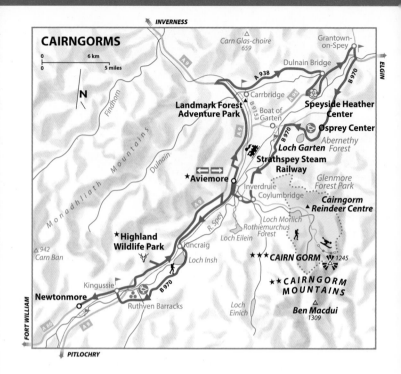

CAIRNGORMS

INVERNESS

Carn Glas-choire 659

Grantown-on-Spey

Dulnain Bridge

ELGIN

Carrbridge

Landmark Forest Adventure Park

Boat of Garten

Speyside Heather Center

Osprey Center

Loch Garten

Abernethy Forest

Strathspey Steam Railway

★ Aviemore

Inverdruie Coylumbridge

Glenmore Forest Park

Cairngorm Reindeer Centre

Loch Morlich

Rothiemurchus Forest

★ Highland Wildlife Park

Kincraig

Loch Eilein

Loch Insh

★★★ CAIRN GORM 1245

△ 942 Carn Ban

★★ CAIRNGORM MOUNTAINS

Kingussie

Newtonmore

Ruthven Barracks

Loch Einich

Ben Macdui 1309

PITLOCHRY

FORT WILLIAM

Findhorn

Dulnain

Monadhliath Mountains

R. Spey

🕑 In order to protect the plateau, funicular passengers are not permitted to exit the top station to go onto the mountain unless they are booked on a guided walk or a guided mountain bike descent. If you want to visit the summit of Cairn Gorm you must walk up from the car park.

🚗 DRIVING TOURS

🚗 1 THE SOUTHERN CAIRNGORMS★
42mi/68km.

A drive upstream beside the Spey.

◯ Leave Aviemore by the B970. Before reaching the charming small town of Kingussie, stop off at the ruined 18C Ruthven Barracks.

Highland Folk Museum, Newtownmore
♿🕑*Daily: Apr–Aug 10.30am–5.30pm; Sept–Oct 11am–4.30pm.* ✖ ☎*01540 673 551. www.highlandfolk.com.*

Within sight of the Cairngorm mountains, this 1mi/1.6km long, 32ha site is devoted to living history. In addition to relocated and re-created buildings and architectural features, there are working demonstrations and actors interpreting the past. It includes a township from the 1700s, an 1800s farm (reinterpreted for

Male capercaillie displaying, Cairngorm Mountains

© ClawsAndPaws/iStockphoto.com

Red squirrel, Cairngorm Mountains

the 1930s), a school house, church, clockmaker's shop, tailor's shop, joinery, the estate sawmill and more. A vintage bus covers the site.

▷ Leave Newtonmore on the A86 or the A9, cross Kingussie and head towards Kincraig.

👥 Highland Wildlife Park★

🕐Daily (weather permitting in winter) Apr–Oct 10am–5pm (Jul–Aug 6pm; Nov–Mar 4pm). 🕐25 Dec. ⊜£17.95 (child 3–15, £9.95) – online discounts available. ✖ ☎01540 651 270. www.highlandwildlifepark.org.

The Highland Wildlife Park was opened in 1972 and, like Edinburgh Zoo, is run by the Royal Zoological Society of Scotland A drive-through area includes herds of free-ranging European bison, red deer, wild horses, Soay sheep from St Kilda, ibex (wild goat) and shaggy Highland cattle. In the walk-about section are wild cats, badgers, polecats, pine martens, beavers, golden eagles, wolves, grouse and capercaillie.

▷ Return to Aviemore on the A9.

🚗 2 THE NORTHERN CAIRNGORMS★
41mi/61km.

▷ Leave Aviemore on the A9 heading north towards Inverness. The Landmark Forest Adventure Park is at Carrbridge.

👥 Landmark Forest Adventure Park

🕐Daily Apr–mid-Jul and mid-Aug–Oct 10am–6pm; mid-Jul–mid-Aug 10am–7pm; Oct–Mar 10am–5pm. 🕐25 Dec, 1 Jan. ⊜£21.45 (child £19.20) – low-season £7.25, child £6.10. ✖ ☎01479 841 613. www.landmarkpark.co.uk.

This is where traditional forestry heritage park meets modern theme park with a treetop trail, huge slides, a water-coaster adventure playground and various white-knuckle experiences themed to fit in with the beautiful surroundings.

▷ Continue on the A938 east to Dulnain Bridge and the local road to Skye of Curr.

The Speyside Centre

🕐Apr–Sept Mon–Sat 9am–5.30pm, Sun 10am–5pm; Oct–Mar daily 10am–4pm. 🕐25 Dec, 1 Jan. ✖ ☎01479 851 359. www.heathercentre.com.

A colourful display of over 300 varieties of heather in a beautiful setting near the River Spey is the main draw here. An exhibition in the visitor centre presents the historical and modern uses of heather: thatching, basketware, wool dyeing. An art gallery, garden centre, restaurant and gift shop complete the visit. Also a good place to spot red squirrel.

▷ Follow signs towards the village of Grantown-on-Spey. At Boat of Garten take the B970 south towards Loch Garten.

Osprey Centre (Loch Garten)★

Access to the Royal Society for the Protection of Birds' hide within the sanctuary area is by a clearly marked path only 5min walk. The hide is equipped with binoculars and telescopes.

Apr–early Sept 10am–6pm. £5 (child, £2). 01479 821 409. www.rspb. org.uk/reserves.

In 1954, after an absence of 38 years, ospreys returned to breed in Britain choosing a nest site by Loch Garten, within the ancient Abernethy pine forest. Operation Osprey was started to give total protection during the breeding season, and the area round the tree-top eyrie was declared a bird sanctuary. In 1975, the nesting area, and surrounding woodland, loch and moor, was declared a nature reserve with open access to visitors, and includes a Visitor Centre.

▶ Return to Aviemore on the B970

ADDRESSES

STAY

AVIEMORE

Ardlogie Guest House – *Dalfaber Road.* 01479 810 747. www.ardlogie. co.uk. 5 rooms. This cosy guesthouse enjoys a quiet location with attractive light and airy bedrooms, two of which offer wonderful mountain views. There is a terrace with seating overlooking the garden. This is excellent value, plus there are free passes available to the local golf and country club.

GRANTOWN-ON-SPEY

The Grant Arms Hotel – 0800 043 8585. www.grantarmshotel.com. 50 rooms. Queen Victoria and Prince Albert stayed here in 1860, but the hotel has been significantly improved since then! This is the base of the Birdwatching and Wildlife Club, and the perfect base for anyone with a keen interest in low-level walks and birdwatching. The integral **restaurant** () serves local produce to good effect.

Elgin★

Set in the rich agricultural area known as the Laich of Moray, the attractive market town of Elgin, famous for its cathedral, stands on the banks of the Lossie and is the administrative centre for the Moray district.

SIGHTS
Elgin cathedral★

Daily: Apr–Sept 9.30am–5.30pm; Oct–Mar 10am–4pm. 1–2 Jan, 25–26 Dec. £9. 01343 547 171. www.historicenvironment.scot.

Once one of the most beautiful cathedrals in Scotland, today the biscuit-coloured ruins still stand, majestic, evocative and rich in style, characteristic of the 13C, a period of intensive church building.

The creation of the diocese dated back to 1120 when the Celtic churches of Birnie, Kinneddar and Spynie had served as episcopal seats prior to the final

▶ **Population:** 24 760.
ℹ **Info:** Elgin Library; 01343 562 608.
▶ **Location:** The medieval plan has been preserved and the High Street links the cathedral to the former site of the castle.
Don't Miss: The cathedral chapter house.
Timing: Allow half a day, longer if taking the Glen Moray distillery tour.
Kids: Older ones may enjoy the Moray Motor Museum.

move in 1224 to the Church of the Holy Trinity at Elgin. Both the town and the cathedral suffered ignominious destruction in 1390 at the hands of the **Wolf of Badenoch**, otherwise known as Alexander Stewart, the second (and illegitimate) son of King Robert II, who

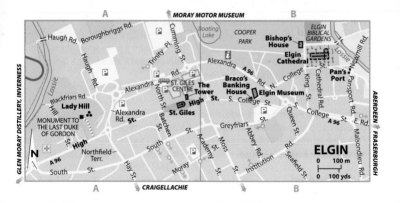

MORAY MOTOR MUSEUM

Haugh Rd. Boroughbriggs Rd.

GLEN MORAY DISTILLERY, INVERNESS

Haugh Rd.

Trinity Pl.

Cumming St.

Boating Lake

COOPER PARK

ELGIN BIBLICAL GARDENS

Bishop's House

Alexandra

A 96

Rd.

N. College Rd.

Elgin Cathedral

King St.

Cathedral Rd.

Lossie

Pan's Port

Newmill Rd.

ABERDEEN // FRASERBURGH

Blackfriars Rd.

Lady Hill

Alexandra Rd.

North St.

Batchen St.

ST. GILES CENTRE

The Tower

High St.

Braco's Banking House

S. College St.

Elgin Museum

Queen St.

S. College

A 96

Pansport Rd. E. Rd.

Maisondieu Rd.

MONUMENT TO THE LAST DUKE OF GORDON

High St.

St. Giles

High St.

Northfield Terr.

A 96

South St.

South

Hay St.

Moray St.

St.

Academy St.

Greyfriars

St.

Moss St.

Abbey Rd.

Institution Rd.

Seafield St.

ELGIN

0   100 m
0   100 yds

CRAIGELLACHIE

burned the place down in retaliation for having been excommunicated by the Bishop of Moray when he left his wife. Although duly repaired, the cathedral suffered gradual deterioration after the Reformation. This was in part due to the fact that it was no longer in use as a place of worship and also due to the protracted struggle over the ownership of church property after the Reformation. In 1711 the collapse of the central tower wreaked much damage and the ruins became a quarry for building materials. Conservation began in the early 19C by the determined efforts of one man.

Between the buttressed twin towers of the west front is a deeply recessed portal with large windows above. Intricate vine and acorn carving frames the doorways. On the internal face is an attractive arcade marking the passageway between the towers at first floor level. This feature is also found at Arbroath (⌖ *see ARBROATH*). The view of the town from the top of the south tower (*134 steps*) is screened by the trees of Cooper Park, although the Duke of Gordon (⌖ *see High Street, below*) can be seen on his column on Lady Hill. The transepts are the oldest parts. The two figures in the south aisle originally adorned the outer walls of the central tower. The east end is an impressive arrangement of two rows of five lancets crowned by a rose window. The piers of the choir have unusual spire-like terminations.

Elgin cathedral

O. Forin/MICHELIN

The octagonal 13C **chapter house★★** was reconstructed in the 15C when it was provided with elaborately rich vaulting and carved bosses. The stone benching is discontinued for the five canopied seats.

Standing within the former cathedral precincts are **Pann's Port**, a former gateway and in the corner of Cooper Park, the ruins of one of the manses, miscalled the **Bishop's House**.

Elgin Museum

&⚬*Apr–early Nov Mon–Fri 10am–5pm, Sat 11am–4pm.* ✆*01343 543 675. www.elginmuseum.org.uk.*

This purpose-built Italianate building (1843) houses the local history museum, independently run since its opening in 1842, making it Scotland's oldest independent museum. Items of particular interest are the local fossil fish and reptiles and incised Pictish stones, especially the **Burghead Bulls**.

High Street

Wynds and pends link the main thoroughfare to the north and south. **Braco's Banking House**, marked by street-level arcades, was the banking house of William Duff of Dipple. His son William Duff of Braco and later Earl of Fife invested the accumulated fortune in the building of Duff House. Farther along on the right as the street widens is a 17C **tower**, now offices.

The handsome **Church of St Giles** designed in the Classical style by the Aberdonian Archibald Simpson, is greatly enhanced by its mid-street site. The steepled tower and fluted columned portico dominate the façades. **Lady Hill** at the far end of the street was the site of the medieval castle.

Today it is dominated by the monument to the last Duke of Gordon (d.1836) with his Grace above.

Moray Motor Museum

Bridge Street. &⚬*Daily Easter–Oct 11am–5pm.* ⚬*£7.* ✆*01343 544 933. https://moraymotormuseum.org.*

Classic cars and motorcycles here include: a Ford Model "T"; a 1937 Bent-

ley; a Bristol 403 (1953); a 1929 Rolls Royce Phantom I adapted as a shooting vehicle, with a large spotlight for night hunting; and a 1968 E-Type Jaguar.

Glen Moray Distillery

Bruceland Road. ⚬*May–Sept Mon–Fri 9am–5pm, Sat 10am–4.30pm; Oct–Apr Mon–Fri 9am–5pm.* ⚬*Tours Mon–Fri 9.30am, 11am, 12.30pm, 2pm, 3.30pm. Sat 10.30am, noon, 1.30pm, 3pm.* ⚬*£5.* ✖ ✆*01343 550 900. www.glenmoray.com.*

Glen Moray single malt whisky has been distilled on the banks of the River Lossie since 1897 at this small friendly distillery. The tour ends with a tasting.

🚗 DRIVING TOUR

🚗 THE MORAY COAST★
34mi/55km.

This drive from Elgin to Forres takes you along one of the UK's most important whale and dolphin observation points.

▶ Leave Elgin on the A941 and at Lossiemouth turn left and follow the coast road to Burghead and then the B9089 to Kinloss, and Findhorn on the B9011.

Findhorn

The internationally renowned New Age community **Findhorn Foundation** (founded in 1962) is focused on **Universal Hall**, a strikingly unconventional structure in timber and stone.

The **village** of Findhorn overlooks the bay of the same name. Its tidal water, sand dunes, fine beach, mud flats and saltmarsh is used for watersports but is also of international significance for wading birds and migrant geese, while seals haul out close to the mouth of the bay.

The **Heritage Centre** (&⚬*2–5pm: daily Jun–Aug; May and Sept Sat–Sun only;* ✆*01309 690 659; www.findhorn-heritage.co.uk*) occupies an old store building and a former ice house.

West of Findhorn Bay lies an extensive area of dunes, the famous **Culbin**

Sands, which were originally held by marram grass. The effects were devastating when the grass was widely removed for thatching in the 17C. Fertile land and the village of Culbin were covered by sand. In 1922 the Forestry Commission started afforestation with Corsican pine, and the **Culbin Forest**, a site of special scientific interest.

▶ Leave Findhorn with the bay on your right.

Sueno's Stone★★
Outskirts of Forres, close to the Findhorn road, B9011.
A legacy of the enigmatic Picts, this sandstone cross slab (6m high, now protected by glass) is superbly carved on all sides and probably dates from the 9C. The purpose of this stone, which has no parallel in Scotland, remains uncertain. It was unearthed in 1726 and mistakenly named after Swein Forkbeard, the Danish king. Three sides including the one with the wheel cross are decorative. The fourth, the most spectacular, is narrative, depicting horsemen, armed warriors and headless corpses. The theory is that this outstanding piece of craftsmanship represents a commemorative monument to a battle, probably between the local people and Norse invaders.

Forres
This royal and ancient burgh is situated south of Findhorn Bay. Both the tolbooth and mercat cross are 19C. The lively **Falconer Museum** (*Tolbooth Street;* ◷ *Apr–Oct Mon–Sat 10am–5pm, Sun 1–5pm;* ☏ *01309 696 261; www.falconermuseum. co.uk*) interprets the town of Forres and is dedicated to Hugh Falconer, a local 19C scientist and discoverer.

▶ Head south on the A940 for 1.2mi/2km, then minor roads.

Dallas Dhu Distillery
♿◷ *Daily Apr–Sept 9.30am–5.30pm; Oct–Mar Sat–Wed 10am–4pm.* ◷ *25–26 Dec and 1–2 Jan.* ⬤£6. ☏ *01309 676 548. www.historicenvironment.scot.*

Sueno's Stone
© Vipersniper/iStockphoto.com

Built in 1899, this picturesque distillery in stone and slate was closed in the early 1980s, but now provides a fascinating and well-documented experience of the processes involved in producing the "sovereign liquor". After learning about the history of whisky from its monastic beginnings, visitors take a self-guided tour which ends with the customary "wee dram".

▶ 4mi/6.4km from Forres on the A96 towards Nairn is Brodie Castle.

Brodie Castle★
✗◷ *Mar–Jun and Sept–late Oct daily 10am–5pm; Jul–Aug daily 9.30am–6pm; Nov–Feb daily 10am–4pm.* ⬤£11. ☏ *01309 641 371. www.nts.org.uk.*
This castle was the seat of the Brodies right up until the late 20C. What visitors see today began in 1567, as a fortified house built by the 12th Earl. Additions were made in the 17C and alterations were made in 1824.
These days Brodie Castle is famous for its garden and in particular its daffodils, which are a picture in the spring.
The house contains fine French furniture including an ingenious Louis XV bedside table, plus English, continental and Chinese porcelain, and a remarkable collection of clocks. The Red Room, for-

Brodie Castle

© Andrea Pistolesi/hemis.fr

merly the Great Hall, boasts many fine paintings, including 17C Flemish and Dutch art (Gerard Dou, Mytens), and 18C and 19C English watercolours. Scottish painting by the likes of Peploe, Gillies and MacTaggart and early 20C works are also represented. The Dining Room dates back to the 17C extension and is notable for its plaster ceiling which was painted over in the 19C and only later rediscovered. The magnificent 19C Library contains some 6,000 volumes. The 19C Salon, with its intricate ceiling comprising delicately decorated compartments, features several interesting pictures including Charles I by Van Dyck. Below stairs is a huge Victorian kitchen and servants' quarters to explore.

Dufftown

The old local rhyme, "Rome was built on seven hills, Dufftown stands on seven stills", is still valid today as Dufftown remains capital of the malt whisky industry. The trim little town was laid out in 1817 by James Duff, 4th Earl of Fife, initially to give employment to local peple after the Napoleonic Wars. Glenlivet, the first of Dufftown's numerous distilleries, was established in 1823.

SIGHTS
Glenfiddich Distillery★
North of the town centre on the east side of the A941. ⌖✕ ➤⚑*Visit by guided tour only, Apr–Oct:* ⊜*Explorers Tour (1h30) 10.30am–4pm, £10; Spirit of Innovation Tour (2h) daily at 11am, 1pm and 3pm, £25; Solera Tour (2h30) 10am and 2pm, £50; Pioneers Tour (4h) once daily at noon, £95.* ⌚*Two weeks at Christmas.* ☎*01340 820 373. www.glenfiddich.co.uk.*
Set in the heart of the Highlands, Glenfiddich (meaning "Valley of the Deer" in Gaelic) is a place of great beauty, as well as the brand name of the world's best-selling single-malt whisky. The film and tour provide an excellent introduction

▶ **Population:** 1 610.
ℹ **Info:** Clock Tower. ☎01340 820 501. www.dufftown.co.uk.
▶ **Location:** Dufftown is 17mi/27km south of Elgin on the A 941.
⊗ **Don't Miss:** If you see only one distillery make it Glenfiddich.
⌚ **Timing:** There are the two whisky festivals, one in early May and the other in September. The Highland Games take place on the last weekend in July. You will need a car to explore the many distilleries.

to this family firm's history (founded in 1886) and the art of malt whisky distilling through all the stages from malting to bottling.

Balvenie Castle
Behind Glenfiddich Distillery. ⌚*Apr–Sept daily 9.30am–5.30pm.* ⊜*£6.* ☎*01340 820 121. www.historicenvironment.scot.*

Glenfarclas Distillery

© Peter Burnett/iStockphoto.com

Whisky Trail

This signposted tour (*about 70mi/113km*) takes in eight malt whisky distilleries. The following are suggested highlights:

The Glenlivet Distillery *Glenlivet, Ballindalloch.* ⚒️🕐*Mid-Mar–early-Nov daily 9.30am–6pm.* 🎫*Classic Tour £12.50; Dram of Distinction Tour £40.* 🖉*01340 821 720. www.maltwhiskydistilleries.com.* This was the first licensed distillery in the Highlands (1824). The original maltings are the setting for the visitor centre.

Glenfarclas Distillery *Marypark.* ⚒️🕐*Oct–Mar 10.30am, noon, 1.15pm, 2.30pm.* 🎫*£7.50; Connoisseur's Tour & Tasting Fri 2pm Jul–Sept,* 🎫*£40.* 🖉*01807 500 345. www.glenfarclas.com.*

Cardhu Distillery *Knockando. Tours from* 🎫*£8–£25 – Nov–Feb Mon–Fri 10am–4pm; Mar and Oct Mon–Sat 10am–5pm; Apr–Sept daily 10am–5pm.* 🖉*01479 874 635. www.malts.com.*

Set on a strategic route from Donside to Moray, this now ruined courtyard castle was successively the seat of Comyns, Douglases and Stewarts. The initial structure with its massive curtain wall is a rare example of 13C military architecture in Scotland. The moat dated from the period of Comyn ownership in the late 13C and early 14C. In the mid 16C the 4th Earl of Atholl, a Stewart, built a fine Renaissance dwelling. The latter, along the entrance front, is clearly distinguished by itd richer architectural ornament: carved armorial panels, mouldings and corbellings.

Speyside Cooperage
About 4mi/6km NW to Craigellachie on the far bank of the Spey by A941. ⚒️✖️🕐*Mon–Fri 9am–5pm;* 🥃*tours every half hour starting 9am.* 🎫*£4.* 🕐*2 weeks over Christmas period.*

🖉*01340 871 108. www.speysidecooperage.co.uk.*

Since 1947, this family-owned Speyside Cooperage (barrel makers) has produced the finest casks from American oak. Today it is the only working cooperage in the UK where visitors can experience the ancient art of coopering still using traditional methods and tools.

A viewing gallery allows visitors to enjoy the sights, smells and sounds of coopers making and repairing some of the 100 000 barrels that the workshop turns out annually. Although they may be shipped across the world, many of the casks remain in Scotland, for the maturing of the area's whiskies.

THE HIGHLANDS

If there was only one region that could fly the flag for Scotland abroad, then it would probably be the Highlands. It not only boasts Scotland's most awe-inspiring landscapes of dark lochs and snow-capped peaks, but also some of the most remote and extensive wilderness in Europe. There is history aplenty (Glencoe, Bonnie Prince Charlie, standing stones), legends (Nessie), wildlife (dolphins, whales, eagles and deer), and a whole host of sporting opportunities in both summer and winter. The Highlands are an historic region of Scotland, culturally distinct from the Lowlands, but the term is here used to refer to the vast, largely wilderness area north and on either side of the Great Glen, but excluding the islands. The area is sparsely populated, with mountain ranges dominating, including the highest in Britain. It is also the region that saw most depopulation during the infamous Highland Clearances.

Highlights

The Great Glen: Around Inverness and Fort William

The gateway to the far north is Inverness where Loch Ness to the south, with or without its monster, is a star attraction. Nearby, the very names Culloden and Cawdor castle are powerful siren calls. Some 70mi/113km southwest along the Great Glen, the area of Fort William, Ben Nevis and Glen Nevis styles itself the outdoor capital of Britain, offering hill walking, ice climbing, skiing, snowboarding, canyoning, canoeing, paragliding and mountain biking. It peaks in every sense at Ben Nevis, Britain's highest mountain while a few miles south, the landscapes Glencoe – perhaps the most infamous name in Scottish history – are equally awe inspiring.

From Fort William, the Road to the Isles and the Ardnamurchan peninsula – wild, and sometimes desolate, but always spectacular – are driving highlights if, in places, demanding for the driver. Ardnamurchan proves to be the westernmost point of the British mainland.

Wester Ross

The northwest Scottish seaboard is quintessential coastal Highland Scotland, combining mighty mountains, inspiring seascapes, glistening lochs with picture-postcard island castles, tiny crofter cottages and mysterious offshore islands.

From Ullapool you can explore Scotland's finest lochs – Maree, Broom and Assynt – drive the Bealach-na-Bo pass with its unsurpassed views, and enjoy the Falls of Measach.

There are surprises too, such as the world-class gardens of Inverewe, where palms flourish at a latitude north of Moscow and waves lap white sand beaches that wouldn't look out of place in the Caribbean. And then there are golf courses, such as the world-famous Royal Dornoch.

The Scottish mainland ends with a bang: northwest at wild, and difficult of access, Cape Wrath, and northeast – beyond the tourist fripperies of John o' Groats – with the 60m high exclamation marks of the Stacks of Duncansby.

Easter Head on the Dunnet Head peninsula is the northernmost point of the British mainland, and a certain target for all visitors this far north.

Inverness★

and around

Inverness stands at the northern end of the Great Glen, astride the outlet of Loch Ness. At the very hub of the Highlands roads and rail network, it has long been known as the capital of the Highlands and makes an ideal touring centre for much of the region.

A BIT OF HISTORY

Hub of the Highlands – The strategic importance of this site has been appreciated from earliest times as testified by the existence in the vicinity of a variety of ancient sites and monuments. St Columba is said to have visited Brude, King of the Picts, at his capital beside the Ness, although the exact site is unsure. By the 11C, King Duncan (c.1010–1040), made famous by Shakespeare, had his castle in the town. But the town's strategic importance was its downfall in later times when it suffered variously at the hands of the English, Robert the Bruce, turbulent Highland clans, the Lord of the Isles, Mary, Queen of Scots' supporters, and the Jacobites. The post-1715 Rising law and order policy for the Highlands, enacted by General Wade, included the creation of a citadel in Inverness, as one of several strategic strongholds in the Highland fringes.

Such a troubled history means that there remain few historic buildings in town. The architecture today is largely that of the 19C, one of expansion due in large to Telford's construction of the Caledonian Canal (1803–22) and the arrival of the railway.

SIGHTS

Inverness Castle

Several earlier castles have preceded the present 19C building which now serves as court house and administrative offices. The red sandstone structure evident today was built in 1836 by architect William Burn on the site of an 11C defensive structure.

The esplanade with the **statue** of Flora MacDonald affords a good **view** of the Ness and the town.

▶ **Population:** 63 220.

Info: 36 High Street ✆01463 252 401. www.inverness-scotland.com.

Don't Miss: A cruise on Loch Ness; "monster hunting" trips depart from Inverness and Fort Augustus. Northern Meeting Piping Competitions (*see Calendar of Events*) are held annually in Eden Court Theatre and are the oldest of all piping contests, dating back to 1781.

Kids: North Kessock Dolphin and Seal Visitor Centre; Loch Ness Monster Exhibition Centre.

Inverness Museum and Art Gallery★

Castle Wynd. ⏰*Apr–Oct Tue–Sat 10am–5pm; Nov–Mar Tue–Thu noon–4pm, Fri–Sat 11am–4pm.* ⏰*25–26 Dec, 1–2 Jan.* ✆*01349 781 730. www.highlifehighland.com.*

The imaginative and well-presented exhibition "Inverness, Hub of the Highlands" interprets the rich heritage of the Highlands. Topics of special local significance range from the Great Glen; the vitrified Fort Craig Phadrig (visible from the window); the Picts and their surviving works; the engineering feats of more recent times, such as the military roads of General Wade, Telford's Caledonian Canal and the Kessock Bridge. Exhibits on the Highland way of life include the former silver-producing centres of Inverness, Tain and Wick and there are a presentation pair of **Doune pistols** (*see DOUNE*) by John Murdoch. These guns of exquisite craftsmanship are dated c.1790.

Town House

At the foot of Castle Wynd.

This was the scene in 1921 of the first ever cabinet meeting outside London. The base of the mercat cross incorporates the

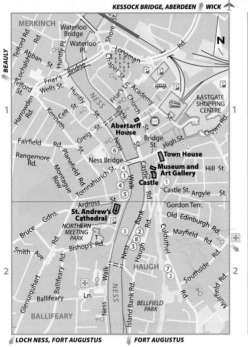

Clach-na-Cuddain or "stone of the tubs" used as a resting place by washerwomen on their way to and from the Ness. As long as the stone remains Inverness will continue to flourish. Along Church Street lies **Abertarff House**, a renovated 16C house which is the oldest in Inverness.

Inverness Cathedral

Ardross Street. ⏰*Daily 8am–5.30pm.* 📞*01463 237 503.*
www.invernesscathedral.co.uk.
This imposing richly decorated neo-Gothic edifice was built 1866–69 for the diocese of Moray, Ross and Caithness. The nave piers are columns of polished Peterhead granite. The choir screen and rood cross are by Robert Lorimer. A lack of funds precluded the construction of the two giant spires of architect Alexander Ross' original design.

Kessock Bridge

1.25mi/2km north on the A9.
Opened in 1982 this suspension bridge spanning the Beauly Firth carries the A9 north to the Black Isle. With a total length of 1 052m the bridge's main span has a clearance of 29m above high water. There is a good **view★** of Inverness from the bridge.

ADDITIONAL SIGHT

The **Scottish Dolphin Centre** at Spey Bay (*46mi/75km to the east*) ♿📇⏰*Daily: Apr–Sept 10.30am–5pm; Nov–mid-Dec Thu–Mon 10am–3pm; mid-Feb–Mar Thu–Mon 10.30am–3.30pm;* 📞*01343 820 339; https://dolphincentre.whales. org*) gives information on the marine life of the Moray and Beauly Firths. Bottlenose dolphins, harbour porpoises and upwards of 1 000 grey and common (harbour) seals inhabit these waters. You can not only watch seals and dolphins through binoculars, but, if you are lucky, you can also hear the seals' mating roars and the mysterious sounds emitted by the dolphins, with the aid of the centre's sophisticated listening equipment. The centre also suggests the best places to watch dolphins and seals nearby.

🚗 DRIVING TOURS

🚗 **1** LOCH NESS AND THE GREAT GLEN★
66mi/105km.

The geological fault of the Great Glen slices across the Highlands. From Loch Linnhe in the south, a series of freshwater lochs linked by stretches of the Caledonian Canal lead northwards to the Moray Firth. This corridor divides the Central and Northern Highlands.

Loch Ness provides the major tourist attraction, and this route along the shores of the loch from Inverness to Fort William can easily be followed in reverse.

Natural Avenue – From earliest times this route has been used to penetrate inland. Columba visited the Pictish King Brude at Inverness. Bruce appreciated the importance of its strongholds and in the 18C General Wade exploited this natural line of communication when he proposed a military road network linking the key garrison posts at Fort William, Fort Augustus and Inverness. Today the glen is one of the busiest tourist routes to the north.

Caledonian Canal – This feat of civil engineering was built between 1803 and 1822 to connect the North Sea and Atlantic Ocean and save vessels the treacherous waters of the Pentland Firth and the long haul round Cape Wrath. Initially proposed and surveyed by James Watt, the work was later supervised by **Thomas Telford** (1757–1834). The canal has a total length of 60mi/96km; lochs account for 38mi/61km while the remaining 22mi/35km were man-made.

Twenty-nine locks were required to deal with the varying levels of the lochs. The most spectacular series, known as **Neptune's Staircase** (⚫️*see FORT WILLIAM: Driving Tour*), is at Banavie near Fort William.

⊳ Leave Inverness to the southwest on the A82.

Loch Ness★★
Measuring some 23mi/37km long and with a maximum depth of 230m, it is

Nessie

The initial sighting of a large snake-like, hump-backed monster with a long thin neck in Loch Ness was made in the 6C by a monk. Despite various expeditions, using highly equipped submarines and state-of-the-art underwater surveillance, the loch has failed to reveal its secret. The exhibition centre at Drumnadrochit provides a good introduction both to the loch and to the Nessie story.

perhaps little wonder that Nessie (*see below*) has never been found in its dark waters. When the wind blows there are real waves on the loch which can make for very uncomfortable sailing for the many holiday cruisers who come here. However, in good weather its pastoral wooded shores are a beautiful sight. You have to be on the water to appreciate the loch however as a thick tree screen hides much of it (prior to Drumnadrochit) from the road.

Drumnadrochit
This neat little lochside village is best known for the **Loch Ness Exhibition Centre★**👥👤 (♿🕐*daily Apr–Jun and Sept–Oct 9.30am–5pm; Jul–Aug 9.30am–6pm; Nov–Mar 10am–3.30pm;* ⊕*£8.45; child 6–15, £4.95;* ✕🅿️; ✆*01456 450 573; www.lochness.com*), a hi-tech multi-media presentation through seven themed areas of the loch's history, mystery and legend.

Examine the evidence (or lack of) and judge for yourself. There are, of course, the famous fake monster photographs and all kinds of scientific and non-scientific theories.

Urquhart Castle
Fairly steep path and stairs down to the castle. 🕐*Daily Apr–Sept 9.30am–6pm (Jun–Aug 8pm); Oct 9.30am–5pm; Nov–Mar 9.30am–4.30pm.* 🕐*25–26 Dec.* ⊕*£12.* ✆*01456 450 551. www.historicenvironment.scot.*

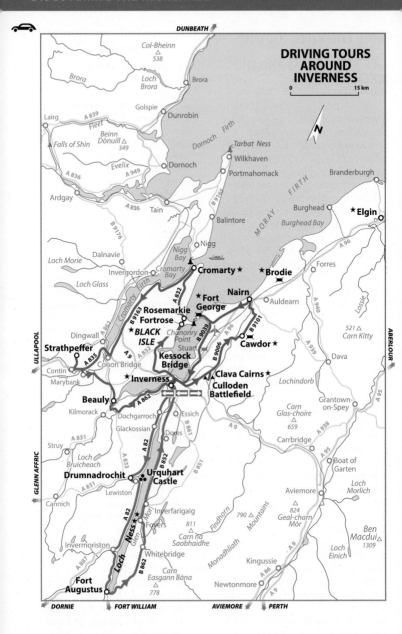

DRIVING TOURS AROUND INVERNESS

0   15 km

These much-photographed castle ruins are strategically set on a rocky promontory jutting into Loch Ness.

Urquhart was one of a chain of strongholds garrisoning the Great Glen, a fact which gave it a turbulent history which is interpreted in the exhibition and audio-visual display in the new visitor centre, alongside medieval artefacts found at the castle.

Seen from the roadside, the various parts are easy to distinguish. The gatehouse on the landward side gives access to a double bailey courtyard. To the right the Norman motte is encircled by walls. On the seaward side, beyond the water

Loch Ness and Urquhart Castle

© Jiangli/iStockphoto.com

gate are the basements of a domestic range and on the left the four-storeyed tower house.

From the viewing platform (*50 steps*) there are good views of the castle's layout and up and down Loch Ness. There is a good view of the northern part of Loch Ness as the road descends to Drumnadrochit.

Fort Augustus

This busy little town at the southern end of Loch Ness sits astride the Caledonian Canal and its many locks.

It's a good place to come and watch the boats crossing the staircase of locks but its swingbridge is a bottleneck for road traffic.

▶ From Fort Augustus, return to Inverness along the eastern shore of Loch Ness on the B862 and B852, via Foyers.

🚗 2 AROUND NAIRN

43mi/69km.

Culloden is signposted from Inverness city centre. The site of the battlefield, however, lies to the south of the B9006.

Culloden

♿ 🕐 *Visitor centre: daily: 27 Dec–Feb and Nov–23 Dec 10am–4pm; Mar–May and Sept–Oct 9am–6pm; Jun–Aug 9am–7pm: Battlefield: daily, all year.*

🕐 *24–26 Dec, 1–2 Jan.* 🎧 *£11 (inc. audio tour).* ✕ ☎ *01463 796090. www.nts.org.uk.*

On 16 April 1746 this bleak moor saw the end of the Jacobite Rising of 1745 when Prince Charles Edward Stuart's army was defeated by a government army under the Duke of Cumberland, the younger son of King George II. After months in hiding as a fugitive the prince escaped to France and lifelong exile.

A dynamic **visitor centre** features interactive characters that witnessed or were involved in the battle. In the Battle Immersion Theatre a 4-minute, 360-degree film relives the horror of the battle. There are also exhibits of weapons and artefacts found on the battlefield.

The **Old Leanach Cottage** – which survived the battle – has been restored as it was at the time of the battle. Stones and monuments mark the graves of

Boat Trips

The Caledonian Canal is used principally by pleasure craft and is operated by the British Waterways Board. Enquire locally about cruiser operators: some offer monster hunting systems as an option. Several companies operate cruises on Loch Ness with departures from Inverness and Fort Augustus.

the clans. A hand-held audio device is available to take onto the battlefield to help you further understand the armies' manoeuvres and tactics.

▶ From the visitor centre, follow the signs to Clava Cairns.

Clava Cairns★

Head east on the A9 and the B9006. Turn right at the Cumberland Stone then continue for 1mi/1.6km.

This impressive site includes three cairns, girdled by stone circles, and a small ring of boulders. The middle cairn was a ring-cairn with its centre always open to the sky. The two others, now unroofed, had entrance passages leading to a burial chamber. Some of the stones of the cairns bear cup marks. The complex dates c.4400–2000 BCE, and each cairn and stone ring formed a single design.

▶ From Culloden, drive towards Croy on the B9006, then follow signs to Clephanton and Cawdor.

Cawdor Castle★

◷*Daily mid-Apr–early Oct 10am–5.30pm.* ☞*£12.50.* ✗ ✆*01667 404 401. www.cawdorcastle.com.*
Cawdor is the title that Shakespeare's witches promised to Macbeth. The Thanes of Cawdor built the castle and lived in it from the late 14C.

Cawdor Castle

© Salvatore Conte/iStockphoto.com

The Scottish Play – William Shakespeare wrote *The Tragedie of Macbeth* in 1606. Its narrative of witches, prophecy, treason, execution and murder were topics that fascinated King James VI of Scotland. This opportunity was not lost on the Bard, who put the finishing touches to his script in time for a special royal performance at Hampton Court that summer to entertain the king. The history books tell us that Macbeth did indeed slay King Duncan, but as Cawdor Castle was not built until the late 14C and Macbeth was born c.1005 then it is impossible for Duncan to have lost any blood or Lady Macbeth to have lost much sleep in this particular castle!

Exterior – The approach to the castle from the drawbridge side gives a view of the central tower, which is the 14C keep with the 17C wings to the right. Later additions and transformations created the fairy-tale-like castle of today.

Interior – In the Drawing Room, the original great hall, Francis Cote's **portrait of Pryse Campbell**, 18th Thane of Cawdor, shows him resplendently attired in an assortment of tartans. This ardent Jacobite defied all by having himself portrayed thus in 1762, during the period of Proscription of Highland dress. The painting also helps to prove that the idea of one clan, one sett (pattern) was in reality a concept of the 19C. Emma Hamilton, a friend of John, 1st Lord Cawdor and his wife, is portrayed by Romney.

The **Tapestry Bedroom** is so named after the set of 17C Flemish tapestries depicting events from the life of Noah. The imposing 17C Venetian four-poster retains its original velvet hangings. The Yellow Room is a good example of Jacobean design. The centre window of the Tower Sitting Room was the original, and only, entrance to the castle in the 14C, served by removable wooden steps. The fine set of 17C Bruges tapestries is after designs by Rubens on the theme of the house's thorn tree legend. The **Thorn Tree Room** is a vaulted chamber, where the remains of a holly tree have been carbon dated back to 1372. By legend it is the original marker for the site of the castle and is also an ancient pagan symbol to ward off evil.

Antwerp tapestries grace the front stairs while the Dining Room has English panels (c.1690) showing scenes from Cervantes' *Don Quixote* and a most unusual carved stone fireplace.

The walled **garden, flower garden and wild gardens** are well worth a visit as is the **Big Wood** which is particularly lovely in spring. Red deer occasionally enter the wood.

▶ Take the B9090 north to Nairn.

Nairn

This favourite seaside resort, on the southern shore of the Moray Firth, is popular thanks to a combination of sun (it is one of the driest and sunniest places in Scotland), sea, sand and golf (two good courses). It is an ideal touring centre.

▶ Leave Nairn on the A96; at the golf course take the B9092.

Fort George★

&⊙*Daily: Apr–Sept 9.30am–5.30pm; Oct–Mar 10am–4pm.* ⊙*25–26 Dec, 1–2 Jan.* ⊛*£9.* ✕ ☎*01667 460 232. www.historicenvironment.scot.*

Set on a peninsula jutting into the Moray Firth, this outstanding artillery fortress was built 1748–69 to serve as a stronghold for the troops of George II. It is impressive both in its size and its elaborate defences. Although Fort George is a working army barracks, the public may visit several of its buildings, where displays and audiovisual presentations give a glimpse into the living and working conditions in an 18C fort. Beyond the emblazoned main gate and entrance tunnel are **guardrooms** for the officers and regular soldiers. The **historic barrack rooms** show the evolution in living conditions with two rank and file rooms from 1780 and 1868. The 1813 Officer's Room is surprisingly spartan. The **grand magazine** was the store for 2 500 powder barrels. A plain galleried **chapel** stands on its own. The Lieutenant-Governor's and fort major's houses are now occupied

by the **Queen's Own Highlanders Regimental Museum** (⊙*daily Apr–Sept 9.30am–5.30pm; Oct–Mar 10am–4pm; www.thehighlandersmuseum.com*). The history of the regiment is evoked through displays of uniforms, colours, weapons, campaigns, medals, and militia silver.

⟵ ③ BLACK ISLE AND STRATHPEFFER★

75mi/120km.

Despite its name, the Black Isle is actually a verdant peninsula of fertile farmland surrounded by the Cromarty, Beauly and Moray Firths. Allow at least a day in Cromarty, and try to stay overnight to appreciate the peace of the town.

▶ Leave Inverness on the A9, heading north. Turn right onto the B9161.

Fortrose

This busy little town is Black Isle's chief community of the. Away from the bustle of the main street, the remnant of the **cathedral church** makes an attractive picture in its peaceful **setting★** of green lawns enclosed by the charming red sandstone houses of the former close. The remaining south aisle has attractive vaulting and the damaged tomb of its builder, Euphemia, Countess of Ross, widow of the Wolf of Badenoch. The detached two-storey building may have been a sacristy and chapter house.

▶ About one minute's drive along the A832 northeast of Fortrose is the village of Rosemarkie.

Rosemarkie

The Black Isle has a concentration of prehistoric and Pictish sites and **Groam House Museum** (⊙*early Apr–Oct Mon–Fri 11am–4.30pm, Sat–Sun 2–4.30pm; Nov Sat–Sun 2–4pm;* ☎*01381 620 961; www.groamhouse.org.uk*) displays 15 intricately carved Pictish standing stones including the famous Rosemarkie Cross Slab. All the stones on display originated in Rosemarkie, some dating back to the 8C, when it was an important centre of early Christianity.

▶ Head north along the A832 to Cromarty.

Cromarty★

Dramatically sited on the northern tip of the Black Isle the tiny port of Cromarty has been described as "the jewel in the crown of Scottish (18C–19C) vernacular architecture".

Cromarty was a 13C Royal Burgh, but owes much of its present appearance and allure to its development in the late 18C by Sir George Ross, who encouraged a high standard of building and rebuilding, improved the harbour, and established industries, including a ropeworks (now housing) and a brewery (now a university study centre). A ferry, once used by royal pilgrims to the shrine at Tain, still operates across the deep water of the Firth, but since the building of the railway and the improvement of roads, Cromarty no longer lies on the main route north. Today it is little more than a village and popular holiday backwater.

Hugh Miller Museum & Birthplace Cottage

&⊙*End Mar–Sept daily 1–5pm; Oct Tue, Thu–Fri 1–5pm.* ⊛*£6.50.* 🅿 ℘*01381 600 245. www.nts.org.uk.*
Cromarty's most famous son, **Hugh Miller** (1802–1856), was a mason turned writer and geologist. His birthplace, a thatched cottage with crow-step gables, is now a museum, with a collection of geological specimens (including some outstanding fossils) and souvenirs.

Cromarty Courthouse Museum

⊙*Apr–mid-Oct daily noon–4pm.* ℘*01381 600 418. www.cromarty-courthouse.org.uk.*
Built by Sir George Ross in 1773, the courthouse is a splendid five-bay structure dominated by an octagonal clock tower. The interior gives a good account of local history, while courtroom scenes are brought to life by talking figures.

Ecoventures

⊙*Trips (2h) depart Cromarty Harbour Apr–Oct. Call for sailing times.* ⊛*£31 (child 5–12, £24.* ℘*01381 600 323. www.ecoventures.co.uk.*
High speed RIBs (rigid inflatable boats) scoot out to visit the most northerly colony (around 130 in total) of bottlenose dolphins in the world, one of only two resident populations in the UK.

▶ Leave Cromarty on the B9163 along the north coast of the Black Isle. At Conon Bridge, the view back out along the Cromarty Firth (and its oil rigs beyond) is magnificent.

▶ At Conon Bridge take the A835 towards Ullapool and at Contin turn right along the A834 to Strathpeffer.

Strathpeffer

Framed by monkey puzzle trees and other exotic conifers, the ornate villas and hotels of this delightful Victorian spa town adorn the slopes at the head of a lush valley. Strathpeffer had its heyday in the years before World War when a branch railway line up the valley from Dingwall enabled well-heeled visitors to arrive by direct sleeping car express from London. A small pump room and the spa pavilion survive, and the water may be "taken" in The Square.

Highland Museum of Childhood

&⊙*Apr–Oct Tue–Sat 10am–5pm, Sun 12.30–4pm.* ⊛*£3.* 🅿 ℘*01997 421 031. https://highlandmuseumofchildhood. org.uk.*
Strathpeffer's pretty station building, complete with a glazed canopy on ornate cast-iron columns, survived the closing of the railway in 1951 and part of it now houses a charming little Museum of Childhood including a fine collection of doll's houses.

▶ Return towards Contin, and retrace your route along the A835. At Marybank take the A832. At Muir of Ord follow the A862 to Beauly.

Beauly

In a sheltered position at the head of the Beauly Firth this delightful village takes its name *Beau Lieu* from the 13C Burgundian monks who founded a priory here.

▶ The A862 follows the south bank of the Beauly Firth and returns you to Inverness.

ADDRESSES

🛏 STAY

MacDonald House Hotel – *1 Ardross Terrace. ☎01463 232 878. www.macdonaldhouse.net. 11 rooms.* The MacDonald House is family owned and is more a B&B/guest house than hotel. It enjoys a superb situation in one of the most picturesque areas of Inverness, on the banks of the River Ness.

Premier Inn, Inverness – *www.premierinn.com.* There are four Premier Inns in Inverness, all less close to the city centre: Millburn Road, River Ness, West (on the Caledonian Canal) and East. All offer standardised accommodation at seasonal prices, with a budget eatery adjoining or nearby.

Glen Mhor Hotel – *7–17 Ness Bank. ☎01463 234 308. www.glen-mhor. com. 110 rooms and apartments.* Beneath the castle and on the river, this very smart hotel consists of eight Victorian town houses and offers a range of trad-contemporary rooms, each with their own character and varying prices. It has a particularly good bar and the excellent **Nicky Tam's restaurant and Bar** 🍽🍽 serving classic Scottish dishes.

Glenmoriston Town House – *20 Ness Bank. ☎01463 223 777. www. glenmoristontownhouse.com. 30 rooms and 3 apartments.* A 5min walk from the town centre, this first class luxury town house hotel offers trad-contemporary bedrooms (some with river views); a piano-bar offering 260 malt whiskies and over 50 artisanal gins. Restaurant (🍽🍽) – 👍*see right.*

Inverness Palace Hotel & Spa – *8 Ness Walk. ☎01463 223 243. www. invernesspalacehotel.co.uk. 88 rooms.* This Victorian Baronial-style pile sits on the river opposite the castle, offering individually designed contemporary and classically styled bedrooms. All Best Western mod cons and luxuries including a health club and a beauty spa with pool.

The Waterside – *19 Ness Bank. ☎01463 233 065. www.thewaterside inverness.co.uk.* This is a privately owned hotel in Inverness which comprises two river side properties located on the beautiful banks of the River Ness. The integral à la carte **restaurant** serves a delicious menu using local produce sourced for its taste and freshness.

Rocpool Reserve – *14 Culduthel Road. ☎01463 240 089. www.rocpool.com. 11 rooms.* A stylish boutique hotel with a chic lounge and minimalist bedrooms, some with terraces, hot tubs or saunas. **Chez Roux Restaurant** (🍽🍽) – 👍*see below.*

Columba Hotel – *7 Ness Walk. ☎01463 231 391. www. columbahotelinverness.co.uk. 82 rooms.* This grand historic hotel with bright airy rooms enjoys views of the river and castle, but is blighted by road traffic.

🍴 EAT

Café 1 – *Castle Street. ☎01463 226 200. www.cafe1.net.* Busy, popular bistro opposite the castle. Good value set lunches and à la carte menu.

Chez Roux – *Rocpool Reserve Hotel, 14 Culduthel Road. ☎01463 240 089. www. rocpool.com.* French inspired menu in this small, modern restaurant in the Rocpool Reserve Hotel (👍*see above*).

Rocpool – *1 Ness Walk. ☎01463 717 274. www.rocpoolrestaurant.com.* Well-run and deservedly popular restaurant on the banks of the River Ness, serving dishes with a Mediterranean edge (*Booking essential*).

Contrast Brasserie – *Glenmoriston Town House Hotel, 20 Ness Bank. ☎01463 223 777. www. glenmoristontownhouse.com.* Arguably the finest restaurant in town, where a French team serves up gourmet modern French cuisine; and a chic yet relaxed brasserie, **with** two- and three-course lunches and pre-theatre menus (*5–6.30pm*) Mon–Fri year-round.

Fort William★

Fort William lies on the shore of Loch Linnhe below Britain's highest mountain, Ben Nevis. The town developed around a succession of strategically sited strongholds and forts at the southern end of the Great Glen and today it is still the main town of the Lochaber District. In summer Fort William is crowded with holidaymakers as it makes an ideal touring centre from which to discover the beauty of the surrounding countryside. Highlights of the tourist calendar are the Ben Nevis Race and the Glen Nevis River Race. The Nevis Range ski resort brings the town to life during the winter months.

▶ **Population:** 10 340.
🖫 **Info:** 15 High Street. ℘01397 701 801. www.visitfortwilliam.co.uk.
⌖ **Don't Miss:** Glen Nevis; the Road to the Isles; the Glenfinnan Gathering and Highland Games; the Ardnamurchan Peninsula.
🕐 **Timing:** Allow at least 3 days.
👪 **Kids:** The Silver Sands of Morar.

SIGHT

West Highland Museum

Cameron Square. 🕐*Jan–Apr and Oct– Dec Mon–Sat 10am–4pm; May–Sept Mon–Sat 10am–5pm (Jul–Aug also Sun 11am–3pm).* 🕐*25–26 Dec.* ℘*01397 702 169.* *www.westhighlandmuseum.org.uk.* This local museum covers a wide variety of topics, including the Caledonian Canal, Ben Nevis, the former fort, crofting and Jacobite relics. From soldiers to crofters, princes to clergymen, all sections of the West Highlands community are represented.

EXCURSIONS

Ben Nevis★★

4mi/6.4km to the southeast. *Start of the footpath: Parking area at Achintee Farm. Access by footpath: 4h–5h ascent and 3h descent by a well-marked but very rugged path.* This rather shapeless granite mass (*alt. 1 345m*), is Britain's highest peak, extremely popular with climbers and walkers. Prospective walkers should be appropriately experienced, clad (boots and waterproofs) and equipped (whistle, map, food, etc). At the summit, with its war memorial, once stood a hotel (closed in 1915) and an observatory. There is an annual fell race to the summit and back, held in September. The current records – men, 1hr 25min 34sec; women, 1hr 43min 25sec – have not been bettered since 1984.

Jacobite Steam Train

© Thomas Heymann/imageBROKER/age fotostock

Glen Nevis★

The road follows the south bank of the River Nevis for 10mi/16km round the foot of Ben Nevis (though there is no view of the summit). The glen road terminates at a parking area from which a pleasant 🚶 walking path continues through a narrow rocky gorge into the upper glen and the Steall waterfall. The "bridge" across the Water of Nevis is not for the faint-hearted.

Nevis Range

Torlundy. 4mi/6.4km north by A82.
This well-designed resort is the newest of the five Scottish Ski Centres, and boasts the most modern facilities for learning to ski and snowboard. Moreover it offers the highest skiing in Scotland, with an enviable record for good snow conditions running late into the season.

A **gondola** (cable-car) service (♿ ⏰ *Apr–Jun daily 10am–5pm; Jun–Sept daily 9.30am–6pm; weather permitting; check website for winter hours (Dec–Mar) and charges for gondola passes; ⏰Nov; ☎01397 705 825; www.nevisrange.co.uk*) makes the 655m up the slope of Aonach Mor to the ski resort in just 12 minutes. There are great **views★★** of Skye, Rhum, the Great Glen and the surrounding mountains. The **Mountain Discovery Centre**, located at the top station, interprets the wildlife, mountain habitat and landscape with interactive displays and video footage.

In summer the resort also offers many activities such as dry slope skiing, mountain biking, and mountain and forest walks.

Jacobite Steam Train★★

Departs from Fort William. ⏰Late Apr–late Oct Mon–Fri 10.15am and 2.30pm, plus Sat–Sun May–Sept. ⊗£37.75 (child £20.75) return, standard class. ☎0844 850 4685. www.westcoastrailways.co.uk.
Operated by West Coast Railways, the Jacobite steam train links Fort William and Mallaig, an 45-mile journey through magnificent scenery and crossing the Glenfinnan Viaduct (Ḃ*see below*) that

features in several *Harry Potter* films, and visits Morar and the silvery beaches used in the films *Highlander* and *Local Hero*.

Commando Memorial★

The monument, to the left of the A82, northeast of Fort William, is a memorial to all Commandos who lost their lives in the World War II. The site overlooks their training area at Achnacarry Castle. The memorial was inveiled by the Queen Mother in 1952, and it has become one of the country's best-known monuments both as a war memorial and as a tourist attractrion. It commands as splendid view: Ben Nevis can be seen to the southwest rising above the domes of Aonach Mor.

🚗 DRIVING TOUR

🚗 1 ROAD TO THE ISLES★★
43mi/69km, one way.

This scenic route, often very busy, passes through landscapes rich in historical associations to the town of Mallaig, one of the ferry ports for Skye and other Inner Hebridean isles.

▶ Leave Fort William by the Inverness road, A82, passing on the way the ruins of Inverlochy Castle. Turn left to Mallaig taking A830.

Neptune's Staircase

This flight of eight locks at Banavie was designed by Telford as part of the **Caledonian Canal** to raise the water level 19m in 457m.

From Corpach, with its paper mill (pulping operations ceased in 1980), there are magnificent retrospective **views★★** of Ben Nevis.

Treasures of the Earth

Corpach. ⏰Daily: Mar–Jun and Sept–Oct 10am–5pm; Jul–Aug 9.30am–6pm; Nov–Feb 10am–4pm. ⊗£6 (child 5–15, £4). ☎01397 772 283; www.treasuresoftheearth.co.uk.
Experience a fine private collection of crystals, gemstones and fossils, housed

in an atmospheric simulation of caves, caverns and mining scenes.

▷ The road follows the northern shore of Loch Eil, the westward continuation of Loch Linnhe.

Glenfinnan Monument Visitor Centre

🕐 *Daily: Nov–Feb 10am–4pm; Mar and Oct 9.30am–5pm; Apr–Sept 9am–7pm.* 🚗*£4.* ✕ 📞*01397 722 250. www.nts.org.uk.*

In a glorious setting at the head of **Loch Shiel** stands the monument (built 1815) to commemorate those who died while following Prince Charles Edward Stuart in the 1745 rising.

Here, five days after the prince's landing at nearby Loch nan Uamh, the standard was raised before a 1 300-strong army of Highlanders. The "Year of the Prince" ended 14 months later when he left for France from near the same spot.

From the top of the tower (🚶 *61 steps with an awkward trap door exit to viewing area*) there is a splendid **view** of Loch Shiel framed by the mountains, and northwards over the much photographed, many spanned **Glenfinnan Railway Viaduct** made famous by the flying car sequence in the *Harry Potter* films as part of the Hogwarts Express train route.

The **Glenfinnan Gathering and Highland Games** is held annually at the foot of the monument on the second or third Saturday in August.

▷ Beyond Glenfinnan, the road and railway part company to go either side of landlocked Loch Eilt. After the Lochailort turn-off, the road passes the head of the sea loch, Loch Ailort, before rising to cross the neck of the Ardnish peninsula.

The road runs along Loch nan Uamh, (*pronounced loch nan oo-av*) providing a seaward **view★** of the Sound of Arisaig. Down on the foreshore of the north side a **cairn** marks the spot where Prince Charles Edward Stuart came ashore on 19 July 1745.

▷ The road then follows Beasdale valley, and soon crosses to Borrodale valley.

Arisaig★

This scattered community looks over the **Sound of Arisaig**. Cruises leave from the pier for Rhum, Eigg and Muck. Beyond Arisaig, the rocky shore is interrupted by a series of sandy bays, the most famous being the **⚑▲White Sands of Morar★**, known for their white silica sand, which featured prominently in the 1983 cult film *Local Hero*.

A number of the houses in the area were used as training schools by the Special Operations Executive during the Second World War, and the **Land, Sea and Islands Centre** (🕐*Apr–Oct Mon–Sat 10am–6pm, Sun 11am–5pm; Nov–Mar Mon 10am–1pm, Sat 10am–4pm, Sun 11am–4pm.* 📞*01687 450 771; www.arisaiginfo.org.uk*) has changing displays on the connection between the area and military activities.

Morar

The village lies at the entrance to Loch Morar, the deepest inland loch (over 305m deep), inhabited by a monster Morag, "sister" to Nessie.

Morar was a popular holiday base for the English composer, **Sir Arnold Bax** (1883–1953), who spent time here in the 1930s working on his Third Symphony.

Mallaig★

The houses spill down the slopes overlooking the bay, sheltered by two headlands. This fishing port is the terminal for the Skye and Small Isles ferries.

🚗 ② ARDNAMURCHAN PENINSULA★★★

150mi/240km. Allow two days if intending to complete the whole itinerary. It is a long and demanding journey for the driver. There are several places en route where accommodation is available, but booking in advance is essential at any time of year.

Ardnamurchan is a 50 sq mi/130 sq km peninsula noted for its unspoilt and undisturbed remoteness, accessed only by a single track road with passing places.

The lighthouse (✗café nearby) lies beyond a surprise, and arguably Britain's most remote, set of traffic lights, and is commonly regarded as the westernmost point of the British mainland, although Corrachadh Mòr, a kilometre to the south, is a little further west.

Since it was first surveyed in 1932 the area of Ardnamurchan has been of great interest to scientists from all over the world who come to study its remarkable cratering record.

☺ Anyone visiting the Isle of Mull can reach Ardnamurchan directly by car ferry from Tobermory to Kilchoan (*www.calmac.co.uk*).

◖ Follow the A830 to Lochailort (as above), then branch south onto the A861, skirting the Sound of Arisaig with views of Eigg and Muck. Continue past Loch Moidart and the tip of Loch Shiel to Salen, then on the B8007 along Loch Sunart and on by a devious route to Ardnamurchan Point.

Ardnamurchan Natural History Centre, Glenmore

🕐*Apr–early Nov Sun–Fri 8.30am–5pm.* 🕐*Sat.* ✗ ✆*01972 500 209. www.ardnamurchannatural historycentre.co.uk.*

A fascinating introduction to Ardnamurchan's wild landscape, flora and fauna including the chance to view golden eagles. Free wildlife exhibition.

Ardnamurchan Point★★

Crowned by a lighthouse, Ardnamurchan Point offers dramatic **views★★** out across the Atlantic.

From the Ardnamurchan road, a minor road leads out to **Sanna Bay** ♣♣, one of Scotland's finest strands with pure white beach and turquoise seas. This is remarkable countryside, wild, rugged, almost primeval, indeed at Sanna, is a so-called "impact" crater, although in fact the product of volcanic activity rather than spacial impact.

◖ Return to Salen and bear right onto the A861 for a scenic run via the village of Strontian and through Glen Tarbert to Corran. Keep north along the west shore of Loch Linnhe and later the south bank of Loch Eil to Kinlocheil. Then take the A830 back to Fort William. ✆*There is an alternative, route back to Fort William by using the ferry at Corran to Inchtree and then the A82 north. This will reduce the distance by 23mi/37km, but probably not much saving in time if you have to wait overlong for the ferry.*

⊂⊐ ③ GLENCOE★★

28mi/44km, to Kingshouse on the edge of Rannoch Moor – one way.

This short tour follows the A82 from Fort William through the glen to the the wild expanse of Rannoch Moor. The splendid glen with its stark and grandiose mountain scenery lies on the principal tourist route from Glasgow to the north. The glen is splendid in either direction, so this tour runs as far as Kingshouse, where there is a hotel, and returns from there. Awe inspiring in sunshine, Glencoe is dramatically more memorable in menacing weather.

Glencoe village

On the shores of Loch Leven the village boasts a small museum, **Glencoe Folk Museum** (🕐*Apr–Oct Mon–Sat 10am–4.30pm;* ✺*£3;* ✆*01855 811 664; www.glencoemuseum.com*). Note the glassware engraved with the white rose of the Jacobites, the museum's Lochaber war axes – introduced to Scotland around 1300, some were still in use in 1745 – and the exhibit on the local slate industry.

Glencoe Visitor Centre

♿🕐*Apr–Oct daily 9am–6pm; Nov–Mar daily 10am–4pm.* 🕐*24–26 and 31 Dec, 1–2 Jan.* 🅿*£4.* ✗ ✆*01855 811 307. www.nts.org.uk.*

The Visitor Centre provides a good introduction, both historical and geological, to the famous glen and its environs. Guided walks and Land Rover safaris

Buachaille Etive Mor, Glen Coe

© Denis Palanque/hemis.fr

are available and a ranger will help with advice on hill walking and climbing.

Glen Coe

Glen Coe is a vast and narrow glaciated valley, although originally the product of an ancient super volcano active about 420 million years ago. The road through the glen is the main road north, and so popular on that account alone. But the scenery is everything here whether entering the glen from the west, from the village of Glencoe or from the east, when the most distinctive herald is the mass of Buachaille Etive Mor.

On the northern flank of the glen the great unbroken and serrated ridge of **Aonach Eagach** (The Notched Heights) continues for 3mi/5km. One local climber warns that there are no other ridges in the area that are "...so narrow and so difficult to escape from once committed. Some sections are extremely exposed". On the southern side are the so-called Three Sisters, outliers of the great nine-peaked **Bidean nam Bian** (*Peak of the Bens: alt. 1 150m*). The Sisters lie from east to west: Beinn Fhada (The Long Mountain), Gearr Aonach (The Short Ridge) and Aonach Dubh (The Black

The Massacre of Glencoe

Highland loyalties ran deep to the Stuart cause and when James VII's short reign (1685–88) ended in flight, the clans were reluctant to renounce the cause. After the Convention had offered the Scottish crown to William and Mary in March 1689, John Graham of Claverhouse rallied the Highlanders. But despite victory at Killiecrankie on 27 July 1689, defeat came a month later at Dunkeld. William proposed a pardon to all clans willing to take an oath of allegiance by 1 January 1692. Alastair Maclain, chief of the MacDonalds of Glencoe, arrived in Fort William within the deadline, only to be sent to Inveraray where he finally took the oath on 6 January. Paperwork confirming that the oath had been sworn on time however was mislaid and a plot was hatched to make an example of Maclain and his clan.

At the beginning of February a force of 120 men, under Campbell of Glenlyon, was billeted on the MacDonalds of Glencoe and for 12 days all cohabited peacefully. Treachery struck on the 13th with the slaughter of 38 of their hosts, including Maclain, and the burning of their homes. Another 40 subsequently perished of exposure out in the winter wilds. An official enquiry confirmed that although the king had given orders to punish the clan, his minister, the Master of Stair, undoubtedly exceeded them. Murder was common in these times but even then, "Murder under Trust" was a most heinous crime.

Ridge). Between the first two, although not visible from the glen, is Coire Gabhail (Hidden Valley) where the MacDonalds hid plundered cattle.

The eastern end of the glen is occupied by the conically shaped Buachaille Etive Mor (*alt. 1 022m*), which guards the entrance to the glen and offers a challenge to the rock climber.

Across the glen from Buachille Etive Mor, the zigzags of the **Devil's Staircase**, a series of hairpin bends on the old military road leading over to Kinlochleven, is regularly followed by walkers undertaking the West Highland Way. The Devil's Staircase was given its name by soldiers working on the road building programme of General Wade, because of the difficulties of carrying building materials up that stretch of the road.

At the eastern end of the glen traces can still be found of the old road, followed by William Wordsworth and his sister Dorothy on their "holiday" to Scotland in 1803.

Rannoch Moor

Other than the A82, no road disturbs the isolation of this desolate moorland, and few routes exist through its convoluted and marshy expanse. This expanse was at the heart of the last significant icefield in the UK during the Loch Lomond Stadial at the end of the last ice age. Rannoch Moor is designated a Site of Special Scientific Interest (SSSI) and a Special Area of Conservation.

Kingshouse

Kingshouse is the name of the place; Kings House, the hotel thought to be one of Scotland's oldest licensed inns, originally built in the 17C. It was sited at the head of Glen Coe for travellers crossing Rannoch Moor.

Dorothy Wordsworth, however, was not impressed, writing: *"Never did I see such a miserable, such wretched place, – long rooms with ranges of beds, no other furniture except benches, or perhaps one or two crazy chairs, the floors far dirtier than an ordinary house could be if it were never washed."*

ADDRESSES

🛏 STAY

FORT WILLIAM

🛏🛏 **Lawriestone Guest House** – *Achintore Road.* 𝄞*01397 705 849. www. lawriestone.co.uk. 4 rooms.* This Victorian house, just a 5min walk from the town centre, enjoys views over Loch Linnhe and has spacious airy rooms.

🛏🛏 **Premier Inn** – *Loch Iall, An Airds Way.* 𝄞*0871 527 8402. www.premierinn.com.* A chain hotel with standardised rooms. Brewers Fayre **Restaurant** (🛏🛏) next door. Close by the railway/bus station.

🛏🛏🛏 **Ashburn House** – *18 Achintore Road.* 𝄞*01397 706 000. www.ashburn house.co.uk. 7 rooms.* This luxury Victorian B&B overlooks Loch Linnhe, a 5min walk from the town centre. Bedrooms are beautifully furnished; comfortable conservatory lounge.

GLENCOE

🛏🛏 **The Glencoe Hotel** – *Tyndrum Road.* 𝄞*01855 811 245. www.crerarhotels.com/ the-glencoe-inn. 15 rooms.* This hotel has a stunning setting in the shadow of the Pap of Glencoe and surrounded by the beautiful Ardgour Hills.

🛏🛏🛏 **Kings House Hotel** – *Glencoe.* 𝄞*01855 851 259. www.kingshousehotel. co.uk.* Long-established inn/hotel at the easterly entrance to Glen Coe, and directly on the West Highland Way. Bunkhouse (🛏). **Restaurant** and bars.

🍴 EAT

FORT WILLIAM

🛏 **The Grog and Gruel** – *66 High Street.* 𝄞*01397 705 078. www.grogandgruel.co.uk.* This traditional alehouse and restaurant is in the centre of Fort William and provides a warm and friendly atmosphere.

🛏🛏 **Garrison West** – *4 Cameron Square.* 𝄞*01397 701 873. www.garrisonwest.co.uk.* This town centre restaurant is good for lunch and dinner in hearty portions.

🛏🛏 **Lime Tree Restaurant** – *Achintore Road.* 𝄞*01397 701 806. www. limetreefortwilliam.co.uk.* Housed in the Lime Tree Hotel (accommodation 🛏🛏) this rustic dining room has exposed beams and an open kitchen.

Thurso

Most visitors use this small town as a gateway to the Orkneys, from Thurso's car ferry port, Scrabster, to Stromness. Busy in summer, it also makes a good centre for visiting the very scenic north coast, from Durness to Duncansby Head.

The origins of this north-facing **Caithness** town go back to Norse times, but the oldest (and most interesting) part of the present town is medieval, and overlooks the harbour at the mouth of the River Thurso.

There are many dignified late Georgian/ early Victorian houses, many of them built with thick walls of blue Caithness flintstone. In the 1950s and 60s the town expanded threefold in response to the construction of the nearby Dounreay nuclear power station (♨ *see Box, below*).

🚗 DRIVING TOURS

🚗 ① NORTHEAST COAST THURSO TO WICK★
75mi/120 km.

This excursion takes in the northeastern tip of the Scottish mainland, notable for its magnificent coastal scenery.

▷ Leave Thurso on the A836 east.

Sheltered coves and sandy bays alternate with giddily steep cliffs, rock stacks, natural arches and bridges, and narrow inlets, known locally as goes.

▷ **Population:** 7 610.
🛈 **Info:** http://thursotown.co.uk.
◉ **Location:** Thurso is 20mi/32km west of John o' Groats on the A 836.
☺ **Don't Miss:** The views from Strathy Point; the views of the Kyle of Tongue from Torrisdale Bay; view of Loch Eriboll.
👫 **Kids:** The beach at nearby Dunnet Bay.

Rock ledges are the home of guillemots, shags, fulmars, kittiwakes, a variety of gulls and other species.

Castletown
London's famous Strand was paved with Caithness flagstones, exported from the little harbour at Castletown. Other reminders of the more prosperous times of the 19C and early 20C are the stump of a windmill, a dam, and the quarry workers' cottage. The industry was killed off by the introduction of concrete paving slabs.

▷ Continue on the A836 8.5mi/13.7km eastwards to the village of Dunnet.

Mary-Ann's Cottage
Westside Dunnet. ♿ 🕙 *Daily Jun–Sept 2–4pm (Tue 10am–4.30pm).* 📞 *01593 721 325. www.caithness.org.*
The home of Mary-Ann Calder, born here in 1897, this typical crofting cottage,

---

Dounreay

Nuclear energy came to Scotland in August 1957 – its fast reactor was the first of its kind. For over 40 years, the coastal landscape around Sandside Bay has been dominated by the futuristic dome of this nuclear power station, but it is now in the process of decommissioning, set to finish by 2025. The public are no longer allowed near the plant but its story is told as part of the lively new **Caithness Horizons** in the former Thurso Town Hall (🕙 *Mon–Fri 10am–6pm, Sat 10am–5pm, Sun noon–5pm (Winter Mon–Sat 10am–5pm);* ✗ 📞 *01847 893 155; www.caithnesshorizons.co.uk*) which relates the history of the local area.

together with its outbuildings, is being actively conserved as an important social document. Far from being a static exhibit, it shows the evolution of this type of habitat, with modern developments like the 1950s kitchen as well as a wealth of indicators of the traditional, pre-Improvement, rural way of life.

Dunnet Head

Reached by a single-track road across a wild landscape with lochans, Dunnet Head is the most northerly point on the British mainland, almost 2.5mi/4km further north than John o' Groats, which is traditionally known as the northernmost point.

The lighthouse, which stands on the 90m clifftop of Easter Head, is 105m tall and it was built in 1831 by Robert Stevenson, the grandfather of Robert Louis Stevenson.

The buildings nearby (bunker, radar and montoring stations, etc.) date from World War II and were part of the protection of the naval base at Scapa Flow. The cliffs are rich in sea birds.

Castle of Mey

○Apr We–Thu 11am–3pm; May–Sept daily 10.20am–4pm. ⊜£11.95 (gardens only, £6.50). ✗ ℘01847 851 473. www.castleofmey.org.uk.

The castle was built 1566–72 by George Sinclair, Earl of Caithness, and occupied by his descendants for three centuries. Seen from a distance, its turreted aspect is very striking.

In 1952 the late Queen Mother, Her Majesty Queen Elizabeth, saw the castle. Falling for its isolated charm and hearing it was to be abandoned, she decided to save it. Having acquired the most northerly inhabited castle on the British mainland, The Queen Mother renovated and restored the house and created the beautiful gardens visitors see today.

For almost half a century she spent many happy summers here and shorter visits at other times of the year.

▷ Return to the coastal road (A836) to John o' Groats.

John o' Groats

Traditionally this is the northernmost extremity of the mainland United Kingdom. In fact that particular honour goes to Dunnet Head (also known as Easter Head) some 11mi/18km northwest of here, though John o' Groats is certainly the northernmost settlement. It lies 876mi/1 410km from its southern counterpart, Land's End in Cornwall and is the starting or finishing point for various feats of endurance, usually undertaken for charity, with the challenge of going from one end of the country to the other in a certain time, or even non-stop.

The scattered community takes its name from a Dutchman, Jan de Groot, who started a regular ferry service to the Orkney Islands in the 16C. The octagonal tower of the hotel recalls the story of the ferryman, who, to settle problems of precedence among his seven descendants, built an eight-sided house with eight doors and an octagonal table. A passenger boat service operates day trips from the harbour to Burwick on South Ronaldsay, May to September (℘01955 611 353; www.jogferry.co.uk).

▷ Take the road to the east to Duncansby Head, 2mi/3.2km away.

Duncansby Head★

From around the lighthouse, which commands this northeastern headland of mainland Scotland, there is a good view across the Pentland Firth, a channel (7mi/11.3km wide) notorious for its treacherous tides. A path leads to another clifftop viewpoint overlooking the Stacks of **Duncansby★★**. Standing offshore these pointed sea-stacks rise to a spectacular height of 64m.

▷ Return to John o'Groats. Follow the signs south to Freswick and Wick.

Caithness Broch Centre

The Old School House, Auckengill. ○Apr–Sept Mon–Fri 10am–4.30pm; also Sat during Jul–Aug. ℘01955 631 377. www.thebrochproject.co.uk.

This museum is centred around **brochs** (ᒪsee SHETLAND) –Caithness boasts

100-plus Iron Age brochs – and the communities, ancient and modern, associated with them.

As you travel south, the road climbs and once over the rise, South Ronaldsay, the southernmost isle of Orkney, can be seen in the distance.

Pass on the way the tall remains of **Old Keiss Castle**, occupying a dramatic location at the top of sheer cliffs overlooking the sea.

Beware, the castle is in a dangerous state. There have been collapses and under no circumstances should the structure be entered.) Standing nearby is the white form of its successor, New Keiss Castle, remodelled in 1860 (*private*).

Wick

Standing on the river of the same name, Wick (takes its name from the Norse term vik, meaning bay. A small fishing fleet operates out of the harbour and is a reminder of past glories; in its heyday over 1 000 boats operated out of Wick and the neighbouring port of Pulteneytown.

Wick was one of the first towns to develop the herring fishery on a large scale and by the early 19C was the largest herring fishing port in the country.

The British Fisheries Society commissioned Thomas Telford to draw up the plans for this new fishing settlement, attempting to bring some order to the jumble of undecked boats and mass of masts all over the harbour.

The quays and all available dockside space spilled over with the paraphernalia of the curing industry. Curing, which had to be done within 24hrs of landing the catch, entailed gutting the fish, salting and packing them in barrels and was carried out by large teams of itinerant workers, mostly women.

Wick Heritage Centre

Easter–Oct Mon–Sat 10am–5pm. 01955 605 393. www.wickheritage.org. A number of fully furnished rooms take visitors back in time to typical local houses between 1900 and 1925.

Other displays and exhibits trace the town's history and heritage, most notably: a model of the herring port; the complete optical and mechanical working of Noss Head Lighthouse; a fine display of Caithness glassware which was produced in Wick between 1960 and 2005, when the business moved away from the area.

From Wick follow signs to Noss Head to the northeast of the airport. It's a 15min walk to the castle ruins.

Girnigoe Castle and Sinclair Castle

The jagged ruins of two adjacent castles are dramatically set on a peninsula, overlooking the great sandy sweep of Sinclair's Bay on one side and a typical geo on the other. Nearest to the point of the peninsula is the late-15C Castle Girnigoe with its evil-looking dungeon. The part known as Castle Sinclair, an early-17C addition, stands to the left beyond a ditch. Both were the seat of the Sinclair Earls of Caithness, a clan with a dark and often violent history in these parts. The castles are currently being restored.

From Wick take the A99 to Ulbster and then signs direct you to the Hill o' Many Stanes.

The Hill o' Many Stanes★

To the right off the main road.
With its 22 rows of small stones this is a Bronze Age monument (c.1850 BCE). The purpose of the fan-shaped arrangement may have been astronomical.

Continue south along the A99. Just before Lybster turn away from the coast heading N along a narrow road with passing places for 7.5mi/12km.

Grey Cairns of Camster★

This is typical Highland crofting country – a bleak expanse of moorland dotted with small cultivated areas and crofts. The first of the two cairns is the **Round Cairn** with its entrance passage (*6m long, can only be negotiated on hands and knees*) and chamber. The much larger second one, the **Long Cairn★★**, is 60m long by 10m wide. This long-horned structure incorporates two earlier beehive cairns. The main chamber is tripartite, subdivided by large slabs. The chambered cairns of the area date from the Neolithic period (4000–1800 BCE).

2 NORTH COAST: THURSO TO DURNESS
74mi/119km via the A836 and the A838.

Bleak moorland scenery gives way to the glories of coastal scenery beyond, with an ever-changing pattern of sandy bays, lochs and headlands.

▶ Leave Thurso on the A9, then A836.

Scrabster
This is the terminal port for the car ferry to Stromness in Orkney.

▶ Go back to turn W on the A836.

Melvich Bay
From the war memorial behind the hotel in the crofting community of Melvich, there is a splendid **view** over Melvich Bay with the sand bar. The island of Hoy is visible in the distance.

▶ The road beyond Melvich is single track with passing places. Cross the River Strathy which opens into another sandy estuary, Strathy Bay. Then turn right to Strathy Point.

Strathy Point★
🏃 *15min walk from the car park to the point.*
There are excellent **views★★★** along the coast to the east of Strathy Bay in the foreground, with Dounreay and Hoy in the distance.
The landscape then becomes scoured and hummocky with the stately outline of the granite peaks of **Ben Loyal★★** (763m) ahead, rising above the plateau.

Bettyhill
This is one of the crofting communities which originated at the time of the Highlands Clearances when crofters were evicted, in this case from Strathnaver, to make way for sheep.
The story of the Highlands Clearances is one of several subjects in the **Strathnaver Museum** (🕐Apr–Oct Mon–Sat 10am–5pm; ✆£3; ✆01641 521 418; www. strathnavermuseum.org.uk).
The road then follows the sandy estuary of **Torrisdale Bay★**, crosses the river, then climbs out of Strathnaver to ascend to the scoured plateau surface dotted with reed-choked lochs.
Go round Cnoc an Fhreiceadain and just before reaching Coldbackie there are excellent **views★★** of the Kyle of Tongue sea loch.

Tongue
This small village lies on the shores of the sea loch. The Kyle of Tongue is bridged by a causeway which offers a new **view** inland towards Ben Loyal and, ahead, a ruined Mackay stronghold perched on an eminence.
Beyond Tongue the road becomes double track and the outline of Ben Hope appears on the horizon. Peat banks are visible from time to time. On the descent there are glimpses of Loch Hope stretching away to the left. From the west side of Loch Hope, there are fine views of the loch stretching away to **Ben Hope★** (*alt. 927m*) in the background. A little farther on, a magnificent **view★★★** unfolds of Loch Eriboll, another deeply penetrating sea loch.

▶ The road becomes single track on the east side. Go round the loch. Sangobeg has a lovely sandy beach.

Durness★
This small hardy village, once a crofting community, is the most northwesterly community in mainland Britain. It now thrives as a stopping-off place for travellers rounding the northwest corner of Scotland.

Smoo Cave
An outcrop of limestones accounts for the presence of this, Britain's largest sea cave and the sandy beaches. The waters of the Allt Smoo river plunge down a

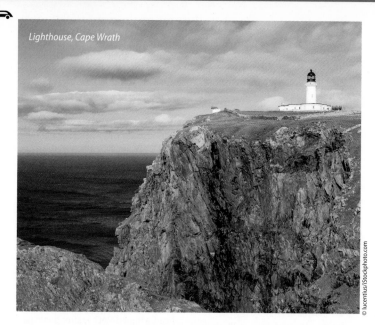

Lighthouse, Cape Wrath

© lucentius/iStockphoto.com

sink-hole to reappear at the mouth of the outer cave. The two inner caves are accessible only to potholers.

Balnakeil Craft Village

1mi/1.6km west by a local road.
This former radar station is now occupied by a community of craftspeople, at work making and selling ceramics, jewellery, weaving, bookbinding, leatherwork and more.

Cape Wrath★★★

Accessible by ferry, from Keoldale slipway 0.5mi/800m south of Durness.,

In My Life

In the garden of Durness Village Hall is a monument to John Lennon; three stones engraved with the lyrics of the Beatles classic song *In My Life*, recalling the many happy holidays John spent at his cousin's Durness croft. Every year until he was 17, John would make the long journey here by bus and spend three weeks enjoying the fresh air and gardens.

then minibus. ⏱*Ferry and bus operate Easter–mid-Oct. Call or see website for times* ⊜*£20.50 (bus £13, and ferry £7.50, return).* 𝄞*01971 511 284. www.visitcapewrath.com.*

The bus takes 40min for the trip (11.5mi/18.5km) through bleak moorland country, now MOD territory, to the lighthouse, which marks the most northwesterly point on the British mainland. The lighthouse was built by Robert Stevenson (the father of Robert Louis Stevenson) in 1828; the name Wrath comes from the Norse for turning point, as it was here that the Norsemen turned their ships to head for home. Near the lighthouse are the ruins of a coastguard station, built by Lloyds of London to watch over ships, and the Ozone Café, the most remote café in mainland Britain.

To the east – above the bay of Kearvaig – the Clo Mor Cliffs have a dizzying drop of 281m, making them the highest sea cliffs in main-land Britain.

The totally exposed cape offers a variety of vantage points affording outstanding **views★★** – especially eastwards and particularly from Clo Mor Cliffs. The churning seas and superb coastal scenery is an unforgettable sight.

Wester Ross★★★

The Atlantic seaboard of Wester Ross includes the finest Highland scenery in Scotland: the splendour of majestic mountains such as Beinn Eighe, Liathach, Slioch and An Teallach; the beauty of Lochs Maree, Broom and Ewe; the rugged beauty of wild and rocky Torridon and the fastness of the Applecross peninsula; and not forgetting the charm of small isolated communities like Plockton, Poolewe, Kinlochewe and Applecross.

🚗 DRIVING TOURS

🚗 1 GLEN SHIEL TO GAIRLOCH

The itinerary described covers 113mi/180km although there are alternatives that reduce the distance to 74mi/119km. Allow at least 1 day.

This is the quintessential Scottish Highland landscape where mountains, lochs, seashore, woods and moorland all come together in the correct proportions. Parts of the route are busy in the tourist season but other stretches still permit the luxury of enjoying it all in solitude.

Glen Shiel★

This grandiose V-shaped valley passes from the head of Loch Duich through to Loch Cluanie. Stretching 6mi/9.7km down the left side of the Glen are the **Five Sisters of Kintail**. Rising up from the lochside some of the peaks top 914m. The valley was the site of the **Battle of Glen Shiel**, which ended the Jacobite rising of 1719. The battle is sometimes considered an extension of the Jacobite rising of 1715, but is more correctly a separate rebellion, and the only rising to be extinguished by a single military action. This battlefield has been included in the Inventory of Historic Battlefields in Scotland.

Info: 13 Strath, Gairloch. ☏01445 712 085. www.visitwester-ross.com.

Location: Explore the area from any one of the main touring centres, Kyle of Lochalsh, Gairloch or Ullapool.

Don't Miss: The views from Bealach-na-Bà; Loch Maree; the view of Loch Maree from the A832.

Drivers: Keep the petrol tank well topped up.

Timing: Allow at least two days for sightseeing, but to enjoy this glorious area to the full, take extra to walk, climb, sail or fish.

Eilean Donan Castle★

9mi/14.5km east by the A87.
🕐*Daily: Feb–late Mar 10am–4pm; late Mar–Oct 10am–6pm.* ✆£10. ✖ ☏01599 555 202.
www.eileandonancastle.com.
One of the most iconic images of Scotland, Eilean Donan has an idyllic island **site★★** (today linked by a bridge) with a picture-postcard mountain and loch setting. It has starred many times on TV and on the movie screen. Following the abortive Jacobite rising of 1719 the ruins were abandoned for 200 years until the 20C when a complete reconstruction was undertaken. The Banqueting Hall, bedrooms and kitchen (as it would have looked in 1932) as well as courtyard are open to visitors. The outer ramparts offer excellent **views** of the three lochs.

Kyle of Lochalsh

Famous as the original ferry port for Skye and the "Welcome" mat for the island – before the bridge was built in 1995 – this small town is still a busy place in summer.

▶ Leave Kyle to the north by the coast road, enjoying the views

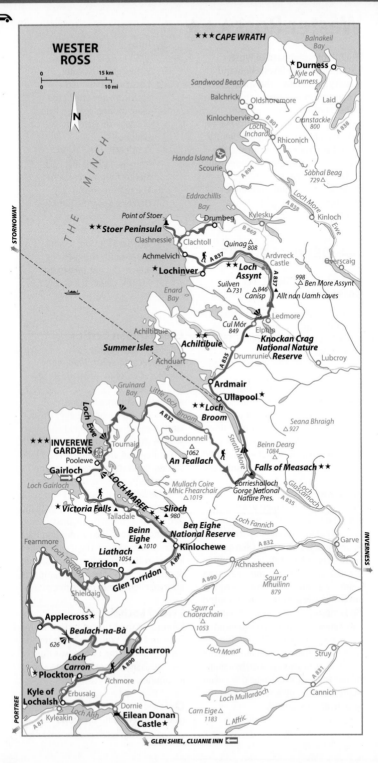

Eilean Donan castle and Loch Duich

seawards to Skye, with the Cuillin on the skyline.

Plockton★

This lovely village, with its palm tree-lined main street, has an ideal **site** facing east overlooking a sheltered bay. Originally a refugee settlement at the time of the clearances, it is now a holiday centre popular for yachting and windsurfing.

▷ At Achmore join the A890, turning left.

Down on the shore, pass Stromeferry, a former railhead and ferry point. The lochside road on the southern shore has fine **views** of the loch.

Loch Carron

This sea loch has two branches, Loch Kishorn and Upper Loch Carron, backed by the glen of the same name.

▷ At Strath Carron junction take the A896 left.

Lochcarron

This is a small strip settlement down on the loch shore.

▷ Follow the A896 as it branches to the right beyond Lochcarron and rises to cross moorland, then take a narrow valley down to the shore of Loch Kishorn.

On the far side are the Applecross mountains; from left to right are Meal Gorm (*alt. 710m*), Sgurr a' Chaorachain (*pronounced Skoor a Koo-ra-ken; alt. 792m*), forming the sides of the valley to be ascended, and Beinn Bhan (*alt. 896m*).

▷ The A896 is a possible short cut to Shieldaig. The itinerary, however, follows the narrow road to the left to cross the Applecross peninsula via Bealach na Bà (Pass of the Cattle). *This route has hairpin bends and steep gradients and is not recommended for learner drivers, caravans or heavy vehicles. The pass is closed to traffic in wintry conditions. However, the splendid views make it all worthwhile at other times.*

Bealach na Bà

The road over this pass, historically a drovers' road, is one of few in the Highlands that is engineered similarly to roads through the mountain passes in the Alps, with very tight hairpin bends that switch back and forth up the hillside and gradients that approach 20%. It boasts the greatest ascent of any road climb in the UK, rising from sea level at Applecross to 626 metres, and is the third highest road in Scotland.
Striated rock and scree slopes are overlooked by rocky overhangs. Hairpin bends allow the final ascent of the back wall of the corrie. The **vista★★** framed by the hanging valley is spectacular

with Loch Kishorn, Loch Carron, Loch Alsh and the Isle of Skye below in the distance.

The rocky moorland surface is dotted with lochans. From the car park there are superb **views★★★** westwards of Skye, the Cuillin, and the fringing islands.

The descent to Applecross and the coast is more gradual.

Applecross★

This picturesque village is situated on a bay with a popular red sandy beach. This was the site in the 7C of St Maelrubha's monastery.

The coastal road has good **views** across the Inner Sound to Raasay and Rona with Skye beyond.

▷ Continue round the south shore of Loch Torridon, Loch Shieldaig and Upper Loch Torridon, rejoining the A896 at Shieldaig; turn left.

Torridon

The village lies at the foot of Liathach at the head of Upper Loch Torridon. The **Torridon Countryside Centre** (& ☉ *Apr–Sept Sun–Fri 10am–5pm; estate, deer enclosure and deer museum (unstaffed) open daily;* ☎*01445 791221; www.nts.org.uk*) offers an audiovisual introduction to the Torridon area, including information on climbing and walking routes.

☺*Remember, these mountains can be very dangerous and are only for experienced, fit and properly equipped explorers. Changeable weather makes them treacherous. Always leave behind a detail of routes and objectives with an estimated time of return.*

▷ The A896 through Glen Torridon is single track with passing places.

Glen Torridon

The glen leads through a flat-bottomed glacial valley. The lower part of the glen is overlooked to the north by **Liathach**, "Grey One" (*alt. 1 055m*); with its seven peaks it is an impressive sight. The valley to the south, containing Loch Clair, leads

through to Glen Carron (*no through road for cars*).

The imposing range of **Beinn Eighe** (*alt. 1 010m*) to the north is a long ridge also of seven peaks; the most easterly ones have a whitish quartzite capping.

Kinlochewe

The village has retained the loch's original name and is known as a good centre for climbing, hill walking and fishing.

▷ Take the A832 to the left.

Beinn Eighe Visitor Centre

Anancaun. & ☉*Daily Mar–Oct 10am–5pm.* 🅿 ☎*01445 760 258. www.nnr.scot.*

This is the gateway to the **Beinn Eighe National Nature Reserve**, a 5 000ha mountain area of Caledon pinewoods (one of the few remaining fragments of the native Scots Pine Forest), barren moors and lochans with breathtaking views over Loch Maree and Torridon. Among the wildlife can be found pine marten, red deer and the more elusive wildcat. Nature is all around you here; take the time to appreciate it.

A number of short trails suitable for all (including a wheelchair-friendly route) set off from the centre. All routes have descriptive panels giving an insight into the surroundings.

A roadside picnic area makes an ideal vantage point for viewing the loch and Slioch (the Spear) on the far side. This is also the starting point of a nature and mountain **trail** (4mi/6.5km) on the lower slopes of Beinn Eighe. This is a 4–5hr hike, and it is advisable to wear boots.

Loch Maree★★★

This magnificent loch epitomises the rugged grandeur of the west coast. Measuring 12mi/19km long and 3mi/5km wide, it is ensconced between the towering form of **Slioch** (980m) to the north and a shoulder of Beinn Eighe. At its widest point the loch is studded with isles and it was on **Isle Maree** that St Maelrubha set up his cell in the 7C. The isle became a popular place of pil-

Loch Maree with a view to Slioch

© David Woods/iStockphoto.com

grimage and Loch Ewe was rechristened Maree, a corruption of Maelrubha.
Less spiritually, in the 17C the lochside slopes were the site of iron smelting.

Victoria Falls★
Car park off the main road.
A viewing platform and riverside path afford good views of the falls as they drop in two stages over great slabs of rock. They are named after Queen Victoria who visited the area in 1877. A roadside viewing point overlooks the dammed Loch Bad an Sgalaig. The surrounding country is hummocky and dotted with small lochs.

▶ Pass the bay of Charlestown.

Gairloch
As a holiday centre for the Northern Highlands, Gairloch lies at close proximity to the majestic mountain scenery of the Torridon area and the splendid sandy beaches of the immediate coastline. At the head of Loch Gairloch the pier still has the lively bustle of a fishing port.
The **Gairloch Heritage Museum** (*Achtercain*. ♿ 🕐 *Mon–Wed, Fri–Sat 10am–6pm, Thu 10am–8pm;* 🎟 *£5;* 🅿 *℘ 01445 712 287; www.gairloch heritagemuseum.org*), has won national awards and illustrates all aspects of life in the past in a typical West Highland parish. Visitors to this new purpose-built

museum (*opened 2019*) will experience 7 000 years of local history, from evidence of Gairloch's earliest settlers to the twentieth century engineering marvels of the Rubh Re lighthouse lens. Established in 1989, **Gairloch Marine Life Centre & Cruises** (🕐 *depart Charleston Harbour daily Mar–Oct; two-hour cruises 10am, 12.30pm, 3pm;* 🎟 *£20; ℘ 01445 712 636; www.porpoise-gairloch. co.uk*) is one of the longest running marine wildlife operators in Europe and has the longest running porpoise survey world-wide. On any cruise you might expect to see harbour porpoises, minke whale, common and grey seals, common dolphins, bottlenosed dolphins, Risso's dolphins and basking sharks, all of which swim in the area. More unusual visitors to these waters include killer whales, white beaked dolphins and even sun-fish, all spotted in recent years.

🚗 2 GAIRLOCH TO LOCHINVER
85mi/136km – one way. Plus the Stoer Peninsula extension.

This excursion reveals the scenic coast-line to the north where bays, beaches and headlands succeed one another. The hinterland is breathtaking mountain scenery. Take the A832 northeastwards across the rock-and-moorland neck of the Rubha Reidh peninsula.

Anthrax Island

In 1942, the island of Gruinard gained notoriety as a biological weapon testing ground for anthrax. Its guinea-pig victims: a flock of sheep. In 1986, a clear-up was mounted, and, controversially, the island was declared "safe" in 1990. Since then sheep have been kept on the island and closely monitored. None has shown signs of anthrax contamination. Landing here, however, is still forbidden.

▷ Pause at the viewpoint before descending to Loch Ewe.

The roadside viewpoint has a superb **view★★★** of Loch Maree with its forested islands and majestic mountain flanks. **Loch Ewe** stretches ahead enclosed by the peninsulas of Rubha Reidh and Rubha Mor. **Poolewe** is the small village at the head of Loch Ewe.

Inverewe Gardens★★★

&⊙*Visitor centre: daily: Apr and Sept 10am–5pm; May–Aug 9.30am–6pm; Oct 10am–4pm. Gardens, all year.* ⊙*May be closed during periods of inclement weather.* ⊕£12.50. ✗ ℘01445 712 952. www.nts.org.uk. Enjoying a magnificent west coast setting, these outstanding gardens are a

source of pleasure and an unrivalled display of beauty in all seasons.

In 1862, the founder, **Osgood Mackenzie** (1843–1922), bought a barren Wester Ross estate including Am Ploc Ard, "the high lump" in Gaelic. The peninsula was exposed to Atlantic gales and salt spray with an acid peaty soil devoid of vegetation. Initial work included rabbit fencing, the creation of a Corsican pine and Scots fir windbreak and the transportation of soil for bedding the plants. A lifetime of patient planning, judicious planting and careful tending, aided by the tempering effects of the Gulf Stream, produced the delightfully informal gardens of today. Osgood's cherished work was continued by his daughter Mrs Sawyer who, in 1952, handed the gardens over to the National Trust for Scotland.

Visitors are free to wander at will but a suggested route is indicated by arrows and numbers. Each species is labelled and the guidebook contains a list of the more interesting plants. Half of this 26ha site is woodland.

Here, on a latitude similar to that of St Petersburg, flourish some 2 500 species, many of which are exotic but flourish in some sheltered corner. Colour is to be found in most seasons: mid-April to mid-May (rhododendrons), May (azaleas), June (rock garden, herbaceous and rose borders), early autumn (heathers) and November (maples).

The twisting paths give unexpected and ever-changing **vistas** of garden, sea and mountain. The high viewpoint affords a **view** back towards Poolewe in its head of the loch setting with the Torridon peaks in the background.

A vantage point on the A832 north of Tournaig towards Ullapool has a lovely **view★** of Loch Thurnaig in the foreground, the Inverewe Gardens promontory behind, then Loch Ewe backed by Rubha Reidh, and the Isle of Ewe just to the right.

Second viewpoint

The Isle of Ewe is straight ahead while Aultbea shelters in a bay to the right.

Inverewe Gardens

© Peter Baker/International Photobank/age fotostock

Falls of Measach

© font83/iStockphoto.com

▶ The road rises up and over Rubha Mor Peninsula.

The descent offers a wide **view** over Gruinard Bay and Island of the same name, once the scene of an anthrax experiment (👆*see box left*).

As the road follows the southern shore, straight ahead is **An Teallach** (*pron. An Challoch; alt. 1 062m*) with, away to the left, the twin peaks of Beinn Ghobhlach (*pron. Ben Vol-vok*), the Forked Mountain.

At the head of the loch the road follows the wooded Strath Beag up to the moors of Dundonnell forest. This stretch of the road, known as Destitution Road, was made during the potato famine of 1851 to give work to starving men.

There is an excellent roadside vantage point with a **view**★ over the farmland and woodland of Strath More at the head of Loch Broom.

▶ Not far from the crossroads with the A835 (Braemore Junction), follow signs to the Falls of Measach.

Falls of Measach★★

The road follows the northern shore of **Loch Broom**★★ (21mi/34km long) in a beautiful mountain setting. The loch sides are dotted with houses and traces of former field patterns are visible on the south side. From a point near the head of the loch there are particularly fine **views**.

In the wooded cleft of the mile-long **Corrieshalloch Gorge National Nature Reserve**★ (🕐*all year, daily. ☎01445 781 229, www.nts.org.uk*) the waters of the River Droma make a spectacular sight as they drop over 46m. The bridge over the chasm and a viewing platform (👓*honesty box*) provide excellent vantage points.

▶ Take the A835 north.

Ullapool★

Set on the shore of Loch Broom, the white houses of the fishing port and resort of Ullapool make an attractive picture. In summer the waterfront is a lively throng of yachtsmen and holiday-makers. Ullapool makes an ideal touring centre for the Wester Ross coast and is an unrivalled centre for sea angling.

The village was laid out in the late 18C by the British Fisheries Society and flourished as a fishing port during the herring boom. Fishing is still an important activity, based on the Minch fishery, and in season the trawlers anchor in the loch while a fleet of factory ships can usually be seen in attendance at the mouth of Loch Broom.

The port is also the terminal for the car ferry to Stornoway (the capital of the Isle of Lewis in the Outer Hebrides) and

The Road to the Middle of Nowhere

The road from Lochinver to Ullapool (and vice versa) – via Achiltibuie★★, the Coigach peninsula and Enard Bay – is one of the most scenic Wester Ross routes even in this region of stunning drives. En route you can gaze on lochs backed by mighty peaks, the Summer Isles on the horizon, beaches, bays, inlets, moors, waterfalls, forests, tiny villages and, of course, lots of sheep. At Altandhu, make a detour to this small Highland village and its locally renowned smokehouse (*01854 622 353; www.salmon-from-scotland.com*). Achiltibuie and the other villages on the Coigach peninsula enjoy some of the most spectacular views anywhere in the Highlands and on a clear day the Cuillin of Skye (65mi/105km away) are clearly visible.

Despite, or perhaps on account of, its remoteness there are several places to stay in this wonderfully out-of-the-way place; for more information visit *www.coigach.com*.

a haven for many small pleasure craft in summer.

Ullapool Museum
8 West Argyle Street. ⏱*Apr–Oct Mon–Sat 11am–4pm.* ⬧*£4.* *01854 612 987. www.ullapoolmuseum.co.uk.*
Housed within a restored Thomas Telford church, built in 1829, this award-winning museum tells the story of Ullapool and Lochbroom through a mix of traditional and multimedia displays. It includes natural history and the story of Ullapool as a gateway for emigrants from Scotland to Nova Scotia. The so-called klondyking era was a unique period in the history of Ullapool and Lochbroom. Between the late 1970s and mid-1990s, flotillas of factory processing ships spent the long winter months in Lochbroom drawn by the boom of the mackerel fishery.

Summer Isles
⏱*Apr–Sept. Cruises (2h15) depart 10am and 1.30pm.* ⬧*£35.* *01854 612 472. www.summerqueen.co.uk.*
The *Summer Queen* sails to this group of offshore islands where dolphins, seals and seabirds are the principal attractions.
Tanera Mhor, the last inhabited Summer Isle, is one of the few places in Britain to print its own stamps, on sale at the post office. All letters posted on Tanera Mòr must bear two stamps: a

Summer Isles stamp to carry it from Tanera to the mainland and a Royal Mail stamp for the rest of the journey.

▷ Take the A835 north.

Ardmair
A hamlet on the shore of Loch Kanaird. Before entering the small valley look back to the view over Isle Martin in Loch Kanaird, and farther out to sea. The road crosses Strath Kanaird, and Ben More Coigach (*alt. 743m*) rises sheer to the left as if it were a cliff wall.

Knockan Crag National Nature Reserve
⏱*Unstaffed visitor centre, open all year.* *01463 701 600. www.nature.scot.*
The centre is on the edge of the Inverpolly National Nature Reserve covering an area of 10 867ha. This glacially scoured countryside with its many lochs and lochans, the largest of which is Loch Stonascaig, has three important landmarks, the peaks of **Cul Mor** (*alt. 849m*), **Cul Beag** (*alt. 769m*) and **Stac Pollaidh** (*pron. Stack Polly, alt. 613m*), once described as an "irascible porcupine".
These upstanding masses of Torridonian sandstone lie on a base of Lewisian gneiss. The geological sequence exposed at Knockan Cliff is explained on the nature-cum-geological **trail** from the centre. From the centre there is a **view** across the main road of the main peaks,

with, from left to right, Cul Beag, Stac Pollaidh and Cul Mor with its whitish quartzite summit.

Before reaching Ledmore junction there is a **view** to the left over the waters of Cam Loch to the sheer slopes of **Suilven** (*alt. 731m*), a twin-peaked mountain when seen from the north or south.

The road passes Loch Awe and its outlet, the River Loanan with, to left and right, the majestic forms of **Canisp** (*alt. 846m*) and the rounded outliers of **Ben More Assynt** (*alt. 998m*). The Inchnadamph area at the head of Loch Assynt is a Cambrian limestone outcrop noted for its underground features. At the **Inchnadamph Nature Reserve** a track leads to the **Allt nan Uamh caves**, where human remains at least 4 500 years old, along with the bones of animals now extinct in Scotland, have been found.

Loch Assynt★★

The road along this loch (6mi/10km long) is wonderfully scenic. Just before the fork in the lochside road there is a splendid **view** of the ruins of Ardvreck Castle, a 16C MacLeod stronghold. The waters are flanked to the left by Beinn Gharbh, with Canisp peeping from behind, and to the right lofty **Quinag** (808m). The road follows the loch's change of direction and then the winding River Inver.

Lochinver★

Set round the head of a sea loch, this attractive village with its mountainous backdrop is best seen from the sea. It has a dual identity: as a busy holiday centre and haven for many pleasure boats, and, quite separately, it is the second largest fishing port in Scotland.

 ◗ It is well worth taking the short detour on the B869 to explore the Store Peninsula.

Stoer peninsula★★

The Stoer peninsula is renowned for its beautiful scenery, charming crofting communities and sandy coves. At the isolated hamlet of **Achmelvich**, there

is a gorgeous white-sand beach where it is not uncommon to see seals and dolphins. There is more white sand at the attractive bay of Clachtoll.

The narrow roads lead you to the lighthouse, built by the Stevenson family in 1870 (and automated in 1978) at **Point of Stoer**. From here there is a footpath (2mi/3.2km) to see the mighty 61m high twisted sea stack of red sandstone known as the **Old Man of Stoer**.

Back on the B869, go through Clashnessie and its beautiful beach, and continue via the villages of **Drumbeg** and Nedd. Don't miss the **Little Soap & Candle Company** with its charming tea garden (◷*10am–5pm: Apr and Sept Sun–Thu; May–Aug Sat–Thu; Oct times vary; ✆01571 833 263; www.thelittlesoapand-candlecompany.co.uk*) who offer homebaking and cream teas.

ADDRESSES

⌂ STAY

ULLAPOOL

🛏🍴 **Lochview** – *Garve Road. ✆01854 612 333. https://lochviewullapool.scot. 7 rooms.* This guesthouse on the village outskirts overlooks Loch Broom.

🛏🍴 **Ferry Boat Inn** – *Shore Street. ✆01854 612 431. www.fbiullapool.com. 9 rooms.* Charming small pub, regarded by many as the best in town. The **Blue Kazoo Seafood Restaurant** (🍴🍴) on site serves local fish and shellfish.

🛏🍴 **The Sheiling** – *Garve Road. ✆01854 612 947. www.thesheilingullapool.co.uk. 6 rooms.* In an acre of grounds, and including a sauna, this guesthouse enjoys views of Loch Broom and the mountains.

🛏🍴 **Westlea House** – *2 Market Street. ✆01854 612 594. www.westlea-ullapool. co.uk. 5 rooms.* Boutique B&B, open all year; stylish and comfortable rooms.

☝ EAT

APPLECROSS

🍴🍴 **The Potting Shed Café** – *Applecross Walled Garden, Strathcarron. ✆01520 744 440. www.applecrossgarden.co.uk.* This delightful, quirky place on the beautiful Applecross peninsula is one of the best places to eat in the Highlands.

The Scottish Islands

There are hundreds of offshore islands around the coast of Scotland, collected easily enough into four main groups: those in the Firth of Clyde, among which Arran is the largest; the Hebrides, sub-divided into the Inner Hebrides and the Outer Hebrides; Shetland and Orkney. Of these, the 2011 census recorded 93 offshore islands as having a usually resident population that since the previous census in 2001 has been seen to grow by 4%, to bring the total estimated "island" population to almost 104 000. Only 4 islands have a population greater than 10 000. An island, for statistical purposes, is "land that is surrounded by seawater on a daily basis, but not necessarily at all stages of the tide, excluding human devices such as bridges and causeways".

The Clyde islands

The largest and most populous of the Clyde islands are Arran and Bute, along with the smaller island of Great Cumbrae.

Arran is the most accessible of all Scotland's major islands and is nicknamed "Scotland in Miniature" because it is cut in two by the Highland Boundary Fault and therefore has both Highland and Lowland landscapes; this also makes it a geologist's paradise. However, it isn't just the lie of the land that draws thousands of visitors each year. Other typical Scottish/Gaelic features include a fine sturdy baronial castle, stone circles, a whisky distillery, and no fewer than seven golf courses.

Serious walkers head to the north of the island with the peak being Goat Fell (*alt. 874m*); on a clear day this offers wonderful views across the Firth of Clyde.

Great Cumbrae the larger of the two islands known as The Cumbraes, home to the National Watersports Centre, the Cathedral of the Isles and the University Marine Biological Station. The popular holiday island has a golf course that rises almost to the summit, and a great round-island road much favoured for family cycle runs.

The Inner Hebrides

The islands of the Inner Hebrides are by far the most fragmented of the island groups, forming an archipelago of islands of varying sizes that cling to the west coast of Scotland. There are 25 inhabited islands, and more than 40 that are uninhabited.

The Isle of Skye is the largest of these. True romantics eschew the new bridge

Highlights

1 Drive round the **Trotternish peninsula on Skye** (p383)

2 Enjoy the colourful waterfront of **Tobermory** on Mull (p394)

3 Take the boat trip to see **Fingal's Cave** on the island of Staffa (p396)

4 Step back in time at **Skara Brae** on Orkney (p413)

5 Take a boat trip to **Mousa broch** (p424)

and take the "bonnie boat ... over the sea to Skye". Colourful Portree and the beautiful Trotternish peninsula are highlights for many visitors while the ever-changing weather and the jagged Cuillin offer challenges to walkers and climbers alike.

Located west of Oban, across the Firth of Lorne, Mull is the third largest Scottish island, so large in fact that it is easy to forget that it is an island. The island has a ragged 300-mile coastline, a mess of inlets and lochs and glorious vistas whether you travel the northern part, the great wedge of high ground in the middle or drive the long route down the Ross of Mull to sail across to the island of Iona. Satellites of Mull include the pilgrimage island of Iona, but equally worthy escapes like Staffa, home of Fingal's Cave, the Treshnish Isles (superb for seeing puffins up close), and the less well-known islands of Ulva and Gometra (no cars allowed, but bikes are welcome). With few 'Collachs' remaining on the island, Coll, is rapidly becoming an island economy of holiday homes, especially popular with those who seek out flora and fauna. Nearby, a dark sliver of land marks the location of low-lying Tiree, renowned for the sandy miles of its beaches that each year see the International Windsurfing Championships. For good measure Tiree holds Britain's sunshine record.

Invariably overlooked, and not far from the busy seaport of Oban, the Slate Islands (Seil, Easdale and Luing) really should command everyone's attention. Likewise the islands of Kerrera, and Lismore, at the southern end of Loch Linnhe.

The last islands lie along the Firth of Lorne, which embraces the whisky-producing island of Islay, the George Orwell favoured island of Jura, and the seldom visited Colonsay and Oronsay.

The Outer Hebrides

Also known as the Western Isles, the Outer Hebrides form a massive archipelago that stretches for 130mi/213km and looks west to the Atlantic Ocean rather than eastwards to mainland Scotland. Here on the edge of Europe is a striking mix of landscapes from windswept golden sands to harsh, heather-backed mountains and peat bogs. An elemental beauty pervades the Hebrides, which remain the heartland of Gaelic culture, with the language still spoken by the vast majority of islanders.

Lewis and Harris (the latter famous for its tweed) are the main settlements while North Uist, Benbecula, South Uist and Barra possess long wild breezy beaches. In keeping with the frontier spirit of the islands, on Barra the beach doubles as a landing strip for scheduled flights from the mainland!

Further west, and proving a challenge for most tourists, is the remarkable island group of uninhabited St Kilda, abandoned by its people in the 1930s in the hope of a better life.

Orkney

For centuries, Orkney lay beyond the boundaries of civilisation, islands so remote that visitors rarely went there. Today it is known that Orkney contains some of the oldest and best-preserved Neolithic sites in Europe, and the "Heart of Neolithic Orkney" is a designated UNESCO World Heritage Site, and that brings in tourists by the shipload.

The islands have been at the crossroads of history in northern Europe for more than 7 000 years, and for the Norsemen who settled here, they were an important staging post.

Shetland

On a parallel with the southern tip of Greenland, and as close to Norway as it is to the Scottish mainland, Shetland lies almost 100 miles north of the mainland, a fascinating, sprawling, convoluted landscape where land and water intermingle.

Bolstered by almost 100 smaller islands, the mass of Shetland comprises the Mainland and three northerly islands – Fetlar, Yell and Unst. Collectively they enjoy a coastline that is breathtakingly stunning, a confusion of gloups, sounds, wicks, geos and voes that make for a bewildering geography.

Man has lived on Shetland since the Mesolithic period; the earliest written references to the islands date from Roman times.

The early historic period was dominated by Scandinavian influences, especially Norway, and the islands become part of Scotland only in the 15C.

The Clyde Islands★★

Lying in the Firth of Clyde between Ayrshire and Argyll, the Clyde islands comprise as many as forty islands and skerries, although most are uninhabited. The influence of the Atlantic Ocean and the North Atlantic Drift give the islands a mild but damp oceanic climate. The larger islands – Arran in particular – have been inhabited since Neolithic times, and their history has been influenced by the emergence of the kingdom of Dál Riada from about the year 500, and later absorbed into the emerging Kingdom of Alba. They experienced Norse incursions during the early Middle Ages and then became part of the Kingdom of Scotland in the 13C. The islands offer a diverse landscape influenced by the fact that the geological feature known as the Highland Boundary Fault runs past Bute and slices through Arran, giving the island group characteristics both of the Highlands and the Central Lowlands.

Isle of Arran★★

Arran, the largest of the Clyde islands, with an area of 165sq mi/427 sq km, measures 20mi/32km long and 10mi/16km wide. "Scotland in miniature", the island is cut in two by the Highland Boundary Fault. The mountainous northern part, with Goat Fell (*alt. 874m*) the highest peak, has deep valleys and moorland while the southern half has more typically Lowland scenery. Around the coast, sheltered sandy bays, rugged cliffs and small creeks alternate. Protected by the arm of the Kintyre peninsula, the island has a particularly mild climate. As you approach the isle by steamer one of the first things you can pick out against the towering backdrop of Goat Fell is the red sandstone mass of Brodick Castle, over the bay.

▶ **Population:** 5 058.

🗓 **Info:** The Pier, Brodick. 📞01770 303 774. www.ayrshire-arran.com.

▶ **Location:** The Isle of Arran lies 14mi/22.5km off the Scottish mainland in the Firth of Clyde.

🌼 **Don't Miss:** Brodick castle garden in bloom (*late spring*).

🌼 **Drivers:** Make sure the petrol tank is full before setting out on an island tour, as there are few filling stations.

🕐 **Timing:** Allow at least 2 full days to look around (👀*see suggested Driving Tour*)

👫 **Kids:** Sandy beaches.

A BIT OF HISTORY

Set on the main migration route on the western seaboard the island has a rich prehistoric heritage, including the long cairn collective tombs of the Neolithic agriculturalists, standing stone circles of the Bronze Age (Machrie Moor) and Iron Age forts. Elsewhere are monopliths and chambered cairns, and the glens reveal the remains of ancient chapels, blackhouses and turf dykes, while the hilltops reveal traces of fortifications.

ARRAN TODAY

Although promoted as one of the 'Clyde islands', Arran's characteristics are distinct, and more truly reflect those of the Inner Hebrides, geologically, culturally and historically. Much of the superficial landscape is the product of the Highland Clearances in the 18C and 19C, and there is a definite Celtic influence underpinning ancient links with Ireland and the legendary Irish king, Fionn McCool. Yet it is the language of the Norse people that comes alive in placenames and features across the landscape: Brodick derives

Goat Fell viewed from Brodick

from Broad Vik, Sannox from Sandy Vik and Goat Fell, from Geita Fjell.

The modern economy is essentially based on agriculture with large sheep runs on the moorland areas and arable farming or dairying restricted to the improved areas of valleys and coastal fringes. Forestry is on the increase on the east coast but the main industry is undoubtedly tourism, exploiting the isle's natural assets: its scenic beauty and its timelessness. In 1995, adding to the island's economy, a new whisky distillery opened on Arran (&See LOCHRANZA), although in the early 19C there were more than 50 distilleries here, most of them illegal and well concealed, not that such a distinction deterred the gentry, who regularly "took the Arran waters" said to be the best in Scotland at the time, and rivalled only by Glen Livet.

Today, facilities for the visitor include golf, cycle and boat hiring, pony trekking, rock climbing, hill and ridge walking, fishing, sea-angling, yachting, waterskiing and fine sandy beaches with safe bathing.

🚗 DRIVING TOUR

🚗 THE ISLE
56mi/90km. Allow half a day. The visit can be done in either direction or in two trips by taking the road between Brodick and Blackwaterfoot to cut across the waist of the island (10mi/16km).

This mainly coastal route gives a good view of the island and its diversity of scenery, from the moors, glens and mountains of the north to the more pastoral landscapes and rocky cliff coastline of the south.

Brodick
With its sandy beach and many hotels and boarding houses, this is the isle's largest resort and the port of call for the ferry.

Isle of Arran Heritage Museum
1mi/1.6km out of Brodick on the Lochranza road. ⏱Daily late Mar–Oct 10.30am–4.30pm. ⌾£4. ✕ ℘01770 302 636. www.arranmuseum.co.uk.

Visit the blacksmith's shop, milk house, and cottage furnished in late-19C and early-20C styles, alongside an exhibition area with displays of local social history, geology and archaeology.

Paths lead to the castle (*1mi/1.6km*) and Goat Fell (*3mi/5km*).

Brodick Castle★★
&⏱Apr–Oct daily 10am–5pm. ⌾£13.50. 🅿 ✕ ℘01770 302202. www.nts.org.uk.

Teeming with history and surrounded by mountains, Brodick is every inch the quintessential island castle. The present building was fashioned in 1844, but the seat dates back centuries to when it's strategic position overlooking the Firth of Clyde made Brodick a fortress to be reckoned with. The castle was the ancient seat of the Dukes of Hamilton and contains a fabulous collection of valuable artefacts.

A stronghold from earliest times, the castle soon became royal and from 1503 Hamilton property, when the 2nd Lord Hamilton inherited the earldom of Arran. Following the 2nd Duke's death at Worcester (1652), Cromwellian troops occupied the castle and extended it westwards. In 1844, a further extension, complete with a four-storey tower, all in the baronial style, was made by the ageing Gillespie Graham (1776–1855).

Indoors, dark wood, heavy Victorian colours and sporting trophies hark back to an age of aristocratic leisure and luxury. There is an **exhibition room** on the ground floor which houses the impressive Beckford collection. In the Hall and first-floor staircase landing busts portray William the 11th Duke and Princess Marie of Baden who made Brodick their home and for whom Gillespie designed the 19C extensions and decorations. Their son the 12th Duke is also here; gambler, racing man and collector of the many sporting items. Portraits on the landing show the 10th Duke and his Duchess, Susan Beckford, who assembled many of the exquisite treasures now on display. The first and more intimate suite of rooms was that of the Duchess of Montrose, heiress of the

Ferries to the Isle of Arran

Caledonian MacBrayne (*0800 066 5000; www.calmac.co.uk*) links Ardrossan, on the west coast of Ayrshire (55min, up to 10 ferries a day, some only May–Sept), with Brodick; and Claonaig, on the Kintyre peninsula, with Lochranza at the northern tip of the isle (30min, up to 9 ferries a day in summer). Reservations are not required for foot passengers, but online reservation is recommended for vehicles.

12th Duke, who made it her life's work to preserve the house and its collections which are now in the care of the National Trust for Scotland.

After two years of extensive works, the castle now has an exciting new visitor experience, focusing on the fascinating stories of the people who lived here, and with interactive activities to bring the building to life. There are several interactive activities, including the Victorian arcade where you can race a horse on a roll-a-derby or play other traditional Victorian games. These activities, combined with special lighting, audio and costumed interpreters, bring the castle to life.

Brodick castle

Gardens

Within the gardens, visitors can explore the Silver Garden Trail and Plant Hunters' Walk. The **walled garden** provides a sheltered site in which to grow and develop plants that are rarely seen growing outdoors in Scotland. Built in 1710, it's the oldest part of the gardens and has stunning views over Brodick Bay. The walled garden also has a new centrepiece around the sundial, with sandstone paving reflecting outwards. Built in 1845, the Bavarian summerhouse is the only survivor of four similar structures that once graced the woodland here. It was constructed in a Bavarian style as a wedding present for Princess Marie of Baden and holds a prominent position over the coast road and Brodick Bay.

There's so much to see in the **country park**, with over 10 miles of 🚶 waymarked trails. These pass by woodland, waterfalls and bathing pools, all helping to conjure up an island charm that will beguile children and adults alike.

Arran is a fantastic place to spot wildlife, and if you're lucky, you may encounter all of Scotland's 'Big 5' – red squirrels, seals, otters, red deer and golden eagles. Wildlife lovers can visit the new Red Squirrel Hide for a chance to watch this endangered species feed and play, alongside various species of birds.

The **Isle Be Wild adventure play park** is ideal for explorers of all ages to enjoy – one section is for toddlers and younger children and one is for older children. This epic woodland playground features zip wires, high towers, bridges across burns and jungle-style walkways – a real paradise for our younger visitors. Also keep an eye out for fairies on the new Fairies and Legends Trail, where you can also learn about our fascinating early history in a reconstructed Bronze Age roundhouse.

▶ Take the A841 north.

Corrie

This former fishing hamlet consisting of a line of whitewashed cottages makes a convenient starting point for ridge walkers and mountaineers.

Sannox Bay

Another sheltered sandy stretch. From here the road moves inland, up North Glen Sannox climbing to higher, bleaker moorland scenery in the shadow of the surrounding peaks and crests. Once over the watershed, the road drops steeply through Glen Chalmadale towards Loch Ranza.

Lochranza

Once an active herring-fishing village and port of call for the Clyde steamers, this rather scattered community has several holiday homes. The island was once famous for its whisky, favoured by mainland gentry, and in 1995 the **Arran Distillery** (🕐*Mar–Oct daily 10am–5.15pm; Nov–Mar daily 10am–4pm;* 📞*01770 830 264; www.arran-whisky.com*) became the first (legal!) whisky producers to open on the island in over 150 years (🚗*Several tours available – see website for details*). The roofless ruin of 16C **Lochranza Castle** (🕐*Apr–Oct 9.30am–5.30pm; www.historicenvironment.scot*) stands on a spit jutting out into Loch Ranza.

Once round the point the view extends over Kilbrannan Sound to the Kintyre coast.

The road becomes more twisting but remains close to the shore. Beyond is the shingle beach of Catacol bay.

Machrie Moor Stone Circles

🚶*1.5mi/2.4km inland off the road* 🅿.
These five ruined stone circles in an impressive setting date from the Bronze Age. Their exact purpose remains unclear. Four of the five had associated short cist burials and in two cases accompanying food vessels, which have been attributed to the period 1650 BCE–1500 BCE (Stonehenge c.2800 BCE–1550 BCE).

Drumadoon

Along the shoreline at Drumadoon are a series of sea-fashioned caves above a raised beach. Here you will find **King's**

Cave, said to be the place where the future king of Scotland, Robert Bruce, was inspired by the persistence of a spider building a web to return to his quest for the throne of Scotland. Alas, the attribution of the King's Cave is disputed by historians.

3mi/4.7km – King's Cave Trail: A circuit of forest and shoreline with wonderful views inland and across Kilbrannan Sound (*https://forestryandland.gov.scot/visit/kings-cave*).

Whiting Bay

This popular resort enjoys views to **Holy Island**, before the road rounds to **Lamlash Bay** affording the classic view of Brodick Castle, dominated by Goat Fell.

Lamlash Bay

Lamlash is the largest village by population on Arran. A prehistoric ring of stones suggest that an ancient settlement has existed here since antiquity. This is the place, where King Haakon and his Viking fleet dropped anchor en route to engage the forces of Alexander III at the Battle of Largs in 1263. King Haakon was defeated, and this removed the long-standing threat to Scotland. Haakon died in Kirkwall, Orkney on the way home, and three years later his successor ceded all the western isles to the king of the Scots.

Holy Island

This small unspoiled rocky island is home to the wild Eriskay pony, Soay sheep and Saanen goats.

The central summit, Mullach Mor, gives Holy Island an impressive appearance and tempts people across. Known in the Celtic language as Innis Shroin, the island of the water spirits, Holy Island has a long history as a place of spiritual importance.

Today, the island is home to a Buddhist community and a centre for world peace and health. You can spend the night there and attend meditation courses and yoga (*Apr–Oct; ℘01770 601 100; www.holyisle.org*).

From Lamlash, a ferry makes the round trip to Holy Island. Between April and end October, the Holy Isle Ferry (*£12 return; ℘01770 700 463, 07970 771 960*) runs when the tides allow. Times are posted at the jetty.

Lagg

The village of Lagg at the southern end of the island was once a hotbed of whisky making, both legal and elicit. So, it is perhaps not surprising that a new distillery was opened here in 2019. **Lagg Distillery** (*Daily 10am-6pm; ℘01770 870 565; www.laggwhisky.com*).

Bute ★

A wealth of hotels, guest houses and B&Bs, pastel-painted porticoes, curlicues, cast-iron coronets and sundry other Victorian extravagances greet your arrival at Rothesay on the island of Bute, and, bizarre as it may seem, there is often a queue of menfolk (and a few women) trying to see the restored Victorian toilets on the pier! Of course, there is a more substantial island beyond this fulsome and frenetic welcome, a serene place of sandy beaches, forts, Celtic chapels, stone circles and standing stones.

Ferries to the Isle of Bute

Caledonian MacBrayne (*℘0800 066 5000; www.calmac.co.uk*) links Rothesay with Wemyss Bay up to 17 times Mon–Fri, fewer at weekends. Reservations are not required for foot passengers, but online reservation is recommended for vehicles.

VISIT

Discovery Centre Cinema

A short distance up Victoria Street lies the grand cast iron and glass structure of the 1924 winter garden in one of Scotland's most innovative visitor centres. A 90-seat cinema (*01700 507043; https://discovery-centre-cinema.business.site*) shows the latest films and also accommodates the Bute Film Club, who screen arthouse cinema during the winter months.

Rothesay Castle★

🕐*Apr–Sept daily 9.30am–5.30pm; Oct–Mar Sat–Wed 10am–4pm.*
*£6. *01700 502 691.*
www.historicenvironment.scot.
Rothesay castle is unique among Scottish castles, both for its early date and for its unusual circular plan. It is famous for its association with the Stewarts – hereditary high stewards until 1371, and thereafter the royal dynasty. From them is descended Charles, Prince of Wales and Duke of Rothesay.

Bute Museum

🕐*Apr–Sept Mon–Sat 10.30am–3.30pm, Sun 1.30–3.30pm; Oct–Nov and Feb–Mar Tue–Thu and Sat 1.30–3.30pm.*
🕐*Dec–Jan. £4. *01700 505 067.*
www.butemuseum.org.uk.
An independently run museum containing displays on the natural and historical heritage of the island from Mesolithic and Neolithic times to the present day.

St Blane's Chapel

Originally founded in the 6C, the monastery here may well have been a forerunner of the better known monastery on Iona. Today, a wall surrounds the site within which stands a 12C chapel with a Romanesque chancel arch. This is a gentle and serene spot, given to peace and quiet.

Dunagoil Fort

This is one of the most important late prehistoric and early historic sites in Scotland. It can be found on the coastline just west of St Blane's chapel. This impressive fortress pays back the intrepid visitor with dizzying views from the top.

Dunagoil has been occupied from Neolithic time onwards and was probably a central fortress in the southern Dalriadic kingdom, roughly around the 6C.

Mount Stuart House★★

🕐*Apr–Jun and Sept–Oct guided tours daily at 11.30am, 12.30pm, 1.30pm, 2.30pm, 3.30pm; Jul–Aug daily 11am and 4pm, free flow noon–4pm; Jan–Mar pre-booked tours only Mon–Fri.*
*£13 (house and gardens), £8.25 (gardens only). *01700 503 877.*
www.mountstuart.com.
The spirit of 19C invention is embodied in Mount Stuart – a feat of Victorian engineering, this neo-Gothic mansion was one of the most technologically advanced houses of its age.

Mount Stuart is believed to be the first home in the world to have a heated indoor swimming pool, and the first in Scotland to be purpose-built with electric light, central heating, a telephone system and a Victorian passenger lift. Most of which are still in use today.

Cumbrae★

Also known as Great Cumbrae, the island is regarded as Scotland's most accessible island, and a great place for outdoor enthusiasts, and those in search of otherness. Given its small size (4mi/6.5km long and 2mi/3km wide), it is not surprising that Cumbrae is the most densely populated of the Scottish islands and popular since the heyday of the Clyde steamers.

The only settlement on Cumbrae is Millport, which curves around an attractive bay on the south coast, and is home to Britain's smallest cathedral, the so-called **Cathedral of the Isles**, opened in 1851, and the tallest building on Cumbrae.

Millport is a typical seaside resort without the brashness, and easily accessible by a frequent Calmac ferry from Largs (*0800 066 5000; www.calmac.co.uk*).

VISIT

Museum of the Cumbraes

Garrison House, built in 1745, is home to the Museum of the Cumbraes where Objects on display highlight the island's fascinating history and include the Goldie ethnography collection; diaries of Mary Ann Wodrow; 4000 year-old stone coffins – or 'cists' – found on the Cumbraes, and objects from island life over the years (℘01475 531 381).

At the **Robertson Museum and Aquarium**, you can learn about the wide variety of marine life and local habitats on the island. Situated within the grounds of the Field Studies Council building, the Robertson Museum features a reconstruction of part of "The Arc", the first research station ton the island in 1895t.

There is limited accommodation on Cumbrae, so the best idea is just to make a day of it.

Old pier, Millport, Cumbrae

© Ellgemac/iStockphoto.com

ADDRESSES

STAY

ARRAN

Dunvegan House – *Shore Road, Brodick.* ℘*01770 302 811. www.dunvegan house.uk. 9 rooms.* This attractive guesthouse is located on the seafront with fine views over the bay. Guests can enjoy the lawned garden and comfortable lounge. Owners will pick-up from the ferry by prior arrangement.

Lilybank – *Shore Road, Lamlash.* ℘*01770 600 230. www.lilybank-arran. co.uk. 6 rooms.* This whitewashed cottage on the bayfront looks onto Holy Island. Rooms are modern and cosy.

Glenisle – *Shore Road, Lamlash.* ℘*01770 600 559. www.glenislehotel.com. 13 rooms.* Attractive white-washed Victorian property, formerly an inn, with fine views over Lamlash Bay to Holy Island. Home cooking.

Douglas – *Brodick.* ℘*01770 302 968. www.thedouglashotel.co.uk. 22 rooms.* Stylish, modern hotel with pink granite façade, just past the ferry terminal. Integral **bistro** offers classical cuisine with a modern twist.

Auchrannie Resort – *Auchrannie Road, Brodick.* ℘*01770 302 234. www.auchrannie.co.uk. 64 rooms.* Spa resort hotel set in 96 acres, and with a good range of family oriented leisure facilities. **Cruize bar-brasserie** offers fine dining experiences, alongside **Brambles seafood and grill** restaurant, and **Eighteen69** glasshouse restaurant serving Scottish-themes tapas.

BUTE

The Esplanade Hotel and Restaurant – *4 High Street, Rothesay.* ℘*01700 502 001. www.esplanadebute.com. 17 rooms.* A traditional Scottish boarding-house situated prominently beside the harbour with fine views out over Rothesay Bay.

The Victoria Hotel – *55 Victoria Street, Rothesay.* ℘*01700 500 016. www. victoriahotelbute.com. 20 rooms.* Arguably the finest hotel on the island, with a choice of dining in the **Victoria Restaurant** or **Ghillies Bistro**.

EAT

ARRAN

The Lagg Hotel – *Lagg, Kilmory.* ℘*01770 870 255. www.lagghotel.com.* The hotel restaurant looks out over the river and gardens and serves a selection of dishes ranging from pub classics such as freshly battered haddock to more sophisticated dishes such as confit of duck with puy lentils. *13 rooms ( ).*

WHAT'S HAPPENING

Keep up to date with news and views, as well as informative features, on all the Scottish islands by reading the **Scottish Island Explorer** (*www. scottishislandsexplorer.com*) magazine.

The Inner Hebrides★★★

The Inner Hebrides are a motley lot, ranging from the large islands of Skye and Mull to the small, but no less beautiful islands of Lismore, at the southern end of Loch Linnhe and opposite Oban, and Gigha (⌖p258), a tiny island off the western coast of Kintyre. In essence, they are parts of mainland Scotland that became separated with rising sea levels; Kintyre didn't quite make it as an island, although the Vikings dragged their boats across the peninsula to claim it as an island. There are 35 inhabited islands in this group, and even more that are uninhabited. The earliest known settlers were Picts to the north and Gaels in the southern kingdom of Dál Riada prior to the islands becoming part of the Suðreyjar kingdom of the Norse, who ruled for over 400 years until sovereignty was transferred to Scotland by the Treaty of Perth in 1266. Today, the Gaelic language remains strong in some areas; the landscapes have inspired a variety of artists; and there is a magnificent diversity of wildlife, while the main commercial activities are tourism, crofting, fishing and whisky production. It will take many visits to fully appreciate all the islands, but they would be journeys of joy and discovery.

Isle of Skye ★★

The very name – Skye – is enough to evoke the mystery and enchantment of this Hebridean isle, famous for its spectacular scenery and wealth of legends. Its mystic aura has its origins in Norse and Gaelic times when the isle was known variously as the Misty Isle or Winged Isle. This enchantment derives in part from the isle's rapidly changing weather moods. It is hard not to be spellbound when a heavy mist is pierced by fingers of sunshine prior to rolling away, or when persistent rain clears to reveal a landscape of purest sunlit colours. Come to Skye expecting bad weather, and anything else is an improvement; patience will reward.

- ▶ **Population:** 9 232.
- **Info:** Bayfield House, Bayfield Road, Portree. ℘01478 612 992. www.isleofskye.com.
- **Location:** At 48mi/77km long and up to 25mi/40km in breadth, Skye is the largest of the Inner Hebrides group. Portree is the capital. Skye is joined to the mainland by the Skye Bridge at Kyle of Lochalsh.
- **Timing:** At least 2 full days; more if you enjoy hill walking.
- See www.cicerone.co.uk for a guide to walking on Skye.

ISLE OF SKYE TODAY

After much debate a **toll-bridge** opened in 1995, linking the island to the mainland between Kyleakin and Kyle of Lochalsh. It is the longest cantilever bridge (238m main span) in Europe, and aroused controversy on both aesthetic and conservation grounds, and not least for putting ferry operators out of business. People from all over Skye played a prominent part in a long campaign to force the Government to remove the tolls from the Skye bridge. The campaign lasted for more than nine years, with many people charged in the Courts just for refusing to pay the toll; some were arrested and even imprisoned for their opposition to the tolls. In the end they won the day and the tolls were lifted.

Kyleakin

The linear village of Kyleakin is the first port of call on reaching Skye by the bridge, and dominated by the ruined

Ferries to the Skye

Caledonian MacBrayne (*0800 066 5000 or 01475 650 397; www.calmac.co.uk*) operate a ferry between Mallaig and Armadale. Reservations are not required for foot passengers, but reservation is required for vehicles.

A ferry operated by the Isle of Skye Ferry Community (*www.skyeferry.co.uk*) runs between Easter and the end of October, 10am–6pm (7pm in Jun–Aug), from Glenelg and Kylerhea. £15 (car and up to 4 passengers)

Access to Glenelg is from Glen Shiel over the Mam Ratagan pass. The onward journey on Skye is on a rough and undulating single track road through a wild landscape until the main Broadford road is reached.

14C Castle Moil, the ancestral seat of the Clan MacKinnon. It is often written that a Norwegian princess created a toll here, by stretching a chain across the strait and stopping boats getting through without paying. Known as Saucy Mary, her name is reflected in the village today! Tradition says that she built Caisteal Maol when she was married to one of the MacKinnon chiefs, but it is known to have been built around 1490–1500 and was at one time called Dunakin (Hakon's fort).

At the pier is the **Bright Water Centre** (*Easter–Sept Mon–Fri 10am–4pm; *01599 530 040; www.eileanban.org*), an interactive interpretation of the local and natural history of the area, and home to an exhibition about the writer Gavin Maxwell, most famous for his book *Ring of Bright Water*. For a time he lived at the lighthouse on Eilean Bàn, and his writing opened the eyes of many to the beauty of the Highlands, as well as capturing stories of his life with otters.

Sleat★★

Pronounced 'slate', this is the southernmost area of Skye, projecting from the main road between Kyleaking and Broadford. The name derives from *sleibht*, which refers to an extensive tract of moorland, a description well deserved. But this thumb of rocky, lochan-endowed moor, creased into myriad folds, is also known as the 'Garden of Skye', an appellation that comes from Sleat's more sheltered environment, protected from the worst of Skye weather.

The history of Sleat is essentially that of the MacDonalds, in spite of the fact that there was a time when Sleat was Macleod territory.

Once across the initial stretch of moorland, the road draws level with **Ornsay**, a small tidal island, widely acknowledged as one of the most beautiful tidal islands in western Scotland.

Armadale Castle, Gardens & Museum of the Isles

Mar and Nov Mon–Fri 10am–3pm; Apr–Oct daily 9.30am–5.30pm. £8.75. *01471 844 305.* (*01471 844 774) www.armadalecastle.com.*

Only ruins remain of much of the castle, but part of it has been restored so that six interconnecting galleries, each with their own theme, take visitors through 1 500 years of the history and culture of the area once known as the Kingdom of the Isles. The MacDonalds (Clan Donald) were the Lords of the Isles and the museum follows their story and that of the Highlands. There are also special exhibitions that change each year plus children's trails and interactive exhibits. The castle grounds offer 16ha of exotic trees, shrubs and flowers, a selection of woodland walks, nature trails, scenic viewpoints overlooking the Sound of Sleat, and a children's adventure playground.

Broadford

This small village is a key service centre for southern Skye, lying on the edge of Broadford Bay – Breiðafjorðr in the Old Norse.

Broadford functioned largely as a cattle market until the early 19C, when Thomas Telford built the road from Portree to Kyleakin.

Legend has it that the recipe for the liqueur Drambuie was given by Bonnie Prince Charlie to Clan MacKinnon who then passed it onto James Ross in the late 19C. Ross ran the Broadford Inn (now the Broadford Hotel), where he developed and improved the recipe, initially for his friends and then later to patrons. The brand had been owned by the MacKinnon family for more than a hundred years, but was bought by William Grant & Sons in 2014.

Elgol★★

The small dispersed settlement of Elgol lies at the end of a long single-track road that leaves Broadford and starts down the wide glen of Strath Suardal against which there is a fine backdrop of the Red Cuillin.

The road eases past the ruined **Cill Chriosd** (Christ's Church) and its fascinating and superbly located graveyard surrounded by cotoneaster-clad walls and containing a small group of yew trees, said to ward off evil. Cill Chriosd served as the parish church until 1840, and is now a most evocative ruin.

Not far beyond the church, a stunning view opens up of Bla Bheinn, a Black Cuillin outlier and a dramatic image of the difficulties that await anyone considering venturing into the mountains. Elgol itself, however, has its own way of dealing with the Cuillin, offering trips on the *Bella Jane* (◔*Mar–Oct; ℰ01471 866 244 or 0800 731 3089; www.bellajane. co.uk; also booking offices in Broadford and Elgol*) across Loch Scavaig to a landing near the outflow of Loch Coruisk from where it is a short walk into the very heart of the Cuillin. ◔Be sure not to miss the last returning boat.

The Cuillin★★★

These dramatic, often harsh mountains figure large in most views of Skye. The **Black Cuillin** – that's Cuillin, not Cuillins, nor Coolin Hills, just Cuillin – are a horseshoe-shaped range encircling the glacial trough of Loch Coruisk. Gabbro rocks form over 20 sharp peaks, all over 3 000ft/914m with the highest point being Sgurr Alasdair (*alt. 992m*). This ridge, intersected by ravines and vertical gulleys, provides a real challenge for climbers, and with few of the summits accessible to anyone without scrambling ability.

Facing these across Glen Sligachan are the conical summits of the **Red Cuillin**.

Sgurr nan Gillean and the northern Black Cuillin from Sligachan

The pink granite here has weathered to more rounded forms, although Bla Bheinn is an exception.

The Cuillin are a favoured haunt for climbers, geologists and walkers; however, treacherous weather, scree slopes, and steep ascents and descents really do require skill and experience...and, preferably, a guide. For low-level walkers, provided the transport logistics can be resolved, the walk through Glen Sligachan (*pronounced Slig-a-han*) to Camasunary and then to Kilmarie or (much more demanding) to Elgol, is arguably the finest walk on the island.

Sligachan★★★
The drama of Sligachan is evident the moment you arrive. Here is the finest view of the jagged peaks of the Black Cuillin, set against the rounded, smooth-sided domes of the Red Cuillin across the great divide of Glen Sligachan. On the one hand Sgurr nan Gillean marks the northern end of the Cuillin ridge, and on the other the distinct profile of Marsco looms over the glen.

Closer to the road the scree slopes of Glamaig promise nothing but endless toil. Yet in 1899, a visiting Gurkha, Havildar Harkabir Thapa, ran barefoot from the door of the Sligachan Hotel to the top of Glamaig and back in an astonishing 55 minutes. Today (since 2018), the record stands at 44 minutes and 22 seconds (*www.scottishhillracing. co.uk*), and the race is held each year, early in July.

Portree★
Portree is the main town on Skye, a busy port with a thriving culture. It sprawls around a natural harbour fringed by high ground, cliffs and raised beaches. This is the cultural focus of Skye, and the Aros Centre, just to the south of the town, which celebrates the island's Gaelic heritage and runs theatre, concerts and films and incorporates an exhibition capturing the drama of Skye's history, a spectacular RSPB exhibit with live and recorded footage of rare sea eagles.

Old Man of Storr

© lightkey/iStockphoto.com

In the centre of town, the Royal Hotel is the site of MacNab's Inn, the last meeting place of Flora MacDonald and Bonnie Prince Charlie in 1746.

🚗DRIVING TOURS

🚗 1️⃣ TROTTERNISH★★
48mi/77km.

This peninsula (20mi/32km long) to the north of Portree is known for its unusual rock formations. A coastal road (A855) circles it with lovely seascapes over the Sound of Raasay and Loch Snizort.

▶ Leave Portree by taking the A855 north towards Staffin.

The Trotternish ridge★
The Trotternish peninsula is dominated by a ridge rising to 719m at The Storr, and composed of a succession of escarpment summits – 13 in all – fashioned by landslip and erosion. The hills are composed of horizontal flows of basaltic lavas, which built up on top of each other. On the east side the underlying sedimentary rocks have collapsed under the weight of the basalt, tipping everything sideways to form the distinctive landslips we see today.

The most distinctive feature of the ridge is the rock pinnacle **The Old**

The north Trotternish ridge from the Quiraing

Man of Storr, first ascended in 1955 by Don Whillans and James Barber. ⚶ A steep path leads up from the A855 through an area of cleared plantation, and upwards to the base of the Old Man.

Brothers' Point★★

⚶ Rubha nam Brathairean – Brothers' Point in English – is an interesting destination, seldom visited by tourists hastening north, but well worth the short walk from the parking area at Cul nan Cnoc (*Culnacnoc*). The origin of the name is uncertain, but it is thought to have been a place where monks lived and worshiped in safety more than a thousand years ago.

Kilt Rock★

Walk across the car park to the viewing area. There are interesting cliff formations of basaltic columns and an impressive waterfall that sometimes plumes back up into the air drenching the unsuspecting passerby.

An Corran★

A slight detour from the A-road, An Corran may be the oldest human site on Skye, being Mesolithic (8500–5000BP). The first arrivals on the north-west coast were bands of hunter-gatherers known as Mesolithic (Greek meso = 'middle' and lithos = 'stone' or Middle Stone Age people). A shell midden (a heap of food debris consisting mainly of sea shells) found here is generally accepted as the first proof of Mesolithic man on Skye. The site at An Corran has been dated to around 8500BP. Apart from its historical significance, this remote spot, tucked away out of sight and rarely visited by tourists, is quite special for another reason. On the beach at An Corran you may at low tide find footprints left by a family of dinosaurs that walked across the sand 165 million years ago! They were Ornithopods, herbivorous creatures that walked on two legs. The footprints are best seen after a winter storm as they are often covered by the sea at high tide and by sand in the summer.

There is a lovely sandy beach close by – at low tide once a year the local cattle are herded at full gallop down the slope, onto the sand and before they get chance to think about it they are in the sea and swimming to Staffin island for winter grazing.

Quiraing★★

From Staffin Bay, this great ridge with its numerous rocky bastions is clearly visible.

⚶ There is a popular walk into the sanctuary of the Quiraing, which sets off

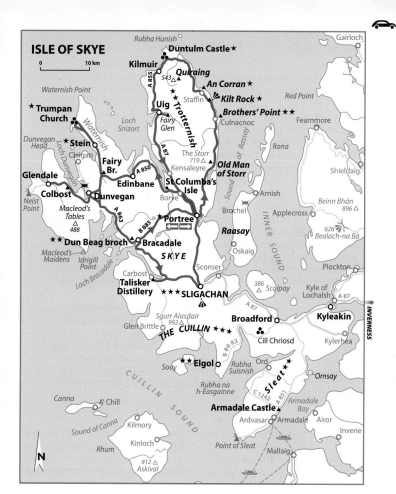

Rubha Hunish
Duntulm Castle ★
Gairloch
Kilmuir
543 △
Quraing
An Corran ★
Waternish Point
Uig
Staffin
Kilt Rock ★
Red Point
Fearnmore
★ Trumpan
Church
Fairy
Glen
Trotternish
Brothers' Point ★ ★
Culnacnoc
Dunvegan
Head
Loch
Snizort
Rona
Fernmore
Stein
Claigan
The Storr
719 △
Sound of Rassay
Shieldaig
Fairy
Br.
A 850
Kensaleyre
Old Man
of Storr
Arnish
Beinn Bhán
896 △
Glendale
Edinbane
St Columba's
Isle
Colbost
Dunvegan
Borve
Brochel
Applecross
626 ⌁
Bealach-na Bà
Neist
Point
Macleod's
Tables
488 △
A 863
B 885
Portree
INNER
Plockton
★★ Dun Beag broch
Bracadale
Raasay
Macleod's
Maidens
Idrigill
Point
SKYE
Oskaig
Sconser
Scalpay
Kyle of
Lochalsh
A 87
Loch Bracadale
Carbost
Talisker
Distillery
★★★ SLIGACHAN
386 △
Plockton
Glen Brittle
Sgurr Alasdair
992 △
THE CUILLIN ★★★
Broadford
A 87
Kyleakin
Cill Chriosd
Kylerhea
INVERNESS
Canna
A' Chill
Soay
★★ Elgol
Rubha
Suisnish
Ord
Sleat
Ornsay
Inverie
Sound of Canna
Kilmory
Rubha na
h-Easgainne
C 1242
Armadale
Bay
Rhum
Kinloch
CUILLIN SOUND
Armadale Castle ▲
Ardvasar
Armadale
Airor
812 △
Askival
Point of Sleat
Mallaig

0   10 km

from the high pass, Bealach Ollasgairte (not named on maps), and follows a clear path all the way. Stout footwear is essential.

Duntulm★

The jagged tooth of a ruined ancient MacDonald stronghold stands on its clifftop site commanding the sea route to the Outer Hebrides. The castle (⊶ *not open to the public*) was built in the 14C–15C, at a time of feuds between the rival MacLeod and Macdonald clans. The defences were improved in the 16C, and by the early 17C the MacDonald's had finally gained the upper hand in the area.

Kilmuir

In the churchyard is a Celtic cross monument to **Flora MacDonald** (1722–1790) commemorating her bravery when she organised the escape of (Bonnie) **Prince Charles Edward Stuart** from the Outer Hebrides dressed as her maid. The Prince was soon to arrive in France and lifelong exile, having spent months wandering the Highlands, a hunted fugitive with £30 000 on his head. A quarter of a century later Dr Johnson and Boswell visited Flora at her nearby home.

Skye Museum of Island Life

♿ 🕑 *Easter–Sept Mon–Sat 9.30am–5pm.* ♿£3. 🅿 ☏01470 522 206. www.skyemuseum.co.uk.

Flora MacDonald

Flora MacDonald (1722–1790), was the daughter of Ranald MacDonald of Milton on South Uist in the Outer Hebrides. Her father died when she was a child, and her mother was abducted and married by Hugh MacDonald of Armadale, Skye. So, she was brought up under the care of the chief of her clan, the MacDonalds of Clanranald her father's cousin, and was partly educated in Edinburgh.

During the Jacobite Risings, in June 1746, at the age of 24, she was living on Benbecula when Bonnie Prince Charlie took refuge there after the Battle of Culloden.

Flora promised to help the prince escape the island. The commander of the local militia was her stepfather, Hugh MacDonald. The commander gave her a pass to the mainland for herself, a manservant, an Irish spinning maid, Betty Burke, and a boat's crew of six men. The prince was disguised as Betty Burke. After a first repulse at Waternish, Skye, the party landed at Kilbride. The prince was then hidden in rocks while Flora found help for him, following which it was arranged that he be taken to Portree and from there to Raasay.

The talk of the boatmen brought suspicion on Flora MacDonald, and she was arrested and brought to London for aiding the prince's escape. After a short imprisonment in the Tower of London, she was allowed to live outside of it, under the guard of a gaoler. When the Act of Indemnity was passed in 1747, she was released.

On 6 November 1750, at the age of 28, she married Allan MacDonald of Kingsburgh, a captain in the army, and the couple lived at Flodigarry where they subsequently became parents to five sons and two daughters.

In 1774, she and her husband emigrated to North Carolina, but in 1779 Flora returned to Scotland. She resided at the homes of various family members, including at Dunvegan, her daughter Anne having married Major General Alexander Macleod. Flora died at Kingsburgh on Skye in 1790, at the age of 68. She is buried in the Kilmuir cemetery.

The museum groups a late-19C crofter house, a weaver's house, a smithy and a ceilidh house. The latter has an interesting display of photographs and documents including newspaper cuttings, which give a flavour of crofting life in the late 19C.

▶ Continue following the A855 towards Uig.

🚶 From the tight hairpin bend above Uig (pronounced Oo-ig) there is a fine, short walk on a good path out to the top of the promontory at Idrigill, a fine **view★** and a good space to watch for eagles. *If you park your car here, do so with consideration; buses travel this road, and take a wide turn at the bend.*

Uig

This sprawling settlement is essentially the ferry port for sailings to the Outer Hebrides, set in a beautiful protected bay, indeed "Uig" is Norse for "sheltered bay". Often it is warm and dry here when there is rain further south. The community makes its living from fishing, crofting, tourism and the ferry.

Around the bay are several crofting townships including Cuil, Rha and Idrgill. The rivers Rha and Conon flow into the bay through wooded gorges. A small area of woodland is managed by the Woodland Trust and is one of the few areas of ancient woodland left in Skye. The **Tower** on the hill to the South of Uig village, opposite the Uig Hotel, is associated with the Highland Clearances. It was a place where the local crofters had to go to pay their rents.

The Fairy Glen – Volcanic activity on northern Skye began about 60 million years ago; it has now stopped, but along the eastern side of Trotternish a vast amount of evident landslip shows that some geological changes are still rumbling on. Some authorities estimate that at one time the lava that covered northern Skye was more than 1 200m thick, with most of the lava flows occurring from what are known as 'fissure eruptions' that happened over a long period of time. Today, the lavas of north Skye dip at a shallow angle to the west, and have an average individual thickness of just 10m. The result of all this flow of geological material is a rather uniform landscape, punctuated by outcrops of harder rocks, such as today take the form of Castle Ewen, in the so-called Fairy Glen, near Uig. To get there, take the minor road along the south side of Glen Uig, and once the isolated farmsteads and crofts are passed, you enter a fantastic wonderland of lumps and bumps and crazy pinnacles. Follow the road with care until the distinctive pinnacle of Castle Ewen comes into view – geologists have one view about this upthrust of rock, but everyone around Uig swears it was created by fairies.

▷ Now simply follow the A87 back to Portree.

② DUNVEGAN★
44mi/70km.

This tour embraces the central part of northern Skye, running out to the MacLeod stronghold at Dunvegan before turning south, with ample opportunity to deviate and explore the crumpled recesses of Duirinish.

▷ Leave Portree on the A87 and at Borve bear left onto the A850. After 3km/2mi turn right (for Peinmore, Tote and Prabost) and immediately left.

St Columba's Isle (Eilean Chaluim Chille)★★
A completely unexpected and little-known spot, St Columba's Isle is an ancient burial ground on a tiny island in the River Snizort. It has a ruined chapel dedicated to St Columba, who visited Skye around 585, and is the site of the cathedral church of the Bishops of the Isles.

Before crossing the footbridge there are a couple of stones with information panels telling you about this and the mortuary chapel where Clan Nicholson have 28 of their Clan chiefs buried. In the early 1500s the area was also the site of the Battle of Trotternish, an important battle between the warring clans of the MacDonalds and the MacLeods.

Edinbane
The name An t-Aodann Bàn is said to be taken from the bog cotton that grows on the hill sides. There has been a settlement here since 1600, but the village, its hotels and **Edinbane Pottery** (℘01470 582 234; www.edinbane-pottery.co.uk) are much more recent, and a pleasant diversion on the way to Dunvegan.

Fairy Bridge
Fairy Bridge at Beul-Ath nan Allt (the Ford of the Three Burns) inspired fear among travellers in the past. Horses were spooked, probably by the dancing fairies, that, or the fact that three murders have been committed there? Whatever it was, men feared to pass that way at night.

This is said to be where the fairy wife of the Chief of Clan MacLeod left him to return to her own people. She left their son wrapped in a silken shawl which became the clan's famous Fairy Flag, to be used just three times to save the Clan when it was in trouble.

Fairy Bridge was a very important place during 1842, when thousands of people came from all over Skye to hear open air sermons being preached during the Skye revival.

⊚ *Note, too, that it is just 'Fairy Bridge', not 'The Fairy Bridge'.*

▷ A deviation north along the B886 leads into Waternish, to the village of Stein on Loch Bay.

Stein★
Previously known as Lochbay, Stein is a crofting township originally intended as a major fishing port. The 18C Stein Inn is

the oldest pub on Skye. The folk singer Donovan had a house in Stein during the 1970s.

In spite of its small size, Stein also boasts art and craft shops, a dive centre, a renowned seafood restaurant, and Skyeskyns an exhibition tannery and shop.

▶ Beyond Stein a narrow road continues further into Waternish to Trumpan.

Trumpan★

The atmospheric ruin of Trumpan church is as far as you can drive into Waternish. The presence of the church indicates that this was once a thriving township. The church has never confidently been dated, but it is thought it may have been on this hilltop spot for 700 years, when it was known to its Gaelic-speaking congregation as Cille Chonain, or St Conan's church. In the graveyard is the Clach Deuchainn (The Trial Stone). Here, an accused person was blindfolded and it was established they were telling the truth if, with ease, they were able to find the aperture in the stone with their hand. If they had to grope they were guilty.

The nearby **Ardmore Bay** is the setting for the infamous, if somewhat fiction-alised, **Battle of the Spoiling of the Dyke** (♻ *See box*).

▶ Return to the main road and turn right.

Dunvegan

This is the main settlement on the west coast, famous for its **castle★** (♿ ⊙ *daily Apr–mid-Oct 10am–5.30pm;* £14; gardens only, £12; seal boat trip, £9.50; ✗; 🕿 01470 521 206; www.dunvegancastle. com) the seat of the MacLeods. This Hebridean fortress is set on a rocky platform commanding Loch Dunvegan and has a fascinating history of personalities, clan legends and mementoes. The most valuable heirloom is the **Fairy Flag**. According to one legend this was the parting gift to Iain, the 4th Chief from his fairy wife with whom he had lived for 20 years. The fabric, thought once to have been dyed yellow, is silk from the Middle East (Syria or Rhodes); experts have dated it between the 4C and 7C. Perhaps it was the robe of an early Christian saint, or maybe the war banner of Harold Hardrada, King of Norway, killed in 1066. It is said that the flag has the power of warding off disaster to the clan and has twice been successfully invoked.

The Battle of the Spoiling of a Dyke

On a Sunday in May 1578, a party of MacDonalds from Uist landed in Ardmore Bay in a fleet of eight ships under cover of mist, and found their way to Trumpan church where they surprised the local people, MacLeods, at worship. In one of the cruellest episodes in the Island's history, the MacDonalds set fire to the thatched church, burning the congregation or putting any that escaped the flames to the sword, save one. The woman, mortally wounded, escaped and raised the alarm, though the flames of the church had been seen by the guards at Dunvegan castle. Vengeance was swift, for the MacLeods, aided by the forces of the Fairy Flag, that changed 'the very grass blades ... to armed men', set about the MacDonalds, forced them back to the bay, where they discovered that their galleys had been beached by a retreating tide. All but a handful of the MacDonalds were slain, and their bodies laid alongside a stone dyke that was pushed over them as a makeshift grave.

The MacDonalds' act was itself a reprisal for an equally savage act, when the MacLeods found hundreds of them hiding in a cave on the island of Eigg, and suffocated them by lighting a fire at the cave entrance.

Neist Point and the lighthouse

© imageBROKER/ hemis.fr

Among other prized possessions is the Dunvegan Cup and Horn of Sir Rory Mor, the 15th Chief. Tradition requires that the heir, on coming of age, quaffs the horn filled with claret without falling down drunk! Family portraits include canvasses by Zoffany, Raeburn and Ramsay. During summer a boat trip runs across Loch Dunvegan to small islets colonised by **seals**, where these playful sea mammals can be observed at close quarters. Herons also nest on these islands and Arctic terns and many other species of bird can frequently be seen.

▶ From south of Dunvegan the B884 crosses the peninsula to Glendale.

Looming large on the horizon are **MacLeod's Tables**, two flat-topped mountains where a MacLeod chief is said to have entertained James V to a torchlit banquet.

Colbost Folk Museum

🕐*Closed until 2020 due to storm damage; call or check website for details.* 𝄢*01470 521 296. www. dunveganmuseums.co.uk/Colbost.html.* The Black House shows a typical abode of the 19C, with the family quarters and byre under one roof. Behind is an interesting example of an illicit whisky still. Documents on display recall how an uprising of local crofters highlighted the problems of 19C crofting. The resultant Croft Act accorded among other things the much-sought-after security of tenure. Today the area around here is popular with "white settlers" from England.

Glendale

This is a typically scattered crofting community with a mill down in the bay. The estate encompasses the small crofting townships of Skinidin, Colbost, Fasach, Glasphein, Holmisdale, Lephin, Hamaraverin, Borrodale, Milovaig and Waterstein.

Over 200 years ago, crofters came with their grain and a supply of peat, some even from the Outer Hebrides, to mill their grain here. The kiln was used to reduce the moisture content prior to grinding.

Beyond Glendale a narrow road presses on to Waterstein and **Neist Point lighthouse**, north of Moonen Bay, sometime shark-hunting ground of Gaving Maxwell (*Harpoon at a Venture*). Neist Point is an atmospheric place, and a great spot to sea watch for dolphins, killer whales, basking sharks and sea birds.

Return to Dunvegan and then follow the coast road (A863) south to Bracadale.

Dun Beag broch★★

A fine example of a Hebridean broch, apparently occupied to the 18C (www.historicenvironment.scot). Dun Beag perches on top of a rocky knoll, a shot uphill walk from the road. The surviving remains of the tower-like structure stand around 2m high, and the interior measures some 11m across within walls about 4m thick.

Bracadale

In itself a small place, Bracadale and its neighbour Struan have little to detain visitors, except those interested in mountaineering. In the churchyard at Struan lies the grave of **Professor Norman Collie**, described by one biographer as one of the four greatest mountaineers of his time. In spite of class distinctions, Collie formed a firm friendship with John Mackenzie, the first native Scot to become a professional guide. Together Collie and Mackenzie were a formidable team and put up many new routes in the Cuillin. In death, they were buried, unusually head-to-toe, in the Struan churchyard.

At Struan turn left onto the B885, a narrow, single-track road that leads across a wide expanse of moorland back to Portree.

For a longer return to Portree, stay on the A863 to the head of Loch Harport, and there deviate right to Carbost.

Talisker Distillery

Nov–Feb Mon–Sat 10am–4.30pm, Sun 10.30am–4.30pm; Mar–Oct Mon–Sat 9.30am–5pm, Sun 10am–5pm. Visit by guided tour only; see website for details. Tours £10–£45. 01478 614 308. www.malts.com. Set on the shores of Loch Harport with dramatic views of the Cuillins this is Skye's only distillery, producing a sweet, full-bodied single malt.

Return to the A863 and turn right, driving as far as Sligachan, and there turn left onto the A87 back to Portree.

EXCURSION

RAASAY

Reached by a regular ferry from Sconser on Skye (www.calmac.co.uk). Raasay lies between Skye and the mainland of Scotland. It is separated from Skye by the Sound of Raasay and from Applecross by the Inner Sound. It is most famous for being the birthplace of the poet Sorley MacLean, an important figure in the Scottish literary renaissance.

About 14mi/23km north to south and 3mi/4.8km east to west (at its widest), Raasay's terrain is varied. The highest point at 444m is Dùn Caan, an unusual, flat-topped peak. The 2mi/3km of road between Brochel Castle and Arnish were built using hand-tools by Calum MacLeod over a period of ten years. Only when complete was the road surfaced by the local council; by then Calum and his wife were the last inhabitants of Arnish. The story of the building of the road is told in Calum's Road by Roger Hutchinson.

Raasay is a splendid place for those in search of peace and quiet, and to look for wildlife, since the island is one of only four of the Inner Hebrides where mountain hares breed. Raasay is regularly visited by white-tailed sea eagles and golden eagles. and there are populations of otter and red deer.

ADDRESSES

STAY

Blà Bheinn B&B – Crossal, Carbost. 01478 640 269. www.blabheinn.scot. 2 rooms. Open Apr–Oct. B&B not far from Sligachan, with fine views of the Red Cuillin and the northern edge of the Black Cuillin. 2 nights minimum stay.

Rosedale – Beaumont Crescent, Portree. 01478 613 131. www.rosedale hotelskye.co.uk. 20 rooms. This converted quayside terrace of former fisherman's houses enjoys views over the harbour.

🛏️ **Marmalade** – *Home Farm Road, Portree. ☎01478 611 711. www.marmalade hotel.co.uk. 8 rooms.* Formerly Portree House, the Marmalade is a small intimate Georgian hotel set in mature gardens, with excellent views overlooking Portree. **Restaurant** (🛏️🛏️).

🛏️ **Edinbane Inn** – *Edinbane. ☎01470 582 414. www.edinbaneinn.co.uk.* Originally built as a farmhouse this established inn has a warming stove and open fire, exposed stone walls, and a friendly atmosphere. **Restaurant** (🛏️🛏️). Music on some evenings.

🛏️ **Glenview** – *Culnacnoc. ☎01470 562 248. www.glenviewskye.co.uk. 3 rooms.* A B&B and yarn shop on the way round Trotternish.

🛏️ **Stein Inn** – *Waternish. ☎01470 592 362. www.stein-inn.co.uk. 5 rooms.* Stay at the oldest inn on Skye, with all rooms offering views out across Loch Bay.

🛏️ **Sligachan Hotel** – *Sligachan. ☎01478 650 204. www.sligachan.co.uk. 21 rooms.* Long-established hostelry with a history of mountaineering exploits. Directly on the main road to Portree. **Seamus's Bar** adjoining, and campsite across the road.

🛏️ **Tigh an Dochais** – *13 Harrapool, Broadford. ☎01471 820 022. www.skyebedbreakfast.co.uk. 3 rooms.* Contemporary 5-star B&B by the sea with fantastic views of Broadford Bay.

🛏️ **Bosville** – *Bosville Terrace, Portree. ☎01478 612 846. www.bosville hotel.co.uk. 25 rooms.* Skye's first boutique-style hotel overlooks the town harbour and hills; rooms are modern and stylish and its award-winning **Dulse and Brose Restaurant** 🛏️🛏️ offers bistro style food.

🛏️ **Cuillin Hills Hotel** – *Portree. ☎01478 612 003. www.cuillinhills-hotel-skye.co.uk. 34 rooms.* Each room is individually styled to a high standard; some traditional, others more contemporary. The **View Restaurant** (🛏️🛏️) offers seafood dishes.

🛏️ **Flodigarry Hotel** – *Flodigarry. ☎01470 552 203. www.hotelintheskye. co.uk. 29 rooms.* The hotel holds special appeal for those with a passion for refined splendour, highland hospitality, comfort, luxury and old-world elegance.

Bedrooms are available in both the main house and Flora MacDonald's Cottage. The **Skye Restaurant** (🛏️🛏️) serves modern Scottish cuisine.

🛏️ **Toravaig House Hotel** – *Knock Bay, Sleat. ☎01471 820 200. www. toravaig.com. 9 rooms.* Individually styled bedrooms using quality materials and furnishings. Two-roomed **restaurant** with classical menu of island produce.

🛏️ **Kinloch Lodge** – *Kinloch Lodge Hotel, Sleat. ☎01471 833 333. www.kinloch-lodge.co.uk. 19 rooms.* 17C hunting lodge with fantastic views and a country house feel; comfy antique-filled lounges and contemporary bedrooms. **Restaurant** (🛏️🛏️).

🍽️ EAT

🛏️ **The Old Inn** – *Carbost. ☎01478 640 205. www.theoldinnskye.co.uk.* A free-house traditional Highland pub set on the shores of Loch Harport. Popular with locals as well as tourists and hill walkers, Dishes with local fish, meat and produce served all day. **Bunkhouse** accommodation (🛏️).

🛏️ **The Old School** – *Dunvegan. ☎01470 521 421. www.oldschoolrestaurant.co.uk.* Lunches and snacks during the day with café style service, and an à la carte evening menu 7 nights a week, all based around local seafood, Scottish beef and game.

🛏️ **Loch Bay Restaurant** – *1 MacLeod's Terrace, Stein, Waternish. ☎01470 592 235. www.lochbay-restaurant. co.uk.* Chef Michael Smith runs a contemporary Scottish restaurant with classic French influences.

🛏️ **Sconser Lodge** – *Sconser. ☎01478 650 333. www.sconserlodge.co.uk.* Housed in the Sconser Lodge Hotel (*8 rooms* 🛏️🛏️) this restaurant, open to non-residents, focuses on meat, game and the finest local seafood. *8 rooms* (🛏️🛏️).

🛏️ **Three Chimneys & The House Over-By** – *Colbost, Dunvegan. ☎01470 511 258. www.threechimneys. co.uk.* This restaurant, with 6 spacious rooms, is set in an atmospheric crofter's cottage on the shore of Loch Dunvegan. It serves accomplished Skye gourmet seafood dishes. The **House Over-By bedroom suites** 🛏️🛏️ are characterful, sumptuous, very romantic and enjoy spectacular views of the sea.

The Small Isles ★

The four "Small Isles" – Eigg, Muck, Rum and Canna – are part of the Inner Hebrides, and lie just off the west coast at the junction of the Sound of Arisaig and the Sound of Sleat. In spite of their apparent 'togetherness', the islands are distinct, each differing in its geography, agronomy and ownership. But collectively they offer a wonderful menu of scenery, lifestyle and wildlife.

ISLE OF EIGG

 www.isleofeigg.org. No visitors' vehicles allowed on the island.

Eigg is dominated by "An Sgurr", a dramatic pitchstone ridge, the largest of its kind in Europe. Laig bay, a large white Atlantic beach, faces the stark outlines of the Cuillin of Rum, a most memorable view.

Further North is the Singing Sands, a musical quartz beach surrounded by outstanding geological formations. Eigg has many cultural and historical attractions, too: Picts and Vikings have left their marks, and its rich history is steeped in clan warfare and the crofting way of life.

In 1997, the people of Eigg set up the Eigg Heritage Trust to buy the island, which had gone through a troubled time with previous owners. Now owned by the Trust, Eigg offers stunning scenery, wildlife and a relaxing get-away-from-it-all feeling for the visitor.

ISLE OF RUM

 www.isleofrum.com.

Managed by Scottish Natural Heritage, Rum is one of Scotland's finest National Nature Reserves. The island is a haven for birds and animals including sea eagles, deer, goats, otters and seals.

The Cuillin of Rum, with their Norse names – Askival, Hallival, Trollaval, Orval – bring an air of mystery to an island once described as the Forbidden Island. These mountains are the remains of a huge, ancient volcano and attract geologists from all over the world.

Rum was the site for the reintroduction of sea eagles in Scotland, which have since flourished and spread to many other parts of the western seaboard. The island once supported a thriving community, but like many places across Scotland was 'cleared' in the 19C to make way for sheep and red deer.

Kinloch Castle

At the head of Loch Scresort, and still very much as it was when the family left, is a time capsule of Edwardian life, including superb furniture and fittings, a marvellous Steinway piano, Lady Bullough was a pianist, and one of the few operating Orchestrions, automated organs operated by paper-rolls, in the world. Guided tours daily Apr–Oct; check website for times. £9. $\mathcal{C}$ 01687 462 026; www.isleofrum.com.

ISLE OF MUCK

 www.isleofmuck.com.

Muck is the smallest of the Small Isles and the most fertile, and possessing a small population, mainly living round the tiny harbour of Port Mor. It has been owned by the same family – the MacEwens – for over 100 years.

In spite of it diminutive size, Muck has a lot to offer; moreover, it is an easy island to explore on foot, and a great place to relax, having wonderful quiet beaches, stunning landscapes and wildlife. Some of the sites include Beinn Airein (138m, the highest point); Camus Mor, a Site of Special Interest (SSSI); Bágh, a renovated croft house with a turf roof;

'A'chille' ('the old village'); Shell Bay, and Caisteal an Duin Bhain, a prehistoric fortified rock.

ISLE OF CANNA

www.theisleofcanna.com.

Canna is the most westerly of the four Small Isles and was previously owned by John Lorne Campbell; it was given to the National Trust for Scotland in 1981, and today the Trust has several working crofts worked by a small population. The island has been a bird sanctuary since 1938 and the 157 different species of birds have been recorded since 1969.

Canna House

Ⓘ *Closed for tours, but gardens are open.* ☎ *01687 462 963; www.nts.org.uk. Access to the walled garden is free at all times.*

Now in the care of the National Trust for Scotland, Canna House was the home of Gaelic scholars, Dr. John Lorne Campbell and his wife Margaret Fay Shaw. She wrote her autobiography in 1995 'From the Alleghenies to the Hebrides' and John Lorne Campbell published 'Canna, the story of a Hebridean Island'.

Isle of Mull ★
and Isle of Iona

The Inner Hebridean island of Mull with its varied scenery and sense of peace is an ideal holiday centre and the stepping-stone for Iona. The sheltered Sound of Mull separates the island (24mi/39km long and 26mi/42km wide) from the mainland. The deeply indented coastline varies from the rocky cliffs of the Ross of Mull, with its offshore skerries, to small creeks and sheltered sandy beaches, such as Calgary Bay. Inland the scenery can be desolate and dramatic, like the moorlands which rise to the island's highest peak, Ben More (*alt.* 966m), or peaceful and pastoral, dotted with crofting townships. As with all the Hebridean Islands, the seaward vistas are superb. But the main reason for visiting Mull must surely be the stunning wildlife: otters, red deer, white-tailed and golden eagles, and a wealth of birdlife.

🚗 DRIVING TOURS

🚗 1 NORTH MULL

44mi/71km circuit departing from Tobermory. Narrow, single-track roads.

▶ **Population:** 2 667.

Info: The Pier, Craignure ☎ 01680 812 377. https://visitmullandiona.co.uk.

Location: Caledonia MacBrayne (CalMac) ferries connect Mull with Oban (40min), Kilchoan and Lochaline on the mainland. If travelling in summer book ahead (*www.calmac.co.uk*). The island roads are for the most part twisting and narrow – but perfectly suited to a leisurely discovery of Mull's charms.

Don't Miss: Calgary Bay; in April the Mull Music Festival; the island of Ulva.

Don't Forget: Petrol stations are few and far between. Keep the tank topped up.

Timing: If you want to experience the island atmosphere allow at least three full days on Mull.

Kids: Calgary Bay beach. Young fans of the TV series *Balamory* will easily recognise Tobermory.

Visit www.cicerone.co.uk for a guide to walking on Mull.

ISLE OF MULL

Starting from Tobermory and calling at the white sand beach of Calgary this excursion is ideal for families.

🧑‍🧒 Tobermory ★

HQ of the Hebridean Whale and Dolphin Trust (Visitor Centre: ✆01688 302 620; www.hwdt.org).

The main town of Mull, Tobermory is famous for the cheerful colours of its waterfront buildings and the yachts bobbing in the natural harbour. This was the setting for the BBC children's TV show *Balamory*. A popular yachting centre, Tobermory Bay is also known as the last resting place of a galleon which sailed with the Spanish Armada and there are tales of treasure deep in the bay.

The town rises steeply from the bay, fronted by the sort of mix of shops you come to expect from island communities, from banks and hotels, pharmacy and supermarket, and a scattering of restaurants, including a pierside chippy where everything is cooked to order.

▶ Take the B8073 past the Mishnish lochs: Pellach, Meadhoin and Carnain an Arnais westwards towards Dervaig.

Kilmore standing stones ★

Until 2015 cloaked in forest plantation, the Kilmore standing stones are a puzzle, but now stand isolated, as presumably they originally were, amid a rash of tree-felling debris. There were formerly five standing stones, but only two remain on their feet, the others being recumbent. It has been suggested that they indicate both the rising southern moon (south-east) and possibly the setting northern moon (north-west)

Dervaig

Dervaig is a charming village with a single street of low white houses and the unusual pencil-shaped tower of Kilmore church. It features superb stained-glass windows by the leading Scottish stained-glass artist, Stephen Adam.

Close by in beautiful Glen Bellart is the **Old Byre Heritage Centre** (🕐*Apr–late Oct Mon–Fri 10.30am–6.30pm*; ✗; 📞*01688 400 229; www.old-byre.co.uk*). The island's history and traditions are related in museum displays while two films illustrate, respectively, Mull's history and its abundant and varied wildlife.

The adjacent tea room is a great place for a lunchtime bowl of soup.

⊙ Continue along the B8073.

🚶 Just before reaching Calgary a minor road runs north and west to Caliach, from where a short walk leads out to the splendid viewpoint of Caliach Point.

👪 Calgary Bay ★★

This unspoiled west coast bay with its white shell sand beach is an ideal spot to search for otters and eagles.

There is a basic campsite here, toilets and a seasonal café a short way along the road towards Dervaig.

⊙ The B8073 bears south along the bay and after 2mi/3.2km runs parallel with the coast and the islands of Gometra and Ulva on your right.

Isle of Ulva ★★

£5 return ferry for foot passengers and cyclists. 📞01688 500 264. www.isleofulva.com.

Once inhabited by several hundred people, Ulva is now almost deserted. A network of footpaths lead to abandoned villages and a variety of landscapes (basalt cliffs, moors, woods).

By the ferry slipway **Sheila's Cottage** is a faithful reconstruction of a traditional thatched croft house which was last lived in early this century by Sheila MacFadyen. With an exhibition on island history, **The Boat House** (*www.theboathouseulva.co.uk*) is outstanding for a simple coffee break or as a lunchtime showcase for Ulva's seafood...and cakes!

🚶 You can walk all the way to the adjacent island of Gometra, but you will need to start early and not dawdle if you don't want to miss the last ferry.

Failing that, there is a good choice of walks around the island, especially that to Ormaig, birthplace of Lachlan Macquarrie (*see GRULINE*).

Eas Fors waterfall ★

Eas Fors Waterfall is one of the most spectacular waterfalls on Mull, with superb views across Loch Tuath to Ulva. It falls in three levels, one above the road, the second immediately below it, and the third – not to be approached – which falls down steep cliffs into the sea. *Children and pets should be kept away from the lower falls. There are no barriers and the grassy ground can be very slippery at times.*

Loch na Keal ★

The meadows, rocks and streams of this west coast sea loch make for a great picnic stop, and attract cyclists and bird-watchers. The loch is a great place to watch for otter and dolphin.

⊙ After Killiechronan, turn left to Salen, and there left again to follow the undulating 'main' road back to Tobermory.

Aros Park ★

This verdant park is within walking distance of Tobermory, by a path along the edge of the bay. Trails wander through attractive woodland, lush with ferns, and there's a waterfall to discover, plus a play trail for children to explore. You can cook a barbecue and even try your hand at trout fishing.

The park has superb views too, looking back to Tobermory and over Calve Island and the Sound of Mull to the craggy profile of Ardnamurchan.

🚗 ② SOUTH MULL ★

35mi/56km.

Starting from Craignure, this tour visits two castles and slips through the great glen before turning north to head to Loch na Keal and Salen. Dramatic landscapes flank the great glen; dramatic driving leads through to Loch na

Keal, and all with a better than average chance of seeing eagles.

▶ Take the A849 south to Torosay. Around 1.5mi/2.5km from Craignure you will pass Torosay Castle (⌖ *closed to the public*) on your left. It was built in 1856 in the Scottish Baronial style.Continue along the A849 for 1mi/1.6km.

Duart Castle★★

ⓣ*Apr 11am–4pm; May–mid-Oct daily 10.30am–5pm.* ⌖£7.50. ✕ ℗ ℘*01688 812 309. www.duartcastle.com.*

Duart Castle, home of the chief of **Clan Maclean**, is on a strategic site perched on a rocky crag, guarding the Sound of Mull. The earliest keep, built c.1250, was extended, only to be stormed in the 17C, garrisoned by Redcoats in the 18C then abandoned to fall into a ruinous condition. The 26th clan chief restored the stronghold to its present-day appearance. Clan and family mementoes are on show. On the upper floor a Scouting Exhibition recalls Lord Maclean (1916–90), 27th clan chief, and his lifetime devotion to the movement and his role as Chief Scout.

The ramparts have good views across to the mainland.

▶ Rejoin the A849 and drive west through Glen More following the course of the Lussa River and then the Coladoir River. At the head of Loch Scridain turn right onto the B8035.

Loch Scridain

The shores of this sea loch are a great place to spend time birdwatching and keeping an eye out for otters. The hills above are popular with eagles, of both varieties.

▶ The ongoing drive across Ardmeanach to Loch na Keal is at its most dramatic beyond the coastal area known as Gribin. There is rather more scope for nature watching on the south side of Loch na Keal than on the north.

🚶 A very agreeable and easy walk can be taken from the River Ba into the vast amphitheatre of Loch Ba; go just as far as the bothy at Knockantivore, then return the same way. Take binoculars and look for deer as well as birdlife.

Gruline

On reaching Gruline, a scattered settlement at the head of Loch na Keal, park the car by the side of the road and walk in to visit the **mausoleum★**. This simple building reveals a remarkable link with Australia, for it is the last resting place of Major General Lachlan Macquarie, who was born at Ormaig on the island of Ulva.

Macquarie served as Governor of New South Wales from 1809 until 1821 and did much to help shape Australia into the country it has since become. He was also the first person to use the name "Australia" in an official document, which he did in 1817. Macquarie later returned to England, and died in London in 1824, following which his body was returned to Mull for burial.

▶ At Salen, turn right and drive back to Craignure.

EXCURSIONS

STAFFA ★★ AND TRESHNISH ISLANDS ★★★

The basaltic island of Staffa, lying on the western seaboard of Mull, beyond Ulva, is a deserted National Nature Reserve run by the National Trust for Scotland. It owes its fame to its unique geological features, immortalised in Mendelssohn's overture *Fingal's Cave,* composed following his 1829 visit.

Further to the northwest lie the Treshnish Islands, an archipelago of small islands and skerries that are part of the Loch Na Keal National Scenic Area. They are also designated as a Site of Special Scientific Interest, a Special Protection Area due to their importance for breeding seabirds and a marine Special Area of Conservation. This is one place where, at the right time of year, you can see puffins literally at your feet, as well as

The Birthplace of Christianity in Scotland

The Columban Settlement – In the year 563, 166 years after St Ninian's mission (see WHITHORN) **St Columba** (521–97) and a group of followers set off from Ireland. Their chosen site, this bare and somewhat inhospitable island, suited the tenets of their monastic traditions. The community flourished and was successful in converting the native people of the mainland. It was from Iona that St Aidan set out to establish Irish Christianity in Northumbria in 636. Even after the death of Columba in 597, the community went from strength to strength and was to become the mother house for the Columban monasteries.

Although nothing remains of St Columba's monastery, the period was one of great artistic achievement. There were beautiful intricately carved crosses and grave slabs, and it has been suggested that the sacred work of art, the *Book of Kells*, was undertaken in whole or in part by the scribes and illuminators of the Iona community. This period was brought to an end by the Norse raids of the 8C and 9C.

Some of the monks accepted refuge at Dunkeld, which became the new centre of the Columban Church. Following a particularly savage raid in AD 803 when 68 monks lost their lives, the remaining members, with the relics of St Columba and perhaps the *Book of Kells*, returned to Kells in Ireland.

hundreds, probably thousands of razor-bill, guillemot, gannet and cormorant. A day spent visiting Staffa and Treshnish will be well spent. Tours are offered by Staffa Tours (*www.staffatours*), Turus Mara (*www.turusmara.com*) and Staffa Trips (*www.staffatrips.co.uk*), all operating from multiple starting points – check their websites for details.

ISLE OF IONA ★

CalMac ferries make the short trip from Fionnphort on the southwest tip of the Isle of Mull (www.calmac.co.uk).

This tiny remote and isolated windswept Inner Hebridean Isle – measuring about 3mi/5km long by 1mi/1.6km wide – is one of the most venerated places in Scotland. The main sights are easily reached on foot from the pier at Baile Mór. Over 1 400 years ago St Columba and his companions landed on its southern shore to establish a monastic settlement. Today, the island remains an important place of pilgrimage although there are few tangible remains.

The **nunnery** was founded at the same time as the monastery and the ruins here are a good example of a typical, small medieval nunnery. The cloister-garth is bordered by the early 13C church and the ranges of the conventual buildings, parts of which date from the late medieval period. Fragments of the cloister arcade are on display in the Infirmary Museum. Beyond the main group is a simple rectangular building, St Ronan's church, with narrow triangular-headed windows.

Across the road, in the old manse, is the **Iona Heritage Centre** (*01681 700 439; www.ionaheritage.co.uk.*) with exhibits on the social history of the isle.

Maclean's Cross★

The cross, which dates from the 15C, is a product of the local school of carvers. On the west face is a Crucifixion while on the reverse the intricately carved patterns maintain the Celtic traditions.

Reilig Odhrian

This early Christian burial ground is reputed to be the last resting place of Scotland's early kings, the Lords of the Isles and other chieftains. The most notable medieval effigies and grave slabs are now in the Infirmary Museum.

St Oran's Chapel★

This is the island's oldest surviving building, dating from the 12C (restored 20C). The simple rectangular structure has a worn but rather fine Norman west door with three arches of beak-head and chevron decoration.

High Crosses

Of the three standing crosses **St Martin's★** (8C), complete and original, displays figure scenes on the west face. Only the truncated shaft of St Matthew's (9C–10C) remains. The third one is a replica of St John's Cross (8C).

Abbey

&♿🕐Apr–Sept daily 9.30am–5.30pm; Oct–Mar Mon–Sat 10am–4pm. 🕐25–26 Dec, 1–2 Jan. 💷£9. 📞01681 700 512. www.historicenvironment.scot.

The present church no doubt stands on the site of its Columban predecessor. The original 13C church was altered towards the end of the century and enlarged in the 15C. Conversion work included the adding of a tower at the crossing and a south aisle to the choir. Fragments of the 13C Benedictine church include the north transept and an arcade of the choir's north wall. The elaborate trefoil-headed doorway below was inserted when the north aisle was converted into a sacristy in the 15C. Note the carved capitals of the arcade and the piers of the crossing.

The pale creamy green communion table is of Iona marble. A door in the north wall of the nave leads into the cloisters with the unusual twin-columnned arcade. There are two originals in the west side.

To the north of the west front is St Columba's Shrine, said to be the original burial place of the saint. The exact whereabouts of the saint's relics remain a mystery.

Infirmary Museum★

🕐Times and charges same as Abbey; admission included on same ticket.

The museum houses an outstanding collection of early Christian and medieval stones. The 8C Celtic **Cross of St John★** has pride of place. The early Christian works (Nos. 1–49) dating from 563 to the second half of the 12C include incised crosses (Nos. 3–33) and ring crosses (Nos. 23–33 and 38–48). The medieval section (Nos. 50–110) has examples of the Iona School of carving (14C–15C). Their work included grave slabs, effigies and free-standing crosses (♿see Maclean's Cross). The group (Nos. 71–83) of grave slabs includes human figures and the distinctive West Highland galleys. Nos 98–101 show the armour of the period.

Michael Chapel

🕐 Times and charges same as Abbey.

This small early 13C chapel was used by the monks as an interim church while they built the new church on the site of the old.

Island Festivals

The **Mull Music Festival** (♿see Calendar of Events) features concerts for accordions, fiddles, pipes and Gaelic choirs. Ceilidhs give summer visitors a chance to participate. The **Tobermory Highland Games** are known for the piping and clan march. The **Mull Theatre** (🕐May–Sept; 📞01688 302 828; www.tobermory.co.uk) has a summer season with plays adapted for a two-person cast. The Mull Theatre is based at Druimfin, just outside Tobermory.

ADDRESSES

🏠 STAY

MULL

🛏🛏 **Brockville** – Raeric Road, Tobermory. 📞01688 302 741. www.brockville-tobermory.co.uk. 2 rooms. This modern house is set a 5min walk from the harbour. Its breakfast room has sea views and there is a lovely outdoor terrace.

🛏🛏 **Harbour Guest House** – 59 Main Street, Tobermory. 📞01688 302 209. www.harbourguesthouse-tobermory.com. 7 rooms. Originally a fisherman's cottage, Harbour Guest House is one of the colourful buildings situated on the water front of the harbour.

Mishnish Hotel – *Main Street, Tobermory.* ✆*01688 302 500. www.themishnish.co.uk. 12 rooms.* Open all year and something of an institution offering great accommodation, bar meals and the touch of class that is the **Mishdish Restaurant**. If you fancy a pizza, try the upstairs **Amaretto Restaurant**. You can't go wrong here.

Highland Cottage – *Raeric Road. (by Back Brae), Tobermory.* ✆*01688 302 030. www.highlandcottage.co.uk. 6 rooms.* This modern small luxury hotel by the harbour has lovely individually styled bedrooms, two of which have four-poster beds and offer sea views.

Tobermory Hotel – *53 Main Street, Tobermory.* ✆*01688 302 091. www.thetobermoryhotel.com.* Boutique-style hotel offering quality service and a warm highland welcome.

Park Lodge Hotel – *Western Road, Tobermory.* ✆*01688 302 430. www.park-lodge-tobermory.co.uk.* A local family run hotel offering affordable modern accommodation on three floors, but no lift.

IONA

Ardoran House B&B – *Iona.* ✆*01681 700 070. www.ardoranhouse.co.uk.* A modern bed and breakfast guest house with spacious well appointed twin or double bedrooms.

Skerryvote B&B – *Iona.* ✆*01681 700 776. www.skerryvore-iona.co.uk. 2 rooms.* Skerryvore is open year-round and provides evening meals in winter. Alternatively, you can cook for yourself in the guest kitchen. The owners run the island taxi and guests and their luggage can be picked up on arrival and dropped off on departure, at Iona Pier free of charge.

Argyll Hotel – *Iona.* ✆*01681 700 334. www.argyllhoteliona.co.uk. 20 rooms.* A small owner-operated hotel in the village street overlooking the Sound of Iona. Integral **restaurant** serving local produce.

St Columba Hotel – *Iona.* ✆*01681 700 304. www.stcolumba-hotel.co.uk. 27 rooms.* Originally built as a Manse in 1846 and since extended, the hotel stands on rising ground to the north of the village.

ⴵ/ EAT

Fisherman's Pier Fish and Chip Van – *Main Street, Tobermory.* ✆*01688 301 109. tobermoryfishandchipvan.co.uk.* A legend, where everything is cooked to order, fresh and delicious. Don't be shy about standing in the street eating your supper; cruise ship travellers often make a beeline for this little place.

Duart Castle Tearoom – *Duart, Craignure. Open Apr–mid-Oct 10.30am–5pm (11am–4pm in Apr).* A great spot for a light lunch of soup and roll, snacks and traditional baking using home-grown ingredients.

Café Fish – *The Pier, Tobermory.* ✆*01688 301 253. www.thecafefish.com. Open mid-Mar–Oct.* Small and very popular eatery at the far end of the harbour. Very much seafood specialists, and a good place to go for the freshest oysters and mussels. Reservations strongly advised. Can get noisy.

The Old Pier Restaurant – *Craignure Inn, Craignure.* ✆*01680 812 305. www.craignure-inn.co.uk.* The best of local produce: scallops from the Sound of Mull, mussels farmed at Inverlussa on Loch Spelve, crabs from Croig on the west coast of the island and Highland beef and Hebridean lamb from the Lagganulva farm near Ulva Ferry. Also has **3 rooms**.

Mishdish Restaurant – *Main Street, Tobermory.* ✆*01688 302 500. www.themishnish.co.uk.* Seafood restaurant and oyster bar with a touch of class, and a decent wine list. For something Italian, try the upstairs **Amaretto Restaurant**. For something a bit more rustic, try the **Mish Bar**. There's accommodation, too – **12 rooms** (see above).

Highland Cottage – *Raeric Rd. (by Back Brae), Tobermory. Open Mid-Mar–late-Oct.* ✆*01688 302 030. www.highlandcottage.co.uk.* Set by the harbour, the cosy Highland Cottage features a pretty dining room and a locally sourced menu.

Ninth Wave Restaurant – *Bruach Mhor, Fionnphort. Open May–Oct.* ✆*01681 700 757. www.ninthwaverestaurant.co.uk.* Award-winning game and seafood restaurant down the Ross of Mull. Home-grown produce, fresh-caught seafood and organic meats from Mull.

Islay and Jura ★★

Although lying close together and seemingly with the same geological pedigree, Islay (pronounced Eye-la) and Jura are remarkably different. For the most part, Islay is low-lying with moorland and a few small hills buttressed by sea cliffs. Jura, in contrast, is rugged and hilly, an island wilderness rising to the impressive summits of the Paps of Jura. The two are separated by the Sound of Islay.

ISLAY ★★

Islay is the southernmost island of the Inner Hebrides, and its capital is Bowmore, although Port Ellen is the main port.

Islay has a long and rich human pre-history, evidence having been found to show that the island has been inhabited since Mesolithic times.

Standing stones, crannogs, duns, fort and chambered cairns proliferate, but few compare with the **Kildalton High Cross** close by Ardmore Point. Carved by a sculptor from Iona around the year 800, the cross ranks among the finest Celtic relics in Scotland.

Islay used to be the seat of the Lordship of the Isles in the 14C and 15C, and a power-base sufficiently strong to enter into its own treaties with England, Ireland and France.

Whisky

For many, the island is synonymous with the distillation of whisky. Indeed, Islay is one of five whisky distilling localities and regions in Scotland whose identity is protected by law. There are eight active distilleries and the industry is the island's second largest employer after agriculture.

Those on the south of the island produce malts with a very strong peaty flavour, considered to be the most intensely flavoured of all whiskies. From east to west they are Ardbeg, Lagavulin, and Laphroaig. On the north of the island Bowmore, Bruichladdich, Caol Ila and Bunnahabhain are produced, which are substantially lighter in taste.

Kilchoman is a microdistillery opened in 2005 toward the west coast of the Rinns. All the distileries have shops and visitor centres and organise tours.

Wildlife

The island is also renowned for its wildlife and its floral diversity, having as much in common with Ireland as with Scotland; at the Mull of Oa it is almost equidistant between the two.

Lochs Gruinart, Loch Gorm and Loch Indaal host to as many as 35 000 over-wintering Barnacle geese and 12 000 Greenland white-fronted geese which appear in great number, while at the cliffs of the Mull of Oa choughs share the territory with snow bunting, purple sandpiper and a herd of feral goats. Other waterfowl include whooper and mute swan, eider duck, Slavonian grebe, goldeneye, long-tailed duck and wigeon. Several thousand red deer inhabit the moors and hills; fallow deer can be found in the southeast, and roe deer are common on low-lying ground. Otters are frequently seen around the coasts along Nave Island, where common and grey seals breed. Offshore, minke whales, pilot whales, killer whales and bottle-nosed dolphins are regularly recorded.

Ferries to Islay and Jura

Caledonian MacBrayne (✆ *0800 066 5000; www.calmac.co.uk*) operates a 2-hour crossing from Kennacraig to Islay several times per day throughout the year.

To reach Jura from Islay, a small car ferry run by ASP Ship Management Ltd. on behalf of Argyll & Bute Council sails from Port Askaig on Islay to Feolin on Jura, the journey takes only 10 minutes. ✆ *01496 840 681 for enquiries; www.islayjura.com*. There are around 14 ferries a day Mon-Sat with about half that number on a Sunday.

Cupstones

Associated with various Islay churches are **cupstones** of uncertain age; these can be seen at Kilchoman church, where the carved cross there is erected on one, and at Kilchiaran Church on the Rhinns. In historic times some may have been associated with pre-Christian wishing ceremonies or pagan beliefs in the "wee folk".

JURA ★★

Underlying metamorphic rock produces a dour moorland landscape on Jura, devoted almost entirely to deer farming. This is by far the wildest island among the Inner Hebrides, and much of the island of roadless and uninhabited, with vast areas of blanket bog, heather, bracken and rock that culminate in the three Paps of Jura, summits almost as high as those on Arran: Beinn an Òir (*alt. 785m*); Beinn Shiantaidh (*alt. 757m*) and Beinn a' Chaolais (*alt. 733m*).

Only one road penetrates the island, with rather more ambition that realism. Beyond Lealt the road degenerates into a rough track that leads past Barnhill, sometime home of Eric Blair, aka **George Orwell**, who lived here during the final years of his life, while writing his prophetic novel 1984, and described the island as "extremely ungetatable".

Off the northern end of the island is the Gulf of Corryvreckan, where strong Atlantic currents and unusual underwater topography conspire to produce a particularly intense tidal race, and the third largest whirlpool in the world.

EXCURSIONS

COLONSAY★★ AND ORONSAY★★

Linked by a tidal strand, Colonsay and Oronsay have resplendent golden beaches with few rivals. Halfway across the strand is the sanctuary cross, which it is said if reached by any Colonsay miscreant, gave immunity from punishment provided he or she remained on Oronsay for a year and a day.

Kildalton High Cross

© Jaime Pharr/iStockphoto.com

Both islands have been occupied since at least 5 000 BCE, and Oronsay has a number of Mesolithic shell middens and numerous duns and forts.

Most visitors are attracted to Colonsay for the tranquility and raw natural beauty. It may be one of the smallest of the Hebridean islands, but Colonsay offers the visitor a very wide variety of natural attractions in its varied habitats. In a great environmental project started in 2013, Colonsay and Oronsay became the first Hebridean islands to be clear of litter. Each year, volunteers go out to clean up the 50 miles of coastline, and now have the annual task under control; visitors are invited to join in the effort (*http://colonsaycc.org.uk/Litter.htm*). The project has been extended to 2022.

Colonsay is served by a CalMac Ferries Ltd. from Oban five times a week in summer, four times a week in winter. The journey takes just over 2 hours and passes the islands of Kererra and Mull and then sailing south and west past the islands of Seil, Luing, Scarba and Jura.

In both summer and winter, there is an extra option. This is a ferry that originates at Kennacraig or Port Askaig, makes its way north via Islay and Colonsay to Oban, then pauses before re-tracing the route. If you want a day trip to Colonsay from Islay, this is only possible on a Wednesday or Saturday in summer (www.calmac.co.uk.

The Outer Hebrides★★★

The chain of islands known as the Outer Hebrides, or Western Isles, extends some 130mi/209km from the Butt of Lewis in the north to Barra Head in the south. The islands – Lewis, Harris, North Uist, Benbecula, South Uist, Barra and Vatersay – buffeted by the Atlantic waves, may be treeless and windswept, but boast beautiful moorlands, glistening lochans, superb sandy beaches and crystal clear water. Isolation has helped to preserve the islands' cultural identity; Gaelic is widely spoken and many islanders are bilingual.

Lewis★★★ and Harris★★

Athwart Atlantic fury, the Outer Hebrides are often referred to as the Long Island, as if they were one continuous island. In fact, they are many islands, with a distinctive culture that has the Gaelic language and traditions are its roots. In addition to the main components there are several groups of even more remote islands that roam the seas, access to most of which is just something to dream about: the Shitants, the Monachs, Flannan Isles (which featured in Peter May's 2016 novel *Coffin Road*), North Rona, the St Kilda group and far flung Rockall.

To visit any of these islands, large or small, needs rather more ingenuity than the ability to read a ferry timetable. These are lonely, remote places, that will appeal to lovers of wild places frequented by wildlife for which they provide safe and peaceful havens. It was not always the case: in times past almost all the islands were inhabited, and the seas around them frequented by trawlers from as far south as Fleetwood in Lancashire that sailed north to fish the Atlantic depths. For many, the light of life has gone forever, but they remain places of fascination for the curious and intrepid voyager.

The largest islands are deeply indented by arms of the sea such as Loch Ròg, Loch Seaforth and Loch nam Madadh. There are also more than 7 500 freshwater lochs in the Outer Hebrides, and the interplay between water and sky is endlessly fascinating,.

▸ **Population:** Lewis 19 658; Harris 1 916.

▪ **Info: Stornoway, Lewis:** 26 Cromwell Street, ☎01851 703 088 **Tarbert, Harris:** Pier Road, ☎01859 502011 **Lochmaddy, North Uist:** Pier Road. ☎01876 500 321 **Lochboisdale, South Uist:** Pier Road. ☎01878 700 777 www.visithebrides.com.

▶ **Location:** Lewis and Harris are one island, roughly 26mi/43km distant from the Scottish mainland.

◉ **Don't Miss:** Callanish Standing Stones.

◷ **Timing:** Allow at least 2–3 days, longer if you can. ◔ There is much to be said, if time allows, for beginning a Western Isles journey in Stornoway and ending it in Castlebay on Barra (allow 7–10 days, plus sailing time from and back to the mainland).

▲▪ **Kids:** To the east of Stornoway the Eye Peninsula has some fine sandy beaches; Barra is also renowned for its sandy beach, which is used as the airport runway – when the tide is out.

Stornoway

The capital and only town of any size lies on a narrow neck of the Eye Peninsula. The main shopping area fronts the landlocked harbour, which is also overlooked by the 19C castle (now a technical college) and its wooded grounds. A good view of the town can be had from the foot of the war memorial on the hill behind the hospital. Stornoway makes a good base.

An Lanntair "The Lantern"

&♿🕐*Mon–Sat 10am–late; last Sun of month 1.30–5pm.* ✗; *℘01851 708 480. www.lanntair.com.*
On the Stornoway waterfront, near the ferry terminal, this arts centre is a fine introduction to the island's arts and culture with all-day food, exhibitions, live music and events, and a craft shop.

Lews Castle

Designed by Glasgow architect Charles Wilson, and standing across the harbour at Stornoway, Lews Castle was built in 1847–1857 as a country house for Sir James Matheson, who had previously bought the whole island with his fortune from the Chinese opium trade. *The grounds are open to the public.*

LEWIS

Arnol Black House – *signposted off the A858.* ♿🕐*Apr–Sept Mon–Sat 9.30am–5.30pm; Oct–Mar daily except Wed and Sun 10am–4pm.* 🎫*£6. ℘01851 710 395. www.historicenvironment.scot.*

This traditional, fully furnished, straw-thatched house shelters under one roof a sleeping area with box beds, a living area, and a byre and stable-cum-barn. This type of dwelling, known as a Black House – due to its open hearth – was common up until 60 to 70 years ago. Beside the Black House, a furnished 1920s croft house can also be viewed.

Callanish Standing Stones★★★

Calanais: signposted off the A858; Visitor centre★. 🕐*Apr–May and Sept–Oct Mon–Sat Mon–Sat 10am–6pm; Jun–Aug Mon–Sat 10am–6pm; Nov–Mar Tue–Sat 10am–4pm.* ✗ *℘01851 621 422. www.callanishvisitorcentre.co.uk.*
This famous group of stones (the locals say you never count the same number twice!) forms a circle with alignments radiating outwards at the compass points. The site is one of a series in the vicinity and it is generally assumed they were used for astronomical observations. It dates from the late Stone Age and early Bronze Age (3000 BCE–1500 BCE), making it over 4 000 years old and roughly contemporary with Stonehenge. Composed of Lewisian gneiss the stones were once partially buried under peat. The central cairn or burial chamber was a later addition by the Neolithic people (2500–2000 BCE). A smaller set of stones★ stands just off the A858 to the southeast, and is also worth a visit.

Dun Carloway Broch★★

(Dùn Chàrlabhaigh: signposted from the A858). www.historicenvironment.scot.
Although not a complete example (♿*see Mousa, SHETLAND*), enough remains of this structure to intrigue. The galleried walls and entrance guard chamber are still visible, making this one of the best-preserved examples of a broch.

Callanish Standing Stones
© kippiss/iStockphoto.com

Garenin

Found at the end of the Garenin road beside the village bay, Garenin is most famous for the **Blackhouse Village**, which consists of nine restored traditional thatched cottages. These houses were lived in till 1974 and were the last group of blackhouses to be inhabited in the Western Isles. Some now serve as holiday cottages.

Uig

Pronounced "oo-ig", this township is famed on two counts, as the home of the Brahan Seer, a legendary 17C clairvoyant, and as the place where the world-famous Lewis Chessmen (&*see Box, opposite*) were found in 1831. Uig is well off the beaten track, but its beach, sand dunes and machair grasses make it well worth the effort.

HARRIS
Leverburgh

The township of Obbe was renamed by the English soap magnate Lord Leverhulme in 1920. He had acquired Harris in 1918, and Lewis – for £167 000 – later the same year, and dreamed of developing the islands. However, his grand schemes, including a project to make Leverburgh an important fishing port, failed.

The **An Clachan** community shop (&*01859 520 370; www.harriscommunityshop.co.uk*) displays the **Millennium Tapestry** (©*Mon–Sat 9am–5.30pm*) a series of tapestries depicting scenes from Harris, and created by members of the community The tapestries in this project are a mix of quilting, embroidery, cross-stitch and needlepoint.

Harris Tweed

The **orb** trademark guarantees that this fine quality cloth is handwoven by the islanders in their homes. Weaving tweed originated in Harris and in the mid-19C it was commercialised in Lewis where today all processes after weaving are done in the mills of Stornoway, Carloway and Shawbost. In the mid- to late-20C the industry went into decline, due in no small part to its antiquated looms which are costly to maintain and produce cloth of a width not suitable for modern cutting equipment. The recent invention of a new loom, which is easier to operate, and weaves cloth twice as wide as previously, as well as producing more intricate designs, has helped to stem the decline, thus reducing a threat to the way of life of whole communities.

The Lewis Chessmen

The **Lewis Chessmen**, a unique hoard of 80 pieces carved from walrus ivory, are of Norse origin and date from the mid-12C. Most of the pawns are missing but the superbly crafted main pieces include the kings, queens, knights and bishops with their distinctive attributes: crowns, shields, swords and croziers. The demonic expressions of the gaming pieces, uncovered by a storm, terrified the finder who suspected witchcraft. According to tradition a curse is attached to the chessmen and previous owners have met horrible deaths. The pieces changed hands several times until they were acquired by the British Museum. Some are also displayed at the Museum of Scotland in Edinburgh.

St Clement's church

In the township of Rodel near the southern tip of Harris is a church with the outstanding **tomb★** of the 16C builder Alexander MacLeod (d.1546).

Splendid carvings decorate the arch and the back of the recess above the effigy of the 8th Chief of MacLeod.

Shawbost School Museum (*Apr–Oct Mon–Sat 10am–5pm. 01851 710 212; www.visitouterhebrides.co.uk*). This small folk museum gives an insight into the life and customs of the past.

Tarbert

With a good range of facilities, the main community of Harris, Tarbert, sits on the isthmus between West and East Lochs. It is the ferry terminal for Skye and North Uist, and for boat tours to the Shiant Islands.

North Uist, Benbecula and South Uist

Bridges and causeways link the islands, which offer spectacular land and seascapes: rolling hills and moorland, white sand dunes and beaches, sparkling sea lochs and pounding waves. This is a very uncomplicated landscape, geologically interesting, but for the general visitor a place to relax and explore.

The chambered cairns and stone circles, castles and chapels attest to the islands' rich history. There is a rich birdlife and in summer a profusion of wild flowers, good walking and fishing.

Barpa Langass★ on North Uist is a Neolithic chambered cairn, about 5 000 years old. It can be reached by a short walk from the A867, about 5mi/8km southwest of Lochmaddy. Excavation has found evidence of burnt burials as well as pieces of pottery.

Benbecula is a low-lying jigsaw of lochans; Rueval its only hill of note. Such action as there is takes place at Balivanich, fuelled by the nearby military base. With the rugged heights of Hecla and Beinn Mhor to the east and fertile machair to the west, **South Uist** is scenically the finest of the southern group. Just south of Cill Donnain, the **birthplace of Flora Macdonald** lies in sad ruins down a side road.

Eriskay and Barra

Between South Uist and Barra, the tiny island of **Eriskay** seems inoccuous enough. But it has its place in history for two important events; one rather more long-lasting in popular memory than the other.

On the 23 July 1745, at Coilleag a'Phrionnsa on the west coast, less than nine months before defeat at Culloden, Prince Charles Edward Stuart (Bonnie

Village Street, St Kilda

© Warwick Lister-Kaye/iStockphoto.com

Prince Charlie) stood for the first time on Scottish soil, having landed from France. Two hundred years later, at the height of the Battle of the Atlantic, with German U-boats exacting a terrible toll on merchant shipping, New York-bound steamship *The Politician*, endeavouring to evade detection by slipping through the notorious Sound of Eriskay, foundered near the tiny island of Calvay (Calbhaigh).

On board, among motorcycle parts, silks and plumbing were more than 250 000 bottles of whisky. Once the crew were saved, the islanders turned their attention to this bounty, steadily removing the bulk of the cargo. When Excise officers appeared on the scene, every available orifice and container from hot-water bottles to rabbit holes concealed the whisky. The event gave rise to the hilarious account in book and film by Sir Compton Mackenzie as *Whisky Galore*. It is said that even today bottles turn up in the most unexpected places, but read *Polly* by Roger Hutchinson for the true story.

Barra – The romantic small island, which takes great pride in its Norse heritage, is famous for its fine beaches. Blue waters surround the island, the bluest of blue. The beaches here are magnificent, none more so than Traigh Mhor, which serves as the island's airfield.

North of the airfield, the tiny cemetery of Cille-bharraidh is the last resting place of the MacNeils, clan chiefs of the island with their stronghold in Kisimul Castle in Castle Bay. Among the tombstones is the grave of Compton Mackenzie, who made Barra his home.

EXCURSION
ST KILDA

Getting to St Kilda is not easy, nor is it what might be regarded as on the conventional tourist trail; these islands (although only one can be routinely visited) are for hardy souls with a romantic and nostalgic leaning, and those who love to explore wild and inaccessible places. St Kilda is a far-flung domain of islands, 41mi/65km west of North Uist, surrounded by implacable, uncompromising seas, around which the air is frantic with converging armies of seabirds: gannet, fulmar, razorbill, guillemot, puffin and Leach's petrel. The sheer sea cliffs and sea stacks around the coast provide a magnificent breeding ground for these birds, up to half a million birds visiting each summer.

These sea-girt islands were once home to a race of people who tolerated unimaginable hardships, and, no doubt, joys, too, of a kind. But in August 1930, the few remaining St Kildans, no longer able to sustain their lifestyle, left the islands. But they had evolved a rich cultural heritage, which contributed to the islands being awarded World Heritage Status,

406

one of fewer than 30 places in the world with mixed heritage status.

There is no tourist accommodation on Hirte, the main island, and the only visitors who get to stay do so as part of National Trust for Scotland volunteer work parties, and pay for the privilege (www.hiort.org.uk).

Cruise ships call into Village Bay from time to time, and there are charter boats operating from the Western Isles and the Isle of Skye, including

- www.gotostkilda.co.uk
- www.integrityvoyages.co.uk
- www.kildacruises.co.uk
- www.seatrek.co.uk
- www.seaharris.com
- www.northernlight-uk.com

ADDRESSES

STAY

LEWIS

Royal Hotel – *Cromwell Street, Stornoway.* 01851 702 109. *www.royalstornoway.co.uk. 24 rooms.* Just a few steps from the centre of Stornoway. The informal **Boatshed Restaurant** offers modern creative cuisine.

Caladh Inn – *James Street, Stornoway.* 01851 702 740. *www.caladhinn.co.uk. 68 rooms.* Very close to the port and centre of town this three-storey hotel is the largest in Stornoway and has a good restaurant.

Broad Bay Guest House – *Back, Stornoway.* 01851 820 990. *www.broadbayhouse.co.uk. 4 rooms.* Probably the finest 'small' place to stay on Lewis. High levels of soundproofing, luxury mattresses, fine Egyptian cotton bedlinen and goosedown duvets help to ensure you have a peaceful and relaxing stay. Informal 3-course evening meal 3 nights of the week and a lighter supper platter on the other 3 nights of the week (excluding Monday).

Cabarfeidh Hotel – *Manor Park, Perceval Road South, Stornoway.* 01851 702 604. *www.cabarfeidh-hotel.co.uk. 46 rooms.* This modern, comfortable hotel is in a quiet area, less than a mile from the town centre of Stornoway. **Solas restaurant**.

HARRIS

Harris Hotel – *Tarbert.* 01859 502 154. *www.harrishotel.com. 23 rooms.* The hotel facilities include a television lounge, library, drying room, bicycle storage. Integral **restaurant**, and over 100 whiskies, and several Scottish gins.

Ardhasaig House – *South, near Tarbert.* 01859 502 500. *www.ardhasaig.co.uk. 5 rooms.* Set against the Harris Hills with stunning views across West Loch, this hotel has traditional comforts, modern facilities and an excellent **dining room** (reservations essential).

Hotel Hebrides – *Pier Road, Tarbert.* 01859 502 364. *www.hotel-hebrides.com. 21 rooms.* Sublime comfort, top quality beds, great food, late breakfasts and checkouts, an excellent range of drinks and friendly staff. **Restaurant** and bar.

NORTH UIST

Temple View Hotel – 01876 580 676. *www.templeviewhotel.co.uk. 10 rooms.* Temple view is a delightful family hotel, highly praised for food service and comfort, welcoming all ages.

Langass Lodge Hotel – 01876 580 285. *www.langasslodge.co.uk. 11 rooms.* This former shooting lodge is set on the edge of Loch Eport, a comfortable and small hotel with an excellent integral **restaurant**; booking essential.

BENBECULA

Isle of Benbecula House Hotel – *Creagorry.* 01870 603 046. *www.isleshotelgroup.co.uk. 20 rooms.* This former inn enjoys wonderful sea views. Its pleasant conservatory **restaurant** serves contemporary dishes.

Dark Island Hotel – *Liniclate.* 01870 603 030. *www.isleshotelgroup.co.uk.* Enjoy a striking destination inspired by the extraordinary landscape. Located on the Benbecula Coastal Machair. Bar and Restaurant.

BARRA

Isle of Barra Beach Hotel – *Tangasdale Beach.* 01871 810 383. *www.isleofbarrahotel.co.uk. 39 rooms.* By a white-sand beach this hotel enjoys superb Atlantic views. Bar, cinema room **restaurant** all on site. Car hire also available.

Orkney★★

The archipelago of the Orkney islands is located off the northeast tip of Scotland – the nearest island is just 6mi/10km offshore – where the North Sea and the Atlantic Ocean meet. Orkney spans 70 beautiful islands, about half of which are inhabited, and many thousands of miles. The largest island, known as "Mainland", is home to most of the population. The islands are mainly low lying, with a gently rolling landscape of green fields, heather moorland heaths and lochs; only on Hoy is there any significant elevation.

Highlights

1 The sense of Orcadian history at **St Magnus cathedral** (p410)

2 Discovering the Stone Age settlement of **Skara Brae** (p413)

3 Stepping inside prehistoric **Maes Howe** (p414)

4 Visit the **Broch of Gurness** (p414)

5 Visiting the **Italian Chapel** (p417)

Prehistory

The first settlers were established on the islands by the 4th millennium BCE and the island has a great wealth of impressive prehistoric remains, including the Neolithic settlement at Skara Brae, the outstanding tomb of Maes Howe, the Bronze Age stone circle of Brodgar, the Iron Age brochs (ancient roundhouses) of Birsay and Gurness, and the Pictish earth houses. Not surprisingly, under the name 'Heart of Neolithic Orkney', the islands were awarded World Heritage status in 1999. Individually, the sites are magnificent, but collectively they represent one of the richest Neolithic landscape in western Europe.

The Golden Age – With the arrival of the Norsemen in the 8C and 9C this Pictish land became Scandinavian. The Norse settlement was a peaceful and gradual process and in due course Orkney, as part of a Norse earldom, became the pivot of Viking Britain. It is this Norse heritage (traced in *The Orkneyinga Saga*) which differentiates the Orkney and Shetland Islands from the rest of Scotland. Even today the imprint is clear in place names, and in literature much influenced by the sagas, as well as in artistic designs and in time-honoured traditions. As late as the 19C, Norn – a form of Norse – was the language spoken rather than Gaelic.

Surety for a Dowry – The late medieval period brought Scottish rule when the islands were given in security for the dowry of Margaret of Denmark, future bride of James III. The period is often associated with misrule and the despoiling of Orkney lands by Scottish overlords, and with tyranny, in particular that of the Stewart Earls of Orkney.

The 18C was an era of prosperity with the making of **kelp**. Seaweed was burned to obtain an ash residue rich in potash and soda, in demand for the glass and soap manufacturing industries. The kelp industry brought great prosperity to the local nobility who were nicknamed the "Kelp Lairds".

Today – In these low-lying islands agriculture is the main economy with the cattle rearing and dairying the main activities. Distilling and tourism follow in order of importance, with these three industries employing much of the 19 000 inhabitants. The traditional crafts, such as knitwear and straw-backed Orkney chairs, continue to flourish.

😊 And if that's not enough, Orkney was voted the most romantic destination in the UK by publishers Mills and Boon at its prestigious 2015 Romantics Awards.

© Hartmut Krinitz/hemis.fr

Old Man of Hoy

GETTING THERE

Allow at least three days to visit Mainland Orkney, which is divided into East Mainland and West Mainland with the capital, Kirkwall, the dividing point. The principal tourist information office is in Kirkwall (*West Castle Street. ℘01856 872 856; www.orkney.com*).

BY SEA

John o' Groats Ferries (*℘01955 611 353; www.jogferry.co.uk*) Operate May–Sept from John o' Groats (40min) to Burwick – No Vehicles.

Pentland Ferries (*℘01856 831 226; www.pentlandferries.co.uk*) between Gills Bay, near John o' Groats and St Margaret's Hope (~1h).

Northlink Ferries (*℘0845 6000 449; www.northlinkferries.co.uk*) has services from Scrabster (Thurso) to Stromness (90min); from Aberdeen to Kirkwall (6h); and from Lerwick to Kirkwall (5h30).

BY AIR – Fly to Orkney with Loganair (*℘0344 800 2855; www.loganair.co.uk*) from Inverness, Glasgow, Edinburgh and Sumburgh (Shetland). Check website for flights from other UK airports, which mainly fly into the above city hubs.

GETTING AROUND

Causeways link a few of the islands, with inter-island ferries connecting 13 others (*Orkney Ferries; ℘01856 872 044; www.orkneyferries.co.uk*).

Loganair (reservations: *℘01856 873 457; www.loganair.co.uk*) services the other principal inhabited islands from Kirkwall (*Connections are dependent on the weather*).

Stagecoach bus service operates in Orkney and links Kirkwall, Stromness and St Margaret's Hope (*℘01856 878014; www.stagecoachbus.com*). You can also explore the islands by car or bike. For a list of local car and cycle rental locations, visit *www.visitorkney.com*.

The relatively flat landscape of the Orkney Islands makes cycling an option, but remember, it can be very windy, and rain heavily, at any time of year.

BY CAR – Travelling by car is the best way to get around the islands. Most of the roads are wide and in good condition, although there are still many minor single-track roads to contend with. Fuel stations are few and far between, so it is always a good idea to fill up whenever possible.

Kirkwall★★

Kirkwall spreads up the hillside from the harbour and is dominated by its splendid 800-year-old cathedral. The town has been the island fulcrum since it was a Norse trading centre and today it combines its role of capital with that of shopping and business centre. The central situation of Kirkwall makes it an ideal touring centre.

MAIN STREET

Stroll along the town's main thoroughfare, a narrow stone-flagged way that incorporates **Broad Street**, **Albert Street** and **Bridge Street**, and ends at the harbour. Former town houses of country lairds, now occupied by shops, some still emblazoned with coats of arms, provide the main points of interest, along with pends leading to attractive paved courtyards.

SIGHTS

St Magnus Cathedral★★

Apr–Sept Mon–Sat 9am–6pm, Sun 1–6pm; Oct–Mar Mon–Sat 9am–1pm, 2–5pm. Call for tours of the cathedral and general enquiries. ℘01856 874 894. www.stmagnus.org.
The founder, Earl Rognvald, started to build his new cathedral in 1137 with the

▶ **Population:** 9 293.
Info: West Castle Street. ℘01856 872 856. www.visitorkney.com.
▶ **Location:** At the northern end of the Kirkwall–Scapa isthmus that divides Mainland in two.
Advice: If intending to visit a number of the Historic Environment Scotland properties, it is worth getting an Orkney Explorer Pass, £27 for 7 sites.

intention of dedicating it to his murdered kinsman, **Earl Magnus**. Building operations supervised by the earl's father Kol were completed rapidly in 1152. Two years later the Orkney see became part of the Norwegian diocese centred on Trondheim, an arrangement that was to continue until 1472. The cathedral is Norman in character and contemporary with two other masterpieces of this style, Durham and the nave of Dunfermline abbey. The exterior, severe and quite plain, is dominated by the tower and steeple. The three west front doorways added later, are very beautiful, although much weathered, and show originality in the alternate use of red and yellow sandstone.

Doors, St. Magnus Cathedral, Kirkwall

© Peter Giovannini/imageBROKER/age fotostock

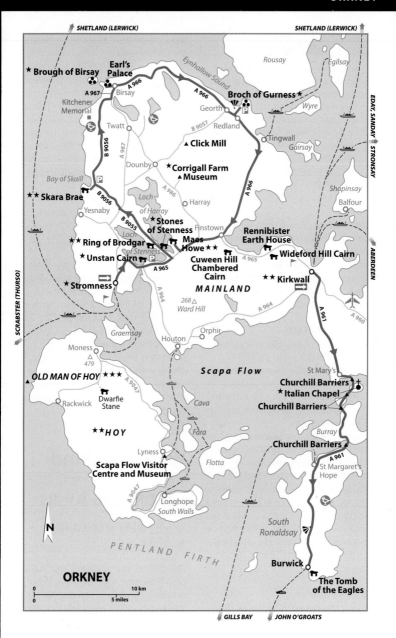

Rousay

Egilsay

★ Brough of Birsay   Earl's Palace

A 967   Birsay

A 966

Eynhallow Sound

Broch of Gurness ★

Kitchener Memorial

Georth   Wyre

EDAY, SANDAY STRONSAY

Twatt   B 9057   Redland

Tingwall

Gairsay

★ Click Mill

B 9056   A 967   Dounby

★ Corrigall Farm Museum

A 966

A 986   Harray

Shapinsay

Balfour

Bay of Skaill

P

★★ Skara Brae   B 9056

Loch of Harray

Yesnaby   B 9055

★ Stones of Stenness   Finstown

Rennibister Earth House

ABERDEEN

★★ Ring of Brodgar   Loch of Stenness   P

Maes Howe ★★

A 965   Wideford Hill Cairn

★ Unstan Cairn   A 965

Cuween Hill Chambered Cairn

★★ Kirkwall

★ Stromness

A 964   MAINLAND

A 964

268 △ Ward Hill

SCRABSTER (THURSO)

Graemsay   Houton

Orphir

A 961   A 960

Moness △ 479

Scapa Flow

St Mary's

▲ OLD MAN OF HOY ★★★   A 9047

Churchill Barriers

★ Italian Chapel

Rackwick   Dwarfie Stane   Cava

Churchill Barriers

★★ HOY   Fara

Burray

Churchill Barriers

Lyness   Flotta

A 961   St Margaret's Hope

Scapa Flow Visitor Centre and Museum

A 9047   Longhope South Walls

South Ronaldsay

N

Burwick

PENTLAND FIRTH

The Tomb of the Eagles

ORKNEY

0   10 km
0   5 miles

Interior – The initial impression is one of vastness although the dimensions of this cruciform church are relatively small. The admirable proportions, strong sense of unity, and warm tones of the red stone make for a pleasing result. The **view** is best from the west end. The design of the nave elevation moves eastwards in seven bays as slowly as it moves upwards through the triforium and clerestory, where there is no quickening of the rhythm. Ornamental detail is confined to decorative mouldings on the recessed arches of the main nave arcade, the interlaced wall arcading of the nave aisles and transepts and

Ba' Games

Kirkwall is famous for its Christmas and New Year's Day Ba' Games (ball games) when the Uppies play the Downies in an anything-goes (within reason!) football-cum-rugby match. Historically, it symbolises the rivalry between the bishop and the town's secular authorities. *www.orkneyjar.com/tradition/bagame.*

the grotesque heads of the choir consoles. The square pillars on either side of the organ screen enshrine the relics of St Magnus (right), slain in 1115, and his nephew Earl Rognvald, the builder. *The other main sights stand within what must have been the cathedral precinct.*

Bishop's Palace

Watergate, Kirkwall. ◷*Apr–Sept daily 9.30am–5.30pm.* ᵴ£6. ℘*01856 871 918. www.historicenvironment.scot.*
A new episcopal palace was built in the 12C alongside the new cathedral, the original seat having been at Birsay (Ⓒ*see p414*).
It was in the original palace that the Norwegian King Haakon died in December 1263 after the Battle of Largs. His death and the palace are described in one of the Sagas. Two rebuildings followed in the 16C and 17C, the latter by Earl Patrick as part of his scheme to create a vast lordly residence incorporating his new palace across the road. The round tower on the corner is part of Bishop Reid's 16C remodelling.

Earl's Palace★

Watergate, Kirkwall. ◷*Apr–Sept daily 9.30am–5.30pm.* ᵴ£6. ℘*01856 871 918. www.historicenvironment.scot.*
Although in ruins, this early-17C palace still displays much architectural sophistication and beauty. The refinement is all the more surprising in that the builder was the villainous despot **Patrick Stewart**, Earl of Orkney (d.1615). Like his father he was executed, but only after the final hour had been postponed to allow the condemned man time to learn the Lord's Prayer.
The palace, built 1600–07, is an early example of Renaissance style. Details of interest on the exterior include the corbelling of the windows, chimney breast and corbel course, the sculptured panel above the main entrance and the oriel windows. Inside, a splendidly spacious staircase with straight flights rises to the Great Hall and the other principal apartments. The vaulted chambers on the ground floor have exhibits on Orkney's other historic monuments and sites.

Orkney Museum

Broad St. Tankerness House.
◷*Mon–Sat: May–Sept 10.30am–5pm; Oct–Apr 10.30am–12.30pm, 1.30–5pm.* ℘*01856 873 191. www.orkney.gov.uk.*
This fine 16C town mansion houses a well-presented museum portraying life in Orkney from its prehistoric beginnings to present day.
Don't miss the St Magnus Reliquary, a simple wooden casket. Exhibits portraying domestic life include an example of a typical draught-excluding straw-backed Orkney chair.

West Mainland

⌂DRIVING TOURS

⌂ 1 WEST MAINLAND★★
46mi/74km

This driving tour combines important prehistoric sites with the tranquil agricultural landscape of the interior and dramatic coastal scenery. The tour may be taken in either direction, starting from Stromness.

▷ Leave Stromness along the A965, and drive to Stennes. Turn left on the B9055.

Stones of Stenness★
These standing stones, of which only four remain, originally formed an ellipse,

although it is suggested that the monument, up to 6m high, was once made up of 12 megaliths. Radiocarbon dating from excavations carried out in the 1970s show that the site dates from earlier than 3100 BCE. At the centre of the ring, is a large stone hearth, similar to those found in Skara Brae and other Neolithic settlements (*www.orkneyjar.com*).

Ring of Brodgar★★

This Bronze Age stone circle stands in an impressive site on a neck of land between the lochs of Stenness and Harray. Of the original 60 stones 27 remain upright. Two entrance causeways interrupt the encircling ditch, and the whole comprises a massive ceremonial enclosure and stone circle probably dating from between 2500 and 2000 BCE. Around it are at least 13 prehistoric burial mounds and a stone setting (2500 BCE–1500 BCE).

▶ Continue along the B9055 for Skara Brae, and then, at Loch of Skaill, turn right onto the B9056.

Skara Brae★★

🕑*Daily: Apr–Sept 9.30am–5.30pm; Oct–Mar 10am–4pm. ✎£9 (Skara Brae and Skaill House); Oct–Mar £7 (Skara Brae only). ✕. 𝒥01856 841 815. www.historicenvironment.scot.*

On the west coast, overlooking the Bay of Skaill, clusters a group of Stone Age dwellings. Long protected by sand, this is one of the best-preserved groups of prehistoric houses in Western Europe and provides a vivid picture of life in Neolithic times; the two main periods of settlement are between c.3100 BCE and c.2500 BCE.

The first inhabitants grew grain and kept cattle, sheep and pigs. They fished in the sea, which at that time was much farther than it is now from the village. To supplement their diet they hunted deer. Their tools were of wood, stone, bone and horn. They dressed in skin clothing, and had shell and bone necklaces and ornaments. Their pottery, heavily decorated, ranges from small fine cups to large coarse storage vessels. They belonged to a culture which buried its dead in tombs like Maes Howe.

The Settlement (*0.5mi/800m walk from the car park*) – Today several dwellings (Nos. 1–10) remain, linked by once-covered passageways (A, B and F). Seven are well preserved; remains of several others are less prominent. Only driftwood and scrubby trees were available for timber and even the furniture was built of stone.

Rectangular in shape with rounded corners, the huts had regularly coursed flagstone walls. Each dwelling had a

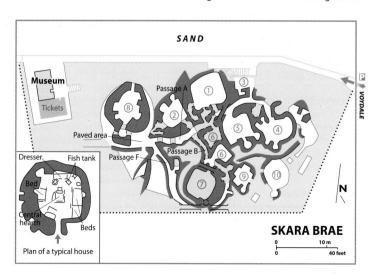

SKARA BRAE

short entrance passage guarded by a door at the inner end. The hearth for the fire was in the middle and smoke was allowed to escape by a hole in the roof. Privies were connected to a sophisticated underground sewer system. The boxes lined with clay, which are let into the floor, may have served as tanks for bait. The best-preserved house (No. 7) has been roofed over.

▶ Continue on the B9056, through Quoyloo, and on to join the A967, then left on the A966, and follow a minor road to the car park overlooking Birsay Bay.

Brough of Birsay★

The island can only be reached at low tide. For tide times, ask at the local tourist offices in Stromness or Kirkwall.
🕐*Mid-Jun–Sept daily 9.30am–5.30pm (tides permitting).* ⊜*£6.* ✆*01856 841 815. www.historicenvironment.scot.*
Set around scenic Birsay Bay are the remains of a complex of Pictish, Norse and later settlements. A small visitor centre on the island contains important early sculptures and Viking artefacts.

Pictish metalworkers

The earliest remains are houses and metalworking debris of the Pictish period. There is also a replica of a fine Pictish symbol stone.

Norse occupation

A group of 10C and 11C farmsteads marks this period. The Norse Earls made Birsay one of their principal seats in Orkney.

Norse church

The 12C remains are set within an enclosure representing the **Norse graveyard**. Both Pictish and Norse graves have been uncovered. An important example of the former is the **Birsay Stone** (replica).

Norse long houses

To the southwest and higher up the slope are typical Norse houses with the living quarters at the upper end and byre lower down. The walls had cores of turf.

▶ Return to the A966.

Earl's Palace

In the village of Birsay are the ruins of a once sumptuous residence built by the late-16C Earls of Orkney around three sides of a courtyard.

▶ Leave Birsay on the A966, as far as Redland, and turn left on minor road to the Broch of Gurness.

Broch of Gurness★

🕐*Apr–Sept daily 9.30am–5.30pm.* ⊜*£6.* ✆*01856 751 414. www.historicenvironment.scot.*
At the point of the Aikerness promontory are the remains of a broch (a tall circular Iron Age tower) and subsequent phases of occupation, which together make up one of the most outstanding surviving examples of an Iron-Age settlement in northern Scotland.
The road offers fine **views** across the Sound of Rousay and to the island of Eynhallow.

▶ Follow the A966 to Finstown, turn right.

Maes Howe★★

🍴*Guided tours only from Skara Brae centre: daily: Apr–Sept 9.30am–5pm; Oct–Mar 10am–4pm. Advance booking required.* ⊜*£9 incoudes coach transfer.* 🚫*Do not park at Maes Howe.* ✆*01856 761 606. www.historicenvironment.scot.*
The Neolithic chambered cairn of Maes Howe (which means great mound) is the finest chambered tomb in northwest Europe. It was built prior to 2700 BCE (around the time when Stonehenge began) and the ingenuity of construction and quality of workmanship are such that it has been suggested this was the tomb of a chieftain or ruling family. The whole is covered by a mound 8m high and 35m in diameter, and was encircled by a ditch.
Interior – A passage (12m long) leads to the inner chamber, off which open three burial cells. The tomb was pillaged in the 12C by Norsemen, and according to the rich collection of runic inscriptions

The Churchill Barriers

The Churchill Barriers are a series of four causeways with a total length of 1.5mi/2.3km linking the Orkney Mainland to the island of South Ronaldsay via Burray and two smaller islands, Lamb Holm and Glimps Holm.

The barriers were built during the Second World War primarily as naval defences to protect the anchorage of Scapa Flow. In October 1939, the Royal Navy battleship HMS *Royal Oak* was sunk at her moorings within Scapa Flow in a nighttime attack by the German U-boat U-47. Shortly before midnight on the 13 October, the U-47 had entered Scapa Flow through Kirk Sound between Lamb Holm and Orkney Mainland. Although the shallow eastern passages had been secured with measures including sunken block ships, booms and anti-submarine nets, the U-boat commander was able to navigate the U-47 around the obstructions at high tide. He then launched a surprise torpedo attack on the unsuspecting Royal Navy battleship while at anchor. The U-47 then escaped seaward using the same channel by navigating between the block ships.

In response, Winston Churchill, then First Lord of the Admiralty, ordered the construction of several permanent barriers to prevent any further attacks. Work began in May 1940 and was completed by September 1944. However the barriers were not officially opened until 12 May 1945, four days after the end of World War II in Europe. The work was undertaken by Italian prisoners of war.

to be found within, there was so much treasure to remove, it took them three nights to accomplish the robbery.

VISITS

Rennibister Earth House
Between Kirkwall and Finstown. Leave the car on the road up to the farm. The site is behind the farmhouse.
This earth house, or souterrain, consists of an oval chamber with five wall recesses and an entrance passage. Human bones were found in the chamber, but its original purpose is uncertain.

Cuween Hill Chambered Cairn
Above Finstown. Short walk from parking area. Access is on hands and knees through a low tunnel. Take a torch.
Discover a 5 000-year-old Neolithic tomb where bones of men, dogs and oxen were found buried. The cairn attests to a belief in an afterlife 5 000 years ago.

Wideford Hill Cairn
1mi/1.6km on foot from the road. The site is on the flank of the hill, follow the path. Access is by a trap door and ladder.
This chambered tomb, within its cairn, dates from between 3500 BCE and 2500 BCE and has a main chamber with side cells. From the hillside there is a fine **view** northwards over the Bay of Firth.

Kirbuster Museum★
Near Birsay. Mar–Oct Mon–Sat 10.30am–1pm, 2–5pm, Sun noon–5pm. 01856 771 268; www.orkney.gov.uk.
This is the last un-restored example of a traditional "firehouse" in northern Europe, occupied until the 1960s, and a perfect to learn what life was like in the past in these remote communities.

Corrigall Farm Museum★
Near Dounby. Mar–Oct Mon–Sat 10.30am–1pm, 2–5pm, Sun noon–5pm. 01856 771 411. www.orkney.gov.uk.
This group of 18C buildings has been restored to its mid-19C appearance to form a delightful museum of farming and rural life. The original "firehouse"

has been subdivided by a gable fire-place into "in-by" and "oot-by". The out-by included pig stalls and recessed goose nests. The in-by was the family room with sleeping area beyond. The present exhibition area was the byre, which was later replaced by a separate building with flagstone stalls. Another building contains the stable for the working Clydesdale horses.

▶ Continue along the A986 to Dounby, turn right onto the B9057.

Click Mill
NE of Dounby on B9057. 🕐*All year.*
This is the last and best surviving example in Orkney of a watermill with a horizontal paddle wheel.

Stromness★
The second Mainland centre and principal fishing port, Stromness is many visitors' first view of the islands as it is the terminal for the boat service from the Scottish mainland.
Although used as a haven by the Norsemen, the settlement only really developed in the 18C as a trading centre and the last port of call for the Hudson Bay Company's ships. Whaling and herring fishing then took over as the principal activities.
The dominance of the sea in the past is reflected in the physical layout. A long, winding and paved main street is overlooked on the seaward side by gable-ended dwellings, each with their own jetties.

The Pier Arts Centre
&🕐*Tue–Sat 10.30am–5pm.* ℘*01856 850 209. www.pierartscentre.com.*
This "glowing postmodern shed of dark metal and glass" was voted best building of the year in 2007 by the Royal Incorporation of Architects in Scotland. It features a permanent collection of **abstract art★** highlighted by some of the greatest works of the 1929–63 period, including early work by Ben Nicholson and Barbara Hepworth, together with canvases of other St Ives

painters including Peter Lanyon, Patrick Heron and Naum Gabo.

Stromness Museum
🕐 *Daily 10am–5pm (Wed 7pm).* ⊜*£5.* ℘*01856 850 025.*
www.stromnessmuseum.co.uk.
Orkney's natural history and maritime museum includes displays on whaling, fishing, the Hudson Bay Company and the scuttled German Fleet in Scapa Flow.

Unstan Chambered Cairn★
🕐 *The key hangs in a box at the back door.* ℘*01856 841 815.*
The cairn on the edge of the Loch of Stenness contains an excellent example of a communal tomb typical of Neolithic times. The main chamber is divided by upright slabs into compartments. The pottery found here gave rise to the name Unstan Ware, which dates from the middle of the 4th millennium BCE.

East Mainland and South Ronaldsay

🚗DRIVING TOUR

🚗 ② SOUTH RONALDSWAY★
20mi/33km each way

This excursion offers the opportunity to visit more of the Orkney Islands (Lamb Holm, Glims Holm, Burray and South Ronaldsay) without taking a boat or plane.

▶ Take the airport road out of Kirkwall then fork right onto the A961, South Ronaldsay road.

The early stretch has a good view of **Scapa Flow**, the famous naval base where on 21 June 1919 the trapped German Grand Fleet was scuttled. Activity has most recently returned with the island of Flotta being used as a pipeline, landfall and tanker terminal for gas and oil from the Piper and Claymore Fields. Lyness on Hoy serves as a supply base and is also home to the **Scapa Flow Visitor Centre and Museum** (*see below*), which includes extensive photographic displays, many artefacts and an impressive audiovisual display sited inside a huge oil tank.

○ Follow signs to St Margaret's Hope.

Beyond is the first of the **Churchill Barriers** linking Mainland to three outlying islands (*see box above*).

○ Turn left immediately after crossing the first causeway.

Italian Chapel★

Lamb Holm. Daily: Apr and Oct 10am–4pm; May and Sept 9am–5pm; Jun–Aug 9am–6.30pm; Nov–Mar 10am–1pm. 1 Jan, 25 Dec. £3. 01856 781 580. www.italianchapel.co.uk.

This famous chapel comprises two Nissen huts, converted into a chapel with whatever materials were at hand, by Italian prisoners of war who were working on the construction of the causeways in 1943–45. With its rood screen and fresco paintings, it stands as a testimony to faith in times of adversity. On either side of the following two causeways there are rusting hulks which are valuable as scallop breeding grounds.

On the island of South Ronaldsay a roadside viewpoint with indicator offers **views★** across the Pentland Firth of Dunnet Head and John o' Groats on the Scottish mainland.

Burwick

In summer a passenger ferry operates between Burwick and John o' Groats. Nearby, in South Liddle is the **Isbister Chambered Cairn**, better known as **The Tomb of the Eagles**. (*It is a walk of about 1 mile to the tomb; the passageway into the tomb is only 70cm wide and 85cm high so visitors have to lie on a trolley and pull themselves in. Inside there is limited headroom, but there is light.*)

Mar 10am–noon; Apr–Sept 9.30am–5.30pm; Oct 9.30am–12.30pm; £7.80; 01856 831 339; www.tomboftheeagles.co.uk). The cairn is estimated to have been built around 3000 BCE, and used for approximately 800 years. It is over 3.4m high and consists of a rectangular main chamber, divided into stalls and side cells. The bones of around 340 people, plus 70 talons from the white-tailed sea eagle and the remains of at least 14 birds (hence inspiration for the tomb's popular name) were discovered here.

Once common in Orkney, it is thought that the sea eagle was perhaps a totem of the people who built the tomb.

EXCURSIONS

HOY★★

A short ferry ride from Houton Pier takes you across to the island of Hoy to Lyness and the **Scapa Flow Visitor Centre** (*closed until 2020 for renovations; 01856 791 300, www.orkney.gov.uk*). The museum is centred around the former fuel oil pumping station at Lyness Naval Base (*HMS Proserpine*). The fascinating exhibition illustrates the importance of Scapa Flow as a base for the British fleet throughout history, concentrating on its role during two world wars. It includes photographs, text, artefacts, films and an audio exhibition, plus a collection of large military vehicles, cranes and artillery. A new World War 1 exhibition has been installed for 2016.

The road wanders roughly northwards, following the coastline, before turning left to cross the moors to Rackwick Bay, on the way passing the start of a ⚐ path that leads across moorland to the **Dwarfie Stane**, a huge block of red sandstone that had been the subject of folklore long before Walter Scott immortalised it in *The Pirate*, as the favourite residence of Trolld, a dwarf famous in the northern sagas. The stone is arguably the most unconventional chambered cairn in Britain.

⚐ From Rackwick a path climbs across the base of Moor Fea to an abrupt end overlooking the **Old Man of Hoy★★★**, a 137m sea stack created by erosion of the cliff, and seeming to be under perpetual threat of collapse. The stack was first climbed by mountaineers Chris Bonington, Rusty Baillie and Tom Patey in 1966.

Lancashire-born composer and Master of the Queen's Music, Sir Peter Maxwell Davies CH CBE (1934–2016) moved to live on Hoy in 1971. Orkney (particularly its capital, Kirkwall) hosts the St Magnus Festival, an arts festival founded by Davies in 1977. He frequently used the festival to premiere new works. Since his move to Orkney, Davies drew on Orcadian or more generally Scottish themes in his music, and he sometimes set the words of Orcadian writer George Mackay Brown. His short piano piece *Farewell to Stromness* entered the Classic FM Hall of Fame in 2003, his first ever entry, and was at that time the fastest-rising new entry in the chart's history. Davies died at his home on Hoy on 14 March 2016.

ADDRESSES

🛏 STAY

⊜⊜ **Polrudden** – *Peerie Sea Loan, Kirkwall.* ℘*01856 874 761. www. polrudden.com. 7 rooms.* This is a large modern house outside the town centre with picture windows overlooking quiet fields.

⊜⊜ **Houton Bay Lodge** – *Houton Bay, Scapa Flow, Orphir.* ℘*01856 811 320. https://houton-bay-lodge-orphir.hotelmix. co.uk. 8 rooms.* �. With great views of Scapa Flow and the southern Islands, this modern house in a rural setting offers bright and spacious bedrooms.

⊜⊜⊜ **Albert Hotel** – *Mounthoolie Lane, Kirkwall.* ℘*01856 876 000. www. alberthotel.co.uk.* Ideally situated in the centre of Kirkwall, offering boutique style hotel rooms with luxury furnishings and a contemporary design.

⊜⊜⊜ **The Creel** – *Front Road, St Margaret's Hope, South Ronaldsay.* ℘*01856 831 311. www.thecreel.co.uk.* This B&B has stylish **rooms**, on the waterfront of the bay.

⊜⊜⊜ **Merkister Hotel** – *Loch Harray, East Mainland.* ℘*01856 771 366. www. merkister.com. 16 rooms.* Sited on the edge of a loch, this peaceful family-run small hotel offers trim bedrooms, a lively public bar, and the **Skerries Restaurant**⊜⊜⊜ offering an extensive Scottish menu.

⊜⊜⊜ **Sands Hotel** – *Burray.* ℘*01856 731 298. www.thesandshotel.co.uk. 6 rooms.* A former fishing store, totally modernised with six stylish sea view rooms, a popular bar and spacious **dining room**⊜⊜ also with bay views.

🍴 EAT

⊜⊜ **Foveran Restaurant with Rooms** – *St Ola, Kirkwall.* ℘*01856 872 389. www. thefoveran.com. Dinner only.* Enjoy an aperitif with a beautiful view of Scapa Flow in the lounge. Meals are exclusively fresh local produce specialising in seafood. Stay overnight in one of their **8 rooms**⊜⊜⊜.

⊜⊜ **Skerries Bistro** – *Banks of Orkney, Banks, Cleat, South Ronaldsay.* ℘*01856 831 605. www.skerriesbistro.co.uk. Open Apr–Sept.* Specialising in local seafood. Food served daily except Sat noon–4pm; Mon, Wed, Fri–Sat from 6pm (reservations advised). A bit way out, but well worth tracking down.

⊜⊜ **Lynnfield** – *Lynnfield Hotel, St Ola, Kirkwall.* ℘*01856 872 505. www.lynnfieldhotel.com.* Modern traditional cuisine, championing the very best of Orcadian produce. Also **10 rooms** ⊜⊜⊜.

⊜⊜ **The Storehouse Restaurant with Rooms** – *Bridge Street Wynd, Kirkwall.* ℘*01856 252 250. www. thestorehouserestaurantwithrooms.co.uk.* Stylish B-Listed Storehouse converted into Kirkwall's first hotel for 80 years with a ground floor **restaurant** with comfy bar seating infront of a log fire and **8** individually designed luxury **bedrooms**.

⊜⊜ **Kirk Gallery and Café** – *Tankerness.* ℘*01856 861 203. https://sheilafleet. com.* You track this place down for its excellent lunches and very naughty cakes. But you'll get drawn into Sheila Fleet's artisan jewellery displays and workshop, too. Be warned!

Shetland★★★

This windy archipelago shaped by the sea possesses a wildly indented coastline with a savage beauty, in places rugged and rocky, elsewhere sandy and smooth. Here on the very edge of the British Isles you will find remains of the earliest human settlements and a Viking heritage that is still alive today. The islands are closer to the Arctic Circle than to Manchester, closer to Bergen in Norway than to Edinburgh, and many aspects of the local culture feel more Scandinavian than Scottish.

A unique natural environment

Shetland offers probably the best wild-life-watching in Scotland. This includes over a million breeding seabirds, the highest density of otters in Europe, regular sightings of killer whales and superb displays of rare subarctic flora. The cliffs around **Sumburgh Head**, a protected RSPB reserve, attract thousands of summer breeding seabirds, including puffins, guillemots, shags and fulmars. On Mousa, Arctic and Great skuas and Arctic terns defend their nesting grounds by dive-bombing all intruders, people included, so if visiting there do try to walk round the breeding colonies, for their sakes as well as yours. For more details on all Shetlands wildlife including specialist holidays and tours visit *www.shetlandwildlife.co.uk*.

The Old Rock

Shetlanders know their islands as 'The Old Rock'; and a rocky landscape it is, too. Bolstered by 100 smaller islands, Shetland lies almost 100 miles north of the Scottish mainland, and extend over 70 miles from north to south, making this a sprawling, convoluted and fascinating landscape where land and water mingle. Few realise that Shetland lies north of the 60th parallel, which puts it as far north as Hudson Bay in Canada and the southernmost tip of Greenland. This is the land of the 'Simmer dim', the land of light nights, where anyone hoping to catch both sunset and sunrise may have only a few hours to wait.

Highlights

1. Discovering both old and new at the **Shetland Museum** (p422)
2. Stepping back into several time periods at **Jarlshof** (p423)
3. A sunny afternoon on the white sand **St Ninian's Isle beach** (p423)
4. Deciphering the meaning and purpose of **Mousa Broch** (p424)

Sullom Voe

35mi/56km north of Lerwick. From the main A970 the only indication of this major oil terminal is the flame on the flare stack. The decisive factors in siting an oil terminal and accompanying port facilities at Sullom Voe were the presence of a deep sheltered inlet and its proximity to the oilfields in the East Shetland Basin. The port with its four specialised jetties can berth ships of up to 300 000t, and at its peak it once handled a staggering 1.4 million barrels of oil a day. The oil arrives via two pipelines from over a dozen offshore oilfields some 100mi/160km to the northeast. The gases (propane and butane) are separated from the oil and then stored prior to shipment. The terminal has no refining facilities. Calback Ness Peninsula is the site for 16 huge storage tanks.

Lerwick

The port capital of Lerwick is set on a promontory overlooking the natural harbour, sheltered by the island of Bressay. The town has always been important as a fishing port, and the oil boom has brought new activities.

A BIT OF HISTORY

By contrast with Orkney, Shetland has few tracts of flat land. It is deeply penetrated by the sea and until recently had an economy dominated by fishing and crofting. The oil boom of the 1970s led to the disruption of this traditional and well-balanced economy but although it has one of the largest oil ports in Europe (at Sullom Voe), the oil industry still comes second after fishing. Thankfully for visitors oil-related industrialisation is limited to **Sullom Voe** and oil revenues do, indirectly, help bolster the traditional industries (crofting, fishing, fish processing and knitwear). Elsewhere the islands retain their attractions of wild beauty, solitude and empty spaces. In Mainland with all its coastal indentations, the sea is ever present. The long coastline is varied and of outstanding beauty, be it rocky and

- ▶ **Population:** 7 500.
- ? **Info:** The Market Cross, Lerwick. ☎01595 693 434; www.shetland.org.
- ◑ **Location:** The capital Lerwick, the islands' hub, is on the east coast of the largest island, known as Mainland.
- ◉ **Don't Miss:** Jarlshof, Mousa Broch.
- ◉ **Weather warning:** Be prepared for poor weather at any time of year.
- ◔ **Timing:** Allow at least three days.

rugged or sandy and smooth. Wildlife is varied and plentiful.

The archaeological treasures of the Shetland Islands, often preserved by the shifting sand dunes, reveal fascinating information on early human settlements. Recent excavations have uncovered an Iron Age village at Sumburgh.

A Port through the centuries – As a haven, Lerwick provided shelter for King Haakon's and other Viking fleets. In the early 17C, it became an illegal market-

GETTING THERE

BY SEA – Northlink Ferries (☎0845 6000 449; www.northlink ferries.co.uk) has services from Aberdeen to Lerwick (12-13 hours, arriving 7.30am, although you don't have to leave the ship until 9.30am.

BY AIR – Fly to Shetland with **Loganair** (www.loganair.co.uk) from Aberdeen, Edinburgh, Glasgow, Inverness, Orkney (Kirkwall) and Manchester.

GETTING AROUND

For widespread exploration, the car is the best option, but be sure to keep the fuel tank topped up as filling stations are few and far between. The inter-island flight service (www.

airtask.com) makes it easy to go 'island-hopping' to some of Shetland's more remote locations, such as Fair Isle, Foula, Foula and Papa Stour. Shetland Islands Council operates an inter-island ferry service (www. shetland.gov.uk/ferries) linking the larger islands with the Shetland Mainland. The services are fast and frequent, and passenger fares are very reasonable.

Shetland has an excellent public transport infrastructure, which visitors can use to explore every corner of the islands (http://travel.shetland.org).

Car rental and **bike hire** are possible at Lerwick and/or Sumburgh (www. shetland.org/plan/travel/car-and-bike-hire).

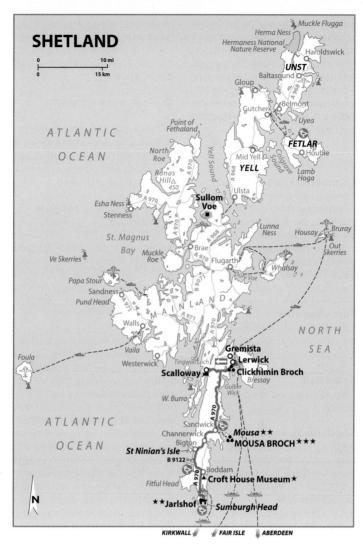

place servicing the Dutch herring fleets before being demolished by order of the Scalloway court. The Dutch burned the fort in 1673 and the French set fire to Lerwick in 1702. Both the German and British navies sheltered here in the 20C and now there is an assorted flotilla of oil vessels.

Most of the sandstone buildings on the waterfront date from the 18C although a few, such as No. 10 Commercial Street, are older. The narrow main street still follows the old shoreline but modern harbour works have been built out in front of shops and warehouses that once stood in the sea. Perched on a hillside overlooking the harbour – now home to pleasure boats – the town's lanes retain their charm and their shelter from the prevailing southwesterly gales.

Up Helly Aa★★

Held annually on the last Tue in January to mark the end of the yule season, Up Helly Aa is a tradition that originated in the 1880s, one that continues to this day as a community procession celebrating the islands' historical links with the Viking legacy. The procession culminates in the torches being thrown into a replica Viking longship or galley. The event happens all over Shetland and is currently celebrated at ten locations – Scalloway, Lerwick, Nesting and Girlsta, Uyeasound, Northmavine, Bressay, Cullivoe, Norwick, the South Mainland and Delting.

AROUND LERWICK

Commercial Street

Known simply as The Street, this paved and twisting thoroughfare winds its way along the shore. Steep lanes lead off uphill. At the southern end of the street are the lodberries, where 18C warehouses still stand with the foundations in the sea. This area featured in the TV detective-drama *Shetland*.

Fort Charlotte

From the walls of this 17C fort, rebuilt in the 18C, there is a good view of Bressay Sound and island of the same name.

Town Hall

Stained-glass windows depict Viking history.

Shetland Museum

&⊙*Early Oct–Apr Tue–Sat 10am–4pm; May–early Oct Mon–Sat 10am–5pm, Sun noon–5pm;* ⊙*over Christmas;* ✖; ℘*01595 695 057. www.shetlandmuseum andarchives.org.uk.*

Set in a stunning modern-traditional harbourside building, this landmark project displays over 3 000 artefacts on two floors, a wealth of easily accessible archive material, a temporary exhibition area, a boat hall and sheds, an art gallery, auditorium, shop and the excellent **Hay's Dock café-restaurant.**

🚗 DRIVING TOUR

🚗 LERWICK TO JARLSHOF★
20mi/32km.

This tour takes in various aspects of Shetland. Discover its desolate moorland scenery (at times interrupted by peat cutting), the varied and attractive shoreline with crofting townships down by the sea, and the numerous vestiges of man's occupation in the past.

▶ Leave Lerwick by the A970.

The main road, before the turn-off for Scalloway, provides a good **view★** of the inlet of Gulber Wick. Such deeply penetrating arms of the sea (known as *voes*) are typical of Shetland.

▶ Take the B9076 to the right to rejoin the A970.

On the right is the valley which is the setting for Tingwall Loch, the head of which is reputed to be the site of the Law Ting Holm or meeting place of the old Norse Parliament.

Scalloway

Attractively set round its bay, Scalloway was the former islands capital and is still dominated by the ruin of **Scalloway Castle**, built in 1600 (℘*01856 841 815; www.historicenvironment.scot*).
This was the principal island seat of **Patrick**, **Earl of Orkney** (⌖*see ORKNEY*), renowned for his cruelty, and the castle was constructed by forced labour. This grand example of a Scottish fortified house is just as splendid as his other residences and attractive details include the corbelling of the corner turrets, sculptured panel above the entrance doorway and sandstone window, door and angle trims. It was occupied for less than a century and is now roofless. Beneath the grand banqueting hall are large kitchens and a dungeon where 17C "witches", condemned to die on nearby Gallows Hill, awaited their fate.

▶ Go back along the B9073 to return to the A970. Turn right, and follow the road in the direction of the airport; it provides a succession of fine views of the east coast all the way. Mousa Broch is visible on its island site. At Channerwick, turn right to take the B9122, and right again in Bigton.

St Ninian's Isle

An attractive beach links this idyllic island to the mainland. It was in the ruins of an early Christian church that **St Ninian's Treasure**, one of the most important troves of silverware ever found in Britain, was discovered. The originals are now in the Museum of Scotland in Edinburgh while the Shetland Museum has replicas.

The B9122 offers views of a succession of small bays sheltered by headlands.

▶ Return to the A970.

Croft House Museum★

Boddam. ⏱*Daily May–Sept 10am–1pm, 2–5pm.* ✆*01950 460 557. www. shetlandheritageassociation.com.*
Set in the typical crofting township of Boddam, this farmhouse grouping reproduces an accurate picture of rural life in the mid-19C. The croft steading itself comprises kitchen, sleeping accommodation and byre with the barn behind and a small horizontal watermill down by the stream. Note the roofing of cured turf with straw on top.

▶ Return to the main road, heading south again towards the site of Sumburgh airport.

Jarlshof★★

25mi/40km from Lerwick.
⏱*Apr–Sept 9.30am–5.30pm; Oct–Mar restricted hours, call 01856 841 815 (Skara Brae, Orkney) for details. (During winter opening hours tickets are only available from the Sumburgh Hotel).* ⏱*25–26 Dec, 1–2 Jan.* ✦*£6.* ✆*01950 460 112. www.historicenvironment.scot.*
Set on the seashore not far from Sumburgh airport is the prehistoric site of Jarlshof The sequence of occupation is clearly distinguished, from the mid-2nd millennium BCE to the 17C.

Stone Age – Only fragments remain of the earliest settlers' village, contemporary with Skara Brae (⏱*see ORKNEY*), on the landward side.

Bronze Age – Six oval-shaped houses with cubicles built into the walls. Later settlement of the early Iron Age period brought about the alteration of the original plan including the addition of earth houses.

Late Iron Age – This settlement is clustered around the ruins of a broch, partly eroded by the sea. The broch itself is equipped with a well. The complex includes a completely preserved example of a wheelhouse (a circular hut divided radially).

Viking Era – Remains include numerous long houses, the layout of which reflecting various centuries of occupation.

Medieval Farmstead – Only parts of the original house and barn, from the 13C to 16C, are preserved.

Jarlshof – The 16C New Hall was built for Earl Robert Stewart. It was converted into kitchens when a new Laird's House was added in the early 17C.

Museum – This displays finds from excavations and a plan of the entire Jarlshof site.

EXCURSIONS

Shetland Textile Museum

Gremista: 1.2mi/2km north of Lerwick.
⏱*Tue–Sat noon–5pm.* ✦*£3.*
✆*01595 694 386;*
www.shetlandtextilemuseum.com.
This typical 18C booth (*böd*) at Gremista, 1.2mi/2km north of Lerwick, once provided family accommodation as well as a working store for the nearby fish drying beach. Remarkably this was the birthplace of Arthur Anderson (1792–1868), co-founder of what is now P&O Ferries, and is furnished in a basic Shetland style. It features displays on the life and times of Anderson. but is now largely dedicated to Shetland's textile cultures and heritage.

Clickimin Broch★

1mi/1.6km southwest of Lerwick.
Built on an island in a small loch and accessible by a stone causeway, at its peak around 60 people would have lived at this small settlement. Although only 5m high, the characteristic layout of this defensive structure can be seen as evidence of successive occupations.

MOUSA★★

Mousa is a small island, uninhabited since the 19C, but renowned both for its Iron Age round tower, and as a Special Protection Area for almost 7 000 breeding pairs of European storm-petrel. Mousa is mentioned in the *Orkneyinga Saga* as a place of defence during invasions – as well as a lovers' hideout.

The island is accessible during summer months by a passenger-only ferry which operates from the Shetland Mainland from Sandsayre Pier, Leebitton (✆*07901 872 339; www.mousa.co.uk*). Storm petrel dusk trips are also available *late May–Jul, 10.30pm, Mon, Wed and Sat.* ✆*£25 (booking essential).*

Mousa Broch★★★

Brochs are the culmination of a tradition of small stone fortified farms, sometimes referred to as towers, stretching back to 500 BCE. Mousa Broch, probably dates back to the first two centuries of our era, the finest surviving example and may have been more strongly built than the other 500 known brochs in Scotland, most of which are found in the Highlands and Islands.

Ingeniously constructed, the tower (13m high and 15m in diameter at the base) swells out at the base like a bottle kiln. Enter by a passage (5m long) which had a door midway along. The courtyard, with a central hearth, was surrounded by lean-to timber structures supported by the scarcements (ledges) still visible on the inner faces of the walls. Three doorways lead to mural chambers; a fourth opens into a staircase, again with a mural, which leads to the wallhead. Above the uppermost scarcement, the hollow wall is divided by stone slabs into galleries which open onto the courtyard by means of three sets of ladder-like openings.

YELL

The appellation 'Gateway to the Northern Isles' says much about Yell; its face is a plain canvas of blanket peat, yet it is an island that blends tradition with modernity.

The Old Haa at Burravoe dates from the 17C, and was opened as a museum in 1984 to house a permanent display of material depicting the history of Yell. Such action as there is occurs at Mid Yell, the main centre of the population; there is a fine natural harbour here.

UNST

Unst is the most northerly inhabited island in Britain, and one of the most unique islands in Europe. The island holds scenic beauty, rich history, heritage and traditions alongside a mystical charisma, and is well worth the effort of journeying here. Its rugged landscape will charms visitors, and the golden, often empty, beaches leave you feeling in awe of such a wonderful space. National Nature Reserves provide excellent wildlife opportunities

At the far northern tip of Unst, Herma Ness looks out across to the lighthouse on Muckle Flugga. Beneath your feet the sea cliffs are host to thousands upon thousands of sea birds, mostly gannets, and for many years a black-browed albatross, half a hemisphere away from home.

This is a most dramatic location, and one you will have had to dodge Great skuas, bonxies in the local dialect, which will dive at you if you pass by in the breeding season.

At Baltasound, a bus shelter has been 'improved', by the addition of seats, curtains and information leaflets. For a time, it even served as a two-person cinema, showing short videos compiled by local school children.

FETLAR

Fetlar – The Garden of Shetland – is for birdwatching...and doing not much.

A large stone wall known as Finnigert Dyke divides the island in two, north to south, and is arguably Fetlar's oldest surviving man-made structure, believed to date from the Bronze Age.

The northern part of Fetlar is a RSPB reserve, home to Arctic skua and whimbrel. The Lamb Hoga peninsula and nearby Haaf Gruney have some of the largest colonies of storm petrel. But of greatest importance are red-necked phalaropes, for which the Loch of Funzie is an important breeding site.

FAIR ISLE★★

Equidistant from Shetland and Orkney, 25mi/40km southwest of Sumburgh Head, Fair Isle is Britain's most isolated inhabited island. Norse settlers named the island Fridarey, the island of peace. Fair Isle is magically fair; a resilient place, with resilient people, who mostly live in traditional crofts on the more fertile southern part of the island.

Famous for birds, knitwear and more than a hundred shipwrecks, Fair Isle is a tiny gem in the jewellery of the northern isles. The island is one of Britain's most successful small communities, pioneering projects in wildlife tourism, windpower and sustainable management of the environment.

Fair Isle is renowned for its birdlife, but the ever-popular observatory and guesthouse was destroyed by fire in 2019 – check website for updates (*www. fairislebirdobs.co.uk*).

🕊*There are daily return flights from Tingwall on Shetland (✆01595 840 246 www.airtask.com).*

ADDRESSES

🏠 STAY AND 🍴 EAT

🍽🍽 **The Dowry** – *98 Commercial Street, Lerwick. ✆01595 692 373.* The new kid on the block. The Dowry is a trendy bar-bistro open daily except Sun from 10am–11pm. Vegetarian and vegan options.

🍽🍽 **The String** – *88 Commercial Street, Lerwick. ✆01595 694 921. Open for lunch Wed–Sun and dinner Tue–Sat. Closed Mon.* The emphasis is on local seafood and meat, along with craft beer, gin, wine and artisan coffee.

🍽🍽 **Bonhoga** – *Weisdale. ✆01595 745 750. Open Mon–Sat 10.30am–5pm, Sun 11am–5pm.* Bonhoga was a meal and barley mill from 1855 until the early 20C, then a butchery and tannery before falling into dereliction in the 20C The building was renovated and opened as Bonhoga Gallery in 1994. Exhibitions; **café**.

🍽🍽🍽 **Burrastow House** – *Walls. ✆01595 809 307. www.burrastowhouse. co.uk. 6 rooms.* Located on the remote west side of Shetland, where you can find spectacular scenery, peace and the ideal refuge for the escapist.

🍽🍽🍽 **Queens Hotel** – *Commercial Street, Lerwick. ✆01595 692 826. www.kgqhotels.co.uk.* Set in Lerwick Harbour, and originally built in the 1860s as seafront warehouses. **Restaurant** 🍽🍽.

🍽🍽🍽 **Grand Hotel** – *Commercial Street, Lerwick. ✆01595 692 826. www.kgqhotels. co.uk.* Sister hotel to the Queens, centrally placed in Lerwick, and also boasting a fine seafood and local produce **restaurant**.

🍽🍽🍽 **Kveldsro House** – *Greenfield Place, Lerwick. ✆01595 692 195. www.shetlandhotels.com. 17 rooms.* Spacious Georgian house in the town centre, with integral **restaurant** offering mainly island produce.

🍽🍽🍽 **The Lerwick Hotel** – *15 South Road, Lerwick. ✆01595 692 166. www. shetlandhotels.com. 34 rooms.* Ten minutes from the town centre, with unrivalled views of Brewick Bay and the island of Bressay. **Bay Brasserie** serves seasonal seafood.

🍽🍽🍽 **The Shetland Hotel** – *Holmsgarth Road, Lerwick. ✆01595 695 515. www.shetlandhotels.com. 64 rooms.* Spacious and modern en suite bathrooms with baths and showers. The **Waterfront Bar and Grill** is a modern informal eatery open for lunch and dinner.

SHOPPING

Mirrie Dancers – *Commercial Street, Lerwick. ✆01595 690 592. www. mirriedancers.co.uk.* Luxury hand-made and bespoke chocolates, pralines and truffles.

The Original Cake Fridge and Tea Room - *East Burrafrth (B9071); ✆01595 810911.* A fabulous repository of all things cake and fudge (and fresh eggs), located in a beautiful corner of Mainland, Shetland. Tearoom open all year 10am-4pm; the external cake fridge is a drive-by, with honesty box for payment.

INDEX

INDEX

INDEX

INDEX

INDEX

INDEX

INDEX

INDEX

🏨 STAY

INDEX

♀/EAT

MAPS AND PLANS

THEMATIC MAPS

MAPS

MAP LEGEND

★★★ **Worth a special journey**

★★ **Worth a detour**

★ **Interesting**

Tourism

Sightseeing route with departure point indicated	AZ B Map co-ordinates locating sights
Ecclesiastical building	Tourist information
Synagogue – Mosque	Historic house, castle – Ruins
Building (with main entrance)	Dam – Factory or power station
Statues, small building	Fort – Cave
Wayside cross	Prehistoric site
Fountain	Viewing table – View
Fortified walls – Tower – Gate	Miscellaneous sight

Recreation

Racecourse	Waymarked footpath
Skating rink	Outdoor leisure park/centre
Outdoor, indoor swimming pool	Theme/Amusement park
Marina, moorings	Wildlife/Safari park, zoo
Mountain refuge hut	Gardens, park, arboretum
Overhead cable-car	Aviary, bird sanctuary
Tourist or steam railway	

Additional Symbols

Motorway (unclassified)	Post office – Telephone centre
Junction: complete, limited	Covered market
Pedestrian street	Barracks
Unsuitable for traffic, street subject to restrictions	Swing bridge
Steps – Footpath	Quarry – Mine
Railway – Coach station	Ferry (river and lake crossings)
Funicular – Rack-railway	Ferry services: Passengers and cars
Tram – Metro, underground	Foot passengers only
Bert (R.)... Main shopping street	Access route number common to MICHELIN maps and town plans

Abbreviations and Special Symbols

C	County council offices	U	University
H	Town hall		Park and Ride
J	Law courts	M3	Motorway
M	Museum	A2	Primary route
POL.	Police		Hotel
T	Theatre		Battlefield

COMPANION PUBLICATIONS

A map reference to the appropriate Michelin map is given for each chapter in the Sights section of this guide.

MAPS

Regional map – Scotland

The **Michelin map 501** (Scale 1 : 400 000 – 1cm = 4km – 1in : 6.30miles) covers Scotland, the network of motorways and major roads and some secondary roads. It provides information on shipping routes, distances in miles and kilometres, town plans of Edinburgh and Glasgow, services, sporting and tourist attractions, a list of Unitary Authorities of Scotland and an index of places; the key and text are printed in four languages.

Country maps

The **Michelin Tourist and Motoring Atlas – Great Britain & Ireland** (Scale 1 : 300 000 – 1cm = 3km – 1in : 4.75 miles – based on 1 : 400 000) covers the whole of the United Kingdom and the Republic of Ireland, the national networks of motorways and major roads. It provides information on route planning, shipping routes, distances in miles and kilometres, over 60 town plans, services, sporting and tourist attractions, and an index of places; the key and text are printed in six languages.

The **Michelin map 713 – Great Britain & Ireland** (Scale 1 : 1 000 000 – 1cm = 10km – 1in : 15.8 miles), on one sheet, covers the whole of the United Kingdom and the Republic of Ireland, the national networks of motorways and major roads. It provides information on shipping routes, distances in miles and kilometres, a list of Unitary Authorities for Wales and Scotland; the key and text are printed in six languages.

ROUTE PLANNING

Michelin is pleased to offer a route planning service at **www.viamichelin.com**.
Personalised route plans, comprehensive maps, addresses of hotels and restaurants featured in *The Red Guides* and practical and tourist information.